PRACTICAL BANKING
AND
BUILDING SOCIETY LAW

To my girls — Amy & Nicola

PRACTICAL BANKING
AND
BUILDING SOCIETY LAW

Professor Anu Arora
Faculty of Law, University of Liverpool

BLACKSTONE
PRESS LIMITED

First published in Great Britain 1997 by Blackstone Press Limited,
Aldine Place, London W12 8AA. Telephone 0181-740 2277

© A. Arora, 1997

ISBN: 1 85431 628 1

British Library Cataloguing in Publication Data
A CIP catalogue record for this book is available from the British Library.

Typeset by Style Photosetting Ltd, Mayfield, East Sussex
Printed by Ashford Colour Press, Gosport, Hants.

Contents

Classification of financial institutions — Deposit-taking institutions — Investing institutions — Specialised financing agencies — Institutional diversification — International markets — The Single European Market — The EC 'passport' — Freedom of capital movements — Banking — Insurance — Investment services — Development of the building society sector

Relationship between the common law and the Banking Act 1987 — The banking sector — Common law definition of 'bank' and related expressions — Structure and functions of banks — Bank of England — Commercial banks — Merchant banks — Overseas and foreign banks — Trustee Savings Bank — National Girobank — Building societies — Building Societies Act 1986 — Trading powers under the 1986 Act — Supervision of building societies — Building Societies Commission — Functions of the central office — Amendments to the Building Societies Act 1986

Need for control — Regulatory function of the Bank of England — Banking Act 1987 — Duties of the Bank of England as a general supervisor — Board of Banking Supervision — Regulation of deposit-taking — Restriction on the acceptance of deposits — Meaning of deposit — '. . . in the course of carrying on a business' — '. . . whether there or elsewhere' — '. . . a deposit-taking business' — Exempted persons and transactions — Authorisation — Application for authorisation — Statutory criteria for authorisation — The Bank's interpretation of the schedule 3 criteria — Applications by overseas institutions — The Bank's informal requirements — Granting of authorisation — Refusal of an application — Revocation and restriction of authorisation — Directions in order to safeguard assets — Enforcement — Offences — Profits from unauthorised deposits — Supervisory information and statistics — Power to obtain specific information — Power to appoint investigators — Accounts and auditors — Auditors and the duty of confidentiality — Banking names and descriptions — The £5 million threshold — Banking descriptions — Overseas institutions and representative offices — Use of name by a representative office — Changes in control — Objection to new or increased control — Objection by the Treasury — Restrictions and sale of shares — Advertisements for deposits — Deposit Protection Scheme — Deposit Protection Board — Deposit Protection Fund — Large exposure — Appeals

Part 3

requirements — Duration of negotiability — Conditions for incurring liability on a bill of exchange — Delivery of the instrument — Capacity and authority of the parties to a bill of exchange — Forged or unauthorised signatures — Capacity to draw a bill of exchange — Effect of incapacity — Consideration — Holder in due course — Holder who has taken the bill — Completeness and regularity of the bill — Overdue bills and notice of dishonour — Necessity for value and good faith — Title of the holder in due course — Defects of title from which the holder in due course takes free

negotiable stocks and shares as securities — Life policies as security — The assignment

Preface

This book is written at a time of considerable change in the banking and building society sector. The face of banking regulation continues to change and become more complex. The collapse of BCCI has resulted in considerable litigation. Considerable changes are likely as a result of the deregulation of the Bills of Exchange Act in 1996. Building societies have seen a rush for mutuals to convert to company status and acquire recognition as banks. To stem the tide two new building societies acts have received Royal Assent in 1997. In May 1997, the Chancellor announced changes in the role of the Bank of England. Although legislation will follow in the future, Appendix 1 of this book outlines the proposed changes.

Meanwhile, the phase of banking business and practice has continued to evolve rapidly. This book examines the scope of bank and building society regulation, the banker–customer relationship and payment instruments including the changes resulting from the Cheques Act 1992. Where banking practice diverges from the practice followed by building societies this is highlighted. Forms of finance available to customers are also examined, including enforcement of security. The book concludes with an examination of what was traditionally considered the role of building societies — mortgage lending for house purchase.

I would like to record my thanks and gratitude to Ann Porter who very patiently typed up the manuscript for me, Professor R. R. Pennington for giving me his comments on the manuscript, Richard Tyson-Davies of APACS and the Building Societies Commission. My thanks, of course, are due to Alistair MacQueen, Heather Saward and Paula Doolan for their great patience.

Finally, my thanks go to my family.

Anu Arora
Faculty of Law
University of Liverpool
July 1997

Table of Cases

Table of Statues

Table of Statutory Instruments

PART 1

1   The City of London as a Financial Centre

The UK has evolved a sophisticated financial system, which comprises a large number of diverse institutions. Since 1975 the financial sector has been one of the fastest growing areas of the UK economy. Alongside this growth there has been considerable innovation and structural change.

The City of London, sometimes known as the 'square mile', accommodates the head offices of many financial institutions and so can be thought of as the nerve centre of the UK financial system. However, there is more to the financial system than the City. There are branch offices of banks, building societies, insurance companies etc., and many financial institutions have their head offices in provincial cities.

The activities of financial institutions located in the City are not necessarily restricted to the UK. The City has a long-established role and reputation as a world financial centre. This role developed when the City evolved as a centre for international trade and then as a centre for international finance. The current success of the City is based, in particular, on the nineteenth century when sterling and bills of exchange drawn and discounted on London were widely used.

After the First World War and with the gradual decline of sterling as an international currency the City's role as a major financial centre declined.

The 1960s and 1970s saw a resurgence of the City with the rapid development of the Euromarkets. The Eurocurrency market involved banks physically located in London accepting foreign currency deposits, mainly in dollars from foreign residents, which were lent to foreign borrowers. In effect London became an offshore centre for foreign currency transactions, which were often intended to circumvent regulations imposed on institutions in their home countries.

The development of the Eurocurrency market resulted in a substantial increase in the number of foreign banks with a physical presence in London (the numbers grew from around 80 foreign banks in the late 1950s, to over 300 by the end of 1979). In recent years the significance of the Eurocurrency market has declined in relation to the Eurobond market, which represents the internationalisation of the issue of and dealings in securities. Thus, in addition to the role of the City institutions in the domestic financial sector there is an extensive offshore business in banking and securities. Prior to 1979, it was possible to demarcate clearly between the domestic and international activities of the City, since exchange control prevented UK financial institutions from fully participating in the Eurocurrency market; that demarcation is now less distinct.

The City accommodates many institutions other than purely financial ones: it is a major international centre for non-life insurance business, it houses various organised markets for spot and futures trading in a variety of commodities and also serves as an international shipping centre.

CLASSIFICATION OF FINANCIAL INSTITUTIONS

Several classifications of institutions and their businesses are possible, e.g., according to the type of commodity produced, the turnover of the business, or number of employees. A classification of financial institutions according to such criteria would not give any cohesive idea of the nature of the business activities they undertake. As early as 1959, the Radcliffe Committee (Committee on the Working of the Monetary System, *Report* (Cmnd 827) (London: HMSO, 1959) concluded that although the various markets for credit functioned in the economic sense as a single unified market, there were a great many differences in the activities of particular financial institutions. Each type of institution had 'its special type of business and by tradition or commercial arrangement a preference for one form of lending rather than another'. Since the Radcliffe Committee Report the nature and degree of specialisation of the activities of individual institutions have altered dramatically. Not only has the degree of specialisation in the activities of individual institutions changed but the diversification of functions undertaken by them makes classification considerably more difficult. Nevertheless, it cannot be denied that many financial institutions can now be described as multi-product firms. Moreover, many institutions form part of a much larger conglomerate consisting of companies which offer many varied products. The present structure of the financial institutions inhibits the use of any simple classification, especially as some institutions referred to under a specific category may span a variety of financial categories. The discussion here of the role of financial institutions is, therefore, organised along the lines of the classification adopted in the Wilson Committee Report (Committee to Review the Functioning of Financial Institutions, *Report* (Cmnd 7937) (London: HMSO, 1980).

The Wilson Committee distinguished between three types of financial intermediaries: deposit-taking institutions, investing institutions and specialised financing agencies.

Deposit-taking institutions

The common feature ascribed to deposit-taking institutions is that they accept deposits which constitute liquid and nominal capital. These institutions then make loans or acquire other assets with longer maturity dates. In the UK all institutions deemed to be engaged in banking activities are included in a subset of deposit-taking institutions termed the UK monetary sector. The classification of certain deposit-taking institutions as 'banks' is based on authorisation under the Banking Act 1987 (see chapter 3). Within the UK monetary sector the institutions which correspond most closely to banks in the traditional sense are termed 'retail banks', i.e., banks which have an extensive branch network or which participate in the clearing system. Such banks are prepared to accept deposits in small amounts from a variety of business and personal customers. Retail banks are distinguished from 'wholesale banks', which deal with large commercial or industrial companies with large or bulk deposits.

An alternative nomenclature commonly used to distinguish between the various institutions included in the UK monetary sector is to describe them as 'primary banks' and other banks as 'secondary banks'. The main deposit-taking institutions classified as being outside the UK monetary sector are building societies.

Until recently there was some justification for classifying the building societies separately from other institutions such as banks, because of the specialised types of loans. Until very recently, the traditional function of the building societies was that of mortgage finance for the purchase of domestic housing, and their major source of funding was retail savings deposits. However, building societies have evolved their activities in a way which blurs the distinction between them and the traditional banks — a trend which has intensified since the changes in the legislation controlling their activities under the Building Societies Act 1986. A further extention in the activities of building societies will occur when the Building Societies Act 1997, which amends the powers given to building societies under the 1986 Act, comes into effect. This is likely to be at the end of 1997.

Apart from building societies, the other main deposit-taking institutions are the National Savings Bank (previously known as the Post Office Savings Bank), operated through post offices, and certain finance houses whose main business is the direct financing of instalment credit sales of motor vehicles and consumer durable products to individuals, and plant and machinery to businesses.

Investing institutions

Investing institutions are institutions which specialise in collecting funds from individuals, mostly on a longer-term basis, and investing the pooled funds in long-term securities or, sometimes directly, in property. In the UK investment institutions can further be divided into: (a) contractual savings institutions; and (b) portfolio institutions.

Contractual savings institutions obtain funds from personal savers under long-term contractual arrangements, whereby savers make regular contributions over a period of years in return for a terminal lump sum in the future, or in return for a future annuity. Long-term contractual savings in the UK are mainly made through savings schemes linked to life assurance policies and pension funds.

Portfolio institutions permit individuals to participate in pooled investment funds, which are used to acquire portfolios of marketable securities. Investing in this way can reduce investment risks by portfolio diversification. In the UK two major types of such institutions are unit trusts and investment trusts.

Specialised financing agencies

Specialised financing agencies are institutions created to fill gaps in financial markets with respect to the requirements of certain types of borrowers. Such institutions may be public-sector agencies financed by the government, or private-sector agencies set up with official support, raising funds from banks, other financial institutions or by directly issuing securities. Their common feature is the provision of finance in situations where the risk factor or the time period before there is a return on the investment is unacceptable to other providers of finance. The main areas where these providers have identified and exploited a gap is in the provision of equity finance and loan capital to small firms and the funding of new enterprises.

In an effort to remedy the lack of funds in the small-business sector two private-sector institutions were established. In 1945, at the request of the government, the Industrial and Commercial Finance Corporation (ICFC) was incorporated by the London and Scottish clearing banks and the Bank of England. The Finance Corporation for Industry was also established under the ownership of the Bank of England and a range of insurance companies and unit trusts. In 1973, a single holding company was established, Finance for Industry, which again was reorganised in 1983. The bulk of ICFC's finance for small firms consists of medium and short-term loan capital. Another example of a specialist financing institution is Equity Capital for Industry, which was established at the instigation of the Bank of England and a consortium of financial institutions. It aims to provide equity capital and a continuing involvement with the companies in which it invests.

The largest public-sector institution is the British Technology Group, formed in 1981, whose function is the exploitation of innovations. In addition finance is provided directly by the government for firms in certain regions under the terms of the Industry Act 1971 and through the Scottish and Welsh Development Agencies.

INSTITUTIONAL DIVERSIFICATION

Financial institutions have diversified both by extending the traditional lines of business they normally undertake and also by mergers and takeovers. Indeed, takeovers and mergers have not merely been on a national basis but on a global basis as the financial markets have expanded, an example is the merger of the Midland Bank Group with the giant Hongkong and Shanghai Bank. The history of the Midland Bank itself clearly shows the marked change in the nature of the banking business. In the mid 1950s the Midland Bank, the largest bank at the time, had five subsidiary companies. Two of the subsidiaries were banks in Scotland and Northern Ireland undertaking fairly traditional banking activities, while the remaining three were set up to undertake executor and trustee work for the bank's customers. Nowadays, all the major banks have diversified to such an extent that either directly or through subsidiaries they carry a vast range of activities. Since 1971, when certain controls on their activities were relaxed, they have further extended their activities on both the deposit and lending side; they compete with secondary banks for wholesale deposits in both sterling and foreign currency; and they now make short and long-term loans to businesses. Significantly, they also compete with building societies in the provision of loans to home purchasers. The building societies have retaliated by expanding their business in general deposit taking and other activities usually thought to be within the remit of the banking business. Banks are now engaged in a number of activities including hire-purchase finance, leasing, credit cards, accepting bills of exchange, unit trust and pension fund management, insurance, personal investment management, and arranging and underwriting new issues of shares on the capital market. More recently, following a relaxation of the membership rules of the Stock Exchange, banks have either set up companies or acquired existing Stock Exchange firms to undertake the function of broker-dealer in securities in the secondary market.

A similarly wide range of activities is undertaken by merchant banks, of which there are approximately 100 in the City. The majority are included as banks in the UK monetary sector. Among this group there are a number of banks which have for a long period been referred to as 'accepting houses'. The original function of these institutions was the accepting of bills of exchange for domestic and foreign borrowers. In the nineteenth century they extended their activities to include bond issues in London for foreign governments and later to arranging new issues of shares and debentures for domestic companies. In the 1960s they expanded into wholesale banking, both in foreign currency and sterling, and they now do considerable business in unit trust, pension fund and personal investment management. An important element of their work now involves financial advisory services to non-financial companies, e.g., handling large takeover bids.

INTERNATIONAL MARKETS

Advances in international communications and the automation of the financial sector have resulted in the collapse of international barriers to the operation of financial institutions. Internationalisation has been aided by the relaxation of exchange control and other regulations, and is shown by the number of financial institutions which have subsidiaries and branches in the UK, and the extent of the presence that UK institutions have abroad.

As global barriers have been removed there has been coordination of regulation on an international basis. The Basle Committee on Banking Supervision, established in 1975 and consisting of representatives from the central banks and supervisory authorities in the Group of Ten (G10) major industrialised countries, has aimed to establish principles for international cooperation between banking supervisors to cover banks operating in a number of countries. The Basle Concordat, published at the end of 1975, set out understandings about the division of supervisory responsibility for such banks. The Concordat was revised in 1983 to introduce the principle of consolidated supervision, under which a single supervisory authority takes responsibility for the overall supervision of all subsidiaries of a bank. Further principles for the exchange of information between supervisors were published in 1990 and 1992, setting out minimum standards for the supervisory responsibilities and powers of home and host country authorities.

A further initiative in 1987 by the Committee led to agreement on a common risk-weighted approach to the measurement of capital. The Basle Capital Accord, formally adopted in 1988, set out an agreed framework for capital measurement for internationally active banks and established a minimum 8 per cent for the ratio of bank capital to weighted-risk assets. EEC Directives correspond closely to the requirements of the Basle proposals and other international banks were expected to observe the ratio by the end of 1992.

The removal of barriers in the EU has allowed banks to move freely within the member States.

THE SINGLE EUROPEAN MARKET

The basic elements of a common market for financial services were contained in the Treaty of Rome, namely: the right to establishment (art. 52), the freedom to supply services across borders (art. 59), and the free movement of capital (art. 67). The financial services sector was slow in working towards a comprehensive common market and in 1985, the Cockfield Report (European Communities Commission, *Completing the Internal Market*, COM (85) 310 final, 14 June 1985) gave priority to the freeing of international capital movements.

The Cockfield Report outlined a new strategy in the establishment of the single market. The report rejected the proposition that a commitment to a common market in financial services could not be achieved until regulatory arrangements had been harmonised between members. This had delayed the evolution of a single market in financial services as national authorities sought to impose their own regulation on other member States. The Cockfield Report concluded that 'experience has shown that relying on a strategy based totally on harmonisation would be over-regulatory, would take a long time to implement, would be inflexible, and would stifle innovation'.

The new strategy proposed by Cockfield required a distinction to be drawn between what was essential to harmonise, and what was to be left to mutual recognition by national regulations. This strategy represented a completely new approach to achieving the single market in financial services and was based on three main features:

(a) There would be an agreed set of minimum harmonised regulations.

(b) Operating outside this set of minimum regulations there would be mutual recognition of the regulatory arrangements of other member States.

(c) Regulation would be based on home-country requirements.

It was recognised that it would no longer be necessary to harmonise all regulatory requirements. National authorities would be left to regulate other areas, but on the basis of mutual recognition of each member State's regulatory and supervisory systems.

The Cockfield Report was followed by the Single European Act 1986, which committed the European Community to the completion of an internal market in 'goods, persons, services and capital'. It was accepted that harmonising the laws of member States was not necessarily the best way to achieve this. Only essential matters would be harmonised, leaving others in the hands of national governments, but on the basis of mutual recognition. It was also agreed that regulation would be based on home-country requirements. In the banking sector, for example, common regulation relates to authorisation criteria, minimum capital requirements, the definition of own funds (equity capital), large exposure limits, deposit protection arrangements, control of major shareholdings in banks and recognition that sound accountancy and internal control mechanisms must exist.

The effect of the new approach is that if an institution is authorised in one member State, it is deemed to be similarly authorised in all other member States, with the result that an institution authorised in one State does not need separate authorisation when either locating in another member State or providing cross-border services.

The EC 'passport'

The idea of mutual recognition had been firmly accepted by the mid 1980s and creating a single market in financial services meant removing regulatory barriers to EC firms operating outside their country of origin. EC member States agreed to 'mutually recognise' (accept as adequate) the regulatory standards of other member States. Consequently, authorisation in one country in the Community would also constitute authorisation to conduct business in all Community member States. Thus, an EC firm authorised in one member State ('home State') and wishing to operate in other member States ('host States') can choose whether to supply services through branches or on a cross-border basis without having a physical presence in the host State.

The passport Directives in the different areas of financial services have a number of aspects in common.

Each passport Directive, or set of Directives, defines its scope in terms of type of institution and activities carried out. This is significant because the activities covered by a specific type of authorisation may vary from State to State.

The Directives require firms to be authorised and have established the conditions which must be satisfied for initial and continuing authorisation. These authorisation requirements generally relate to three main areas: the need for adequate management and controls (e.g., accounting procedures); minimum levels of capital a firm must have for initial and continuing support of its business; and the 'fitness' requirements of shareholders and controllers (including directors and managers) of the institution. The Directives emphasise the division of responsibility between home and host States. In general, the home State takes responsibility for the prudential supervision of a firm and all its branches and the 'fitness' of its controllers and major shareholders. The conduct of a firm's business with customers, however, is largely the responsibility of the authorities in the host State.

The Directives also address relations with third countries. The intention is to allow firms from third countries access to European markets on the same terms as European firms if similar access is permitted by third countries to European firms.

Freedom of capital movements

The full benefits of a common market in financial services cannot be achieved without freedom of capital movements. Capital controls impede the optimum distribution of savings and investments. Exchange controls limit the extent to which savers can invest in other countries and borrowers can finance their investment by gaining access to the savings of residents in other countries. Exchange control prevents consumers from taking advantage of more efficient services offered in other countries and cross-border trade in some financial services such as life assurance is affected. All member countries had various degrees of exchange control after 1945, and it was only during the 1960s that they began to dismantle these controls. The Commission's first Directive aiming at freeing capital movements within the EC was issued in May 1960, and its scope was widened by another Directive in December 1962. The fluctuations experienced by the currency markets during the 1970s and the wide-ranging repercussions of the increases in the price of oil led some member States to invoke art. 108 of the Treaty of Rome. This, together with arts 109 and 73, left open the possibility of using measures to safeguard and protect a country's external position. Consequentially, even the most liberalising requirements contained in these Directives did not have any practical impact. However, after 1989 there was a gradual easing of exchange controls in most EC member States and most had been eliminated by the end of 1989.

Free movement of capital did not become a reality between persons resident in member States until the Capital Liberalisation Directive (Council Directive for the Implementation of art. 67 of the EEC Treaty: Liberalisation of Capital Movements (OJ L178/5, 88/361/EEC 8.7.88, p. 5). Since 1 January 1994, however, the provisions which regulate the free movement of capital are arts 73b to 73g of the EC Treaty (inserted by the Treaty of European Union). Article 73b appears to guarantee free movement of capital and payments not merely between member States but also between member States and non-member States. However, the guarantee is qualified and art. 73d sets out the grounds on which member States can restrict free movement of capital between themselves. Article 73d(1)(b) provides that member States have the right to:

> . . . take all requisite measures to prevent infringements of national law and regulations, in particular in the field of taxation and the prudential supervision of financial institutions, or to lay down procedures for the declaration of capital movements for purposes of administrative or statistical information, or to take measures which are justified on grounds of public policy or public security.

This provision reiterates art. 4 of Directive 88/361/EEC (OJ 88/361/EEC, 8.7.88, p. 5) and adds public policy and public security as new grounds for restrictions on capital movements.

The art. 73d restrictions apply equally to movements of capital between member States and non-member States. In addition, art. 73c permits the retention of any national or Community law measures that existed on 31 December 1993 restricting the movement of capital to or from third countries 'involving direct investment (including investment in real estate), establishment, the provision of financial services or the admission of securities to capital markets'.

Banking

In general, barriers to the supply of cross-border banking have been more onerous than those related to location. However, since the acceptance of the Cockfield strategy several banking Directives have been adopted with the aim of creating a single European market in the banking sector. It is intended merely (at this stage) to outline the scope of the main EC Directives:

(a)   The First Banking Coordination Directive was adopted in 1977 (77/780/EEC, OJ L322, 17.12.77, p. 30). This applied to 'credit institutions' (banks and building societies) and required all of them to be authorised. In the UK, the Directive was given effect by means of the Banking Act 1979 (repealed by the Banking Act 1987). Authorisation by the host State of branches of credit institutions from other member States was made compulsory.

(b)   The second major step towards a single market came in 1989, with the adoption of the Second Banking Coordination Directive (89/646/EEC, OJ L386, 30.12.89, p. 1). This was given effect in the UK on 1 January 1993, together with the Own Funds Directive and the Solvency Ratio Directive (see (c) and (d) below). The Second Banking Directive provided for a passport for Community credit institutions. The scope of the Directive includes deposit-taking, lending, and money transmission services.

(c)   The Directive on Own Funds (89/299/EEC, OJ L124, 5.5.89, p. 16) establishes EC-wide definitions of capital for prudential supervision and follows closely the Basle Convergence Agreement on Capital Standards. The Own Funds Directive applies to all credit institutions as defined in the First Banking Directive.

(d)   The Solvency Ratio Directive (89/647/EEC, OJ L386, 30.12.89, p. 14) establishes a framework of activities, setting a minimum ratio of 8 per cent for own funds to weighted-risk assets. The Directive must be read together with the Own Funds Directive. The purpose of the Solvency Ratio Directive is to ensure that every credit institution authorised under the Second Banking Directive has sufficient and sound capitalisation to withstand losses caused by risks inherent to banking.

(e)   The Directive on the Supervision of Credit Institutions on a Consolidated Basis (92/30/EEC, OJ L110, 28.4.92, p. 52) requires the consolidated supervision of the financial condition of a credit institution. Consolidated supervision means considering the financial data of the whole group in monitoring compliance with supervisory standards.

(f)   The Directive on the Monitoring and Control of Large Exposures of Credit Institutions (92/121/EEC, OJ L29, 5.2.93, p. 1) was implemented in January 1994. At the same time the Bank of England undertook a review of its policy on large exposures. The Bank requires each UK authorised institution to set out its policy on large exposures.

(g)   The Directive on the Annual Accounts and Consolidated Accounts of Banks and Other Financial Institutions (86/635/EEC, OJ L372, 31.12.86, p. 1) enables borrowers, creditors, shareholders and the public to compare annual and consolidated accounts by requiring Community-wide harmonisation of accounting standards.

Other Directives have been adopted and will be discussed later (see p. 70).

Insurance

In contrast to the banking and securities sector, and with the exception of reinsurance, the insurance industry in the EC (with the exception of the UK) has been relatively protected from outside competition and has not seen any general globalisation. Indeed, member States have imposed a multitude of restrictions on insurance services provided through branches or agencies and on services provided across borders. In many EC countries there are legally imposed constraints on taking out insurance policies with a foreign insurer. Several countries retain strict systems of prior host-country authorisation and control over foreign insurance companies, and their soliciting of business, and many require a foreign insurance company to establish a branch before offering services. Most EC countries require life insurance companies to set up permanent subsidiaries in order to conduct business with host-country residents and some member States require approval for, or prohibit, insurance policies in foreign countries. In general the UK is the only member State in which foreign life insurance companies are allowed to compete freely, that is, without being required to establish a subsidiary, as well as without being subject to any restriction on the currency in which the contract is denominated.

The EC arrangements in the insurance sector are complex but some progress has been made. The Freedom of Services Directive for Non-Life Insurance adopted in 1988 (Second Directive on the Coordination of Laws, Regulations, and Administrative Provisions Relating to Direct Insurance other than Life Assurance, 88/357/ EEC, OJ L172, 4.7.88, p. 1) gives non-life insurers licensed to write insurance business in any EC member State the right to offer 'large risks', including all marine, aviation and transport risks, and 'mass risks' including small commercial risks and personal insurance. For large risks the home-country principle was applied, whereas for mass risks the rules of the country in which the policyholder resides applied. Similarly, the principle of the Second Life Directive of 1988 (Second Council Directive on the Laws, Regulations and Administrative Provisions Relating to Direct Insurance other than Life Insurance and Laying Down Provisions to Facilitate the Effective Exercise of Freedom to Supply Services, OJ L12, 4 July 1988) enabled a customer to purchase at his own initiative life assurance on a cross-border basis, but the customer had to accept the degree of protection and supervision prevailing in the insurer's home country; in other words the home-country principle would apply in such unsolicited cross-border trade. If, however, a policy were concluded outside the country of residence at the initiative of the insurance company, the provisions applicable would be those of the country where the risk was situated. The Second Directive remains largely in force, but from a practical point of view the provisions have substantially been overtaken by the third pair of Directives.

In July 1992, the Council of Ministers adopted the Third Non-Life Insurance Directive (92/49/EEC, OJ L228/1, 11.8.92, p. 1) (Directive on the Coordination of Laws, Regulations and Administrative Provisions Relating to Direct Insurance other than Life Assurance) and the Third Life Directive (Directive on the Coordination of Laws, Regulations and Administrative Provisions Relating to Direct Life Assurance (92/96/EEC, OJ L360, 9.12.92, p. 1)). These take freedom of services to its conclusion by introducing the single European licence. An insurer authorised in any member State will automatically be allowed to sell most types of non-life insurance anywhere in the Community, either through a branch or agency in the host State, or by direct selling in the host State. The home State will control all its activities and its solvency. In the UK these Directives were implemented by the Insurance Companies (Third Insurance Directives) Regulations 1994 (SI 1994/1696).

Investment services

Investment services cover a heterogeneous area of finance and includes securities trading, unit trusts, securities broking, portfolio management, underwriting and investment advice. The category also includes issues related to the access of companies to foreign stock exchanges and the quotation of securities on foreign stock exchanges. In this area, in particular, arrangements for completing the internal market are closely related to the issue of freedom of capital movements within the EC.

The EC made initial efforts to harmonise the different regulations of the member States on the admission of securities to stock-exchange listing and to harmonise the information to be provided to investors. In 1972, in a proposal for a first Directive in this area the Commission stated that the omissions and differences in the information provided to the public regarding securities constituted a barrier to capital movements between member States. Since 1979 the Council of Ministers has adopted a series of Directives in this area, the first being the Directive Coordinating the Conditions for the Admission of Securities to Official Stock Exchange Listing (79/279/EEC, OJ L66, 16.3.79, p. 21). The Directive set out conditions to be met by those issuing securities, including minimum issue price, a company's period of existence, free negotiability, sufficient distribution, and the provision of appropriate information for investors. Member States were, however, free to impose stricter requirements. Additionally, in 1980, a Directive on Coordinating Requirements for Drawing Up, Scrutiny and Distribution of Listing Particulars to be Published for the Admission of Securities to Official Stock Exchange Listing (80/390/EEC, OJ L100, 17.4.80, p. 1) was adopted. The Directive laid down the many items of information to be published when shares, debt securities and certificates representing shares were admitted to stock-exchange listing, dealing with the content, checking and publication of listing particulars prior to the official quotation of securities on an EC stock exchange. This was followed, in 1982, by a Directive on Information to be Published on a Regular Basis by Companies the Shares of which have been Admitted to Official Stock Exchange Listing (82/121/EEC, OJ L48, 20.2.82, p. 26). The Directive required quoted companies to make available on a half-yearly basis sufficient information to enable the public to evaluate the financial position of the company and the general progress of business.

A similar strategy has been applied to the marketing of unit trusts and investment funds based on mutual recognition, minimum harmonisation, and control by the country of registration or origin. A 1985 Coordination Directive provided for home-country authorisation of unit trusts (Council Directive on the Coordination of Laws, Regulations and Administrative Provisions Relating to Undertakings for Collective Investment in Transferable Securities (UCITS) (85/611/EEC, OJ L375, 31.12.85 p. 3)), so that any unit trust authorised by a member country may operate throughout the Community, but must comply with any relevant laws and regulations in force in the host country, even if these do not apply in the home country. A major consumer protection provision was that the management company of a unit trust must act 'solely in the interest of the unit holders'. This was followed by a Council Recommendation of 1985 (85/612/EEC, OJ 1985 L375; 31.12.85, p. 19) which sought to extend the scope of the 85/611 Directive.

The new strategy was also applied to earlier Directives on listing requirements. Directive 87/345/EEC (OJ L185, 4.7.87, p. 81) amended earlier Directives on listing particulars to ensure compliance with the earlier Directives, and to ensure that if approved in one member State, listing particulars would automatically be recognised on the stock exchanges of other member States without the need for additional approval.

In 1989 a Directive was issued coordinating the requirements for the drawing up, scrutiny and distribution of prospectuses to be published when transferable securities are offered to the public (89/298/EEC, OJ L124, 5.5.89, p. 8).

The Investment Services Directive (93/22/EEC, OJ 1993/L141/27, 11.6.93, p. 23) provided for the removal of barriers to both the provision of cross-border services and the establishment of branches throughout the Community, based on the principles of harmonisation of essential standards, mutual recognition and home-country control. Investment firms would be able to establish branches throughout the Community without obtaining prior authorisation from the host country for each branch. Once an investment services firm had been authorised in its home country, it would be able to operate throughout the EC. In order to ensure that these branches were able to compete effectively in the host country, the Directive also provided for liberalisation of rules governing access to stock exchanges, financial futures and option exchanges.

In 1993, the Commission adopted a Directive (93/22/EEC, OJ 1993, L141/1, 15.3.93) on the capital adequacy of investment firms aimed at establishing minimum amounts of initial capital and defining a common framework for supervising market risks.

The Investment Services Directive (93/22/EEC, OJ 1993/L141/27, 11.6.93, p. 27) also provided for liberalisation of access to stock-exchange membership in countries throughout the Community for investment firms authorised in their home member States. Price Waterhouse (European Communities Commission, *Research on the 'Cost of Non-Europe', Basic Findings, vol. 9, The Cost of Non-Europe in Financial Services* (Luxembourg: Office for Official Publications of the European Communities, 1988) suggested that the major problem in establishing a presence in a foreign securities market would appear to be regulations preventing foreigners being licensed as brokers. A host State is required to ensure that an investment firm that is authorised to provide brokerage, dealing, or market-making services in its home State may enjoy the full range of trading privileges normally reserved to members of the stock exchanges and organised securities markets of the host country. To meet this obligation the host State is required to ensure that such an investment firm has the option to become a member of the host country's stock exchange or organised securities markets by setting up branches or subsidiaries in the host State or by the acquisition of an existing member firm.

DEVELOPMENT OF THE BUILDING SOCIETY SECTOR

Building societies, like banks, are deposit-taking institutions. They are distinguish-able from banks in that their purpose and powers are defined by statute. Building societies began in the eighteenth century, as people moved from the country to the towns during the industrial revolution. Initially, they were 'terminating' societies: a group of perhaps 10 or 20 people contributed regularly until they had saved enough to buy land and start building. Members would draw lots to decide who was housed first. Payments continued until all the members were housed and the society then terminated. In the nineteenth century, there emerged societies which paid interest to attract investors who did not want a house, and permanent societies which did not cease to exist when all members were housed, but continued to borrow money from savers to lend to prospective house owners.

Building Societies were first recognised by statute in 1836, when provision was made for the application of the friendly societies legislation to them. In 1874, following the report of the Royal Commission on Friendly Societies, a separate legal framework was established for them. This defined the purpose for which a building society could be established as that 'of raising by the subscriptions of the members a stock or fund for making advances to members out of the funds of the society upon security of freehold, copyhold, or leasehold estate, by way of mortgage' (Building Societies Act 1874, s. 13). The effect of this statutory definition of their purpose with the powers permitted them by legislation was to confine societies to a narrow range of relatively low-risk activities, i.e., making advances on the security of mortgage, raising funds from which advances could be made and activities ancillary to these purposes. Subsequent amendments to the legislation resulted in still further restrictions on the activities building societies were allowed to undertake. The Building Societies Act 1960, for example, was enacted following the exposure of malpractice at the State Building Society. This was one of a number of rogue building societies which presented themselves to potential investors as normal building societies but which used the money invested with them to finance property transactions not considered within the normal range of building society lending (see E. J. Cleary, *The Building Society Movement* (London: Elek, 1965)). The 1960 Act, therefore, limited the amounts societies could lend to companies and the amount they could lend in any single loan.

Building societies continued to be governed by the narrow definition of their purpose under the 1874 Act. It was not until the Building Societies Act 1986 that the powers of the societies were redefined and their legal framework recast. The 1986 Act was passed largely in response to the increased competitive pressures to which the building societies found themselves exposed, in particular in what was traditionally their markets, i.e., the markets for housing finance and personal savings. Faced with increased competition from the banks and National Savings, the Building Societies Association argued that its members were prevented from responding to the pressures by offering a full range of financial services. It therefore sought freedom for its members to compete on more equal terms with other providers of financial services (Building Societies Association, *New Legislation for Building Societies*, 1984).

The Building Societies Act 1986 loosened the restrictions the building societies had been subject to and empowered them to hold new forms of assets and to provide new types of services. The Act did not, however, remove all restrictions. In its response to the Building Societies Association, the government agreed that societies should be allowed to diversify their business but insisted that their primary function should continue to be that of specialists in housing finance and personal savings (*Building Societies: A New Framework* (Cmnd 9316, 1984), p. 1). The Act therefore made it a condition of the establishment of a building society that its primary purpose must continue to be that 'of raising, primarily by the subscriptions of the members, a stock or fund for making to them advances secured on land for their residential use'.

No sooner had the Building Societies Act 1986 come into force than criticisms of the narrowness of the terms in which the powers to provide new services were expressed and a comprehensive review was undertaken. This review led to a further increase in the range of services that societies were allowed to provide so that a society may now, subject to certain limitations, provide banking, investment, insurance, trusteeship, executorship and land services (Building Societies (Commercial Assets and Services) Order 1988 (SI 1988/1141); amended by the Building Societies (Provision of Services) Order 1989 (SI 1989/839)). It did not, however, result in any basic alteration to the primary purpose of a building society, i.e., to raise funds from individual members for lending to other members on the security of first mortgages on owner-occupied residential property. However, in order to preserve building societies and to stem the tide of conversion of such societies to banks, the Building Societies Act 1997 (which amended the 1986 Act) removed the remaining restrictions on the activities of building societies, provided they continued their mortgage lending business.

2 What is a Bank or Building Society?

RELATIONSHIP BETWEEN THE COMMON LAW AND THE BANKING ACT 1987

The Banking Act 1987 provides that all institutions which undertake a deposit-taking business are required to obtain authorisation. The wording of the Act is such that it applies not only to credit institutions as defined in the EC First Credit Institutions Directive (77/780/EEC) but also to institutions which finance any activity of their business, other than lending, to any material extent from deposits or from interest earned on deposits. The authorisation requirement is therefore wide and extends to institutions beyond those commonly described as banks.

The words 'bank' or 'banker' may bear different shades of meaning in different periods of history (*Bank of Chettinad Ltd of Colombo* v *Commissioner of Income Tax, Colombo* [1948] AC 378) but facilitating the transmission of money (either through the cheque account facility or other electronic means) must be an integral part of the banking business.

THE BANKING SECTOR

The UK banking industry is divided into a number of sectors, each of which has its own characteristics and can therefore be distinguished from others. At common law various attempts were made to give a definition of what is a 'bank', but the courts were largely concerned with treating as a bank an institution engaged in the banking business. Even now the law does not attempt to define the term 'bank', but establishes a number of characteristics which must be complied with if an institution is to be treated as carrying on a banking business. It is also interesting to note that many of the requirements imposed by the courts as characterising a bank or banker have been adopted by the Banking Act 1987. The early definition is still relevant for two reasons:

(a)   There exist several statutes which use one or more of the expressions 'bank', 'banker' or 'banking business' without any useful definition. Some of these statutes are examined below.

(b)   There exist a number of rights which are available to an institution by virtue of being a bank or banker, e.g., the banker's lien, and the banker's right to set off.

The importance of the common law definition has undoubtedly declined since the introduction of statutory regulations in the form of, originally, the Banking Act 1979, and now the Banking Act 1987. The Banking Act 1979 introduced a two-tier system comprising recognised banks and licensed deposit takers. Since then the Banking Act 1987, has superseded the 1979 Act with the introduction of a single system of authorisation of deposit-taking institutions. Consequently, a number of pre-1979 statutes, including the Bankers' Books Evidence Act 1879, the Agricultural Credits Act 1928 and the Solicitors Act 1974, were amended to provide that the expression 'bank' or 'banker' should include an institution authorised under the Banking Act 1987.

In addition to these pre-1979 statutes, there are a number of important statutes which avoid using the expression 'bank' and instead refer to institutions authorised under the Banking Act 1987, for example, the Companies Act 1985, the Insolvency Act 1986, the Building Societies Act 1986 and the Financial Services Act 1986. These statutes were originally enacted with references to recognised banks and authorised deposit-taking institutions under the Banking Act 1979, but were amended to refer to authorised institutions by the Banking Act 1987, sch. 6. This tendency towards clarity of expression is not universal and there still exist several statutes where the expression 'bank' or 'banker' is used without proper definition. In relation to these statutes the common law remains of paramount importance. They include a number of statutes regulating the liability of banks to their customers, for example:

(a)   The Bills of Exchange Act 1882, s. 2, provides that:

'Banker' includes a body of persons whether incorporated or not who carry on the business of banking.

(b)   The Cheques Act 1957, s. 6(1), is to be construed as one with the Bills of Exchange Act 1882.

COMMON LAW DEFINITION OF 'BANK' AND RELATED EXPRESSIONS

The common law did not attempt to define the term 'bank' but *United Dominions Trust Ltd* v *Kirkwood* [1966] 2 QB 431 established a number of characteristics of the business of banking. Lord Denning MR, in the Court of Appeal, accepted the view expressed by Paget (*Paget's Law of Banking*, 6th ed., p. 8), who said that bankers have three essential characteristics, namely:

(a)   the acceptance of money from and collection of cheques on behalf of customers and placing them to the credit of the customer;
(b)   honouring cheques presented or orders drawn on them by their customers;
(c)   they must keep current accounts or something of that nature in their books in which the credits and debits are entered.

The Court of Appeal held that banking need not be the only activity undertaken by a company to qualify it as a bank but it must be a substantial activity (*Re*

Shields' Estate [1901] 1 IR 172). However, in *Re Roe's Legal Charge* [1982] 2 Lloyd's Rep 370 at 381 the court emphasised that it was not concerned with the size of clearing activities of an alleged bank in comparison to the number of clearings of other recognised banks.

Where the usual characteristics associated with the banking business were not satisfied the court could take into account the commercial reputation enjoyed by the institution; if the institution was treated as a bank within the commercial community then the courts would recognise it as such. On that approach the evidence produced by UDT in *United Dominions Trust Ltd* v *Kirkwood* was sufficient to establish its status as a bank.

The words 'bona fide' carrying on of the business of banking were held in *United Dominions Trust Ltd* v *Kirkwood* to involve two requirements:

(a) the banking transactions must not be negligible in size when compared to the rest of the business;

(b) the transactions relied on must genuinely be banking transactions and not merely a disguise for other transactions of a different legal nature.

STRUCTURE AND FUNCTIONS OF BANKS

The United Kingdom banking system is not a symmetrical or logical structure; it has grown up gradually over the last 300 years and is constantly undergoing change. Although there is some overlap in the work of the different types of banks the structure allows for flexibility and change.

Bank of England

The Bank of England stands at the head of the banking system. Until 1946 the Bank existed as a corporation owned by private stockholders in whom was vested the power to appoint the governors and directors. Its rights and obligations were prescribed by charter and by a series of statutes. By the Bank of England Act 1946, the whole of the capital stock of the Bank of England was transferred to the Treasury against compensation in the form of government stock (see the Radcliffe Report, Committee on the Working of the Monetary System, *Report* (Cmnd 827, 1959), ch. 9). It has been a public corporation since the compulsory acquisition of its share capital by the Treasury. Constitutionally, the Bank is not a Department of State administered by a Minister, but it is a public corporation with the right to manage its internal affairs independently.

The Bank is administered by a Governor and Court of Directors presided over by the Governor. The Governor and the directors are appointed by the government. They act independently but in close consultation with the Chancellor of the Exchequer and the Treasury. The only legal power which the Treasury have over the actions of the Bank is to give it general or specific directions, in the public interest after consultation with the Governor; a power which has in fact never been exercised (Bank of England Act 1946, s. 4(1)). More recently, the Banking Act 1987 gives the Treasury powers to direct the Bank to object to applications for authorisation under the Act in respect of institutions whose country of origin does not have reciprocal facilities for UK-registered authorised institutions.

The functions of the Bank of England are numerous and traditionally summarised under a number of headings.

Bankers' bank   The holding of balances at the Bank serves as a convenient method for settling inter-bank indebtedness arising from payment transactions between customers of different banks or for payment to the Exchequer. The clearing mechanism works in essentially the same way today as when it was formally instigated in 1773, except that much of it is now computerised. At the end of clearing each bank has a net position with every other bank, and this has to be settled by the transfer of bankers' balances at the Bank of England. However, not all the institutions in the UK monetary sector maintain deposits at the Bank as a means of effecting inter-bank settlements; secondary banks maintain balances for this purpose with the clearing banks.

It is through its role as the bankers' bank that the Bank performs its function as the central note-issuing authority in England and Wales. Its notes and coins are legal tender (and must be accepted in payment of debts) and its £1 notes are also legal tender in Scotland and Northern Ireland (Bank Currency Act 1844, ss. 10–16; Currency and Bank Notes Act 1954, s. 1(2)). This is now an administrative rather than a policy-making role. An increase in the demand for cash from the general p iblic (through increased withdrawals from banks) is reflected in a decrease in the stock of notes held in the tills of the banks. In order to meet the increase in demand and to replenish their stock of notes the banks will then make drawings, in the form of notes, from their deposits at the Bank of England. The stock of notes held as a reserve in the Banking Department will decline. If the Banking Department wishes to replenish its own reserves of notes, a change in the fiduciary issue has to be authorised and the Issue Department will then provide more notes to the Banking Department. The Banking Department then 'pays' for the additional notes by transferring securities of equivalent value to the Issue Department providing it with additional assets to match the increase in its liabilities. The total volume of bank note issue is determined by the Treasury; part of the note issue is backed by gold, coin and bullion held by the Issue Department, but the greater part, known as the 'fiduciary issue', is covered by securities issued to the Bank by the Treasury on behalf of the government (Currency and Bank Notes Act 1954, s. 2).

The Issue Department is for accounting purposes a part of the central-government sector. The accounts and resources of the Issue Department are kept distinct from those of the Banking Department of the Bank of England, which operates in much the same way as a commercial bank.

Lender of last resort   The stability of the banking sector ultimately rests on the confidence reposed in it by the public and that, in part, derives from the ability of the banks to redeem bank deposits for notes and coins on demand. In response to a number of periodic crises, the Bank has evolved the role of supplying its notes freely to other banks to maintain the general convertibility of bank deposits. Since around 1870, the Bank has underpinned the stability of the system by acting as lender of last resort. The Bank will dictate the rate of interest payable on money so borrowed and the period for which the cash may be borrowed. As a matter of policy it always makes these terms 'penal' and it also defines the classes of bills which are acceptable for re-discount and the types of bonds which are eligible as collateral security for loans. The rate of interest payable on loans or re-discounts by the Discount Office is known as the base Rate, which may more strictly be defined as the minimum rate at which the Bank of England stands ready to lend at last resort.

Regulation of the banking sector   The fact that the Bank of England is willing to act as lender of last resort may lead to banks taking unreasonable risks. As a cost of relying on the ability of a lender of last resort to come to the aid of the banks, some prudential supervision and regulation of banks can be justified. The Bank's general powers of regulation were enshrined in the Banking Act 1946, which gave the Bank powers to give directions of a general character and to make recommendations. However, for a long period supervision was restricted to the large clearing banks and carried out on an informal basis. However, the experience of the secondary banking crisis (see chapter 3) and the need to comply with the requirements of the European Community resulted in steps being taken to strengthen the legal basis of the Bank's regulatory powers and these culminated in the Banking Act 1979, now the Banking Act 1987. Recently, in view of the growing internationalisation of banking, the Bank and other central banks have sought to harmonise their criteria for the assessment of banks and liquidity ratios (see chapter 5).

Banker to the government   The Bank of England has, from its inception, acted as the primary banker to the central government. The Exchequer, the central account of the government, is kept at the Bank of England, as are several other accounts. They all appear in the Bank's published accounts under the single heading, 'Public Deposits'. The services which the Bank performs from day to day are in essence like the services of any bank to a customer with a current account: the receipt of moneys due, transfers of payments out, advice and assistance to the customer on the conduct of the account, and occasional overnight assistance if the account goes temporarily 'in the red'.

The Bank of England also manages the borrowing from the market which is the residual method of financing the Exchequer. The Bank receives the tenders for each week's issue of Treasury bills, opens the tenders, issues and allots the bills, receives the subscriptions and credits them to the Exchequer. The Bank also manages new issues of government bonds and stock, whether for cash or conversion; it advises the government on the terms appropriate for an issue, publishes a prospectus, receives applications, issues and allots stocks or bonds and organises the 'underwriting' of the issue. The Bank keeps a register of stockholders and is responsible for the payment of dividends to stockholders on the due dates.

At the heart of its work as the central bank lies the Bank's open market operations in government debt, including both operations in Treasury bills in the course of management of the money market and operations in government bonds. The Bank of England operates almost daily in the money market by buying Treasury bills from the market (thus putting money into circulation) or selling Treasury bills to the market (thus taking cash in), to smooth out shortages and surpluses of funds, which mainly arise due to the uneven incidence of payments by and into the Exchequer. The purpose of these operations is to maintain an orderly market. The Exchequer needs the money market to take care of its cash requirements; but the amounts of cash that pass through the Exchequer and the banking system if left alone would create either shortfalls or excesses of cash in the market and wide fluctuations in the price of borrowing. It is in the government's interest, as the largest borrower in the money market, that the money market operates in an orderly manner; and that requires that the short-term rate of interest does not vary on a day-to-day basis.

Exchange Equalisation Account   The Bank manages, on behalf of the Treasury, the Exchange Equalisation Account, which does not form part of the Bank's own balance sheet. This account, originally established in 1932, is the official repository of the nation's gold and foreign currency reserves. The function of the account is to implement any chosen official policy with regard to the sterling exchange rate, i.e., to sell foreign currency for sterling whenever the volume of foreign currency demanded exceeds the supply at a chosen rate and vice versa.

The account was especially significant from 1945 to 1972 during the operation of the Bretton Woods system, under which governments were committed to maintaining the value of their currencies against the US dollar. It was also significant when the UK was a member of the exchange rate mechanism of the European monetary system.

Commercial banks

In evidence submitted by the Committee of London Clearing Bankers to the Committee established to Review the Functioning of the Financial Institutions (November 1977) it was submitted that the role of the clearing banks is primarily that of financial intermediation; that is, they channel funds from those who have them to those who need them. This is done through the extensive network of branches operated by the main clearing banks (Barclays, National Westminster, Lloyds and Midland; the Scottish banks also have a considerable presence throughout the country). It was also said that what distinguishes these banks from other banks is the extent to which this role is based on the provision of current account facilities and money transmission services. The transmission of payments is facilitated by the participation of these banks in the daily clearings. Non-clearing banks also provide current account facilities but these form a minor part of their business. By providing these money transmission services banks have not only provided much of the infrastructure on which the nation relies for the conduct of its financial transactions but they have ensured their facility to provide the lending and other services based on the ability to attract deposits.

There are four major payment clearings in the UK undertaken by the three companies working under the umbrella of APACS. The Cheque and Credit Clearing Company undertakes two daily clearings, i.e., one for cheques and one for paper credits. BACS (a single bulk electronic clearing) handles credit transfers, direct debits and standing orders. The CHAPS Clearing Company manages high-value same-day settlement clearing, i.e., the electronic CHAPS systems for credit transfers throughout the UK (the Town Clearing which handled paper debit instruments within the confines of the City of London was abandoned in February 1995). There is no common clearing for credit card, debit card or ATM transactions and payment obligations are settled by bilateral or card scheme arrangements. Many of the payments can be made from, and be directed to, anywhere in the country. If cheques are processed and physically presented to the paying bank, it can take up to four days for the payment process to be completed.

Commercial banks faced with competition, especially from the building societies, have diversified into a whole range of business activities not traditionally viewed as part of their business. Banks have extended their business into lending for house purchase and lending generally, executor and trusteeship, foreign exchange, short and medium-term borrowing for businesses etc. During the 1960s and 70s, the clearing banks bought up the main hire-purchase companies, and then broadened them into finance houses. Unit trust offshoots were similarly added, as well as insurance and credit card services. During the 80s the big clearing banks have extended their networks abroad and although there have been some disastrous loans to Third World countries, clearing banks have continued to extend their international business.

Banks have also tried to extend the banking habit in the 'unbanked' part of the population. This received a considerable boost when the inhibitions on non-cash wages payments were removed by the repeal (by the Wages Act 1986) of the Truck Acts 1831 to 1940, and paying wages into bank accounts was made cheaper by technology.

Merchant banks

Merchant banks provide the same services as commercial banks for a deliberately restricted range of customers (e.g., companies and other business customers for whom they provide other services). Their principal activities range from the finance of imports and exports and world trade generally by the acceptance of bills of exchange or otherwise, to arranging the issue or sale to the public of shares and other securities of companies and public authorities and to advising on takeovers of companies.

Although merchant banks act as intermediaries between the interested parties, they also take an extensive stake in commercial ventures themselves, either by medium or long-term loan or by subscribing or underwriting issues of securities. Many merchant banks engage in the whole range of merchant banking activities, but most specialise in a particular area of business, or undertake work originating from the part of the world with which the bank has historical connections.

The merchant banks which engage in the acceptance of bills of exchange are represented on the Accepting Houses Committee, and enjoy the privilege of knowing that bills accepted by them which are held by other banks or discount houses may be discounted at the Bank of England. These merchant banks specialise in the work of marketing securities issued by companies and public authorities, which are usually listed on the London Stock Exchange. Other merchant banks have extended their activities into Europe.

Overseas and foreign banks

London is one of the major centres for international banking and most of the world's major banks have a presence in the City. There are a number of organisations which represent these banks. Foreign banks which operate in their own name are entitled to full membership of the Foreign Banks Association. Some banks provide current account facilities to their customers but most of them furnish travel facilities and deal in foreign currency and securities. Most of them are also involved in Eurodollar transactions. Membership of the British Overseas and Commonwealth Banks Association is open to any bank in the UK although historically its membership has consisted of banks whose main business was in the Commonwealth countries and British protectorates.

Consortium banks are banks incorporated in the UK by foreign banks and, although distinct from the parent company, nevertheless reflect the interests of the parent company. Many of them carry out the functions associated with foreign banks; many are involved in the flotation of bonds and shares issued for the purposes of the countries to which they are affiliated.

The existence of so many banks and of associations representing them resulted in the need for an additional organisation that might be regarded as a coordinator. That function is performed by the British Bankers Association. The main objects of the Association are to provide facilities for the discussion of matters of interest to the British banks and to make representations on their behalf.

Trustee Savings Bank

The establishment of trustee savings banks was sanctioned by a series of Acts starting in 1817. Their initial object was to provide facilities for the savings of the working classes, who for a long time were unable to open bank accounts. The bank was restructured under the Trustee Savings Bank Act 1985, and the Act provided for a reorganisation of these banks as a group of companies under the umbrella of a holding company. This resulted in the Trustee Savings Bank of England and Wales, with similar banks in Scotland and Ireland. The Trustee Savings Bank is a member of the clearing house. The Trustee Savings Bank is authorised under the Banking Act 1987. More recently it was acquired by Lloyds Bank plc when further restructuring was undertaken.

National Girobank

The National Girobank was established by the Post Office Act 1969. The Act authorised the Post Office to provide such banking services as it thought fit and deemed it for 'all practical purposes to be a banker and to be carrying on the business of banking' in the exercise of its powers. The National Girobank was privatised at the end of the 1980s and became Girobank plc, which was acquired by the Alliance & Leicester Building Society. Girobank plc is now authorised by the Banking Act 1987 (see p. 27). The bank maintains branches through the Post Office. Initially, it offered its customers mainly the use of money transfers but these activities have now been broadened so that it now offers full current account facilities, deposit account facilities, overdrafts, personal loans and credit card facilities. Money can also be transferred overseas in many post offices through giro accounts.

BUILDING SOCIETIES

Unlike banks, there has never been a problem in defining a building society. A building society is a society incorporated under the Building Societies Act 1986, or under one of the predecessor Acts. A building society is a statutory corporation, whose powers derive entirely from the Building Societies Act 1986. Its corporate capacity is limited to what the legislation permits. However, a building society is not only empowered to undertake anything expressly permitted by the statute, but can also do that which is necessary or proper for carrying out the express purposes of the society, and anything which may be regarded as incidental or ancillary to powers which are expressly authorised.

A building society may be established if its purpose or primary purpose is that of raising, primarily by subscriptions from members, a fund for making to them advances secured on land for their residential use (Building Societies Act 1986, s. 5(1)). Members subscribe to a society by investing in its shares and interest is paid in accordance with the society's rules. Unlike a registered company with a share capital the share capital of a building society is subject to fluctuation, and a building society has no fixed amount of authorised share capital. A society may accept deposits or loans from members or non-members, to be applied for its purposes. Out of the funds so acquired advances may be made to members secured on land for their residential use. However, the funds may be used for other purposes and building societies are given powers, for example, (a) to make secured loans for the purchase of mobile homes; (b) to make loans, whether secured or unsecured, for other purposes; (c) to offer 'facility accounts', under which overdraft facilities may be provided, as well as credit or debit cards etc.

Building Societies Act 1986

The Building Societies Act 1986 represents the first comprehensive review of the legislative framework regulating the building society sector for over a century. Although the Act gives added scope for business to building societies, it also ensures that the building societies do not stray too far from their traditional areas of business. The problems faced by the Grays Building Society in 1978, and then by the New Cross Building Society, pointed to defects in the regulation of building societies. The 1986 Act therefore seeks to rationalise the control powers available against building societies. The Act is concerned with three main topics: trading powers, supervision and constitution of building societies. The Building Societies Act 1986 was amended by the Building Societies Act 1997 which removed many of the restrictions on the trading powers of such societies and gave the Building Societies Commission further powers (see p. 65).

Trading powers under the 1986 Act

The Building Societies Act 1962 was a consolidating statute and did not represent any significant appraisal of the role of the industry. Section 1(1) of the 1962 Act has been referred to as a 'statutory straitjacket', as it laid down the objects of a building society. This provision, basically, allowed a building society to raise a fund from the subscriptions of its members and to use this to make advances on the security of freehold or leasehold estate. Although the 1962 Act allowed a limited lending power it restricted advances to first charges only (except in very limited circumstances). However, even before the 1986 Act, building societies undertook a wider range of activities than merely taking money from savers to make advances on first mortgage. Ancillary powers were exercised where they related to the attainment of the main objects. For example, they acted as agents in respect of the insurance of the mortgage security or the life of the mortgagor but where the property was not in mortgage to the society or the life insured not a borrower, the position was different.

The straitjacket of the 1962 Act has been replaced by s. 5(1) of the Building Societies Act 1986 which provides that:

A society may be established under this Act if its purpose or principal purpose is that of raising, primarily by the subscriptions of the members, a stock or fund for making to them advances secured on land for their residential use.

The words 'principal purpose' have been taken to indicate that building societies are not wholly confined to their old trading activities. However, secondary powers are not limited to just those incidental to the main object and sch. 8 to the 1986 Act specifically lists areas of business which societies may undertake. The financial services within that list include: money transmission services; foreign exchange services; making or receiving payments as agents; management, as agents, of mortgage investments; provision of services relating to the acquisition or disposal of investments; arranging for the provision of credit; administration of pension schemes; and arranging for the provision of insurance of any description.

As a result of the 1986 Act, building societies have the power to offer a full money transmission service with chequebooks, cheque guarantee cards and overdraft facilities. Although not listed as a service, some of the larger building societies can offer unsecured loans and credit card facilities. The power to make unsecured loans is also important in that it enables building societies to help first-time homebuyers with the cost of furnishings, carpets etc. The power to make or receive payments as agents is extremely useful to societies, their customers and customers of other organisations. It means that building societies can accept payment for certain utility companies, e.g., gas, electricity etc.

Supervision of building societies

Building societies are regulated separately from banks. Building societies, unlike banks, are subject to two systems of control. One is the system of prudential supervision similar to that applied to banks, which, because of the diversification of societies into more risky kinds of business, is designed to ensure that they remain a safe place for investors' money. Hence, it was said that any move by societies into the provision of new services should not detract from their traditional security for investors (*Building Societies: A New Framework* (Cmnd 9316, 1984), para. 1.11). Although the prudential regime operated by the Registry of Friendly Societies had been strengthened prior to the 1986 Act, the Registry's powers were in some respects deficient. The Act, therefore, gave the Building Society Commission powers 'to complete the shift of the Registry's prudential system from a "reactive approach", with the supervisor only intervening when something had started to go wrong, to the more positive approach implicit in an authorisation system' (*Annual Report of the Building Societies Commission*, 1986–87, para. 2.8). The second system of control, which has no counterpart in relation to banks, is a system of 'nature limits' designed to preserve the distinctive character of building societies as member-based institutions, primarily engaged in raising funds from their members and lending them to other members for the purpose of owner-occupation. These limits have been described as the price which a building society must pay to retain its mutual status and the right to call itself a building society. An alternative to retaining mutual status is, subject to the agreement of members, for a building society to convert to the status of a deposit-taking business and to regulation by the Bank of England (the Alliance & Leicester, Northern Rock, the Woolwich and the Halifax will all convert from building societies to banks in 1997).

Building Societies Commission

Building societies are supervised by the Building Societies Commission, a body corporate established under the Building Societies Act 1986, s. 1(1). According to s. 1(4) of the Act the general functions of the Commission are (a) to promote the protection by each building society of the investments of its shareholders and depositors, (b) to promote the financial stability of building societies generally, (c) to secure that the principal purpose of building societies remains that of raising, primarily from their members, funds for making advances to members secured on land for residential purposes, (d) to administer the system of regulation of building societies provided for under the Act, and (e) to advise and make recommendations to the Treasury or other government departments on any matter relating to building societies. The Commission consists of not less than four and not more than 10 members appointed by the Treasury, one of whom is appointed to be the Chairman and another to be Deputy Chairman.

The expenses of the Commission are recovered from charges on building societies and fees payable in respect of the exercise of certain of its functions (s. 2). The Commission must keep proper accounting records and must prepare in respect of each accounting year a statement of accounts in the form the Treasury directs (s. 3(1)). The Commission must lay before the Treasury and Parliament an annual report of the discharge of its functions, including a record of the terms of every determination of the powers of a building society made by it during the year. The Commission may lay before Parliament such other reports relating to the discharge of its functions as it thinks fit.

The Building Societies Commission has wide powers to enforce the limitations of the Building Societies Act 1986 on the powers of the building societies. The Commission's powers include: (a) powers in relation to asset and liability structure requirements; (b) powers to determine the extent of building society powers; (c) powers in relation to authorisation; (d) powers to control advertising; and (e) powers to obtain information.

Functions of the central office

The central office (i.e., the central office of the Registry of Friendly Societies) retains certain powers and duties with respect to building societies under the Building Societies Act 1986. The central office retains functions relating to: (a) registering memoranda (s. 5) and rules (sch. 2) of societies; (b) registering amalgamations, transfers of engagements and dissolutions (ss. 93, 94, 97); (c) registering recognised schemes for the investigation of complaints (s. 83); and (d) maintaining the public records of societies (s. 106). The central office must prepare and maintain a file relating to each building society, known as the public file, which must contain copies of any documents and records of any matter directed by or under any provision of the Act to be kept in the public file of the society and must be available for inspection on reasonable notice by members of the public.

The Chief Registrar of Friendly Societies may give directions about the form of and particulars to be contained in any document to be issued by or sent to the central office.

Amendments to the Building Societies Act 1986

The Building Societies Act 1986 prevents building societies from offering a range of financial services that other competitor institutions, e.g., banks, can offer. The Act, therefore, unfairly restricts the mutual sector. In order to stem the number of mutuals converting to banks the Building Societies Act 1997 will give greater commercial freedom to societies to offer a wider range of services to their customers. The 1997 Act provides that a society can carry on any business set down in its memorandum, subject to keeping within the nature limits. However, the primary purpose of building societies will still continue to be that of making loans which are 'secured on residential property . . .' (Building Societies Act 1997, s. 1(1)). The powers of the Building Societies Commission are also strengthened (see p. 65).

PART 2

3 Regulation of the Banking Sector

NEED FOR CONTROL

The business of banking has been, and will always be, a precarious one. Often due to no fault of its own, a bank will find itself caught up in events which adversely affect its business, but over which it has no control. The bank's business may be overtaken by national or international events, or merely by questionable management. There have been many bank failures, including some very recently. Indeed the Bank of England in 1696, merely two years after its foundation, was facing a financial crisis due to the war in Flanders (J. Giuseppi, *The Bank of England: A History from its Foundation in 1694* (Evans Publishers)). Again some 20 years later a shortage of funds resulted in a widening of the Bank's borrowing powers (Bank of England Act 1716). Probably, the most well remembered recent crises were the Wall Street crash in 1929 and the depression of 1929 to 1933 which led to the collapse of many banks. More recently, the depression in 1973–6 and the collapse of the property market led to the 'secondary banking' crisis when many fringe banking institutions collapsed, and some medium and larger banks faced financial strain. To prevent a general loss of trust in the financial sector the Bank of England and the major retail banks launched the 'lifeboat' operation which successfully bailed out a number of institutions which were facing difficulties (see 'The secondary banking crisis and the Bank of England's support operation', *Bank of England Quarterly Bulletin*, June 1978, p. 230 at 233; M. Reid, *The Secondary Banking Crisis 1973–75* (London: 1983)). The secondary banking crisis was triggered by the collapse of London and County Securities Ltd in November 1973, as a result of investing short-term deposits in long-term transactions and the consequent, and unexpected, failure of the short-term deposits not being renewed. This led to a liquidity problem for the institution and because of the disastrous effect of a collapse of a bank on the economy generally the Bank of England launched a rescue of several institutions (the Bank of England had experienced such crises with the Overend Gurney crash of 1866, the Baring crisis of 1890 and the prolonged international crisis of 1929–33). Whilst the Bank of England was involved in a crisis at home, similar bank crises were occurring in Europe. In Germany, the Bankhaus Herstatt was facing considerable problems and a similar rescue operation was launched. Even where the banking and financial sector is not generally facing a crisis, the collapse of one bank can have international ramifications. The closure of the Bank of Credit and Commerce International had global repercussions for both individual and business customers. More recently, the collapse of Barings Bank led to a further reconsideration of bank regulation (Bank of England, *The Board of Banking Supervision's Report on Barings: The Post-Barings Recommendations – a Report*, Press Notice, S.S.D, 11 January 1996).

The possible loss of customer confidence, the trend towards the regulation of the financial sector and other external factors, the most important being UK membership of the European Community, have resulted in an increased regulation of the banking sector.

REGULATORY FUNCTION OF THE BANK OF ENGLAND

The task of supervising the banking sector has traditionally been in the hands of the Bank of England. The idea of giving the Bank supervisory powers was first mooted in the nineteenth century. Prior to that the Bank had indirect control of the banking system by its ability to influence interest rates and through its established function of lender of last resort (W. Bagehot, *Lombard Street* (London: 1873)). The Bank's role as the venue for the settlement of the daily balances between the trading banks also became entrenched in the nineteenth century and contributed towards the already considerable influence it exercised over the clearing banks.

Although the Bank of England had considerable informal powers over the clearing banks and has acted at many times in its history to counter an impending banking crisis, it was only under the Bank of England Act 1946 that it was given a statutory supervisory function. Section 4(3) of the Act provided that:

> The Bank, if they think it necessary in the public interest, may request information from and make recommendations to bankers, and may, if so authorised by the Treasury, issue directions to any banker for the purpose of securing that effect is given to any such request or recommendation:
>   Provided that:—
>   (a)   no such request or recommendations shall be made with respect to the affairs of any particular customer of a banker; and
>   (b)   before authorising the issue of any such directions the Treasury shall give the banker concerned, or such person as appears to them to represent him, an opportunity of making representations with respect thereto.

Under s. 4(4) of the Act, a direction could be issued by means of a secret document.

By 1976 the dangers of a banking sector which thrived on the informal means of supervision available to the Bank of England and Treasury were apparent. The memory of the secondary banking crisis and the first Banking Directive issued by the Council of Ministers led to the government producing a White Paper entitled *The Licensing and Supervision of Deposit-Taking Institutions* (Cmnd 6584, 1976). The Banking Act 1979 enacted the changes set out in the White Paper, and, giving effect to the First Banking Directive (77/780/EEC), a system of control was introduced whereby all credit institutions were required to be licensed by the Bank of England. The Act, however, did not introduce a single uniform system of authorisation. It divided deposit-taking institutions into four groups, namely: (a) the Bank of England; (b) recognised banks; (c) licensed institutions; and (d) institutions listed in sch. 1 to the Act. The sch. 1 institutions were exempt from the regulatory provisions of the Act and included central banks of EC member States and institutions regulated under other statutory provisions, such as building societies. Additionally, certain types of transactions were exempted from the scope of the Banking Act 1979. The Act also introduced the Deposit Protection Scheme and generally considerably increased the regulatory powers of the Bank of England. However, the collapse of the Johnson Matthey Bank in October 1984 and the subsequent investigation of what went wrong at the bank exposed major deficiencies in the system of UK banking supervision. The Banking Act 1987 (repealing the 1979 Act) was intended to remedy the serious defects highlighted by the Johnson Matthey affair.

Banking Act 1987

The Banking Act 1987 in form closely follows the scheme of supervision laid down in the 1979 Act and the prime motive remains the same, namely, to protect depositors. The authorisation criteria remain the same as under the 1979 Act but certain aspects of the regulatory provisions are reinforced and spelled out in greater detail. Significantly, the flexible nature of supervision is maintained by the new Act, which does not purport to regulate every aspect of prudential supervision.

Duties of the Bank of England as a general supervisor

The position of the Bank of England as the general supervisor and regulator of deposit-taking institutions has been strengthened and more clearly defined under the Banking Act 1987. In addition to the powers of authorisation conferred on the Bank, it has two other main duties, namely:

(a)   to supervise the institutions authorised by it (Banking Act 1987, s. 1(1)); and
(b)   to keep under review the operation of the Act and developments in the field of banking which appear, to the bank, to be relevant to the exercise of its powers and functions (s. 1(2)).

The Act imposes, for the first time, an express duty on the Bank to supervise authorised institutions. The additional duty on the Bank to keep under review developments in the banking sector is an admission of the rapid and increasingly sophisticated developments taking place in the banking sector and the Bank must have regard to these developments in the discharge of its duties. The government White Paper published prior to the Act (*Banking Supervision* (Cmnd 9695, 1985)) placed considerable emphasis on the flexible nature of the UK banking system and the requirement on the Bank of England to have regard to the changing nature and structure of the banking sector.

The Bank of England is under a legal duty to report annually to the Chancellor of the Exchequer on the exercise of its functions under the Act (s. 1(3)) and the Chancellor is required to lay copies of the report before Parliament. The first such report was published in May 1988 and contains, amongst other matters, details of operational supervision under the Act and information on the organisation and staffing of the Banking Supervision Division. The report must contain a statement of any material change in the principles that the Bank will apply in interpreting the criteria in sch. 3 to the Act.

Section 1(4) of the Banking Act 1987 follows the Financial Services Act 1986, s. 187, in giving the Bank and its staff protection from suit for liability in damages arising from anything done in the discharge of the Bank's functions under the Act. The immunity also extends to cover acts or omissions by members of the Board of Banking Supervision but it will not extend to any acts or omissions done in bad faith. However, although auditors play a greater role in the supervisory process, they are not immune from action for their conduct acting as the Bank's agent.

The question whether a supervisory body owes a depositor a duty of care in the exercise of its regulatory functions has been considered by the courts. In *Yuen Kun Yeu* v *Attorney-General of Hong Kong* [1988] AC 175 the Privy Council concluded that since the Commissioner of Banking (the supervisory body in Hong Kong) had no power to control the day-to-day activities of the deposit-taking institution whose liquidation had caused loss to the plaintiff, the Commissioner owed no duty of care since there were not such close and direct relations between the Commissioner and the plaintiff as to give rise to a duty of care. It was also alleged on behalf of the plaintiff that registration of the deposit-taking institution amounted to a seal of approval, and by allowing that registration to stand, the Commissioner made a statement about the continuing creditworthiness of that institution. The Privy Council held that the Hong Kong Banking Ordinance placed a duty on the Commissioner to supervise deposit-taking institutions in the general public interest, but there was no assumption of any special duty of care towards individual members of the public.

Yuen Kun Yeu v *Attorney-General of Hong Kong* was reviewed by Saville J in *Minories Finance Ltd* v *Arthur Young* [1989] 2 All ER 105, which arose out of the collapse of Johnson Matthey Bank (JMB). Saville J held that the Bank of England was under no duty to exercise reasonable skill and care in exercising its supervisory function in order to prevent losses which arose as a result of imprudent or careless management of JMB. The learned judge said that the principles of common sense did not indicate that this obligation existed and therefore there was no cause of action against the Bank. The action by JMB's parent company was based on the proposition that it was a depositor and the Bank owed a duty to depositors to exercise reasonable care and skill in its supervision of banks such as JMB. The Bank, relying on *Yuen Kun Yeu* v *Attorney-General of Hong Kong*, argued that it did not owe a duty of care to depositors in the UK. Saville J accepted that the decision in the *Yuen Kun Yeu* case presented strong evidence in favour of the Bank's submission, but not so strong as to dismiss the action as unsustainable. The two cases involved two independent and separate supervisory bodies operating under different legislation. Under the Banking Act 1979 (the case was decided under the 1979 Act, although issues relating to the definition of the term 'deposit' are still relevant under the 1987 Act), it could not be argued that the Bank owed a duty of care to the parent company as depositor, because s. 1(5)(d) of the 1979 Act excludes from the definition of deposit any sum paid by one company to another at a time when one is a subsidiary of the other or both are subsidiaries of another company. The statutory prohibition on accepting deposits in the course of a deposit-taking business without authorisation could not apply to money deposited by the parent company. Consequently, the Bank did not owe a duty of care to persons making deposits if they did not fall within the ambit of the Banking Act.

In *Three Rivers District Council* v *Bank of England (No. 3)* [1996] 3 All ER 558 the court held that a plaintiff has a sufficient interest to maintain an action of misfeasance where it was established that the defendant was a public officer who intended to injure him and who knew he had no power to do what he did and that the plaintiff would probably suffer loss, and the plaintiff did suffer a loss resulting from the wrongful act. This case should be distinguished from earlier cases. In *Three Rivers* the plaintiff's claim was for misfeasance or positive wrongful conduct, not a failure to act or to act with due care as in *Yuen Kun Yeu*.

Board of Banking Supervision

An important innovation under the Banking Act 1987 is the establishment of an advisory committee to the Bank known as the Board of Banking Supervision. The Board was in fact created in May 1986 and the Act merely gave it statutory force (s. 2(1)). The government White Paper gave consideration to separating the supervisory authority from the Bank but concluded that any advantages outweighed the major upheaval involved. A compromise was thus proposed in the form of a new Board of Banking Supervision.

The Board consists of three ex officio members, namely, the Governor of the Bank, who is the Chairman of the Board, the Deputy Governor of the Bank and the Executive Director of the Bank, and six independent members appointed jointly by the Chancellor of the Exchequer and the Governor of the Bank. The White Paper envisaged the independent members would comprise senior bankers, either recently retired or with no executive duties, and members of the legal and accountancy professions. The Act imposes a statutory duty on the independent members to advise the ex officio members on the exercise by the Bank of its supervisory functions and any matters arising from the exercise of such a function. The White Paper sets out some of the areas on which advice will be provided:

(a) broad issues involving the supervision of institutions authorised under the Act;
(b) the development and evolution of supervisory practice;
(c) the administration of the new Act;
(d) the structure, staffing and training of the Banking Supervision Division.

In addition, any member of the Board may raise any matter of concern in the field of banking supervision and discuss with and provide advice to the Governor of the Bank on such matters.

In order to enable the independent members to discharge their statutory duty, the Bank must make regular reports to the Board with such information as the Board may reasonably require (s. 3(4)). The ex officio members are not bound to follow the advice of the independent members of the Board but they must give notice to the Chancellor of the Exchequer whenever it is decided that the advice of the independent members shall not be followed. The independent members then have a right to notify the Chancellor of their reasons for the advice (s. 2(5)). The Board is required to prepare an annual report of its activities to be published together with the report prepared by the Bank (s. 1(3)). Members of the Board are given immunity from liability for any acts or omissions unless such conduct is affected by bad faith.

REGULATION OF DEPOSIT-TAKING

The main focus of the Banking Act 1987 is the regulation of deposit-taking institutions in the UK and consequently the general prohibition on the acceptance of deposits, and the definitions of 'deposit' and 'deposit-taking' business are fundamental to the new legislation.

Restriction on the acceptance of deposits

Section 3 is fundamental to the Banking Act 1987, because the system of banking supervision derives from the need of deposit-taking institutions to obtain authorisation. This is achieved by placing an absolute prohibition on the acceptance of deposits unless authorised by the Bank of England. The section abolishes the distinction between recognised banks and deposit-taking institutions introduced by the Banking Act 1979. Instead, the Banking Act 1987 introduces a single supervisory regime and a single set of criteria for authorisation, though some vestige of the two-tier system is retained, e.g., only an institution with a paid-up equity capital of at least £5 million will be permitted to use a name indicating that it is a bank or banker or is carrying on a banking business (s. 67).

Meaning of deposit

The term 'deposit' is defined by the Banking Act 1987, s. 5, which virtually repeats the wording used in the Banking Act 1979. Almost any form of borrowing from the general public is a 'deposit' for the purposes of the Act. Indeed, this has been considered necessary 'in order to prevent deposit-takers disguising their activities by dressing up their deposit-taking in such a way as to take it outside the scope of the controls' (see Morison, Tillett and Welch, *Banking Act 1979*). A deposit is defined in s. 5(1) as:

a sum of money paid on terms—
(a) under which it will be repaid, with or without interest or a premium, and either on demand or at a time or in circumstances agreed by or on behalf of the person making the payment and the person receiving it; and
(b) which are not referable to the provision of property or services or the giving of security.

The exclusion of certain types of payments from the definition of deposit is qualified by s. 5(2)(a), which provides that a payment will be referable to the provision of property or services or the giving of security if the money is paid under a contract for the sale, hire or other provision of property or services and will be repayable only if the property or services are not provided. The provision re-enacts s. 1(6)(a) of the 1979 Act with altered wording, which places beyond doubt that a sum of money will be excluded from the definition of 'deposit' only if there is a contract for the sale of specific goods or services. The Bank interprets

s. 5(2)(a) as referring to advance or part payment for a specific item of property or service. In the view of the Bank (*Banking Supervision Guide*, p. 1–1), s. 5(2)(a) does not exclude from the definition of a deposit credit balances maintained by customers in a budget account where the balances are held for the credit of the customer for the purchase of unspecified goods or services in the future.

Section 5(2)(b) provides that a payment will be referable to the provision of property or services and, therefore, not a deposit, if the money is paid by way of security for the performance of a contract or services supplied or to be supplied. This covers the sort of advance 'deposit' required by gas suppliers or British Telecom, before services are provided. Section 5(2)(c) deals with a situation where a sum is paid as security for the safe return of property, e.g., caution money required by 'landlords'. In *SCF Finance Co. Ltd* v *Masri (No. 2)* [1987] QB 1002 the court had to decide whether moneys paid to the plaintiff in connection with dealings in commodity futures undertaken by the plaintiffs amounted to a deposit for the purposes of the Banking Act 1979. The court concluded that the sum paid out by the defendant was 'paid by way of security for payment for the provision of property or services' and was therefore not a deposit under the 1979 Act.

Section 5(3) excludes from the scope of the Act certain other payments which might otherwise come within the definition. These exclusions cover:

(a)   A sum paid by the Bank of England or an authorised institution (i.e., a loan made by an authorised person or authorised institution in the course of a business or into an account kept by it with another person, whether or not authorised);

(b)   Any sum paid by a person specified in sch. 2 to the Act. The schedule covers a wide range of institutions which, for a number of reasons, are considered as unnecessary to bring within the regulatory powers of the Bank of England. The schedule includes four categories of institutions namely:

(i)   those which are considered to be adequately regulated under other legislative provisions, e.g., building societies, friendly societies, authorised insurance companies and credit unions;

(ii)   those which could be described as part of the public sector, e.g., National Savings Bank, local authorities, municipal banks and Crown Agents;

(iii)   those which are relatively small and which do not pose a risk to the public, e.g., penny savings banks and school banks; and

(iv)   those which could be described as international or supranational bodies, including the European Atomic Energy Community, the International Monetary Fund, and the International Finance Corporation.

The schedule also excludes the EC central banks, but not the central banks of non-EC countries. This is in accordance with the First Banking Coordination Directive.

(c)   Any sum paid by a person (not falling within (a) or (b)) in the course of carrying on a business consisting wholly or mainly of lending money. The exemption would cover, for example, a payment by an overseas bank which is not authorised under the Act (*Banking Supervision Guide*, p. 1–2).

(d)   Any sums paid by one company to another at a time when one is a subsidiary of the other or both are subsidiaries of another company, or the same individual is a majority or principal shareholder controller of both of them. This exception was discussed by the court in *Minories Finance Ltd* v *Arthur Young* [1989] 2 All ER 105 where it was held that the Bank of England owed no duty of care to the depositor where that depositor is a parent company and the banking business is carried on by a subsidiary.

(e)   Where the sum is paid by a person who, at the time of payment, is a close relative of the person receiving it, or was a close relative of a director, controller or manager of that person. Section 5(5) defines a 'close relative' of a person as meaning that person's spouse, children, stepchildren, parents, step-parents, brothers, sisters, stepbrothers, stepsisters and the spouse of any of these children. Relatives such as cousins, nieces and nephews do not count within the definition and therefore any moneys accepted from them would be classed as 'deposits' for the purposes of the Act if the funds are accepted on terms which fall within s. 5(1) of the Act.

'. . . in the course of carrying on a business'

The restriction on deposit-taking as defined in s. 3(1) applies only if the deposit is accepted in the course of carrying on a business. The Act gives no definition of the words 'in the course of carrying on a business', although the courts have examined the word 'business' in several cases. In *Town Investments Ltd* v *Department of Environment* [1978] AC 359 it was said that the word business 'suits its meaning to the context in which it is found'. In *Rolls* v *Miller* (1884) 27 ChD 71 the dictionary definitions were found to be far too wide-ranging to be of any significant use, and the court said 'the word means almost anything which is an occupation, as distinct from a pleasure — anything which is an occupation or duty which requires attention is business'. In *Graham* v *Lewis* (1888) 22 QBD 1 the court was of the view that carrying on a business is a narrower concept than merely occupying oneself with a business; it implies carrying on a regular business undertaking. What is therefore necessary is that the deposits are accepted in the ordinary course of the banking business. In *Premor Ltd* v *Shaw Brothers* [1964] 1 WLR 978 at p. 983 Lord Denning MR suggested that for something to be 'in the course of' a business requires the transaction must be connected with transactions forming part of the business or designed to promote the business.

The court will undoubtedly look at the facts of the case and the purpose for which the definition is required and decide what is reasonable in the circumstances, having regard to the intentions of Parliament, i.e., in the case of the Banking Act 1987 the intention must be to protect the interests of the depositors against loss arising from a poorly regulated banking sector.

'. . . whether there or elsewhere'

The Act applies to the carrying on of a deposit-taking business anywhere in the world provided that the deposit is accepted in the UK. The wide scope of the Act is reinforced in s. 6(3) which provides:

For the purposes of subsection (1) above all the activities which a person carries on by way of business shall be regarded as a single business carried on by him.

The effect of s. 6(3) is that an institution can qualify as a deposit-taking business by virtue of its activities outside the UK and the Bank of England will consider the worldwide activities of such a business in order to determine whether the business falls within the remit of the Bank's supervisory function.

'. . . a deposit-taking business'

Whilst the Act restricts the circumstances in which a person may accept a 'deposit', it does not per se make unlawful the carrying on of a deposit-taking business. Section 6(1) provides that a business is a deposit-taking business if, in 'the course of the business money received by way of deposit is lent to others', or where 'any other activity of the business is financed, wholly or to any material extent, out of the capital of or the interest on money received by way of deposit'.

Section 6(1) recognises the traditionally held view at common law that a person who deals with other people's money to make a profit is carrying on the business of banking (a 'deposit-taking business' under the Act). The *Banking Supervision Guide* (p. 1–2) also points out that the wording of s. 6(1) is such that the provisions of the Act do not apply merely to credit institutions which finance any activity of their business (other than lending) from deposits or from interests earned on deposits. The prohibition on deposit-taking goes beyond institutions commonly regarded as banks. It extends to any institution which takes deposits and uses them to finance lending or other related activity.

With regard to the words 'any material extent' in s. 6(1)(b), the Bank has indicated that it will have regard to the absolute value of the sums involved in the financing of any activity of the business, and to the proportion of the total financing of the activity provided by the sums in question (*Banking Supervision Guide* pp. 1–3).

A business does not, however, fall within the definition of deposit-taking 'if the person carrying it on does not hold himself out as accepting deposits on a day-to-day basis' (s. 6(2)(a)) and if deposits are accepted on particular occasions only, whether or not they involve the issue of debentures or other securities (s. 6(2)(b). Given the broad definition of deposit it is likely that many institutions will seek to rely on these exceptions in order to keep outside the scope of the Act. To fall within the exemption of the Act both the requirements must be satisfied. An institution which holds itself out to accept deposits on a 'day-to-day' basis would be caught under the Act even if in fact it only accepted deposits on 'particular occasions', as would an institution which, despite not holding itself out to accept deposits on a 'day-to-day' basis, accepted deposits more frequently than on 'particular occasions'. Section 6(4) provides that in determining whether deposits are accepted only on 'particular occasions' regard may be had to the frequency of those occasions and to any distinguishing characteristics (compare the statutory requirements with requirements laid down in *United Dominions Trust Ltd v Kirkwood* [1966] 2 QB 431). *SCF Finance Co. Ltd v Masri (No. 2)* [1987] QB 1002 examined the words now contained in s. 6(2)(a) (originally s. 1(2) of the 1979 Act) and held that on the ordinary meaning of the words, a person holds himself out to accept deposits on a day-to-day basis only if (by way of an express or implicit invitation) he holds himself out as being generally willing on any normal working day to accept such deposits from those persons to whom the invitation is addressed who may wish to place moneys with him by way of deposit. Section 6(4) of the Act allows the court to look at the frequency of the 'occasional deposits' and to any characteristics distinguishing them from each other.

Exempted persons and transactions

The restriction on the acceptance of deposits under the Banking Act 1987, s. 3, is subject to s. 4 of the Act, which exempts certain persons, institutions and transactions from the need to obtain authorisation. Under s. 4 the Treasury is empowered, after consultation with the Bank of England, to amend the list of exemptions in sch. 2. The exemption from authorisation by the Bank of England extends to credit institutions authorised by the State authorities of the European Union, EU central banks, certain other international bodies, e.g., the IMF etc. Additionally, the section enables regulations to be made by the Treasury exempting certain transactions from the s. 3 prohibition. The Treasury made the Banking Act 1987 (Exempt Transactions) Regulations 1988 (SI 1988/646), which came into force on 29 April 1988. The list of exempt transactions in these Regulations includes: charities; church deposit funds; industrial and provident societies; agricultural, forestry and fisheries associations; retail and other cooperative societies; solicitors; deposits accepted in the course of estate agency work; certain public undertakings; the National Children's Charities Fund; sterling debt securities; sterling commercial paper; and authorised and exempted persons under the Financial Services Act 1986.

Not all types of deposits which may be accepted by the persons or bodies mentioned in the list are necessarily exempted and there are a number of requirements which have to be satisfied before a transaction can achieve the status of an 'exempt' transaction. The Regulations should be consulted for the details.

AUTHORISATION

Application for authorisation

The Bank of England, as the institution responsible for supervision, is responsible for handling all applications for authorisation under the Banking Act 1987. The statutory procedure for the grant, refusal, restriction or revocation of authorisation is contained in ss. 8 to 14 of the 1987 Act. Section 8 provides the formal mechanism for the applicant to achieve authorisation and requires the application to be in such manner as directed by the Bank. In addition, the application must be accompanied by:

(a)   a statement setting out the nature and scale of the deposit-taking business which the applicant intends to carry on, any plans of the applicant for future development of that business and the particulars of the applicant's arrangements for management of the business; and

(b)   such other information or documents as the Bank may reasonably require for the purpose of determining the application.

The other information which may be required will be such as will enable the Bank to assess the risks arising from the operations of other companies in the group

(*Banking Supervision Guide*, p. 11–6). Further, under s. 8(5) of the Act, the Bank may require the applicant (or a controller) to provide a report from an accountant (or other expert) on any specific aspect of the information so provided.

The Bank may, at any time after receiving an application, require by written notice further information or documents from the applicant (or controller) before determining whether or not to grant the application. The maximum penalty for knowingly or recklessly furnishing any information in connection with an authorisation application which is false or misleading in a material particular, is imprisonment for a term of up to two years or a fine (s. 94(2) and (5)).

Statutory criteria for authorisation

The Bank of England must not grant authorisation unless it is satisfied that the minimum criteria laid down in sch. 3 are fulfilled. However, the Bank may (subject to the right of appeal) refuse authorisation even if the applicant has satisfied the minimum requirements in sch. 3. The importance with which the Bank views its discretion to refuse authorisation was emphasised in its *Statement of Principles* (1988) published in accordance with s. 16 of the Act. In that statement, the Bank stressed that, notwithstanding compliance with the sch. 3 requirements, it may still refuse authorisation if it considers for any reason that there are 'any significant threats to the interests of depositors and potential depositors'. Other factors which will influence the discretion of the Bank in the exercise of its power to refuse authorisation will be its ability to monitor the institution in connection with the sch. 3 requirements after authorisation, and its ability to assess any risks or threats to the interests of depositors.

The Bank's interpretation of the schedule 3 criteria

The sch. 3 criteria (which closely follow those found in the Banking Act 1979, with the exception of the minimum net assets requirements) have regard to quality, rather than quantity or type of activity. The Bank monitors their fulfilment as part of its regular supervisory functions. The minimum requirements imposed in sch. 3 are discussed in the following paragraphs.

Directors etc. to be fit and proper persons Paragraph 1(2) of sch. 3 to the Act provides that every person who is, or is to be, a director, controller or manager (s. 105) of an authorised bank must be a fit and proper person to hold the particular position which he holds or intends to hold. With regard to a person who is a director, executive controller or manager of the institution the Bank will have consideration, amongst other things, to the individual's probity and whether he has sufficient skills, knowledge, competence, soundness of judgment and experience to undertake and fulfil his particular duties and responsibilities properly. The diligence with which he is fulfilling or the time he is likely to devote towards fulfilling his responsibilities will also be taken into consideration. Additionally, the Bank may have regard to a person's reputation and character, including such matters as whether he has a criminal record, including certain spent convictions. Any convictions for fraud or other dishonesty or violence are relevant; any convictions with regard to contravention of any banking, insurance, investment or other financial services legislation designed to protect members of the public from financial loss due to dishonesty, incompetence or malpractice will be especially relevant. The Bank will also have regard to the person's record of non-compliance with various non-statutory codes, e.g., the Takeover Code.

Once an institution has been authorised the Bank will continue to monitor the individuals concerned with the management of the institution with regard to the 'fit and proper' requirement. In this respect the Bank will look for an understanding of the institution's business, and future development and for evidence of sound judgment with regard to commercial and administrative matters in connection with the business.

In respect of shareholder controllers, the Bank will take into account their business interests, their financial soundness and strength, and in the case of bodies corporate, the nature and scope of their business. The Bank will have regard to the influence of the shareholder on the authorised institution and in particular to any threat which holding the position may have to the interests of depositors or of potential depositors. For example, a financially weak shareholder controller would not be a fit and proper person if his financial condition was likely to undermine confidence in the authorised institution.

The Bank will also make enquiries of outside sources about the person concerned and it may consult other regulatory authorities.

Business must be directed by two persons   Paragraph 2 of sch. 3 provides that at least two individuals must effectively direct the business of an authorised institution; commonly referred to as the 'four eyes' principle. It will, therefore, not be sufficient for the business to be carved up so that one person deals with certain specific aspects of the business only. These provisions are intended to ensure that at least two minds are directed to the formulation and implementation of the policy of the institution. Both persons 'must demonstrate the qualities and application necessary to influence strategy, day-to-day policies and their implementation' (Bank's *Statement of Principles*, para. 2). In addition both persons must have sufficient experience and knowledge of the business and the necessary authority to detect and resist any imprudence, dishonesty or other irregularities in the institution. Paragraph 2 requires that such persons must 'effectively direct' the business and that has been interpreted by the Bank to mean that executive authority must be vested in at least two individuals. They need not be on the board provided they report directly to it.

Composition of board of directors   In the case of a UK authorised institution, the directors must include such number (if any) of directors without executive responsibility for the management of its business as the Bank considers appropriate, having regard to the circumstances of the business and the nature and scale of its operations. The Bank attaches considerable importance to the role of non-executive directors, placing some importance on their ability to bring an 'outsider's independent perspective to the running of the business and in questioning the approach of the directors' (*Statement of Principles*, sch. 3, para. 3). The Bank considers that non-executive directors have an important role as members of an institution's audit committee.

Business to be conducted in a prudent manner   Paragraph 4(1) of sch. 3 requires that an authorised institution must conduct, or in the case of one which is not yet authorised, will conduct, its business in a prudent manner. Whilst the Bank will have regard to other factors, it reviews all applications for authorisation with this paragraph in mind. The prudent manner criterion is the one which in the Bank's judgment is most relevant to the interests of depositors. It is also relevant in determining whether directors, controllers and managers are fit and proper persons to hold their respective positions. Subparagraphs (2) to (8) specify a number of conditions which are to be taken into account in deciding whether a particular institution is conducting its business in a fit and proper manner. However, these requirements are not exhaustive and other matters may be considered, such as the institution's management arrangement, the institution's general strategy and objectives, planning arrangements, policies on lending and other exposure, and bad debt and taxation provisions.

It is required by para. 4(2) and (3) that an authorised institution maintain a level of capital commensurate with the nature and scale of its operations, and sufficient to safeguard the interests of its depositors and potential depositors. In deciding whether adequate net assets are maintained the nature and scale of the institution's operations, the risks inherent in those operations, and any other business taken by the group of companies, in so far as they may affect the deposit-taking institution, are taken into consideration.

In assessing capital adequacy, the Bank will take into account all risks of loss to which the institution may be exposed, including credit risks, foreign exchange risks, interest rate and position risks, operational risks, and contagion risks arising from subsidiaries and other associated companies. Therefore, the minimum net asset requirement of £1 million, will operate as a minimum guide to the Bank. In assessing the institution's risk potential the Bank will take into account management expertise, experience and record, its internal controls and accounting procedures and its size and position in the market.

An institution will not be regarded as conducting its business in a prudent manner unless it maintains adequate liquidity. Each institution will be assessed in the light of its own particular circumstances, including potential liquidity problems which could arise because of its connection with other companies. The Bank will take into account factors similar to those relating to capital adequacy in order to judge the issue of adequate liquidity.

Paragraph 4(6) requires the institution to make adequate provision for the depreciation or diminution of the value of its assets. The Bank, therefore, expects an institution to make provision for liabilities which are or will be expected to be discharged and for any losses which it will or expects to incur. In examining the institution's provision for depreciation etc., the Bank will look at the institution's internal system for monitoring the recoverability of loans, the frequency with which provisions are reviewed, and the institution's policy in valuing security.

The Bank also requires 'adequate records and control systems for sound banking practice' and prudential returns made to the Bank should be complete, accurate and timely. The Bank must therefore be satisfied that these requirements are likely to be fulfilled by the applicant should authorisation be granted. The Act gives no guidance on what is meant by 'adequate records'. The *Statement of Principles* indicates that an individual institution's needs and circumstances will be taken into account, but the records and systems in question must be sufficient to protect the interests of depositors and potential depositors.

Business must be conducted with integrity and skill   Paragraph 5 requires the business of the institution to be conducted with such integrity and professional skill as is appropriate to the nature and scale of its activities. Again the Act gives no indication of the meaning of these terms but the *Statement of Principles* emphasises that the Bank considers integrity and skill as distinct elements. The first requirement refers to the ethical standards of business, which could be called into question, e.g., contravention of statutory provisions designed to protect the public against dishonest conduct, incompetence and malpractice. The Bank will judge these indiscretions against the criteria set out in sch. 3, together with the interests of depositors and potential depositors.

Minimum net assets   The minimum net asset requirement of £1 million sterling for all institutions applies at the time of authorisation. The Treasury may, after consultation with the Bank, by order vary the minimum net asset requirement. In addition, s. 67 restricts the use of a name which indicates the institution is a bank, banker or carrying on banking services to institutions with a minimum paid-up capital (or equivalent) of £5 million.

Applications by overseas institutions

Section 9(3) of the Banking Act 1987 provides that where an applicant for authorisation has its principal place of business in a country outside the UK, the Bank of England must satisfy itself that the requirements of paragraphs 2, 3 and 6 of sch. 3 are satisfied. For paras 1, 4 and 5, the Bank must rely on information provided by the national supervisory authority in the country in which the applicant has its principal place of business, provided the Bank is satisfied with the nature and scope of the supervision exercised by that authority. The *Banking Supervision Guide* indicates that the Bank will make such enquiries of the overseas supervisory authority as it considers necessary (pp. 11–18). There is no requirement for the applicant to supply references from the home supervisor, although it should consult the home supervisor before making a formal approach to the Bank. If the Bank is not satisfied with the level and adequacy of supervision by any authority in the applicant's principal place of business, the difficulties the Bank has in satisfying itself with respect to the management and overall financial soundness of the applicant institution will be increased.

It is essential that the Bank be satisfied about the respectability and adequate supervision of the overseas applicant as a branch is an integral part of an overseas institution to which it belongs, and authorisation granted by the Bank will extend to the whole institution. Therefore, a separate authority is not required for the overseas institution to extend its business by opening other branches.

The Bank's informal requirements

In addition to the statutory requirements which have to be satisfied when an application is made under the Banking Act 1987, the Bank of England will expect an applicant to be introduced to it by a well-known bank or professional adviser. A series of discussions may take place to clarify the applicant's business plans and a detailed feasibility study of the institution's business may be required by the Bank.

Granting of authorisation

If the Bank decides to grant authorisation, it will notify the institution in writing of that decision, and authorisation will take effect from notification (s. 10(1)). An announcement of the Bank's decision to grant authorisation will also be published simultaneously in the *London Gazette*, or in the *Edinburgh Gazette* or *Belfast Gazette* in the case of institutions from Scotland or Northern Ireland.

Refusal of an application

Where the Bank proposes to refuse an application for authorisation, it is required by s. 10(2) to give the applicant notice in writing of its intention to refuse, together with notice of the grounds on which it proposes to refuse, authorisation. The Bank must also give the applicant details of its right to make written representations to the Bank, and where such representations are made, the Bank must take them into consideration before reaching a decision on the application. Where the ground for the Bank's refusal to grant authorisation is that sch. 3, para. 1 (fit and proper person requirement) is not satisfied in relation to any person, the Bank must also give notice of its intention to refuse an authorisation to that person, together with reasons for the refusal and that person's right to make representations under s. 10(4).

Revocation and restriction of authorisation

In order to protect the interests of depositors and potential depositors, and to enable the Bank of England to carry on its continuous supervisory function, the Bank is given powers by the Banking Act 1987, ss. 11 and 12 to revoke or restrict authorisation. The Act sets out guidelines identifying when the Bank may revoke authorisation, and specific instances where it must do so. In addition, the Bank has published its own interpretation of the guidelines.

The statutory grounds for revocation contained in the 1987 Act broadly follow those established in the Banking Act 1979 with the addition of two new provisions in s. 11(1)(c) (where a person becomes a controller etc. in contravention of s. 21 or has become or remains a controller despite being served with a notice of objection under ss. 22–4), and s. 11(4) (where it appears that the institution has ceased to be an 'authorised institution' under the Financial Services Act 1986 or has had its consumer credit licence revoked under the Consumer Credit Act 1974).

Many of the grounds for revocation reflect the requirements of the First EEC Banking Directive. However, the circumstances in which authorisation can be revoked go further than the Directive since they include a 'catch-all' provision in s. 11(1)(e) which allows the Bank to revoke authorisation where the interests of the depositors or potential depositors are 'in any other way threatened, whether by the manner in which the institution is conducting or proposes to conduct its affairs or for any other reason'.

Where an authorised institution has its principal place of business in a country outside the UK, the Bank may revoke its authorisation (and it must do so if that country is an EC member State) if it appears to the Bank that the home supervisory authority has withdrawn deposit-taking authorisation for that institution.

The making of a winding-up order against an authorised institution requires the Bank to revoke its authorisation (s. 11(6)), but the Bank has a discretion whether or not to withdraw authorisation in other events akin to insolvency, namely: when a composition or arrangement is entered into by the creditors of the institution; when a receiver or manager is appointed over the institution's undertaking; or possession is taken, pursuant to a debenture, over any property of the institution (s. 11(7)). Section 11(8) gives the Bank a discretionary power to revoke authorisation where it appears that an administration order has been made in relation to the institution.

Restriction of authorisation   Section 12 of the Act provides that the Bank has further discretionary powers enabling it to impose restrictions on an authorised institution where it appears to the Bank:

(a)   that there are grounds on which the Bank's power to revoke an institution's authorisation are exercisable; but

(b)   that the circumstances are not such as to justify revocation.

An authorisation may be restricted by imposing such limits on its duration as the Bank thinks fit, or by imposing such conditions as the Bank thinks desirable for protecting the institution's depositors or potential depositors, or by imposing both such restrictions. A restriction on the duration of an authorisation cannot allow the authorisation to continue for more than three years from the imposition of the restriction. The Bank is also empowered to vary or withdraw any condition imposed on an authorised institution, and to vary any limit on the duration of an authorisation. Where revocation of an institution's authorisation is mandatory under s. 11 or where the Bank considers the imposition or variation of a restriction on an institution's authorisation a matter of urgency (s. 14(1)), it need not give the notice required under s. 13 of its intention to revoke, vary or impose a restriction or authorisation.

The Bank's interpretation of its power of revocation and restriction of authorisation   In the *Statement of Principles*, published by the Bank of England in May 1988, the Bank issued guidelines on how it would interpret its powers of revocation and restriction of authorisation under the Act. Whether or not grounds for revocation or restriction exist will depend on the Bank's judgment of the institution's circumstances and whether or not the relevant provisions of the Act apply to the circumstances in question. The Bank takes the view that its powers become exercisable whenever there is a threat to the interests of depositors, or potential depositors, and may be exercised even though the Bank is of the opinion that the threat is only slight or remote. However, the severity of the action taken by the Bank and any restrictions it imposes on the institution will vary with its perception of the gravity of the threats. The *Statement of Principles* indicates that the Bank perceives that its powers to revoke or restrict an authorisation are sufficient to enable it to intervene before the deterioration of the institution's condition is such that there is a threat of loss resulting to depositors. Where it considers that the institution itself will take sufficient remedial action to avert loss and to protect its depositors, the Bank will generally be reluctant to restrict or revoke authorisation. Where the bank takes the view that remedial action by the institution concerned will result in the authorisation requirements being fulfilled, the Bank may restrict revocation; such a restriction normally being without time limit.

Notice of revocation or restriction Where the Bank proposes to restrict, revoke or vary the restrictions on an authorisation, it must give written notice to the institution concerned of its intentions. The notice must include full details of the proposed restrictions together with grounds upon which the Bank proposes to act, and the institution's right to make representations to the Bank within 14 days beginning with the day on which the notice is given. However, the Bank need not give this notice where it considers the revocation to be mandatory, or where the Bank considers the imposition or variation of restriction to be a matter of urgency. Section 15 provides that an authorised institution may surrender its authorisation by giving written notice to the Bank. The surrender of the authorisation will take effect from the giving of notice, or from any later date specified in the notice.

Directions in order to safeguard assets

The Bank is empowered to issue directions to an institution with a view to safeguarding that institution's assets, when the Bank intends to give notice of its intention to revoke or restrict authorisation. The Bank may also give directions for any of the reasons specified under s. 19. The Act imposes few constraints on the Bank's freedom to decide what directions to give an institution, except that they must be such as 'appear to the Bank to be desirable in the interests of the institution's depositors or potential depositors, whether for the purpose of safeguarding its assets or otherwise' (s. 19(2)). The Bank may in particular require an institution to take certain steps, or to refrain from adopting or pursuing a certain course of action, or to restrict the scope of its business in a specific way. The Bank may impose limitations on the acceptance of deposits, the granting of credit or the making of investments by the institution. It can also prohibit the institution from soliciting deposits, either generally or from persons who are not already depositors, or from entering into any other transaction or class of transactions, or require the removal of any director, controller or manager.

ENFORCEMENT

Offences

If, on an application by the Bank of England, the High Court (or the Court of Session in Scotland) is satisfied that an institution or any other person has accepted deposits contrary to s. 3 of the Act, the court may order that the institution or other person who appears 'knowingly' to have committed a breach of that section, shall repay the deposits immediately or within such time as the court may direct

(s. 48(1)(a)). Alternatively, the court may appoint a receiver of the assets of the institution or of the person to recover those assets.

Profits from unauthorised deposits

Where the High Court (or the Court of Session in Scotland) is satisfied that profits have accrued to any person as a result of his accepting deposits in breach of s. 3, the court may order him to pay any such amounts into court and appoint a receiver to recover from him such sums as appear just, having regard to the profits which appear to have accrued to him. In deciding the terms on which to make the order the court may have regard to the effect that payment in accordance with the order would have on the solvency of the person concerned or his ability to carry on his business in a manner satisfactory to his creditors. The court may require any person, against whom an order is made under this provision, to provide it with such accounts or other information as may be necessary to determine whether any, and if so what, profits have accrued to him and to determine how any such amounts should be distributed. Any amount paid into court or recovered from a person in respect of illegitimate profits will be paid out to such persons or distributed amongst such persons as appear to the court to have made deposits from which the profits have accrued or to such other person or persons as the court thinks fit.

Supervisory information and statistics

In order to fulfil its supervisory function the Bank requires a flow of accurate and up-to-date information and statistics. The government White Paper, *Banking Supervision* (Cmnd 9695), ch. 9, proposed a tightening of the Bank's powers and procedures to ensure that all returns used for supervisory purposes are submitted promptly and contain accurate information. Consequently, the Banking Act 1987 contains a number of new provisions which enable the Bank to request information and documents from authorised institutions, and various connected parties, supported, if necessary, by an accountant's report. The Act also empowers the Bank to appoint investigators to assess the state, conduct, ownership and control of authorised institutions.

Power to obtain specific information

Under the Banking Act 1987, s. 39(3), the Bank of England may require an authorised institution to produce specified documents, and the Bank may copy such documents (s. 39(5)). It may also require the institution and its staff (past or present) to comment upon any of the documents produced (s. 39(5)). If the required documents are not forthcoming, the Bank can compel the person who was required to produce them to state, to the best of his knowledge and belief, what has happened to them (s. 39(5)). Even where the documents are held by a third party, the Bank has the power to require their production unless they are covered by legal professional privilege (s. 39(4) and (13)). The Act includes a definition of documents which is sufficiently wide to encompass computer or other electronic records, since it includes information 'recorded in any form' (s. 106(1)). Where necessary the Bank may request a printout of these records (s. 106(1)). Where an authorised institution does not comply with s. 39 by failing to provide the required information, the Bank may exercise a right of entry to obtain the information or documents required (s. 40).

Power to appoint investigators

The Banking Act 1987, s. 41, gives the Bank of England power, where it appears 'desirable . . . in the interests of depositors or potential depositors of an authorised institution', to appoint one or more competent persons to investigate and report to the Bank on (a) the nature, conduct or state of the institution's business or any particular aspect of it, or (b) the ownership or control of an institution or a former authorised institution.

Investigators are given wide powers including the ability to call for documents, personal attendance and other assistance from staff, agents, bankers, auditors and solicitors of the institution under investigation (s. 41(5)), but any legal professional communication is privileged (s. 41(11)).

Section 41(7) provides that investigators have the power to enter premises occupied by a body which is being investigated after written notice of such an intention is given, except where there is 'reasonable' cause to believe that as a result of giving notice relevant documents would be removed, tampered with or destroyed. The statutory powers of investigation in the Banking Act 1987 are in addition to the investigatory powers of the Department of Trade and Industry under ss. 432 and 442 of the Companies Act 1985.

Accounts and auditors

The collapse of the Johnson Matthey Bankers highlighted the failure of auditors to conduct detailed inquiries relating to the quality of bank loans and the effectiveness of internal controls. The Banking Act 1987 has made it possible for auditors to play a significant role in the supervisory process of authorised institutions and for the Bank of England to be directly involved in the appointment of bank auditors. The Leigh-Pemberton Committee (*Report of the Committee Set up to Consider the System of Banking Supervision* (Cmnd 9550) (London: HMSO, 1985)) commented that if the Bank of England cannot carry out detailed inspections itself, it must be able to rely on the assistance and cooperation of auditors whose duties necessitate first-hand knowledge of an institution's accounts. It therefore recommended that coordination and contact between supervisors and auditors must be improved. The government's White Paper, *Banking Supervision* (Cmnd 9695, 1985), also proposed a strengthening of the links between auditors and the Bank. The government's proposals were given statutory effect in ss. 39 and 47 of the Banking Act 1987. Consequently, bank auditors are now directly involved in the bank supervisory process.

Section 39 empowers the Bank to call for such information as the Bank may reasonably require from an authorised institution. This power is supported by the right to require an authorised institution to provide a report from an accountant containing any information which the Bank may require. The Bank's *Guidance Note on Reporting Accountants' Reports on Accounting and Other Records and Internal Control Systems* (BSD/1994/2 March 1994) provides detailed guidance to institutions and to reporting accountants appointed under s. 39 on the scope of the report, and requires reporting accountants to have a proper understanding and working knowledge of (a) the returns submitted by an authorised institution as well as the Bank's current reporting instructions and ad hoc rulings; (b) policy notices published by the Bank which relate to the returns; (c) the Bank's guidance note on accounting and other records and internal control system and reporting accountants' reports thereon; and (d) the Bank's consultative paper on its relationship with auditors and reporting accountants issued in March 1994. In normal circumstances, the auditors of authorised institutions are expected to double as reporting accountants.

Reporting accountants will be required to form an opinion on whether the information contained in the returns is complete and accurate in all material respects, has been prepared in accordance with the Bank's current reporting instructions and any further ad hoc rulings which apply specifically to the institution in question, and has been prepared using the same accounting polices as those applied in the institution's most recent statutory audit.

Auditors and the duty of confidentiality

An auditor's primary duty is owed to the institution for which he or she acts and to its shareholders. It is unlikely that this duty of care is owed to depositors and account holders of a bank on the liquidation of a bank. In *Caparo Industries plc* v *Dickman* [1990] 2 AC 605 the House of Lords held that in deciding whether auditors owed a duty of care to persons who rely on the published accounts in buying shares the proximity of the relationship is vital. It must be shown that the auditors knew the accounts or any statement made in connection with them would be communicated to the investor either as an individual or as a member of a group. The *Caparo Case* was applied in *Al-Nakib Investments (Jersey) Ltd* v *Longcroft* [1990] 1 WLR 1390 where the court concluded that the defendants did not owe a duty of care to the plaintiffs in respect of transactions involving the purchase of shares in the market. The prospectus and interim reports had been issued for a particular purpose (a rights issue) and were used for a purpose not intended, i.e., buying shares on the open market.

The duty to disclose information to the Bank, even in its supervisory role, has in the past been limited by the Banking Act 1979. Section 47 of the Banking Act 1987 overrides an auditor's duty of confidentiality and enables such an individual to pass information to the Bank concerning the business affairs of the client (see *Price Waterhouse* v *BCCI Holdings (Luxembourg) SA* [1992] BCLC 583, where Millett J held that it was in the public interest to disclose confidential information to the Bank of England in furtherance of its supervisory functions, but it was also in the public interest to disclose information to an inquiry set up to investigate the BCCI collapse). Section 47 is drafted so as not to impose a statutory duty on auditors to disclose information to the Bank, but they may be liable in negligence if they fail to communicate with the Bank when circumstances indicate that they ought reasonably to have done so. The information communicated must be acquired either as an auditor, accountant or in some other professional capacity, in respect of an authorised institution and must be acquired in the relevant professional capacity and be communicated to the Bank in good faith.

Section 47(5) requires accountants' professional bodies to introduce non-statutory rules or guidelines specifying the 'circumstances' in which matters are to be communicated to the Bank. Guidelines issued in February 1988 by the Auditing Practices Committee of the Consultative Committee of Accountancy Bodies stress that the principal source of information for the Bank will be the management of the authorised institution but that auditors or reporting accountants should take the initiative in making ad hoc reports when they 'consider it expedient to do so in order to protect the interests of depositors because there has been a material loss or there exists a significant risk of material loss'. Such circumstances may arise where there has been an adverse occurrence, or adverse change in the auditors' or reporting accountants' perception of the institution and the occurrence has given rise to a material loss or indicates that a reasonable probability exists that a material loss may arise and that the interests of depositors might be better safeguarded if the Bank were made aware of the occurrence or change of circumstances. In order to preserve relations with the institution concerned, auditors or reporting accountants should encourage the institution itself to report matters of concern to the Bank. However, where the institution fails to respond to such a request, or the situation is an exceptional one, in so far as the interests of depositors are concerned, the auditors or reporting accountants should report to the Bank direct.

In addition the Bank of England has issued a notice to all authorised institutions outlining the circumstances in which auditors and reporting accountants are able to communicate with the Bank and vice versa, and the arrangements for three-way discussions between the Bank, authorised institution and reporting accountants; and the circumstances in which the Bank will expect auditors and reporting accountants to report to the Bank.

In giving recognition to the expanded role of auditors under the 1987 Act, s. 46 requires authorised or former authorised institutions incorporated in the UK to give the Bank written notice 'immediately' if they decide to remove an auditor before, or replace an auditor after, his term of office has expired, or if an auditor ceases to act in an investigation. Additionally, the auditor must give immediate written notice to the Bank if he resigns, does not seek reappointment or if he decides to qualify his opinion on the institution's accounts.

Failure to comply with the requirements in s. 46 is an offence under the Act.

BANKING NAMES AND DESCRIPTIONS

The government White Paper, *Banking Supervision* (Cmnd 9695, 1985) acknowledged that the word 'bank' evoked an image of an institution of substance and security and took the view that the expression should remain a privilege of those institutions whose status justified it. For that reason it is accepted that supervisory authorities must be empowered to control the use of names or descriptions incorporating terms such as 'bank', 'banker' or 'banking'.

The Banking Act 1987, s. 67(1) provides that no institution may use any name which indicates or may reasonably be understood to indicate (whether in English or any other language) that it is a bank or carrying on banking business, unless it is authorised under ss. 67 or 68. The inclusion of a test of reasonableness prevents bottle banks, blood banks or similar entities falling foul of the legislation. The restriction in the use of such descriptions applies to any persons or authorised institutions (Banking Coordination (Second Council Directive) Regulations 1992 (SI 1992/3218), reg. 47 and sch. 8, para. 18, the regulation to authorised institutions includes a reference to a bank authorised in another EC member State) carrying on a business in the UK, and therefore the use of such words in a foreign language will be caught by the prohibition under the Act. The restriction does not apply to overseas institutions with representative offices in the UK (see p. 49).

The £5 million threshold

The Banking Act 1987, s. 67, provides that authorised institutions incorporated in the United Kingdom with paid-up share capital of more than £5 million, may use a name which indicates that the institution is a bank, banker or carrying on a banking business. There are detailed rules which are applied to determine whether this threshold is reached, for example, redeemable share capital is not taken into the calculation (s. 67(3). The share capital may be denominated wholly or partly in a currency other than sterling. Companies which do not have £5 million in paid-up share capital may include their undistributable reserves (s. 264(3) of the Companies Act 1985) to reach the £5 million figure. An authorised institution which is a United Kingdom partnership may use a banking name if one or more designated fixed capital accounts are credited with at least £5 million and these accounts are covered by the partnership agreement and indicate the capital contributions of each partner (s. 67(4)). The partnership agreement must also provide that the capital of a retiring partner will be replaced by an equivalent amount, either by the continuing partners or any incoming partner (s. 67(4)(c)).

Where the share capital is denominated in a currency other than sterling and fluctuations in exchange rates lead to the £5 million threshold not being satisfied, the institution concerned will only be prevented from using a banking name if the situation persists for more than three months (s. 67(5)).

Existing institutions which had already called themselves banks but which did not satisfy the requirements of s. 67 were allowed to continue calling themselves banks. Schedule 5, para. 13(2), provides that a UK-incorporated institution which was either recognised or licensed under the Banking Act 1979 may retain the name under which it was registered immediately before Part III of the 1987 Act came into force (1 October 1987). However, a corporate institution will no longer be able to use that name if the total value (in sterling) of its issued share capital and undistributable reserves falls below their value on 1 October 1987.

Section 68 contains a list of institutions which are exempt from the provisions of s. 67. The list is similar to that found in the Banking Act 1979, s. 36, but certain additional institutions are exempted. The National Savings bank, municipal bank or school banks may use a banking name provided the name contains an indication that it is a savings, municipal or school bank, as necessary (s. 68(1) and (2)). An authorised institution incorporated under the law of a country or territory outside the UK, or formed under laws of another EC State may use the name 'under which it carries on business in that country or territory or state' (s. 68(3)). Under the Banking Coordination (Second Council Directive) Regulations 1992 (SI 1992/3218), reg. 47 and sch. 8, para. 17, the reference to authorised institutions includes a reference to a bank authorised in another EC member State. A similar exemption is granted to a representative office (see p. 50) and authorised institutions which are wholly owned subsidiaries of institutions which meet the criteria under s. 67 or the immediate parent company of such an institution. Finally, certain banks, e.g., EC central banks and the European Investment Bank, are expressly exempted (s. 68(6)) from s. 67.

Banking descriptions

Although the use of banking names is restricted under ss. 67 and 68, the following section (s. 69) commences by permitting all authorised institutions to describe themselves as banks. Apart from authorised institutions a number of exempted institutions may describe themselves as banks. Section 69(1) provides that 'No person carrying on any business in the United Kingdom shall so describe himself or hold himself out as to indicate or reasonably be understood to indicate (whether in English or in any other language) that he is a bank or banker or is carrying on a banking business unless he is an authorised institution' or is otherwise exempted. The section then provides that if an institution is prohibited from using a banking name, it may not use a banking description in such immediate conjunction with its name that the description might reasonably be thought to be part of its name. The section contains certain exemptions to the general restriction on the use of banking descriptions by unauthorised institutions, e.g., a building society under the Building Societies Act 1986 may describe itself as providing 'banking services', provided that the description is not used in such immediate proximity with its name as to be reasonably thought to be part of its name.

Overseas institutions and representative offices

Part IV of the Banking Act 1987 regulates overseas institutions with representative offices in the UK. Many of the statutory provisions follow the proposals in the government White Paper, *Banking Supervision* (Cmnd 9695, 1985), and the White Paper highlighted the concern of the government with regard to representative offices. The government wanted to avoid the situation:

> in which offices of dubious institutions may abuse their position in this country — the London address — to carry out illegal or undesirable activities outside the United Kingdom and outside the jurisdiction of the United Kingdom authorities. There is also the risk that once established as a representative office, an institution will begin to expand its activities and effectively operate as a 'branch' of its parent institution, i.e., by taking deposits in the United Kingdom, but without having obtained the necessary authorisation (*Banking Supervision* (Cmnd 9695), ch. 13.5).

The government was so concerned about these risks that it considered the possibility of requiring representative offices in the UK to obtain authorisation. Instead, the Banking Act 1987 requires that notice of intention to establish a representative office must be given to the Bank of England two months prior to establishing such an office. The Bank is entitled to reasonable access to any information and documents from an overseas institution that has established, or is about to establish, a representative office, that the Bank may reasonably require. The *Banking Supervision Guide* states that the Banking Supervision Division of the Bank will expect to be consulted by overseas institutions well in advance of any notice of intention to establish a representative office. It also expects to be assured that the proposal has the approval of the supervisory authorities in the country of incorporation. The notice of intention must be in the manner directed by the Bank, and the Bank expects a period of consultation between the overseas institution and the Bank.

Use of name by a representative office

As a general rule an overseas institution which has its principal place of business in a country outside the UK may use the banking name it uses in that country (or an approximate English translation) in the UK, provided it is qualified by the words 'representative office' in immediate conjunction with its name and these words are as prominent as the name (Banking Act 1987, s. 68(5)).

The terms 'overseas institution' and 'representative office' are defined in the Act. An overseas institution is a body incorporated in a country or territory outside the UK or a partnership or association formed under the law of such a country or territory, or a person who has his principal place of business in such a country or territory, and which satisfies one of a number of requirements in s. 74. The meaning of representative office has been extended to signify premises from which the deposit-taking, lending or other financial or banking activities of the overseas institution are promoted or assisted. The *Banking Supervision Guide* states that the Bank of England expects the business of representative offices to be restricted to representative activities in 'a narrow sense' and the Bank's interpretation of such activities includes 'the reporting back to head office on such business trends and opportunities in the UK and generally representing the interests and promoting the banking services of an overseas institution'. An overseas institution will need to establish a branch if it intends to engage in significant banking activities or if it proposes to extend the functions undertaken by the representative office.

CHANGES IN CONTROL

The White Paper, *Banking Supervision* (Cmnd 9695) noted that s. 14 of the Banking Act 1979 required licensed deposit-takers (but not recognised banks) to notify the Bank of England within 21 days of changes in control, but that the Bank did not have a power of objection to such a change before the event. The provisions contained in the Banking Act 1987, ss. 21 to 26, extensively increased the powers of the Bank to protect the UK banking sector from aggressive foreign control or other undesirable takeovers. Certain defined persons are required to give notice to the Bank before changes in individual shareholdings can be effected in authorised institutions.

Under s. 21 of the Act no person may become a minority (controls 15 per cent or more but less than 50 per cent of the voting rights), majority (controls 50 per cent or more but less than 75 per cent of the voting rights), or principal (controls 75 per cent or more of the voting rights) shareholder controller or an indirect controller (person in accordance with whose directions or instructions directors of the institution act etc.) of an authorised institution incorporated in the UK unless he has served written notice to the Bank to that effect and the Bank consents to his becoming such a controller or does not object within three months. (The definitions of the various kinds of controller are in s. 105.)

The requirement in s. 21 applies not merely to a person who seeks to become a shareholder controller or an indirect controller of an institution but also to a person who proposes to increase a shareholding beyond 50 per cent or 75 per cent of the voting rights in an institution. Fresh notice is required to be given whenever any transaction relating to shares of an authorised institution changes the percentage of voting rights of any shareholder from 50 or less to more than 50, or from 75 or less to more than 75 and the Bank then has the opportunity to object.

The notice required by s. 21(1)(a) from a prospective controller must contain such information as the Bank directs, and the Bank may, after receiving it, call for such additional documents or information as it may reasonably require in order to determine whether or not to serve a notice of objection.

Objection to new or increased control

Section 22 of the Banking Act 1987 enables the Bank of England to object to new or increased shareholder control. The Bank is required to send a preliminary written notice to the person seeking control specifying the grounds for objection and then a notice of objection. The Bank may object within three months of the prospective controller's written notice unless it is satisfied that (a) the person concerned is a fit and proper person to become a controller of the institution; (b) the interests of depositors and of potential depositors would not be threatened in any manner by the acquisition in question; and (c) that having regard to the person's likely influence as a controller the sch. 3 requirements will continue to be fulfilled. The general presumption is that the greater the influence on the authorised institution by a potential controller the more stringent the requirement relating to fitness. The Bank will also take into consideration the ability and willingness of the authorised institution to undertake remedial action in the event that sch. 3 is not satisfied.

The Bank has wide powers to object to a proposed controller and the Bank must be able to assess the suitability of a prospective controller and his intentions regarding the institution of which he proposes to acquire control.

Where a person becomes a controller without giving the required notice under s. 21, the Bank may serve him with notice of objection at any time within three months of becoming aware of the failure to give notice (s. 22(6)).

Objection by the Treasury

The Treasury are empowered to direct the Bank of England to serve a notice of objection (s. 23) to a person who has given notice of intention to become a controller or who has become a controller without giving the relevant notice. The grounds for objection are not specified but are regulated by s. 183 of the Financial Services Act 1986, which empowers the Treasury to disqualify or restrict the authorisation on the ground that the institution is connected to a country which does not offer equal treatment to UK persons or institutions in the investment, banking or insurance fields. The s. 23 provision was introduced as an amendment to the Banking Bill and it was made plain that it was aimed specifically at Japan, as part of a concerted campaign by the UK and USA to gain access to the Tokyo market.

The power to object is given to the Treasury rather than the Bank, which indicates that political and economic reasons may dictate its usage.

Restrictions and sale of shares

Where a person becomes or continues as a shareholder controller having received a notice of objection, s. 26 empowers the Bank to serve a notice of objection on the person concerned and direct the shares to be subject to one or more restrictions, namely: (a) any transfer or agreement to transfer shares will be void, including any agreement relating to a rights issue; (b) no voting rights will be exercisable in respect of such shares; (c) no rights offer will be made in respect of such shares; and (d) except in a liquidation, no payments of any nature will be made in respect of such shares.

ADVERTISEMENTS FOR DEPOSITS

The Banking Act 1979 empowered the Bank to control and regulate advertisements for deposits by licensed institutions and deposit-takers. The 1987 Act has strengthened these powers and extended them to all authorised institutions. However, the flexible approach adopted elsewhere in the Act enables the Treasury to make regulations for 'regulating the issue, form and content of deposit advertisements' (s. 32(1)). A 'deposit advertisement' is defined by s. 32(5) as an advertisement containing an invitation to make a deposit, or any information 'which is intended or might reasonably be presumed to be intended to lead directly or indirectly to the making of a deposit'. An advertisement also includes any other means of bringing such an invitation or information to the notice of any persons to whom it is addressed.

For the purposes of the Act, an advertisement inviting deposits with a specified person will be presumed (unless the contrary is proved) to have been issued by the order of that person. Thus, it is the principal who is deemed to have issued the advertisement. However, a person who publishes or arranges for the publication of an advertisement in the ordinary course of his business will not be guilty of an offence under s. 32 if he can show he received the advertisement for publication in the ordinary course of his business and that the advertisement (either in part or whole) was not devised or selected by him, or by his agent, servant, or employee and that he did not know or believe that its publication would constitute an offence (s. 32(4)).

Where the Bank of England considers any deposit advertisement which is proposed to be issued by or on behalf of an authorised institution is misleading it may by written notice under s.33:

(a) prohibit the institution from issuing advertisements of a specified kind;

(b) require that advertisements of a particular description be modified in a specified manner;

(c)   prohibit the issue of any advertisements which are wholly or substantially repetitions of a prohibited advertisement; or

(d)   require the institution to take all practical steps to withdraw from display any advertisements, or any advertisements of a particular description, specified in the direction.

DEPOSIT PROTECTION SCHEME

The Deposit Protection Board and Deposit Protection Fund were established under s. 21 of the Banking Act 1979 and continue to exist under s. 50 of and sch. 4 to the Banking Act 1987. The basic approach adopted by the Banking Act 1979 and continued under the 1987 Act involves levying contributions at a flat percentage of each contributory institution's 'deposit base'. The scheme is similar to that established under the Policyholders Protection Act 1975, which contains provisions for indemnifying policyholders out of a fund financed and levied on the insurance industry itself. A fund for the protection of depositors was also set up under the Building Societies Act 1986.

Deposit Protection Board

The Deposit Protection Board was set up as a body corporate, and it has power to hold, manage and apply the Deposit Protection Fund in accordance with the Act. It can levy contributions for the fund from authorised institutions and carry out any other functions conferred on it. The Banking Act 1987, sch. 4, deals with the constitution, proceedings, accounts, audit and annual report of the Deposit Protection Board. The Board consists of three ex officio members, namely, the Governor, the Deputy Governor and Chief Cashier of the Bank of England, together with three ordinary members appointed by the Governor of the Bank from time to time. The ordinary members must be persons who are directors, controllers or managers of contributory institutions, but not persons who are officers of the Bank of England.

Deposit Protection Fund

The Board's primary function is to maintain and continue the Deposit Protection Fund. By the Banking Act 1987, s. 51, the Fund consists of (a) any money which formed part of the Fund when s. 51 came into force; (b) initial, further and special contributions levied by the Board on contributing institutions under the Act; (c) money borrowed by the Board under the Act; and (d) any other money required by the Act to be credited to the Fund or received by the Board and directed by it to be so credited. Initial contributions are levied under s. 53 of the Act with the Board having power to levy further (s. 54) or special (s. 55) contributions if payments out of the fund in any one year are likely to result in the amount standing to the credit of the fund falling below £3 million, or where such payments are likely to exhaust the Fund. The amounts credited to the Fund are placed by the Board in an account with the Bank of England (s. 51(2)), and the Bank invests the money placed with it in Treasury bills (s. 51(3)). Any income from the money so invested is credited to the Fund (s. 51(3)).

Payments chargeable to the fund under s. 51(4) include (a) repayments of the special contributions under s. 55(2); (b) payments of compensation under s. 58; (c) money required for the repayment of, and the payment of interest on, money borrowed by the Board; and (d) the administrative and other incidental expenses incurred by the Board. The amount of the initial contribution levied from a contributory institution must not exceed £300,000 (s. 56(2)). A contributory institution will not be required to make a further or special contribution if the amount of its contribution, together with any previous initial, further or special contributions will amount to more than 0.3 per cent of the institution's deposit base (s. 56(3)).

If a formerly authorised institution at any time becomes insolvent, the Board must, as soon as practicable, pay out of the Fund to each depositor who has a protected deposit (s. 60) with that institution, an amount equal to 90 per cent of the protected deposit, with a maximum payment of £20,000 (s. 58). Where an administration order is made in respect of the institution under s. 8 of the Insolvency Act 1986, the payment must be made as soon as practicable after the date it becomes due and payable under the terms of the deposit, or if later, on the approval of the administrator's proposals under s. 24 of the Insolvency Act (s. 58(2)). A protected deposit includes accrued interest on the relevant deposit, including all interest which is due to the depositor (s. 60(2)). Section 60(6) excludes secured deposits, which are undefined but which would appear to be deposits on which a deposit-taking institution has given some form of security, and deposits which have an original term of maturity of more than five years. Section 60(6) also provides that the deposit is not protected unless it was made whilst the relevant institution was authorised or at a time when the depositor did not know, or could not reasonably be expected to have known, that it was not so authorised. Deposits placed with UK branches of exempt overseas institutions are no longer excluded from the scheme and they cannot obtain exemption from the Treasury.

Where the Board is satisfied that a payment has been, or will be, made in respect of a protected deposit under any other comparable scheme for protecting depositors or investors, or under a government guarantee or other authority, the Board may deduct an amount equal to the whole or part of that payment from the amount payable out of the Fund (s. 58(3)). When the Board does make a deduction of any amount payable to the depositor under any other scheme it may agree with the authority responsible for the scheme that it will reimburse that authority to the extent of the deduction or any lesser sum agreed. Alternatively, the Board may, by agreement with the authority responsible for the scheme, or the authority by which the guarantee was given, make the full payment required and recoup from that authority the agreed contribution (s. 58(3)(b)).

LARGE EXPOSURE

Although the issue of large concentrated loans has caused concern for some time the Banking Act 1987 contained no specific provisions covering large scale exposures. This concern was highlighted in April 1983 when the Bank of England issued a notice (BSD/1983/1) covering, amongst other things, the size of individual exposures and the need to keep within prudent limits. These guidelines, although not having legal force, were supposed to prevent an institution lending over 10 per cent of its capital base to one customer. The collapse of the Johnson Matthey Bank is proof that these guidelines were being ignored; a small number of Johnson Matthey loans were identified as considerably higher than 10 per cent. The potential seriousness of concentrations of lending and other exposures to individual or economic borrowers was emphasised by the Leigh-Pemberton Committee report (*Report of the Committee Set up to Consider the System of Banking Supervision* (Cmnd 9550, 1985), ch. 5), which drew attention to the fact that such concentrations have, in recent years, been one of the most important causes of difficulties to banks. The report also noted that many countries have imposed specific limits on large exposures to individual borrowers, although it recommended against imposing such lending limits in the UK. The government accepted the case against statutory limits but was also of the view that the issue of individual exposures to non-bank customers was of sufficient importance to justify some form of statutory limitation.

The recommendations contained in the White Paper, *Banking Supervision* (Cmnd 9695, 1985), are reflected in s. 38 of the Banking Act 1987. The section provides that an authorised institution (other than one whose principal place of business is outside the UK) must submit a report to the Bank of England if it enters into any transaction or transactions relating to one person (defined as including a partnership, a corporation and a government) the result of which would leave it exposed to losses in excess of 10 per cent of its available capital resources, or if it proposes to enter into a transaction or transactions relating to one person, which (alone or together with previous transactions with that person) would risk it being exposed to losses in excess of 25 per cent of its available capital resources.

Section 38 also applies to any transaction or transactions relating to persons or institutions connected in such a way that the financial soundness of any one of them may affect the financial soundness of some or all of them (e.g., where the financial soundness of the parent company may affect the soundness of its subsidiaries or vice versa).

The Bank of England has made it clear that all banks must stand behind their subsidiaries and a bank should not hide behind the limited liability principle should its subsidiary become insolvent. Consequently, large exposures will only pose a threat if they are large in relation to the capital base of the group of companies. Thus, the supervision of large exposures should be carried out at group level. Section 38(3) provides that if an authorised institution to which s. 38(1) applies has subsidiary companies which are not authorised institutions, the Bank may by notice in writing to that institution direct that s. 38 will apply to it as if the transactions and available capital resources of the subsidiaries, or such of them as are specified in the notice, were included in those of the parent company. Section 38(3) applies only to subsidiaries which are not authorised institutions.

The question whether an institution is or would be exposed to the type of risk provided for under s. 38(1) will be determined in accordance with principles published by the Bank or notified to the institution concerned (s. 38(6)). Any such principles may provide for determining the amount at risk in particular circumstances or the extent to which any such amount is taken into account (s. 38(6)), and may exclude from any consideration, either wholly or in part, risks resulting from transactions of a particular description or entered into in particular circumstances or with persons of particular descriptions (s. 38(8)). The principles applied by the

Bank may be varied from time to time. An institution guilty of an offence under s. 38 is liable on summary conviction to a fine. Under s. 38(11), the Treasury may (subject to an annulment by a resolution of either House of Parliament) in consultation with the Bank amend s. 38. (See 'Barings: The Bank of England's First Report to the Board of Banking Supervision', *Journal of International Banking and Financial Law*, vol. 11 (March 1996), pp. 128–30 at 129.)

APPEALS

An appeal from a decision of the Bank of England under certain provisions of the Banking Act listed in s. 27 is to a tribunal constituted under s. 28. Where the ground or one of the grounds for the Bank's decision relates to ss. 10(3) or 13(4)(a) (i.e. the minimum criterion under sch. 3 is not satisfied), or the effect of the Bank's decision is to require the removal of a person as director, the person to whom the Bank's decision relates may appeal to the tribunal against the finding that there is a ground for the decision or against the decision requiring his removal (s. 27(2)). Section 27(3) extends the right of appeal to individuals whose status as 'fit and proper persons' is rejected by the Bank.

The Banking Act 1979 enabled an aggrieved person or institution to appeal to the Chancellor of the Exchequer against a decision of the Bank and the Chancellor in turn would refer the matter to persons appointed for such purposes. The grant of a right of appeal was a new departure under the 1987 Act, since the Bank's supervisory role was, up until that time, largely non-statutory and informal. The rights of appeal under the Banking Act 1987 are both reinforced and extended, and appeals are decided by an impartial tribunal. Section 29 deals with the powers of the tribunal to determine appeals. The section is a considerable extension on s. 11(3) of the 1979 Act. In *Shah* v *Bank of England* [1994] 3 Bank LR 205 (the first case to be decided under ss. 13 and 27 of and sch. 3 to the 1987 Act), Vinelott J examined the scope of the jurisdiction of the tribunal. He took the view that an appeal against a decision of the tribunal under the Banking Act 1987 was analogous to an application for judicial review. A tribunal constituted under the Act must form its own view on whether the Bank's decision or finding was justified by the evidence on which it was based. The tribunal is to form its view on objective criteria, although it is entitled and likely to give the policies and approach 'of the Bank of England as the statutory regulator with unrivalled experience in the field very considerable weight'. Although the tribunal must make its own evaluation of the evidence and of the inferences to be drawn from the facts, the Bank is charged with the duty of regulating the conduct of banking business, and it is not the function of the tribunal to substitute its own decision as to the steps which need to be taken in the discharge of that duty.

4   Regulation of Building Societies

AUTHORISATION

A building society requires authorisation to raise funds and to borrow money.
Authorisation is therefore fundamental to building societies, and particularly to the
new structure of prudential control and supervision introduced by the Building
Societies Act 1986. The system introduced by the Building Societies (Authorisation) Regulations 1981 (SI 1981/1488) and the Building Societies (Authorisation)
Regulations (Northern Ireland) (SR 1982/155) was much developed by the 1986
Act. In particular the so-called 'criteria for prudent management' laid down in
s. 45 of the 1986 Act are a yardstick by which to measure the directors and other
officers, and generally the direction and management of every building society. A
comparable regime applies in relation to other deposit-taking institutions, particularly through the provisions of the Banking Act 1987 (chapter 3). Like the 1981
Regulations, the authorisation provisions of the 1986 Act were implemented in
order to give effect to Directive 77/780/EEC.

Section 9(1) of the 1986 Act provides that, subject to certain specified
exceptions, a society 'shall not raise money from members or accept deposits of
money unless there is in force an authorisation of the Commission'. A breach of
this prohibition is a criminal offence punishable in the case of the building society
by an unlimited fine and in the case of its officers by imprisonment for up to two
years or an unlimited fine or both (s. 9(11)).

The Act provides that applications for authorisation must be made in the
following three circumstances:

(a)   where a newly formed society seeks authorisation for the first time (s. 9);
(b)   where an authorised society is directed by the Commission to seek renewal
of its authorisation (s. 41); and
(c)   where a society's authorisation has either expired, following a refusal by
the Commission to renew it, or been revoked on any one of the discretionary
grounds provided by s. 43(1) of the Act.

In all three cases, authorisation may be granted unconditionally or subject to conditions. As with the Bank of England's powers to grant conditional authorisation,

the Building Societies Commission is relieved of making a difficult choice between refusing to grant or renew authorisation where it has reservations about the security of investments placed with societies under its supervisory control. It can therefore address its prudential concerns by attaching suitable conditions to the society's authorisation (s. 42).

Initial authorisation

Section 9(4) of the Building Societies Act 1986 sets out four requirements which an applicant for authorisation must satisfy, namely:

(a) *Minimum qualifying capital*
The society must have a qualifying capital of an amount which is not less than the prescribed minimum, which is currently set at £100,000 (s. 9(13)). This amount represents a compromise between the minimum capital requirement of £1m for deposit-taking institutions under the Banking Act 1987, and the need in the case of mutual societies, without access to the conventional methods of raising capital, not to set a threshold so high that it is impossible for a new society to become authorised in future (Chief Registrar of Building Societies, *Building Societies Act 1986: Capital Adequacy* (1986) para. 8.13). In the absence of access to outside capital, provision is made for this sum to be raised by the issue of deferred shares without prior authorisation up to a maximum of £250,000 (Building Societies (Deferred Shares) Order 1991 (SI 1991/207)).

(b) *Fit and proper persons*
The holders of certain key posts in relation to the direction and management of the society (e.g., chairman of the board of directors and any executive directors, the chief executive, the secretary and managers) must each be fit and proper persons. In common with other investor protection legislation, the concept of a fit and proper person is not defined, but in considering whether this requirement is satisfied, the Commission will take account of both the context, including the nature and scale of the business proposed to be conducted, and the specific duties, responsibilities and powers designated to a particular post. Personal factors of the individuals concerned, ranging from their integrity, reputation and character, through to their qualifications, experience, competence and commitment will be taken into consideration.

(c) *Prudent management*
The third requirement is that the board of directors, together with the chief executive and secretary, must have the capacity and intention to direct the affairs of the society in accordance with 'the criteria of prudent management'. The criteria for 'prudent management' are set out in s. 45(3) of the 1986 Act. Like the 'prudent management' requirements applicable to banks, the 1986 Act requires societies to satisfy specific rules relating to capital and liquidity, structure of commercial assets, arrangements for assessing the adequacy of securities for advances secured on land, records and systems of control, direction and management and the conduct of their business. These requirements constitute the core of continuing prudential obligations on authorised building societies. A failure by an authorised building society to satisfy any of these requirements entitles the Commission to assume that it has prejudiced the security of the investments of shareholders and depositors, so that it may intervene to protect the interests of investors.

(d) *Depositors*

The fourth requirement is that the investments of depositors will be adequately protected without the imposition of any conditions.

Unconditional authorisation will be granted by the Building Societies Commission if it is satisfied that the above requirements are satisfied. Conditional authorisation may be granted if the capital adequacy and fit and proper persons requirements are satisfied and the imposition of certain conditions would secure the protection of the investments of shareholders and depositors. If, however, the Commission is not satisfied that the capital adequacy and fit and proper person requirements are satisfied, or that the imposition of conditions would secure the protection of depositors and investors, it must refuse to grant authorisation (s. 9(5)(a)).

Renewal of authorisation

Under the Building Societies Act 1986, sch. 20, para. 6, societies which were already authorised when the Act came into force were not required to seek fresh authorisation. Most of these societies had been automatically authorised when the requirement of authorisation was first introduced in implementing the First Banking Directive in 1981 (Building Societies (Authorisation) Regulations 1981 (SI 1981/1488)).

To safeguard against the possibility that some of these societies may not satisfy the authorisation requirements, the 1986 Act gave the Commission the power (initially for five years and extended for a further five years under the 1986 Act) to direct any society whose business it has reason to believe is being conducted in a manner which does not protect the investments of shareholders and depositors adequately to apply for renewal of its authorisation. If the society fails to apply for authorisation within the permitted period allowed, its authorisation must be revoked (s. 43(3)(c)). The same requirements as apply for initial authorisation apply to applications for renewal of authorisation. Authorisation must be renewed unconditionally if the Commission is satisfied that all the necessary requirements are satisfied.

Reauthorisation

Where the authorisation of a building society has expired under s. 41(7) or been revoked under s. 43(1) the Building Societies Act 1986 allows for the possibility of reauthorisation (s. 44). Applications for reauthorisation fall to be assessed against the same requirements as applications for renewal of authorisations. Authorisation must be granted unconditionally if all the requirements are satisfied, and subject to conditions if the Commission is satisfied that the minimum capital and fit and proper persons requirements are satisfied and that the imposition of conditions would secure the protection of the investments of shareholders and depositors (s. 44(4)).

Conditions

The Building Societies Commission may impose conditions on a society's authorisation. Conditions may relate to any of the society's activities and not just those for which authorisation is required (i.e., the raising of money from members and the acceptance of loans and deposits). The society may be required to take certain steps or to refrain from adopting a particular course of action or to restrict the scope of its business in a particular way. The Commission may impose limitations on the issue of shares, acceptance of deposits or the making of advances or other loans or require the removal of any director or other officer (ss. 9(6), (7); 41(9); 44(6)). A failure to comply with conditions to which its authorisation is subject renders a society liable to have its authorisation revoked.

Authorisation procedure

Applications for initial authorisation or reauthorisation must normally be determined within six months but where additional information is required this period may be extended to a maximum of 12 months (Building Societies Act 1986, sch. 3, para. 2(7) and (8)). The society must be notified of the Commission's intention either to refuse or to grant authorisation subject to conditions and the reasons for it (sch. 3, paras 2(4) and 4(1).

The society must be given an opportunity to make representations, which the Commission must take into consideration before reaching its final decision (sch. 3, paras 2(6) and 4(3)).

FINANCIAL REGULATION

Building societies, like banks, are required to observe specific capital adequacy and liquidity requirements. The sole reference to the capital adequacy in the Building Societies Act 1986 is found in the criteria for prudent management, the first of which requires the society to maintain reserves and other designated capital resources at an adequate level, having regard to the range and scale of the current and future business of the society including the business of any subsidiaries or other associates (s. 45(3)). A building society's capital consists of its reserves, i.e., the excess of its assets over its liabilities, accumulated from operating surpluses over the years. Traditionally, a building society's sole source of capital was its reserve but provision has been made for the issue of subordinated long-term debt and permanent interest-bearing shares (PIBS) by societies, which may be aggregated with their reserves for the purpose of assessing capital adequacy.

The Commission's approach to capital adequacy is set out in a series of prudential notes issued after consultation with the industry. Like the Bank of England's approach to capital adequacy for deposit-taking institutions, on which it is modelled, it is designed to ensure that the various financial risks to which building societies are exposed are taken into account in assessing their capital adequacy (discussed in Prudential Note 1987/1, s. 3). Capital adequacy requirements for building societies are set on an individual basis. Two requirements are established for each society: the 'minimum acceptable level', below which a society and the investors in it will be at risk, and the 'desired capital', which is a higher figure intended to reduce the risk of the minimum acceptable level being breached.

The prudent management criteria require a building society to maintain adequate assets in liquid form (s. 45(3)). The terms 'adequate' and 'liquid' are defined with reference to s. 21(1) of the Act, which provides that a 'building society shall secure that, of its total assets, it keeps such a proportion of them having such a composition as will at all times enable the society to meet its liabilities as they arise'. In deciding the actual amount and composition of its liquid assets, a society must have regard to the range and scale of its business, including business it proposes to carry on (s. 21(3)). The scale and nature of business, and the composition and character of the assets and liabilities of any associated bodies must also be taken into account (s. 21(4)). Liquidity margins are established by the building societies themselves in the light of guidance issued by the Commission.

A building society may keep a greater proportion of its assets in liquid form than is required for the purpose of meeting its liabilities (s. 21(2)). The proportion must not, however, exceed one third of its total assets (s. 21(3)(a)), although this is a 'nature' rather than a prudential limit, intended to ensure that the bulk of the society's funds are applied for its primary purpose (i.e., the provision of housing finance) rather than investment in gilt-edged stocks or other money market instruments (*Building Societies: A New Framework*, para. 2.10).

A building society is also restricted in the investment of its liquid funds, whether held for the purpose of meeting its liabilities as they arise or otherwise, to assets of a character authorised by the Commission (s. 21(3)(b)). The liquid assets which a society may hold are prescribed by the Building Societies (Liquid Asset) Regulations 1991 (SI 1991/2580) and include Treasury bills, gilt-edged securities, bank deposits, certificates of deposit and floating rate notes issued by a bank or building society, and local authority securities and loans.

Auditors

Auditors of a building society are entitled under the Building Societies Act 1986, s. 82(8), to furnish information obtained during the course of their audit work to the Commission when either they or the Commission are satisfied that it is expedient for them to do so in order to protect the shareholders and depositors. In certain circumstances the Commission expects the auditors to take the initiative and approach it with information in order to protect the investments of shareholders and depositors (s. 82(8) and Building Societies (Auditors) Order 1994 (SI 1994/525)). They should do so where there has been an occurrence, including a change in circumstances, or a change in the auditor's perception of an existing situation, which involves an actual or potential risk which is or may be relevant to the security of investments of shareholders and depositors. The section envisages that the auditor should first seek to persuade the society itself to inform the Commission, but in exceptional circumstances the auditor may notify the Commission, if necessary, without the knowledge of the society.

Portfolio regulation

To retain its mutual status and the right to describe itself as a building society a society must confine its activities to those allowed by the Building Societies Act 1986. It must also observe limits on its pattern of business as expressed in certain balance sheet ratios. Their purpose is to ensure that the mainstream business of building societies continues to be that of raising funds from the public and lending them for the purpose of enabling individuals to acquire residential property for owner occupation. They also contribute to the prudential strengths of building societies in that they limit the society's exposure against the riskier forms of borrowing and lending.

On the assets side of the balance sheet, these ratios are expressed in the form of commercial asset structure requirements.

Asset structure

Building societies are required to maintain a structure of commercial assets which satisfies Part III of the 1986 Act. Class 1 assets consist entirely of class 1 advances (s. 11(8)). A class 1 advance is one made to an individual whose loan is fully secured against a property which is to be used for residential purposes and which is not subject to a prior charge in favour of another lender (s. 11(2)). This is a typical building society loan for the purposes of homebuying. Section 11(3) provides that, to qualify as being for residential purposes, at least 40 per cent of the area of the property must be so used by the borrower or a prescribed dependant. Further, the Building Societies Commission is empowered to make regulations laying down situations where land may be taken to be for residential use. The importance of the asset classification is that not less than 75 per cent of commercial assets (the total of class 1, 2 and 3 assets) must be in the form of class 1 loans (s. 20(2)). Class 2 assets are defined by s. 11(4) as being advances secured on land where the requirements for a class 1 (s. 11(2)) advance are not met, e.g., property that will not be used for residential purposes or where an advance exceeds the value of the security, additional security, e.g., guarantees, indemnities or other contractual promises made by a public body established under any statute, is required (s. 11(4)). Class 3 assets are limited to 15 per cent of a building society's assets. Investment in this class is limited to societies which have the qualifying asset holdings (defined by s. 118 as commercial assets of £100 million). The Commission can extend the list of class 3 assets.

On the liabilities side of the balance sheet, the 1986 Act introduced a limit on the proportion of its funds a building society may raise from the wholesale markets. This limit was intended to maintain the traditional role of building societies as a home for personal savings, and not to limit their exposure to a more volatile source of funding. A society which wishes to raise more than 5 per cent of its funds from wholesale sources is required to agree with the Commission a limit on the proportion of non-retail funds it may hold and to satisfy it that the society has the necessary management capacity and expertise to operate that policy.

The 1986 Act also stipulates that at least 50 per cent of a building society's funds must be subscribed in the form of shares rather than deposits (s. 8(1)). The significance of this requirement is that shareholders are members of the building society, with a voice in the running of its affairs.

The choice of the figure of 50 per cent as the dividing line between mutuality and non-mutuality is to some extent arbitrary, but in the government's view a building society which has raised less than 50 per cent of its funds in the form of shares could no longer be said to be based on the concept of mutuality.

A building society whose pattern of business does not conform to these limits may be required by the Commission under s. 36 to submit for its approval a restructuring plan which will bring its business back within the relevant statutory limits, or to submit the necessary resolutions to its members for the transfer of its business to a company. If the society fails to comply, or if the restructuring plan or transfer resolutions are not approved or implemented, the Commission may either present a petition to the court for the winding up of the society or apply for a court order directing the society to carry out the restructuring plan (s. 37). The Commission may also apply for an order directing a society to modify its business, where the Commission has reason to believe that the society's purpose or principal purpose has ceased to be that of raising, primarily by the subscription of the members, a stock or fund for making to them advances secured on land for their residential use (s. 37).

The maintenance of a structure of commercial assets which satisfies the statutory requirements is also one of the prudent management criteria. A failure to maintain the requisite structure may therefore lead to the imposition of conditions on a society's authorisation.

INFORMATION AND INVESTIGATIONS

The Building Societies Act 1986, s. 52, gives the Building Societies Commission extensive powers to obtain information and to appoint investigators. These powers are modelled on those conferred on the Bank of England under the original Banking Act 1979 (now the Banking Act 1987, ss. 39, 41). The Commission's powers to obtain information extend to any information, documents or explanations of matters relating to the existing business or future plans for development of a building society or its associated bodies. The Commission can also require information or documents to be accompanied by a report from an accountant approved by it (s. 52(5)(d)). A failure to comply with a requirement imposed in the exercise of these powers is an offence, as is the provision of false or misleading information (s. 52(10)).

Investigations are normally carried out on a voluntary basis but s. 55 empowers the Commission to appoint one or more persons to investigate and report on any aspect of a building society's business. Officers, employers and agents of the society (and of its associated bodies) may be required to produce documents, to attend before investigators and otherwise give full assistance in connection with the investigation (s. 55(3)). A failure without reasonable cause to comply with a requirement, including a requirement to answer any questions, is an offence.

In addition to its power to appoint investigators, the Commission also has a more general power under s. 56 of the Act to appoint inspectors to investigate and report on the affairs of a building society. Investigators may be appointed on an application of the members of a society, as well as on the Commission's initiative. The main difference between inspectors' powers and those of investigators appointed under s. 55 of the Act is that the former have power to examine witnesses on oath.

POWERS OF INTERVENTION

The ultimate sanction available to the Building Societies Commission is the revocation of a building society's authorisation under the Building Societies Act

1986, s. 43. A society's authorisation may be revoked at the direction of the Commission on one of four grounds: (a) that it has failed to make use of it; (b) that it has failed to send a copy of its annual accounts to the Commission within six months of the end of its financial year; (c) that it has failed to comply with a condition to which its authorisation is subject; and (d) that the Commission 'considers it expedient to do so in order to protect the interests of shareholders and depositors'. In certain circumstances revocation is mandatory, e.g., where a society fails to apply for renewal of its authorisation within the period allowed (s. 43(3)(c)).

Section 45 of the 1986 Act applies to determine whether intervention is 'expedient' to protect investors. It provides that a failure by a society or its directors to satisfy one or more of the criteria entitles the Commission to assume that it has prejudiced the security of the investments of shareholders or depositors, and so to intervene to protect those investments (ss. 43(2) and 45(1)). In *R* v *Chief Registrar of Friendly Societies, ex parte New Cross Building Society* [1984] QB 227 the Court of Appeal concluded that the words 'expedient . . . in the interest of investors and depositors' under the Building Societies Act 1962 conferred a wide discretion on the Chief Registrar to intervene whenever there was a risk of loss to investors.

Section 45 of the Building Societies Act 1986 provides that the Commission may take account of factors other than the criteria of prudent management in deciding whether to revoke a building society's authorisation. However, except where revocation is mandatory, a building society must be given notice of the Commission's intention to revoke authorisation. An opportunity must be given to the building society to make representations, which the Commission must take into consideration before reaching a final decision to revoke authorisation. Revocation does not become effective until the end of the period during which an appeal may be brought or determined.

IMPOSITION OF CONDITIONS ON AUTHORISATION

The Building Societies Commission also has a power under the Building Societies Act 1986, s. 42, to impose conditions on a building society's authorisation, which complements its power to grant or renew authorisation subject to conditions. The only ground on which this power is exercisable is that the Commission 'considers it expedient to do so in order to protect the investments of shareholders or depositors' (s. 42(1)). Section 45 applies for the purpose of determining whether the application of conditions is expedient, so that the imposition of conditions is likely (but is not limited) to follow a failure by a society or one of its directors to satisfy one or more of the prudent management criteria.

The conditions which may be imposed are the same as may be imposed on the initial grant or renewal of authorisation. They need not be confined to the raising of funds or deposits, and they may require the society to take certain steps to adopt or refrain from adopting a particular course of action. A failure to comply with conditions imposed on its authorisation renders the building society liable to have its authorisation revoked.

The building societies legislation does not, unlike the banking legislation, provide any guidance on when the imposition of conditions is to be preferred to the revocation of authorisation. However, the decisive factor is likely to be the prospect of the building society taking remedial action, so that where there is no realistic prospect of remedial action the Commission is likely to revoke authorisation. The Commission's power of intervention does not preclude other action from being taken, e.g., merger with another society.

APPEALS

A building society which is aggrieved by a decision of the Building Societies Commission to refuse or revoke authorisation or to impose conditions may appeal to a tribunal under the Building Societies Act 1986, s. 46. The scope of the appeal is confined to the legality of the Commission's decision. The question for the determination of the tribunal is whether, for the reasons adduced by the appellant, the decision was unlawful or not justified by the evidence on which it was based (s. 47(4)). The tribunal may confirm or reverse the Commission's decision, or vary it where the decision was to refuse or revoke authorisation by directing it should be granted or continued subject to conditions; it may also direct the Commission to grant or continue authorisation subject to different conditions from those imposed (s. 47(6)). Where the tribunal's determination is that authorisation should be granted or continued subject to conditions, it is for the Commission to determine the conditions to be imposed (s. 47(7)).

COMPENSATION

The Building Societies Act 1986, Part IV (ss. 24–33) established an investor protection scheme, administered by a separate Building Societies Investor Protection Board under which payments will be made to investors with failed societies. This scheme replaced a non-statutory scheme established by the building societies in 1982. The measure of compensation payable under the scheme is 90 per cent (s. 27(2)) of the first £20,000 of an investor's protected investment. In contrast to the banks there is no standing fund and contributions are only levied if a building society becomes insolvent. Contributions will be levied at a fixed percentage of each society's share and deposit base. As with the banking scheme (Banking Act 1987, s. 58(5)), the Board may decline to make contributions to any person who, in its opinion, has any responsibility for, or may have derived a profit from, circumstances which gave rise to a society's financial difficulties (Building Societies Act 1986, s. 27(4)).

BUILDING SOCIETIES ACT 1997

The Building Societies Act 1997 (the '1997 Act') (which received Royal Assent on 21 March 1997), will amend the Building Societies Act 1986. The Act is likely to come into force by the end of 1997, but two provisions were given immediate effect on the Act receiving Royal Assent. The effect of the Building Societies Act 1997 will be to ensure that building societies which decide to remain mutual will be able to develop their business without the constraints of the current legislation. The new legislation aims to increase competition, create a level playing field by removing restrictions currently placed on building societies and increase the commercial freedom of societies to undertake a wider range of activities.

The 1997 Act provides that a building society may carry on any business activity set out in its memorandum, subject to complying with the nature limits. However, the nature of business activities a building society may undertake are not free from all limitations. The 'purpose or principal purpose' of a society will continue to be 'the making of loans secured on residential property' (s. 1(1)(a)). Neither a building society, nor its subsidiaries, is permitted to act as a market maker in securities, commodities or currencies; trade in commodities or currencies; or enter into any transaction involving derivative instruments over £100,000 (s. 10).

The capacity of a building society to enter into binding contracts, however, is not limited by its memorandum (1997 Act, sch. I (to be implemented as Part II of sch. 2 of the Building Societies Act 1986). Schedule I of the Building Societies Act 1997 applies to mutuals rules similar to those found in s. 35 of the Companies Act 1985. The validity of an act done by a building society cannot, therefore, be called into question due to 'lack of capacity by reason of anything included in the society's memorandum' (para. 16). This rule applies to any limitations contained in the company's constitution by reason of resolutions passed at a general meeting, or a special meeting or a postal ballot of the members, or resulting from agreement between the members.

A member of a building society may bring proceedings to prevent a society from entering into a transaction or act beyond its capacity. As with shareholders of a limited company any right to bring such proceedings is lost where the act or transaction is entered into in pursuance of a legal obligation already entered into by the society (para. 16).

Moreover, any person dealing with a building society in good faith is not bound by limitations on the powers of the board of directors to bind the society (or any limitations placed on the authority of others) contained in the company's constitution (i.e., in the memorandum and rules of the society). A person will be deemed to have acted in good faith, and unless the contrary is proven bad faith will not be established by such a person 'knowing that the act is beyond the powers of the directors under a society's constitution' (para. 17).

Powers and functions of the Building Societies Commission

The functions and powers of the Building Societies Commission have been reinforced under the 1997 Act. Many of the extended powers relate to the supervision and control of building societies. Section 22 (the 1997 Act inserts a new s. 45AA into the 1986 Act) provides that the Commission will publish, in such detail as it thinks appropriate, a statement of principles in accordance with which it purposes to exercise its powers of control and interpretation of the criteria of prudent management. The Commission is given powers to require a building society to submit a restructuring plan where the society fails to comply with the requirements imposed under s. 5 (i.e., the purpose or principal purpose, and principal office provision), or where s. 6(1) (the lending limit – at least 75 per cent of its business assets must by loans fully secured on residential property) or s. 7(1) (the funding limit – at least 50 per cent of its funds must be raised in the form of shares held by individual members) requirements are not satisfied.

The Commission may also serve to a society notice of its intention to serve a prohibition order (1997 Act, s. 14 inserts a new s. 36A into the 1986 Act). Such an order may prohibit either absolutely (or subject to conditions) the power of a building society to continue a certain activity, or during a specified period the disposal of assets acquired by the society by virtue of undertaking the prohibited activity. Where a society contravenes a prohibition order the Commission may petition for a winding up order, but failure to comply with such an order will not invalidate any transaction or act entered into by the society. A winding-up order may also be made if the court is satisfied that s. 5(1)(a) has not been complied with.

The Commission's power to impose conditions on a building society, subject to written notice being given to the Society (1986 Act, s. 42 and sch. 3, Part III) are extended under s. 16 of the 1997 Act (which inserts a new s. 42A into the 1986 Act). Section 16 provides that where the Commission considers that conditions should be imposed as a matter of urgency then the requirement of written notice need not be complied with. A building society on whom conditions are imposed may, however, make representations to the Commission.

In order to protect the investments of members and depositors the Commission may direct a building society to transfer its business to one or more building societies or to an existing company (1997 Act, s. 17). The Commission's power to revoke authorisation is also reinforced by the 1997 Act (s. 19 inserts a new s. 43A into the 1986 Act).

Accountability to members

The 1997 Act makes building societies more accountable to members. On a members' requisition a building society must call a special meeting of its members. Such a meeting must be instigated by the requisite number of members (100) or fewer if permitted by the society's rules. The requisition must state the objects of the meeting, be signed by the requisitionists and be deposited at the society's principal office. The meeting can deal only with such business as is stated in the notice calling the meeting (1997 Act, s. 25 which inserts a s. 20A into the 1986 Act).

It is important that a society should not change its strategic direction without consulting its members. Any proposal to expend more than 15 per cent of a mutual society's own funds on the acquisition or establishment of a business outside the society's core activity of mortgage requires the approval of the members (1997 Act, s. 29 which inserts a new s. 92A into the 1986 Act).

Any individual who saves with a building society will have a membership account.

Protection of investors

The Treasury is given power (after consultation with the Building Societies Commission, the Bank of England, the Building Society Investor Protection Board and the Deposit Protection Board) to establish a single board known as the Deposit Protection Board. Authorised building societies will become contributory institutions and in the event of either a bank or building society becoming insolvent the Board will operate a compensation scheme for depositors (1997 Act, ss. 32 and 33).

Investigation of complaints

The new s. 34 of the 1997 Act introduces a new s. 83 to the 1986 Act. All authorised building societies are required to be members of a recognised complaints scheme. A complaint may be brought for investigation by any:

(a) individual;
(b) partnership, club or other unincorporated association if the turnover does not exceed £1 million;
(c) body corporate where the complainant is not a member of a group whose turnover does not exceed £1 million, or where the turnover of the group does not exceed £1 million.

A complaint may relate to action taken by a building society in relation to a relevant service provided by it, and which affects the complainant in certain prescribed respects. Any service provided by a connected undertaking of a building society may also have a complaint investigated. Consequently, building societies are required to ensure that any connected undertakings belong to one or more of the recognised schemes for complaints handling.

Business names

Every building society must display outside every office or place of business its registered name in legible characters. Its name must be set out, in legible form, on a number of business documents, e.g., business letters, statements of account, passbooks, all notices and publications including all documents sent out to members, all invoices and receipts etc.

As with registered companies the new Act requires that building societies will not, without the prior written approval of the Building Societies Commission, undertake any business which creates the impression that the business is connected with HM's government or with any local authority, or include any word or expression set out in regulations.

Transactions with directors and persons connected with them

A building society which enters into a transaction with either a director, or person connected with such a director in circumstances where the Board of Directors exceed the limitations placed on them by the society's memorandum and rules, is voidable at the instance of the society (1997 Act, s. 38 inserts a new s. 66A into the 1986 Act). Any director who authorised the transaction is liable to account for any gain made either directly or indirectly from the society and to indemnify the society for any resulting loss or damage (s. 38(3)). This obligation of the director to compensate the society arises whether or not the transaction is avoided. However, under s. 38(4) the transaction may cease to be voidable if restitution is no longer possible, or the society is indemnified for any loss or damage resulting from the transaction, or where an innocent third party who gave value acquires an interest, or the transaction is ratified by the society in a general meeting either by an ordinary or special resolution.

Transfers of a building society business to a company

Section 30 and sch. 5 of the 1997 Act amend s. 98 and sch. 17 of the 1986 Act relating to the giving of information to members about a proposed transfer of a building society's business to a company. A building society is permitted to send to its members a summary of its transfer statement. A full transfer statement must be made available to those members who request it. A society must notify its members at the next annual general meeting of any non-confidential proposals received by the society for it to transfer its business to a company.

Where the remuneration of directors or other officers of a building society is to increase, in consequence of the transfer of its business to a company, that must be approved by the members of the society by ordinary resolution.

Sections 40 and 41 of the 1997 Act came into effect on 21 March 1997. Section 40 amends s. 100 of the 1986 Act to remove a requirement under which building societies converting to public limited companies had to maintain a priority liquidation distribution right for depositors who were members of the former society. The effect of the provision under s. 100 was to treat every member of the society who held shares in the society on the day preceding the transfer of business to be treated as if he had a deposit with the successor of an amount equal to the value of his shareholding. That right no longer exists.

Section 41 replaces s. 101 of the 1986 Act which provides for the protection from takeover, previously enjoyed by a successor company to a building society which transfers its business to a specially formed successor for five years after conversion, to be removed if, during that period, the successor company or a subsidiary undertaking takes over, or acquires the business of, another financial institution, or if its shareholders holding 75 per cent of the shares, vote to waive the protection.

THE BUILDING SOCIETIES (DISTRIBUTIONS) ACT 1997

The Building Societies (Distributions) Act 1997 has also received Royal Assent, and came into force on 21 March 1997. This Act introduces new ss. 102B to 102D to the 1986 Act to provide that where a building society transfers its business to a company, and proposes to make a cash or share distribution to members, it must also make a distribution in respect of certain trust accounts (where the beneficiary cannot act in relation to the account because of ill-health or old age etc.) The provisions extend to borrowers and investors, and apply to decisions to transfer business made public after 22 January 1997.

5 Banking and the Single European Market

In the EC, financial integration is, and has always been, an important part of the Community's stated objective of a European internal market. The financial sector represents an important and substantial share of the economies of all EC member States. The creation of the European market requires that the free movement of goods and persons, the freedom of establishment, and the freedom to provide services throughout the market be accompanied by the free supply of financial services. In addition, the free movement of capital is essential. Article 8 of the Treaty of Rome called for the common market to be 'progressively established' during the following 12 years. Impetus was given to this by the Single European Act 1986, which added art. 8a to the Treaty of Rome and provided for the completion of the internal market 'over a period expiring on 1 January 1992' (European Communities Commission, *Completing the Internal Market*, COM (85) 310 final, 14 June 1985. The Act also implemented the *Cassis de Dijon* principle (*Rewe-Zentral AG* v *Bundesmonopolverwaltung für Branntwein* (case 120/78) [1979] ECR 649) or the principle of mutual recognition of national standards. Adopting this approach would have meant that the sale of a product or service which was lawful in one member State could not be prohibited in another member State, unless it was in the 'public interest'. The Single European Act introduced a more expedient system of qualified majority voting on various pieces of EC legislation instead of the requirement of unanimous agreement. The creation of the single market was intended to allow all of the following: (a) the free movement of capital; (b) the right to sell financial services across frontiers without a local establishment; and (c) the right of establishment in other member States without prior authorisation by the host country regulators.

With these objectives in mind, the European Council passed a number of Directives specifically aimed at deregulating the banking industry in member States.

SECOND BANKING COORDINATION DIRECTIVE

The Second Banking Coordination Directive (89/646/EEC, OJ L386, 30.12.89, p. 1) came into force on 1 January 1993 (SI 1992/3218, implemented on 1 January 1993). The purpose of the Directive was to remove the obstacles left by the First

Directive (77/780/EEC) to the free provision of banking services on a cross-border basis and to assist in the EC-wide establishment of credit institutions.

The Second Directive has resulted in fundamental changes in the legal framework of banking business in the Community, with the purpose of creating a single banking market with no internal barriers to the movement of banking services and the establishment of branches but not subsidiaries within the Community. (The distinction between a branch and subsidiary has been criticized: see W. van Gerven, 'The Second Banking Coordination Directive and the Case-law of the Court of Justice' 10 YEL 1991 57, 59). This has been made possible by the creation of a 'single banking licence' through 'mutual recognition' and the application of a minimum of Community standards on prudential supervision.

The Second Directive applies to 'credit institutions' (as defined in the First Banking Directive (see art. I of Directive 77/80/EEC)). Such an institution is defined as an 'undertaking whose business is to receive deposits or other repayable funds from the public and to grant credits for its own account'. The Second Directive also applies to 'financial institutions' (i.e., subsidiaries 90 per cent owned by one or more credit institutions and complying with certain conditions, including a guarantee from a parent company (arts 1(6) and 18(2))). Activities which are not authorised in the annex to the Directive and entities that are not authorised and supervised as credit institutions (i.e., as deposit-taking institutions) will not benefit from mutual recognition. Thus, the single banking licence is valid in other member States only with respect to banking activities that are enumerated in the annex to the Directive. The annex therefore defines the scope of the principle of mutual recognition. Credit institutions authorised in their home member State will be entitled in each of the other member States:

(a)   to establish branches (arts 18 and 19); and
(b)   to offer their services freely to individuals and businesses without the need for any further authorisation by the host member State.

Mutual recognition is extended to a branch but not to a subsidiary of a credit institution. A subsidiary, being a separate legal entity, is required to obtain its own licence before it can engage in banking activities.

A host member State may subject a credit institution from another member State to licensing and supervision requirements if it wishes to undertake any services in addition to those specified in the annex. The requirements must satisfy the following conditions:

(a)   credit institutions from the host member State must be subject to the same requirements;
(b)   the imposition of licensing and supervision requirements in the host member State in addition to those already imposed by the home member State must be justified on grounds of public policy; and
(c)   the likelihood of causing harm to the public must justify the licensing requirements or other restrictions in question.

Although mutual recognition permits a Community credit institution to provide its services anywhere in the Community the Second Directive prevents 'forum shopping'. It states that the principle of mutual recognition requires that member

States do not grant an authorisation or withdraw an existing authorisation where it appears that the institution has opted for the legal system of one member State for the purpose of evading the stricter standards of supervision in other member States (Second Banking Coordination Directive, 8th recital). The power to refuse or withdraw an authorisation is only given to home member States. Host member States do not have the power either to refuse, or to withdraw an authorisation to operate a branch of a credit institution from another member State.

The annex (reproduced in sch. I to the Second Banking Coordination Directive Regulations) to the Second Directive enumerates activities which, in the opinion of the Commission, are considered to be 'integral to banking' and which constitute the provision of traditional banking services in the Community, namely:

(a)   acceptance of deposits and other repayable funds from the public;
(b)   lending, including consumer and mortgage credit, factoring and financing of commercial transactions;
(c)   financial leasing;
(d)   money transmission services;
(e)   issuing and administering means of payment (e.g., cheques, credit cards, money orders);
(f)   guarantees and commitments;
(g)   trading for customers or for own account in:

(i)   money market instruments (cheques, bills, certificates of deposit etc.),
(ii)   foreign exchange,
(iii)   financial futures and options,
(iv)   exchange and interest rate instruments,
(v)   transferable securities;

(h)   participation in share issues and the provision of services related to such issues;
(i)   advice to undertakings on capital structure, industrial strategy and related questions, and advice and services relating to mergers and the purchase of undertakings;
(j)   money broking;
(k)   portfolio management and advice;
(l)   safekeeping and administration of securities;
(m)   credit reference services;
(n)   safe custody services.

The agreed list of banking activities has been drawn up on a liberal universal banking model. The most important and far-reaching aspect of the list is the inclusion of all forms of transactions in securities. The Commission recommends that the annex be updated under a flexible procedure so that it can respond to changes in banking services and practice.

Branch establishment

A credit institution which wishes to establish a branch in another member State is required to inform the authorities of its home member State of its intention to establish a branch in the host member State (arts 19(1) and 20). The notification must be accompanied by certain information concerning the credit institution and the branch, in particular information relating to the operations and structure of the branch (art. 19(2)). The home member State authorities must communicate this information, together with information on own funds and solvency ratio of the credit institution, to the authorities in the host member State within three months (art. 19(3)). The only action open to the authorities of the home member State is to refuse a referral to establish a branch to the authority in the host State. In such a situation the home member State must give reasons for such a refusal, which is subject to appeal in the courts of the home member State (art. 19(3)).

Role of supervisors

The Second Directive is based on the principle of 'home country control' under which each credit institution will be supervised by the authorities of the home member State, even in connection with activities carried out across the border in another member State (Second Directive, 4th and 10th recitals, arts 13 and 15). Consequently, the various supervisory functions to be exercised over a bank's activities, including the activities of its branches in other member States will fall to the authorities of the member State where the bank has its head office. The Second Directive, however, provides some exceptions to this rule, for example, the host member State will retain primary responsibility for the supervision of liquidity of the branches of credit institutions and exclusive responsibility for the implementation of monetary policy. Therefore, the authorities in the host country no longer have competence over solvency regulation; this transfer of power has been achieved by the simultaneous entry into force, along with the Second Banking Directive, of the Community Directives concerning solvency ratios (89/647/EEC, OJ L386, 30.12.89, p. 14) and own funds (89/299/EEC, OJ L124, 5.5.89, p. 16).

Creation of Community-wide barriers to non-EC banks

The preamble to the Second Banking Directive indicates that the rules of reciprocity set out in the First Directive governing the authorisation of branches of credit institutions from non-EC countries will continue to apply. Consequently, it was originally thought that all banks incorporated in non-EC countries would be precluded from opening up branches within the EC or even from setting up a banking business if their home country failed to provide the same opportunities to EC banks. However, the actual practical implications of reciprocity have changed from time to time, largely due to lobbying by non-EC banks. On 13 April 1989, the European Commission issued a statement clarifying the situation. The statement was adopted on 29 May 1989, and accepted by the Council on 19 June 1989. The drafting of art. 9 was revised as a result and now provides that where the Commission finds that a third country is not granting the Community's credit institutions market access and competitive opportunities comparable to those granted by the Community to non-EC banks (equivalent treatment), the Commission may submit suitable proposals to the Council for negotiations with the third country in question (art. 9(4)). Moreover, where the condition of effective market access has not been secured, the Commission may 'limit' or 'suspend' new authorisations and acquisitions by institutions governed by the laws of the third country (art. 9(4)). It is therefore important for non-EC banks to devise a strategy with regard to the entry barriers to the EC member States.

Foreign banks and the single market

Whilst the Second Banking Directive created the single market in banking services for EC countries, it also affected the position of non-EC banks.

Community legislation makes a distinction between the establishment of a subsidiary within the Community by a foreign bank and the establishment of a branch. Subsidiaries of foreign banks incorporated in any member State of the EC are legally independent entities subject to Community law and to the national legislation of the country of incorporation. They are considered Community credit institutions and have the same rights and obligations as other 'domestic' EC credit institutions (Second Directive, arts 18(1) and 19(1)). Once authorised by the supervisory body of the country of incorporation, such subsidiaries enjoy the same freedom under the Second Banking Directive to establish branches as institutions originating from within the EC member States. The main issue for foreign banks is the conditions for entry into the Community market, embodied in the notion of 'reciprocity'.

In contrast to subsidiaries, branches of non-EC banks do not qualify for the EC-wide licence and will not benefit from mutual recognition and the privileges attached to it. The activities of a branch of a foreign bank will be limited to the territory of the member State where it is located and will be subject to the national legislation of that country.

The 'reciprocity' issue

The move to a single licence represents a major change in entry to the EC markets for foreign banks. The consequence of the single market is that one member State (country A) will have to permit the operation of a subsidiary of a foreign bank from a third country licensed in another member State (country B), although the licence would not have been issued to that subsidiary by member State A because of lack of a reciprocal arrangement with the foreign government. National reciprocal arrangements are ineffective; instead the Second Banking Directive evaluates reciprocity on a Community basis.

The reciprocity clause in the Second Banking Directive must be read in the light of the Commission's consistent statements that European markets should remain open. However, the Community negotiates from a position of strength with reciprocity being looked at on a Community-wide basis. Applications from non-Community institutions for the establishment of a subsidiary within the Community are suspended whilst the Commission investigates whether EC credit institutions in the Community enjoy reciprocal treatment in the third country from which the institution originates. If reciprocal arrangements are found to be lacking then the Commission undertakes negotiations with the third country to remedy the situation (Second Directive, art. 9). In the original proposal, the term 'reciprocal treatment' was not defined and this led to fears that 'mirror treatment' would be insisted upon by the Commission. The proposal was criticised as in some non-EC countries banks would have found it difficult to respond on such a basis, e.g., in the USA where the then Glass–Steagall Act and the then barriers to interstate banking would preclude 'mirror treatment', and so it was argued that reciprocity should be based on 'national treatment', i.e., according foreign institutions the same treatment given to domestic institutions. The Commission was accused of creating 'Fortress Europe', although the Commission's intention was to open up the banking markets by liberalising the institutions from national restrictions. However, the Commission acknowledged that the proposed regulation was too cumbersome for foreign institutions and a revised proposal was put forward in early 1989, which more clearly indicated the treatment it wished third countries to provide for EC credit institutions defining the circumstances in which sanctions would be triggered. The amended proposal was further revised by the European Council of Ministers, and adopted as part of the Second Banking Directive. Moreover, the title to the reciprocity provisions has been changed from 'Reciprocity' to 'Relations with Third Countries', signalling that retaliation was not the main objective.

Branches of foreign banks and EC regulation

A branch of a foreign bank is a dependent unit of the credit institution incorporated in a non-EC country. Branches of non-EC banks are licensed within the Community by the national authorities of each member State only for the territory of the particular country. They do not enjoy the rights guaranteed by the Treaty of Rome to freedom of services throughout the Community. Since branches of foreign banks are not legally independent entities, they cannot establish sub-branches. Branches of foreign banks are not governed by the Second Banking Directive but by the national law of the member State in which the branch operates. Since 1977, member States have been obliged to notify the Commission and the EC Banking Advisory Committee of all authorisations granted to subsidiaries of foreign banks (art. 8(a)).

The First Banking Directive states that member States 'shall not apply to branches of credit institutions having their head office outside the Community . . . provisions which result in more favourable treatment than that accorded to branches of credit institutions having their head office in the Community' (art. 9(1)). This provision applies both to the initial authorisation of such branches and to the rules relating to their continuing business. This principle is also expressed in art. 5(2) of the original Recommendation on Large Exposures (87/62/EEC, OJ L33, 4.2.87, p. 10) and in the Council Directive on the disclosure requirements for branches of banks having their head office outside the member State of incorporation of that branch (89/117/EEC, OJ L44, 16.2.89, p. 40).

In discussions prior to the adoption of the Second Banking Directive, the European Parliament and some member States advocated the harmonisation of supervision of branches of foreign banks in the Community, notably the requirements for capitalisation. The European Parliament was concerned that branches of third-country banks might receive an unfair advantage in some member States once the single market was achieved, and, in the first and second readings of the proposal, the Parliament voted in favour of far-reaching amendments as 'an indispensable adjunct to a soundly conceived principle of reciprocity'.

The Commission and the majority of the member States repeatedly rejected the need for harmonisation and reciprocity clauses covering such branches since the branches of foreign banks do not enjoy the benefits of single licence. However, the First Banking Directive provided, as early as 1977, that 'the Community may through arrangements concluded in accordance with one or more third countries, agree to apply provisions which, on the basis of the principle of reciprocity, accord to branches of a credit institution having its head office outside the Community identical treatment throughout the territory of the Community'.

OWN FUNDS DIRECTIVE

The Directive on Own Funds (89/299/EEC, OJ L124/16, 17.5.89, p. 16, implemented in the UK in December 1990 (BSD/1990/2)) establishes standard EC definitions of capital for prudential supervision purposes and follows closely the Basle Convergence Agreement on Capital Standards, which was implemented in the UK from the end of 1989. The Own Funds Directive applies to all credit institutions as defined in art. 1 of the First Banking Coordination Directive (77/780/EEC), including building societies. Although the provisions of the Own Funds Directive are applied on a consolidated basis in the UK, the Bank of England or Building Societies Commission will nevertheless assess capital adequacy on an unconsolidated basis to ensure a reasonable distribution of capital within a group. The own funds of a credit institution can serve to absorb losses and therefore serve as a yardstick for the regulatory authorities of the solvency of a credit institution.

Until the adoption of the Directive there were no EC-wide definitions of own funds. Own funds are the most expensive funds for a company and therefore it is important to identify the extent to which equity substitutes are being recognised as own funds for this will reflect on the competitiveness of the credit institution. The Own Funds Directive only defines a maximum list of such items and qualifying amounts to be included in the own funds calculation, allowing member States to use their discretion as to whether all or some items will be recognised, and enabling them to use lower ceilings for the qualifying amounts. This will enable member States to influence the competitive position of their credit institutions.

Own funds serve as the reference basis not only for the solvency ratio, but also for a number of other supervisory standards like capital adequacy, the limitations on large exposures and the limitations of participations in non-bank entities.

A credit institution's own funds consist of its capital elements, similar to those agreed under the Basle Agreement and the US risk-based Capital Adequacy Guide-lines. According to the Own Funds Directive, the member State may recognise the following as to be included in the 'Own Funds' calculation (art. 2):

(a) paid-up capital plus share premium accounts;
(b) reserves;
(c) revaluation reserves;
(d) funds for general banking risk;
(e) value adjustments;
(f) certain other funds and securities, fixed-term cumulative preferential shares and subordinated debt; and

(g) commitments of the members of credit institutions set up as cooperative societies and of the borrowers of certain institutions organised as funds.

A distinction is made between 'original own funds' and 'additional own funds'.

The Directive provides for certain limits on additional own funds and provides that the amount of additional own funds or 'soft capital' (items (c), (e), (f) and (g) in the above list) by comparison to the original own funds or 'core capital' (items (a) and (b)) mean that the total amount of soft capital taken into account may not exceed 100 per cent of the amount of core capital, and subordinated loans and fixed-term preferential shares may not exceed 50 per cent of the core capital.

DIRECTIVE ON CONSOLIDATED SUPERVISION

The Council Directive on the Supervision of Credit Institutions on a Consolidated Basis (92/30/EEC, OJ L110, 28.4.92, p. 52, implemented in the UK in 1993 (BSD/1993/1)) replaces Directive 83/350/EEC. Directive 92/30/EEC requires the consolidated supervision of the financial condition of a credit institution, including credit or financial institutions in which it holds a participation. Consolidated supervision means that the authority supervising the parent credit institution will apply the financial data of the whole group in monitoring compliance by the credit institution with its supervisory standards (e.g., solvency ratio; lending limits and restrictions on investments by credit institutions in the non-trade sector). Consolidated supervision must be distinguished from the principle of home member State supervision as provided for under the Second Banking Directive. The consolidated supervision will be the responsibility of the regulatory authorities in the home member State where the parent credit institution has its head office (art. 3(8)). Whenever possible supervision by the home member State will be exercised in consultation with the regulatory authorities of the member States of the subsidiary institutions, so that distortions of competition between the consolidated group and the domestic credit institutions of the countries in which the members of the group are established will be avoided. However, the Directive on Consolidated Supervision does not preclude concurrent supervision of a subsidiary by the authorities where the subsidiary is authorised.

The concept of the Directive on Consolidated Supervision is that a credit institution's financial status should be assessed realistically. Equity investments in other credit or financial institutions require particular attention, because a subsidiary's financial difficulties may affect the financial stability and soundness of the credit institution being assessed ('contagion risk'). Equity investments also constitute a long-term freezing of the assets of the investing credit institution. Only consolidated supervision prevents a credit institution from escaping compliance with supervisory standards by moving assets or activities into subsidiaries. For these reasons subsidiaries will be supervised by the parent credit institution's home member State.

The Directive on Consolidated Supervision only applies where a credit institution, i.e., deposit-taking institution, is the parent company. Consolidated supervision extends to credit and financial institutions in which a credit institution has a participation (art. 2). 'Financial institution' is defined as an 'undertaking, not being a credit institution, whose principal activity is to grant credit facilities (including guarantees), to acquire participations or to make investments'. 'Participation' means ownership, directly or indirectly, of 25 per cent or more of the capital of another credit or financial institution (art. 1, indent 6). Where ownership is between 25 and 50 per cent of the capital of another credit or financial institution, there is discretion as to whether and how consolidation may be effected.

Consolidated supervision is not limited to participations in credit and financial institutions located in the Community but an exemption is given to credit or financial institutions located in a non-Community country where there are legal restrictions to the transfer of the necessary information. An application of the principle of supervision on a consolidated basis to credit institutions whose parent companies have their head office in non-Community countries and to credit institutions situated in non-Community countries whose parent credit institutions have a head office in a member State will be made possible by reciprocal bilateral agreements to be entered into between the competent authorities of the member States and the non-Community countries concerned. Within the EC, and to enable the home country State to perform the necessary consolidated supervision, all member States are directed to ensure that the necessary information for consolidated supervision can be exchanged.

The Solvency Ratio Directive (89/647/EEC, OJ [386, 30.12.89, p. 14, implemented in the UK in December 1990 (BSD/1990/3)) and the Owns Funds Directive (89/299/EEC, OJ L124, 5.5.89, p. 16, implemented in the UK in December 1990 (BSD/1990/2)) apply to consolidated supervision of the whole group, even to those affiliates that are involved in market risks rather than credit risks. The dual regulation results in a competitive disadvantage for banks which have to maintain capital to cover both credit risks (under the Solvency Ratio Directive) and market risks (under the Capital Adequacy Directive).

Supervision of control of large exposures is proposed to be carried out on a consolidated basis in accordance with a Council Directive on Monitoring and Controlling Large Exposure of Credit Institutions.

SOLVENCY RATIO DIRECTIVE

The Solvency Ratio Directive (89/647/EEC, OJ L386, 30.12.89, p. 14, implemented in the UK in December 1990 (BSD/1990/3)) must be read together with the Own Funds Directive (89/299/EEC, OJ L124, 5.5.89, p. 16, implemented in the UK in December 1990 (BSD/1990/2)). The aim of the Solvency Ratio Directive (given effect in the UK in 1990) is to ensure that every credit institution authorised under the Second Directive has sufficient and sound capitalisation to withstand losses caused by the realisation of risks inherent to the banking business. The Solvency Ratio Directive represents the Community's version of the capital adequacy rules of the Basle Committee on Banking Regulations and Supervisory Practices that were proposed by the 'Basle Agreement' (Committee on Banking Regulations and Supervisory Practices, International Convergence of Capital Measurement and Capital Standards, July 1988). The Solvency Ratio Directive requires the member States to adopt the measures necessary to comply with its provisions, which in turn will satisfy the Basle Agreement.

The Solvency Ratio Directive is applicable to all credit institutions as defined by art. 1 of the First Banking Directive. If a credit institution is a parent undertaking and to be included in the consolidated supervision of a banking group, the solvency ratio is to be calculated on a consolidated basis in accordance with the provisions of the Directive on Consolidated Supervision and the Bank Accounting Directive (86/635/EEC, OJ L372, 31.12.86, p. 1).

The Solvency Ratio Directive addresses only the credit risk incurred by a credit institution. It provides a formula to compute a credit institution's solvency ratio. The Bank of England's capital requirements will continue to be specified as target and trigger risk-asset ratios. The 8 per cent minimum standard required by art. 10(1), remains the base line for the Bank's discretion in setting the requirements at both consolidated and solo (or solo consolidated) levels.

LARGE EXPOSURES DIRECTIVE

The Commission issued a Recommendation on Monitoring and Controlling Large Exposures of Credit Institutions (87/62/EEC; OJ L33, 4.2.87. p. 10, implemented in the UK in October 1993 (BSD/1993/2)) in 1987. It was intended to prevent excessive exposure concentrations to a single creditor or group of creditors. The Commission's reason for choosing a recommendation rather than a binding Directive was that the banking systems of member States could be adjusted more gradually at the discretion of each member, whereas a Directive would have to be implemented by a given date.

The annex to the Large Exposures Recommendation contained a detailed outline of what was considered to be a 'large exposure' and how such exposures should be controlled. A 'large exposure' was defined as one equal to or exceeding 15 per cent of a credit institution's own funds. The annex proposed an amount equal to 40 per cent of the own funds as the maximum acceptable amount of exposure to a single client or group of clients. The total of a credit institution's large exposures could not be more than 800 per cent of its own funds and these limits should be exceeded only in extraordinary circumstances.

The Large Exposures Recommendation suggested that supervision should be achieved through the introduction of a reporting requirement for large exposures and member States should require Community credit institutions to report any large exposure to the competent home member State authorities at least once a year. In the case of non-Community credit institutions, the annex proposed that the branch's large exposures should be reported to the authorities of the host member State.

However in January 1994, the UK implemented the Council Directive on the Monitoring and Control of Large Exposures of Credit Institutions (92/121/EEC, OJ L29, 5.2.93, p. 1). At the same time the Bank of England undertook a review of its policy on large exposures. The mandatory imposition of large exposure limits is based on the idea that the controlling of exposure is an integral part of prudential supervision, and excessive concentration of exposures to a single client or group of connected clients might result in an unacceptable danger of loss. The Directive is intended to neutralise distortions of competition arising from differing large exposure limitations in the various member States. The Bank of England requires each bank to set out its policy on large exposures, including exposures to individual customers, banks, countries and economic sectors, in a policy statement. In the case of UK-incorporated banks, this policy should be formally adopted by the bank's board of directors. The Bank of England expects banks not to implement significant changes in these policies without prior discussion with it. Significant departures from a bank's stated policy may lead the Bank of England to reconsider whether the bank satisfies the statutory minimum criteria for authorisation.

The Large Exposures Directive contains basically the same definitions as other Directives but the term 'exposure' includes all risks defined in the Solvency Ratio Directive.

The Large Exposures Directive also provides for a reporting requirement of large exposures. The definition of large exposure is consistent with the definition in the Large Exposure Recommendation but a special limit will apply to exposures by a credit institution to its affiliates other than own subsidiaries which will be 30 per cent of own funds in the aggregate. The Directive also grants member States' authorities the right to exempt certain exposures fully or partially or apply a weight to a large exposure. Such exempted exposures include loans to certain affiliates of credit institutions and claims against central governments, central banks and European Communities. The control of large exposures will be effected on the basis of a consolidated supervision.

BANK ACCOUNTING DIRECTIVE

In 1986, the Council of the European Communities adopted the Directive on the Annual Accounts and Consolidated Accounts of Banks and Other Financial Institutions (86/635/EEC, OJ L372 31.12.86, p. 1 which came into force in the UK under the Bank Accounts Directive (Miscellaneous Banks) Regulations 1991 (SI 1991/2704), the Companies Act 1985 (Bank Accounts) Regulations 1991 (SI 1991/2705) and the Companies Act 1985 (Bank Accounts) Regulations 1994 (SI 1994/233)). In order for borrowers, creditors, shareholders and the public, from different member States, to be able to compare the annual accounts and the consolidated accounts, this Directive provides for Community-wide harmonised accounting standards for credit and financial institutions. The provisions governing annual accounts of credit institutions are also necessary to provide a uniform basis for the coordination of supervisory standards for authorisation requirements and other purposes. The Directive addresses the specific problems of credit institutions and requires broader publication of their financial status than is required for other companies. The Directive is currently being revised (see *Journal of International and Banking Financial Law*, January 1997, p. 97).

RECOMMENDATION AND DIRECTIVE ON DEPOSIT GUARANTEE SCHEMES

The Recommendation Concerning the Introduction of Deposit Guarantee Schemes (87/63/EEC, OJ L33, 4.2.87, p. 16) suggested the Community-wide introduction and harmonisation of deposit guarantee schemes. These are schemes designed to guarantee appropriate compensation for depositors in order to protect them against losses. As a mere recommendation the member States were not required to conform to it but it was seen as an inducement for the voluntary introduction of deposit guarantee schemes. The Deposit Guarantee Recommendation suggested certain minimum standards for existing and future schemes throughout the Community.

A Directive on Deposit Guarantee Schemes (94/19/EC, OJ L135, 31.5.94, p. 5) was adopted by the European Community in May 1994 and it has been implemented in member States. Under changes proposed to the UK scheme (Credit Institutions (Protection of Depositors) Regulations 1995 (SI 1995/1442) implemented on 1 July 1995), qualifying deposits placed with the UK branch of a bank from another EEA country will be covered by the bank's home country deposit protection arrangements, rather than by the UK scheme. The cover of the UK scheme was widened to branches of UK-incorporated institutions throughout the EEA. The other main changes introduced were the extension of the UK scheme to include deposits in other EEA currencies as well as sterling, and to increase the level of cover offered by the UK scheme from 75 per cent to 90 per cent of the first £20,000 of the deposit.

There are no changes to the structure of the Deposit Protection Scheme nor the way it is funded. However, the UK scheme will 'top up' cover to UK branches of EEA banks whose home State cover is less generous than that offered here, with branches which choose to pay for this option given the same total level of cover as is offered to depositors with UK-authorised institutions.

Guarantee schemes exist in most member States but they differ widely in their legal structure and in the scope of protection they confer.

PRUDENTIAL SUPERVISION DIRECTIVE

Agreement was reached among member States on a Directive to reinforce prudential supervision within the European Community following the collapse of BCCI (95/26/EC, OJ 1995 L168/7, 18.7.95). It came into effect on 16 July 1996 (Bank of England Notice, 55/1996/9). It covers not only credit institutions but also investment firms and insurance companies. The Directive has four main provisions:

(a)   It requires supervisors to refuse authorisation where group and ownership links preclude effective prudential supervision.

(b)   Member States must require that a financial undertaking has its head office in the same State as the registered office.

(c)   It allows member States to widen the range of disclosure gateways, to allow supervisors to provide confidential information to, amongst others, those supervising the accountancy profession, and to bodies responsible for the detection and investigation of breaches of company law (including external inspectors).

(d)   Member States are required to place a duty on auditors, and experts (e.g., reporting accountants) appointed by supervisory authorities, to report material breaches of law and certain other concerns to the supervisory bodies.

PART 3

6 Customers

WHO IS A CUSTOMER?

Why the question is important

Although there is no statutory definition of the term 'customer' it may be of paramount importance to determine whether in a given situation a person or institution is a 'customer' within the banker and customer context. In fact the term 'bank' or 'banker' cannot be defined without reference to the term 'customer'.

The question may be of practical significance because it may be necessary to decide whether a banker and customer relation exists for the purposes of various statutory provisions. For example, s. 75(1) of the Bills of Exchange Act 1882 deals with the customer's right to countermand payment of cheques; whilst s. 75(2) deals with the termination of the banker and customer relationship on the customer's death; s. 1 of the Cheques Act 1957 deals with the paying banker's liability regarding endorsements on cheques and s. 4 deals with the collecting banker's liability where it receives payment for a customer other than the true owner.

The nature of the contract entered into between the bank and its customer imposes certain contractual duties between the parties, for example, the bank will owe its customer a duty to conform to the customer's mandate, to exercise reasonable skill and care (this is reinforced under the Supply of Goods and Services Act 1982) and the duty of confidentiality. The law may also hold that the bank owes certain fiduciary duties to its customer.

A number of remedies are available to the bank where its customer becomes overdrawn or does not keep up with repayments (e.g., right to combine or consolidate accounts).

Case law

A number of cases have examined the features of the banker and customer relationship which would be indicative of a person being a customer of a bank:

(a)   The banker and customer relationship does not come into existence unless the parties intended to enter into that relationship. In *Robinson* v *Midland Bank Ltd* (1925) 41 TLR 402 it was said that a person does not become a customer of a bank unless he opens an account personally or instructs an agent to act for him. In *Barclays Bank Ltd* v *Okenarhe* [1966] 2 Lloyd's Rep 87 it was suggested by Bailhache J that a mere offer to open an account, and its acceptance by the bank, will create a binding contract on the basis of the general law of contract.

(b)   There must be an account held by the bank, whether that be a current or deposit account, to make a person a customer. In *Great Western Railway Co* v *London and County Banking Co. Ltd* [1901] AC 414 the House of Lords held that cheques (which the bank had cashed for a man who had obtained them fraudulently were not cashed for a customer since the man did not maintain an account with the bank and nothing was put to the debit or credit of an account for him. The bank had merely collected the money for itself and since it had a defective title to the cheques the bank was liable to the true owner.

(c)   Duration is not of the essence to the existence of the banker and customer relationship (*Commissioners of Taxation* v *English, Scottish and Australian Bank Ltd* [1920] AC 683). A person whose money has been accepted by a bank on the footing that the bank undertakes to honour cheques up to the amount of the credit balance standing on his account is a customer of the bank 'irrespective of whether his connection is of short or long standing'. A person will be a customer although he has never drawn on the account; the mere fact that an account facility has been opened for him by the bank is sufficient (see *Ladbroke* v *Todd* (1914) 111 LT 43).

(d)   The general rule that a customer of a bank must hold an account with a bank may be qualified to the extent that a person who merely agrees to open an account may be treated as a customer. In *Woods* v *Martins Bank Ltd* [1959] 1 QB 55 the plaintiff was given certain investment advice by the defendant's bank manager. The plaintiff signed a letter instructing the bank to deal with amounts previously held in a building society account. Any credit balance was to be held by the bank for the account of the plaintiff. It was held that the banker and customer relationship existed from the date the bank accepted instructions contained in the letter, even though the account was not actually opened until later. The imposition of liability for negligent advice would not now be dependent on establishing a banker and customer relationship since a duty of care is owed by the bank in undertaking its business activities (*Barclays Bank plc* v *Quincecare* [1988] FTLR 507; see p. 150).

(e)   A person is not a customer of a bank if the bank merely 'performs some casual service' for him (*Great Western Railway Co* v *London and County Banking Co. Ltd*; *Barclays Bank Ltd* v *Okenarhe* [1966] 2 Lloyd's Rep 87). Merely cashing cheques over the counter does not make the recipient of the payments a customer. In practice banks will often cash a cheque over the counter if accompanied by a cheque card for a person who is not a customer, and that does not make the recipient of the payment a customer of the bank. Even a course of casual dealings will not be sufficient to create a banker and customer relationship (*Ladbroke* v *Todd*; *Commissioners of Taxation* v *English, Scottish and Australian Bank Ltd*).

(f)   A bank may be a customer of another bank if it has an account with that other bank. Since the clearing banks maintain accounts with the Bank of England there exists a banker and customer relationship between them and the Bank.

Alternatively, where a bank which is not a member of the clearing system uses that bank to clear its cheques the banker and customer relationship is established (*Importers Co. Ltd* v *Westminster Bank Ltd* [1927] 2 KB 297). Consequently, the expression 'customer' is not restricted to the individual customers of a bank. The same reasoning would apply to a building society which, not being a member of the clearing system, employs a bank to clear cheques drawn on accounts held with banks paid into the credit of its customer's account. In practice some building societies notify their customers that such cheques paid to the credit of the customer's account will take anything between eight and 10 days to be credited to the customer's account.

(g)   The opening of an account by a person who purports to act with the authority of another, but in fact does not do so, will not create a contractual relationship between the bank and the person purported to be represented or between the bank and the actual applicant.

(h)   Where, however, the person who opens an account impersonates another with a view to committing a deception he may still become a customer of the bank if the bank manager intended to deal with the person before him and not the person he represented himself to be (see *Barclays Bank Ltd* v *Okenarhe*; *Ladbroke* v *Todd* in which Bailhache J held that a rogue who pretended to be the person named on a cheque tendered by him to the defendant bank was, for the purposes of the banker and customer relationship, its customer).

(i)   In the case of forgery, however, the alleged customer cannot ratify the agent's acts. As bank accounts can easily be used for fraudulent acts the authority of a person who purports to act as an agent in opening the account must be clearly checked and verified. In *Stoney Stanton Supplies (Coventry) Ltd* v *Midland Bank Ltd* [1966] 2 Lloyd's Rep 373 it was held that a banker and customer relationship had not been entered into when it was discovered that the bank's mandate to open the account had been forged. This was despite the fact that the bank had opened an account relying on the mandate and the account had actually been operated.

SPECIAL TYPES OF CUSTOMER

The discussion so far has concentrated on the relationship which must subsist for a person to be treated as a customer of the bank. Once that relationship is established there exists a single contract which binds the bank and its customer. Moreover, by the nature of the relationship which exists any sums paid to the credit of the customer's account become the property of the bank. Consequently the customer has a right to sue in debt for any balance standing to the credit of his account (*Foley* v *Hill* (1848) 2 HL CAS 28). By complying with the payment mandate the bank satisfies two distinct functions: (a) it repays the debt owed to the customer, and (b) it acts as an agent in complying with the customer's mandate.

The performance of these functions does not usually cause any problems in the course of the banker and customer relationship, but problems may arise if the account has been opened by an individual other than in his or her personal capacity, e.g., as trustee or on behalf of a partnership. In connection with special accounts the bank must safeguard its position and ensure that (a) the person giving the mandate has the authority to act in that capacity, and (b) that the payment mandate is issued in favour of the person entitled to the money. If the bank fails to act properly with regard to either of these obligations it may find itself liable to the true owner of the funds either because the mandate was defective and the bank has acted without authority, or payment is made to someone other than the true owner.

The following discussion examines the types of special accounts which banks may open and the consequences of opening such accounts.

JOINT ACCOUNTS

A joint account is one which is opened in the name of two or more persons in their own capacity. Although any one or more of the joint account holders may be authorised to draw against the account, each account holder acts for himself or the other joint holders and this distinguishes joint account holders from other account holders who act in a representative or fiduciary capacity, e.g., directors of a company.

One of the main concerns of joint account holders will be who has authority to draw against the account. When a joint account is opened with a bank the account holders will give instructions to the bank which will authorise it to honour instructions drawn either by any one of the joint account holders, by two or more of their number or by all of them. A bank may find it has failed to comply with the payment mandate either where a cheque does not bear the authorised signature or because the authorised signature is forged. In *Jackson* v *White* [1967] 2 Lloyd's Rep 68 the plaintiff entered into negotiations with a view to entering into a partnership with the first defendant. The plaintiff paid into a joint account £2,000 and instructed the bank that cheques could only be drawn against the signatures of both himself and the first defendant. The first defendant forged several cheques which were honoured by the bank. The first defendant refused to repay the money misappropriated from the joint account when negotiations with the plaintiff to join the business broke down. The plaintiff applied for an injunction against the bank compelling it to re-credit the account with the amount of the forged cheques and for an order requiring the bank to honour cheques drawn by the plaintiff alone. Parke J (following *Welch* v *Bank of England* [1955] Ch 508; *Twibell* v *London Suburban Bank* [1869] WN 127 and the Australian case of *Ardern* v *Bank of New South Wales* [1956] VLR 569) held that the bank entered into both a joint agreement to honour cheques drawn jointly by the plaintiff and first defendant, and a separate agreement with each of them not to honour cheques improperly drawn. As the bank had honoured cheques not signed by the plaintiff, the plaintiff was entitled to sue for breach of that separate agreement.

A similar view was expressed in *Catlin* v *Cyprus Finance Corporation (London) Ltd* [1983] QB 759 where the bank honoured instructions given by one of the joint account holders, in breach of its mandate. The court held that although the account was a joint account the bank owed a separate duty to conform to the mandate of each joint account holder. Bingham J said that a duty owed to the joint account holders which could only have been enforced jointly would be worthless where the purpose of the account was to safeguard against the misconduct of one of the account holders.

The nature of the bank's liability to joint account holders was cast in doubt by *Brewer* v *Westminster Bank Ltd* [1952] 2 All ER 650 where it was held that an action on a joint account could only be brought by the joint holders, and therefore an action against the bank failed because one of the account holders had in fact forged the signature of the other. However, in the light of the *Jackson* and *Catlin* cases, *Brewer* v *Westminster Bank Ltd* cannot be regarded as good law.

In both the *Jackson* and *Catlin* cases the plaintiffs established that funds paid into the accounts were their property. Consequently, both plaintiffs were entitled to recover the full amounts of the cheques which should have been dishonoured (see *Welch* v *Bank of England*). However, where the action is based merely on breach of contract by the bank (*Twibell* v *London Suburban Bank*) the court held that the proper measure of damages 'was a moiety of the sum for which the cheque was drawn'.

A defrauded joint owner of an account may not be allowed to recover the amount of an unauthorised cheque if the payment discharges a valid debt. The equitable principle of subrogation would apply to discharge the debt owed to a third party and to that extent the bank stands in the position of the debtor. In *B. Liggett (Liverpool) Ltd* v *Barclays Bank Ltd* [1928] 1 KB 48 a bank, contrary to its mandate, honoured a company's cheques signed by a single director. The cheques were drawn in favour of, and paid to, the company's trade creditors. The company brought an action against the bank to recover the amount of the defective cheques. In normal circumstances there would undoubtedly have been liability imposed on the bank but for the principle of subrogation, which enabled the bank to enforce the rights of the trade creditors for payment. Wright J was of the opinion that in such cases the customer is really no worse off because his legal liability is discharged to the debtor, although in circumstances which at common law would not entitle the bank to debit the customer's account. The principle was followed in *Jackson* v *White* and enabled the court to mitigate the rule that at common law a bank which makes a payment against an invalid mandate cannot debit the customer's account or if so debited must re-credit the account. An innocent joint account holder who seeks to recover the amount of an unauthorised cheque by virtue of the joint ownership can only recover one half of the account.

The problem which arose in the *Jackson* and *Catlin* cases does not arise where either, or any, of the joint holders can draw against the account for their own purposes. However, in *Re Bishop* [1965] Ch 450 the fact that investments purchased sometimes in the names of a husband and wife jointly and sometimes in the sole name of one or other of them were paid for out of a joint account to which both the husband and wife credited funds did nothing to displace the legal titles indicated by the purchase transactions. Stamp J held that where a joint account is opened then, in the absence of facts or circumstances which indicate that the account was intended, or was kept, for some specific or limited purpose, each account holder can draw upon it not only for the benefit of both account holders but for his or her own benefit. Each account holder, in drawing money out of the account, is to be treated as doing so with the authority of the other (see also *Re Young* (1885) 28 ChD 705; *Pettitt* v *Pettitt* [1970] AC 777).

Where one of the joint account holders dies the question which inevitably arises is who is entitled to the credit balance in the joint account. In most cases the modern bank mandate form will contain a survivorship clause and the contract will thus specify the person or persons to whom the bank may pay the credit balance on the joint account. But even failing a survivorship clause it is well established that legal title in the deceased's share of the credit balance vests in the survivor (see *Russell* v *Scott* (1936) 55 CLR 440 at 451). Indeed, *McEvoy* v *Belfast Banking Co. Ltd* [1935] AC 24 shows how imprudent it may be for the bank to ignore a survivorship clause. In that case a customer whose health was failing deposited £10,000 with the bank in the joint names of himself and his son. He specifically instructed the bank that the amount deposited was payable to either of joint holders or to the survivor. The purpose of the transaction was to avoid death duties which would become payable on the father's death if the amount deposited formed part of the father's estate at the time of his death. The balance of the father's estate was left to the executors in trust for his son, who would acquire the property on his 25th birthday. On the father's death the executors transferred the £10,000 from the joint account into their own names and frequently used the balance in the course of a business left by the father. All this was done with the knowledge of the son who took an active part in the business. However, on the business going into liquidation the son demanded the amount of £10,000 from the bank under the rights of survivorship attached. The majority of the House of Lords concluded that the executors were entitled to receive the money and apply it under the father's will as the father had not manifested an intention to make a gift of it to the son. Lord Thankerton took the view that the contract was solely between the father and the bank, and although made for the benefit of the son, being a mere volunteer, he could not enforce the contract.

Lord Atkin disagreed with the reasoning of Lord Thankerton and said that not only had the father clearly manifested an intention of advancement but that the contract was actually between the bank and the two parties in whose name the account had been opened, i.e., the father and son jointly. However, in order to make himself a party to the joint account contract, the son had to ratify the agreement and that he had failed to do. On the contrary, the son's knowledge that the £10,000 had been used in the father's business and his active involvement in that business indicated that he approved the action taken by the executors.

Although the bank succeeded in the *McEvoy case* on its facts, the bank was criticised by the House of Lords. Nevertheless, the bank is within its rights in paying out to the survivor of a joint account the balance of any money held to the credit of the account. Disputes may arise about the equitable title (i.e., whether the survivor is entitled to keep the money absolutely or whether he holds it on trust, e.g., for the personal representatives for the beneficiary). The presumption is that equitable title follows the legal title but this presumption may be rebutted by showing a different intention, e.g., where the joint account is not truly joint and has only been opened as a matter of convenience. The court will take into consideration the whole history and conduct of the joint account. Thus, in *Marshall* v *Crutwell* (1875) LR 20 Eq 328 it was held that the presumption of survivorship was displaced when it was shown that the joint account had been opened by the husband, who was in poor health, transferring the credit balance from his personal account to a joint account in the name of himself and his wife (see also *Husband* v *Davis* (1851) 10 CB 645; *Williams* v *Davies* (1864) 3 Sw and Tr 437). Although the bank was instructed to pay cheques drawn by either of the account holders, the wife had restricted her withdrawals from the joint account to payment of household expenses. When the husband died disputes arose concerning the credit balance between the widow (the surviving joint account holder) and the remaining heirs.

Jessel MR held that it was never intended to make a gift of the credit balance to the wife and the husband's estate was beneficially entitled to the credit balance.

However, there must be clear evidence of the ownership of the money and in *Hirschorn* v *Evans* [1938] 2 KB 801 Greer LJ held that in the circumstances a garnishee order against the husband could not attach to a joint account, because there was no clear evidence of the beneficial ownership of the money.

On the other hand, in *Jones* v *Maynard* [1951] Ch 572 a husband and wife had a joint account into which the husband's salary and investment income was paid. The wife contributed a little investment income of her own and the rental from a jointly owned property was credited to the account. The surplus credit balance from the account was invested regularly in the husband's name alone. When the parties divorced, the wife claimed that she was beneficially entitled to half of the investments. The husband argued that the wife was only entitled to such investments as were proportionally represented by her own contributions to the account. Vaisey J held in favour of the wife and concluded that when the spouses have a common purse and pool their resources then the money which goes into the pool becomes joint property. (See also *Rimmer* v *Rimmer* [1953] 1 QB 63 and *Young* v *Sealey* [1949] Ch 278 where an account was opened by a lady in the joint names of herself and her nephew, and which could be drawn on by either of the account holders was sufficient to give the nephew a beneficial and legal title to the moneys.)

PARTNERSHIP ACCOUNTS

A partnership account resembles a joint account in that it will be opened in the name of more than one person. Unlike a registered company a partnership does not enjoy separate legal status and the account is in effect a joint account of the specified partners. By s. 5 of the Partnership Act 1890 each partner acts as the agent of his co-partners and the partnership business. Thus, a partner can open an account on behalf of the partnership in the partnership name but he cannot open a partnership account in his own name. In *Alliance Bank Ltd* v *Kearsley* (1871) LR 6 CP 433 Montague Smith J said that an account opened by a man in his own name is prima facie his private account.

Not only must a partner act within the scope of the authority conferred on him but the bank must conform to the strict terms of the mandate given to it with regard to the operation of the account.

Under s. 6 of the 1890 Act a partner has authority to operate the partnership account in his own right. A partner in a trading partnership also has implied authority to draw, accept and endorse bills of exchange or other negotiable instruments on behalf of the business (*Harrison* v *Jackson* (1797) 7 TR 207 at 210; *Williamson* v *Johnson* (1823) 1 B and C 146). A partner has implied authority to borrow money for the purposes of the partnership if the business is one which cannot be carried on in the usual way without such power (*Bank of Australasia* v *Breillat* (1847) 6 Moo PC 152 at 194 where a partner was held entitled to overdraw on a bank account; and *Fisher* v *Tayler* (1843) 2 Hare 218).

However, a partner will not be deemed to have authority to open a bank account in his own name for partnership purposes. In *Ringham* v *Hackett* (1980) 124 SJ 201 Megaw LJ held that a partner who dishonestly wrote his signature in manuscript below the printed name of his firm nevertheless bound the partnership.

The *Ringham* case was followed in *Central Motors (Birmingham) Ltd* v *P.A. and S.N.P. Wadsworth* (1982) 133 NLJ 555) where an account was opened in the partnership name, with both partners being required to sign the cheques drawn on the account. One of the partners drew a cheque for the purchase of a car without the consent of the other. The court rejected the attempt to distinguish the *Ringham* case and held that s. 5 of the Partnership Act 1890, together with ss. 23(2) and 91(1) of the Bills of Exchange Act 1882 were sufficient to impose liability on the partner who had not signed.

In *United Bank of Kuwait Ltd* v *Hammound* [1988] 1 WLR 1051 the Court of Appeal held that an undertaking given as security for a loan was within the ordinary course of a solicitor's business where there was an underlying transaction of a solicitorial nature. For the purposes of establishing ostensible authority the question whether or not an undertaking was given in the usual course of a solicitor's business was to be considered on the basis of the transaction as it appeared objectively, irrespective of its true nature.

It is imperative for a partner to act within the course of the express or implied authority conferred on him. Additionally, the bank must conform to the mandate given, and any decision regarding the mandate includes a judgment on the part of the bank as to the validity of the mandate given by the partner. In *Forster* v *Mackreth* (1867) LR 2 Ex 163 a partner endorsed some bills of exchange on behalf of the firm. He also drew a number of post-dated cheques in the partnership name. The Court of Exchequer held that it was not in the ordinary course of the partnership business to deal in bills of exchange and therefore endorsing such bills was outside the scope of the partner's authority. Drawing post-dated cheques was also outside the scope of the business and outside the scope of the authority conferred on the partner. Martin B reached this decision on the basis that 'we cannot in substance distinguish this [post-dated] cheque from a bill of exchange . . .'. However, recent cases treat post-dated cheques as both valid and regular (see pp. 182–3).

The powers conferred by the Partnership Act 1890 upon a partner may be varied by agreement between the partners. In practice most partnership agreements will deal with the issue of the authority of a partner to operate a bank account and if the bank is given specific instructions it should require all partners to sign the mandate given.

Death of a partner

Unless a partnership agreement expressly provides to the contrary the death of a partner dissolves the firm. There is no rule of survivorship in the operation of the partnership account. Section 38 of the Partnership Act 1890 provides that the surviving partners have the power to continue to act for the partnership firm for the purposes of winding up the affairs of the partnership. For the purposes of winding up the affairs of the partnership a surviving partner has, in law, the authority to complete unfinished transactions, including the authority to sell the whole or part of the partnership property in order to pay off partnership debts (*Barton* v *North Staffordshire Railway Co* (1888) 38 ChD 458) and draw upon the partnership bank account (*Backhouse* v *Charlton* (1878) 8 ChD 444). In *Backhouse* v *Charlton* Malins V-C took the view that a bank which pays against cheques drawn on the partnership account after the death of a partner can assume that the surviving partner acts within his authority when drawing on the account. In that case it was held that the bank was not required to make any enquiry concerning the payment of cheques drawn after the death of the deceased partner. Indeed the bank was bound to honour all of the cheques in question. Similarly, in *Re Bourne* [1906] 2 Ch 427 a partnership was carried on by Grove and Bourne. On the death of Grove, the remaining partner, Bourne, continued the business in the partnership name until his death. At the time of Grove's death, the partnership account was overdrawn by £6,476. Bourne deposited with the bank, as security, title deeds over certain partnership assets in order to secure a further overdraft. At the time of Bourne's death the bank account was overdrawn by £4,463. Bourne's estate being insolvent, the question that arose was whether the bank or Grove's executors had priority to the proceeds of sale of the property charged in favour of the bank. The Court of Appeal held for the bank and said that the surviving partner had the power to give a good title to purchasers and mortgagees. Romer LJ said:

> The account with them [the bank] was a partnership account. It was continued under the partnership name, and apparently for the purposes of the partnership, and it appears to me impossible to say that it is not or may not be reasonable for a surviving partner to continue the partnership account for the purpose of winding up the estate.

Bankruptcy of a partner

The bankruptcy of a partner dissolves the firm in the absence of a provision to the contrary in the partnership articles. The bankrupt partner then has no authority to bind the partnership (ss. 33 and 38 of the Partnership Act 1890). A bank has no lien on a partner's private account for an overdraft on the partnership account unless either the partnership agreement so states or the terms of the overdraft supplied by the bank so provide. In *Watts* v *Christie* (1849) 11 Beav 546 a partnership account was overdrawn although one of the partners maintained a private account with the same bank which was in credit. The bank failed and the partner holding the credit balance assigned to the partnership the amount of the credit due to him from the bank in order to facilitate a set-off of the credit balance against the partnership's debit balance. If such a set-off were permitted the partnership firm would recover the net credit balance resulting from the assignment and would not be obliged to pay the amount due under the overdrawn partnership account prior to the assignment to the bank's trustee in bankruptcy. Lord Langdale MR held that the purported assignment was ineffective. At law a separate debt cannot be set off against a joint debt; neither can it in equity or in bankruptcy (see *Ex parte Christie* (1804) 10 Ves Jr 105 and *Addis* v *Knight* (1817) 2 Mer 117).

MINORS' ACCOUNTS

A bank's obligations to a minor customer are the same as to any other customer and the minor's self-regarding duties must be the same as those for adult customers since these duties merely operate as defences which the bank can rely upon if the customer challenges the bank's right to debit his account.

The Family Law Reform Act 1969 reduced the age of majority from 21 years to 18. By s. 1(2) of the Act this applies for the purposes of any rule of law and generally. By s. 12 a person who is not of full age may be described as a 'minor'.

Until recently, the obligation owed by a minor under contracts entered into by him was governed by a combination of the common law and the Infants Relief Act 1874. These rules remain applicable to contracts entered into before June 1987, but contracts entered into thereafter are subject to the Minors' Contracts Act 1987, s. 1.

Contracts for necessaries

Contracts for necessaries continue to be subject to the common law and are not affected by the Minors' Contracts Act 1987. Therefore, a minor is bound by a contract under which he is supplied with goods and services that constitute necessaries (*Nash* v *Inman* [1908] 2 KB 1) and loans granted to enable a minor to acquire necessaries are also recoverable (*Re National Permanent Benefit Building Society* (1869) LR 5 Ch App 309 at 313; *Lewis* v *Alleyne* (1888) 4 TLR 560). A minor is bound to pay a reasonable price for goods and services suitable to his station in life and needs.

Contracts valid unless repudiated at majority

Certain contracts made by minors are voidable, but will become valid when the minor attains majority, unless repudiated at the time. The rules governing such contracts are unaffected by the Minors' Contracts Act 1987, and continue to be governed by the common law.

Contracts of a continuous nature, e.g., a tenancy or a partnership, are binding on a minor unless he repudiates the contract during his minority or within a reasonable time after attaining his majority. Although a minor may repudiate such contracts and avoid future liability, he cannot recover back money already paid unless he can establish a total failure of consideration (see *Steinberg* v *Scala (Leeds) Ltd* [1923] 2 Ch 452). A minor who voluntarily carries out a contract which could not have been enforced against him cannot later repudiate the contract and compel the other party to return any benefits already conferred on him (*Valentini* v *Canali* (1889) 24 QBD 166). A debt paid to a minor during his minority cannot be treated as a defective payment so as to allow the minor to insist on payment again when he attains majority (*Re Brocklebank* (1877) 6 ChD 358).

The scope of the protection conferred on the minor was illustrated in *R. Leslie Ltd* v *Sheill* [1914] 3 KB 607 where it was held that a loan obtained by a minor was irrecoverable although obtained as a result of the minor misrepresenting his age. The court held that the amount could not be recovered by bringing an action in deceit or in quasi-contract for that would enable the lender to obtain an indirect remedy not available in contract. To off-set the sort of situation which arose in *Leslie* v *Sheill* equity developed a doctrine of restitution which applied the principle that an infant should not be enriched by his own fraud. In addition to the equitable remedy of restitution it is to obtain relief under the Minors' Contracts Act 1987. Where a contract is unenforceable against a person because he was a minor or where the minor repudiates the contract the 1987 Act (s. 3(1)) provides the court has the power where it thinks it is 'just and equitable' to require the minor to return the property, or property representing that which was acquired by him.

Operation of a bank account by a minor

The Bills of Exchange Act 1882, s. 22(1), provides that a person's capacity to issue a negotiable instrument is the same as his capacity to enter into a simple contract; thus, a person's capacity to incur liability on a bill is coextensive with his capacity under the rules of contract. A minor may sue on a bill (*Warwick* v *Bruce* (1813) 2 M and S 205) but he cannot be made liable on a bill or other negotiable instrument either as drawer, acceptor or endorser. A holder in due course is not in any better position than a holder for value of the bill of exchange (*Re Soltykoff* [1891] 1 QB 413; *Levene* v *Brougham* (1909) 25 TLR 265). But it may be possible to hold a minor liable for necessaries supplied to him under the sale contract for the value of goods supplied to him.

A minor is not liable for a post-dated cheque although its date of payment is subsequent to his attaining the age of majority (*Hutley* v *Peacock* (1913) 30 TLR 42; cf. *Belfast Banking Co.* v *Doherty* (1879) 4 LR Ir 124 where the court held a holder in due course may sue the acceptor of a debt incurred during infancy, but accepted after attaining majority). The signature of a minor does not, however, invalidate the whole bill. Section 22(2) provides that 'Where a bill is drawn or endorsed by an infant [or minor] . . . the drawing or endorsement entitles the holder to receive payment of the bill, and to enforce it against any other party thereto'.

Loans or other financial accommodation for a minor

Problems may arise when a minor requires financial accommodation. There is no legal bar to a bank or building society permitting a minor to overdraw on a current account or to granting a loan facility. Contracts which are not for 'necessaries' and which are not 'voidable' are unenforceable against a minor. However, such contracts are enforceable at the suit of the minor (*Bruce* v *Warwich* (1815) 6 Taunt 18). The minors' immunity under such contracts may be removed by ratification of the contract by the minor reaching majority (Minors' Contracts Act 1987). Although these contracts are unenforceable against a minor, property may pass from the minor to the other party.

Where a bank does advance credit to a minor it may require a guarantee to be given by a person of full age. A guarantor is personally liable to the bank if the principal debtor to whom the loan is made defaults. A guarantee is therefore an undertaking to be secondarily or collaterally answerable for the debt on default by the principal debtor. However, the issue which has arisen is whether a guarantee given by a person of full capacity can be enforced if the principal debtor on the account is himself a minor. There was a dearth of authority in English law until *Coutts and Co.* v *Browne-Lecky* [1947] KB 104 where the repayment of a minor's overdraft was guaranteed by two persons, both of whom enjoyed full capacity. The fact that the debtor was of the age of minority was known to all the parties, including the bank. Oliver J held that the guarantors could not be liable in an action to recover the amount of the guarantee. The learned judge relied on *Swan* v *Bank of Scotland* (1836) 10 Bli NS 627 where a father who had guaranteed his infant son's overdraft could not be sued on the guarantee, even though all the parties were aware of the incapacity. Oliver J also relied on the principle established by Pothier and quoted in de Colyar's *Law of Guarantees and Principle and Surety*, 3rd ed. (1897), p. 210:

As the obligation of sureties is according to our definition an obligation accessory to that of a principal debtor, it follows that it is of the essence of the obligation that there should be a valid obligation of a principal debtor; consequently if the principal is not obliged, neither is the surety, as there can be no accessory without a principal obligation.

The law, however, was changed by the Minors' Contracts Act 1987, which repealed the Infants Relief Act 1874. Section 2 of the Minors' Contracts Act 1987 provides that where a guarantee is given in respect of an obligation of a party to a contract made after the commencement of the Act, and the obligation is unenforceable against him because he was a minor when the contract was made, the guarantee is not, for that reason alone, to be unenforceable against the guarantor. The section ensures that the guarantee of an unenforceable minors' contract is as effective as if the guarantee has been given in respect of a contract entered into by a person of full capacity.

Alternatively, a bank may require a person of full capacity to give an indemnity for the debts of the minor. With an indemnity, the surety agrees with the lender that he will be legally liable for the existing or future indebtedness of the minor. Thus, the surety is primarily liable for the indebtedness of the minor and his liability is not dependent on the default by the minor (for a discussion of the difference between an indemnity and guarantee see *Moschi* v *Lep Air Services Ltd* [1973] AC 331).

A bank may obtain a valid undertaking from a person of majority for a facility granted to a minor, because of is a joint undertaking of a nature which holds the person of majority separately liable. In *Wauthier* v *Wilson* (1912) 28 TLR 239 a father and son jointly issued a promissory note in order to obtain a loan for the son. When the son defaulted on the loan the bank sued the father on the promissory note. Pickford J held that the transaction was in reality one where the father acted as a guarantor. The Court of Appeal affirmed the decision of the trial court but held that the father entered into a joint and several liability to repay the amount of the loan facility issued in favour of the son. Although the bank was unable to recover the amount of the loan from the son, because of his minority, the father was liable. Joint and several liability can be imposed not merely under a negotiable instrument but in any case where one of the recipients of a loan is not of the age of majority.

COMPANY ACCOUNTS

A company registered under the Companies Act 1985 (as amended) enjoys separate legal status from its members (*Salomon* v *A. Salomon and Co. Ltd* [1897] AC 22, reversing the judgment of Vaughan Williams J, and the Court of Appeal). Consequently, the company can enter into contractual obligations in its own right and give a valid discharge for any indebtedness incurred on its behalf. However, because the company is an artificial legal entity it must act through properly appointed agents. In the case of a company, that is likely to be persons appointed to the board of management.

Until recently, a bank dealing with a registered company would have to satisfy itself that a transaction was not *ultra vires* the company (*Ashbury Railway Carriage and Iron Co.* v *Riche* (1875) LR 7 HL 653). The memorandum of association of the company is a public document and anyone dealing with the company was deemed to have notice of the contents, and, significantly, notice of any limitations on the capacity of the company to enter into certain transactions. Any contracts in excess of the company's capacity were deemed to be *ultra vires* and void (*Re Jon Beauforte (London) Ltd* [1953] Ch 131; *Re David Payne and Co. Ltd* [1904] 2 Ch 608). The *ultra vires* rule led to considerable problems and calls for the reform of the rule were made as long ago as 1945. The recommendation of the *Report of the Company Law Committee* (Cmnd 1749) in 1962, that the *ultra vires* rule should be abolished, was never implemented. However, s. 9 of the European Communities Act 1972 (consolidated as s. 35 of the Companies Act 1985, which in turn was amended by the Companies Act 1989) gave effect to the First Directive issued by the Council of Ministers of the European Communities on the Harmonisation of Company Law (68/151/EEC). Section 35 of the Companies Act 1985, as originally enacted, provided that a company was bound by the decisions and acts of its directors even in connection with matters outside the objects of the company, unless the third party had notice of want of authority on the part of the directors. The section also provided that the third party was presumed to have acted in good faith unless the contrary was proved. The powers of the directors to bind the company were deemed to be free of any limitations in the articles or memorandum of the company, and the third party was relieved from any obligation to enquire into the capacity of the company. Section 35 of the Companies Act 1985 gave rise to a number of difficulties, including those of interpretation (see *International Sales and Agencies Ltd* v *Marcus* [1982] 2 All ER 551; *TCB Ltd* v *Gray* [1986] Ch 621; *Barclays Bank Ltd* v *TOSG Trust Fund Ltd* [1984] BCLC 1).

At the end of 1985, the government appointed Dr Dan Prentice to conduct a study of the 'legal and commercial implications of abolishing the *ultra vires* rule as it applies to registered companies' (see Department of Trade and Industry, *Reform of the ultra vires Rule: A Consultative Document* (London: DTI, 1986) which includes Dr Prentice's report. The report recommended that a company should have the same capacity to enter into contracts as natural persons and a third party dealing with the company should not be deemed to have constructive notice of the memorandum and articles. The report also recommended that it should be possible for a company to ratify a contract in excess of a director's authority even where the third party had actual knowledge of the want of authority.

Purpose of the new rules

The purpose of the new rules is to validate transactions entered into by a company, although they are *ultra vires* or beyond the capacity of the company's objects and powers. At the same time personal liability will continue to be imposed on company directors for loss caused by them to their company by entering into *ultra vires* transactions (Companies Act 1985, s. 35(3)). The new rules also preserve the rights of individual members of the company to seek injunctive relief to prevent the company and its directors from entering into *ultra vires* transactions (Companies Act 1985, s. 35(2)).

Where a company acts outside the scope of the objects clause the new s. 35(1) (amended by s. 108 of the Companies Act 1989) provides:

The validity of an act done by a company shall not be called into question on the ground of lack of capacity by reason of anything in the company's memorandum.

The section does not provide that companies shall have full and unlimited legal capacity, so as to overrule the decision in *Ashbury Railway Carriage and Iron Co. Ltd* v *Riche* (1875) LR 7 HL 653. Instead the section provides that neither the company nor the third party to a contract or transaction can question its validity on the ground that it is outside the objects or powers of the company.

The old s. 35 has been replaced by a new s. 35A, which is worded differently. It does not require the third party or the company to have acted in 'good faith', but the third party is deemed to have acted in good faith even though he has knowledge that the contract is outside the scope of the objects clause (s. 35A(2)(b)). The company's lack of authority cannot be relied on by either the company or the third party. The new section applies to any transaction or other act and will therefore extend, for example, to gifts made to a charity. There is no requirement in s. 35A that the act should be one which is 'decided on by the directors' as there was in s. 35 as originally enacted.

A member of a company has always had a right to sue for an injunction to restrain the company or its directors from doing an *ultra vires* act. This right is preserved and the Companies Act 1985, s. 35(2) now provides that any member, regardless of the size of his holding, may 'bring proceedings to restrain the doing of an act' which but for the new s. 35(1) would be beyond the company's capacity. However, no such proceedings may be brought in respect of an act to be done in fulfilment of a legal obligation arising from a previous act of the company. The new s. 35(2) confers shareholder protection in respect of prospective acts to be entered into by the company. Once the transaction has been concluded and a legal obligation is imposed on the company then the shareholder's right to object no longer exists.

The directors remain under a duty to 'observe any limitations on their powers flowing from the company's memorandum' (s. 35(3)). If, therefore, directors cause their company loss by entering into transactions which are beyond their powers then they may be held in breach of their fiduciary duties and liable to compensate the company. Any transaction in excess of the directors' powers may be ratified by a special resolution of the shareholders (s. 35(3)).

Limitations on directors' powers

A company, unlike individuals, must act through human agents, whose authority may however be limited. Directors, or officers, of the company may have limitations imposed on them in a number of ways (e.g., restrictions imposed in the memorandum or articles, by the general meeting etc.) In order to make these limitations ineffective against persons who deal with the company's directors, or officers in good faith, the Companies Act 1985, s. 35A(1) provides that in favour of a person dealing with a company in good faith, the power of the board of directors to bind the company, or authorise others to do so, shall be deemed to be 'free of any limitation under the company's constitution'.

Problems affecting banks

A number of issues will affect the way in which a bank handles and operates an account maintained by a company. Some of the issues which may influence the bank are now examined.

Lending to a company   Prior to the changes introduced by the Companies Act 1989, which amended the Companies Act 1985, a bank which lent money to a customer which was a registered company had to determine whether the company had the capacity to borrow. Generally, such a power was expressly given in the memorandum or articles of the company and the bank was deemed to have constructive notice of any limitations on the authority to borrow (*Re Jon Beauforte (London) Ltd* [1953] Ch 131). Even if such a power were not expressly conferred on a trading company, the power to borrow was implied by the courts and such an act was considered incidental to carrying out its objects. If the power could not be implied then the act was considered *ultra vires* and ratification was not possible unless s. 9 of the European Communities Act (consolidated as s. 35 of the Companies Act 1985, and now amended by the Companies Act 1989) applied to protect the third party.

The combined effect of the new ss. 35 and 3A (which allows a company to register with a general objects clause allowing it to undertake general commercial activities) of the Companies Act 1985 is to allow a company to have the full contractual capacity of natural persons. The issue of whether a trading company can borrow certainly presents no problems.

A non-trading company whose sole function is to own property for its share-holders does not have an implied power to borrow. Non-trading companies do not usually require the power to borrow and despite the new s. 35 a bank is advised to scrutinise a non-trading company's memorandum and articles, although the bank is no longer deemed to have constructive notice of any limitations of authority contained in such documents (s. 35B).

Form of company contracts   Companies registered under the Companies Act 1985 have always been able to execute contracts in the same way as individuals. This has been reinforced by the fact that a company need no longer have a seal (s. 36A(3)). However, if a contract made by an individual has to be by deed (a legal conveyance, mortgage or lease of land) then a company, too, must make it by deed. This does not prevent verbal contracts being enforced against a company when the plaintiff has performed his obligations. Again, if the contract is one which must be in writing, it may be made on behalf of the company in writing and signed by a person authorised by it. This, however, applies not only to contracts which the law requires to be made in writing (e.g., hire-purchase and consumer credit agreements) but also to contracts which are merely evidenced by a written memorandum and signed (e.g., contracts of guarantee). In this case it is not necessary that the memorandum should be prepared as part of the transaction or that the person authorised to sign it should be the agent who negotiated the contract (*Jones* v *Victoria Graving Dock Co.* (1877) 2 QBD 314).

Current account operations   The transactions which are most likely to involve a bank in the current account operations of the company (customer) are the discounting or negotiation of bills of exchange or the payment of cheques drawn on behalf of the company. The purpose of discounting or negotiating a bill of exchange is to enable the bank's customer to obtain funds against an instrument which will mature at a future date. To that extent the bank may provide credit for the customer. Alternatively, the bank may be involved in honouring cheques on behalf of the customer against any credit balance on the customer's account or if the amount of the cheque is within an agreed overdraft limit. In both these instances the bank will act as an agent in carrying out the customer's instructions. The bank is, therefore, under an obligation to ensure that it acts within the mandate conferred by the customer.

Directors' actual liability   Under the general law directors can act on behalf of a company only at board meetings at which their collective decisions are expressed by resolutions. They have no power to act individually as agents of the company. The board may not delegate any of its powers to one or more members of the board unless the articles expressly permit (*Re County Palatine Loan and Discount Co., Cartmell's Case* (1874) 9 Ch App 691). But in practice the articles of the company will contain the widest powers of delegation both to individual directors (Table A, art. 72) and to other agents chosen by the board (Table A, art. 71). The articles of most companies empower the board of directors to appoint one or more of their number to be a managing director and to delegate to him any powers either concurrently with or to the exclusion of the board (Table A, art. 72). A managing director is vested with apparent authority to carry on the company's business in the usual way and to do all acts necessary for that purpose. Thus, he may sign cheques and bills of exchange on behalf of the company (*Dey v Pullinger Engineering Co* [1921] 1 KB 77), even in favour of himself (*Bank of New South Wales v Goulburn Valley Butter Co. Pty Ltd* [1902] AC 543), borrow money on the company's account and give security over the company's property for its repayment (*Biggerstaff v Rowatt's Wharf Ltd* [1896] 2 Ch 93), receive payment of debts owed to the company even by cheque made payable to him personally (*Clay Hill Brick and Tile Co. Ltd v Rawlings* [1938] 4 All ER 100), guarantee loans made to the company's subsidiaries and agree to indemnify persons who have given such guarantees themselves (*Hely-Hutchinson v Brayhead Ltd* [1968] 1 QB 549). The apparent authority of a managing director is confined to commercial matters (*George Whitechurch Ltd v Cavanagh* [1902] AC 117). An ordinary non-managing director or secretary has no power to act as an agent of the company by virtue of his or her office. At one time the law held that a person who negotiated a contract with a secretary or non-managing director acted at his own risk. However, under the changes introduced by the Companies Act 1989, it is no longer possible for a company to raise the director's lack of authority. The issue of personal liability being imposed on directors, or officers, as signatories of the company will be examined later (p. 204).

7 The Bank Account

The extension of banking activities and the ensuing competition has benefited the customer not only in the form of additional services being supplied by banks and building societies, but also in the nature of the accounts available to the customer.

SAVINGS ACCOUNTS

The savings account remains, along with the current account, one of the commonest types of account facility. The customer can pay in any amount he chooses and is entitled to withdraw any sums without having to give notice. Interest is usually paid on the lowest balance in each calendar month, although with some accounts interest may be calculated on a daily basis. Higher rates of interest may be earned on some accounts if the customer is willing to give notice prior to a withdrawal, for example, several building societies have accounts which give a higher interest if the customer is willing to give seven days' or 30 days' notice. Another common form of account is the fixed deposit; here the customer deposits a given amount for a specified period of time either at a fixed or variable rate of interest. In most cases it will be possible to withdraw the amount deposited before the date for maturity but the customer is then likely to lose part of the interest. It is possible to renew the deposit on maturity at the then prevailing rates of interest. Other types of interest-bearing accounts may be available to customers.

Although it was common practice to provide the customer with a passbook giving a record of his deposit and withdrawal transactions, this facility is now largely provided only by the building societies. With some deposits a deposit receipt may still be issued by the banks. The reasons for the disuse of pass books was that customers frequently lost them or did not understand their purpose and attempted to effect an assignment of the credit balance by physically handing over the passbook to a creditor.

There are two separate questions which need to be examined with regard to the status of the deposit receipt or passbook. First, the courts have had to determine whether a deposit receipt or passbook can be negotiated or used to transfer title to the credit balance it represents. A deposit receipt is not a negotiable instrument and in *Akbar Khan* v *Attar Singh* [1936] 2 All ER 545 at 548 Lord Atkin pointed out that, unlike a promissory note, a deposit receipt did not include an express promise by the bank to pay the amount involved. The sole object of the deposit receipt was to constitute a record of the transaction and evidence the indebtedness (see also *Hopkins* v *Abbott* (1875) LR 19 Eq 222; *Moore* v *Ulster Banking Co* (1877) IR 11 CL 512). The same purpose was accorded to the passbook in *Birch* v *Treasury Solicitor* [1951] Ch 298. It may be possible for a bank to issue deposit receipts which are made expressly negotiable (*National Bank of Australasia Ltd* v *Scottish Union and National Insurance Co.* (1951) 84 CLR 177). Nevertheless, the delivery of a deposit receipt or passbook does not, in itself, confer on the transferee any rights of ownership. To confer such rights the credit balance must be validly assigned. Although in *Birch* v *Treasury Solicitor* the Court of Appeal held that deposit books are 'essential indicia of title' and their 'delivery a transfer of the chose in action to found a good *donatio mortis causa*'.

A customer who has handed over a deposit receipt or passbook will still be able to obtain payment and convince the bank that it has been lost unless it is a condition precedent to the repayment of the deposit that the deposit or passbook be produced. In *Wood* v *Clydesdale Bank Ltd* 1914 SC 397 the court was of the view that a bank which has paid an impostor who produces a passbook or deposit receipt will still be liable to pay its customer. It is submitted that this must necessarily be correct unless the customer can be estopped from claiming payment from the bank. It is then for the bank to seek any money paid to the impostor.

The second question which needs to be answered is whether the credit balance in favour of the customer and as evidenced by the passbook or deposit receipt is capable of assignment. The money which stands to the credit of the customer's account and the transaction which is evidenced by the passbook or deposit receipt is a chose in action which is assignable, independent of the receipt and despite any restrictions found in that receipt. A chose in action can be assigned both in equity and under the Law of Property Act 1925. To be a legal assignment the assignment itself must be in writing under the hand of the assignor, it must be absolute and not be by way of charge, it must relate to the whole of the fund (*Forster* v *Baker* [1910] 2 KB 636; *Re Steel Wing Co. Ltd* [1921] 1 Ch 349) and it must be notified to the debtor. An assignment which fails to meet any of these requirements will take effect in equity.

The rules for an equitable assignment are more relaxed than those required to be satisfied for a legal assignment. All that is required is that the creditor should manifest a clear intention to make an irrevocable transfer of the debt. The assignment will be effective as between the assignor and assignee even if notice is not given to the debtor, although the debtor will not be affected by the assignment until notice is given to him. An equitable assignment may take place in one of three ways namely:

(a)   When the creditor either signs a written transfer and sends it to the assignee or makes a binding agreement for assignment which will be given effect in equity. Neither writing nor signature is required by equity, and an equitable assignment will be effective if made by conduct or orally. All that is required is an intention, manifested to the intended assignee to make a present assignment (*William Brandt's Sons and Co.* v *Dunlop Rubber Co. Ltd* [1905] AC 454).

(b)   When the creditor declares himself to be a trustee for the intended assignee. Such a trust may be express or implied from the agreement, e.g., where the assignor undertakes to account to the assignee for sums paid to him by the original creditor (see *International Factors Ltd* v *Rodriguez* [1979] QB 351).

(c) When the creditor notifies the debtor directing him to make payment to the third party who is the intended assignee. In *Re Kent and Sussex Sawmills Ltd* [1947] Ch 177 it was held that such a direction must be given in pursuance of a prior agreement between the creditor and the third party, or be communicated to the third party subsequently (*Curran* v *Newpark Cinemas Ltd* [1951] 1 All ER 295. A direction to the debtor which has not been assented to by the third party nor subsequently notified to him is merely a revocable authority to pay, even if it is expressed as being irrevocable. The direction to the debtor must also make it clear that the right to receive payment has become vested in the assignee and the creditor is no longer entitled to receive payment (*James Talcott Ltd* v *John Lewis and Co. Ltd* [1940] 3 All ER 592).

Where a legal assignment cannot effectively take place, the courts may hold that the assignee has acquired an interest in equity. Where the assignor hands over a deposit receipt or passbook, and indicates orally his intention to assign the balance, the transferee may acquire rights in equity (see *Re Griffin* [1899] 1 Ch 408). In *Re Pinto Leite* [1929] 1 Ch 221 it was emphasised that an equitable assignment becomes effective when the assignor loses his rights over the debt and the bank is not entitled to refuse to accept the deposit receipt or passbook from an assignee (*Woodhams* v *Anglo-Australian and Universal Family Assurance Co.* (1861) 3 Giff 238).

CURRENT ACCOUNTS

A current account is one where the customer maintains liquid funds for his daily use. The main feature of such accounts is that money can be withdrawn not only in cash for use by the customer himself but the customer can draw cheques against the account in favour of a third party to pay his creditors. The customer can also request the bank which maintains his account to collect cheques drawn in his favour and credit them to his account. The customer will also have access to the giro system, standing order and direct debit facilities available against the current account in order to enable the payment of bills. Probably the most significant advantage of the current account is that the customer may, with either the express or implied consent of the bank, overdraw on the current account. An overdraft is money lent, usually in the form of a loan on a current account (see *Re Hone* [1951] Ch 85 at 89).

The drawing of a cheque or accepting a bill of exchange payable at the bank, when the drawer knows he has insufficient funds to meet it may be taken as a request for an overdraft facility. The customer is liable to pay interest on an overdraft from the moment the overdraft accrues. Interest is calculated on overdrafts at an agreed rate or, if there is no agreement, at the bank's currently published lending rate. This is fixed by reference to the base rate (uniform for all major banks) plus a number of percentage points over the base depending on the customer's creditworthiness (see chapter 16).

Representations made on drawing a cheque

Although banks, and indeed customers, tend to be concerned with the civil consequences of improperly drawing cheques there are also consequences in criminal law. At common law it was never an offence, as such, to obtain property by deception (*R* v *Jones* (1704) 2 Ld Raym 1013) but by 1757 a statutory offence of obtaining property by false pretences had been created. The offence is now defined in s. 15 of the Theft Act 1968 and is supplemented by the offences of obtaining a pecuniary advantage by deception (s. 1 of the Theft Act 1978), evasion of liability by deception (s. 2 of the 1978 Act), and obtaining a pecuniary advantage by deception (s. 16 of the 1968 Act). Beyond these lie offences of fraud, some of them in the Theft Act 1986, e.g., false accounting, false statements by company directors, procuring the execution of a valuable security by deception; others in the Forgery and Counterfeiting Act 1981 and others in the companies legislation. All of these offences are based on the idea of an intention to defraud.

The deception may take the form of either words or conduct and will usually involve an express assertion of a fact which is untrue, although, on occasion, conduct may be intended to imply certain facts. An example is where goods or services are paid for by a cheque. The drawing of a cheque implies a number of representations namely (a) that the drawer has an account at the bank on which the cheque is drawn; and (b) that the cheque will be met on presentation, which may mean that there is a sufficient credit balance standing in the account to meet the cheque, or that there is an arrangement with the bank for a sufficient overdraft facility (*R* v *Giltmartin* [1983] QB 953).

In *Metropolitan Police Commissioner* v *Charles* [1977] AC 177 it was held that the use of a cheque card with a cheque implies not only that the bank will honour the cheques (provided that certain relevant conditions are satisfied) but also that the drawer has the authority to use the cheque card in the manner represented. Similarly, in *R* v *Lambie* [1982] AC 449 it was held that the use of a credit card implies not only that the credit-card company will ensure that the money is paid, but that the person using the card has the authority to use it in the manner represented.

An offence of obtaining something by deception is not committed unless the deception causes the obtaining.

DISTINCTIONS BETWEEN CURRENT AND DEPOSIT ACCOUNTS

There are a number of distinctions between interest-bearing accounts and current accounts. Savings accounts all earn interest for the customer. Although some banks pay interest on current accounts maintained with a minimum credit balance, a number of banks do not provide this facility (where interest is payable on current accounts banks used to require a minimum current account balance of £500, although this figure now varies considerably).

The amount deposited by the customer to the credit of his current account may be withdrawn by cheque. Cheques are not provided with a deposit account and there is no modern authority to suggest that cheques can be drawn against a savings account. Although in *Hopkins* v *Abbott* (1875) LR 19 Eq 222 and *Stein* v *Ritherdon* (1868) 37 LJ Ch 369 Malins V-C suggested that a deposit at call may be liable to be drawn on by cheque there is no modern authority to support this view.

A current account may be in credit or may, with either the express or implied consent of the bank, be overdrawn. Where the customer's account is overdrawn, the nature of the banker-customer relationship is reversed with the customer being the bank's debtor. In *Barclays Bank Ltd* v *Okenarhe* [1966] 2 Lloyd's Rep 87 the view was expressed that an overdrawn deposit account cannot exist in law.

Another distinguishing feature between a deposit and current account is that a withdrawal from a deposit account may be subject to a condition precedent and no cause of action will arise against the bank until that condition has been satisfied (*Re Dillon* (1890) 44 ChD 76). In the case of building society passbooks or other cases where a deposit receipt is issued by a bank the institution may require the production of such a receipt or passbook before the amount can be withdrawn (see *Re Tidd* [1893] 3 Ch 154 at 157), although a bank or building society may make payment to a customer against an indemnity. The courts may in equity order repayment to be made to the customer in the event of the deposit receipt or passbook being lost.

The distinction between current and deposit accounts was explained in *Re Head (No. 2)* [1894] 2 Ch 236 at 238.

Another major distinction between current and deposit accounts is that the balance on a current account is payable to the customer on a nationwide basis. The customer can not only draw cheques payable to a third party who may be located anywhere in the country but can also withdraw cash from his account by drawing a cheque at any branch of his bank which will normally be paid if backed by a cheque card. Alternatively, the customer can withdraw cash from an automated teller machine (ATM), and not merely one operated by his bank but from ATMs operated by other banks with whom he will probably not have an account. A credit balance maintained in a deposit account can be withdrawn at the branch where the account is kept or, subject to reasonable notice, the customer may be permitted to withdraw the balance at a different branch.

INCIDENTS OF THE BANKER AND CUSTOMER RELATIONSHIP

Once an account is opened with a bank, whether it is a deposit or current account, certain distinctive features arise. Where the customer is overdrawn on his account the very nature of the banker and customer relationship allows the bank to exercise certain remedies, which will be examined in this section of the chapter.

Appropriation of payments

One of the features of the overdrawn current account is that the debit balance will alter on an almost daily basis because mutual dealings will be transacted through it. For most purposes it is adequate to determine the net credit or debit balance on the account, although in some cases it may become important to determine which of the debit entries have been discharged by the credit entries that have taken place. This may be important, for example, where the bank seeks to enforce a security in relation to the overdrawn current account or where the issue is that of a partner's liability on the dissolution of the firm.

A situation may arise where a third party guarantees an overdraft facility for an agreed period. On the expiration of that agreed period the bank decides not to freeze the account on the final date for which the security is given and the account is continued in the ordinary manner with further credits and withdrawals being made against the account. Where, in that situation, the bank subsequently seeks to enforce the guarantee a dispute will probably arise about the extent of the debts covered by the guarantee. The bank will undoubtedly argue that the guarantee extends to the full amount overdrawn including any amounts withdrawn after the account should have been frozen or ruled off, whilst the guarantor will seek to reduce the amount of his liability by any sums paid to the credit of the account after that date.

If a partnership firm is dissolved, for example, on the retirement of a partner, and the partnership account continues to be operated in the ordinary way, the liability of the retired partner for partnership debts incurred after his retirement and after notice of retirement has been published in the *London Gazette* will have to be determined.

The principle used by the courts to solve disputes of this nature is known as 'the rule of appropriation of payments' or as 'first incurred first discharged'. The effect of this rule is that each item paid to the credit of the customer's account is deemed to discharge the earliest of the debit items on the account. The rule was established in *Devaynes* v *Noble*, *Clayton's Case* (1816) 1 Mer 572 where one of the partners in a banking partnership died, and consequently the partnership was dissolved. The remaining partners continued to carry on its business as a going concern. Eventually the bank became insolvent and a customer, Clayton, sought to recover the balance due to him from the deceased partner's estate. There was a substantial credit balance on Clayton's account at the time of the partner's death, but during the period following it Clayton withdrew amounts exceeding the credit balance. However, Clayton also paid in numerous items during that period, so that the balance standing to the credit of the account was higher than the original credit balance in favour of Clayton at the time of the partner's death. Grant MR held that the deceased partner's estate was not liable for debts incurred by the bank in respect of money deposited by the customer to the credit of the account. The money paid out by the bank had discharged the initial balance due to the customer at the date of the partner's death. The learned judge examined the general area of appropriation of payments and distinguished those situations from one where the question of appropriation relates to a bank account (see p. 609).

The rule in *Clayton's Case* is based on a presumption about the probable intention of the parties and a creditor who has a different intention must make it clear to the debtor. In *Clayton's Case* there was no indication of any different intention and the amounts paid out by the bank after the death of the partner had discharged the initial balance due to the customer. The presumption of intention on which the rule in *Clayton's Case* is based is not readily displaced. In *Deeley* v *Lloyds Bank Ltd* [1912] AC 756 a bank obtained from its customer a first mortgage to secure an overdraft. When the bank received notice that the customer had granted a second mortgage over the property, it failed to freeze the balance as it stood, and instead allowed the customer to continue operating the account in the ordinary manner. The amounts paid in by him were higher than the balance of the overdraft at the date of the notification of the second mortgage although further fresh withdrawals had left the account in debit. The second mortgagee claimed that he had priority to the bank, as credits (applying *Clayton's Case*) to the customer's account had discharged the earlier indebtedness. The Court of Appeal upheld Eve J at first instance in favour of the bank. It held that the rule in *Clayton's Case* had been displaced by the intention of the parties and Fletcher Moulton LJ contended that it was absurd to attribute to a bank an intention to appropriate payments in to a secured rather than unsecured debt. He ridiculed the recognition of a legal rule which the bank could circumvent by the 'simple formality of drawing two horizontal lines in their books and making believe to commence a new account'. The House of Lords, however, reversed the decision on the grounds that the rule in *Clayton's Case* was not excluded by the conduct of the parties. It held that primarily the right to appropriate a payment made to the credit of an account rested with the debtor but if he did not evince an intention, the creditor ought to do so and in the absence of a specific appropriation the position was governed by the rule in *Clayton's Case*. Indeed, if either the bank or creditor had intended to appropriate the payments made to the credit of the account after notification of the second mortgage, it should always rule off the account where it is desired to preserve a security on which further advances cannot be charged (see per Lord Shaw of Dunfermline; [1912] AC 756 at 785). An alternative course of action would be for the bank to strike a balance in the account and then open a fresh account in the name of the customer (see *Royal Bank of Canada* v *Bank of Montreal* (1976) 67 DLR (3d) 755).

The rule in *Clayton's Case* has also been applied in cases where a partnership firm is dissolved. In *Royal Bank of Scotland* v *Christie* (1841) 8 Cl & F 214 a partner in a trading firm mortgaged his own land to secure advances made to the firm by its bank. At the date of the partner's death the firm had overdrawn on its account but on the death of the partner the account continued unbroken. The surviving partners paid into the account amounts which exceeded the debit balance at the deceased partner's death, and then withdrew an even larger balance. The court held that the rule in *Clayton's Case* required payments into the account by the surviving partners to be credited first against the earlier debit items in the account so that the payments into the account after the death of the partner went to pay off the mortgage.

In *Re Yeovil Glove Co. Ltd* [1965] Ch 148 a company created a mortgage over the whole of its assets by way of a floating charge to secure its existing and future indebtedness to the bank. The company went into liquidation within 12 months of the creation of the charge with the result that the charge was void except as security for 'cash paid to the company at the time of or subsequently to the creation of, and in consideration for, the charge' (Companies Act 1948, s. 322(1)). The Court of Appeal held that the floating charge was valid security for advances made by the bank after it was created, but not for earlier advances. However, because the company had paid amounts into its current account since the creation of the charge, those amounts went towards satisfying its existing indebtedness under *Clayton's Case* and the advances made since the creation of the floating charge were still owing and secured by the charge.

The rule in *Clayton's Case* applies only to current accounts (*Cory Brothers and Co. Ltd* v *Owners of Turkish Steamship Mecca* [1897] AC 286) and there are a number of instances where it is likely to be displaced namely:

(a)   Slade J expressed the view in *Siebe Gorman and Co. Ltd* v *Barclays Bank Ltd* [1979] 2 Lloyd's Rep 142 at p. 164 that the opening of a fresh account displaces the rule in *Clayton's Case*. He also recognised two further exceptions to the rule. First, the rule does not apply in respect of secured transactions where the second mortgagee agreed to the making of fresh advances by the first mortgagee.

Secondly, the rule does not apply where the fresh advances are made under a contractual obligation arising under the mortgage deed.

(b)   The rule does not apply where a trustee pays trust money into his personal account, thus mixing trust funds with his own funds. In *Re Hallett's Estate* (1880) 13 ChD 696 a solicitor who misappropriated funds from a client account and had them transferred into his account (so that trust and personal funds were mixed in the account) was deemed to withdraw his personal savings first; thus leaving the trust funds intact.

(c)   The rule does not apply to separate bank accounts even if maintained with the same bank. In *Bradford Old Bank Ltd* v *Sutcliffe* [1918] 2 KB 833 a customer had a loan account and a current account and it was held that payments to the credit of the current account must be appropriated to that account. Accordingly, a guarantor for the loan account could not claim that such payments should be used to reduce the loan account (see Scrutton LJ p. 847).

The rule does not apply where the account has been stopped, i.e., where payments in and out do not take place.

(d)   The rule does not apply where the parties have merely entered into a series of transactions without a current account. In *Cory Brothers and Co. Ltd* v *Owners of Turkish Steamship Mecca* [1897] AC 286 it was said that the rule in *Clayton's Case* does not apply where there is no current account between the parties, nor where it is clear from the circumstances that the creditor intended to reserve the right to appropriate when necessary.

(e)   The rule does not apply where the bank agrees not to apply the first-in first-out rule. Thus, in *Westminster Bank Ltd* v *Cond* (1940) 46 Com Cas 60 the guarantor argued that because the bank had continued the account unbroken after making a demand on him, the loan had been paid off by subsequent payments into the account. The court rejected this argument on the grounds that the guarantee form contained an express clause to prevent the operation of the rule.

Combination of accounts

A customer may maintain more than one account with a bank for a number of reasons, for example, a person acting in a fiduciary capacity will be required to keep client funds separate from his own, e.g., a solicitor or trustee will be required to keep client or trust funds in separate accounts from his own. A customer may decide to maintain separate accounts for personal reasons, e.g., the customer may maintain a current and a deposit account with the bank.

Despite operating separate accounts for a customer, the bank may decide to treat all the customer's accounts as one and combine the balances so as to produce a single debit or credit balance payable to, or from the customer. The situation is likely to arise where, for example, the customer is either unwilling or unable to repay the overdraft on one of his accounts although he has another account which is in credit. This may arise where the customer is bankrupt or insolvent. The bank may decide to combine two or more accounts where a customer draws a cheque against an account with an insufficient credit balance but the deficiency can be met by combining the balances standing to the credit of the other account.

Where the bank decides to combine two different accounts on the bankruptcy or insolvency of the customer, it basically acts for its own benefit to reduce the amount of the overdraft on one account against the credit balance standing against another account. This is especially significant where the insolvent customer has an overdraft of, for example, £500 on account A, but at the same time he has a credit balance on account B of, for example, £1,000. If, on the insolvency or the bankruptcy of the customer, the bank were to hold the credit balance of £1,000 for the trustee in bankruptcy, the bank would clearly be disadvantaged. The bank would merely be an unsecured creditor of its customer and be repaid a dividend with the other general creditors of the customers. In that situation the bank is very likely not to recover the full amount of the debit balance on the overdrawn account. If the bank, however, were to combine the accounts it would be entitled to set off the entire amount of the overdrawn account against the credit balance on account B immediately and the bank is then under an obligation only to pay the remaining £500 to the trustee in bankruptcy. The bank will, therefore, receive payment in full of the amount of the overdraft in priority to the other unsecured creditors.

Where a customer draws a cheque in excess of the credit balance standing to the credit of his current account or where the amount of the cheque is in excess of an agreed overdraft limit, the bank would clearly be entitled to dishonour the cheque. Combining the current account with another account so as to pay the cheque means that a cheque which would otherwise be dishonoured will actually be paid and that the bank acts in favour of the customer.

There are a number of issues which have to be resolved in respect of the bank's right to combine the accounts:

(a) Does the bank have a right to combine?
(b) Should the bank give notice of its intention to combine?
(c) Is combination of accounts forbidden by statute?

Before these issues are discussed it is necessary to settle the terminology which should be applied to this right of the bank to apply the credit balance on one account against a debit balance of the same customer against another account.

Terms commonly used   The terms used to describe the bank's right to combine one or more accounts have rarely been consistently used. Although the terms 'combination' or the 'right to combine' are probably the most frequently used, the right has also been referred to as a 'set-off', 'a right to consolidate', 'a right to confound' and 'a lien'. These terms have often been used interchangeably and not always in their correct legal context. Some authors view the right to combine as a set-off and Professor Ellinger (Ellinger and Lomnicka, Modern Banking Law, 2nd ed. (Oxford: Clarendon Press, 1994, p. 184), expresses the view that '. . . the bank's right to combine the balances of all the accounts of a single customer is to be regarded [as] a right of set-off'. Professor Goode, in *Legal Problems of Credit and Security*, 2nd ed. (London: Sweet and Maxwell, 1988), takes a narrower view and states, at p. 147:

This right of combination would seem to be merely a particular form of contractual set-off, the only difference being that the term 'combination' (or 'consolidation') is usually employed where the right to combine is implied from usage or course of dealings, as in the case of the banker's right of combination, whereas the term 'contractual set-off' tends to be reserved for express contractual provisions allowing the combination of accounts.

However, some authors draw a clear distinction between the two concepts and it has been said that:

Combination of accounts is not a set-off situation, because this postulates mutual but independent obligations between the two parties. Rather, it is merely an accounting situation, in which the existence and amount of one party's liability to the other can only be ascertained by discovering the ultimate balance of their mutual dealings. (Everett and McCracken, *Financial Institutions Law* (Sydney: Serendip Publications, 1987), pp. 223–4)

Others take the view that 'combination' is merely a specialised term for a set-off peculiar to banks (Penn, Shea and Arora, *The Law Relating to Domestic Banking*, (London: Sweet and Maxwell), pp. 143–7; see also *Re K (Restraint Order)* [1990] 2 QB 298 at 303–5).

The right to combine the accounts The basic rule is that a bank may combine two or more accounts at any time without notice to the customer, even though the accounts are maintained at different branches of the same bank. The rule was explained in *Garnett v M'Kewan* (1872) LR 8 Ex 10, where it was held that the bank was justified in dishonouring cheques because the customer was not entitled to expect his cheques to be honoured at one branch of a bank where he had an account in credit if the credit balance was counterbalanced by a debit against him at another branch. Kelly CB thought it important that there was a course of mutual dealings between the bank and its customer and as the customer had the power to order the bank to transfer amounts from one of his accounts to another, so the bank had a similar right. In such a case, although the bank cannot be said to be acting under express instructions from the customer, such a mandate may be implied by the fact that as a customer is assumed to know the state of his accounts; drawing a cheque on an account which is overdrawn implies an instruction to the bank to transfer funds from the account in credit to the overdrawn account. The rule in *Garnett v M'Kewan* has been approved in a number of cases including *Halesowen Presswork and Assemblies Ltd v Westminster Bank Ltd* [1971] 1 QB 1, *Barclays Bank Ltd v Okenarhe* [1966] 2 Lloyd's Rep 87, *Re K (Restraint Order)* [1990] 2 QB 298 and in *Hongkong and Shanghai Banking Corporation v Kloeckner and Co. AG* [1990] 2 QB 514. In the *Halesowen* case Lord Denning MR in the Court of Appeal answered the question whether the bank was entitled to combine accounts so as to be liable only for the remaining balance and held that the bank has a right to combine the two accounts whenever it pleases, and to set off one against the other, unless it has made some agreement, express or implied to keep them separate.

In *Re K* it was said that the bank could exercise its right to combine accounts without infringing a restraining order under the Drug Trafficking Offences Act 1986. More recently, in the *Hongkong and Shanghai Banking Corporation* case Hirst J rejected the argument that the doctrine of the autonomy of the letter of credit of necessity led to the conclusion that a set-off could not be permitted.

There can, therefore, be no doubt that the bank has a right to combine accounts and to discharge its obligation to the customer for the repayment of the credit balances. Any doubts raised by the judgment of Swift J in *W.P. Greenhalgh and Sons* v *Union Bank of Manchester* [1924] 2 KB 153, in which he rejected the possibility of any right to combine two or more accounts, have clearly been settled. However, whilst doubts persisted banks attempted to preserve their rights to combine accounts by taking letters of set-off signed by customers relying on credit balances for borrowing on other accounts, although in *Midland Bank Ltd* v *Reckitt* [1933] AC 1 Lord Atkin indicated that he could not comprehend how the document increased the bank's rights.

Does notice have to be given?   The question whether a bank is required to give notice to the customer of its intention to combine the accounts was considered in *Garnett* v *M'Kewan* (1872) LR 8 Ex 10 where the court unanimously answered it in the negative. Kelly CB (at p. 13) said:

> In general it might be proper or considerate to give a notice to that effect, but there is no legal obligation on the bankers to do, arising either from express contract or the course of dealing between the parties.

A somewhat different conclusion may be reached if there is an agreement with the customer not to combine the accounts. In *Buckingham and Co.* v *London and Midland Bank Ltd* (1895) 12 TLR 70 the plaintiff had a current account, and a loan account secured against his house. The bank manager had the property re-surveyed, and decided that the amount of the loan should be reduced. The bank therefore set off the credit balance on the current account against the amount outstanding on the loan account without giving notice to the customer. Consequently, cheques drawn by the customer on the current account were dishonoured. The jury found that there was a consistent course of dealings between the bank and the customer which enabled the customer to draw on the current account without regard to the state of the loan account (see also *Bradford Old Bank Ltd* v *Sutcliffe* [1918] 2 KB 833). An agreement not to combine accounts may be displaced by reasonable notice or subsequent developments affecting the banker and customer relationship. Thus, in *British Guiana Bank* v *Official Receiver* (1911) 104 LT 754 it was said that the agreement to keep the accounts apart remained in effect only whilst the accounts were 'alive' and was terminated if the customer became insolvent. The issue was discussed in *National Westminster Bank Ltd* v *Halesowen Presswork and Assemblies Ltd* [1972] AC 785 and the House of Lords held that an agreement not to combine accounts had only been intended to be operative during the existence of the banker and customer relationship and, that relationship having terminated with a winding-up resolution having been passed by the company customer, the bank could combine the accounts without giving notice. A requirement imposing notice of the intention would have served no purpose since the banker and customer relationship had been terminated. Viscount Dilhorne approved *British Guiana Bank Ltd* v *Official Receiver* where Lord Macnaghten, having examined the nature of the agreement entered into with the customer, concluded that there was nothing 'in it to exclude the operation of the right of set off'.

When a bank combines a customers' accounts, is it required to honour cheques drawn by the customer but not yet presented? A period of notice could in fact defeat the advantages gained by the bank combining credit and debit balances. A customer who receives notice of the bank's intention to combine accounts may decide to withdraw the credit balance against which combination is sought. To protect the bank against this situation arising, Lord Cross of Chelsea in *National Westminster Bank Ltd* v *Halesowen Presswork and Assemblies Ltd* expressed the view at p. 810 that:

> The choice . . . lies between a notice taking immediate effect and no notice at all. On any footing the bank would be obliged to honour cheques drawn up to the limit of the apparent credit balance before the company became aware that the bank was consolidating the accounts and so it might be said that notification to the customer was not a condition precedent to the exercise by the bank of its right of consolidation but only a measure of precaution which the bank might take to end its liability to honour cheques.

Special rules relating to insolvency   Probably, the most frequent use by banks of the right to combine a credit balance with a debit balance is where a customer is declared bankrupt (Insolvency Act 1986, s. 323) or becomes insolvent (Insolvency Rules 1986, r. 4.90). In such circumstances the right to combine accounts exists not merely at common law but also under statute, namely s. 323 of the Insolvency Act 1986 (which replaced s. 31 of the Bankruptcy Act 1914) or under the Insolvency Rules 1986. In both cases a set-off is permitted between amounts due to the creditor from the bankrupt individual or insolvent company and vice versa provided there has been a course of 'mutual dealings' between the parties, including 'mutual credits, mutual debts or other mutual dealings'.

The effect of the bank's right to combine accounts in the event of the customer's insolvency was discussed in *National Westminster Bank Ltd* v *Halesowen Presswork and Assemblies Ltd* [1972] AC 785. The bank sought to set off the credit balance on the No. 2 account (a trading account opened for the company) against the debit on the No. 1 (current) account. The liquidator argued that it had been agreed to keep the accounts separate and that by agreement the bank had contracted out of s. 31 of the Bankruptcy Act 1914 (the predecessor to s. 323 of the Insolvency Act 1986). The House of Lords dealt with two main issues, namely:

(a)   Were the dealings between the bank and its customer 'mutual'? Lord Simon of Glaisdale (at p. 808) took the view that:

> . . . 'mutual dealings' would not cover a transaction in which property is made over for a 'special (or specific) purpose' (see *Re Pollitt, ex parte Minor* [1893] 1 QB 175 and 455; *Re Mid-Kent Fruit Factory* [1896] 1 Ch 567 and *Re City Equitable Fire Insurance Co. Ltd* [1930] 2 Ch 293).

He took the view that every payment of money, or contractual provision, is for a special or specific purpose in the ordinary sense of those words and something else is required to take the transaction out of the concept of 'mutual dealings'. He then went on to define the concept of 'mutual dealings' as follows:

> . . . money is paid for a special (or specific) purpose so as to exclude mutuality of dealing within section 31 if the money is paid in such circumstances that it

would be a misappropriation to use it for any other purpose than that for which it is paid.

The law is the same under the Insolvency Act 1986, s. 323, although the new section provides that any sums due from the bankrupt to the party seeking to exercise the set-off are not to be included in the account if the other party had 'notice at the time they became due that a bankruptcy petition relating to the bankrupt was pending'.

(b)   Was it possible to contract out of s. 31 of the Bankruptcy Act 1914? The majority of the House of Lords (Viscount Dilhorne and Lords Kilbrandon and Simon of Glaisdale) concluded that it was not possible because the section was mandatory. They based their decision on the wording used in the section and took into account that the change in terminology between the Bankruptcy Act 1849 (12 and 13 Vict, c. 106), s. 171, and the Bankruptcy Act 1869 (32 and 33 Vict, c. 71), s. 39) from 'may' to 'shall' must have been intended to avert doubts. Lord Cross, however, reached a different conclusion and said that the word 'shall' was intended to give the creditor a definite right to 'set off' as opposed to giving s. 31 a mandatory effect. Section 323 of the Insolvency Act 1986 supports the view that the right to set off is mandatory in subsection (2), which provides that an account 'shall' be taken of what is due from each party to the other. It therefore follows that a set-off follows automatically regardless of any agreement to the contrary between the parties.

A question which did not arise in the *Halesowen* case is whether allowing a bank a right of set-off actually amounts to a voidable preference under ss. 239 or 340 of the Insolvency Act (s. 239 applies to the winding up of companies and s. 340 applies to the bankruptcy of individuals). Where a preference is given to a creditor within the 'relevant time' (normally within six months of the winding up or bankruptcy) the court has the power to set aside the preference if the debtor was desirous of conferring a benefit on the creditor. Where the customer arranges for a sum to be credited to his account under pressure the rule is inapplicable.

Limitations on the right to combine   Mocatta J recognised the following exceptions to the bank's right to combine in *Barclays Bank Ltd* v *Okenarhe* [1966] 2 Lloyd's Rep 87:

(a)   There is no right to combine in relation to accounts maintained with a bank by one person but in two different capacities, e.g., where the customer maintains an account in his personal capacity and also holds a trust account. In *Union Bank of Australia Ltd* v *Murray-Aynsley* [1898] AC 693, however, the Privy Council held that where there are several accounts in the name of the same customer with a bank, but the customer does not make it clear to the bank and the bank does not know which of those accounts is a trust account, the bank is entitled to combine all the accounts.

(b)   The right to combine does not arise if there is an express or implied agreement not to combine the accounts. For example, in *Bradford Old Bank Ltd* v *Sutcliffe* [1918] 2 KB 833 set-off was not permissible where the bank had agreed with the customer that the two accounts would be kept separate. In that case the bank had opened a current account and Scrutton LJ said that amounts paid into that account could not be used by the bank in discharge of the loan account without the customer's consent. Similarly, in *Buckingham and Co.* v *London and Midland Bank Ltd* (1895) 12 TLR 70 it was held that the bank had no right to combine a loan account (secured) with a current account. Again, in *Re E.J. Morel (1934) Ltd* [1962] Ch 21 the court recognised the right of the bank to combine, but this time only to a limited extent as the bank was not allowed to combine all three accounts. In the *Morel* case a company maintained a No. 2 account and a wages account, and the arrangement was that the credit balance on the No. 2 account would always be sufficient to cover the wages account. It was held that the No. 2 account and the wages account were in substance one as between the bank and the company.

(c) If money is deposited with the bank for a special purpose the bank cannot combine. In *W.P. Greenhalgh and Sons* v *Union Bank of Manchester* [1924] 2 KB 153 the bank had knowledge of the ultimate destination of the proceeds of certain bills deposited by the customer to the credit of his account and for that reason the court held the bank had no right to combine accounts. In *Barclays Bank Ltd* v *Quistclose Investments Ltd* [1970] AC 567 it was held that money paid into a bank account was paid in with the knowledge of the bank for a specific purpose, i.e., payment of a dividend, and, that purpose having failed due to the liquidation of the customer, the bank could not claim a set-off against other indebtedness of the customer.

(d) Combination is not possible for contingent liabilities. In *Jeffryes* v *Agra and Masterman's Bank Ltd* (1866) LR 2 Eq 674 a customer who was indebted to the bank handed to it certain bank receipts issued by another bank representing deposits lodged with that other bank. The court held that the bank could only set off such sums as were due and payable immediately and it could not retain the balance as security for amounts the customer might owe the bank in future.

(e) Set-off is not available where there is any doubt as to the identity of the account holder. In *Bhogal* v *Punjab National Bank* [1988] 2 All ER 296 it was held that the right of set-off against funds held in several different accounts depends on the several different accounts belonging to the same person. See also *Uttamchandani* v *Central Bank of India* (1989) 139 NLJ 222 where the Court of Appeal held that:

> Set-off has never been allowed save where the accounts are of the same customer, held in the same name, and in the same right. Even then, the right of set-off may be excluded by agreement express or implied. What is unusual about the present case is that the bank is seeking to set off accounts held in different names.

More recently, in *Re Bank of Credit and Commerce International SA (No. 8)* [1996] Ch 245 it was held that there could be no set-off under r. 4.90 of the Insolvency Rules 1986 (SI 1986/1925) where a bank advanced money to a borrower company, the principal debtor, and repayment was secured by a charge granted to the bank by a third-party depositor on a deposit made by him with the bank, and before the loan was repaid the bank went into liquidation, unless the security documents were such as to impose a personal liability on the third party.

POSITION OF THE BANK AS A CONSTRUCTIVE TRUSTEE

The banker-customer relationship is based on an implied contract (see chapter 8) and although in many instances the bank will act as an agent of the customer (e.g., where the bank holds deeds for safe-keeping; in carrying out the payment mandate) the relationship in respect of the operation of the current account is that of debtor and creditor (see *Foley* v *Hill* (1848) 2 HL Cas 28). However, a bank may find itself in the position of a constructive trustee as a result of handling money belonging to a third party and it is intended to concentrate on this aspect of the relationship in the remaining section of this chapter.

Consequences of liability as a constructive trustee

(The discussion in this section on liability as a constructive trustee is based on A.J. Oakley, *Constructive Trusts*, 2nd ed. (London: Sweet & Maxwell, 1987), pp. 4–10.)

A person who is made a constructive trustee has liabilities of both a proprietary and a personal nature. Where the property which is the subject of the constructive trust is still identifiable in the hands of the constructive trustee, both proprietary and personal remedies may be available to the beneficiary, who will be able to choose which to pursue, or whether to pursue both. In the majority of cases where a constructive trust is imposed, the beneficiary is held to have an absolute interest in the subject matter of the trust and is therefore entitled to call for the property to be transferred to him, together with any profits made as a result of the breach of trust (*Re Duke of Marlborough* [1894] 2 Ch 133). Alternatively, the beneficiary may be held to have less than an absolute interest in the property subject to the trust. In that case he will have rights in proportion to his beneficial interest (see *Bannister* v *Bannister* [1948] 2 All ER 133).

If the beneficiary elects to rely on the personal remedy of the constructive trustee to account, he will in effect be claiming damages for breach of trust from the constructive trustee (Oakley, op. cit., p. 5). In such a situation the beneficiary will seek to recover the value of the misappropriated assets and once that sum is paid, 'the constructive trust will be discharged and the constructive trustee will thereafter be absolutely beneficially entitled to the property upon which the constructive trust was imposed' (ibid., loc. cit.).

Where the constructive trustee is solvent both the remedies will enable the beneficiary to recover his interest in the property. However, if the beneficiary seeks to recover the assets misappropriated and any profits arising whilst the property was in the hands of the constructive trustee then the appropriate remedy would seem to be the proprietary. Where, however, the value of the property has fallen whilst in the hands of the constructive trustee, an action based on the personal liability of the trustee will enable the beneficiary to recover the value of the property when it reached the constructive trustee, and so ignore the fall in the value.

Where the constructive trustee is insolvent, the election between the two remedies will be significant. If the beneficiary relies on the proprietary remedy he will take in priority to the general creditors of the insolvent constructive trustee, whereas if he chooses to rely on the personal remedy the beneficiary will rank equally with the general creditors. In such a situation the beneficiary is likely to rely on the proprietary remedy in order to obtain priority. If such an action is successful it will inevitably result in a smaller share of the assets being available to the general creditors of the constructive trustee; their only remedy then is to attempt to have the imposition of liability as a constructive trustee set aside on the basis that it amounts to a preference.

The remedies so far discussed are available if the property is identifiable in the hands of the constructive trustee. If the property is no longer identifiable in the hands of the constructive trustee, it may nevertheless be possible to trace the property into the hands of a third party (unless the third party is a bona fide purchaser of a legal interest in the property).

Where a bank is held liable as a constructive trustee the extent of its liability will depend on the nature of assistance rendered by the bank. Where the bank 'knowingly assists' a breach of trust its liability will extend to all the losses to the fund caused by the dishonest trustee, whether the funds actually came into the hands of the bank or not, whereas in the 'knowing receipt' cases the bank will be liable to account only for those funds it receives or deals with in breach of trust.

Bank's liability as a constructive trustee

A bank may have imposed on it liability as a constructive trustee, if the bank, taking into account either its actual or constructive knowledge and its conduct, has become involved in a breach of trust by another, or if, taking into account the knowledge of the bank, it has become involved in a breach of fiduciary duties owed by another. The bank may, therefore, find itself liable either to the extent of the default of the trustee, or to the extent of its involvement in the breach of trust. However, it may be possible to mitigate the bank's liability by reducing the amount recoverable by the beneficiary because of his contributory negligence.

Barnes v *Addy* classification

In *Barnes* v *Addy* (1874) LR 9 Ch App 244 the court held that a stranger to a trust may make himself liable to the beneficiaries of the trust in two circumstances namely:

(a)   where he knowingly assists the dishonest trustee in breach of trust;
(b)   where he knowingly receives or deals with a trust fund in breach of trust.

The facts of the case were that the two surviving defendants, who were solicitors, had participated in bringing about a disposition of trust property in breach of trust and the question was whether such a person could be made liable for breach of trust. Lord Selborne LC said that the duties of a trustee may be imposed on others who are not properly appointed trustees, but the law must safeguard against strangers, such as agents, being made constructive trustees, unless they receive trust property or assist in the dishonest act of the trustees.

Lord Selborne was concerned to protect agents who, although acting honestly, act in a manner so as to assist in a disposition of trust property in breach of trust. His lordship was not concerned to protect either persons who 'receive and become

chargeable with some part of the trust property' or persons who induce the trustees
to make the disposition in question, or agents who engage in activities beyond the
scope of the authority conferred on them. The agent must therefore act in a
'dishonest and fraudulent design'. These words must bear their plain and natural
meaning and do not encompass conduct which may amount to constructive fraud
in equity: what is required is a deliberate contravention of, or reckless indifference
to, the rights of the beneficiary. Moreover the agent must have acted with
'knowledge' of the design. Although Lord Selborne did not intend the test of
knowledge to be entirely subjective (see (1874) LR 9 Ch App 244 at 252) he was
insistent that the agent should not be liable if he acted honestly and without fraud.
These remarks cannot have been intended to apply to an agent who has obviously
instigated a breach of trust. It would be contrary to authority to say that such an
agent could not be liable simply because the breach of trust that he had induced
was not a fraudulent and dishonest one (*Eaves* v *Hickson* (1861) 30 Beav 136).
The latter view was confirmed in *Royal Brunei Airlines Sdn Bhd* v *Tan* [1995] 2
AC 378 where the Privy Council decided that where a third party assists a trustee
to commit a breach of trust or procures him to do so, then that third party is liable
to the beneficiary for the loss occasioned to the beneficiary. This is so where the
third party does not receive the trust property and irrespective of whether the
trustee has been dishonest or fraudulent.

The nineteenth-century cases decided after *Barnes* v *Addy* did not treat the two
categories of cases separately but applied the spirit of the decision in that case.
They were concerned with the element of benefit and whether the trustees did
anything out of the ordinary which amounted to a breach of trust (see *Gray* v
Johnston (1868) LR 3 HL 1; *Foxton* v *Manchester and Liverpool District Banking
Co* (1881) 44 LT 406; *Coleman* v *Bucks and Oxon Union Bank* [1897] 2 Ch 243).
In terms of the test of liability the most significant point in this group of cases is
that the knowledge required to affix liability was the actual knowledge of the
existence of a trust and of a breach of trust. It was not enough to know that the
trustees had committed a breach of trust but to be unaware that trust property was
applied in a breach of trust. The misapplication of the trust money had to be in
breach of trust if the stranger was to be held liable and liability could not be
imposed merely because of a general knowledge that the trustees had breached
some conditions of the trust. The cases also required the plaintiff to show 'bad
faith' on the part of the stranger or a want of probity; mere negligence would not
therefore suffice to impose liability on a stranger.

However, with the development of the law there was less emphasis on whether
there was a 'benefit' to the stranger or whether the transaction was 'in the ordinary
course of business'. As the law developed the question of 'knowledge' became
significant.

Type of knowledge for the purposes of imposing liability as a constructive trustee

In order for a stranger to be held liable as a constructive trustee in the 'knowing
assistance' cases the act of assisting requires a mental state on the part of the
stranger which amounts to 'dishonesty' or 'fraudulent design' (*Baden* v *Société
Générale pour Favoriser le Développement du Commerce et de l'Industrie en*

France SA [1993] 1 WLR 509) or 'lack of probity' to such an extent that he becomes a party to the dishonest conduct but he does not necessarily receive the funds, although the two are not necessarily mutually exclusive. The scope of knowing assistance under the *Barnes* v *Addy* classification is narrow but, in recent years, there has been a resurgence of interest.

The next group of cases are more recent twentieth-century cases. Most of them deal with the unauthorised disposition of company assets by the directors of the company. The *Selangor*, *Baden* and *Karak* cases form the core of this group.

Many of the cases have concerned schemes involving a company in buying its own shares. In *Selangor United Rubber Estates Ltd* v *Cradock (No. 3)* [1968] 1 WLR 1555 a bank provided financial assistance in connection with a takeover bid, and because of the inexperience of its officials it was not realised that the company which was its customer was indirectly financing the acquisition of its own shares. The court held that where a bank knowingly participates in a breach of trust by which the trustee wrongfully disposes of the credit balance of an account the bank will be liable to compensate the beneficiary. Ungoed-Thomas J said that for 'knowing assistance' cases an agent who had assisted in bringing about a disposition of trust property in breach of trust will be liable if he 'knew or ought to have known' that the act or transaction in which he participated amounted to a breach of trust, in other words the stranger had to have knowledge of the circumstances which made the design dishonest and fraudulent, but that a dishonest intention on his part was unnecessary (*Bodenham* v *Hoskins* (1852) 21 LJ Ch 864 and *Shields* v *Bank of Ireland* [1901] 1 IR 222). The learned judge said that the 'knowledge required to hold a stranger liable as constructive trustee in a dishonest and fraudulent design, is knowledge of circumstances which would indicate to an honest, reasonable man that such a design was being committed or would put him on inquiry, which the stranger failed to make, whether it was being committed'. The expression 'dishonest and fraudulent design' was to be understood in accordance with 'equitable principles for equitable relief' although such conduct would have to be 'morally reprehensible'. The words 'dishonest and fraudulent design' are to be given a broad meaning.

As a result of the *Selangor* case liability could be imposed on a stranger not only for actual involvement in a breach of trust but for the fact that he had notice of a breach of trust. What is, therefore, significant is the stranger's knowledge of a breach of trust or his failure to inquire. The case appears to have been decided on the principles of the 'knowing receipt' cases rather than the 'knowing assistance' cases.

The *Selangor* case appears to have held the bank liable for what in fact was an act of negligence and not for dishonesty. Similarly, in *Karak Rubber Co. Ltd* v *Burden (No. 2)* [1972] 1 WLR 602 (the facts of which are similar to those of the *Selangor* case) Brightman J held that although to establish liability as a constructive trustee on the part of a third party (who had assisted in a breach of trust) it was necessary to show that the third party has assisted with knowledge of a dishonest and fraudulent design on the part of the trustee, it was not necessary to show that the third party had actual knowledge. It was sufficient to show that the third party had knowledge of circumstances which would have indicated to an honest and reasonable man that such a design was being committed or would have put him on inquiry whether it was being committed. Brightman J said that an objective test for knowledge was applicable to cases of knowing receipt and he could not see any justification in 'denying it a similar role' in knowing assistance cases. He concluded that a person may have knowledge of an existing fact because, in a subjective sense, he is actually aware of that fact, but in an appropriate case the law may attribute knowledge of an existing fact because, in a subjective sense, he has knowledge of circumstances which would lead a reasonable and conscientious man to the conclusion that the fact exists.

Both the *Selangor* and *Karak* cases were decided on the basis of 'knowing assistance' when it is submitted that they should have been decided on grounds of 'knowing receipt'. In *Rowlandson* v *National Westminster Bank Ltd* [1978] 1 WLR 798 the plaintiffs brought an action for a declaration to the effect that a sum of £2,000 deposited with the Curzon Street branch of the defendant bank was held by the bank as a trustee and it was liable as a constructive trustee in allowing the account holder, fraudulently, to draw against the amount. The court held that although no express trust had been declared, created or accepted by the bank when an account described as a 'trust account' had been opened for the plaintiffs, the bank came under a fiduciary duty to the plaintiffs in respect of that account and was liable if it knowingly assisted in a dishonest and fraudulent design on the part of the trustees. The court specifically followed the *Selangor* and *Karak* cases and held the bank liable as a constructive trustee when it cashed cheques improperly drawn on the trust account. Although the case would appear to be correctly decided it is submitted that it was unnecessary to resort to the law of trusts. The case could have been decided on the grounds of breach of mandate by the bank. The *Rowlandson* case was decided without the advantage of the Court of Appeal judgment in *Belmont Finance Corporation Ltd* v *Williams Furniture Ltd* [1979] Ch 250 where the defendant company owned all the shares in City Industrial Ltd which in turn owned all the shares in Belmont. The chairman and controlling shareholder of City and Belmont entered into an arrangement with the chairman and controlling shareholder of Maximum Finance Ltd (Maximum) whereby Belmont would purchase all the shares in Maximum for £500,000 in cash, at a grossly inflated price. The chairman of Maximum in turn would buy from City all the shares in Belmont. The transaction was held to be unlawful under s. 54 of the Companies Act 1948, and in the subsequent insolvency of Belmont, the receiver claimed damages for conspiracy and sought to recover from City and its directors the amount received from the sale of shares on the grounds that the amount had been received by the directors in breach of their fiduciary duties. The Court of Appeal affirmed that the basis of liability for knowing assistance cases is the knowing involvement of the stranger in the fraud of the trustee. To establish that involvement requires proof that the stranger subjectively knew or wilfully shut his eyes to the fraud. If a stranger has acted honestly he cannot be made liable but he may, where relevant, be liable for breach of fiduciary duty.

The extent of knowledge required to impose liability was re-examined in *Baden* v *Société Générale pour Favoriser le Développement du Commerce et de l'Industrie en France SA* [1993] 1 WLR 509 where the plaintiffs sought to recover a substantial sum of money held by the defendants in an account designated a trust account by the customer, a Bahamian bank. The defendant transferred that sum, on its customer's instructions, to an account not so designated with a bank in Panama, and the moneys were subsequently spent by its customer for its own use. The plaintiffs claimed that the moneys belonged to them and that in making the transfer the defendant bank had become a constructive trustee liable in equity to account to them, or alternatively the defendant owed them a duty of care and was negligent when making the transfer. The court held that a stranger to a trust who knowingly assisted in a fraudulent design on the part of the trustees may incur liability as a constructive trustee. To be liable under the category of 'knowing assistance' cases in a breach of trust four requirements have to be satisfied namely:

(a)   The existence of a trust must be shown. It has, however, been held that it will not be necessary to show that a formal trust existed. It is sufficient that there was a fiduciary relationship between the property of another and the trustee.

(b)   The existence of a dishonest and fraudulent design on the part of the trustee must be established (in *Belmont Finance Corporation (No. 2) v Williams Furniture Ltd* [1980] 1 All ER 393 it was said that the words dishonest and fraud have the same meaning and signify something more than misfeasance or a breach of trust). What is required is the taking of a risk to the prejudice of another's rights; a risk which there is no right to take.

(c)   The assistance by a stranger in the fraudulent design or dishonest act. This is simply a question of fact.

(d)   The knowledge of a stranger of the dishonest act. It was accepted that there was no major difference in the degree of knowledge required for liability in the knowing assistance and knowing receipt cases.

It is this last element which has provoked considerable discussion.

Types of knowledge relevant for the purposes of constructive trusteeship

Some of the cases where liability has been imposed as a constructive trustee have given impetus to the idea that mere negligence would suffice to impose liability.

Probably the most significant case on the issue of the degree of knowledge required to hold a stranger who brings about a disposition of trust property liable as a constructive trustee is *Baden v Société Générale pour Favoriser le Developpement du Commerce et de l'Industrie en France SA* [1993] 1 WLR 509. Peter Gibson J held that for an agent of a trust who has assisted in bringing about a disposition of trust property in breach of trust liability will be imposed on the agent if any of five types of knowledge exist namely:

(a)   actual knowledge or notice of the trust and awareness of the breach;

(b)   knowledge that he would have obtained but for wilfully shutting his eyes to the obvious;

(c)   knowledge which he would have obtained but for wilfully failing to make such inquiries as an honest and reasonable man would;

(d)   knowledge of circumstances which would indicate that there has been a breach to an honest and reasonable man;

(e)   knowledge of circumstances which would put an honest and reasonable man on inquiry.

Although in *Selangor United Rubber Estates Ltd v Cradock (No. 3)* [1968] 1 WLR 1555 Ungoed-Thomas J held that the last category of knowledge would render an agent liable, Peter Gibson J thought that only in exceptional circumstances should this type of knowledge be imputed to an agent acting honestly in accordance with the instructions of the trustee. Thus, it would appear that liability would be imposed under the last of the five categories if failure to inquire amounts to gross negligence, i.e., the failure amounts to somewhere between fraud and negligence, but not where it amounts to negligence sufficient to impose liability under the ordinary tort of negligence.

The next category of cases covers the same period of time as the earlier group of cases, although they were all decided before the *Baden* case.

Although since the *Selangor* case there have been a number of cases which have expressed the view that liability could be imposed as a constructive trustee for conduct which amounts to mere negligence, there are also a number of cases which are contrary to this view. The prevailing view appears to be that mere negligence is not sufficient to impose liability as a constructive trustee. A number of cases have held that liability for negligence does not equate with liability as a constructive trustee and in cases such as *Carl Zeiss Stiftung* v *Herbert Smith and Co. (No. 2)* [1969] 2 Ch 276 and *Competitive Insurance Co. Ltd* v *Davies Investments Ltd* [1975] 1 WLR 1240 the issue of 'lack of probity' was discussed. In *Carl Zeiss Stiftung* Sachs LJ took the view that in order to impose liability an element of dishonesty or of consciously acting improperly, as opposed to an innocent failure to make what a court may later decide to have been proper inquiry, is required. That would entail both actual knowledge of the trust's existence and actual knowledge that what is being done is improperly in breach of that trust. Thus negligent, if innocent, failure to make inquiry is not sufficient to attract constructive trusteeship.

Edmund Davies LJ took the view that although not every situation where probity is lacking gives rise to a constructive trust, the authorities appear to show that nothing short of it will do. Not even gross negligence will suffice. In *Polly Peck International plc* v *Nadir (No. 2)* [1992] 4 All ER 769 Scott LJ took the view that liability as a constructive trustee in a 'knowing receipt' case does not require that the misapplication of the trust funds is fraudulent. It does require that the defendant should have knowledge that the trust funds were being misapplied or for the defendant to be shown to have wilfully and recklessly failed to make such inquiries as an honest and reasonable man would have made.

The final group of cases follow the line of reasoning that of the five types of knowledge in *Baden* only the first three types will suffice to impose liability for having brought about a disposition of trust property in breach of trust. This view was expressly followed in two recent cases. In *Re Montagu's Settlement Trusts* [1987] Ch 264 and in *Lipkin Gorman* v *Karpnale Ltd* [1989] 1 WLR 1340 it was held that the degree of knowledge required before a person could be made liable as a constructive trustee was the same whether that person received trust property in breach of trust or whether he assisted in a fraudulent scheme of the trustee. In both cases it was necessary to show that the person had actual knowledge, or shut his eyes to the obvious, or had wilfully or recklessly failed to make such inquiries as a reasonable man would make. The common element was a want of probity. In *Lipkin Gorman* an action was brought against the first defendant, which operated a gambling casino, and the second defendant, Lloyds Bank plc, to hold them liable as constructive trustees for funds misappropriated by a partner in a firm of solicitors from the firm's client account for gambling purposes. Alliott J, at first instance ([1987] 1 WLR 987), held that whilst the court's approach to the two types of constructive trusteeship may vary (i.e., in knowing receipt cases fraud is irrelevant and the recipient will be liable if with want of probity on his part he had actual or constructive knowledge that the payer was misapplying trust money and that the transfer to him was in breach of trust, but in knowing assistance cases, the stranger to the trust must be proved to know subjectively of the fraudulent scheme of the trustee when rendering assistance, or to shut his eyes to the obvious, or to have wilfully and recklessly failed to make such inquiries as a reasonable and honest man would make), there is no suggestion that different degrees or standards of knowledge should apply in respect of the different categories of constructive trustee.

When the alleged constructive trustee is a bank, the court's approach must reflect the established contractual duties of a bank and the judge accepted five propositions put forward by counsel for the second defendants namely:

(a) The bank is entitled to treat the customer's mandate at its face value save in extreme cases.

(b) The bank is not obliged to question any transaction which is in accordance with the mandate, unless a reasonable banker would have grounds for believing that the authorised signatories are misusing their authority for the purpose of defrauding their principal or otherwise defeating his true intention.

(c) It follows that if a bank does not have reasonable grounds for believing that there is fraud, it must pay cheques drawn against the account which are apparently regular.

(d) Mere suspicion or unease do not constitute reasonable grounds and are not enough to justify a bank in failing to act in accordance with a mandate.

(e) A bank is not required to act as an amateur detective.

If the bank has reasonable grounds for believing that the solicitor is operating the client's account in fraud of the plaintiffs, then it is the duty of the bank not to honour cheques drawn by him on the client account, even when drawn within the mandate. The question of whether the bank acts on reasonable grounds must be construed in the light of the first three types of knowledge expressed in *Baden*.

The Court of Appeal allowed an appeal by Lloyds Bank plc against the finding that it was liable to the plaintiffs as a constructive trustee. May LJ rejected the contention that the bank was aware of the fraud in that its manager had actual knowledge of it, or had wilfully shut his eyes to the obvious, or had wilfully or recklessly failed to make such inquiries as an honest and reasonable man would have made. The bank argued that this contention was not open to the plaintiffs since from *Belmont Finance Corporation Ltd* v *Williams Furniture Ltd* [1979] Ch 250 it was clear that where fraud or dishonesty was material, it had to be clearly pleaded and where an element in the alleged fraud or dishonesty was the other party's knowledge of a given fact or state of affairs, that had to be explicitly pleaded. If fraud and negligence were pleaded as alternative contentions they should be pleaded separately. In the *Lipkin Gorman* case, even if the fraud and/or negligence contentions were properly pleaded, a finding of fraud or dishonesty could not be upheld.

May LJ held that negligence on the part of the bank was not sufficient to make it liable as constructive trustee; some want of probity had to be shown. It is wrong to equate the duty to inquire where there has been fraud and the bank is aware of factors which indicate fraud with an allegation of negligence on the part of the bank.

The court reinforced the view expressed in the *Selangor* and *Karak* cases that the common law duty of the paying bank in the usual case where a current account is operated has been placed at a higher level than it should. The bank is under an implied duty to exercise care in paying cheques drawn against the customer's account and when presented with a cheque drawn in accordance with the terms of the mandate a bank must, save in exceptional circumstances, honour the cheque. May LJ took the view that only 'where any reasonable cashier would hesitate to pay a cheque at once and refer it to his superior, and where any reasonable superior would hesitate to authorise payment without inquiry, should a cheque not be paid immediately and such an inquiry be made'.

The trial judge had therefore been wrong to conclude that the bank had acted in such a way as to render itself a constructive trustee for the plaintiffs, or had committed any other breach of the limited duty of care owed to them as its current account customers.

There is a conflict of authority about the remaining two types of knowledge, i.e., knowledge of circumstances which would indicate the fact of a breach of trust to an honest and reasonable man and knowledge of circumstances which would put an honest and reasonable man on inquiry. In *Selangor United Rubber Estates Ltd v Cradock (No. 3)* and the cases which follow that authority it has been suggested that these two further heads of knowledge will suffice to impose liability as a constructive trustee; the remaining authorities suggest that the last two heads will not suffice.

The conclusion therefore seems to be that in relation to the knowing assistance cases where liability for all the trust fund's losses is sought to be imposed, something approaching complicity in the dishonest behaviour is required and Alliott J in *Lipkin Gorman* referred to the first three types of fault expressed in the *Baden* case and appeared to exclude the other categories. It is not clear from the *Lipkin Gorman* case whether lack of probity can be equated with gross negligence but following the earlier cases the answer appears to be in the negative.

Knowing receipt

A person who receives trust property for his own benefit, with notice that it is transferred in breach of trust, will be liable in breach of trust. Liability, therefore, arises where property which is subject to a trust is received by a bank in a manner which is inconsistent with the trust. Consequently, although trust property is received in a manner which is inconsistent with the original trust, a trust arises by operation of law to protect the interests of the beneficiary. In *Rolfe* v *Gregory* (1865) 4 De G J and Sm 576 Lord Westbury LC stated that the 'wrongful receipt and conversion of trust property place the receiver in the same situation as the trustee from whom he received it, and . . . he becomes subject . . . to the same rights and remedies as may be enforced by the parties beneficially entitled against the . . . trustee himself' (see also *John* v *Dodwell and Co. Ltd* [1918] AC 563;

Corser v *Cartwright* (1875) LR 7 HL 731 at 741, where it was said a recipient of trust property will take the property subject to a trust unless (a) he is beneficially entitled to receive it under the terms of the trust; or (b) the disposition is the proper exercise by the trustee of his powers; or (c) the transfer is in breach of trust but the recipient is a bona fide purchaser without notice of the trust).

In *Westpac Banking Corporation* v *Savin* [1985] 2 NZLR 41 the New Zealand court held that for a stranger to be liable within the category of 'knowing receipt' cases he must set up a title of his own to the funds he has received and not act as a mere depository. This offers to draw a distinction between a banker who receives trust funds for his own benefit (e.g., principal) and where he acts as a depository (e.g., agent).

It is difficult to draw any conclusions from the law on constructive trusts as it stands at present. The distinction between 'knowing assistance' and 'knowing receipt' has become blurred as the principles of knowing receipt cases have been applied indiscriminately. Moreover, it should be remembered that the 'knowing assistance' category of cases is intended to apply to cases where the stranger either never receives the trust property or its receipt is irrelevant. The stranger is only liable where he knowingly becomes a party to the fraud, or if he wilfully shuts his eyes to the fraud.

8 Creation of the Banker and Customer Relationship

FORMATION OF THE CONTRACT

In *Joachimson* v *Swiss Bank Corporation* [1921] 3 KB 110 the court took the view that the contract on which the banker–customer relationship is founded comes into existence in the same way as any other contract, i.e., by an offer and acceptance. An offer is made by the person who seeks to open an account, whether a current or deposit account, and an acceptance takes place when the bank opens an account or agrees to open an account. Lord Chorley, giving the Gilbart Lectures in 1955, took the view that once there is a valid offer and acceptance a banking contract is entered into, and an account exists on behalf of the customer on the conclusion of that agreement. That agreement is then binding in law and continues until the banker–customer relationship is terminated either by consent or otherwise.

Although there is a course of dealings between the bank and its customer, there is a single contract between the parties. Although in the normal course of events several amounts are paid into the credit of the customer's account and several withdrawals are made there is a single and indivisible contract entered into between the parties (see *Joachimson* v *Swiss Bank Corporation* [1921] 3 KB 110 per Lord Atkin; *Hart* v *Sangster* [1957] Ch 329 per Lord Goddard CJ; these views were accepted in *Barclays Bank Ltd* v *Okenarhe* [1966] 2 Lloyd's Rep 87). Where the account is in the name of joint account holders a single contract is created although independent obligations are owed to each joint account holder to conform to the mandate. In some instances liability may be imposed on a bank as a trustee but in the normal course of events the bank does not act as a trustee (see p. 112).

ATTEMPTS TO IMPOSE EXPRESS OBLIGATIONS

A person who opens an account with a bank in the UK will normally be asked to complete and sign a bank mandate form instructing the bank to open an account. Whilst the mandate form will contain some of the terms of the contract such forms do not attempt to define the features of the banker and customer relationship. Indeed, the Jack Committee (*Banking Services: Law and Practice* (Cm 622, 1989)) rejected the idea of a 'model contract', even for business customers, on the grounds that the general mandate form signed by the customer on opening his account gives the banks flexibility to respond to competition.

Where a customer is given special facilities, e.g., a cheque guarantee card or a term loan facility, the customer will enter into a separate agreement with the bank which will govern the provision of such services. Such an agreement will generally be evidenced in writing and a customer who signs a written document will be bound by the terms of the agreement, whether or not he has read the document (*L'Estrange* v *F. Graucob Ltd* [1934] 2 KB 394). Where a contract is entered into on the written standard terms of another, or the customer enters into the contract as a consumer (if he does not make the contract in the course of business), any terms which seek to exclude or limit the liability of the bank or which seek to restrict the rights of the consumer are subject to the Unfair Contract Terms Act 1977. The Act applies to the provision of goods or services, including banking services, where one of the parties is a 'consumer' of those services. An exclusion clause under s. 3(2) of the Act is any clause which excludes or restricts liability in respect of a breach of contract. It is submitted that the Act would apply to a clause where the bank seeks to limit the right of the customer to notify the bank of any errors on his bank statement to a certain period. Any such clause will only be valid if it is reasonable. Moreover, if the bank is negligent (whether in breach of its contractual obligations or tortious duty of care) then any term excluding liability is also subject to the test of reasonableness. The test applies not merely to terms defining the bank's duties but also to terms excluding liability for breach.

The onus of proving reasonableness is on the bank, and the court may have regard to a number of facts set out in s. 11 of the Unfair Contract Terms Act 1977, including the bank's resources and ability to underwrite its losses. The section also provides that whether or not a contractual term is reasonable will depend on the circumstances which were or ought reasonably to have been known to the parties at the time the contract was entered into.

The Unfair Terms in Consumer Contracts Regulations 1994 (SI 1994/3159), which came into force on 1 July 1995, implement the Unfair Contract Terms Directive (93/13/EEC, OJ L95/29) provide an extra measure of consumer protection. Businesses are excluded from protection altogether. The Directive effectively provides that the 'small print' in consumer contracts must be fair. This is an important extension of the UK regulations providing protection for the consumer who enters into standard-term contracts where the offending term has not been individually negotiated. A term shall always be regarded as not individually negotiated where it has been drafted in advance and the consumer has not been able to influence the substance of the term. If the term has been individually negotiated, the Regulations may apply to other terms. The Directive is narrower than the Unfair Contract Terms Act 1977 in some ways, e.g., in determining the class of parties to contracts entitled to protection. Under the Regulations an unfair term 'means any term which contrary to the requirement of good faith causes a significant imbalance in the parties' rights and obligations under the contract to the detriment of the consumer'. The Regulations do not apply to the main terms of the contract, e.g., with regard to the adequacy of the price or remuneration or to any term which defines the main subject matter of the contract. The only sanction under the Regulations for a seller or supplier including terms which are not in plain intelligible language is that any ambiguity will be construed in favour of the consumer and the offending term struck out. The remaining terms of the contract continue in existence without the offending term.

Subject to these rules, a bank may by express agreement seek to impose obligations and liabilities on the customer which are outside the scope of the implied contract. Most recently, some banks have attempted to impose obligations on the customer to check his bank statement and to notify the bank of any errors. In *Tai Hing Cotton Mill Ltd* v *Liu Chong Hing Bank Ltd* [1986] AC 80 the Privy Council examined the nature of express written terms on the basis of which three banks sought to impose obligations on a customer who maintained accounts with each of them. Unknown to the customer, forged cheques had been drawn on these accounts, by a dishonest employee, over a period of six years. All three banks carried on business under terms which required the customer to verify the monthly bank statements sent by each bank, within a certain period and unless the respective banks were notified of any error on the account within an agreed time the monthly statements were deemed to be correct.

The Privy Council, overruling the Court of Appeal of Hong Kong, held that although under the general law the customer's accounts could not be debited with the amount of the forged cheques, the effectiveness of the express terms agreed between the parties had to be examined. Their lordships concluded that although the terms which sought to impose a positive obligation on the customer to check his statements and to notify the relevant bank of any error were contractual terms, they did not constitute what had come to be called 'conclusive evidence clauses', since the terms were not expressed in language which was sufficient to bring home to the customer either the intended importance of the inspection he is being expressly or implicitly invited to make or that they are intended to have conclusive effect against him if he raises no query, or fails to raise a query in time, upon his bank statements.

IMPLIED OBLIGATIONS UNDER THE BANKING CONTRACT

In addition to any express terms agreed between the parties the common law recognises that a number of obligations arise when a current or deposit account is opened. In *Joachimson* v *Swiss Bank Corporation* [1921] 3 KB 110 Atkin LJ held that a number of implied terms arise as a result of entering into the banker and customer contract. Two duties are imposed on the bank, namely:

(a) the duty of confidentiality; and
(b) the duty to account to the customer.

The customer on his part undertakes to exercise reasonable care in executing his written orders so as not to mislead the bank or facilitate forgery. The courts have on several occasions rejected the idea of imposing an implied obligation on the customer to exercise reasonable care in the operation of his account (*Kepitigalla Rubber Estates Ltd* v *National Bank of India Ltd* [1909] 2 KB 1010; *Wealden Woodlands (Kent) Ltd* v *National Westminster Bank Ltd* (1983) 133 NLJ 719; *Tai Hing Cotton Mill Ltd* v *Lui Chong Hing Bank Ltd* [1986] AC 80).

It is now intended to deal with the implied duties in some detail.

DUTY TO CONFORM TO THE CUSTOMER'S MANDATE

The bank's duty to its customer to fulfil the customer's mandate, either with regard to the payment of cheques or the collection of such instruments, has both negative and positive aspects. The bank must pay a cheque or other instrument drawn by the customer if it appears to be proper (i.e., it is properly drawn and dated by the customer) and there is a sufficient credit balance on the customer's account or the amount of the instrument is within any agreed overdraft limit. It was, therefore, held in *Fleming* v *Bank of New Zealand* [1900] AC 577 that a bank was guilty of wrongful dishonour, and thereby guilty of a breach of duty when it dishonoured a cheque drawn by its customer who had overdrawn on his account with the bank's consent and who specifically paid into the credit of his account cash and cheques for the purpose of meeting the cheque drawn shortly before the dishonour. The bank could not set off the amount of the payments into the account against the overdraft because the payments were made to the credit of the account for the specific purpose indicated by the customer. The fact that the bank received no consideration for providing the overdraft facility was irrelevant, in particular, where the bank had either expressly or implicitly acquiesced to the customer overdrawing on the account or where the bank had accepted instructions which were inconsistent with an immediate reduction of the overdraft.

The negative aspect of the bank's duty to conform to the customer's mandate requires the bank to ensure that it does not exceed the customer's mandate. It is imperative that the bank does not exceed the customer's mandate, because a failure to comply with the mandate will prevent the bank from debiting the customer's account with the amount of the payment. An obvious example of where the bank has exceeded its mandate and, therefore, cannot debit the customer's account is where it pays a cheque or bill of exchange on which the drawer's signature has been forged (see *Orr and Barber* v *Union Bank of Scotland* (1854) 1 Macq 512 and *Greenwood* v *Martins Bank Ltd* [1933] AC 51). More recently, in *Barclays Bank plc* v *Quincecare* Ltd [1992] 4 All ER 363 the bank was held to be under a duty to refrain from executing an order to transfer funds from the customer's account if it had reasonable grounds to believe that the customer's funds were being misappropriated.

Another example where a bank may discover that it has exceeded its authority is where cheques are drawn by an agent in excess of his authority. In the same way as with forged cheques the customer is not liable if an agent exceeds his authority. Whether an agent acts within the scope of his authority in drawing cheques will depend on the extent of actual or ostensible authority conferred on him by the principal (the bank's customer). Where the bank pays cheques drawn in excess of the agent's actual or ostensible authority, the bank may be liable for breach of contract and for negligence. A bank will be liable in negligence for paying a cheque which, although drawn within the scope of the agent's actual authority (e.g., the amount of the cheque is within express limits imposed on the agent and notified to the bank), is in excess of the agent's ostensible authority (e.g., where the amount of the cheque is paid into the agent's private account).

In *B. Liggett (Liverpool) Ltd* v *Barclays Bank Ltd* [1928] 1 KB 48 it was held that a bank exceeded its mandate when paying a cheque drawn on a company's account signed merely by one director although the company had given express instructions to the bank only to honour cheques signed by two directors. The court rejected the contention that the bank could rely on the rule in *Royal British Bank v Turquand* (1855) 5 El and Bl 327 on the grounds that the bank was put on inquiry by the circumstances of the case and was negligent in not investigating the position before it accepted and acted on the notice of the appointment of a new director.

In *Lloyds Bank Ltd* v *Chartered Bank of India, Australia and China* [1929] 1 KB 40 cheques fraudulently drawn by employees of the plaintiff bank who had ostensible authority were held to have been paid negligently and in excess of the mandate conferred on the defendant bank. Scrutton LJ said that a third party dealing in good faith with an agent acting within his ostensible authority is not prejudiced by the fact that, as between the customer (principal) and his agent, the agent is using his authority in such a way that the customer (principal) can complain that the agent acts for his own benefit. However, where the third party has notice of the irregularity or is put on inquiry as to whether the agent is exceeding his ostensible authority, then the paying bank is not protected. In *Morison* v *London County and Westminster Bank Ltd* [1914] 3 KB 356 the court concluded that the issue of the bank's negligence is one of fact. The court then established guidelines which assist in determining whether or not the bank is guilty of negligence namely:

(a)   the question should in strictness be determined separately with regard to each cheque;

(b)   the test of negligence is whether the transaction of paying any cheque was so out of the ordinary course that it ought to have aroused doubts in the bank's mind and given cause to make inquiry; and

(c)   in order for the bank to raise estoppel against the customer negligence must be the proximate cause of the loss.

Damages for wrongful dishonour of a cheque

If the bank fails to conform to the customer's mandate, and either makes payment when it should not have or fails to make payment when payment should have been made, the customer is entitled to sue the bank for breach of contract. In *Gibbons* v *Westminster Bank Ltd* [1939] 2 KB 882 an action for breach of contract was brought against the defendant bank which wrongfully dishonoured a cheque drawn by the plaintiff on the grounds that there was an insufficient credit balance. The court awarded nominal damages and took the view that a person who is not a trader is not entitled to recover substantial damages for wrongful dishonour of a cheque, unless particular damage is both alleged and proved (e.g., the failure of a transaction in respect of which the cheque was drawn causing loss to the plaintiff) (see also *Rae* v *Yorkshire Bank plc* (1988) *The Times*, 12 October 1988). This rule was first recognised in *Rolin* v *Steward* (1854) 14 CB 595 where it was laid down that there is an irrebuttable presumption in favour of a trader that his commercial reputation is damaged if the bank wrongfully dishonours cheques drawn by him. For these purposes the term 'trader' has not been defined but it would include all merchants in the business of buying and selling goods. In *Baker* v *Australia and New Zealand Bank Ltd* [1958] NZLR 907 it was held that a substantial shareholder and a working director of a company was not a trader, and therefore not entitled to recover substantial damages for the wrongful dishonour of cheques.

However, a non-trader or private customer may recover substantial damages as a result of a wrongful dishonour of his cheque if the loss was reasonably foreseeable by the bank as likely to occur. Consequently, the damages recoverable will depend on who the customer is, and on his being able to show the existence of special circumstances of which the bank was aware at the time the contract was entered into which might cause special loss.

Alternatively, a domestic customer may sue for substantial damages by bringing an action in defamation. Defamation requires an untrue statement which would lower the plaintiff in the estimation of right-thinking members of society. Where a bank wrongfully dishonours a cheque the plaintiff's claim is based on the fact that the defamation (i.e., plaintiff does not have sufficient funds to meet the cheque) is published to a third party by the bank's conduct of returning the cheque unpaid. The bank will be justified in returning a cheque if the customer has an insufficient credit balance or the amount of the cheque is in excess of any agreed overdraft limits and true statements cannot be defamatory. Where, however, due to an error a cheque is wrongfully returned, the bank will be liable if it gives a reason for the dishonour and that reason turns out to be defamatory. A bank will therefore be advised to use a form of wording which does not confer a defamatory meaning when returning unpaid cheques. In *Davidson* v *Barclays Bank Ltd* [1940] 1 All ER 316 a cheque dishonoured due to a mistake and marked 'not sufficient' (i.e., funds) was held to convey a defamatory meaning. Similarly, where a cheque is returned with the words 'present again' (*Baker* v *Australia and New Zealand Bank Ltd* [1958] NZLR 907) or 'refer to drawer' (*Jayson* v *Midland Bank Ltd* [1968] 1 Lloyd's Rep 409) such words can be held to convey a meaning that the customer does not have sufficient funds standing to his credit. However, in *Frost* v *London Joint Stock Bank Ltd* (1906) 22 TLR 760 the defendant bank returned a cheque with the words 'reason not stated' stamped on it. In an action for defamation the court held that the plaintiff had failed to prove the words would naturally be understood as conveying a defamatory meaning since the words were equally capable of some other innocent meaning. In practice, however, banks are required to give a reason for the dishonour of a cheque and so will not return a cheque marked 'Reason not stated'. A bank returning a cheque must ensure that any reason given conveys only an innocent meaning.

Where a bank decides to dishonour a cheque it may protect itself against the possibility of an action for defamation and wrongful dishonour by ensuring that:

(a) the credit balance standing to the customer's account is insufficient;

(b) the amount of the cheque is not within any agreed overdraft limits;

(c) all items have been properly credited to the customer's account;

(d) the cheque about to be dishonoured is not guaranteed by a cheque card;

(e) no post-dated cheques have been paid out of the customer's account thereby erroneously reducing his credit balance; and

(f) the reason for dishonour does not, in so far as possible, convey a defamatory meaning.

Duty to obey the customer's countermand

The bank has a duty to conform to the customer's mandate not merely in making payment but also by acting in accordance with any countermand given by the customer. The customer's instructions to countermand payment must be clear and unambiguous so that where a customer who countermands a cheque gives the wrong cheque number by mistake, the bank can pay the cheque intended to be countermanded and debit the customer's account. In *Westminster Bank Ltd v Hilton* (1926) 43 TLR 124 the court held that in making payment from the customer's account the bank acts as the customer's agent. Where, therefore, the customer gives instructions which are equally capable of interpretation in several ways, the bank is not liable if it adopts an interpretation which is reasonable although not the one intended by the customer.

For the countermand to be effective it must come to the knowledge of the branch manager where the customer's account is maintained. In *Curtice v London City and Midland Bank Ltd* [1908] 1 KB 293 a notice of countermand sent by telegram was placed in the bank's letter box but it was missed when clearing the letter box and so did not come to the attention of the branch manager until after the cheque had been paid. The doctrine of constructive notice does not apply to a countermand of a cheque; only actual notice will suffice with the result that Curtice's cheque was properly paid and the cheque was not countermanded until the countermand was brought to the attention of the branch manager. The bank, however, will be liable for negligence for failing to ensure that its letter box is regularly checked and cleared. In *London Provincial and South-Western Bank Ltd v Buszard* (1918) 35 TLR 142 a countermand sent to another branch of the bank which held the customer's account was held to be ineffective until it came to the attention of the branch where the cheque was drawn (cf. *Burnett v Westminster Bank Ltd* [1966] 1 QB 742).

A bank will not usually act on an unauthenticated notice to countermand payment. Whilst a bank may accept a countermand by telephone it will usually ask for written confirmation of the verbal countermand. Indeed, since the bank is required to act in accordance with a customer's mandate it need not accept an unauthenticated communication. This view was accepted by the court in the *Curtice* case although Cozens-Hardy MR said that the telegram might 'reasonably and in the ordinary course of business, be acted upon by the bank, at least to the extent of postponing the honouring of the cheque until further inquiry can be made'.

A countermand will only be effective if it is given by the drawer or his agent. A countermand will only be effective if it is given before the cheque is paid and within a reasonable time prior to payment in order to enable the bank to take appropriate action. The bank will not, however, accept a countermand of a cheque guaranteed by a cheque card. The whole system of cheque cards is based on the principle that a guaranteed cheque will not be countermanded if the amount does not exceed, in most cases, £50 (see chapter 13).

The Jack Committee on Banking Services was of the view that there was considerable uncertainty and confusion of the paying customer's right to countermand a cheque (*Banking Services: Law and Practice* (Cm 622, 1989), para. 7.80). The Committee recognised that with many of the modern methods of payment the right of the customer to countermand payment may become difficult to preserve but, nevertheless, it recommended that the right to countermand should be protected, when possible. It recommended that a standard of best practice should require banks to make available an explanation of the rights and obligations of the parties to transactions effected through the Bankers' Clearing Company, including the rules of countermand. This recommendation was given effect in the Code of Banking Practice (3rd ed., effective from 1 July 1997) which applies equally to banks, building societies and card issuers and states that banks and building societies will provide customers with details of how their accounts operate, including information about how and when a countermand can be effected. The Midland Bank plc attempts to explain the right of a customer to countermand a cheque in its 'Express Contract for Account Holders' (issued April 1987) under Part 1 of the contract. Paragraph 7 states that:

> You may 'stop' a cheque if you let us know before it is paid by us. We will require details of the cheque and an authorisation signed by you. You cannot 'stop' a cheque that has been guaranteed for payment by a cheque card.

Under the terms of this provision the countermand must be notified to the bank in writing. In practice banks will normally accept a verbal instruction to countermand a cheque if the instruction is subsequently confirmed in writing.

DUTY TO COLLECT INSTRUMENTS

The bank's second duty is to collect amounts payable to the customer by the use of normal banking instruments when he delivers them for collection and to credit the customer's account with the proceeds when they are received (*Joachimson* v *Swiss Bank Corporation* [1921] 3 KB 110, 127 per Atkin LJ). Such instruments obviously include cheques (even those drawn on a bank which is not a member of Bankers' Clearing Company), bills of exchange accepted by another bank, credit transfers, direct debits, payments made through electronic funds transfers and payments made through the Post Office Giro services.

In *Hare* v *Henty* (1861) 10 CB NS 66 the court held that a bank which receives from a customer an instrument for collection must present it for payment by the bank or other institution on which it is drawn or which issued it as expeditiously as possible. If the instrument is to be presented through the London Daily Clearing it is sufficient for the bank to present it or send it to its head office or clearing agent in London for collection through the clearing either on the day it receives the instrument from its customer or on the following day. The bank is only under an obligation to allow the customer to draw against a cheque once it has been cleared but if the bank voluntarily credits the customer's account with the amount of an unpaid cheque the customer may draw against the uncleared amounts immediately (see Lord Lindley in *Capital and Counties Bank Ltd* v *Gordon* [1903] AC 240). The Code of Banking Practice recommends that banks and building societies should explain to their customers when funds can be withdrawn after a cheque or other payment has been credited to the account. Both banks and building societies have attempted to explain this to their customers but there appears a considerable inconsistency in the information given to customers. For example, Barclays Bank plc, *Cash Dispensers* leaflet (issued October 1988) states:

> It is important to remember, however, that . . . cheques paid into your current account will not become cash you can take from the [automated teller] machine

for up to six working days. (This is roughly how long it takes to clear a cheque and credit your account).

Lloyds Bank plc, *Making Your Money Go Round* (August 1988) states:

It takes four working days for a cheque to be cleared through the bank system.
If you make payments or draw cash from your account in the meantime for an amount greater than your total credit balance, you may find interest and account charges are payable.

National Westminster Bank plc, *Personal Current Accounts* (February 1988) states:

When you pay a cheque into your account it takes time — normally three working days — to 'clear it'. That is actually to collect the funds stated on the cheque. Until then it will not affect your balance for the purpose of working out the interest charges you pay if you are overdrawn.

The building societies actually take a longer period to credit a customer's account with the amount of cheques collected on their behalf. The added delay in crediting the customer's account arises because some building societies are not members of the Bankers' Clearing Company and they must employ a bank as an agent to collect cheques on their behalf. The express terms employed by building societies tend to indicate that a longer period is required to credit the customer's account with amounts paid to the credit of his account. For example, the Halifax Building Society, *Welcome to the Halifax* (September 1987):

Please note withdrawals cannot be made against a cheque until it has been presented and clearance has been notified. This normally takes 10 days.

BANK'S DUTY TO RENDER AN ACCOUNT

A bank is under a duty to render accounts to its customer either on demand or periodically, as agreed. Although the intervals between statements are at the discretion of the bank, generally statements of account are sent quarterly unless the customer expressly requests that they are sent more frequently. If a bank fails to supply the customer with a statement of account the customer's legal remedy is to seek a mandatory injunction, or if the account is a current account to close his account and demand immediate payment of his credit balance, so compelling the bank to give an account. A failure to make immediate payment will entitle the customer to sue the bank in debt.

A more significant question is whether a bank, or indeed the customer, is bound by a statement which is incorrect. This arises where, for example, amounts which should have been debited have not been deducted so the credit balance is erroneously increased in favour of the customer, or the value of a cheque has been debited twice so that the credit balance is erroneously reduced. Whilst attempts have been made to render a statement of account conclusive and to restrict the right of the customer to check and verify statements within an agreed time the courts are reluctant to hold such terms valid (*Tai Hing Cotton Mill Ltd* v *Liu Chong Hing*

Bank Ltd [1986] AC 80). Nevertheless, clauses which restrict the right of the customer to notify his bank of any errors on his bank statement may be held to be effective, in the future, if sufficient notice is given to the customer.

Under the existing law a credit or debit entry in a statement of account is not conclusive; it is merely prima facie evidence of the state of the account and it can be rebutted by proof to the contrary. Additionally, the rules of estoppel apply to the correctness of bank statements. In *Holland* v *Manchester and Liverpool District Banking Co. Ltd* (1909) 25 TLR 386 the court held that where the customer acts in good faith on a wrong entry made in a passbook and alters his position accordingly the bank is estopped from claiming that the error be rectified. In the *Holland* case the plaintiff, relying on a statement of his credit balance, drew a cheque which was in excess of his actual credit balance. The bank dishonoured the cheque on the ground of insufficient funds and the customer brought an action for breach of contract. Although the court recognised the bank's right to have an error on the customer's bank statement rectified it held that the bank had no right to dishonour cheques drawn under the belief that the statement was correct. The bank was, therefore, liable for breach of contract. Where the bank discovers a mistake in the customer's statement of account it may correct the error, provided the customer has not already acted under the belief of the correctness of the statement but the bank should also notify the customer so that he does not begin to act on the correctness of the statement. Similarly, in *Skyring* v *Greenwood* (1825) 4 B & C 281 the bank over-credited the customer's account with salary payments over a number of years and the plaintiff accordingly maintained a higher standard of living than he would have done if the mistake had not been made. It was held that it would be prejudicial to the customer to allow the bank to recover the amounts of the mistaken credits.

The customer's belief in the accuracy of the statement is essential so that if the customer is aware of the bank's mistake, the bank is not estopped from adjusting the error. In *British and North European Bank Ltd* v *Zalzstein* [1927] 2 KB 92 the court held the customer could not object to having his account debited with amounts of which he was unaware until after his account had been debited. The bank is only estopped from disputing the accuracy of the statements of account where the customer honestly believes the statement to be correct and acts on it accordingly.

A customer is not guilty of negligence in not realising that a mistaken entry has been made to his account. In *Tai Hing Cotton Mill Ltd* v *Liu Chong Hing Bank Ltd* [1986] AC 80 the Privy Council affirmed the view that the customer is under no duty to check his statements and that an estoppel cannot arise against him for his failure to do so. The Privy Council held there was binding authority in the form of *London Joint Stock Bank Ltd* v *Macmillan and Arthur* [1918] AC 777 in which the House of Lords appeared to reject the idea of an implied contractual duty of a customer to verify his bank statements. But if the customer does realise and is aware that the credit balance on his bank statement is erroneous he cannot then rely on estoppel to prevent the bank from rectifying the error. In *United Overseas Bank* v *Jiwani* [1976] 1 WLR 964 the defendant customer was wrongfully advised of the credit balance on his account. The defendant, being aware of the bank's mistake, used the money towards the completion of a transaction which he had already entered into and with which he would have proceeded in any event. The bank sought to recover the amount wrongfully credited to the customer. The court held that the defendant customer was in a position to repay the money without any hardship being imposed on him and without prejudice to him. For a bank to be estopped from reclaiming the amount wrongfully credited to the customer's account three conditions had to be satisfied namely:

(a)   the bank must be under a duty to give accurate information about the state of the customer's account and in breach of that duty give inaccurate information or in some other way misrepresent the state of the customer's account;
(b)   the customer must show that the inaccurate information misled him about the balance standing to the credit of his account; and
(c)   the customer must show that because of his mistaken belief he changed his position in such a way as would make it inequitable to require him to repay the money wrongly credited to his account.

A statement of account is, therefore, not a final settlement of the account between the bank and its customer. It is only conclusive against the bank if the customer has relied on the statement to his detriment.

BANK'S DUTY OF CONFIDENTIALITY

Many countries have a statutory law relating to the banker's duty of confidentiality. In the UK the duty is implied and the common law imposes a duty of secrecy or non-disclosure in respect of the customer's affairs. The Jack Committee recommended that the duty of confidentiality should be codified in statute and at the same time the exceptions to the rule should be updated. The recommendation to codify the *Tournier* rule was rejected in the government White Paper, *Banking Services: Law and Practice* (Cm 1026, 1990), which took the view that adoption of the rule in a voluntary Code of Banking Practice (published in December 1990; 3rd ed., effective from 1 July 1997) would safeguard the position of customers. Where a breach of the duty of confidentiality is threatened by the bank the customer can obtain an injunction to prevent the bank from disclosing information relating to the customer's affairs but where disclosure has already been made without authorisation the only remedy available to the customer is to sue for damages for breach of contract.

In *Tournier* v *National Provincial and Union Bank of England* [1924] 1 KB 461 the plaintiff was a customer of the defendant bank. In April 1922, the customer's account being overdrawn, he signed a document to pay off the amount owed to the bank by weekly instalments. On the document the plaintiff inserted the name and address of a firm, Kenyon and Co., with whom he was about to enter into employment. The plaintiff failed to make the regular weekly repayments and the bank manager telephoned the plaintiff's employers in order to ascertain his private address. In the course of the conversation the manager disclosed to Kenyon and Co. that the plaintiff was indebted to the bank and that although several demands had been made for repayment of the amount the account was still overdrawn. As a result of the conversation with the bank manager the plaintiff's employers terminated his employment after the initial trial period and the plaintiff brought an action for breach of duty of secrecy. At first instance, judgment was entered for the bank and the plaintiff appealed.

The Court of Appeal allowed the appeal and held that there is an implied term of the contract between a bank and its customer that the bank will not divulge to a third party, without the express or implied consent of the customer, information either about the state of the customer's account or about any transactions entered into with the bank. Any disclosure constituted a breach of the bank's duty to the customer not to disclose information in respect of the customer and acquired in the course of the banker–customer relationship.

Exceptions to the *Tournier* rule

In *Tournier* v *National Provincial and Union Bank of England* [1924] 1 KB 461 Bankes LJ examined the limits and qualifications of the implied duty of secrecy. He said that although there was no authority on this point the exceptions to the duty of secrecy could be classified as follows:

(a) where disclosure is under compulsion by law;
(b) where there is a duty to the public to disclose;
(c) where the interests of the bank require disclosure;
(d) where the disclosure is made by the express or implied consent of the customer.

Where disclosure is under compulsion by law

The duty of confidentiality is a contractual obligation which arises from the implied contract. A contractual duty is unenforceable if there is a statutory duty to the contrary; thus where a statute can compel disclosure any contractual agreement to the contrary will not be enforced. This exception can be examined in two categories namely:

(a) compulsion by order of a court; and
(b) compulsion by statute.

Compulsion by order of a court An order of a court will usually take the form of a subpoena *duces tecum* which when served on a bank official orders him to attend court and to bring with him books, documents or letters relating to the customer's affairs specified in the subpoena.

In *Robertson* v *Canadian Imperial Bank of Commerce* [1994] 1 WLR 1493 the Privy Council held that as a bank manager had disclosed information about one of its customers under a subpoena it had not acted in breach of the duty of confidentiality although the manager had failed to notify the customer of the subpoena ordering the bank to give evidence and to produce bank statements in respect of the customer's affairs. The bank was not under an absolute duty to inform the customer of the subpoena.

An alternative to a subpoena is an order under s. 7 of the Bankers' Books Evidence Act 1879. The section provides that:

On the application of any party to a legal proceeding a court or judge may order that such party be at liberty to inspect and take copies of any entries in a banker's book for any of the purposes of such proceedings.

The Act aims to prevent a bank from being compelled to produce its books in legal proceedings to which it is not a party. The rules of evidence normally require the 'best evidence' to be produced and this would be verbal testimony verified by the written records themselves. A banker's books include ledgers, daybooks, cash books, account books and other records, e.g., computer or microfilm or record, and all other books used in the ordinary business of banks for record-keeping purposes (s. 9(2)). The Act defines 'legal proceedings' as any 'civil or criminal proceedings or inquiry in which evidence is or may be given, and includes an arbitration' (s. 10). The purpose of the Act was primarily to relieve the bank or its officials from having to appear in court to give evidence personally. Section 3 of the Act states that a copy of any entry in a banker's book is receivable as prima facie evidence not only of the entry but of the matters, transactions and accounts recorded in it (*London and Westminster Bank* v *Button* (1907) 51 SJ 466). It must, however, be shown either orally or by affidavit by an officer of the bank that at the time of making the entry the book was one of the ordinary books of the bank and that the entry was made in the usual and ordinary course of business and that the book or other records remained in the custody or control (s. 6) of the bank when the entry was made (*Asylum for Idiots* v *Handysides* (1906) 22 TLR 573). It must also be proved that the copy has been examined with the original and is correct (s. 5). The power to order inspection is discretionary and will be exercised with caution (*Arnott* v *Hayes* (1887) 36 ChD 731) and only if there are sufficient grounds to show that the evidence will be admissible and relevant in legal proceedings. The order, if made, should be limited to relevant entries. In the Act the term 'bank' includes authorised banks, municipal banks, the National Savings Bank, and the Post Office in relation to its banking activities (s. 9(1)).

An order under the Bankers' Books Evidence Act 1879 can relate to both criminal and civil proceedings. In *Williams* v *Summerfield* [1972 2 QB 512 an order was made compelling disclosure of bank records to enable a police inspector to inspect and take copies of certain bank accounts. Lord Widgery CJ said in respect of criminal proceedings:

> I think that . . . justices should warn themselves of the importance of the step which they are taking in making an order under s. 7; should always recognise the care with which the jurisdiction should be exercised; should take into account among other things whether there is other evidence in the possession of the prosecution to support the charge.

Moreover, the courts should not encourage 'fishing expeditions' such as when 'a police officer seeking to make investigations of a suspect bank account started legal proceedings for that purpose and no other.'

In respect of civil proceedings the Bankers' Books Evidence Act 1879 does not give any new powers of discovery or alter the law or practice of discovery (see *Parnell* v *Wood* [1892] P 137; *South Staffordshire Tramways Co.* v *Ebbsmith* [1895] 2 QB 669; *Waterhouse* v *Barker* [1924] 2 KB 759). Discovery is a pre-trial examination of the evidence and documents by parties to legal proceedings. A bank must comply with an order of discovery made if the information is relevant to the litigation and not privileged from production. In *Bankers Trust Co.* v *Shapira* [1980] 1 WLR 1274 an order for discovery was made against the defendants who held accounts for persons who had fraudulently deprived the plaintiffs of a considerable sum of money and allegedly placed it in those accounts. The court held that a person guilty of fraud cannot rely on the confidential nature of the banker and customer relationship to hide the proceeds of fraud. However, such an order should only be made in exceptional circumstances where strong evidence is available showing that misappropriated funds are held to the credit of a bank account. Moreover, a plaintiff may have to give an undertaking to compensate the bank for any damages it becomes liable to pay to its customers.

Under the Bankers' Books Evidence Act 1879 the definition of the term 'banker' did not include branches of foreign banks carrying on business in the UK. This omission was rectified by the Banking Act 1979 (now the Banking Act 1987). In the criminal case of *R* v *Grossman* (1981) 73 Cr App Rep 302 the Court of Appeal refused an order under s. 7 of the Bankers' Books Evidence Act 1879 which would have required disclosure in England and Wales of a bank's books held in the Isle of Man relating to an account maintained there. One of the grounds for refusal was that the account was outside the jurisdiction and conflicts of jurisdiction should be avoided. More recently, in *MacKinnon* v *Donaldson, Lufkin and Jenrette Securities Corporation* [1986] Ch 482 Hoffmann J said that the courts should not, except in exceptional circumstances, impose on a foreigner and in particular a foreign bank which would owe a duty of confidence to its customer regulated by the law of the country where the customer's account was kept, a requirement to produce documents outside the jurisdiction concerning business transacted outside the jurisdiction. He said that due regard to the sovereignty of others is especially important where banks are concerned and continued:

> If every country where a bank happened to carry on business asserted a right to require the bank to produce documents relating to accounts kept in any other such country, banks would be in the unhappy position of being forced to submit to whichever sovereign was able to apply the greatest pressure.

Compulsion by statute The Jack Committee listed 19 statutory provisions in England which require or permit disclosure of confidential information by banks without the consent of the customer. The list, although not exhaustive, is contained in Appendix Q of the Report and includes the Bankers' Books Evidence Act 1879, the Insolvency Act 1986, the Drug Trafficking Offences Act 1986, the Taxes Management Act 1970, the Income and Corporation Taxes Act 1988, and what is now the Prevention of Terrorism (Temporary Provisions) Act 1994. The majority of these provisions entitle the relevant authority to compel a bank to produce information relevant to any matter which it is authorised to investigate. The penalties for failure to comply with requests for disclosure under the statutory powers will vary with each individual statute. It is intended to consider only some of the statutory provisions compelling disclosure of confidential information. For example, s. 745 of the Income and Corporation Taxes Act 1988 gives the Inland Revenue wide investigatory powers if they suspect that the provisions of the Act preventing the transfer of assets abroad for the purposes of evading UK tax have not been complied with. In such cases banks are under an obligation to furnish particulars of any banking transactions between the bank and the customer. In *Clinch* v *Inland Revenue Commissioners* [1974] QB 76 the court considered the effect of a notice served under s. 481 of Income and Corporation Taxes Act 1970 (the predecessor of s. 745 of the Income and Corporation Taxes Act 1988). Clinch was the managing director of a wholly owned subsidiary in England of N.T. Butterfield and Son (Bermuda) Ltd. He specialised in the management and trusteeship of international funds. Many of his customers were persons who wanted to transfer money to Bermuda to avoid paying UK income tax. The Inland Revenue Commissioners served a notice under s. 481 requiring him, where he had acted for an English customer, to furnish them with details of transactions resulting in the formation or management of a foreign company, partnership, trust or settlement and the names and addresses of such customers. Clinch maintained that the notice was void because it was merely a 'fishing expedition' and did not sufficiently either identify the customers or transactions in which the Inland Revenue was interested. Alternatively, the notice was invalid because compliance with it was unduly burdensome. The court held that the notice served on Clinch was within the powers of the Revenue although the court could intervene if the notice served went substantially beyond the purpose of the section in enabling the Commissioners to decide whether tax had been evaded. A notice served under s. 745 of the 1988 Act can only be served on someone in the UK and in connection with files in his possession in the UK.

Section 236 of the Insolvency Act 1986 applies where an administration order has been made in relation to a company, or where an administrative receiver is appointed, or the company goes into liquidation, or a winding-up order is made in respect of the company. Where any of these events occur the court has the power to summon before it (*inter alios*) any person whom the court thinks capable of giving information concerning the promotion, formation, business, dealings, affairs or property of the company. Under s. 236(3) the court is further empowered to require any such person to submit an affidavit to the court giving an account of his dealings with the company and to produce books and records in his possession or control relating to the company. Failure to comply with the order may result in a warrant being issued for that person's arrest and seizure of any books, papers, records or goods in his possession.

There are a number of sections in the Drug Trafficking Offences Act 1986, which are of significance to banks and other institutions in so far as they undertake any banking business. Section 27(1) of the Act provides that for the purposes of an investigation into drug trafficking, the police and customs may apply to a circuit judge for an order in relation to 'particular material or materials of a particular description'. The judge, under s. 27(2), may order that the person who is in possession of the material to which the application relates must either allow a constable to remove the relevant information or give access to such information within such period as the order may specify.

Once the order has been served on any person that person must comply with it notwithstanding any obligation of secrecy or other restriction on the disclosure of information imposed either by agreement or statute. In the context of the banker and customer relationship a bank would have to comply with an order under the Drug Trafficking Offences Act 1986 regardless of the bank's common law duty of confidentiality to its customer. If an order is not complied with, the constable may apply to a circuit judge for a warrant authorising him to enter and search premises.

More significantly for banks s. 31 of the Act creates a new offence of 'prejudicing an investigation' into drug trafficking. This is intended to deter anyone who might 'tip off' a suspect about an investigation, e.g., where an order has been made under s. 27 of the Act and an officer of the bank alerts a customer that his banking affairs are being investigated. The offence carries a maximum term of five years' imprisonment.

Section 24 of the Drug Trafficking Offences Act 1986 makes it an offence for a person or institution (e.g., a bank) to enter into or otherwise be concerned with arrangements for:

(a) retaining or controlling the proceeds of drug trafficking;
(b) placing funds so obtained at the customer's disposal; or
(c) using funds to acquire property by way of investment.

The section is aimed at anyone, including banks, who assists traffickers or benefits them by 'laundering' the proceeds of drugs. In order for s. 24 to operate it is not essential to know that the customer is a drug trafficker and mere suspicion is enough. However, an offence will not be committed if the belief or suspicion is disclosed to the police as soon as possible. Under the section such disclosure 'shall not be treated as a breach of any restriction upon the disclosure of information imposed by contract'.

The Drug Trafficking Act 1986 was one of the earlier pieces of legislation which requires a bank to disclose information to the police on its own initiative and on mere suspicion.

The Act requires banks to disclose, on suspicion, confidential information concerning the location of funds which might be used or derived from possible terrorist offences. There are two provisions which are of concern to banks. Section 9 of the Act makes it an offence to solicit, receive or accept contributions of money or other property, intending that it shall be used for, or in furtherance of or in connection with, acts of terrorism or having reasonable cause to suspect it may be so used. Section 11 makes it an offence to enter into or otherwise be concerned in an arrangement to control or retain terrorists' funds. However, section 12 provides that an offence is not committed under ss. 9 and 11 if the person who entered into such an arrangement acted either with the consent of the police or promptly and on his own initiative disclosed his suspicions to the police about the money or property. The information can be disclosed notwithstanding any contractual agreement concerning the disclosure of information.

The Jack Committee recommended that all the existing statutory exceptions to the duty of confidentiality should be consolidated in a single new Act.

Duty to the public to disclose

In *Weld-Blundell* v *Stephens* [1920] AC 956 Viscount Finlay said that:

Danger to the State or public duty may supersede the duty of the agent to his principal.

In *Tournier* v *National Provincial and Union Bank of England Ltd* [1924] 1 KB 461 Bankes LJ said that these words summarised the circumstances in which a bank has a duty to the public justifying disclosure of a customer's affairs. If the bank has information which leads it, with some confidence, to believe that the customer is using his account for the purpose of committing criminal acts then it must decline to hold the account and it must notify the proper authorities.

The Jack Committee recommended that this exception to the *Tournier* rule should no longer be recognised and that the exception had been affected by legislation to such an extent that it could not envisage a situation where it might be relied upon. Nevertheless, the exception was raised and relied on in *Libyan Arab Foreign Bank v Bankers Trust Co.* [1989] QB 728. The case concerned the United States Presidential Order of 8 January 1986 freezing Libyan assets under the control of overseas branches of US banks. The case arose because Bankers Trust in New York had discussions with the Federal Reserve Board on 8 January concerning accounts maintained with it by the Libyan Arab Foreign Bank. One of the claims made by the plaintiffs involved the scope of the duty of confidentiality and the bank relied on three of the four *Tournier* exceptions, including the obligation to make disclosure in the interests of the public. Staughton J rejected the first two grounds for justifying disclosure but said:

> But presuming (as I must) the New York law on this point is the same as English law, it seems to me that the Federal Reserve Board, as the central banking system in the United States, may have a public duty to perform in obtaining information from banks.

This exception continues to be recognised (despite the recommendation of the Jack Committee) and appears in the voluntary Code of Banking Practice

Where interests of the bank require disclosure

In *Tournier v National Provincial and Union Bank of England* [1924] 1 KB 461 Bankes LJ said that a simple illustration of the third category of disclosure which is justified is 'where a bank issues a writ claiming payment of an overdraft stating on the face of the writ the amount of the overdraft'. Obviously, disclosure by the bank of the customer's affairs will be justified if the bank is a party to legal proceedings either against the customer or a third party, e.g., where the bank sues the guarantor on the amount of the guarantee.

A bank may also be justified in disclosing its customer's affairs if the disclosure is necessitated by an attack on its reputation. In *Sunderland v Barclays Bank Ltd* (1938) 5 LDB 163 it was held that the bank was justified in disclosing confidential information relating to the customer's account to her husband in circumstances where the bank's reputation was clearly under attack. Moreover, the customer had implicitly consented to the disclosure. It is clearly in the bank's interest to maintain its reputation and if that is being challenged the bank will be justified in making disclosure.

The Jack Committee report recommended that this exception should permit disclosure about the customer's affairs where the bank is a party to legal proceedings, or within the banking group for defined purposes but not for the purposes of marketing banking services. Moreover, the disclosure should be limited to what is necessary for the purposes of protecting the bank and its banking subsidiaries against loss in relation to the provision of normal banking services.

However, the view is not in keeping with *Bank of Tokyo Ltd* v *Karoon* [1984] AC 45 where it was held that each corporate entity within the banking group must be viewed as a separate entity for the purposes of the duty of confidentiality.

The Code of Banking Practice provides that disclosure should be permitted in the interests of the bank, e.g., banks may pass on information about defaulting customers when necessary to recover the money owed. The Code allows disclosure in two additional circumstances namely:

(a) Within the group to prevent loss or fraud. This goes further than the Government White Paper published in response to the Jack Report in which it was proposed that disclosure should be permitted in case of loss or potential loss. The disclosure would not be permitted to a subsidiary outside the banking group.

(b) Banks may pass on information about a customer to banking, financial and investment members of the group so that relevant information about the group's services can be supplied to the customer. Banks are required to ensure that those receiving the information about the customer observe the same degree of confidentiality regarding the customer as banks themselves.

Disclosure with the customer's consent

The customer may, either expressly or implicitly, consent to the disclosure. The customer will be deemed to have given an implied consent where he gives the bank's name for the purposes of taking up a reference. Where the customer, however, expressly prohibits the bank from disclosing any information relating to his affairs, the bank must act accordingly even as regards requests for references. The Jack Committee recommended that this exception should be restricted so that disclosure is only permissible with the express consent of the customer. The express consent should be in writing and the document must state the purpose for which consent is given. Any such consent must not be obtained by the bank in circumstances in which the customer feels under pressure.

Continuation of the duty of confidentiality after the banker and customer relationship has terminated

Atkin LJ, reviewing the scope of the duty of confidentiality in *Tournier* v *National Provincial and Union Bank of England* [1924] 1 KB 461 said the duty 'clearly goes beyond the state of the account, that is, whether there is a debit or a credit balance, and the amount of the balance'. It extends to all transactions that go through the account and to any securities or undertakings given in respect of the account. The duty exists not merely for the duration of the account but even after the banker and customer relationship has ceased. Atkin LJ said that it is inconceivable that the bank be at liberty to divulge confidential information after the termination of the banker and customer relationship.

The duty of secrecy extends to information obtained from sources other than the customer's actual account if the information was obtained in the course of the banker and customer relationship, e.g., where the information is obtained with a view to assisting the bank in conducting the customer's business or in coming to decisions relating to its treatment of the customer.

It is doubtful that the duty of confidentiality imposes a strict liability on the bank. As much of banking business takes place through computers and electronic terminals and banks maintain information about customers on computer files, it would impose an unnecessarily onerous obligation to hold a bank in breach of its duty of confidentiality if the bank was liable for the unauthorised access of properly maintained terminals. The bank can only be under a duty to exercise reasonable skill and care to ensure that its computer terminals which may be used to access confidential information are properly maintained.

Disclosure to credit reference agencies

Credit reference agencies are governed by the Consumer Credit Act 1974 and s. 145(8) provides that a credit reference agent is:

> a person carrying on a business comprising the furnishing of persons with information relevant to the financial standing of individuals, being information collected by the agency for that purpose.

Until recently banks had been able to use information available to such agencies but not to contribute to them. In May 1988, an agreement was entered into between the banks and credit agencies under which (for a period of one year) the banks would make available information about customers who were in default. There was, however, a difference of policy between banks in referrals to credit agencies and in a lecture given to the Chartered Institute of Bankers (29 November 1988) the then Governor of the Bank of England said:

> I hope that, even if it had to await a change in the law, the banks and all other lenders will consider very carefully whether they cannot provide more data, subject of course to proper safeguards about its confidentiality. That, it seems to me, will be the essential step towards ensuring that the consumer credit industry operates in the interests of the lenders, of the borrowers, and thus the community as a whole.

The Jack Committee was concerned with the extent of disclosure, i.e., whether it should be restricted to customers in default (black information) or whether it should be extended to information generally about customers who are not in default. It is difficult to envisage the disclosure of white information (i.e., where the customer is in credit and there have been no problems in respect of the account) about a customer being justified under the *Tournier* exceptions. The President of the Chartered Institute of Bankers (*Banking World*, November 1988) said:

> . . . the further step of providing 'white information' on all customer borrowing was more problematical. . . . Market research had shown that a high proportion of customers might refuse permission for such disclosure if asked to consent to it voluntarily.

The Code of Banking Practice (3rd ed.) which adopted the *Tournier* rule provides that information about personal debts owed to the bank may be disclosed to credit reference agencies where the customer has fallen behind with repayments, where the amount outstanding is not in dispute, satisfactory proposals have not been reached for repayment following a formal demand and the bank has given notice of its intention to make the disclosure (para. 4.2).

Strictly speaking any disclosure of confidential information in relation to a customer's banking affairs to a credit reference agency is a breach of the duty of secrecy until the courts rule that it has become universal banking practice.

DUTY TO EXERCISE REASONABLE SKILL AND CARE

A bank owes to its customer a duty to exercise proper skill and care in carrying out any business it agrees to transact on behalf of the customer. A failure to observe this duty will render the bank liable in tort and in contract. The duties in contract and tort are coextensive (*Barclays Bank plc* v *Quincecare Ltd* [1992] 4 All ER 363). Given that the bank owes a legal duty to exercise reasonable care in executing a customer's order to transfer money, any such duty must be subordinate to its other conflicting contractual duties, e.g., where a bank receives a valid and proper order to make payment it is prima facie bound to execute the order. The question is at what stage should the bank take steps to make inquiries as to legitimacy of the order. In *Barclays Bank plc* v *Quincecare Ltd* Steyn J held that a bank must refrain from executing an order if and for as long as it was 'put on inquiry' in the sense that it had reasonable grounds (though not necessarily proof) for believing that the order was an attempt to misappropriate company funds.

To satisfy the duty of care, the standard of skill and care which bank officials must exhibit when acting on behalf of the bank is that reasonably expected from officials of that standing and competence. Where a bank holds out an employee as having special skill he must also display competence in that particular field, e.g., where a bank receives dividends on behalf of a customer it is bound to discharge that duty with reasonable care but a bank cannot be expected to have knowledge of tax repercussions on the customer. In *Schioler* v *Westminster Bank Ltd* [1970] 2 QB 719 Mocatta J agreed with the judgment in *Taxation Commissioners* v *English, Scottish and Australian Bank Ltd* [1920] AC 683 and held that the question whether there had been negligence or not was a question of fact and that it was really impossible to lay down rules or statements which would determine 'what is negligence and what is not'. Each case must be determined on its own circumstances.

Where, however, a bank gives advice on investment this is likely to be considered as being within the scope of a bank's business so that if a bank is negligent or gives improper advice it is liable to the customer. In *Woods* v *Martins Bank Ltd* [1959] 1 QB 55 the court held the defendant bank was liable for the negligent investment advice given by its manager. It was held that the scope of the bank's business was a question of fact and to advise on investment matters was within the course of that business. The advice having been given without the ordinary skill and care that a bank manager should possess the defendant bank was liable for the loss occasioned to the plaintiff (the court distinguished *Banbury* v *Bank of Montreal* [1918] AC 626). The duty to exercise reasonable skill in giving investment advice will not be imposed if by the exercise of some extraordinary skill and care the bank could have discovered some fact which might have affected the advice it gave. The skill required of the bank depends on the extent of the facts known to it, but if a bank with knowledge of the complexity of the matter undertakes to give advice but entrusts that task to inexperienced officials the bank will be liable for the loss the customer suffers (*Selangor United Rubber Estates Ltd* v *Cradock (No. 3)* [1968] 1 WLR 1555).

In addition to the common law duty of care banks owe a statutory duty of care imposed more generally on traders by s. 13 of the Supply of Goods and Services Act 1982. Although this provision does not extend to Scotland the common law has reached a similar conclusion.

Is the bank under a duty to consider the commercial viability of a banking transaction?

Although a bank owes its customer a duty to exercise reasonable care, it does not owe any duty to the customer to advise him that risks attach to something he wishes to undertake, unless he seeks the advice of the bank on that issue. In *Redmond* v *Allied Irish Banks plc* 1987 FLR 307 the plaintiff had a deposit account with the defendant bank. In two separate transactions the plaintiff paid into the account three cheques amounting in total to over £4,000. The cheques were drawn by Wagon Finance on Williams and Glyn's bank and made payable to G. The cheques were crossed 'not negotiable, account payee only' and they appeared to have been endorsed by G. The plaintiff informed the bank that G did not want to pay the cheques into his account for tax purposes and they were paid into the plaintiff's account with the bank. The plaintiff drew out the value of these cheques and handed the money over to G who absconded. It was eventually discovered that the cheques had been put into circulation through fraud and that at no time did G or anyone else have a valid title to them. The bank settled an action brought against it by the true owner of the cheques and then sought to debit the plaintiff's account with the amount of the cheques. The plaintiff alleged that the loss sustained by him in debiting his account was caused by the bank's failure to warn him that dealing with such cheques was risky. Saville J said that there was clear authority for the proposition that a bank owed its customer a duty to exercise reasonable skill and care in interpreting, ascertaining and acting in accordance with the customer's instructions. However, in this case there was no duty owed to advise or warn the customer against the inherent dangers or risks attendant on something the customer wished to undertake. The claim against the bank failed. Similarly, in *Lipkin Gorman* v *Karpnale Ltd* [1987] 1 WLR 987 May LJ in the Court of Appeal qualified the duty of care on banks as follows:

> The relationship between the parties is contractual. The principal obligation is upon the bank to honour its customer's cheques in accordance with its mandate or instructions. There is nothing in such a contract, express or implied, which could require a banker to consider the commercial wisdom or otherwise of the particular transaction.

To impose a duty on a bank to inform its customer of the commercial wisdom of certain transactions would clearly impose too onerous an obligation on the bank. Whilst banks can be expected to exercise due care in carrying out the customer's mandate they cannot be expected to be the arbitrator of what is, or is not, a wise commercial decision on behalf of customers.

DUTY NOT TO CEASE BUSINESS WITH THE CUSTOMER WITHOUT GIVING PROPER NOTICE

A bank may terminate its contractual relationship with its customer by giving notice to that effect and tendering repayment of the credit balance. In *Joachimson* v *Swiss Bank Corporation* [1921] 3 KB 110 it was said that the basis of the banker and customer relationship is that the bank cannot cease to do business with the customer unless it gives reasonable notice of its intention to close his account. The purpose of requiring reasonable notice is not merely to allow cheques already drawn on the account to be presented for payment but also to allow the customer to complete any pending transactions and give persons with whom the customer has habitual dealings notice of the change of bank with whom he maintains an account, e.g., a third party who receives payment from the customer's bank by means of a standing order. In *Prosperity Ltd* v *Lloyds Bank Ltd* (1923) 39 TLR 372 it was held that a month's notice given by the head office of the defendant bank of its intention to close the plaintiff's account was insufficient notice. The court approved *Joachimson* v *Swiss Bank Corporation* and said:

> . . . it is a term of the contract that the bank will not cease to do business with the customer except upon reasonable notice, but this, of course, is subject to any express or special agreement between the parties to the contract.

The length of notice required to be given depends on the facts and circumstances of each case and the extent of the use of the account. The court also held in the *Prosperity* case that because of the personal nature of the banker and customer relationship an injunction is not an appropriate remedy. Since the effect of a prohibitory injunction would be to compel the bank to continue with a contract for personal services the courts will refuse such an application.

DUTIES OF THE CUSTOMER TOWARDS THE BANK

The implied duties owed by the customer to the bank are fairly certain although attempts have been made in a number of cases to expand the scope of these duties. The only duties which a customer owes to the bank, whether he has a current or deposit account, are:

(a) the duty to pay reasonable charges for the services rendered by the bank; and
(b) where the customer has a current account to repay any sums overdrawn on the current account. This duty, however, is not owed by a customer who has only a deposit account with the bank since by its very nature a deposit account becomes overdrawn.

Both these duties, if owed, can be regulated by express agreement between the parties to the banker and customer relationship. Thus, it may be agreed that the customer can overdraw up to a limited amount and it may also be agreed that the bank will give reasonable notice before demanding repayment. The scale of charges for providing banking services are available on inquiry to the customer and a customer who instructs the bank to undertake business is deemed to have agreed to pay the charges. The majority of banks and building societies, however, do not charge customers for normal banking operations if the current account is in credit or if the customer maintains a minimum credit balance.

The Jack Committee recommended that the customer should be given full details of the method of calculation of fees and charges when these are applied to his account, including where the overdraft occurs without prior agreement. If a customer overdraws without prior agreement of the bank or exceeds an agreed overdraft limit, the bank may charge a 'penalty' rate of interest which will be notified to the customer in writing. The Code of Banking Practice (3rd ed., effective from 1 July 1997, para. 2.1) provides that customers be given details of banking charges in connection with the normal operation of their accounts. Each bank or building society must have a published list of tariffs which will be made available to new customers, and which will be made available to existing customers on request or when a service is provided.

Additional duties

If the customer fails to observe certain additional duties owed by him to the bank, the latter will be provided with a defence to any action by the customer. These self-regarding (to the extent that the customer denies himself the right to bring an action against the bank by providing it with a valid defence) duties are:

(a)   to notify the bank when, and if, the customer discovers that forged cheques have been drawn on his account; and

(b)   to draw cheques in such a way as not to facilitate fraud or alteration.

Duty to notify the bank of forgeries

The paying bank is under a contractual obligation to conform to the customer's mandate, i.e., the bank must make payment in accordance with the customer's mandate if it is to be entitled to debit the customer's account. A forged cheque (whether the forgery consists of a forged drawer's signature or an unauthorised alteration of the amount) is wholly inoperative and the bank will be unable to debit the customer's account. The common law rules of estoppel may, however, protect the bank against an allegation of breach of mandate and thus entitle the bank to debit the customer's account. Where the bank is to rely on the common law rules of estoppel it must be established that the bank was misled into believing, either by the customer's representations or his conduct, that forged or altered cheques were in fact genuine.

Misleading statements   In *Brown* v *Westminster Bank Ltd* [1964] 2 Lloyd's Rep 187 the defendant bank, suspecting an irregularity on its customer's account, requested several times that the customer verify that certain cheques were genuine. The customer, an elderly lady, confirmed some of the cheques as having been properly drawn and bearing her signature and she confirmed other cheques as having been drawn under her authority for cash by her servant. Eventually, the bank became so concerned with the number of cheques being drawn for cash by the customer's servant that the branch manager decided to discuss the matter with the customer's son, who held a power of attorney. The customer brought an action in respect of a large number of forged cheques. The court held the customer was estopped from denying that the cheques were genuine even in respect of cheques drawn on the account before the bank's initial inquiry. The bank relied on her statements and accordingly took no action against the servant.

Where a bank relies on a customer's statements about the authenticity of cheques debited from her account the bank can debit the customer's account. The estoppel is likely to apply not only to forged signatures but to other forgeries or material alterations, e.g., where the amount of the cheque is altered but the bank verifies the amount with the customer who informs it that the altered amount is correct, the bank will be entitled to debit the customer's account with the altered amount of the cheque. Where the alteration is the result of the customer's agent acting in excess of his authority the customer may ratify the agent's conduct anyway.

Duty to tell of known forgeries   There is a duty to inform the paying bank of known forgeries. This duty is imposed on anyone, whether a customer of the bank or not, e.g., an endorser of a cheque who knows that his name has been forged on the cheque. In *M'Kenzie* v *British Linen Co.* (1881) 6 App Cas 82 it was said that:

> It would be a most unreasonable thing to permit a man who knew that a bank were relying upon his forged signature to a bill to lie by and not to divulge the fact until he saw that the position of the bank was altered for the worse.

In *Morison* v *London County and Westminster Bank Ltd* [1914] 3 KB 356 the plaintiff's employee over a number of years paid into his own account cheques drawn for the purposes of the business. The plaintiff eventually brought an action against the bank challenging its right to debit the amounts of the forged cheques. Since the customer had for a considerable length of time known of the forgeries the court held there was a breach of duty in failing to notify the bank of the forgeries and the bank was entitled to debit the customer's account.

Morison's case was affirmed in *Greenwood* v *Martins Bank Ltd* [1933] AC 51. In the latter case the customer's wife had over a period of time forged cheques on his account. When the husband discovered this he failed to notify the bank. He subsequently, however, threatened to inform the bank and the wife committed suicide. The husband then brought an action against the bank to recover the amount of the forged cheques. The court held that although mere silence cannot amount to a representation for estoppel to operate, deliberate silence when there is a duty to disclose may amount to a representation and thereby estop the customer from succeeding against the bank. A customer of the bank who discovers forgeries against his account owes a duty to notify the bank for two reasons:

(a)   to safeguard against further forged cheques or instruments being paid; and
(b)   to enable the bank to take steps towards recovering the money wrongfully paid under the forged instruments.

In the *Greenwood* case a failure by the customer to notify the bank of the forgeries when they were first discovered prevented it from taking steps to recover amounts wrongfully paid. Consequently, the customer was estopped from asserting that the cheques were a forgery. Lord Tomlin rejected the contention that since the bank itself was negligent in making payment on the forged cheques it was not entitled to debit the customer's account. The court instead held that although the original loss was caused by the bank's negligence, the cause of the bank's inability to recover the amount of the forged cheques was the customer's failure to comply with his duty and notify the bank of the forgeries when he discovered them. Lord Tomlin said that for the purposes of estoppel (which is a procedural matter) the cause of the ignorance is an irrelevant consideration.

Duty to draw cheques so as not to facilitate alteration

The customer also owes an implied duty to draw cheques in such a way as not to facilitate fraud or alteration. Failure to comply with this duty will entitle the bank to debit the customer's account with the full amount of the altered cheque provided the paying bank acts in good faith and without negligence. In *Young* v *Grote* (1827) 4 Bing 253 the customer was said to be in breach of a duty of care to ensure that when he draws a cheque he does it in a manner that will not allow subsequent alteration. In *Young* v *Grote* the plaintiff customer left blank cheque forms with his wife. The wife instructed an employee to complete one of the cheque forms. The employee filled in the cheque form and after showing it to the plaintiff's wife altered the amount of the cheque by adding an extra figure between the '£' sign and the first number representing the amount to be withdrawn. He then proceeded to complete the amount of the cheque in words and received payment. The court held that the customer was estopped from denying the bank's right to debit the full amount of the cheque. The customer was in breach of his duty of care to ensure that cheques drawn by him cannot subsequently be altered and was liable for the full amount of the altered cheque. The case was followed in *London Joint Stock Bank Ltd* v *Macmillan and Arthur* [1918] AC 777 where the court said that it is beyond dispute that the customer is bound to exercise reasonable care in drawing the cheque to prevent the bank from being misled. If the customer draws the cheque in a manner which facilitates fraud he is guilty of a breach of duty as between himself and the bank and he will be responsible for any loss sustained by the bank as a natural and direct consequence of this breach of duty.

The courts have, however, refused to extend the application of this rule and in *Slingsby* v *District Bank Ltd* [1932] 1 KB 544 where the fraudulent alteration took the form of inserting the words 'per Cumberbirch and Potts' after the name of the payee, it was said that the form of the alteration could not reasonably be anticipated by the customer who was not negligent in leaving a blank space after the payee's name.

The bank can only rely on its customer's duty to safeguard against a possible alteration if the bank itself acts in good faith and without negligence. If a reasonable inspection of the cheque should reveal any alteration or addition, it must treat the cheque as invalid. In *Kepitigalla Rubber Estates Ltd* v *National Bank of India Ltd* [1909] 2 KB 1010 the court similarly refused to extend the scope of the self-regarding duties owed by the customer and it was held that a customer is not under any duty to take precautions to prevent persons having access to his chequebook from forging cheques by forging his signature.

Is the customer under a duty to refrain from altering the printed parts of the cheque form?

In *Burnett* v *Westminster Bank Ltd* [1966] 1 QB 742 it was established that a customer does not owe a duty to abstain from altering the printed parts of the cheque forms issued to him. In that case a customer held two accounts with different branches of the same bank and because he had no cheque forms issued by the one branch he substituted its name and address on a cheque form issued by the other branch. It was said the customer could validly countermand payment of the cheque he had issued by notifying the substituted branch although the cheque never reached that branch. This was because the cheques were mechanically sorted at the bank's head office after presentation and the machines relied on the magnetic-ink characters pre-printed at the bottom of each cheque, so the cheque in question was sent to the branch whose address was printed on it, which did not dishonour the cheque because the customer's countermand had not been sent to that branch.

The unwillingness of the courts to place a duty on the customer not to make alterations on the face of the cheque places on the bank an express obligation to warn the customer against making alterations. This is sometimes done by placing a warning on the inside cover of the chequebook to the effect that pre-printed cheque forms should not be used for any other account. The inside cover of National Westminster Bank plc chequebooks contain information relating to several matters including the following:

These personalised cheques and credits will be applied to the account indicated — please do not permit their use on any other account.

Whilst the instruction about the permitted use of the cheque forms is clear, whether it forms part of the contractual terms is questionable. The banker and customer relationship is entered into when the bank opens an account or requests the completion of an application form for an account to be opened. This is usually done in person at the bank and since the customer does not normally receive a chequebook until a later stage it is doubtful whether this warning is actually binding on the customer.

Does the customer owe a duty to check bank statements?

The courts have been reluctant to extend the scope of duties owed by the customer to his bank. So much so that the customer does not even owe an obligation to refrain from altering the printed parts of his cheque forms. Against that background the banks have been unsuccessful in imposing a duty on the customer to verify his bank statements and to notify the bank of any errors or omissions. The customer is, therefore, not negligent in not spotting mistakes on his bank statements within a reasonable time and the bank cannot raise estoppel against him. In *Chatterton* v *London and County Bank* (1890) *The Miller*, 3 November 1890 Lord Esher MR expressed the view that customers were not bound to examine their passbooks. This view was approved in *Kepitigalla Rubber Estates Ltd* v *National Bank of India Ltd* [1909] 2 KB 1010 and *Tai Hing Cotton Mill Ltd* v *Liu Chong Hing Bank ltd* [1986] AC 80 where the banks submitted that a customer owes a duty of care to the bank to take such precautions as a reasonable customer would take to prevent forged cheques being presented to the bank for payment, and to check his bank statement for unauthorised debit items. The Privy Council rejected these arguments and held that, unless otherwise agreed, the duty of care owed by a customer to his bank in the operation of the current account was limited to a duty to refrain from drawing cheques in such a manner as to facilitate fraud or forgery and a duty to inform the bank of any known forgery on the customer's account. The Privy Council expressly refused to extend the ambit of these duties.

The *Tai Hing* case followed an earlier decision of the Supreme Court of Hong Kong in *Lam Yin-fei* v *Hang Lung Bank Ltd* [1982] HKLR 215 where the court had to examine the construction of written terms which similarly sought to impose on the customer an obligation to verify statements of accounts and to notify the bank of any errors. The court accepted that generally there is no duty in law on the customer to take precautions to prevent persons who have access to the customer's chequebooks from forging his signature on cheque forms. Moreover, if the bank sends statements of account to the customer, that customer is not under a duty to check them so as to ensure that no forged or unauthorised cheques have been paid (*Kepitigalla Rubber Estates Ltd* v *National Bank of India Ltd* [1909] 2 KB 1010). However, the court said the parties are free to impose any obligations or conditions on each other, provided they both agree and the special terms form part of the contractual terms. However, in light of the *Tai Hing* case such terms will only be effective if they are sufficiently strongly worded to impose a positive duty on the customer to verify his bank statements and the customer understands the effect and the obligation he is being required to undertake (the clause may be ineffective, though, under the Unfair Contract Terms Act 1977 or the Unfair Terms in Consumer Contract Regulations 1994 (SI 1994/3159, p. 123).

There have, however, been a number of Canadian cases where the banks have successfully imposed an express obligation on the customer to verify his statements of account. In *Arrow Transfer Co. Ltd* v *Royal Bank of Canada* (1972) 27 DLR (3d) 81 the court held that the verification agreement which formed part of the express contract was an integral part of the contractual relationship between the bank and its customer and that the agreement imposed a duty on the customer to check the bank statements and to notify the bank of any forged cheques debited to the account. The court relied on *B and G Construction Co. Ltd* v *Bank of Montreal* [1954] 2 DLR 753 and *Syndicat des Camionneurs Artisans du Québec Metropolitain* v *Banque Provinciale du Canada* (1969) 11 DLR (3d) 610 where the banks had effectively placed their respective customers under a contractual obligation to verify bank statements supplied to them and to notify the bank of any errors. Consequently, any failure to comply with the obligation deprived the customers of their normal remedies against the banks.

In the UK, once an agreement has been reduced to writing the courts will give effect to the express terms of the written document, and oral evidence will not generally be permitted in order to establish a different intention. In such circumstances the question arises whether an obligation of verification on the customer which is properly incorporated in the contract with the bank can be challenged.

Effective verification clauses Since the courts appear reluctant to impose a duty on bank customers to verify statements of account in the absence of an effective written agreement it is intended in this part of the chapter to examine some of the clauses that have been used successfully to impose an obligation on the customer to verify his bank statement. Although in *Arrow Transfer Co. Ltd* v *Royal Bank of Canada* ((1972) 27 DLR (3d) 81) Laskin J held that contracts such as bank verification agreements must be narrowly construed, the court did give effect to the express clause in that case. The clause which was successful in imposing liability on the appellants required the customer to verify the bank statements and to notify the bank of any errors or other omissions. Martland J held that the verification agreement was not in any way ambiguous. The customer undertook a duty to the bank to disclose within a limited time, amongst other things, amounts wrongly debited to the customer's account and, having failed to perform his contractual duty, the agreement was conclusive evidence against him.

It is interesting to note exactly the obligations undertaken by the customer under the clause. The customer agreed:

(a)   to verify the correctness of each statement of account received from the bank;

(b)   to notify the bank in writing of 'any alleged omissions from or debits wrongly made to, or inaccurate entries in the account as so stated'; and

(c)   with the exception of any alleged errors notified in writing to the bank, that the bank statement was conclusive as to its correctness and the bank free from all claims.

In *B and G Construction Co. Ltd* v *Bank of Montreal* [1954] 2 DLR 753 the verification clause was also held valid. There was no specific reference to forgery or fraud but in the absence of notice from the customer of any erroneous or fraudulent debits from the account the vouchers were to be taken as 'genuine and properly chargeable' against the customer. The court held that verification receipts were signed as part of the banker and customer relationship and the customer accordingly bound.

Whilst the courts have been reluctant to imply a duty on the customer to check and verify statements of account it is clearly possible to impose such an obligation by express written agreement. If the wording is sufficiently clear and unambiguous the clause may be interpreted as wide enough to exclude the customer's right to have his account re-credited with the amount of any forged cheques that have been paid against his account. Otherwise, any attempt by the bank to apportion or share loss is likely to be held as effective.

The express terms of business imposed by the three Hong Kong banks in *Tai Hing Cotton Mill Ltd* v *Liu Chong Hing Bank Ltd* [1986] AC 80 were far less detailed than the terms in the *Arrow Transfer Co.* and *B and G Construction* cases. In the *Tai Hing* case the express terms of business imposed by the first bank provided:

A monthly statement for each account will be sent by the Bank to the depositor by post or messenger and the balance shown therein may be deemed to be correct by the Bank if the depositor does not notify the Bank in writing of any error therein within 10 days after sending of such statement.

The terms of business with the second bank provided:

> The Bank's statement of my/our account will be confirmed by me/us without delay. In case of absence of such confirmation within a fortnight, the bank may take the said statement as approved by me/us.

The terms of business imposed by the third bank were as follows:

> A statement of the customer's account will be rendered once a month. Customers are desired: (1) to examine all entries on the statement of account and to report at once to the bank any error found therein; (2) to return the confirmation slip duly signed. In the absence of any objection to the statement within seven days after its receipt by the bank, the account shall be deemed to have been confirmed.

It is submitted that in all three cases the attempted imposition of liability on the customer to check his bank statements and to notify the bank of any discrepancies was unsuccessful because the wording of the express terms was not sufficient to place an onus on the customer to check his statements and to notify the bank of any defects. However, there is no reason why in the future, such clauses should not be held valid if they are brought to the notice of the customer and he understands the impact of the clause, and the clause is reasonable under the Unfair Contract Terms Act 1977.

TORTIOUS OBLIGATIONS

Although the banker and customer relationship is entrenched in contract the House of Lords held in *Hedley Byrne and Co. Ltd* v *Heller and Partners Ltd* [1964] AC 465 that, as between a banker and a customer, or as between a banker and a third party who might reasonably be expected to rely on the advice given by a bank (*Woods* v *Martins Bank Ltd* [1959] 1 QB 55), the bank owes a duty of care in tort. Whilst a bank will owe a duty of care to its customers both in contract and in tort it will only owe a duty to non-customers in tort because of the existence of a 'special relationship'. This was recognised in *Hedley Byrne and Co. Ltd* v *Heller and Partners Ltd* where Lord Devlin said (pp. 528–9):

> . . . the categories of special relationships which may give rise to a duty to take care in word as well as in deed are not limited to contractual relationships or to relationships of fiduciary duty, but include also relationships which, in the words of Lord Shaw in *Nocton* v *Lord Ashburton* [1914] AC 932, 972, are 'equivalent to contract', that is, where there is an assumption of responsibility in circumstances in which, but for the absence of consideration, there would be a contract.

The extent of the duty to exercise care in tort will depend on the extent of banking services offered by the bank in the course of its business. It is a question of fact to be decided in each individual case whether a particular undertaking is within the scope of the bank's business. Although a bank must provide certain minimum services, there is no limit on the extent of services it might undertake voluntarily at the request of the customer. The standard of care expected from bank employees will be that which may reasonably be expected from officials of that standing and competence (*Woods* v *Martins Bank Ltd*).

In *Henderson* v *Merrett Syndicates Ltd* [1995] 2 AC 145 the House of Lords held that where a person assumes responsibility to perform professional or quasi-professional services for another who relies on those services, the relationship between the parties is itself sufficient to give rise to a duty of care on the part of the person providing the services to exercise reasonable skill and care. Therefore, the managing agents at Lloyd's owed a duty of care to names who were members of syndicates, since the agents by holding themselves out as possessing a special expertise to advise the names on the suitability of risks to be undertaken assumed responsibility towards the names in their syndicates. Where a tortious duty of care arises, persons relying on it may sue on it irrespective of whether there was a contractual relationship between the parties.

However, in *Caparo Industries plc* v *Dickman* [1990] 2 AC 605 the House of Lords had earlier held that liability for economic loss due to negligent misstatement was confined to cases where the statement or advice had been given to the recipient for a specific purpose and the recipient had relied upon and acted upon it to his detriment. Although the case concerned the negligent liability of auditors, it would appear to establish that a bank will incur no liability to third parties where the information or advice supplied by it to a customer is (without the bank's knowledge) passed on to a third party who relies on it. The *Caparo* case was applied in *El-Nakib Investments (Jersey) Ltd* v *Longcroft* [1990] 2 WLR 1930 where the court concluded that the defendants did not owe a duty of care to the plaintiffs in respect of transactions involving the purchase of shares in the market in that the prospectus and interim reports had been issued for a particular purpose (a rights issue) and were used by the plaintiffs for another purpose (buying shares in the market).

In *T.E. Potterton Ltd* v *Northern Bank Ltd* (1995) 4 Bank LR 179 the Irish High Court held that although as a general rule a bank owes no duty of care to a payee of a cheque drawn on it who is not a customer, where a bank deliberately embarks on a course of action intended to deceive the payee of a cheque so that the payee suffers financial loss, the bank will owe a duty of care and be liable in negligence for breach.

Where an officer of a bank voluntarily undertakes to give advice he must exercise reasonable care. Thus, in *Box* v *Midland Bank Ltd* [1979] 2 Lloyd's Rep 391 the court held that a bank manager was not obliged to predict the outcome of an application for a loan made to the regional head office of the bank. However, if he did predict the outcome, he was under a duty to exercise reasonable care. In such cases the bank may be estopped from denying the effect of the representation. However, merely advising a customer on a loan facility or means of financing a transaction does not place a bank under a duty to advise on the prudence, or otherwise, of an investment (see p. 142).

Although the modern view appears to be that an action should normally be based in contract where possible, nevertheless an action in negligence may be founded against a bank, and indeed at times may be the only remedy possible.

BANKING OMBUDSMAN

The Banking Ombudsman Scheme was established in January 1986, as a result of an initiative of the clearing banks. It exists 'to facilitate the satisfaction, settlement or withdrawal' of complaints about banking services. The Scheme is entirely voluntary (unlike the Building Societies Ombudsman) and comprises a banking ombudsman, with a secretariat, who is appointed by and answerable to an independent council. Membership of the Scheme by banks is voluntary (Code of Banking Practice, 3rd ed., para. 5.9), unlike the Building Society Scheme. Member banks agree to be bound by the awards of the ombudsman, although the complainant has the right to pursue legal action through the courts, if dissatisfied with the outcome. The Scheme is financed by the member banks through a levy in proportion to the number of personal accounts held. The Board of the Office of the Banking Ombudsman exercises budgetary control.

The Jack Committee Report generally approved the Scheme, although a recommendation that the Scheme be placed on a statutory footing was resisted by the Council.

The complainant must be 'an individual', though the term extends to 'small companies, partnerships and unincorporated bodies'. The Scheme only covers claims not exceeding £100,000 and extends to all types of business normally transacted through bank branches, including credit-card services, executor and trustee services, insurance and investments. The ombudsman has no jurisdiction over the commercial policies adopted by banks or the exercise of discretionary powers unless these amount to maladministration. The complaint must involve a breach of an 'obligation or duty' owed to the complainant. The ombudsman's decisions must be based on what is fair in the circumstances and he must have regard to the principles of 'good banking' and the Code of Practice.

The procedure adopted by the Scheme is informal and complainants are required to exhaust the member bank's internal complaints procedures prior to a complaint to the ombudsman. On receiving a complaint the ombudsman will investigate the complaint. Initially, the ombudsman will make an 'informal assessment', by which he will seek to achieve an agreed settlement informally. If this method proves to be unsuccessful the ombudsman, after a further investigation, makes a written 'formal recommendation'. If this is accepted by the complainant but not by the member bank within a month, then the ombudsman has power to make an award of up to £100,000. There is a 'test case' procedure, whereby prior to the making of an 'award', a bank may withdraw the dispute and pursue it in the courts, if it believes that the complaint raises an important point of law.

BUILDING SOCIETIES OMBUDSMAN

The Building Societies Act 1986 requires that every building society be a member of one or more recognised schemes for the adjudication of disputes. The Building Societies Ombudsman Scheme became operational in July 1987 and is provided free of charge to customers and is financed by the building societies. The Scheme may be used by individuals only in connection with complaints relating to: (a) share accounts; (b) deposit accounts; (c) first mortgages; (d) class 2 advances; (e) mobile home loans; (f) banking services, trusteeship and executorship; and (g) other loans. In making an award the ombudsman must have regard to the terms of any written contract, the rules of the building society, any advertisement issued by it, the Code of Good Practice (3rd ed., effective from 1 July, para. 5.7) and any other matter relevant to the complaint.

Although the ombudsman has the discretion to determine the procedure to be followed in the investigation of a complaint, he will not consider a complaint until the building society's internal complaints procedures have been exhausted. There is no time limit in which the customer must take the complaint to the ombudsman, provided that there has not been an 'undue delay' on the part of the customer in having the matter investigated.

Following receipt of a complaint the ombudsman will check that it falls within his terms of reference. If the complaint is within the ombudsman's terms of reference he will obtain authorisation from the customer for release of confidential information. The complaint will then be dealt with in confidence.

Having investigated a complaint, the ombudsman will write to both the society and the customer giving at least 14 days' notice of his intention to make a determination and indicating the nature of his proposed determination (the provisional notification). During this period both the customer and building society may make further representations to the ombudsman in respect of the complaint. After circulation of the provisional notification, the ombudsman will usually make a formal determination. He may order the society not to take any further action and/or order the payment of compensation to the customer.

As in the case of the Banking Ombudsman Scheme, the determination is not binding on the customer, who may reject the determination and pursue the matter through the courts. However, unlike the Banking Ombudsman, the Building Societies Ombudsman has no power to bind the society.

9 Termination of the Banker and Customer Relationship

The banker and customer relationship may be terminated in a number of different ways namely:

    (a) by agreement between the parties;
    (b) by the unilateral conduct of one of the parties, e.g., by the customer giving notice to terminate; or
    (c) by operation of law.

TERMINATION BY AGREEMENT

Where the parties expressly agree to terminate the relationship this will, generally, present no problems and the relationship may be terminated according to any agreement reached between them.

TERMINATION BY NOTICE

The banker and customer relationship may be terminated by one of the parties giving notice of intention to terminate. A demand for repayment of the full credit balance on an account when the customer has no other accounts with that bank will suffice to terminate the banker and customer relationship. If the customer has more than one account with the bank the relationship will not be terminated until all the accounts maintained with it are closed. The effect of the termination is that the bank's mandate to honour cheques and to collect cheques and other instruments is withdrawn and the whole of the credit balance becomes immediately repayable either to the customer personally or in accordance with the customer's instructions. Conversely, on termination of the relationship by the bank any debit balance (e.g., where the customer is overdrawn) becomes immediately payable and the bank can recover the amount by bringing an action in debt. However, where the bank has made a loan to the customer which is repayable in the future, the termination of the relationship does not advance the date for repayment of the loan.

    A demand, by a customer, for the repayment of a credit balance on a current account will normally take effect immediately but if the demand is made at a branch other than where the account is maintained then the balance should be available within a reasonable time. In *Clare and Co.* v *Dresdner Bank* [1915] 2 KB 576 Rowlatt J said (p. 578):

> . . . locality is an essential part of the debt owing by a banker to his customer, and . . . his obligation to pay is limited to the place where the account is kept. As a rule, no doubt, a debtor has to seek out his creditor and pay him; but in the case of a bank with several branches that cannot be the true relation of the parties.

A demand for repayment of the credit balance must be made at the branch where the account is kept if the customer wants repayment of the credit balance immediately (see *Leader, Plunkett and Leader* v *Direction der Disconto-Gessellschaft* (1914) 31 TLR 83).

It is advisable for a bank to obtain in writing any indication of the customer's intention to close the account. In *Wilson* v *Midland Bank Ltd* (cited in Milnes Holden, *The Law and Practice of Banking*, vol. 1, *Banker and Customer*, 5th ed. (London: Pitman, 1991), p. 117) the plaintiff's cheque was wrongfully dishonoured by the defendant bank, which gave the reason for the dishonour as being that 'no account' was maintained for the customer. The bank alleged that in a conversation with the manager the customer had informed him that he was closing his account. The customer had no recollection of the conversation and some time after the alleged conversation the customer arranged for his account to be credited with £403 19s 10d. The defendant bank credited the joint account of another customer bearing the same name as the plaintiff and Sachs J awarded damages for breach of contract and for libel.

A customer who wishes to close a deposit account or other account where notice has to be given must give the necessary notice. If, however, the deposit is for a fixed period then it becomes automatically payable at the end of that period. It is usually possible for a customer to withdraw amounts paid in for a fixed period prior to the expiry of the agreed period subject to loss of interest or other penalty.

A bank may terminate the banker and customer relationship by giving notice to the customer and tendering the credit balance held in favour of the customer. However, unless otherwise agreed, the bank must give a reasonable length of notice of its intention to terminate the account so as to enable the customer to make alternative arrangements and to allow any outstanding instruments to be presented (see *Joachimson* v *Swiss Bank Corporation* [1921] 3 KB 110). In *Prosperity Ltd* v *Lloyds Bank Ltd* (1923) 39 TLR 372 McCardie J held that the bank could not lawfully close an account forthwith but should give the customer sufficient notice of its intention to close the account. His lordship is reported as having taken the view that the question of what constitutes reasonableness:

> must depend on the special facts and circumstances of the case. An account might be a small account drawn upon only by cheques cashed by the customer for his own purposes. In that case a comparatively short notice might be all that was needed.

But if the customer uses the account for cheques which are remitted overseas then a longer period of notice is required to be given by the bank.

If the bank decides to close the account without giving any, or a reasonable period of, notice, the customer's only remedy is to sue for damages for any inconvenience and any loss of business he suffers. The customer cannot obtain an order for specific performance or an injunction to compel the bank to continue with the account or even to continue the account until reasonable notice to terminate the account is given.

This requirement to give notice does not apply to a deposit account and, unless otherwise agreed, a bank may repay a balance on a deposit account at any time. Where notice is required to be given in respect of a deposit account prior to closure of the account, it would appear that the bank satisfies its obligations if, instead of the necessary notice, the bank pays interest for the period of notice.

The Limitation Act 1980, s. 5, provides that an action founded on simple contract may not be brought after the lapse of six years from the date on which the cause of action accrued. In an action for recovery of a debt, however, time does not begin to run until the debt becomes due and owing and that requires the creditor to have made a demand for the amount due. It follows from *Joachimson* v *Swiss Bank Corporation* [1921] 3 KB 110 that time does not begin to run on the current account against the customer until a demand for repayment has been made.

TERMINATION BY OPERATION OF LAW

Death

The death of the customer terminates the contract between him and the bank because of the personal nature of the relationship (*Farrow* v *Wilson* (1869) LR 4 CP 744). The credit balance on the customer's current or deposit account vests in his personal representatives but such persons cannot sue the bank to recover the amount credited to his account until they have obtained a grant of probate. A bank's duty to pay cheques on the deceased's account is terminated when the bank receives notice of the customer's death and not merely by the fact of the death if that is unknown to the bank (*Tate* v *Hilbert* (1793) 2 Ves Jr 111; Bills of Exchange Act 1882, s. 75(2)). This actually increases the period during which a bank is protected if it continues to operate the customer's account after his death but the fact of the death is unknown to the bank.

Although the personal representatives of a deceased customer may demand repayment of the deceased's account, they are not entitled to operate it by drawing cheques on it. They are required to open a fresh account in their own names and on the production of the grant of probate to have the balance of the deceased's account transferred to the new account. If the deceased customer's account was overdrawn the personal representatives must discharge the debit balance out of the estate but they are not personally liable for it, so if the estate is insufficient to discharge the debt, the bank will receive the same dividend in the pound as will all the other creditors unless it has taken a security from the deceased.

Mental illness

If the customer suffers from a mental disorder to such an extent that he is unable to manage his own affairs properly, the banker and customer relationship is terminated, in the same way as if the customer had died. In *Drew* v *Nunn* (1879) 4 QBD 661 Brett J said '. . . where such a change occurs as to the principal that he can no longer act for himself, the agent whom he has appointed can no longer act for him'. The court may appoint a receiver to administer the property of such a person and in England the powers and discretions of such a person are defined by the order appointing him or by a later order of the court (Mental Health Act 1983, s. 99). By such an order the receiver may be empowered to operate the customer's account, and in such a situation the proper course is for a new account to be opened in the receiver's name indicating that it is a fiduciary account and the credit balance in the customer's account is then transferred to this account. In honouring cheques drawn by a receiver the bank must be aware of and comply with any limitations on his powers.

If no receiver is appointed to administer the affairs of the customer of unsound mind, there is no one who can give the bank a good discharge if it closes the account. However, it has been held that if a bank makes advances out of the customer's account at the request of a relative or custodian and the advance is used to pay for goods or services necessary to the customer then the bank is entitled to debit the customer's account with the amount of the advance (*Re Beavan* [1913] 2 Ch 595. In practice the bank is likely to suspend the account until the appointment of an administrator and immediate business is likely to be done through a new account (*Scarth* v *National Provincial Bank Ltd* (1930) 4 LDB 241.

Bankruptcy

If a person is adjudged bankrupt by the court the contract between him and the bank is terminated and all his property vests in the trustee in bankruptcy appointed to administer the estate (Insolvency Act 1986, s. 306). On the production of a certificate of appointment the trustee is entitled to receive the balance standing to the credit of the customer's account. By s. 267 of the Insolvency Act 1986 a person may be adjudged bankrupt if he is indebted to the petitioner for £750 or more and he appears either 'unable to pay or to have no reasonable prospect of being able to pay' his debts. A particular problem which may arise in relation to banks is whether a bank should continue to pay its customer's cheques after it learns that a petition has been presented to the court but before it learns that a bankruptcy order has been made. The answer to this question depends on s. 284 of the Insolvency Act 1986. Where a person is adjudged bankrupt, any disposition of property made by that person in the period to which the section applies is void except to the extent that it was made with the consent of the court, or except to the extent that it is subsequently ratified by the court. The period to which the section applies is the period beginning with the day of presentation of the petition for the bankruptcy order and ending with the vesting of the bankrupt's estate in a trustee. If a bank pays a cheque after learning that a petition has been presented and if eventually a bankruptcy order is made, the trustee in bankruptcy may obtain an order from the court ordering the bank to refund the money to him on the ground that the payment of the cheque was a 'disposition of property' and was void. Consequently, as a matter of banking practice banks tend to refuse to pay cheques after notification that a bankruptcy petition has been filed unless the court gives its consent. Section 284(4) then goes on to provide that the section will not apply if the payment is received by the payee in good faith, for value and without knowledge that a bankruptcy petition has been filed. Although s. 284 will not grant a direct remedy against a bank it does mean that if there is any possibility of the payment being declared void the bank will try and ensure that the proper procedure has been followed.

Where the customer's account is overdrawn the payment of a cheque against the overdrawn account is something the bank could prove against the estate. The Insolvency Act 1986, s. 382, defines a 'bankruptcy debt' in relation to a bankrupt as any debt or liability to which he is subject at the commencement of the bankruptcy.

Section 278 of the Insolvency Act 1986 provides that the bankruptcy of an individual 'commences with the day on which the bankruptcy order is made' and unless the bank obtains an unfair preference from the bankrupt it is not concerned with transactions preceding the date of the bankruptcy order. Section 278 resolves a problem created by the Bankruptcy Act 1914 in respect of the bank's obligation to pay the net balance to the trustee in bankruptcy. The 1914 Act provided that the trustee in bankruptcy's title to the customer's assets related back to, or took effect from, the date of the earliest act of bankruptcy proved to have been committed by him within three months before the presentation of the petition on which the bankruptcy was based. Unless an exception were made to this rule the bank would have to account to the trustee in bankruptcy for all amounts paid out of the customer's account after that date.

Another problem which arises is if a bank pays a cheque drawn by its customer after the bankruptcy order has been made but before it is published in the London Gazette. In *Re Wigzell, ex parte Hart* [1921] 2 KB 835 the court held the bank liable for the full amount of the credit balance standing in favour of the bankrupt customer's account on the day the petition was granted, even though, by the order of the court, notice of the adjudication of bankruptcy had not been immediately published in the *Gazette*. Some protection is given in s. 284(5) of the Insolvency Act 1986, which provides that where a payment is made from an account at the insistence of the customer after the commencement of his bankruptcy, the bank may prove for the payment unless (a) the bank had earlier notice of the bankruptcy or (b) it is not reasonably practicable to recover the amount from the payee. The bank will not be able to rely on s. 284(5) after the bankruptcy order has been advertised (*Re Byfield* [1982] Ch 267).

Termination of a company's account

If a customer of a bank is a company, the mandate given by it to the bank may terminate in one of a number of ways namely, by the board of the company passing a resolution to that effect and notifying it to the bank; or by the appointment of a receiver or administrative receiver; or by the making of an administration order; or by the company going into liquidation.

Resolution of the board of directors   A resolution appointing a bank to act in that capacity for a company usually remains in force until an amending resolution is passed by the board of directors and a copy sent to the bank. Accordingly, the original mandate may be amended or determined by a subsequent resolution.

However, a company may close its account by withdrawing its credit balance or by repaying its overdraft, without formally passing a resolution determining the mandate. In such a situation written evidence should be obtained from those authorised to operate the company's account that the account has been closed.

Winding up The bank's position in respect to the payment of cheques where a company customer is wound up is similar to the position on the bankruptcy of an individual. Section 127 of the Insolvency Act 1986 provides that any disposition of property, including any transfer of choses in action, made after the commencement of the winding up is void. The date of the commencement of the winding up depends on whether the winding up is a voluntary one resulting from a resolution of the company to that effect, or is a compulsory winding up resulting from a creditor of the company or a member of it presenting a petition to the court to wind up the company. In *Re Gray's Inn Construction Co. Ltd* [1980] 1 WLR 711 the extent of the bank's right to operate the customer's account after the commencement of the winding up was examined. The company had a current account with its bank. At the time the winding-up petition was presented (3 August 1972) the account was overdrawn and the overdraft secured by the personal guarantee of the managing director. The petition was advertised on 10 August and the head office of the bank made aware of it on 17 August. A compulsory winding up order was made on 9 October, the account having been continued unbroken until then. Between the presentation of the petition and the winding-up order being made, substantial amounts were credited and then withdrawn from the account, leaving a small credit balance. The liquidator claimed either the amount of the credits paid into the account or alternatively the total amount of the debits as dispositions of the company's property under s. 227 of the Companies Act 1948, which is now s. 127 of the Insolvency Act 1986. However, it was agreed in the course of the proceedings that the loss should be restricted to that suffered as a result of the continued trading, approximately £5,000.

Templeman J held that the credits were not dispositions of the company's property within s. 227, and, exercising his discretion under the section, held that the payments out were valid. However, the Court of Appeal, reversing the trial judge, held that the payments should not be validated as the 'dispositions' involved were effected with the purpose of discharging certain pre-liquidation debts in priority to claims of other creditors. Furthermore, the bank could not set off an overdraft on the account against the amount of cheques collected after the commencement of the winding up. It expressed the view that, whenever possible, any amounts paid out in respect of pre-liquidation debts ought to be recovered from the payee.

Liquidation of the bank

The liquidation of the bank will terminate the banker and customer relationship. In *Re Russian Commercial and Industrial Bank* [1955] Ch 148 the court expressed the view that the relationship is terminated when the legal personality of the body corporate ceases to exist (see chapter 18). The credit balance held on behalf of the customer then becomes payable to him immediately, or to his estate. The termination of the banker and customer relationship does not prevent a customer from recovering any unauthorised debits made against his account (*Limpgrange Ltd* v *Bank of Credit and Commerce International SA* 1986 FLR 36). The customer will, however, be treated as an unsecured creditor of the bank.

CONSEQUENCES OF TERMINATION

The consequence of terminating the banker and customer relationship is that the customer is entitled to demand the immediate repayment of any credit balance due to him.

GARNISHEE PROCEEDINGS AND *MAREVA* INJUNCTIONS

As a general rule, the bank need not have regard to the claims of third parties who claim either the whole, or part, of the credit balance which stands in favour of the customer. Thus, the bank's primary duty is to the customer and third parties cannot intervene to prevent payment to the customer without legal process (*Tassell* v *Cooper* (1850) 9 CB 509). The courts may intervene to protect a third party either by way of a garnishee order or by granting a *Mareva* injunction. The bank is in a somewhat invidious position with respect to such orders because they immediately place it in a position where it is caught between its duty to the customer and its duty to the court.

Garnishee proceedings

A balance standing to the credit of the customer's account can be attached by way of a garnishee order issued under the Rules of the Supreme Court 1965 ord. 49, 4.1) or by means of a garnishee summons issued under the County Court Rules 1981 Ord. 30, r. 1). Such an order is usually obtained by a judgment creditor whose judgment debt has not been satisfied, e.g., A owes money to B and B obtains judgment against A in respect of the debt. A has a bank account in which he maintains a credit balance. B can apply to the court to attach the credit balance with a garnishee order so that once the order is served on the bank, the bank's right to honour transfers from the account is suspended. The order *nisi* will attach the full amount standing to the credit of the customer's account. The bank is unable to make payments out of the account even if the amount of withdrawals would leave an amount sufficient to discharge the amount of the order (*Rogers* v *Whiteley* [1892] AC 118; *Edmunds* v *Edmunds* [1904] P 362). However, in some cases the order *nisi* will specify the amount to be attached, including any amounts necessary to cover costs; in that situation the bank is free to deal with the remaining balance in accordance with the customer's instructions.

The creditor will usually apply to the court for an order under which all debts 'owing and accruing' from the bank to the customer are attached for the purpose of satisfying the judgment debt. The order is obtained by the judgment creditor making an *ex parte* application to the court, that is, without serving a notice of his application to the judgment debtor. Initially, an order *nisi* is made and the bank (the debtor) is given an opportunity to show cause why the order should not be made absolute and why it should not comply with the order and pay the amount owed by the customer. If the bank does not show cause, the order will be made final and will require the bank to make payment of the amount attached. Once a garnishee order *nisi* has been made absolute it will relate back to the date of the order *nisi*. Payment either to the debtor or into court will discharge the order.

All debts due or accruing due from any individual or corporation (excluding the Crown) to a judgment creditor can be attached but if a garnishee order is to be made it is essential that at the time the order takes effect there is a debt owing to the judgment debtor which the law recognises to be a debt (*Webb* v *Stenton* (1883) 11 QBD 518). Originally, there was some doubt about whether garnishee orders could be made against bank accounts since a demand is necessary before any balance on a current account becomes 'due and owing'. However; this was resolved in *Joachimson* v *Swiss Bank Corporation* [1921] 3 KB 110 where Bankes LJ observed that the service of the garnishee notice on the bank operated as a demand. However, money represented by a bill of exchange which has not matured can only be attached on maturity (*Hyam* v *Freeman* (1890) 35 SJ 87).

The position with regard to deposit accounts was more complicated because notice has often to be given in respect of these accounts or the deposit may continue to be held until a fixed period. The law was clarified by the passing of s. 38 of the Administration of Justice Act 1956, under which amounts standing to the credit of savings accounts, deposit accounts, and fixed deposit accounts with banks may be attached. This provision was extended by s. 40 of the Supreme Court Act 1981 to any deposit account with a bank or other deposit-taking institution, or to any 'withdrawable share account with any deposit-taking institution'. Thus, garnishee orders can clearly be made to attach credit balances standing in a building society account.

Moreover, a garnishee order can be made to attach a foreign-currency account maintained by the debtor with a bank in the UK. In *Choice Investments Ltd* v *Jeromnimon* [1981] QB 149 Lord Denning MR held that the English courts could attach not only credit balances expressed in sterling but also credit balances expressed in foreign currencies. In *Choice Investments* the account was a debt in US dollars payable on demand and the judgment debtor could therefore require payment in dollars and not merely its sterling equivalent. The currency in which the credit balance is expressed therefore makes no difference to the power of the court to attach it. Lord Denning expressed the view that since in the case of a sum payable in England in a foreign currency the English courts could give judgment for the amount in that foreign currency (see *Miliangos* v *George Frank (Textiles) Ltd* [1976] AC 443) there was no reason why an amount expressed in a foreign currency standing to the credit of a judgment debtor in the jurisdiction could not be attached. A refusal of the courts to attach such amounts would enable a judgment debtor to avoid a judgment creditor enforcing his judgment by merely converting any credit balance in his bank account into a foreign currency.

Where the deposit is maintained with an overseas branch of a bank established in the UK the position was more complicated. In *Richardson* v *Richardson* [1927] P 228 it was held that a garnishee order did not attach a deposit denominated in foreign currency and maintained with a foreign branch of a British bank. However, ord. 49 of the Rules of the Supreme Court 1965 has been amended so that currently all that is required is that the garnishee himself be within the jurisdiction when the order is served on him and that the debt is due and owing at the time of making the order. Consequently, it was held in *SCF Finance Co. Ltd* v *Masri (No. 3)*

[1987] 1 QB 1028 that if the garnishee was physically present in the UK at the time the order was served and provided the debt could be recovered in the UK a garnishee order could be made in respect of it. However, the court should exercise its discretion to make the order absolute with care and in particular the court should refuse to make the order absolute if there is any danger that the foreign courts might assume jurisdiction and compel payment. In *Interpool Ltd v Galani* [1988] QB 738 it was emphasised that the court should not exercise its discretion to issue an order absolute if the debt is recoverable only in a foreign jurisdiction.

Where an order *nisi* is made in respect of a credit balance expressed in a foreign currency, the bank on which it is served should set aside sufficient foreign currency to satisfy the judgment debt expressed in sterling at the rate of exchange prevailing at the time the garnishee order *nisi* was made. However, the bank should not convert the attached foreign currency into sterling until the order has been made absolute. When that has been done the bank should convert the attached currency into sterling at the then rate of exchange in order to meet the judgment debt; any surplus of sterling from the conversion if the rate of exchange has moved in favour of the foreign currency should be paid to the judgment debtor. A problem may arise if by the time the order is made absolute the rate of exchange has moved in favour of sterling so that the amount of the foreign currency attached is insufficient to satisfy the debt owed to the judgment creditor. However, there is nothing to prevent the judgment creditor from applying to the court for a further garnishee order if part of the debt remains unsatisfied because of movement in the rate of exchange in favour of sterling.

A garnishee order *nisi* attaches the debt in the hands of the third party so that he cannot obtain a discharge by making payment to the judgment debtor. The order does not attach amounts paid into the customer's account after the date on which it was made and, in case of delay, when it was served on the bank. In *Heppenstall* v *Jackson* [1939] 1 KB 585 the Court of Appeal held that in order for an amount to be attached by the order *nisi* there must be a present debt due and accruing at the time of the service of the order and amounts paid to the credit of the account after the service of the order were not accruing (the court approved *Jones* v *Thompson* (1858) El Bl & El 63; *Tapp* v *Jones* (1875) LR 10 QB 591 and *Webb* v *Stenton* (1883) 11 QBD 518, all of which decided that the word 'accruing' did not mean debts which might arise at any time in the future between the judgment debtor and the bank). In *Jones and Co.* v *Coventry* [1909] 2 KB 1029 the court held that amounts of uncleared army pension warrants which had been credited to the judgment debtor's account could not be made the subject of a garnishee order.

Grounds for objection to the order being made absolute   The garnishee order *nisi* gives the bank an opportunity to object to the order being made absolute. The most obvious reason for the court not to make a garnishee order absolute is that the debt has already been discharged. However, there are other objections which a bank can raise to have the order discharged, namely:

(a)   The bank's right to repayment will have priority over the garnishee order where the judgment creditor is indebted to the bank in circumstances which give the bank a right either to set off or to combine the credit balance of the garnished account with a debit balance on another account maintained by the customer (*Tapp* v *Jones* (1875) LR 10 QB 591, which held that debts incurred before the attachment order can be set off because they are readily ascertainable but not those arising after). This right would apply in respect of overdrafts which are repayable on demand and which the bank can readily set off but not loan agreements where the debt does not become payable until a future date.

(b)   A bank should object to the attachment order where the amount sought to be attached is standing to the credit of a trust account. In such a case the bank will be aware that the judgment debtor is not entitled to the credit balance in his own right, as in *Plunkett* v *Barclays Bank Ltd* [1936] 2 KB 107, in which the order was discharged. Du Parcq J emphasised that it is the bank's duty in such a case to make the position known to the court, as well as advising the customer of the receipt of the order (see also *Hancock* v *Smith* (1889) 41 ChD 456).

(c)   An order *nisi* will be discharged where the balance standing to the credit of the customer's account is held in a joint account. In *Hirschorn* v *Evans* [1938] 2 KB 801 the Court of Appeal held that a garnishee order could not attach a joint account of a husband and wife in respect of a debt owed by the husband only. This rule might not apply where it can be shown that the credit balance on the joint account is in reality that of the judgment debtor (*Harrods Ltd* v *Tester* [1937] 2 All ER 236).

(d)   The bank is likely to object to an attachment order where the judgment debtor is described by a name different to that of the account sought to be attached (*Moore* v *Peachey* (1842) 8 TLR 406 and *Koch* v *Mineral Ore Syndicate* (1910) 54 SJ 600). In the latter case the order was in fact amended to comply with the name on the account but the bank was not liable for having paid cheques drawn on the account in the meantime. Moreover, if the bank overlooks the discrepancy in the names and suspends the wrong account, it will find itself liable for breach of contract and wrongful dishonour of cheques.

(e)   A bank may oppose the grant of a garnishee order where there is a possibility that payment of the debt to the garnishor will not be recognised as a discharge in another jurisdiction with the effect that payment may have to be made twice. A UK court will exercise its discretion on the basis of an assessment of the extent of the risk involved and not with regard to the propriety of the possible intervention by the foreign court (*Deutsche Schachtbau- und Tiefbohr-Gesellschaft* v *Shell International Petroleum Co. Ltd* [1990] 1 AC 295).

(f)   A garnishee order *nisi* where the judgment debtor is insolvent and the garnishee order is used to give the garnishor precedence over the other creditors should not be made (*Whitbread Flowers* v *Thurston* (unreported)).

(g)   In *Alcom Ltd* v *Republic of Colombia* [1984] 1 AC 580, the House of Lords held that the credit balance on an account cannot be attached if the account is held by a foreign State, unless the account is used for commercial transactions. The account cannot be dissected and the different purposes for which it is used examined individually so as to enable an attachment order to be made.

(h)   Where the credit balance standing in favour of the judgment creditor has been assigned in favour of a third party the court will object to the garnishee order because of the conflict of priorities. In *Rekstin* v *Severo Sibirsko Gosudarstvennoe Akcionernoe Obschestvo Komseverputj* [1933] 1 KB 47 (a case involving money transfer orders) the court held that once an amount due to the judgment creditor has been effectively assigned to a third party that part of the credit balance cannot be made subject to the garnishee order. However, the Court of Appeal expressed the view that mere book entries without communication to the transferee were recoverable and that a garnishee order *nisi* operated to revoke any such transfer. In *Momm* v *Barclays Bank International Ltd* [1977] QB 790 Kerr J considered that the *Rekstin* case must be confined to its special facts. Thus, where the assignment has been completed before service of the garnishee order *nisi*, the assignee's interest prevails over the judgment debtor. A statutory assignment under s. 136(1) of the Law of Property Act 1925 is complete when notice is served on the debtor (the bank in this situation), and where there is a conflict between the statutory assignment and the garnishee order, priority is determined by the date of notification to the bank. An equitable assignment becomes effective on execution, irrespective of the notification to the debtor and such an assignment would have effect if executed in good faith before the order *nisi* was served on the bank.

Mareva injunctions

An unsecured creditor cannot, pending the outcome of an action brought by him, seek to freeze any assets belonging to the defendant. Until the introduction of the *Mareva* injunction, a defendant was free to transfer his assets abroad or otherwise to dispose of them pending the outcome of proceedings brought by the plaintiff. Consequently, a successful plaintiff might discover that the judgment obtained against the defendant would remain unsatisfied because the debtor has transferred his assets out of the jurisdiction or has otherwise effectively dissipated them. The *Mareva* injunction was therefore devised (see *Nippon Yusen Kaisha* v *Karageorgis* [1975] 1 WLR 1093, which was examined and approved by the Court of Appeal in *Mareva Compania SA* v *International Bulkcarriers SA* [1980] 1 All ER 213) as a means of preventing the debtor from disposing of assets which were the likely subject of a court order. Lord Denning MR, giving judgment in the *Mareva* case itself, said that if it appears that a debt is due and owing and there is a danger that the debtor may dispose of his assets so as to defeat the creditor's expectation of satisfying his judgment by levying execution on assets in this country, the court has jurisdiction to grant an interlocutory judgment so as to prevent disposition of the assets. Section 37 of the Supreme Court Act 1981 gives this form of injunction statutory recognition and extends the power of the High Court to grant an interlocutory injunction by providing that a *Mareva* injunction may be granted in respect of assets located within the jurisdiction regardless of whether or not the party is domiciled, resident or present within the jurisdiction. The *Mareva* injunction is therefore available in disputes relating to both international and domestic transactions.

A *Mareva* injunction will be granted where the plaintiff can show:

(a)   that the action he has brought, or intends to bring, is based on a substantive cause and that it stands a prima facie chance of success (*Z Ltd* v *A-Z* [1982] QB 558; *Ninemia Maritime Corporation* v *Trave Schiffahrtsgesellschaft mbH & Co. KG* [1983] 1 WLR 1412; and

(b)   that there is a real danger that the defendant will transfer his assets out of the jurisdiction or that he may otherwise deal with them so as to make them unavailable or untraceable (*Prince Abdul Rahman bin Turki al Sudairy* v *Abu-Taha*

[1980] 1 WLR 1268; *Searose Ltd* v *Seatrain UK Ltd* [1981] WLR 894). In *Etablissement Esefka International Anstalt* v *Central Bank of Nigeria* [1979] 1 Lloyd's Rep 455 and *Polly Peck International plc* v *Nadir (No. 2)* [1992] 4 All ER 769 it was held that a plaintiff who has established a prima facie cause of action must also show that there are reasonable grounds for believing that the defendant will remove or divert the assets in such a way as to prejudice the plaintiff's chance of enforcing the judgment. In *Etablissement Esefka* the court refused to grant an injunction because it did not believe that there was a danger that the assets would be transferred abroad.

When granting a *Mareva* injunction the court should take care to ensure that the order does not interfere with third-party rights. Thus, a *Mareva* injunction served on a bank does not attach to a joint account except where all the account holders are made co-defendants or the order is so drafted that it applies to accounts to which the defendant is a party (*Z Ltd* v *A-Z* [1982] QB 558) Moreover, even where the account is maintained in the sole name of the defendant a third party may be able to establish a superior title, e.g., where the third party can show that amounts standing to the credit of the defendants account are trust account (*SCF Finance Co. Ltd* v *Masri* [1985] 1 WLR 876).

The *Mareva* injunction acts *in personam*. The order does not confer new rights *in rem* and if other claims are established the court will normally allow them to be discharged. The order does not confer any priority on the plaintiff; the principle is important to banks whose right of set-off against the customer is recognised by the courts (*Oceanica Castelana Armadora SA of Panama* v *Mineralimportexport* [1983] 1 WLR 1294).

Parties to a Mareva *injunction*   The question which arose in *Chief Constable of Kent* v *V* [1983] QB 34 was whether, pending criminal prosecution for forgery and obtaining money by deception on forged instruments, the police could apply for an injunction to freeze amounts obtained by the accused. Lord Denning MR held that the court could grant an injunction in every case in which it appeared to be just and convenient to do so. The court therefore held that money obtained by forgery and paid into a bank account by the accused should be frozen, especially since the accused had been granted bail pending trial and would otherwise be free to draw on the account. Where money obtained dishonestly is mixed with funds obtained honestly by the accused, the *Mareva* injunction should be limited to the amount of the money obtained dishonestly. However, if the stolen money can no longer be identified the court will, if necessary, make an order freezing the whole of the credit balance in the bank until the amount obtained dishonestly may be ascertained.

Practical problems   It is now proposed to identify and deal with some of the problems a bank is likely to face when it is served with notice of a *Mareva* injunction against one of its customers.

(a) *Who is the defendant and where does he hold the account?* If the *Mareva* injunction specifies the name of the customer whose account is sought to be attached and the branch where the account is kept, the bank will have no problem in identifying the account which is subject to the order. If, however, the plaintiff cannot identify the bank account (e.g., where a partnership account is held in a name other than that of the defendant or the partnership), the plaintiff may request the bank to conduct a search to determine whether the bank holds any account for or assets owned by the defendant. There is no doubt that a bank which has to search for the defendant's account is entitled to be reimbursed any expenses incurred, in addition to being paid for carrying out the search.

A problem arises, however, where there are delays in identifying the account with the result that the defendant is given the opportunity of transferring the credit balance in his bank or other items held by the bank outside the jurisdiction and thus defeating the *Mareva* injunction. The identification of the defendant's bank account may be time consuming, since banks do not usually maintain a central index of customer's names and it may therefore be necessary for the bank's head office to instruct a number of its branches to conduct a search for the defendant's account. Whilst a *Mareva* injunction normally operates immediately the order is made, a bank which has not been notified of, or cannot comply with, the order because it has not yet identified the defendant's account, cannot be held guilty of contempt of court if the defendant succeeds in removing his assets whilst the bank is carrying out its search. Lord Denning said that the bank will only be liable for contempt where the bank or any of its officers knowingly assists in the disposal of assets, or if the bank acts with carelessness or recklessness.

(b)   *Pre-injunction transactions*   Where the defendant has drawn cheques on his account before the injunction is communicated to the bank but the cheques are presented for payment after notification, the question arises whether the payee or other holder of the cheque is entitled to be paid out of the account which has been attached. The issue of a cheque by the drawer does not, in English law, amount to an assignment of any part of the drawer's bank account to the payee. The defendant bank should therefore dishonour cheques presented to it after notification of the injunction, even though they were drawn before the order was made and notified to the bank. However, the bank must be cautious in giving reasons for the dishonour and ensure that they are not defamatory (e.g., imply that the drawer has insufficient funds to meet the cheque). However, if the defendant's bank is under a legal obligation to a third party to make a payment then the bank must honour its obligation. Thus, if a cheque is drawn before the *Mareva* injunction is granted or before it is notified to the defendant's bank and is backed by a cheque card, the bank must honour it on presentation because of the guarantee liability which the bank undertakes by means of the cheque card. Similarly, if the defendant's bank has undertaken to make payment against the presentation of shipping documents under a letter of credit.

(c)   *The bank's duty of confidence to its customer*   The bank is bound by the duty of confidentiality except when ordered by a court (e.g., when the bank's duty to its customer is outweighed by its duty to the general public). Where, therefore, the plaintiff is uncertain about the extent of the credit balance on the defendant's account when the injunction is granted, the plaintiff must apply for an order of discovery at the time he applies for the injunction.

A bank which has been served with a *Mareva* injunction is under no obligation to divulge whether the injunction has taken effect. Where the bank cannot give effect to the injunction, e.g., if the defendant does not have an account with the bank on whom the *Mareva* injunction is served or the account has a credit balance less than the plaintiff's claim, the bank is not obliged to give notice to the plaintiff of the absence, or insufficiency of the defendant's account.

(d) *Jurisdictional problems* The purpose of a *Mareva* injunction is to prevent the defendant from removing his assets outside the jurisdiction or disposing of them so as to prevent any judgment in favour of the plaintiff being rendered effective. Even if the judgment of the English courts could be enforced abroad, the removal of the defendant's assets will inevitably result in delays and expense to the prejudice of the plaintiff.

An order of the English courts granting a *Mareva* injunction will not operate outside the jurisdiction. Thus, a *Mareva* injunction granted by the English courts will not have effect on overseas branches of UK banks conducting business abroad. The overseas branches of UK banks will have had to comply with the laws of the countries in which they carry on business, and the plaintiff would therefore have to obtain a *Mareva* injunction, or the equivalent in that country (see *R* v *Grossman* (1981) 73 Cr App R 302). Conversely, a *Mareva* injunction issued by an overseas court does not operate in the UK if the defendant has an account held by a branch of a bank in this country. The plaintiff must in that case obtain an injunction through the English courts.

PART 4

10 Negotiable Instruments and the Cheque as a Bill of Exchange

Negotiable instruments are transferable documents embodying an obligation on the part of one person to pay money to another. As such they take the place of cash, and they have, in turn, been given many of the characteristics of cash, e.g., they are easily transferable and the recipient will receive full value. However, negotiable instruments are not legal tender. A negotiable instrument is a document evidencing an obligation on the part of one person (A) to pay money to another person (B). The obligation is discharged by directing an institution (e.g., a bank, building society or post office) with whom A has a credit balance to make the payment on presentation of the instrument. However, the essence of a negotiable instrument is that B may not wish to receive the payment and may negotiate the instrument to C, who, if he receives the instrument in good faith and for valuable consideration, will take free from any defects of title and acquire a good title even against the true owner of the instrument.

The legal relationship between the person first bound to make payment (A) and the first person entitled to receive payment (B) is based on the general rules of privity of contract and many of the answers relating to the obligations which arise between the parties are to be found in the general law of contract. However, there are many situations where the law relating to negotiable instruments has adopted its own solutions, e.g., with regard to the manner in which the benefit of such an instrument may be transferred and the effect such a transfer has on the parties.

NEGOTIABLE INSTRUMENTS AS CHOSES IN ACTION

Negotiability is in essence a form of assignability with special incidents which improve the position of the transferee of a negotiable instrument as compared to the position of an assignee of a chose in action. The common law refused to give effect to the possibility of debts and other choses in action being assignable. The common law courts did not accept the possibility of transferring rights which were intangible, such as contractual rights (Pollock and Maitland, *History of English*

Law, 2nd ed., vol. 2, p. 226). Later the rule was based on the fear that assignments of choses in action might lead to maintenance (*Johnson* v *Collings* (1800) 1 East 98; *Liversidge* v *Broadbent* (1859) 4 Hurl & N 603; *Fitzroy* v *Cave* [1905] 2 KB 364), i.e., intermeddling in litigation in which the intermeddler has no concern. However, debts due to or from the Crown and negotiable instruments (*Ryall* v *Rowles* (1750) 1 Ves Sen 348) could be assigned at law. The common law also recognised that assignments were effective in equity and thus a promise by the assignee not to sue the debtor was good consideration for a promise by the debtor to pay the assignee (*Forth* v *Stanton* (1668) 1 Saund 210; *Master* v *Miller* (1791) 4 TR 320). Although the assignment did not in law entitle the assignee to sue the debtor it might be binding as a contract between the assignor and assignee; the breach of which the assignee could enforce against the assignor (*Gerard* v *Lewis* (1867) LR 2 CP 305). The common law did enforce three kinds of transactions which to some extent operated as an assignment, i.e., novation, acknowledgement and the power of attorney.

Equity regarded the reluctance of the common law to enforce assignments and its fear of maintenance as unrealistic and took the view that choses in action were property which ought in the interest of commercial convenience to be transferable. The method of enforcing such assignments varied with the nature of the chose in action. A legal chose in action was one which could only be sued for in a common law court, e.g., a debt in contract. An equitable chose in action could only be enforced in the Court of Chancery, e.g., an interest in a trust fund.

There were a number of reasons for equity not allowing the assignee of a legal chose to sue the debtor in the Court of Chancery, e.g., the debtor might suffer a hardship if he were later sued for a second payment at common law by the original creditor (the assignor); or the assignor might wish to dispute the assignment and that might require him to be brought to court. In order to resolve these difficulties it became possible for an assignee to sue the debtor at common law in the name of the assignee. If the assignor refused to cooperate, equity could compel him to do so and in the resulting proceedings the rights of the assignor could be protected. Because the common law and equity are now administered in the same courts the problem of maintaining dual actions no longer persists but it may still be necessary to bring all the parties before the court: an action need no longer be brought in the name of the assignor and he need only be joined as a co-plaintiff if he is willing to cooperate with the assignee and as a co-defendant if he is not, e.g., where he wishes to dispute the validity of the assignment.

Statutory assignments

The Supreme Court of Judicature Act 1873 fused the courts of common law and equity and so made obsolete some of the reasons for the original rules for enforcing equitable assignments of legal choses. There was no longer any difficulty in allowing the assignee to sue in any Division of the High Court. A debtor who was successfully sued by the assignee no longer had to take separate proceedings if he were sued again by the assignor: he could rely on the fact of the payment to the assignee as a defence. Consequently, it was not necessary to bring the assignor before the court unless he retained an interest in the subject matter or wished to dispute the validity of the assignment.

Section 136(1) of the Law of Property Act 1925 (re-enacting s. 25(6) of the Supreme Court of Judicature Act 1873) therefore provides that an absolute assignment in writing under the hand of the assignor (not purporting to be by way of a charge only) of any debt or other legal thing in action of which express notice is given in writing to the debtor or trustee is effective in law to pass legal right to the debt or thing in action to the assignee. The effect of such an assignment is to enable the assignee to sue the debtor in his own name, or to sue in his own right, without joining the assignor as a party to the action. The section then provides for a situation where the assignor challenges the validity of the assignment; if he does so the debtor drops out of the proceedings and the dispute is then between the assignor and the assignee.

A 'debt' under s. 136(1) is a sum certain due under the contract or otherwise (e.g., under statute: *Dawson* v *Great Northern and City Railway Co.* [1905] 1 KB 260). The term 'other legal chose in action' is interpreted to mean any 'debt or right which the common law looks on as not assignable by reason of its being a chose in action' (*Re Pain* [1919] 1 Ch 38) but which a court of equity deals with as being assignable. The term also includes a debt not yet due but accruing due (*Brice* v *Bannister* (1878) 3 QBD 569) and the benefit of an obligation to do something other than to pay cash (*Torkington* v *Magee* [1902] 2 KB 427) or to forbear from doing something (*Jacoby* v *Whitmore* (1883) 49 LT 335).

Title of the assignee

An assignee takes 'subject to equities', i.e., subject to defects in the assignor's title and subject to certain claims which the debtor has against the assignor. He takes subject to such defects and claims whether they arise in law or equity and whether or not he had knowledge of them at the time of the assignment (*Athenaeum Life Insurance Society* v *Pooley* (1858) 3 De G & J 294). The assignee cannot, therefore, recover more than the assignor himself could recover. The object of these rules is to ensure that the debtor is not prejudiced by the assignment.

Defects of title

An assignor cannot confer any title if he himself had a defective title or no title. Thus, if a builder assigns money to become due to him under a building contract and then fails to perform the contract so that no money ever becomes payable, the assignee takes nothing (*Tooth* v *Hallett* (1869) LR 4 Ch App 242). Similarly, the assignee of a contract which is affected by mistake or illegality takes no greater rights than the assignor would have had and the assignee of a contract which is voidable for misrepresentation takes subject to the right of the debtor to set the contract aside. Defences available by the terms of the contract to the debtor against the assignor can also be raised against the assignee (e.g., the right to a set-off or counter-claim). However, the payment of the debt to the assignor is only a defence against the assignee if made before notice of the assignment was given to the debtor.

Claims by the debtor against the assignor

The debtor may have claims against the assignor which he could set up, if he were sued by the assignor, to reduce or extinguish his liability. Whether he can rely on these claims against the assignee depends on the way in which they arise.

Claims arising out of the contract If the debtor has claims arising out of the contract assigned on which he could have relied by way of a defence or set off against the assignor, he can also rely on those claims against the assignee, regardless of whether those claims arose before or after the notice of assignment was given (*Graham* v *Johnson* (1869) LR 8 Eq 36). Thus, if a workman assigns money due to him under a contract and he then commits a breach of that contract the debtor can set off against the assignee the amount of any damages which could have been recovered from the assignor. If the amount exceeds the sum assigned, the assignee will not be entitled to anything; but he is not liable to the debtor for the excess as he himself is not in breach of the contract (*Young* v *Kitchin* (1878) 3 ExD 127). Alternatively, if the debtor has been induced to enter into the contract by a misrepresentation on the part of the assignor, he can raise that defence against the assignee in order to exercise his right to rescind the contract.

Claims against the assignor arising out of other transactions The debtor may have a claim against the assignor out of a transaction other than the contract assigned, e.g., the debtor may owe money under a contract for the provision of services and in turn have a claim against the provider of those services for the price of goods sold and delivered. Such a claim can only be set up against the assignee of the debt under the contract for services if it arose before notice of the assignment was given to the debtor (*Stephens* v *Venables (No. 1)* (1862) 30 Beav 625; *Business Computers Ltd* v *Anglo-African Leasing Ltd* [1977] 1 WLR 578).

Claims against intermediate assignees Where a debt which has been assigned to one person is then assigned again by him to another, the question may arise whether a claim or defence which can be raised against the first assignee can be raised against the second assignee. Such a claim or defence may be available against the second assignee if it arose after the first assignment. See *Re Milan Tramways Co.* (1884) 25 ChD 587 at 593, where according to dicta an ultimate assignee takes 'free from any equities which only attach on the intermediate assignee'. The actual decision can be explained on the grounds that the intermediate assignee's liability to the debtor was not established until after the second assignment had been made. The decision in the *Milan Tramways* case was approved in *Fryer* v *Ewart* [1902] AC 187.

NEGOTIABILITY

The rules of negotiability were adopted as part of the common law from the practices and usages of merchants, and not from the rules of equity. These common law rules in respect of negotiable instruments were adopted in the Bills of Exchange Act 1882. Negotiability is in essence a form of assignability with special incidents which improve the position of the transferee of a negotiable instrument as compared to the assignee of a chose in action. The commonest forms of negotiable instruments are bills of exchange, cheques and promissory notes. A negotiable instrument is actually transferable by mere delivery (an instrument payable to bearer is transferred by handing it to the transferee and an order instrument by endorsement and delivery). The delivery of the document must be accompanied by the intention to transfer title.

Defects of title

An assignee takes subject to defects of title but negotiable instruments can circulate like cash so that anyone who deals with them should be able to rely on their validity. The transferee of a negotiable instrument, therefore, takes free from defects of title of any prior parties (Bills of Exchange Act 1882, s. 38(2)) and free from defects available between them, if he is a holder in due course (Bills of Exchange Act 1882, s. 29). Every holder is presumed to be a holder in due course (Bills of Exchange Act 1882, s. 30(2)) unless the instrument is tainted by fraud, duress or illegality, but even then a holder may still enforce the instrument if he can prove that he gave value for the instrument in good faith. However, a forged or unauthorised signature renders the instrument invalid, even as regards a holder in due course.

Sources and characteristics of negotiability

Whether an instrument is recognised as being negotiable depends on mercantile usage (*Goodwin* v *Robarts* (1876) 1 App Cas 476) and on whether the commercial community treats the instrument as having the characteristics of a negotiable instrument. The classes of instruments recognised as negotiable are not closed (*Goodwin* v *Robarts* (1876) 1 App Cas 476; *Bechuanaland Exploration Co.* v *London Trading Bank* [1889] 2 QB 658; *Kun* v *Wah Tet Bank Ltd* [1971] 1 Lloyd's Rep 439; cf. *Crouch* v *Credit Foncier of England* (1873) LR 8 QB 374 where Kennedy J expressed the view that the class of recognised negotiable instruments was closed with the result that the court refused to recognise bearer bonds or debentures as negotiable) although it has been some time since an instrument was given recognition as being negotiable. The reason for that is that, most probably, the sort of instruments to which the characteristics of negotiability may be attributed have been so recognised, and until a new instrument is recognised by the mercantile community as negotiable the courts are not likely to have the opportunity to decide the issue.

It has been said that there are three essential characteristics which must be satisfied if an instrument is to be recognised as negotiable (Jacobs, *Bills of Exchange, Cheques, Promissory Notes and Negotiable Instruments Generally*, 4th ed. (Sweet and Maxwell, 1943)), namely:

(a)   the terms of the instrument must not be incompatible with or such as to negative the idea of negotiability and there should be no indication that the instrument is only transferable subject to defects of title unknown to the transferee and no indication that it is not transferable by delivery or endorsement and delivery;

(b)   the obligation or rights evidenced by the instrument must be of a nature consonant with the commercial function of a negotiable instrument, namely an obligation to pay; and

(c)   the instrument belongs to a class which is treated by the mercantile community as negotiable.

(Milnes Holden in *The Law and Practice of Banking*, vol. 1, *Banker and Customer*, 5th ed. (Pitman Publishing, 1989) also examines the characteristics of negotiable instruments.)

It is therefore essential that the instrument should be recognised by the mercantile community as negotiable. In *Goodwin* v *Robarts* (1876) 1 App Cas 476 the court concluded that a usage once shown to be universal is entitled to judicial recognition even though it did not form part of the law merchant as previously recognised and adopted by the courts.

The courts have examined a number of instruments which have been held to be negotiable under the common law. *Goodwin* v *Robarts* was followed by *Bechuanaland Exploration Co.* v *London Trading Bank Ltd* [1898] 2 QB 658, where the court held that debentures purporting to be payable to bearer were negotiable instruments, and the earlier decision in *Crouch* v *Credit Foncier of England Ltd* (1873) LR 8 QB 374, where the court refused to recognise bearer bonds and debentures as negotiable instruments, must now be treated as having been overruled.

Exchequer and Treasury bills issued by the government to raise short-term loans have been recognised by the courts as negotiable instruments. A blank exchequer bill is payable to '[space for the payee's name]' or order, and any person who takes the Exchequer or Treasury bill for value and in good faith while the space for the payee's name remains blank will acquire a good title free from defects in the title of the transferor (see *Brandao* v *Barnett* (1846) 3 CB 519). Similarly, *Partridge* v *Bank of England* (1846) 9 QB 396 dividend warrants payable to order or bearer or simply to a named payee were recognised as negotiable instruments.

The courts have recognised a number of other instruments as negotiable under mercantile custom, e.g., banknotes, bankers' drafts, share warrants, dividend warrants and bearer bonds. Travellers' cheques have been recognised in the United States as negotiable instruments (*Mellon National Bank* v *Citizens' Bank and Trust Co.* (1937) 88 F 2d 128; *Emerson* v *American Express Co.* (1952) 90 A 2d 236).

Additionally, there are a number of instruments which have received statutory recognition as possessing the quality of negotiability, namely, cheques and bills of exchange, promissory notes and Bank of England notes. These instruments are negotiable if they are in such a state that the true owner, if he so desires, can pass the property in them by delivery or by endorsement and delivery.

There are a number of other instruments whose status as negotiable instruments has not yet been tested before the courts. It is probable that they would be recognised as negotiable. These include instruments such as unit trust certificates to bearer, depository receipts and certificates of deposit issued by banks and other depositaries in respect of investment certificates (shares and bonds) deposited with them, and certificates of deposit of currency entitling the bearer to repayment on a fixed future date.

In *Gorgier* v *Mieville* (1824) 3 B and C 45 the court looked at the question of the negotiability of a foreign instrument. A bearer bond issued by the King of Prussia which was wrongfully pledged with the defendants was held to be negotiable by the usage of the English market if accompanied by a full set of interest coupons. The fact that an instrument is recognised as negotiable abroad will not automatically make it negotiable in the UK and it must be shown to be negotiable by commercial usage in this country.

The *Banking Services: Law and Practice* report (Cm 622, 1989) expressed the view that there was 'considerable merit' in extending the scope of the legislation 'to include a clear criteria for negotiability across a range of instruments' (para. 8.05). It recognised that the concept of negotiability was developed by the law merchant and in cases dealing with negotiable instruments the common law courts have referred to the customs and practices of merchants. The Committee expressed the view that the 'stand-alone' principle 'was one of the main difficulties we met in attempting to formulate a new test of more general application for negotiability' (para. 8.08), and that many of the instruments currently regarded as negotiable would 'by virtue of the collateral references they contain, fail the test in the absence of any provision to the contrary'.

The Committee concluded that the term 'negotiable' in relation to an instrument means that (para. 8.09):

(a)   the obligation or right represented by the instrument is transferable without notice to the party primarily liable; and (b) is transferable to a holder in due course (a bona fide purchaser who has no notice of any defects in the title of the transferor) vesting in the purchaser a title 'free of equities'.

Is payment by negotiable instrument an absolute discharge?

It is a question of fact whether or not a negotiable instrument, drawn in payment of a debt, amounts to an absolute discharge of the debt. This raises a significant question as to whether or not the payee (creditor) can look to the drawer (debtor) for payment where the instrument is dishonoured because there is an insufficient credit balance, or where payment is refused because the paying bank has become insolvent prior to the presentation of the instrument. The question is relevant to any method of payment other than cash, e.g., it has arisen in respect of payments made under a letter of credit (*W. J. Alan and Co. Ltd* v *El Nasr Export and Import Co.* [1972] 2 QB 189; *Shamsher Jute Mills Ltd* v *Sethia (London) Ltd* [1987] 1 Lloyd's Rep 388) and in respect of payments made by a credit card (*Re Charge Card Services Ltd* [1989] Ch 497). In *Re Romer and Haslam* [1893] 2 QB 286 the court concluded in connection with payments made by bills of exchange that:

. . . the giving of a negotiable security by a debtor to his creditor operates as a conditional payment only, and not as a satisfaction of the debt, unless the parties agree so to treat it. Such a conditional payment is liable to be defeated on non-payment of the negotiable instrument at maturity.

Farwell LJ, in *Marreco* v *Richardson* [1908] 2 KB 584 expressed the view that the giving of a cheque for a debt is conditional payment on the cheque being met, i.e., subject to a condition subsequent, and if the cheque is met it is an actual payment *ab initio* and discharges the debt.

However, the eventual payment of the cheque may not operate, in all cases, to make the initial payment absolute. Thus, between the receipt of the cheque and its payment by the drawee bank, payment may be regarded as still conditional and affected by external events occurring during that period. In *Re Hone* [1951] Ch 85 Harman J held that Farwell LJ's view that once a cheque is paid it amounts to an actual payment *ab initio* cannot apply in all cases. In *Re Hone* a cheque in payment of rates was received on 3 November by the council and paid into their account for collection on the following day. On the same day the debtor filed a petition for her bankruptcy and was adjudicated bankrupt. The argument that payment had been made on 3 November was rejected and payment was therefore affected by the bankruptcy of the drawer. In *Re Owen* [1949] 1 All ER 901 the question of whether estate duty was payable on three gifts made by separate cheques depended on whether payment was treated as being made on the day the cheques were given to the donees or when the cheques were presented for collection. Romer J held that estate duty was payable on the gifts and the gifts were not complete until the cheques had been paid by the drawee bank (see *Parkside Leasing Ltd* v *Smith* [1985] 1 WLR 310).

CHEQUES AS NEGOTIABLE INSTRUMENTS

The cheque serves a dual purpose in the payment process. First, a customer who opens a cheque account can withdraw amounts from his account by means of cheques drawn in his favour. In such a situation the cheque will be drawn in favour of 'self' or 'cash', and it will enable the customer to withdraw funds from the branch where the account is maintained. A cheque cashed at a branch of the bank, other than the branch where the account is maintained will be 'backed' by a cheque card and within the amount of the guarantee.

Alternatively, the cheque may be used to pay a third party to whom the customer (drawer) owes money. In such a situation the cheque is drawn in favour of the creditor (payee) and either sent to him by post, or delivered to him personally. The cheque is a mandate by the customer to the paying bank which is indebted to the drawer for the amount of the credit balance to credit the payee's account with the amount of the cheque. Payment by the paying bank will, therefore, discharge the drawer of the cheque for the amount of the debt due. However, the payment in favour of the payee will also discharge the paying bank's liability to its customer for the amount of the cheque, provided the bank acts in accordance with its mandate.

A number of complexities may be added to this situation. The payee of a cheque may, instead of paying it into his account for collection, wish to use it to make a payment to some further person, e.g., a person to whom the payee owes money. Thus, in the case of an order instrument, the cheque may be endorsed in favour of a third party (X), followed by delivery. Alternatively, in the case of a bearer instrument it may be transferred (negotiated) by delivery to X, with the intention of transferring title to the instrument. The holder of a negotiable instrument thus acquires a right to sue the drawer. It is significant that a 'holder in due course' (i.e., someone who takes the instrument in good faith and for value) of a negotiable instrument may acquire a better title than his transferor and may thus be able to enforce the rights of a true owner (e.g., sue in conversion). The fact that the cheque is countermanded by the drawer does not defeat an action brought against him by a holder in due course (s. 30; see p. 307).

Definition of a cheque

The Bills of Exchange Act 1882 applies to both cheques and bills of exchange and (apart from when otherwise provided) the provisions of the Act relating to bills of exchange payable on demand apply equally to cheques. There are additionally specific provisions, e.g., ss. 60 and 80 of the Bills of Exchange Act 1882, s. 4 of the Cheques Act 1957 and the Cheques Act 1992, which apply exclusively to cheques.

The Jack Committee recommended that, instead of the present Bills of Exchange Act 1882, separate legislation should be enacted dealing with cheques and the bank payment mandate (para. 8.06). The Committee's recommendations in respect of the bank payment mandate have not been adopted.

Section 73 of the Bills of Exchange Act 1882 defines a cheque as a bill of exchange drawn on a banker payable on demand. Section 3(1) then goes on to provide that a bill of exchange is an 'unconditional order in writing, addressed by one person to another, signed by the person giving it, requiring the person to whom it is addressed to pay on demand or at a fixed or determinable future time a sum certain in money to or to the order of a specified person, or to bearer'. Section 3(1) is reinforced by s. 3(2), which provides that an instrument which does not comply with these conditions is not a bill of exchange. Moreover, the instrument must be limited to the payment of money and no other act beyond the payment of money can be required. Thus, an order to pay a specified sum and to deliver up horses and a wharf (*Martin* v *Chauntry* (1745) 2 Str 1271), or to give a real security (*Follett* v *Moore* (1849) 4 Ex 410) is not a bill of exchange.

Although the Bills of Exchange Act 1882 does not require that a cheque must be drawn by a customer of a bank, in practice cheques are normally drawn on a bank with which the drawer has a current account. A person who maintains such an account with a bank is a customer of that bank. A cheque which bears a forged drawer's signature will not create a contractual relationship between the forger and the bank. Although the bank will act without a valid mandate from its customer in making payment on a forged instrument a holder in due course may acquire some rights of payment under the instrument (Bills of Exchange Act 1882, s. 55).

The definition does not require the cheque to disclose the date on which it is drawn. In practice, the date of drawing a cheque could become important because banks tend to refuse payment of cheques drawn more than six months prior to presentation for payment. The cheque is then deemed to have become 'stale' by banking practice and the payee is required to obtain a fresh instrument. An alternative would be for the drawer to amend the date and initial his signature, but for the payee to purport to undertake a similar alteration would amount to a material unauthorised alteration and discharge the instrument (Bills of Exchange Act 1882, s. 64(1)).

A cheque must be an 'unconditional order'. The reason is (and it applies equally to all negotiable instruments) that it would greatly prejudice commercial transactions 'of mankind and diminish and narrow their credit and negotiability, if paper securities of this kind were issued into the world encumbered with conditions, and if the persons to whom they were offered in negotiation were obliged to enquire when those uncertain events would be reduced to a certainty' (Story, *Bills of Exchange*). If the order is subject to any conditions or qualifications, the instrument will not be a bill of exchange and the Act provides that an instrument expressed to be payable on a contingency is not a bill and the happening of the event does not cure the defect. Certain cheques, e.g., those issued by Social Security and other government departments sometimes require a receipt form printed on either the front or back of the cheque to be signed. If the order requiring the receipt to be signed is addressed to the drawee bank and places it under an obligation then the cheque is conditional but if the direction is addressed to the payee alone then that does not render the cheque conditional. In *Bavins Junior and Sims* v *London and South Western Bank Ltd* [1900] 1 QB 270 it was held that an instrument drawn 'Pay to B Bavins the sum of sixty nine pounds provided the receipt at the foot hereof is duly signed, stamped and dated' was a conditional order and therefore not a negotiable instrument. The instrument for the signature of the receipt was in this case addressed to the drawee but if the instruction is not addressed to the drawee the instrument remains unconditional in so far as the bank's payment obligation is concerned. In both *Nathan* v *Ogdens Ltd* (1905) 94 LT 126) and *Thairlwall* v *Great Northern Railway Co.* [1910] 2 KB 509) it was held that instructions given at the foot of each instrument did not render them conditional. The *Bavins* case can be distinguished from the other cases because of the nature of the request. Generally, if the direction to obtain the payee's signature appears above the drawer's signature then the direction will constitute part of the payment mandate given to the bank and will render the instrument conditional. Any instructions appearing below the signature are likely to be treated as a direction merely to the payee and incidental to the drawee's instructions. In some cases the letter 'R' will appear on the face of the instrument and serve as an indication to the bank that its customer (the drawer) requires the bank to obtain the payee's signature. Such instruments are treated as conditional and will probably be dishonoured by the bank if the receipt is not signed. The use of such receipts has declined since the Cheques Act 1957 provided that the paid cheque is prima facie proof of payment, although banks no longer follow the practice of returning paid cheques to their customers.

The instrument must be a mandate requiring the bank to make payment. Thus, a request on the instrument in the form, 'You will oblige your humble servant . . .' was held to be a mere request for payment and not a demand to make payment (*Little* v *Slackford* (1828) Mood and M 171; *Ellison* v *Collingridge* (1850) 9 CB 570).

A cheque must be payable on demand, and post-dated cheques are recognised as valid instruments. Other instruments may be drawn at a determinable time in the future. Section 10 of the Bills of Exchange Act 1882 provides that a bill is payable on demand when it is expressed to be so payable, or is payable at sight, or when no time for payment is expressed (see *Claydon* v *Bradley* [1987] 1 WLR 521; *Korea Exchange Bank* v *Debenhams (Central Buying) Ltd* [1979] 1 Lloyd's Rep 548).

A cheque may be drawn or negotiated for any sum of money but it must be for a sum certain, which is normally expressed in both words and figures. A cheque drawn 'Pay A after deducting what he owes me' was held not to be a cheque since it was not possible to ascertain the amount payable to the payee without looking beyond the instrument (*Barlow* v *Broadhurst* (1820) 4 Moo 471). A cheque drawn for French francs was held to be for a certain sum of money although it had to be paid according to the rate of exchange prevailing at the time when the cheque was presented and the bank had to ascertain that rate of exchange prior to payment.

The definition requires that the cheque must be payable to a specified person or his order or to bearer. Section 7(1) provides that where 'a bill is not payable to bearer, the payee must be named or otherwise indicated therein with reasonable certainty'. In *Chamberlain* v *Young* [1893] 2 QB 206 the court held that an instrument made payable to '. . . order', the blank never having been filled in must be construed as meaning that it was payable to 'my order', i.e., to the order of the drawer.

The method of transferring or negotiating a cheque depends on whether the cheque is made payable to bearer or to order.

A cheque is made payable to bearer if it is either drawn in favour of bearer or if the most recent endorsement is a blank endorsement (Bills of Exchange Act 1882, s. 8(3)). A bill is payable to order either if it is expressed to be so payable or if it is expressed to be payable to a particular person and does not include words prohibiting transfer or otherwise indicating an intention that it should not be transferable (Bills of Exchange Act 1882, s. 8(4)). There are, therefore, two issues which arise namely:

(a)   whether a cheque drawn pay cash can be treated as an order bill; and
(b)   whether a bill or cheque payable to a fictitious or non-existing person is treated as payable to bearer or as an order instrument.

Instrument made payable to cash

A cheque or bill of exchange payable to order must specify the identity of the payee with reasonable certainty (Bills of Exchange Act 1882, s. 7(1)). A cheque which is made out for a specific purpose, e.g., 'pay cash or order' is not a bill of exchange as it is not payable to a specific person. In *Orbit Mining and Trading Co. Ltd* v *Westminster Bank Ltd* [1963] 1 QB 794 Harman LJ upheld McKenna J, at first instance, and expressed the view that an instrument drawn 'pay cash or order' is not a cheque since it is not made payable to a specified person. Neither can such an instrument be made payable to bearer. Further, the Court of Appeal expressly rejected the idea that a 'pay cash or order' instrument could be treated as a bearer instrument within s. 7(3) of the Bills of Exchange Act 1882. In so doing the court approved the judgment in *Cole* v *Milsome* [1951] 1 All ER 311 where it was held that an innocent plaintiff who received an instrument drawn 'pay cash or order' from a fraudulent third party was not entitled to recover from the defendant, as drawer, the amount of the instrument. The court rejected the view taken in *North and South Insurance Corporation Ltd* v *National Provincial Bank Ltd* [1936] 1 KB 328 that an instrument drawn in such a form was payable to bearer. In that case the court held that such an instrument was not a cheque and the words 'or order' were to be disregarded, with the result that the instrument was by implication a bearer bill. However, in *Cole* v *Milsome* the court held that a pay cash document was no more than that, and if the amount of the instrument is paid to the person intended to receive it, the drawer cannot claim it back from the bank. The person who holds the pay cash instrument is not treated as a nominee of the drawer.

Difficulties also arise where the drawer leaves the payee's name in blank. In *Daun and Vallentin* v *Sherwood* (1895) 11 TLR 211 it was suggested that such an instrument should be treated as payable to bearer 'because that is the natural effect'. However, the very nature of the negotiable instrument and its definition militates against such an interpretation. Thus, in *R* v *Randall* (1811) Russ & Ry 195 an instrument reading 'pay . . . or order' was held not to be a bill, although in *Chamberlain* v *Young* [1893] 2 QB 206 the court held that an instrument made payable to '. . . order', the blank never having been filled, must be construed as meaning that it was payable to 'my order', i.e., to the order of the drawer. *Chamberlain* v *Young* could be construed as applying the formula used in personal cheques cashed over the counter, e.g., where the drawer uses the words pay 'myself' or 'self'.

Fictitious or non-existent payee

Although the Court of Appeal in *Orbit Mining and Trading Co. Ltd* v *Westminster Bank Ltd* [1963] 1 QB 794 held that the Bills of Exchange Act 1882, s. 7(3), did not apply to 'pay cash' instruments it may be used to hold otherwise ineffective cheques or bills as payable to bearer. Under s. 24 of the 1882 Act a forged endorsement is a nullity and no one can acquire a good title to a negotiable instrument through such an endorsement. Consequently, any person who acquires the instrument after a forged endorsement has been placed on it cannot sue parties prior to that forged endorsement and, in particular, cannot sue the acceptor and drawer. Section 7(3) will apply where the drawer is induced, due usually to the misrepresentation of another, to draw an instrument under the mistaken belief that he (the drawer) is indebted to a third party (payee). The dishonest person responsible for inducing the mistake and persuading the drawer to draw the instrument will then misappropriate it but in order to receive payment on that instrument he will then forge the payee's endorsement. In such cases the payee is either non-existent or fictitious and the endorsement required on the instrument to transfer it must, of necessity, be a forgery. The non-existent or fictitious payee cannot pay the instrument into his bank account and so the way in which payment may be received on the instrument is by 'transferring' it to someone who gives value for it. That transfer can only take place if the payee's endorsement is forged on the instrument. The effect of the forged endorsement, however, is that parties taking the instrument subsequent to the endorsement cannot sue parties prior to the forged endorsement. To avoid this difficulty the Act provides that the instrument should be regarded as payable to bearer. The forged endorsement can, therefore, be ignored since endorsements on bearer instruments are unnecessary to transfer title to them. The drawer (and acceptor in the case of a bill of exchange) who, usually through negligence, has been responsible for bringing the instrument into being can be sued by a holder in due course. The drawer will then bear the loss arising as a result of the instrument being paid.

In *Bank of England* v *Vagliano Brothers* [1891] AC 107 the House of Lords examined the scope of s. 7(3). In that case Vagliano Brothers employed a dishonest clerk named Glyka, who forged bills which purported to have been drawn by Vucina, in Odessa, on Vagliano Brothers in London, and to be payable to Petridi and Co., an existing company. When Glyka asked for the bills to be accepted, Vagliano accepted them without question, adding to the form of acceptance that they were payable at the Bank of England where Vagliano Brothers had an account. Glyka then forged the endorsement of Petridi and Co. and obtained payment over the counter at the Bank. It was held that Glyka was the real drawer of the bills and since he as drawer never intended Petridi and Co. to obtain payment, they were 'fictitious payees' and the bills were payable to bearer. The bank had acted properly in making payment and could debit Vagliano's account. The loss, therefore, fell on Vagliano, and not the Bank. The House of Lords examined the scope of s. 7(3). Lord Herschell on the meaning of the word 'fictitious' said that where the payee is named by way of pretence and without any intention that he should be the person to receive payment the instrument is drawn in favour of a fictitious payee. Lord Macnaghten took the view that 'the proper meaning of the word fictitious is "feigned" or "counterfeit". It seems to me that the "C Petridi and Co." named as payees on these pretended bills were, strictly speaking, fictitious persons.'

The House of Lords was not united on the meaning of fictitious or non-existent payee. Lords Bramwell and Field were of the opinion that the payees were not fictitious. There was a real firm called Petridi and Co. and Vagliano Brothers were accustomed to accepting bills drawn by Vucina in their favour. In determining whether the payee is fictitious Lord Bramwell said it is not a question of intention but a question of fact and the bills were payable to an existing person. If there were no real payee, and the name was inserted as a mere *nominis umbra* then, and only then, would the payee be fictitious.

The *Bank of England* v *Vagliano Brothers* left a number of questions unanswered, for example, whether the real or fictitious character of the payee depends on the intention of the person who actually drew the bill; whether the intention of other parties should be taken into account in determining the character of the payee; and whether the character of the payee as a real or fictitious person should be linked to the presence or absence of a real transaction in connection with which the bill was issued.

In *Clutton* v *Attenborough* [1897] AC 90 a clerk in the accounts department of the appellants, by fraudulently representing to them that certain work had been done on their account by a person named B, induced them to draw cheques payable to the order of B. The cheques, signed by the appellants, were handed by them to their accounts department for transmission to the payee, B. The clerk obtained possession of the cheques, endorsed the payee's signature on them and negotiated the bills to the respondents, who gave value and took them in good faith. The cheques were paid to the respondents by the appellants' bankers. When the appellants discovered the fraud they brought an action against the respondents to recover the amounts of the cheques as money had and received under a mistake of fact. The House of Lords held that although the cheques were drawn in favour of a named person B and there might be a person of that name in existence, the payee of the cheques was nevertheless fictitious because the name, B, had been provided by the person wishing to commit the fraud and the drawer had no knowledge of anyone by that name. The appellants could not have intended the payee to be a real, identifiable person.

Clutton v *Attenborough* is distinguishable from *Vinden* v *Hughes* [1905] 1 KB 795 where a cashier filled in a number of cheque forms with the names of his employer's customers, as payees, and obtained the signature of his employer as drawer. The cashier then forged the signature of the payee by way of endorsement and discounted the cheques to the defendant who obtained payment from the drawer's bankers.

In an action to recover the amounts of the cheques from the defendant the court held that the payee was not a fictitious or non-existing payee because at the time the cheques were drawn the drawer intended certain identifiable persons to receive the amounts of the cheques.

The importance of the rule that a bill payable to a fictitious or non-existent payee may be payable to bearer is that it enables any forged endorsement purporting to be that of the payee to be disregarded.

However, the decision in *North and South Wales Bank Ltd* v *Macbeth* [1908] AC 137 deprives the *Bank of England* v *Vagliano Brothers* of most of its practical value, since it will rarely happen that the drawer of the instrument will sign it without intending it to be payable to an identifiable payee. Macbeth was fraudulently induced by White to draw a cheque for £11,250 in favour of 'Kerr or order'. Kerr was an existing person known to Macbeth, and Macbeth, although misled by White as to the intended use of the cheque, fully intended that Kerr should receive the amount of the cheque. White obtained the cheque and forged Kerr's endorsement on it. He then paid the cheque into his account with the appellant bank. Macbeth, on discovering the fraud, brought an action against the bank to recover the money on the ground that the collecting bank was guilty of conversion. The bank alleged that the payee was a fictitious payee within s. 7(3) of the Act and the cheque was, therefore, payable to bearer. The House of Lords held that s. 7(3) did not apply because the drawer of the cheque, Macbeth, intended that a real person known to Macbeth should receive the amount of the cheque and so it could not be said that the payee of the cheque was fictitious or non-existent.

The leading cases on s. 7(3) illustrate the meaning of 'fictitious or non-existent payee'. The effect of s. 7(3) is:

(a)   The courts will look at the intention of the creator of the instrument, i.e., the drawer.

(b)   If the drawer does not intend the named payee to receive payment, then the payee is fictitious or non-existent and the instrument is payable to bearer.

(c)   A non-existent person appears to be a mere figment of the drawer's imagination, and is non-existent even though many people of that name may exist. A payee may also be a 'fictitious' person, even though a person of that name exists, if he is not intended by the drawer to receive payment.

(d)   If the drawer intended a named and existing person to receive payment, then there is a real payee, even though the drawer has been misled into believing that payment was due to that person. The instrument will not be a bearer instrument, and if it carries a forged endorsement, anyone taking it subsequent to the forged endorsement will not be able to sue the drawer and other parties prior to the forgery.

(e)   A real payee cannot subsequently be converted into a non-existent or fictitious person. If the drawer intended a named and existing person to receive payment, and the name of the person appearing on the instrument is altered without the drawer's authority, the instrument remains payable to bearer.

In *Royal Bank of Canada* v *Concrete Column Clamps (1961) Ltd* (1976) 74 DLR (3d) 26 at p. 32 Laskin CJC criticised the principles derived from the series of cases dealt with above. In that case a payroll clerk employed by the respondent fraudulently prepared for signature by the respondent's authorised signing officer salary cheques, some of which were payable to fictitious persons and some whose names had been chosen at random, and some of which were payable to real persons who had worked for the respondent in the past but to whom no payment was due. The respondent's signing officer, who handled a large number of cheques, signed them without investigation. The clerk forged the payee's endorsement and obtained payment from the drawee bank. In an action by the respondent against the bank it was argued that all the payees were fictitious or non-existent and consequently the cheques should be treated as payable to bearer. The respondent argued that the signatures were forged and therefore 'wholly inoperative'. The trial judge held that the bank was liable in the case of the cheques made payable to the real persons, but not liable in respect of those payable to fictitious persons or to names chosen at random. The judgment was affirmed by the Quebec Court of Appeal and on further appeal, the Supreme Court of Canada held that the appeal should be dismissed. However, Laskin CJC, dissenting, held that there is no basis for treating fictitious and non-existent payees in a different way according to objective fact, discovered after the event, if the central question is whether the drawer or signing officer of the drawer intended (as is generally the case) to have the cheques (issued as a result of a payroll clerk's fraud) take effect according to their tenor.

Signature

In order for an instrument to be a cheque, the mandate to the bank to make payment must be in writing, which extends to include 'printed' signatures (Bills of Exchange Act 1882, s. 2). The word 'signature' is not defined for the purposes of the Act and signatures by marks (*George* v *Surrey* (1830) Mood & M 516), by print (*Re London and Mediterranean Bank, ex parte Birmingham Banking Co.* (1868) LR 3 Ch App 651) and by pencil will suffice (*Geary* v *Physic* (1826) 5 B & C 234), as well as a signature by initials (*Caton* v *Caton* (1867) LR 2 HL 127 at 143).

In *Goodman* v *J. Eban Ltd* [1954] 1 QB 550 Denning LJ, dissenting, expressed the view that a document could not be signed by means of a rubber stamp, although a mark executed by an illiterate person would suffice. He expressed the view that a facsimile signature, unlike a mark placed by an illiterate person, is a 'thoughtless impress of an automaton, in contrast to the reasoned attention of a sensible person'. However, a facsimile signature imprinted by means of a rubber stamp can be executed with the intention of bringing the cheque or bill of exchange into existence.

Drawer and drawee must be different

A cheque must be drawn by 'one person to another'. This covers the normal situation where the drawer instructs the drawee bank to make payment but s. 5(2) provides that where the drawer and drawee are the same persons the holder may treat the instrument as either a bill of exchange or a promissory note. Where the drawer and drawee are the same person or entity (e.g., a banker's draft drawn by one branch on another branch or on its head office) the instrument is a valid banker's draft and defences normally conferred on the paying and collecting banks are extended to dealings in bankers' drafts.

Post-dated cheques

A bank is bound to pay a post-dated cheque on or after the date of payment. In both *Whistler* v *Forster* (1863) 14 CB NS 248 and *Austin* v *Bunyard* (1865) 6 B and S 687 it was held that the holders of post-dated cheques could recover the amounts for which the cheques were drawn and that the instruments were to be taken to have been drawn according to the date appearing on the face of the instruments.

A somewhat different situation arises under s. 3(4)(a) of the 1882 Act which provides that prima facie the instrument need not be dated. An undated instrument would presumably be payable on demand or on presentation. In practice banks will refuse to pay undated cheques without the drawer's consent and this refusal of the bank to make payment was upheld in *Griffiths* v *Dalton* [1940] 2 KB 264 where the defendant gave the plaintiff an undated cheque and the plaintiff purported to fill in the date some 18 months later. The cheque was dishonoured on presentation for payment and the court held that the delay in completing the cheque under the authority given by s. 20(1) of the 1882 Act was unreasonable and the bank was justified in refusing to make payment.

THE CLEARING PROCESS

The process used for the clearing of cheques is based on a procedure developed in the eighteenth century, when the use of cheques became common. Initially, cheques were paid by each bank presenting the instrument by messenger to the relevant paying bank but a practice developed under which messengers gathered in a meeting place to exchange cheques each morning. They met again each afternoon to return any cheques which were to be dishonoured by the paying bank and a balance was struck between them in respect of the 'cleared effects'. The system was confined to cheques drawn and payable within the boundaries of the City of London. In 1833, the then clearing banks hired a place from which clearing could take place; the system was adapted as required to meet the changing demands of a system which developed through network branches and on which demands grew rapidly. The clearing process remained largely unchanged because of the need for the physical presentation of the instruments, except that all the systems, including paper clearing, became highly automated. In 1984, the then 10 members of the Bankers' Clearing House instituted a major study of the structure of the payment systems. A working party, under the chairmanship of Dennis M. Child was established which recommended that a new structure for the organisation of payment clearing systems be established and new rules regarding membership of such systems be implemented. The report identified three groups of clearings and recommended that each should be owned and operated by an individual clearing company set up as a company limited by shares. The report recommended that membership of the separate companies be open to all appropriately regulated institutions. The Child Report also recommended that an umbrella organisation should be established to oversee the development of the operations of the clearings and of the payment industry as a whole. The Committee recommended that membership of this body should consist of all settlement members of the individual clearing companies and other appropriately qualified institutions. The Child Report was implemented during 1985 and a new structure came into operation on 1 December 1985. An umbrella body, known as APACS (Association for Payment Clearing Services) was set up to oversee the payment industry. The three clearing companies established were:

(a)   Cheque and Credit Clearing Co. Ltd, which has responsibility for the cheque and credit clearings in London.

(b)   CHAPS Clearing Co. Ltd, which has responsibility for high-value clearings. It was decided in February 1995 to close down Town Clearing, the use of which had declined sharply over recent years as customers switched to more efficient electronic payment systems. The decision to close the Town Clearing forms part of an initiative to manage and ultimately to eliminate settlement risk (the risk of a member failing) in high-value clearings. An important element of this strategy is the establishment of a Real Time Gross Settlement System for CHAPS (i.e., payment will be pre-settled over a CHAPS member's settlement account at the Bank of England before transmission between banks).

(c)   BACS Ltd, which has responsibility for the electronic bulk clearings.

Physical presentation and clearing of cheques

The presentation of cheques involves two documents, namely, (a) the payment mandate, i.e., the cheque itself; and (b) the credit slip which gives the amount of the credit payment, the name and account number of the customer, and details of the branch and bank where the customer maintains his account, including the sort code of the bank. In the clearing process the two documents serve different purposes. The credit slip is used to effect a credit entry to the payee's account and remains at the branch, whilst the cheque is used to arrange for the drawer's account to be debited.

The majority of cheques are drawn against accounts in which the drawer and payee maintain accounts with different banks, although a similar clearing procedure is applied where the parties maintain accounts with different branches of the same bank. Thus, where the drawer, A, maintains an account with the Z branch of the South Bank, and the payee, B, has an account with the Y branch of the North Bank, a cheque presented by the payee to the credit of his account will be paid through the clearing system. The paper clearing of cheques involves a three-day clearing cycle. On the first day, the day on which the cheque is paid into the payee's account, the cheque and the credit slip are processed by the collecting bank. This will include encoding the amount of the cheque in magnetic characters in the codeline at the bottom of the cheque. In addition a special crossing in favour of the payee's branch (Y branch) is added on the face of the cheque. This crossing is added even though the cheque paid in for collection is already crossed and its purpose is to identify on the cheque the branch which has arranged collection. The cheque is then placed in a bundle of cheques drawn on the South Bank.

In the evening (end of day 1) all bundles of cheques to be collected for the customers of Z branch are forwarded to the clearing department of the South Bank in London.

In the early hours of the following morning (day 2) cheques are delivered to the members' clearing centres. Each bundle of cheques is examined to ensure that the cheques are not physically damaged and that each item has the necessary encoded details on it. At the clearing centres the cheques are processed by high-speed-reader sorters, which are computer-controlled machines which read the magnetic information at the bottom of the cheques and sort them in separate bundles for the banks on which they are drawn. The sorted cheques are then boxed up and taken from the collecting bank's clearing centre to the Clearing Exchange Centre, where they are exchanged. Thus, the North Bank will hand over all the cheques it has collected and which are drawn on other members of the clearing (including the cheque drawn on the South Bank) and collect all the cheques drawn on North Bank.

The cheque drawn by A, on the Z branch of the South Bank, is now in the hands of South Bank. The South Bank will feed the cheques it has received for payment into its reader-sorter machine, which performs a number of functions, e.g., it places the cheque in a box of items drawn on the Z branch of South Bank; it will read the details encoded by magnetic ink and this information is passed to the bank's computer which will take it into account in the calculation of the balance of the drawer's account at the close of business on the subsequent day (Day 3), unless the Z branch gives instructions to countermand the payment on the cheque; and the reader-sorter machine will verify the volume and value of cheques received for payment by the South Bank each day for every clearing bank in the system. If the balance in the drawer's account is insufficient to meet the amount of a cheque the computer will place the cheque on an 'out of order list', consisting of cheques which have to be drawn specifically to the attention of the manager of Z branch of the South Bank.

The actual settlement between the South and North Banks takes place at the end of each trading day (day 2 in the case of the cheque in favour of B). This figure is confirmed to the presenting bank the following day. This settlement is based on provisional figures and an adjustment may be required to account for any dishonoured items.

The cheque in favour of B is then forwarded by the South Bank to the branch where the drawer maintains his account (Z branch) at the end of the second day. The cheque is processed at the Z branch the following day (day 3) and the staff at that branch will, during the course of the day, make decisions regarding its 'fate', i.e., whether to pay the cheque or to return it unpaid. In theory, the branch is supposed to verify the adequacy of the funds to pay the cheque and the regularity of the cheque, i.e., to verify the signature, the proper dating of the cheque and the correct correspondence between the words and the figures. In reality this is only done in respect of cheques placed in the 'out of order list' or in respect of cheques for unusually large amounts and the manager or other authorised bank officer will then have to decide whether or not to make payment on the instrument. If the cheque is honoured, it is then retained by the Z branch of the South Bank.

If the cheque is dishonoured by the Z branch then it must transmit the necessary information into its computer terminal and return the cheque to the collecting branch (Y branch) by first-class post. If the dishonoured cheque is for £500 or more, the decision to dishonour must be given by midday.

On the third day of the clearing process the banks will agree between themselves the values of cheques exchanged the previous day. Settlement on a net basis is then made across members' accounts at the Bank of England.

The same clearing procedure is followed where the collection and payment process involves two different branches of the same bank. In such a case the cheque is processed by the collecting branch and then, through the clearing centre, forwarded to the drawee branch. Although there is no need for the exchange of the cheque at the clearing house, the processing of the cheque in the bank's own clearing department and its delivery to the drawee bank can take up to three days.

Where both the drawer and payee of the cheque maintain their accounts with the same branch of a bank, the clearing procedure is simplified. In this case, the crediting of the payee's account and the debiting of the drawer's account is done by computer terminal at the branch in question. This takes place on the day on which the cheque is received for payment to the credit of the payee's account.

Cheque truncation

The banks have been aware of the need to solve problems which have arisen from a payment system based on the physical movement of paper (although there has been a decline in the volume of personal cheques; approximately 2.1 billion such cheques were issued in 1995, together with 1.1 billion business cheques over the same period (Payments Market Briefing, APACS: 1996). A system of cheque truncation was introduced, which allowed payment to be made against the electronic presentation of data, including details of the accounts to be credited and debited with each payment. This system was limited to payment between accounts of the same bank; it did not extend to inter-bank transactions. The reluctance of the banks to extend cheque truncation was largely due to the limitations of the Bills of Exchange Act 1882, which, under s. 45, required 'due presentation' of the instrument at the 'proper place'. Further, the payment had to be made in 'due course' under s. 59 of the Act.

Following banking practice the courts adopted the approach that only actual physical presentation would satisfy the requirement of 'due presentation'. Thus, at common law, where the place for presentment is specified on the cheque or other instrument, that is the proper place for presentment. If no place for presentment is specified but the address of the drawee or acceptor is given on the instrument, then that is the proper place of presentment. In *Griffin* v *Weatherby* (1868) LR 3 QB 753 Blackburn J said that 'presentment for payment must mean presentment according to mercantile usage; the document itself must be presented though not the holder'. Similarly, in *Barclays Bank plc* v *Bank of England* [1985] 1 All ER 385 the view was expressed that the collecting bank's duty of presentment is not discharged until the cheque is physically handed to the drawee bank for payment through the clearing system. Further, presentment must be within a reasonable time (*Hare* v *Henty* (1861) 10 CB NS 65).

However, under the Deregulation (Bills of Exchange) Order 1996 (SI 1996/2993, implemented on 28 November 1996), the Treasury introduced amendments to the Bills of Exchange Act 1882 (new ss. 74A-C inserted) and the Cheques Act 1957 (new s. 3(2) inserted) to enable the payment of cheques by the transmission of electronic information between the banks, instead of the physical presentation of cheques. Furthermore, dishonour of a cheque and other negotiable instruments by electronic message or telephone is equally effective.

For inter-bank truncation to be effective the new ss. 74A-C to the Bills of Exchange Act 1882 allow cheques to be presented by electronic data, as an alternative to physical presentation. Transmission of electronic data will, under this method of presentation, replace the necessity of physical presentation of the cheque. Banks are able to agree amongst themselves where electronic data is to be transmitted (provided such notice is given in the London, Edinburgh and Belfast Gazettes and the notice specifies the address at which data may be electronically presented (s. 74A(a)) and when, so proper presentment does not necessarily restrict the bank to normal business hours (s. 74B). The paying bank will update the customer's account on the basis of the electronic data. For practical purposes, the cheque will be retained at some point in the clearing process, e.g., a regional or national centre within the collecting bank, although initially it is likely to be a central point within the paying bank.

The information which will have to be transmitted includes the cheque serial number, the identification code of the branch on which the cheque is drawn, and the account number of the drawer of the cheque and the amount for which the cheque is drawn (s. 74A(6)). Although not specifically required by the Act, similar information will have to be transmitted about the payee. The banks may under an express agreement undertake to transmit further details, if they so decide. A paying bank to which information is transmitted electronically may, by the following business day, request that the cheque be physically presented (s. 74B). If such a request is made the earlier electronic presentation will be disregarded (s. 74B(3)(a)). The right to request physical presentation will act to safeguard a paying bank in cases where fraud is suspected. A request for the physical presentation of a cheque (although a prelude to dishonouring the cheque, e.g., if it is found to be forged) will not amount to a dishonour.

Despite the extension of cheque truncation (the Consultative Document 'Electronic Presentation of Cheques' (the Treasury, January 1996)) three categories of cheque will continue to be physically presented for payment to the paying bank, namely:

(a) high-value cheques;
(b) cheques which the customer has requested to be returned to him after payment; and
(c) cheques which the paying bank wishes to have sight of for management information and customer service purposes.

Customer protection and the implications of cheque truncation

The Deregulation (Bills of Exchange) Order 1996 (SI 1996/2993) expresses the view that electronic presentation of cheques (and other instruments) may be permitted without removing any necessary protection. The following discussion merely summarises the protection given to customers and outlines the obligations banks must continue to comply with.

Banks owe both contractual and tortious duties to their customers. In addition, statutory protection is given to the customer and an issue which will arise is whether, by the introduction of inter-bank truncation, the rights of the customer are eroded to any extent. Banks owe a contractual duty to act with reasonable skill and care in paying cheques for their customers' account. This obligation includes ensuring that any system of payment of cheques, and other instruments, is sound and efficient. Concurrently, the banks owe a duty of care in tort to ensure that the system in which they participate is effective, and that they take steps to guard against reasonably foreseeable loss. A customer who suffers loss from a system failure will be entitled to claim compensation. The degree of liability will not only depend on the circumstances but also on the bank's ability to limit liability for loss, e.g., through terms in the customer contracts (see chapter 8).

In principle banks will be contractually liable to their customers for the consequences of incorrect payment because of system defects, even if there is no operational negligence on the part of the bank. Thus, a paying bank will be liable to its customer for any loss suffered due to a wrong amount being debited, since payment would not conform to the customer's mandate. Conversely, the collecting bank could be made liable to its customer if the wrong amount were credited to the account. Thus, the duty of both the collecting and paying banks is not diminished because of a system of truncation.

Similar considerations apply where the wrong account is debited. The paying bank is liable to the customer whose account is wrongly debited. Where the wrong account is credited the bank will only enjoy the protection of s. 4 of the Cheques Act 1957 if it acts in good faith and without negligence (see chapter 12). The true owner may sue the collecting bank for conversion.

Where a cheque is paid electronically the collecting bank will not transmit information about crossings and endorsements. Banks will be responsible for ensuring that the instructions conveyed by crossings are followed. If a collecting bank makes a mistake and pays contrary to a crossing it will be liable to the drawer who suffers a loss, e.g., where due to a mistake and contrary to the 'account payee' crossing, a cheque is received for the collection of someone other than the named payee.

Forged cheques and forged endorsements

Legal protection against the forgery of cheques is provided under the Bills of Exchange Act 1882 and will essentially be unaffected by truncation. However, banks may have to modify their handling procedures to ensure that they continue to comply with the law. Banks will have to agree how long truncated cheques will be stored and the circumstances in which they will be produced. Such agreements will have to encompass other legal obligations regarding the storage of cheques, e.g., those under the Money Laundering Regulations 1993 (SI 1993/1933). Under the Bills of Exchange Act 1882, s. 24, a cheque on which the drawer's signature is forged is a nullity. The paying bank is unable to debit the customer's account and unless the customer actually facilitates the forgery, the paying bank will suffer the loss. Although this position remains unaltered under a system of truncation, the banks will have to have in place appropriate arrangements to enable them to examine suspect cheques.

Where it is apparent that there has been an unauthorised alteration of a cheque (e.g., a change in the date or amount), under s. 64 of the 1882 Act, the instrument is invalidated, except against the person who made the alteration and subsequent endorsers. The drawer will not, therefore, be liable to make payment. Where a system of truncation is used at the collecting bank, the paying bank could not know of an unauthorised alteration. The collecting bank will, therefore, bear the responsibility of permitting truncation of a cheque where the alteration is obvious. If the alteration is not apparent and the cheque is in the hands of a holder in due course, then the drawer is liable to pay only the original amount of the cheque, and the paying bank will be responsible for any difference in the amount paid and the actual amount of the cheque. The drawer will be liable for the full amount of the cheque only if the cheque is drawn in such a way as to invite alteration. Truncation will not affect the position.

Countermand of a cheque

The right to countermand a cheque may be a useful protection to a customer, e.g., against a trader who fails to deliver goods. The right of countermand is governed by the cheque clearing cycle and contractual arrangements between banks and their customers. The ability to countermand cheques will be unaffected by truncation unless the time taken to make payment is reduced. The basic facility to countermand will remain but customers will have to be notified of any changes in their right to countermand and the time during which this right subsists.

11   Rights and Liabilities of the Parties to a Bill of Exchange

The requirements for incurring liability on a bill of exchange are:

(a)   that the person concerned has contractual capacity;
(b)   that he has placed his signature on the document;
(c)   that it has been delivered to a holder; and
(d)   that consideration was received.

The Bills of Exchange Act 1882 devotes a number of sections (ss. 53 to 58) to the issue of liability. It is intended to explore the question of liability of the parties to the bill in this chapter and then to go on to examine the rules of negotiation. The significant question of capacity to draw a negotiable instrument and the protection given to a holder in due course will be examined.

LIABILITY

Drawer

The drawer is normally the person responsible for bringing the negotiable instrument into existence. He will only incur liability on the instrument if he, in addition to signing the instrument, also delivers it to the payee. The drawer of a cheque remains primarily liable on the instrument throughout because, unlike a bill of exchange, it is never accepted. If a bill of exchange is accepted then the primary liability is that of the acceptor and the drawer in effect becomes the guarantor.

The drawer and endorsers of a bill are jointly and severally responsible to the holder for its acceptance and payment (*Rouquette* v *Overmann* (1875) LR 10 QB 525). If the instrument is dishonoured, the holder may enforce payment from the drawer, or the endorser, or the acceptor (in the case of an accepted bill), or all or any of them at his option. Section 55(1)(a) of the Bills of Exchange Act 1882 deals with the liability of the drawer and provides that the drawer will compensate not only the holder, but any endorser who is compelled to make payment. In the case of cheques the position is simple because the drawer remains primarily liable. In *Starke* v *Cheesman* (1699) Carth 509 it was held that the act of drawing a bill implies a promise from the drawer to pay for it, if the drawee does not. An endorsement by the drawer does not give him a new character as endorser, or divest him of any liability to which as drawer of the bill he is subject, and he remains the ultimate debtor. However, the drawer of a bill may insert an express term either limiting or negativing his own liability to the holder (s. 16(1)). Further, parol evidence is admissible, as between the drawer and endorser (s. 28), to prove that the drawer is not liable, or only has limited liability, to the endorser.

The statutory estoppels available against the drawer are found in s. 55(1)(b) which states that the drawer is precluded from denying to a holder in due course the existence of the payee and his capacity to endorse it. However, s. 7(3) provides that where the payee is fictitious or a non-existing person, the bill is payable to bearer. This means that parties subsequent to a forged endorsement of the fictitious or non-existing payee may sue the acceptor or drawer. The fact that the drawer may not attempt to deny the existence of the payee prevents the drawer making any attempt to escape liability on the ground of the payee's non-existence.

Drawee

The drawee, acting merely in that capacity, does not incur any liability on the instrument. Hence banks, who never accept cheques, do not incur any liability on them to the payee or holder. The drawee may undertake liability on a bill of exchange under a separate agreement with the drawer or payee, and will be liable under that separate agreement if he fails to comply with it (*Smith* v *Brown* (1815) 6 Taunt 340; *Laing* v *Barclay* (1823) 1 B & C 398), but he cannot be sued on the bill of exchange itself. The nature of the banker and customer relationship imposes on the bank a duty to its customer to pay cheques on presentation if the customer has a sufficient credit balance, or if the amount of the cheque is within any agreed overdraft facility.

A bank may also undertake to the holder of a cheque drawn by its customer that the cheque will be paid when it is presented for payment if certain special conditions are satisfied, e.g., where a cheque guarantee card is issued to its customer. The undertaking is not addressed to any particular person or group of persons but to any person who acts on it.

In England, but not in Scotland, the drawing of a cheque or bill does not operate as an assignment of funds in the hands of the drawee and does not entitle the holder of the bill to sue the drawee (*Schroeder* v *Central Bank of London Ltd* (1876) 34 LT 735). The Jack Committee recommended that the rule as applied in Scotland should be abolished. However, it is open to the drawer of a bill to assign to the payee or any other person the whole or part of any funds standing to his credit in the hands of the drawee by either an equitable assignment or a statutory assignment. Such an assignment will bind the drawee from the time he receives notice of the assignment. In *Walker* v *Bradford Old Bank Ltd* (1876) 12 QBD 511 the view was that a credit balance can be assigned even before a demand has been made.

Acceptor

The acceptance of a bill of exchange renders the acceptor primarily liable to make payment. Section 54(2)(a) of the Bills of Exchange Act 1882 provides that the acceptor is precluded from denying to a holder in due course:

(a)   the existence of the drawer;
(b)   the genuineness of the drawer's signature (this is an exception to the rule in s. 24); and
(c)   the capacity and authority of the drawer to draw the bill.

By s. 54(2)(b) of the Act, the acceptor is precluded from denying to a holder in due course:

(a)   the capacity of the drawer to endorse an order bill but not the genuineness or validity of an endorsement; and
(b)   the existence and capacity of the payee to endorse the bill in the case of a bill payable to a named payee or his order but not the genuineness or validity of his endorsement.

Since the acceptor cannot deny the genuineness of the drawer's signature, the courts have held that in an action against the acceptor of a bill the authenticity of the drawer's signature does not have to be proved (*Wilkinson* v *Lutwidge* (1725) 1 Str 648).

Payee

The original payee of a bill, cheque or note in whose possession the instrument remains cannot be a holder in due course since the instrument has not been negotiated to him (*R.E. Jones Ltd* v *Waring and Gillow Ltd* [1926] AC 670). The payee cannot, therefore, claim the protection given to a holder in due course. As a holder, he may sue on the instrument in his own name (Bills of Exchange Act 1882, s. 38(1)). However, the Act does not state what defences may be raised against the payee by the original parties to the instrument, i.e., by the drawer of a cheque or by the drawer or acceptor of the instrument. If the payee procures the issue of an instrument by fraud, duress or other unlawful means then the title of the payee is defective and such a defence can be raised against him. As between immediate parties and subject to the rule that negotiable instruments are to be treated as cash in the hands of the recipient, personal defences arising out of the underlying contract may also be raised.

The position is less clear where the fraud, duress etc. is that of a third party, e.g., where A by fraud procures B to draw a cheque payable to C. As the authorities now stand fraud or duress on the part of the third party cannot be raised against the original payee of the instrument who has received it as holder in good faith and for value without notice of defect (see *Talbot* v *Von Boris* [1911] 1 KB 854; *Hasan* v *Willson* [1977] 1 Lloyd's Rep 431; *Hindle* v *Brown* (1908) 98 LT 791). Moreover, the position of the payee (holder) is more favourable than a holder to whom the instrument has been negotiated as s. 30(2) does not apply in the case of the original payee.

Endorser

The liability of the endorser is similar to that of the drawer (s. 55). In several cases it has been pointed out that the endorser is in effect a new drawer and by his endorsement gives a new order as to the payment of the bill to the drawee or the acceptor (*Penny* v *Innes* (1834) 1 Cr M & R 439; *Steele* v *M'Kinlay* (1880) 5 App Cas 754). Consequently, with regard to an accepted bill of exchange the liability of the endorser is secondary to that of the acceptor, or if the drawer remains primarily liable throughout, then he will pay. The liability of the endorser is conditional and does not arise until the instrument has been dishonoured. However, an endorser who is compelled to pay is entitled to be indemnified by the drawer and, if the bill has been accepted, by the acceptor.

There are important estoppels which bind the endorser. Thus, the endorser is precluded from denying to a holder in due course the genuineness and regularity in all respects of the drawer's signature and all previous endorsements (s. 55(2)(b)), i.e., he cannot allege any defects in the signatures which are, or are normally, on the bill when it leaves his hands. Further, in favour of the immediate endorsee and any subsequent endorsee, the endorser is precluded from denying the genuineness and validity of the instrument at the time of his endorsement and that he has good title to it. These preclusions are not limited to a holder in due course but apply to other parties to the instrument. The Bills of Exchange Act 1882, s. 56, provides that when a person signs a bill without in fact being the drawer or endorser, he incurs the liability of an endorser to a holder in due course. He is sometimes called a quasi-endorser since he does not sign the bill to transfer it.

Transferor by delivery

A bill is payable to bearer which states on its face that it is payable to bearer, or on which the 'only or last endorsement' is in blank (Bills of Exchange Act 1882, s. 8(3)). The Bills of Exchange Act 1882, s. 58, provides that where the holder of a bill payable to bearer negotiates it by delivery without endorsing it, he is called a transferor by delivery and is not liable on the instrument. However, he warrants to his immediate transferee, if he is a transferee for value and not a donee, that the bill is what it purports to be (i.e., it is not a forgery), that he has a right to transfer it and that at the time of transfer he did not know of any fact which rendered it valueless.

These liabilities are less extensive than those of an endorser since an endorser's liability is not limited to his immediate endorsee for value. An endorser may also be held liable when a genuine bill is dishonoured, whereas in the case of a transferor by delivery this liability will only arise where at the time of the delivery he knew the bill to be worthless. However, where the bill is forged, the transferor by delivery may be liable even if he did not know of the forgery (*Jones* v *Ryde* (1814) 5 Taunt 488).

NEGOTIATION OF A BILL OF EXCHANGE

The main characteristics of a bill of exchange are:

(a) it is 'transferable', because rights arising under it can be transferred by delivery (and endorsement) so the instrument can be sued upon by the person in possession of it; and

(b) that it is 'negotiable' in the sense that such a transfer may additionally confer on the transferee a good title notwithstanding any defect in the title of the transferor (*Crouch* v *Crédit Foncier of England Ltd* (1873) LR 8 QB 374 at 381–2).

The Bills of Exchange Act 1882 may have intended to distinguish between the terms 'transferable' and 'negotiable' but the terms have often been used interchangeably (see chapter 10 for the views of the Jack Committee (Cm 622, 1989). Byles (*Byles on Bills of Exchange*, 26th ed. (Sweet and Maxwell), p. 83) points out that the 'terms "transferable" and "negotiable" are hopelessly mixed up in the Act'.

Negotiation defined

Section 31 of the Bills of Exchange Act 1882 provides that negotiation takes place when a bill is transferred from one person to another in such a way that the transferee becomes the holder. The term 'transfer' is not defined in the Act but 'holder' is defined in s. 2 to mean the payee or endorsee of a bill or note who is in possession of it, or the bearer. However, the bill or note is issued to the first payee (although the holder of the instrument) but there is no negotiation to him of the instrument (*R.E. Jones Ltd* v *Waring and Gillow Ltd* [1926] AC 670).

A bill payable to bearer is negotiated by mere delivery and no endorsement is necessary (s. 31(2)). A bill is payable to bearer which is expressed to be so payable, or one on which the only or last endorsement is in blank (s. 8(3)). The terms 'bearer' and 'delivery' are defined in s. 2 of the Act. As between the two parties, an intention to transfer the instrument on the part of the transferor is necessary if the transferee is to have an unassailable title. If the instrument is transferred to a holder in due course, the absence of intent to transfer title as between the immediate parties is only a matter of personal defences as between the immediate parties and will not interfere with the title of the holder in due course. Section 21(2) of the Act provides that in the hands of a holder in due course 'a valid delivery of the bill by all parties prior to him so as to make them liable to him is conclusively presumed'. The subsection also provides that as against a transferor and transferee and some other party (other than the holder in due course) it is possible to prove that the instrument was delivered for some purpose other than with the intention to transfer title. Thus, if the holder (A) of a bearer cheque hands it over to B for safe-keeping for A, A is entitled to recall the cheque at any time. If B refuses to return the instrument, A can sue B for its return because B has possession of it for a limited purpose. If B in turn delivers the cheque to C who knows of the circumstances in which B took possession, C can also be sued for the return of the cheque, even if he gave value to B. However, if C is a holder in due course then, although A can sue B, B cannot sue C. Moreover, if the cheque is countermanded and payment stopped on it, C will be entitled to sue the drawer, A.

A bill payable to order is negotiated by the endorsement of the holder completed by delivery (s. 31(3)). A bill is payable to order which is expressed to be so payable, or which is expressed to be payable to a particular person, and does not contain words which prohibit transfer (s. 8(4)). The term 'endorsement' is defined by s. 2 as an endorsement completed by delivery. 'Delivery' (by the same section) means the transfer of possession, actual or constructive, from one person to another.

The requisites for a valid endorsement are set out in s. 32. The endorsement may be 'full' endorsement, or it may be a qualified endorsement, or a conditional or restrictive endorsement. The endorsement may be special or in blank. The endorsement of the holder is required in all cases for the negotiation of a bill of exchange or promissory note payable to order unless the instrument is made payable to bearer through a blank endorsement.

Formal requirements

An endorsement must be written on the bill itself (Bills of Exchange Act 1882, s. 32(1)). The assignment of an instrument by a separate document is not an endorsement (*Harrop* v *Fisher* (1861) 10 CB NS 196). In *KHR Financings Ltd* v *Jackson* 1977 SLT (Sh Ct) 6 it was said that the 'purpose of the provision is to enable a bill to operate as a negotiable instrument by ensuring that one piece of paper contains all the writing constituting the obligations of the bill and the names of the parties to it'. There are two exceptions to the rule, namely, an 'allonge' may be attached to the instrument if there is no space for further endorsements and an endorsement may be written on a copy of the instrument, in countries where copies are recognised.

Signature The endorsement must be signed by the 'endorser', although it is possible for an agent to sign on behalf of the endorser. However, the name signed by the endorser need not necessarily correspond exactly with the name of the payee or the endorsee of the instrument. In *Arab Bank Ltd* v *Ross* [1952] 2 QB 216 Denning LJ said:

> . . . by a misnomer, a payee may be described on the face of the bill by the wrong name, nevertheless, if it is quite plain that the drawer intended him as payee, then an endorsement on the back by the payee in his own true name is valid and sufficient to pass the property in the bill.

Kinds of endorsements An endorsement may take one of three forms, namely: (a) endorsement in blank; (b) special endorsement; and (c) restrictive endorsement. An endorsement in blank consists merely of the endorser's signature and such an instrument is payable to bearer. A special endorsement will specify the person to whom or to whose order the instrument is to be payable. Although no particular form of wording is required by the Bills of Exchange Act 1882 the form of wording most likely to be used is 'pay X or order', followed by the signature of the endorser. If the endorsement merely used the words 'pay X' followed by the signature of the endorser then s. 8(4) treats this as equivalent to a 'pay X or order' endorsement and X can further endorse the instrument. A special endorsement following an endorsement in blank displaces the previous endorsement in blank.

The Act recognises that the endorsee under a special endorsement is in effect a new payee and the provisions in the Act relating to the payee apply (s. 34(3)). This means that the endorsee must be indicated with reasonable certainty, that a bill may be endorsed to two or more endorsees jointly, or to one or more of several endorsees, but an endorsement only of part of the amount for which the instrument is drawn is invalid.

Section 35 provides that there is a restrictive endorsement where the terms of the endorsement prohibit further transfer of the instrument, e.g., where the endorsement states 'pay X only', or when it clearly states that it is not intended to transfer ownership in the instrument but merely to give the transferee authority to deal with the instrument for some limited purpose, e.g., 'pay X for the account of Z'. Such an endorsement gives the endorsee the right to receive payment and to sue any party whom the endorser could have sued, but it gives the endorsee no power to transfer his rights 'unless expressly authorised'.

Duration of negotiability

Section 36 of the Bills of Exchange Act 1882 provides that when a bill is originally negotiable it continues to be negotiable until it is either restrictively endorsed or discharged by payment or otherwise. Thus, a bill of exchange 'is negotiable ad infinitum' (*Callow* v *Lawrence* (1814) 3 M and S 95). However, a bill ceases to be negotiable once it is discharged by payment by or on behalf of the acceptor, or by cancellation or renunciation. The fact that an action has been brought on a dishonoured bill does not determine its negotiability, although a person who takes with notice of the dishonour will not be a holder in due course. Further, a person to whom an overdue bill is negotiated cannot be a holder in due course (s. 29(1)(a)) and does not take the bill free from any prior defects of title (*London and County Banking Co* v *Groome* (1881) 8 QBD 288).

Section 37 deals with a special situation and provides that where a bill is negotiated back to the drawer, or to a prior endorser, or to the acceptor, such party may reissue and further negotiate the bill but he is not entitled to enforce payment against any intervening party to whom he was previously liable. Thus, where A, an endorser of a bill of exchange, has endorsed back to him the same bill after it has passed through the hands of intermediate parties (e.g., B and C), s. 37 provides that A may reissue the bill to D but if the bill is dishonoured and D exercises his right of recourse against A then A cannot in turn sue B and C by virtue of his second endorsement; if that were permitted, B and C would have a right of recourse against A because of his original endorsement.

CONDITIONS FOR INCURRING LIABILITY ON A BILL OF EXCHANGE

Section 23 of the Bills of Exchange Act 1882 provides that no one is liable as drawer, endorser, or acceptor of a bill who has not signed it. As has already been seen the term 'signature' is not defined but it does include a signature placed on the instrument by an agent. Such a person may simply write his principal's name on the instrument without adding any indication that the instrument is drawn as an agent (s. 91(1)).

If an agent signs in his own name and adds words indicating that he is signing in a representative capacity (e.g., a signature by procuration) then that is sufficient notice to any third party that the agent has restricted authority from his principal and the principal will only be bound if he acts within the limits of that authority (s. 25). In *Morison* v *Kemp* (1912) 29 TLR 70 a clerk employed by the plaintiff firm was authorised to draw cheques 'per pro' his employers for the purposes of their business. The clerk drew a cheque in this form and made it payable to a bookmaker to settle his private betting losses. It was held that the employers could recover the proceeds of the cheque from the bookmakers (see also *Attwood* v *Munnings* (1827) 7 B and C 278 where Bayley J explained the effect of the rule contained in s. 25).

It follows that even a holder in due course of a bill so signed cannot enforce it against the principal if the agent has exceeded his authority (*Morison* v *London County and Westminster Bank Ltd* [1914] 3 KB 356; *Midland Bank Ltd* v *Reckitt* [1933] AC 1). Although it is not entirely clear whether all forms of representative signature fall within s. 25 the view appears (*MacDonald and Co.* v *Nash and Co* [1922] WN 272 per Scrutton LJ) to be that the section is confined to cases where the form of signature shows a special and limited authority (e.g., 'per procuration' or 'under power of attorney') and excludes situations where a general authority is conferred (e.g., signatures 'on behalf of' or 'by' the agent).

Where the agent when signing as drawer, endorser or acceptor, clearly and unambiguously indicates that he is acting merely in a representative capacity, he will not be personally liable on the instrument (*Lindus* v *Melrose* (1857) 2 Hurl & N 293; *Alexander* v *Sizer* (1869) LR 4 Ex 102). However, an agent who signs a bill in his own name, without naming his principal, will incur personal liability even though it is known he signs as an agent (*Thomas* v *Bishop* (1733) 2 Str 955). Consequently, an agent who signs a negotiable instrument on behalf of his principal must clearly use words which indicate that he signs as an agent in order to be released from being made personally liable on the instrument.

It may not be enough to place the words 'agent' or 'director' after the signature since the words merely refer to the office held or occupied by the signatory and not necessarily that he signs in that capacity (see *Parker* v *Winlow* (1857) 7 El & Bl 942 and *Landes* v *Marcus* (1909) 25 TLR 478).

Nevertheless, the imposition of personal liability on the agent is applied less rigorously today than in the earlier cases. The main problem which arises is in reference to the positioning of the name of the principal on the instrument in relation to the signature of the authorised agent, or the omission of words which indicate that the agent signs for or on behalf of a principal, or in a representative character. In *Chapman* v *Smethurst* [1909] 1 KB 927 the placing of the word 'director' after the signature was held to make the instrument a promissory note issued by the company. Another case where the effect of s. 26(2) was examined is *Elliott* v *Bax-Ironside* [1925] 2 KB 301 where two directors of the company endorsed the back of a bill of exchange 'in order to guarantee the liability of the company'. The court held that under s. 26(2) the directors would be treated as having endorsed the bill in their personal capacity since that was the only method of giving the additional guarantee required of them. In *Bondina Ltd* v *Rollaway Shower Blinds Ltd* [1986] WLR 517 it was held that a cheque signed by a director of a company without any indication of the capacity in which he signed the instrument was a cheque drawn by the company because in placing his signature on it the director adopted all the wording on it, including the name of the company.

It is impossible to be dogmatic about the words which suffice to negative personal liability since the court is entitled to look at the document as a whole in order to discover the capacity of the signatory. Where the drawer of the instrument is a company it may be possible to establish the personal liability of the signatory under s. 349(4) of the Companies Act 1985 (formerly s. 108(4) of the Companies

Act 1948). The section provides that if an officer of the company or any person acting on its behalf signs or authorises the signature of a negotiable instrument or order for money or goods which does not mention the company's name in full, he is liable to the holder of the document for the obligation embodied in it if the company fails to satisfy the obligation.

The word 'holder' has been construed to mean the person to whom a payment order is addressed or who stands to benefit by it (*Civil Service Cooperative Society Ltd* v *Chapman* (1914) 30 TLR 679). Personal liability under s. 349(4) attaches not only to the person who signs the irregular document but also to the person who authorises its signature. But a person who gives such an authority is personally liable only if he expressly authorises the signature by another of a document which he knows will be irregular (*John Wilkes (Footwear) Ltd* v *Lee International Footwear Ltd* [1985] BCLC 444).

In *Durham Fancy Goods Ltd* v *Michael Jackson (Fancy Goods) Ltd* [1968] 2 QB 839 the plaintiffs had drawn a bill on the defendants which wrongly named them as 'M. Jackson (Fancy Goods) Ltd' and prepared a form of acceptance in the same style. A director of the company signed the acceptance without noticing the misdescription. The bill was dishonoured. It was held that the director was personally liable on the bill but that the plaintiffs were estopped from enforcing his liability since they were responsible for the error. In *Maxform SpA* v *Mariani* [1979] 2 Lloyd's Rep 385 a director of Goodville Ltd was held personally liable on the bills drawn in its registered business name, Italdesign, without mention on the bills of the name Goodville Ltd. The court said that the word 'name' in s. 108 of the 1948 Act could only mean the company's registered corporate name. In *British Airways Board* v *Parish* [1979] 2 Lloyd's Rep 361 and *Calzaturificio Fiorella SpA* v *Walton* [1979] CLY 23 directors of two companies were held personally liable when the word 'Ltd' had been omitted from the company names. In *Banque de L'Indochine et de Suez SA* v *Euroseas Group Finance Co. Ltd* [1981] 3 All ER 198 it was held that s. 108 of the 1948 Act did not render the company director personally liable because the abbreviation 'Co.' for 'Company' was well established and understood. In *Barber and Nicholls Ltd* v *R and G Associates (London) Ltd* (1981) 132 NLJ 1076 it was held that s. 108 would not apply to impose personal liability on several dishonoured cheques because the bank had omitted the word 'London' from the company's printed name on the cheque forms. The omission was not that of the director but of the bank and s. 108 did not apply.

It should be remembered that the company cannot plead lack of capacity in order to escape its payment obligations on a contract (Companies Act 1985, s. 35, see chapter 6). Further, whenever an agent signs a bill without authority from his principal and a third party suffers loss, the agent may be sued for breach of warranty of authority.

Although a signature, whether personal or written by an agent, is essential to liability on a bill, a person signing as a drawer or endorser may avoid such liability as would normally fall on him by adding words to his signature which expressly negative liability. The usual expression used is 'sans recours' or its English equivalent 'without recourse'. In such a case the drawer's signature serves as an expression of primary liability on the bill and the endorser's signature will convey title to the instrument but the person who signs it 'without recourse' cannot be called upon to make payment (s. 16(1)).

Delivery of the instrument

Although a signature is necessary on a negotiable instrument it is not itself sufficient to render a person liable. Delivery is also necessary (Bills of Exchange Act 1882, s. 21(1)). In *Abrey* v *Crux* (1869) LR 5 CP 37 at 42 Bovill CJ said that to constitute a contract 'there must be a delivery over of the instrument by the drawer or endorser for a good consideration: and as soon as these circumstances take place the contract is complete'. By s. 2 of the Act 'delivery' means transfer of possession, actual or constructive from one person to another. Thus, the drawer will not be liable to the payee of the instrument until it has been handed over to the payee and the acceptor will not be liable to the payee until he has signed the instrument and handed it back to the payee (or, by an exception under s. 21, signed the acceptance and given notice that he has done so) and an endorser will not be liable until he has signed and handed over the instrument to the endorsee.

Constructive possession occurs where one person holds the instrument on behalf of another. Thus, where the drawer signs the instrument and hands it over to an agent of the payee, that will be sufficient delivery.

Delivery is also necessary to pass the property in the bill, i.e., from the drawer to the payee, or from an endorser to an endorsee (*Brind* v *Hampshire* (1836) 1 M and W 365; *Arnold* v *Cheque Bank* (1876) 1 CPD 578). In *Re Deveze* (1873) LR 9 Ch App 27 at 31–2) Mellish LJ said that:

> In order to make the property in the bills pass it is not sufficient to endorse them; they must be delivered to the endorsee or to the agent of the endorsee. If the endorser delivers them to his own agent, he can recover them; if to the agent of the endorsee, he cannot recover them.

There is some uncertainty whether an instrument sent by post is delivered when it is posted or when it is received. Where a cheque is sent by post by a debtor to his creditor in payment of a debt, this does not normally amount to payment if the cheque is lost in the post (*Pennington* v *Crossley and Son* (1897) 77 LT 43; *Baker* v *Lipton Ltd* (1899) 15 TLR 435). However, there is authority to support the view that if the creditor expressly or impliedly requests or authorises payment through the post, the debtor will be discharged if he complies with the request or authority by posting the cheque in a properly addressed envelope even if it does not reach him (*Norman* v *Ricketts* (1886) 3 TLR 182; *Thairlwall* v *Great Northern Railway Co.* [1910] 2 KB 509). These cases are difficult to reconcile with cases which establish that payment made by cheque is effected when the cheque is received and accepted in conditional payment of the debt (*Felix Hadley and Co. Ltd* v *Hadley* [1898] 2 Ch 680; *Marreco* v *Richardson* [1908] 2 KB 584; *The Brimnes* [1975] QB 929) or sometimes only when the cheque is cleared and the proceeds credited to the payee's account (*Re Hone* [1951] Ch 85).

CAPACITY AND AUTHORITY OF THE PARTIES TO A BILL OF EXCHANGE

It is necessary to distinguish between capacity and authority in connection with bills of exchange. The capacity to contract is the creation of the law and means

the power to contract so as to bind oneself. However, authority is derived from the
conduct of the parties themselves and means the power to contract on behalf of
another so as to bind that other.

The authority of a person to sign a cheque or bill of exchange under the Bills
of Exchange Act 1882, ss. 25 (signature by procuration) and 26 (signing as an
agent or in a representative capacity), has already been examined. It is now
intended to examine the effect of a forged or unauthorised signature on a bill of
exchange.

Forged or unauthorised signatures

The Bills of Exchange Act 1882, s. 24, establishes that a forged signature, or a
signature which is placed on a bill without the authority of the person whose
signature it purports to be, is 'wholly inoperative' and no right to retain the bill,
or to give a discharge, or to enforce payment against any party can be acquired
through or under the signature. There are, however, three exceptions to this rule
namely:

(a)   those contained in other provisions of the Act;
(b)   estoppel; and
(c)   the ratification of an unauthorised signature not amounting to forgery.

Section 24 applies to any forged or unauthorised signature on a bill whether it
purports to be that of the drawee, the drawer or an endorser. It also applies to the
signature of the maker or endorser of a promissory note and to that of the drawer
or endorser of a cheque. It does not apply to any fraudulent alteration in the body
of the instrument (although it may constitute forgery), which is dealt with by s. 64
of the Act. The words 'forged' and 'forgery' are not defined by the Act and the
words 'where a signature on a bill is forged' are intended to extend to a situation
where the signature in question is counterfeit or falsely purports to be a genuine
signature. However, it was originally thought that a signature would not be 'forged'
if it was merely placed on a bill without the authority of the person whose signature
it purports to be (*Morison* v *London County and Westminster Bank Ltd* [1914]
3 KB 356).

The Forgery Act 1913 altered and extended the definition of forgery in criminal
law and in *Kreditbank Cassel GmbH* v *Schenkers Ltd* [1927] 1 KB 826 it was held
that in interpreting the Bills of Exchange Act 1882 the court should apply the
Forgery Act 1913 so that a company was not liable on bills drawn and endorsed
by an employee without authority. Scrutton LJ reasoned (at p. 840), '. . . the bills
are clearly forgeries within the Forgery Act 1913, as they contain a false
statement'. The inference would therefore appear to be that the words 'where a
signature is forged' in s. 24 should be interpreted in accordance with the current
statutory definition of 'forgery' for the purposes of the criminal law. The current
definition of forgery is contained in s. 1 of the Forgery and Counterfeiting Act 1981
which provides that a person is guilty of forgery if he makes a false instrument,
with the intention that he or another will use it to induce somebody to accept it as
genuine, or by reason of so accepting it to do some act to his own or any other
person's prejudice. Section 9(1) then goes on to provide the circumstances in

which the instrument will be considered to be false and would appear to extend to the situation which arose in *Morison* v *London County and Westminster Bank Ltd.*

Unauthorised signatures Whether or not a signature is unauthorised will be governed by the ordinary principles of the law of agency. The authority to sign may be actual, express or implied, or an apparent (ostensible) authority. As a general rule an act of an agent within the scope of his actual or apparent authority does not cease to bind the principal merely because the agent has acted fraudulently and in his interests (subject to the Bills of Exchange Act 1882, s. 25).

Where a signature is inserted on behalf of the company, then s. 35A of the Companies Act 1985 provides that in favour of a person dealing with the company in good faith, the power of the board of directors to bind the company, or authorise others to do so, is deemed free from limitations (see chapter 6).

Effect of forged or unauthorised signature Where a signature is forged or unauthorised, the basic rule contained in s. 24 is that it is 'wholly inoperative'. Section 24 therefore treats in the same way an instrument which has been forged and one which bears an unauthorised signature. Thus, if the signature of the drawer is forged on a cheque and his bank makes a payment against it, the bank cannot debit the customer's account, and it can be compelled to re-credit the account. The payee, even if he takes in good faith and has given value, cannot sue the drawer if the drawer stops payment, and if the payee has received the amount of the cheque he can be compelled to repay the money. Similarly, if the drawee's signature is forged as an acceptance on a bill of exchange, the drawee cannot be sued. If the payee's signature or that of an endorsee is forged as an endorsement, then the payee or endorsee cannot be sued. The holder will be able to sue all endorsers whose names appear on the cheque after the forged endorsement, but the forgery breaks the chain of title. All signatures appearing on the cheque before the forged signature, and the person whose signature is forged, will be immune from action. Obviously, the holder of the instrument who acquires it on the strength of the forged endorsement will be able to sue the person responsible for the forgery, but that is of little practical value.

Forgery of an endorsement creates a clear break in the chain of title, but forgery of the signatures of other parties may have a different effect. If a drawee's signature is forged as an acceptance, but the drawer's signature and any endorsements are in order, then the bill will be treated as unaccepted, and the drawer will be liable on the instrument. In such circumstances liability can be traced from the holder through the endorsements and the endorsers treated as guarantors. If the drawer's signature is forged on a bill, but there is a good acceptance and all the endorsements are valid, the holder can trace the chain of title back to the acceptor who will be liable; the endorsers will be liable as guarantors.

Exceptions to section 24 of the Bills of Exchange Act 1882 Although it is clear that the rule which renders forged instruments a nullity has numerous applications, it is subject to a number of important qualifications:

(a) *Instruments endorsed abroad.* Section 24 does not apply where an instrument is endorsed abroad. Under the English rules of private international law, the transfer of 'chattels [including choses in action] must be governed by the law of the country where the transfer takes place' (*Embiricos* v *Anglo-Austrian Bank* [1905] 1 KB 677). Thus, if the forgery took place in a foreign country where title could be acquired, or liability incurred, on a forged signature then the English courts will treat the signature as if it were genuine.

(b) *Estoppel.* The effect of ss. 54(2) and 55(2)(b) is to provide that a party to a bill may be estopped from asserting that the signature of another party to the bill is forged or unauthorised. In addition to the statutory estoppels raised against the acceptor and the endorser of the bill of exchange in favour of a holder in due course and against the endorser under s. 55(2)(c) in favour of his immediate or a subsequent endorsee, the acceptor of a bill may, for example, be estopped from denying the authenticity of the signature of the drawer to any innocent holder for value. The party whose signature has been forged or placed on a bill without his authority may also be precluded from setting up the forgery or want of authority. The drawee of a bill may, e.g., be estopped where he has represented to the holder that his signature as acceptor is genuine (*Leach* v *Buchanan* (1802) 4 Esp 226). In particular the drawer of a cheque may be estopped as against the drawee bank from asserting that his signature on the cheque is forged or unauthorised, with the result that the drawee bank is then entitled to debit his account with the amount which it has paid (*Greenwood* v *Martins Bank Ltd* [1933] AC 51; *Brown* v *Westminster Bank Ltd* [1964] 2 Lloyd's Rep 187). Estoppel may arise by representation or by negligence. The essential features giving rise to an estoppel by representation were stated by Lord Tomlin in *Greenwood* v *Martins Bank Ltd*. The House of Lords held that the husband was under a duty to inform the bank of the forgeries and that the deliberate failure to do so amounted to a representation that the cheques forged by the wife were in fact genuine. Further, by reason of the representation the bank had been deprived of the opportunity of suing him and his wife in respect of the tort committed by his wife before her death. However, silence due to ignorance will not be sufficient (*Tai Hing Cotton Mill Ltd* v *Liu Chong Hing Bank Ltd* [1986] AC 80) and there must be a duty to disclose. If the customer has knowledge then he owes a duty to disclose to the bank that his signature as drawer is forged or unauthorised (see *Greenwood* v *Martins Bank Ltd*; *Brown* v *Westminster Bank Ltd*; *Limpgrange Ltd* v *Bank of Credit and Commerce International SA* 1986 FLR 36). The duty of disclosure is not confined to the banker and customer relationship: any person who becomes aware that his signature on a document has been forged is bound to repudiate the signature if the forgery is brought to his attention. Further, a person who becomes aware that his signature as drawer or endorser has been forged on a bill and who knows that the payee will advance money in reliance on the instrument is bound to warn the payee of that fact, and if the payee's position is prejudiced, he will be estopped from setting up the forgery as against the payee (*M'Kenzie* v *British Linen Co* (1881) 6 App Cas 82).

(c) *Ratification*   The Bills of Exchange Act 1882 provides two important qualifications to s. 24. First, the section does not 'affect the ratification of an unauthorised signature not amounting to a forgery' (proviso to s. 24). Ratification becomes possible under the rules of the law of agency, under which, if a person who is not authorised to enter into some transaction on behalf of the principal, enters into it, professing to act as an agent for an identifiable, existing principal with capacity to enter into the transaction in his own right, then the alleged principal may approve or ratify the transaction. Such a transaction therefore becomes a valid act of the principal just as if the agent had the prior authority from the principal to enter into the transaction. Ratification thus renders an unauthorised act fully valid and operates retrospectively to validate the act from the time it was first entered into by the unauthorised agent. However, a forgery cannot be ratified (*Brook* v *Hook* (1871) LR 6 Ex 89; *Greenwood* v *Martins Bank Ltd* [1932] 1 KB 371). Thus, if a person has no authority to sign a private document as an agent, but signs it with intent to defraud, ratification is not possible. If, however, the professed agent acted under an honest mistake, believing that he had authority to act, or was careless in establishing the limits of his authority, then ratification may be possible. Secondly, although s. 24 provides that ratification is not possible in the case of a forgery, the section permits something superficially corresponding to it when it provides that a forged or unauthorised signature is a nullity 'unless the party against whom it is sought to retain or enforce payment of the bill is precluded from setting up the forgery or want of authority'. A party is 'precluded' when he is 'estopped' in England and Northern Ireland, or 'personally barred' in Scotland. However, it is not entirely clear whether the adoption of a forged signature under this proviso is to be treated as a promise requiring consideration, or as an example of estoppel by express representation, or an independent principle akin to ratification.

Capacity to draw a bill of exchange

Even if a person's signature has been properly placed on a bill of exchange, either personally or by an agent, that person may still not incur liability, or only a limited liability on the instrument, because he belongs to a class of persons on whom the law either confers no capacity, or a limited capacity, to contract by negotiable instrument. The question of capacity is dealt with in the Bills of Exchange Act 1882, s. 22, which provides that capacity to incur liability on a bill of exchange is coextensive with capacity to contract. Thus, s. 22 does not enlarge the capacity of a corporation to incur liability as a party to a bill, which is to be determined by the law relating to corporations. At common law, a corporation incurred no liability by drawing, accepting or endorsing a bill of exchange, unless expressly or implicitly authorised by its constitution to do so. If a company entered into a contract which was in excess of its capacity, the transaction was *ultra vires* and void. In so far as third parties are concerned, the ultra vires rule has effectively been abolished by s. 35(1) of the Companies Act 1985 (see chapter 6). However, the rule continues to apply to the acts of a company which is a charity, except in favour of a person who (i) gives full consideration in money or money's worth in relation to the act in question, and (ii) does not know that the act is not permitted by the company's memorandum, or who does not know at the time the act is done that the company is a charity (Charities Act 1993, s. 65). Further, where the board of directors of a company have exceeded any limitation on their powers under the company's constitution in respect of a transaction where the third party is a director of the company, or is a person connected with such a director or a company with whom such a director is associated; then the transaction is voidable and not void, at the company's option (Companies Act 1985, s. 322A, inserted by s. 109 of the Companies Act 1989 which applies to a wide range of defects in the authority of the directors).

Despite the abolition of the *ultra vires* rule, it does not follow that a bill or note drawn, accepted or endorsed by a company in excess of its powers or for an *ultra vires* purpose will necessarily be enforceable against the company. Section 35(3) of the Companies Act 1985 preserves the fiduciary duties of the directors to observe any limitation on their powers flowing from the memorandum (see chapter 6). The directors may be made personally liable if the instrument is enforceable and the company makes a loss by having to make payment against the instrument.

Instruments signed prior to the incorporation of the company   Where a bill or note is signed by a promoter or other person on behalf of a company before it has been formed, the company will incur no liability on the instrument as drawer, acceptor, or endorser, since it cannot be bound by a contract made when it had no legal existence. Further, it cannot, after incorporation, ratify or adopt the signature of the person who purported to be its agent (*Kelner* v *Baxter* (1866) LR 2 CP 174; *Scott* v *Lord Ebury* (1867) LR 2 CP 255). However, under s. 36C(1) of the Companies Act 1985, a contract which is made on behalf of a non-existing company, has effect, subject to any agreement to the contrary, as one made with the person purporting to act for the company and he is personally liable on the contract. Consequently, despite s. 26(1) of the Bills of Exchange Act 1882, even though a person signing adds words to his signature indicating that he signs for or on behalf of a principal, or in a representative capacity, he is personally liable on the bill or note if he purports to draw, accept or endorse the instrument on behalf of a company which has not been formed (*Phonogram Ltd* v *Lane* [1982] QB 938).

Minors   All persons under the age of 18 years are technically known as minors (or infants) (Family Law Reform Act 1969, s. 1) (see chapter 6). Although by the Bills of Exchange Act 1882, s. 22(1), the capacity of a minor to incur liability as a party to a bill is coextensive with capacity to contract, it has long been established that a minor incurs no liability by drawing, endorsing, accepting or making a bill or note, even to a holder in due course. In *Re Soltykoff* [1891] 1 QB 413 Lord Esher MR said that '[An infant] is not liable upon a bill of exchange or a promissory note under any circumstances'. This statement placed the minor in a more favourable position in respect of bills of exchange than under the general law of contract. Since the repeal of the Infants Relief Act 1874 and the Betting and Loans (Infants) Act 1892, a bill, cheque or note which is drawn, endorsed, accepted or made by a person of full age in respect of a debt contracted during minority will be binding on him, and this will be so whether his signature of the instrument constitutes ratification by him of the debt or a fresh promise, based on new consideration, to pay the debt.

If a minor draws a post-dated cheque, and places a date on it so that it becomes payable after he attains majority, he is not liable on the cheque, even after he has attained majority (*Hutley* v *Peacock* (1913) 30 TLR 42). But if a person of full age accepts a bill drawn on him while still a minor, he will be liable on it (*Stevens* v *Jackson* (1815) 4 Camp 164).

Sovereign immunity   Persons who enjoy sovereign and diplomatic immunity cannot be sued, unless they waive their immunity. This protection extends to foreign States and governmental agencies and may defeat a holder in due course unless the immunity is waived, or unless the case falls within the qualifications introduced in the Diplomatic Privileges Act 1964, or the State Immunity Act 1978. The doctrine of sovereign immunity prior to 1987 was derived largely from international law and until *Trendtex Trading Corporation* v *Central Bank of Nigeria* [1977] QB 529 it was accepted that a foreign corporation owned or controlled by a foreign sovereign State could not be sued in a court of law. However, the Court of Appeal held that the Central Bank of Nigeria was not entitled to plead sovereign immunity as a department or organ of a foreign State. Further, the rule of international law that the doctrine of sovereign immunity was not applicable to ordinary commercial transactions, as distinct from the governmental acts of a sovereign State, was part of English law and should be applied by the court.

The rule that a government department which enters into commercial transactions does not have immunity has been given statutory approval by the State Immunity Act 1978, which placed on a statutory basis the court's decision in the *Trendtex* case. The Act provides that a State is immune from the jurisdiction of the UK courts except as provided for by statute. The Act then enumerates the circumstances in which a sovereign, a State, a constituent territory of a federal State and a separate entity exercising sovereign authority will lose immunity. Under s. 3(1) the Act provides that a State is not immune where proceedings relate to commercial transactions entered into by the State or an obligation of the State which has been performed wholly or partly in the UK. A 'commercial transaction' is defined as being a contract for the supply of goods or services, any loan or other transaction for the provision of finance, or any undertaking of indemnity or guarantee relating to such a transaction or any other transaction or activity into which a State enters otherwise than in the exercise of sovereign authority.

Effect of incapacity

Section 22(2) of the Bills of Exchange Act 1882 deals with a situation where a bill is drawn or endorsed by a person having no capacity or power to incur liability on the instrument. It provides that the drawing or endorsement entitles the holder of the bill to enforce it against any party to the instrument, i.e., against any other party other than one with limited contractual capacity. Thus, if a minor draws a cheque which is subsequently endorsed by the payee, the endorsee may enforce the cheque against the payee, but not against the minor. This provision merely reinforces the general common law rule that the incapacity of one or more of the parties to a bill does not diminish the liability of the other parties (*Burgess* v *Merrill* (1812) 4 Taunt 468; *Wauthier* v *Wilson* (1912) 28 TLR 239). The section also provides that the drawing or endorsement by the minor or other person with limited capacity entitles the holder to claim payment of the bill. Thus, if a bill is drawn payable to the order of the drawer and endorsed by him to a person having no capacity or power to incur liability on the instrument, a subsequent endorsement by that person passes the property to the subsequent endorsee, even though the person who acted with limited capacity may not himself be liable as endorser (*Smith* v *Johnson* (1858) 3 Hurl & N 222).

Subsection (2) is reinforced by certain estoppels which are raised in favour of the holder in due course (see ss. 54 and 55).

CONSIDERATION

The essence of the doctrine of consideration is that a person who wishes to enforce a contractual promise must show that he provided valid consideration for that promise. The law therefore recognises and will give effect to bargains where some value, however small (*Chappell and Co. Ltd* v *Nestlé Co. Ltd* [1960] AC 87) has been provided in exchange for that promise. In *Dunlop Pneumatic Tyre Co.* v *Selfridge and Co. Ltd* [1915] AC 847 consideration was explained to be 'the price for which the promise is bought'. If the plaintiff wishes to sue for breach of a promise for which no consideration has been given, then he must show that the promise was made under seal. The general law of consideration applies to bills, cheques and notes (the Jack Committee Report recommended that the need for consideration as a test for negotiability should be abolished (Cm 622, 5 1990, recommendation 8.4), but this recommendation was not accepted (Cm 1026 (1989)). However, the Bills of Exchange Act 1882 qualifies these rules to some extent. Section 27 adopts the common law rule and provides that consideration for a contract on a bill may be constituted by any 'consideration sufficient to support a simple contract', but it qualifies the common law because s. 27(1)(b) goes on to provide that consideration for a bill of exchange may also be 'an antecedent debt or liability' (*Elkington* v *Cooke-Hill* (1914) 30 TLR 670; *Ayres* v *Moore* [1940] 1 KB 278; see also *Hasan* v *Willson* [1977] 1 Lloyd's Rep 431, where it was said that the words 'antecedent debt or liability' refer to the antecedent debt or liability of the promissor or drawer of the bill). Many cheques and other bills of exchange are given in settlement of existing debts and liabilities so that the rule could not be otherwise. Nevertheless, the rule is treated as an exception to the principle that consideration must not be past. The section goes on to provide that 'Where value has at any time been given for a bill the holder is deemed to be a holder for value as regards the acceptor and all parties to the bill who become parties prior to such time'. This is an exception to the rule that a person must be privy to the consideration before he can sue. Thus, it is not necessary for the holder of a bill who sues on it to show that he provided consideration to the defendant. It is sufficient that consideration was provided by anyone in the chain of title, provided the defendant became a party to the bill before any such consideration was given. For example, A draws a bill on B, who accepts it gratuitously. C gives A value for the bill and endorses it to X as a gift. X can sue B although X gave no value for the bill and B received nothing for his acceptance. X can also sue A, but X cannot sue C, as C did not become a party prior to the giving of value.

Section 2 of the Act defines 'value' to mean valuable consideration. As a general rule of contract law, valuable consideration must move from (be given by) the promisee. In the case of bills, as between immediate parties (i.e., parties in direct relation to each other: normally the drawer and acceptor and the drawer and payee of a bill, or the drawer and payee of a cheque are all immediate parties), value must have been given by the holder who seeks to enforce the obligation. As between remote parties (i.e., if their legal relations as parties to the instrument arise not out of direct dealings with each other, but out of their respective dealings with another party: normally the acceptor and payee of a bill, unless it is drawn payable to the order of the drawer, or an endorsee and drawer of a cheque), value need not have been given by the holder so long as value was given for the instrument after the defendant became a party to it.

A party to a contract who cannot sue on it except by pleading the illegality of the consideration to establish his rights will not succeed in his action and the whole action is contaminated (*Simpson* v *Bloss* (1816) 7 Taunt 246). Moreover, the illegal consideration under the transaction which gives rise to the debt in question may be raised as a defence by the debtor against the innocent assignee of a debt. In the case of a holder for value of a bill of exchange the position is similar and it is of no consequence whether the consideration which moves is illegal or merely void. However, if the holder of the bill is a holder in due course he would be able to sue both the issuer and other parties to the cheque (*Woolf* v *Hamilton* [1898] 2 QB 337). This is reinforced by s. 29 of the Bills of Exchange Act 1882, which provides that if an illegal consideration has been given for the acceptance, issue or subsequent negotiation of a bill, it does not affect the title of a subsequent holder in due course.

Section 27(3) of the Act provides that a holder of a bill who has a lien on it, whether by operation of law or by contract, is a holder for value to the extent of the lien. A lien is a right 'in one man to retain that which is in his possession belonging to another, till certain demands of him the person in possession are satisfied' (*Hammonds* v *Barclay* (1802) 2 East 227 at 235). Bankers have a general lien on all securities deposited with them, as bankers, by customers, unless there is an express agreement to the contrary, or unless it is implicit from the circumstances that a lien was not intended (*Brandao* v *Barnett* (1846) 3 CB 519).

HOLDER IN DUE COURSE

The liability of a party to a bill is contractual and the position of the holder is dependent on whether either he or his predecessor in title has given consideration for the instrument. A holder who has not given value for the bill cannot claim against any person who becomes a party to the bill without receiving consideration unless consideration has been given by an immediate party. This is in accordance with the general rule that, as a bill is a simple contract, consideration is necessary to support it. However, under the Bills of Exchange Act 1882, s. 30(1), every party to a bill is prima facie deemed to be a holder for value (*King* v *Milsom* (1809) 2 Camp 5; *Fitch* v *Jones* (1855) 5 El & Bl 238). Moreover, a holder who has not given value himself will have the benefit of the fact that a previous holder has given valuable consideration. In such a situation he himself will be deemed to be a holder for value as regards parties prior to the one who gave value. For example, B draws a bill payable to himself upon A, who accepts it gratuitously; C gives value for B's endorsing the bill to him, and C further endorses the bill to D by way of a gift. D can sue A on the bill although D gave no consideration for the bill and A did not receive value. This applies even though D knew that A had accepted the bill gratuitously. D can also sue B who received value from C, but D cannot sue C, as C did not become a party prior to the giving of value for the bill himself. The rule applicable is that the holder of a bill who receives it from a holder for value, but does not himself give value for it, has all the rights of a holder for value against all parties to the bill, except the person from whom he received it. A holder for value, on the other hand, will either have given value or be able to rely on the fact that value was given by an earlier party to the bill. A holder for value has a complete title to the bill, although he may not personally have given consideration for it, and his title can only be impeached by proof of a defect in his title, e.g., that the issue or transfer of the bill was void or voidable. Where the issue or transfer of a bill has been obtained by fraud, a holder for value obtains no benefit from the mere fact that he has himself given value for the bill or that he takes through one who has given value. To take free from the defect of title, the holder for value must also be a holder in due course. A holder for value, as such, will not be a holder in due course, either because he is the payee of the instrument, or because he took a bill which suffered from a formal irregularity, or because he did not act in good faith.

The holder in due course enjoys the full extent of the protection conferred on a holder of a negotiable instrument. Subject to certain exceptions the holder in due course is unaffected by any defect in the title of any previous holder, or by any omission on the part of any previous holder, or by any omission on the part of any previous holder to carry out the steps necessary to preserve his rights of recourse.

Nevertheless, it cannot be said that the position of the holder in due course is impregnable. He cannot claim against an apparent party to the bill whose signature was unauthorised or forged, nor can he claim through such an apparent party against parties prior to that apparent party. Moreover, he cannot claim against or through a person who has actually signed the bill but whose signature is a nullity because of a fundamental mistake, nor can a holder in due course claim against a party who lacks contractual capacity. A holder who derives title through a holder in due course has, generally, the rights of a holder in due course.

The Bills of Exchange Act 1882, s. 29, substituted the term 'holder in due course' for the more cumbersome 'bona fide holder for value without notice', and its synonyms 'bona fide holder', 'innocent endorsee' etc. (*Lloyds Bank Ltd* v *Cooke* [1907] 1 KB 794 at 806).

Holder who has taken the bill

To qualify as a holder in due course, the holder must have taken the bill in circumstances which constitute him a holder. Section 2 of the Bills of Exchange Act 1882 provides that a 'holder' means the payee or endorsee of a bill or note who is in possession of it, or the bearer.

A person to whom an unendorsed order bill is delivered, but not negotiated (s. 31(3)), is not a holder and therefore cannot be a holder in due course. However, s. 2 of the Cheques Act 1957 creates an exception by providing that where a banker gives value for, or has a lien on, a cheque payable to order which the holder delivers to him for collection without endorsing it, the banker has such rights as he would have had if the instrument had been endorsed in blank.

As a general rule, a person cannot be a holder of an order bill if he takes the bill under a forged endorsement and consequently he cannot be a holder in due course (unless estoppel can be raised).

The holder must have taken the bill, i.e., received it, by negotiation. Notwithstanding the definition of 'holder' in s. 2, the original payee of a bill in whose possession the instrument remains cannot be a holder in due course although he can, of course, be a holder for value. In *R.E. Jones Ltd* v *Waring and Gillow Ltd* [1926] AC 670 the House of Lords was of the opinion that the expression 'holder in due course' cannot include the original payee of a cheque. The House of Lords overruled the decision in *Lloyds Bank* v *Cooke* [1907] 1 KB 794 that the payee of a negotiable instrument could be a holder in due course. The decision in *Lloyds Bank Ltd* v *Cooke* was doubted even before *R.E. Jones Ltd* v *Waring and Gillow Ltd* came before the courts. In *Lewis* v *Clay* (1897) 67 LJ QB 224 Lord Russell of Killowen CJ held that the plaintiff was not a holder in due course of the note, because he was not a person to whom, after its completion by and as between the immediate parties, the note had been negotiated. This view was accepted in *Smith* v *Prosser* [1907] 2 KB 735 and *Herdman* v *Wheeler* [1902] 1 KB 361 although in the latter case the court added that it was not prepared to hold that the payee of a note can never be a holder in due course. However, because of the inconsistency of certain sections of the Bills of Exchange Act 1882 either conclusion may be reached. Section 29(1) enacts that a holder in due course must have had the bill negotiated to him, since the section uses the word 'negotiated', and not 'issued or negotiated'. It therefore becomes necessary to determine the meaning of 'negotiation'. Those in favour of the view that the original payee can be a holder in due course rely on s. 31(1) which enacts:

> A bill is negotiated when it is transferred from one person to another in such a manner as to constitute the transferee the holder of the bill.

Since a holder is defined by s. 2 as including the 'payee or endorsee', s. 29(1) could be satisfied by a transfer of the bill to the payee, who therefore could become a holder in due course. Those who oppose this line of argument rely on s. 31(3), which provides that:

> A bill payable to order is negotiated by the endorsement of the holder completed by delivery.

Since the original payee does not become a holder by endorsement he cannot be a holder in due course.

The further reason given by the House of Lords in *R.E. Jones Ltd* v *Waring and Gillow Ltd* why a payee is not considered to be a holder in due course is that the definition section of the Bills of Exchange Act 1882 (s. 2) draws a distinction between the issue and the negotiation of a bill and thus shows that the two concepts must be mutually exclusive. This is not necessarily so, however. The issue of a bill, cheque or promissory note is defined by s. 2 as the: 'first delivery of a bill or note . . . to a person who takes it as a holder'.

The decision in *R.E. Jones Ltd* v *Waring and Gillow Ltd* has been accepted without question as correct in subsequent cases, namely in *Ayres* v *Moore* [1940] 1 KB 278 and *Arab Bank Ltd* v *Ross* [1952] 2 QB 216.

Completeness and regularity of the bill

A holder of a bill may be a holder in due course only if the bill is complete and regular on the face of it (and this includes the back) when he takes it. If the bill itself conveys a warning of possible defects because of its own formal irregularity, the rule of the overt market, caveat emptor, applies, and the holder, however honest, can acquire no better title than that his transferor has (*Awde* v *Dixon* (1851)

6 Ex 869). Consequently the holder takes, at his own risk, a blank acceptance or a bill which has been torn and the pieces pasted together. However, this situation has to be contrasted with that where the appearance of the bill is consistent with an accidental tearing. In *Ingham* v *Primrose* (1859) 7 CB NS 82 the acceptor of a bill, with the intention of cancelling it, tore it into two pieces and threw them into the street. The pieces were picked up by the endorser, joined together and the bill put into circulation. The acceptor was held liable to a bona fide holder for value because, although the acceptor had intended to cancel the bill, yet he did not in fact cancel it. The decision has been criticised and it is submitted it would now be differently decided although on the facts it was probably correct. It was accepted by the court in evidence that there was a common practice at the time, the mid 19th century, to provide against the loss of a bill in the post by dividing it in two and sending the pieces by successive posts (rather like the later practice of issuing bills in a set) and the payee joined the pieces again on the receipt of both. The court might, therefore, reasonably have held that there was nothing irregular on the face of the instrument.

The effect of s. 29(1) was discussed in *Arab Bank Ltd* v *Ross* [1952] 2 QB 216 where the plaintiff bank sued as holder in due course of two promissory notes made by the defendant in favour of 'Fathi and Faysal Nabulsy Company' which were endorsed on the reverse 'Fathi and Faysal Nabulsy'. The Court of Appeal held that the endorsements were sufficient to pass title to the bank but the bank did not become a holder in due course because the endorsement was irregular in that it did not set out the name of the endorser, the company, in full. The need for regularity was examined by Denning LJ, who stated an irregularity in the endorsement will deprive a subsequent holder of the rights of a holder in due course.

There is an exception to this rule of regularity where a bill is endorsed by a person for the purpose of making himself liable on the bill (e.g., to guarantee its payment). The signature of such a person raises the question whether the bill is complete and regular and whether there can be a holder in due course.

Overdue bills and notice of dishonour

A holder in due course must have taken the bill he holds before it was overdue and without notice of any prior dishonour which had taken place (Bills of Exchange Act 1882, s. 36). When a bill is overdue it remains transferable but it cannot be negotiated so as to confer a title on a subsequent holder free from defects affecting it when it became due (s. 36(2)). On the other hand, where a party takes a bill which has previously been dishonoured by non-acceptance with knowledge of that fact, he cannot be a holder in due course, but if a bill payable on demand is taken by A before it has been in circulation for an unreasonable time, although it has in fact already been presented for payment and dishonoured, A can still be a holder in due course if he does not have knowledge of the dishonour.

Necessity for value and good faith

A holder in due course must himself have given value or derive title through a prior holder in due course. He cannot take the benefit of the fact that he takes through a holder for value who was not a holder in due course. For example, A gives value for a bill with notice of a defect in the prior title and A endorses the bill to B who takes it gratuitously but without knowledge of the defect. B cannot be a holder in due course. The conditions for holding in due course cannot be split up among successive holders, and value and good faith must proceed from the same person to constitute a holder in due course. However, once this has happened, the benefits of being a holder in due course are enjoyed by subsequent holders of the bill and they therefore take free from defects which do not affect him. In order to be a holder in due course it is essential that the holder should act in good faith. Section 90 of the Bills of Exchange Act 1882 provides that a thing is done in good faith where it is in fact done honestly, whether or not it be done negligently. It is therefore a question of the state of mind of the person who takes the instrument at the time he takes it. A party who has not taken the bill in good faith, whether or not he gives value, will not therefore be able to retain it and will obtain no better a title than the person who negotiates it. In *Clarke* v *Shee* (1774) 1 Cowp 197 the plaintiff's clerk received notes and money for his master and with the defendant purchased illegal insurances and lottery tickets. The master was able to prove their identity and was entitled to recover.

Someone who buys a bill from a person who he realises is not its true owner cannot be a holder in due course and similarly a person who wilfully shuts his eyes to the existence of a defect of title which is apparent cannot be a holder in due course. Once the taker of the instrument has a suspicion that something is wrong with the bill, he is put on inquiry. In *Jones* v *Gordon* (1877) 2 App Cas 616 a London agent of a firm drew bills on the firm for £1,727. The firm accepted the bills. At the time both the drawer and acceptors were insolvent and contemplating bankruptcy, and the transaction was concocted in order to defraud the creditors of the acceptors. The drawer offered the bills to the plaintiff, who knew that the acceptor was in financial difficulties but thought that he might be able to pay part of the face value, and so purchased them for £200. Before the purchase the plaintiff also knew someone from whom he could acquire further information, but he made no inquiries. The acceptor subsequently became bankrupt and the plaintiff brought an action to recover the full amount of the bills. The court held that the plaintiff had sufficient knowledge of the affairs of the acceptor to realise that he was, or might be, a party to the fraud and he therefore could not prove for the full amount of the bills. Lord Blackburn examined the meaning of good faith (p. 629) and two important points arise out of his judgment, namely:

(a) If a man suspects something is wrong with a negotiable instrument, that is enough to prevent him from taking it in good faith. The suspicion need not be accurate, provided it is near the truth.

(b) If a man admits that he was careless in not discovering a defect in the title to the bill, he is entitled to be treated as having acted in good faith, but when a man says he was careless, the court may conclude that he was not in fact merely careless, but did suspect something to be wrong and wilfully closed his eyes to it. In that case he has not acted in good faith.

In *Bank of Credit and Commerce International SA* v *Dawson and Wright* 1987 FLR 342 it was held that a bank manager's conspiracy with a fraudulent customer may constitute lack of good faith and knowledge of a defective title on the part of the bank. The court therefore held that the plaintiff bank was not a holder in due course of three cheques either by taking them for collection or by having a lien, the bank being tainted by the knowledge of the bank manager.

It is more difficult to determine the question whether the doctrine of constructive notice can be applied to negotiable instruments, and here two issues have to be looked at, namely:

(a)   whether the person taking the instrument knows of facts which would make a reasonable business person suspicious and

(b)   even if he had no knowledge of such facts whether he was grossly negligent in not discovering the defect and whether in consequence he must be treated as having acted in bad faith.

On the former point, a direction was given to the jury in *Gill* v *Cubitt* (1824) 3 B & C 466 that they were to find a verdict for the defendant acceptor if they thought the plaintiff holder took the bill: 'under circumstances which ought to have excited the suspicion of a prudent and careful man'. This ruling was followed in *Down* v *Halling* (1825) 4 B & C 330. Had it been adhered to it would have created an objective standard for judging a holder's good faith and the standard of behaviour of a reasonable business person would have determined whether a holder was in fact a holder in due course. However, the courts rejected this line of reasoning in favour of a subjective test and the relevant question is not whether the person who took the instrument ought reasonably to have suspected a defect in the title to it but whether he must in fact have suspected it in the light of the knowledge he actually possessed.

The good faith requirement was discussed again in *London Joint Stock Bank* v *Simmons* [1892] AC 201 where a broker defrauded the owner of negotiable securities by pledging them, with other instruments belonging to other persons, to a bank as a security for a personal advance. The bank did not know whether the instruments belonged to the broker or other persons, or if they did belong to other persons whether the broker had any authority to deal with them. The bank made no inquiries. The broker absconded with the advance and when the bank realised the securities the plaintiff sued it for conversion. It was contended on behalf of the plaintiffs that the bank was under a duty to inquire as to the title of the person with whom it dealt, or alternatively as to the authority he possessed to deal with the instruments on behalf of his principals. The bank having failed to do this it could not be a holder in due course since it had not acted in good faith. The House of Lords, however, rejected this reasoning and said there were no circumstances known to the bank to cause it to entertain suspicions, and so the bank was entitled to retain and realise the securities, having taken the instruments in good faith and for value.

The theory of constructive notice has thus been rejected. Any views to the contrary that had arisen in the earlier House of Lords decision of *Earl of Sheffield* v *London Joint Stock Bank Ltd* (1888) 13 App Cas 333 were rejected. The facts of that case were that a money dealer had advanced large sums against securities belonging to the Earl of Sheffield, and pledged on his behalf by his agent. The money dealer then pledged these (and other securities) with the London Joint Stock Bank as security for certain advances. When the money dealer went into liquidation the owner of the securities and his agent brought an action against the bank to recover the stocks or their value. The House of Lords, reversing the Court of Appeal and the court of first instance, held the bank was not entitled to retain the securities. In *London Joint Stock Bank* v *Simmons* it was held that the *Earl of Sheffield's* case turned on its own special facts. The bank knew that the Earl of Sheffield's money broker pledged securities from time to time on both his own account and on behalf of his principals, and so the securities pledged could well have been those of his principals, whereas the bank honestly believed that Mr Simmons's stockbroker was authorised by his client to pledge securities in which they had authorised him to deal. In *Raphael* v *Bank of England* (1855) 17 CB 161 it was said that for the purposes of the rule contained in s. 29 constructive notice is not sufficient. Notice means actual notice, although it need not be specific or complete and so knowledge of the suspicious facts or a suspicion of something wrong combined with a wilful disregard of the means of knowledge will amount to notice.

Once a holder for value of instruments has notice that the person from whom he took them was not the unencumbered owner of them but had only a qualified, conditional or voidable interest, then, however honestly he may have acted in taking the instruments, he will acquire a limited interest equivalent to that which the person with whom he dealt could lawfully transfer. If, however, the holder for value deals with an agent with authority to deal in any way with the instruments in his possession, and the holder believes that the agent has full authority to deal with the particular instruments in question in that manner, and has no suspicion that his powers may be restricted, the holder is entitled to retain the instruments as owner, notwithstanding any fraudulent act of the agent committed on his principal.

The situation of the holder who is grossly negligent in taking the bill from the transferor remains to be dealt with (see *Snow* v *Peacock* (1826) 3 Bing 406. The transferee's title would be affected by a failure to take due caution if the circumstances indicate that inquiry is called for. This is consistent with the subjective test of good faith which now prevails. If a man takes a negotiable instrument honestly believing that he is acquiring a good title to it, even though that belief is negligent, he does acquire a good title unless he is so grossly negligent that he does not follow up suspicions which he must have entertained (see *Goodman* v *Harvey* (1836) 4 Ad & El 870).

It is therefore not sufficient to establish negligence or carelessness, however serious, on the part of the holder of a bill to deprive him of the status of a holder in due course. He must have appreciated from the circumstances that the title of his transferor was suspect and he must have failed to satisfy himself by inquiry that his suspicions were groundless. The most important case on this point is probably *Raphael* v *Bank of England* (1855) 17 CB 161, where bank notes which had been stolen and on which payment had been stopped were paid although a circular notifying the theft and giving a list of the stolen notes was sent to bankers and money changers, including St Paul and Co. One of the notes was changed by a partner in St Paul and Co., who gave evidence that he did not recall that the number of the note corresponded to one listed in the circular at the time the note was changed but he also did not look at the file of notices of lost and stolen notes. This was accepted as a fact at the trial and it was held that the note was therefore taken bona fide within the meaning of the rule. On appeal the Court of Commons Pleas upheld the decision. Cresswell J said:

214 Rights and Liabilities of the Parties to a Bill of Exchange

A person who takes a negotiable instrument bona fide for value has undoubtedly a good title, and is not affected by the want of title of the party from whom he takes it. His having the means of knowing that the security had been lost or stolen, and neglecting to avail himself thereof, may amount to negligence.

However, it is new settled law that if a person takes an instrument honestly, he has a good title to it although he may have acted negligently, unless there is gross negligence.

The case was accepted as good law in *Venables* v *Baring Brothers and Co.* [1892] 3 Ch 527, where American railway bonds, acknowledging indebtedness 'to bearer' and promising to pay the holder the principal sum and the interest on presentation of coupons, were stolen and came into the hands of the plaintiff for value. The theft had been advertised and the plaintiff would have known of it had he not been negligent in failing to check the bond numbers against the advertisement giving notice of the theft. It was held that since the instruments were negotiable the plaintiff's negligence did not disentitle him from asserting a title to the bonds as a bona fide holder.

Title of the holder in due course

The general rule is that if a person's title to a bill is defective, the person to whom he transfers it will obtain no better title to it than he himself has, and the true owner of the bill can, therefore, enforce his rights notwithstanding any ineffective transfers of the title to it by other persons. Thus, if someone forges an endorsement of a bill to a person who believes the endorsement to be genuine, the endorsement is a nullity and the true owner may recover the bill and enforce it himself. In *London Joint Stock Bank* v *Simmons* [1892] AC 201 Lord Herschell observed that:

> The general rule of the law is, that where a person has obtained the property of another from one who is dealing with it without the authority of the true owner, no title is acquired as against that owner, even though full value be given, and the property be taken in the belief that an unquestionable title thereto is being obtained.

It was said by Willis that if the holder for value of a negotiable instrument took it with actual notice that the person with whom he was dealing had only a limited interest, however honestly he may have acted in so doing, he cannot acquire a greater interest in it than that which the person with whom he dealt could lawfully confer (see Willis, *Law of Negotiable Securities*, 5th ed. (London: Sweet & Maxwell, 1930).

If an endorser is induced to endorse a bill by mistake, the negotiation of the bill is void, and the endorsee obtains no title to it despite his good faith. If an endorsement is merely voidable by the transferor (e.g., if it is induced by misrepresentation or undue influence), the title of a subsequent holder in due course is unimpeachable and this applies also to any person who acquires the bill for value subsequent to the voidable endorsement without notice of the endorser's right to avoid it. In *London Joint Stock Bank* v *Simmons* Lord Herschell said:

There is an exception to the general rule, however, in the case of negotiable instruments. Any person in possession of these may convey a good title to them, even when he is acting in fraud of the true owner, and although such owner does nothing tending to mislead the person taking them.

Defects of title from which the holder in due course takes free

A holder in due course of a bill of exchange, in addition to having all the rights and powers of a holder is provided by the Bills of Exchange Act 1882 with certain additional protection. Section 38(2) of the Act provides that a holder in due course holds the bill free from any defect of title of prior parties, as well as from mere personal defences available to prior parties.

Defects of title are enumerated, although not exhaustively, in s. 29(2) of the Act which provides that the title of a person who negotiates a bill is defective when he obtains the bill or the acceptance by fraud, duress, or force and fear, or other unlawful means, or for an illegal consideration, or when he negotiates it in breach of faith, or under such circumstances as amount to a fraud.

The expression 'personal defences' in s. 38(2) refers to such defences as set-off and counterclaim and probably covers defences such as omission of the duties of presentation. The operation of the section may be exemplified as follows: A, the holder of a bill, endorses it to B, who is a person who cannot be made liable on a bill (for example, a minor or a member of a foreign embassy who enjoys diplomatic immunity). The bill is stolen from B by C, who forges B's endorsement and disposes of the bill to D, who fulfils the conditions to be a holder in due course. D endorses the bill to E and E to F, who is also a holder in due course. F can sue D and E on the dishonour of the bill, and it makes no difference if E obtained the bill from D by fraud. But F cannot sue A or B, who became parties to the bill before the forgery of the forged endorsement of B, which is, of course, a nullity.

The list of defects in s. 29(2) of which the holder in due course takes free is not exhaustive; the section states 'in particular' that the title of a transferor is defective when affected by fraud, duress or one of the other specified defects. The holder in due course will be able to enforce the instrument despite these defects although, if duress, fraud or illegality is proved, he will have to prove positively that he took the bill in good faith without notice of such defects. Duress is a common law concept and is supplemented by the equitable doctrine of undue influence, which renders a contract voidable if a party is induced to enter into it by the improper influence of the other. The fact that undue influence is not mentioned specifically in s. 29(2) does not mean that a party who obtains the transfer of a negotiable instrument by such means acquires an unimpeachable title, although a subsequent holder in due course may do so. The words 'or other unlawful means' in s. 29(2) probably cover undue influence. Similarly, the section makes no mention of transfers procured by misrepresentation and once again it is clear that the words 'or other unlawful means' cover misrepresentations and that the subsequent holder in due course would take free from such a defect.

The wording of ss. 29 and 38 is in fact confusing because s. 29 refers to defects in the title of a person who negotiates a bill, whereas s. 38(2) speaks of a holder in due course, who takes free of any defect of title of prior parties, and s. 38(3) refers to defects in the holder's title. These modes of reference must be assumed to refer to the same thing, i.e., title and the difference between the reference to the transferor's defective title and the reference to a holder in due course acquiring free from all defects of title must be considered insignificant.

The Act provides that every holder is prima facie deemed to be a holder in due course but if it can be proved or admitted that the acceptance, issue or subsequent negotiation of a bill was affected with fraud, duress, or force and fear, or other unlawful means, or an illegal consideration, the burden of proof is shifted, and the holder who sues on the bill must prove that value has been given in good faith for the bill subsequent to the fraud or illegality (s. 30(2)). It will be observed that in s. 29(2) there are six listed defects but s. 30(2), which imposes the onus of proving that a defect of title has occurred, lists only five defects (the reference to 'or other unlawful means' is omitted from s. 30(2) and 'illegality' is included generally, whereas under s. 29(2) 'illegal consideration' is specifically recognised); while in connection with the consequent onus of proof on the holder who sues on the bill to prove that value has subsequently been given for the bill in good faith, only two defects are specified, namely fraud and illegality. This makes no difference in substance since the principle is clear and an enunciation of the defects of title from which a holder in due course takes free is unnecessary. The intention of the Act, like the common law decisions on which it is based, is that a holder in due course takes a bill free from all defects of title with the exception of those to which he is made specifically subject, e.g., forgery.

12 Cheques on a Banker and the Protection of the Paying and Collecting Banks

A cheque is an instrument of payment and it instructs the bank on which it is drawn to make payment to the named payee from funds standing to the credit of the customer. The cheque is usually drawn payable on demand and it is dated so it will be payable immediately or within a reasonable time. Although cheques are negotiable instruments they are usually presented by the payee to his bank for collection and are rarely endorsed in favour of a third party. Indeed, many banks have adopted the practice of printing cheque forms for the use of their customers crossed 'account payee' with the result that the collecting bank will only receive it for the credit of the named payee (see pp. 219–21).

Although the law relating to cheques has closely followed that relating to bills of exchange it has been necessary to enact specific provisions for cheques. In *Ramchurn Mullick* v *Luchmeechund Radakissen* (1854) 9 Moo PC 46 at 69 Parke B expressed the view that a cheque seemed to be '. . . a peculiar sort of instrument, in many respects resembling a bill of exchange, but in some entirely different'. It might, therefore, be feasible to have a separate regime dealing with cheques. This view is supported by the Jack Committee Report on Banking Services (Cm 622, 1989). The UNCITRAL Convention on Bills of Exchange and Promissory Notes specifically excludes cheques. The purpose of this chapter is to examine provisions of the Bills of Exchange Act 1882 which apply specifically to cheques, together with the provisions in the Cheques Act 1957 and the Cheques Act 1992.

CROSSED CHEQUES

The practice of crossing cheques originated in the bankers' clearing house in the late eighteenth or early nineteenth century. Clerks who worked for various bankers to whom cheques had been delivered for collection established the practice of writing across the cheques the names of their employers in order to allow payment to be made and for accounts to be settled by the clerks of the clearing house (*Bellamy* v *Marjoribanks* (1852) 7 Ex 389 at 402). The crossing of cheques by the drawer is a later development but it was certainly recognised by the middle of the nineteenth century (Holden, *History of Negotiable Instruments in English Law* (London: Athlone Press, 1995), p. 230).

Crossings were first recognised by statute in the Drafts on Bankers Act 1856, which was supplemented by the Drafts on Bankers Act 1858, which made the fraudulent alteration or obliteration of a crossing a forgery. This was followed by *Smith v Union Bank of London* (1875) 1 QBD 31, where the court held that the negotiability of a cheque was not affected by the crossing on it and the payee had no remedy against the drawee bank although payment on the cheque was made contrary to the crossing. As a result the Crossed Cheques Act 1876 was passed which introduced the 'not negotiable' crossing. The Act also provided a remedy for the true owner of a crossed cheque if it was paid contrary to the crossing and provided protection to a bank which paid a crossed cheque. The Bills of Exchange Act 1882 repealed the 1876 Act and provided for crossings in general in ss. 76–82. Section 82 of the Bills of Exchange Act 1882 has in turn, has been repealed by s. 4 of the Cheques Act 1957, which gives extended protection to the collecting bank. In addition, the Cheques Act 1992 has been enacted to counter the effect, at common law, of the 'account payee' crossing, to which the common law courts failed to give effect literally.

Purpose of the crossing

The purpose of crossing a cheque is to reduce the risk of the instrument being misappropriated, especially where the post is used as a means of delivering the cheque to the payee. The drawee bank cannot pay a crossed cheque over the counter, but only on presentation by a bank. If the drawee bank acts contrary to the mandate given in the form of a crossing then it is liable to the drawer for breach of contract and cannot debit the drawer's account. However, the impact the crossing will have on a cheque will depend on the nature of the crossing itself.

The Bills of Exchange Act 1882 recognises two basic crossings, i.e., the general and the special crossing. In practice, the special crossing is now obsolete. A cheque may be crossed generally by placing two transverse lines across the face of the instrument. Cheques are normally pre-printed in this manner and this in itself is sufficient to constitute a general crossing. However, the two transverse lines may be accompanied by the words 'and company' or an abbreviation, or by the words 'not negotiable', or by the words 'account payee', which have assumed a special status since the Cheques Act 1992.

The special crossing is executed by placing on the face of the cheque the name of a specific bank which is expected to receive payment on behalf of the named payee. The two transverse lines are unnecessary, but may be added to the cheque. This type of crossing is rarely added by the drawer or the holder of the cheque.

Crossed cheques and the words 'not negotiable'

Section 81 of the Bills of Exchange Act 1882 provides for the 'not negotiable' crossing. The words do not have to appear within the crossing, provided they appear on the face of the cheque, although ss. 76–7 refer to the words in the context of the crossing. The Jack Committee on Banking services examined the words 'not negotiable' and concluded that although often used, the words are rarely properly understood. It commented that the 'not negotiable' crossing is often erroneously treated as synonymous with 'not transferable'.

The effect of the crossing is to restrict the negotiability of the instrument but not its transferability. A person who takes a cheque with such a crossing cannot obtain a better title than that of the transferor and hence he in turn can only confer a limited title to a subsequent transferee. Consequently, although a transferee can be a holder for value, he cannot become a holder in due course. In *Great Western Railway Co.* v *London and County Banking Co. Ltd* [1901] AC 414 the Earl of Halsbury LC (at p. 418) discussed the effect of the 'not negotiable' crossing and said that a person who takes a cheque so crossed takes the risk of the person from whom he took it having no title and therefore not being capable of passing a valid title. The effect of the 'not negotiable' crossing and s. 81 had also been examined by the Court of Appeal in *Great Western Railway Co.* v *London and County Banking Co. Ltd* [1900] 2 QB 464, where Vaughan Williams LJ had said (at p. 474) that the transferability of the cheque is not affected by the words 'not negotiable' but only 'its negotiability'. (See also *Universal Guarantee Pty Ltd* v *National Bank of Australasia Ltd* [1965] 1 WLR 691; *Hibernian Bank Ltd* v *Gysin and Hanson* [1939] 1 KB 483.)

Cheques crossed 'account payee'

Although the 'not negotiable' crossing was introduced by an Act of Parliament in 1876 there is evidence to suggest that some time prior to that period, drawers of cheques had devised another way of making cheques secure, in particular from fraud and theft. When the Crossed Cheques Bill 1876 was being debated in Parliament, an amendment was moved which provided that where a cheque was crossed generally or specially, a holder might add to the crossing the words 'For the account of . . .' or any abbreviation, followed by the name of any person to whose account the cheque was to be credited. The amendment was withdrawn and it was not until the Cheques Act 1992 that statutory effect was given to the words 'account payee'.

Although the words 'account payee' originally tended to appear as the only addition to a crossing, the modern practice was to add also the words 'not negotiable'. Although the general understanding therefore was that the words 'account payee' rendered the cheque non-transferable, a number of cases where the words 'account payee' were examined established that the words did not have such an effect. The courts held that the words merely put the collecting bank on inquiry by signifying the account to which the proceeds from the cheque are to be placed. Consequently, if the collecting bank received payment to the credit of anyone other than the named payee without making sure that the payee consented to that payment the bank would be liable in negligence and in breach of s. 4 of the Cheques Act 1957 (see *Akrokerri (Atlantic) Mines Ltd* v *Economic Bank* [1904] 2 KB 465; *House Property Co. of London Ltd* v *London County and Westminster Bank* (1915) 84 LJ KB 1846; *Universal Guarantee Pty Ltd* v *National Bank of Australasia Ltd* [1965] 1 WLR 691).

The courts took the view that the words 'account payee' were not a sufficient indication of any intention to prohibit non-transferability of the cheque. Instead, the courts took the view that it is impossible for a drawee bank to know, when a cheque is passed through clearing, for whose account it is collected and it could not therefore assume responsibility for ensuring that the proceeds are credited to the payee's account. The courts therefore held that the words 'account payee' are not treated as an instruction to the drawee bank but as an instruction to the collecting bank that the proceeds of the cheque are to be applied to the credit of the named payee. The 'payee' is the person in whose favour the cheque is to be drawn and not the holder of the cheque by negotiation (*House Property Co. of London Ltd* v *London County and Westminster Bank*). If the collecting bank collected the cheque for any person other than the named payee then it took the risk of being held liable in conversion if that person had a defective title.

The Review Committee on Banking Services and the Law (Cm 622, 1989) recommended that cheques should remain transferable if the instrument contained an 'account payee' crossing and proposed that a new bank payment order (in addition to the cheque) should be used which, although having the attributes of a cheque, could only be used to make payment to the named payee. Thus, the instrument would be non-negotiable and non-transferable. The use of two separate instruments reflects the approach adopted by the Australian Cheques and Payment Orders Act 1986. This view was rejected in the Government White Paper presented to Parliament in March 1990 (Cm 1026). The White Paper recommended that the natural and common understanding of the 'account payee' or 'account payee only' crossing was that it rendered the cheque non-transferable and this view was given statutory effect by the Cheques Act 1992. The Act amends certain provisions of the Bills of Exchange Act 1882 and introduces a new s. 81A to the 1882 Act. The new section provides:

(1) Where a cheque is crossed and bears across its face the words 'account payee' or 'a/c payee', either with or without the word 'only', the cheque shall not be transferable, but shall only be valid as between the parties thereto.

Section 81A (1) effectively applies s. 8(1) of the Bills of Exchange Act 1882 to the new s. 81A so that cheques crossed 'account payee' are given effect as non-transferable and non-negotiable. Such cheques are only valid as between the original drawer and the original payee. If the payee endorses the cheque in favour of a third party, that person will not acquire a valid title and cannot enforce payment on the cheque. In reality, most UK banks have adopted the practice of having the 'account payee' crossing printed on cheque forms issued not only to customers who are consumers, but also to business customers, who are more likely to use endorsement as a method of transferring title to the instrument.

A further issue which arises is whether a cheque crossed 'account payee' is a bill of exchange under the Bills of Exchange Act 1882. The definition of a bill of exchange under s. 3(2) of that Act requires the instrument (amongst other things) to be drawn 'to or to the order of a specified person, or to bearer'. Clearly, an instrument drawn valid as between the original drawer and payee falls within the definition of a bill of exchange because the instrument is payable to a named person.

The new s. 81A(2) of the Bills of Exchange Act 1882 gives effect to another proposal made in the White Paper. It provides that:

(2) A banker is not to be treated for the purposes of section 80 . . . as having been negligent by reason only of his failure to concern himself with any purported endorsement of a cheque which . . . is not transferable.

The subsection ensures that a drawee or paying bank which pays a cheque crossed 'account payee' in favour of the original payee and ignores any purported endorsement of the cheque will still enjoy the statutory protection conferred on banks under the Bills of Exchange Act 1882 and the Cheques Act 1957.

LIABILITY OF PAYING AND COLLECTING BANKS FOR WRONGFUL PAYMENT

Paying bank's liability in common law

The relationship between a bank and its customer when the bank pays a cheque drawn by the customer is in essence that of agent and principal. The bank must conform to the strict terms of the mandate given to it by the customer; the written cheque itself acting as the mandate to make payment. If the bank makes a payment contrary to the customer's mandate, it acts at its peril and cannot debit the customer's account. The bank will also lose the statutory protection conferred on it. A paying bank may find it has acted without a mandate from the customer in a number of ways, for example, where:

(a)   a cheque form has been stolen and completed so that the drawer's signature is a forgery, or

(b)   there is an unauthorised alteration of the cheque (e.g., where the holder increases the amount of the cheque), or

(c)   where an agent acts in excess of his authority in drawing the cheque.

In all of these cases there is a possibility that the bank may be able to raise an estoppel against the customer where the customer has either facilitated the fraud (although the customer is under no general duty of care) or has misled the bank into believing that the cheques are valid.

The bank may also find itself liable where, for example:

(d)   it makes payment on a cheque which has been countermanded, although the bank will be protected where the customer's instructions are ambiguous or countermand is impossible and payment has been made, or

(e)   payment is made against a cheque on which an endorsement is forged.

The problem of forged endorsements is less likely to arise since banks have adopted the practice of pre-printing cheque forms with the words 'account payee'. However, the problem may still arise where the customer requests open cheques or those not bearing the words 'account payee'. If a cheque drawn on such a form is misappropriated and an endorsement forged then some statutory protection may be available to a paying bank.

Liability in conversion

Where a bank acts in breach of a customer's mandate in connection with the payment of a cheque it may find itself liable not only in contract for breach of mandate but also at common law for conversion. Conversion is a wrongful interference with goods (including documents) by taking, using or destroying them with the owner's right to immediate possession (*Lloyds Bank Ltd v Chartered Bank of India, Australia and China* [1929] 1 KB 40). Conversion is a tort of strict liability and any inconsistent dealing with goods or chattels, however innocent, will suffice to impose liability.

The person to whom the right of action in conversion is available is called the 'true owner' of the bill, cheque etc. in the Bills of Exchange Act 1882, but no definition is given of the term. It would appear to mean a holder of the instrument who can prove that he has (a) ownership and possession of it, or (b) possession of it, or (c) an immediate right to possess it, without either actual ownership or actual possession.

A person will be a true owner of a bill, note or cheque if his title is void.

The old case of *Tate v Wilts and Dorset Bank* (1899) 1 LDB 286 supports the view that there is no conversion of a cheque where the holder has a voidable, and not a void, title. Thus, where the customer has a revocable title which has not been avoided or revoked, at the time the money was received and handed over, an action for conversion will not lie. However, some doubt was cast over the *Tate* case by Sankey LJ in *Lloyds Bank Ltd v Chartered Bank of India, Australia and China*.

The question whether the drawer or payee is the true owner of a cheque may depend on whether the drawer was authorised to make payment in that manner, but even if the drawer retains ownership the payee may be entitled to immediate possession. In *International Factors Ltd v Rodriguez* [1979] QB 351 the plaintiffs and company entered into an agreement under which the plaintiffs agreed to purchase all the company's book debts. It was agreed that if any payment in respect of the assigned debts was paid directly to the company, it would hold the full amount on trust for the plaintiffs. The company received four cheques totalling £11,370 towards payment of debts which were subject to the agreement and arranged for these to be paid into its own bank account. It was held that the plaintiffs were entitled to sue in conversion because the agreement gave them a right to immediate possession of the cheques, since it imposed on the company an obligation to hand over immediately to the plaintiffs any cheques which came into its possession. The court approved *Marquess of Bute v Barclays Bank Ltd* [1955] 1 QB 202, where it was held that the mere fact that cheques were made payable to the defendant was not a sufficient reply to the plaintiffs' claim that they were entitled to the cheques in equity. In order to discharge a cheque, payment by the drawee bank must not only be made to a holder but it must be made in 'due course' (Bills of Exchange Act 1882, s. 59), which means that it must be paid in good faith to the holder without knowledge of any defect in title (ibid.).

The bank's liability for conversion of the instrument is independent of any issue relating to the bank's right to debit the customer's account. The bank may find itself liable in conversion to the true owner of the instrument and also unable to debit the customer's account. It therefore stands to bear a double loss. Where the document converted is a negotiable instrument, the damages are its face value.

A plaintiff who has a remedy in conversion is entitled to 'waive the tort' and sue instead for the same amount as money had and received. By bringing an action for money had and received a plaintiff does not waive the wrong but he waives the form of remedy available in conversion (*United Australia Ltd v Barclays Bank Ltd* [1941] AC 1).

Defences available to the paying bank

Under s. 59 of the Bills of Exchange Act 1882 payment must be made in 'due course' by or on behalf of the drawee or acceptor in order to discharge liability on a bill or cheque. Although the section does not require physical presentation of the instrument there are several requirements which must be satisfied. Payment must be made at or after the maturity of the bill to a holder in good faith and without notice that his title is defective. It follows that if the drawee bank pays a cheque to someone other than the holder that will not discharge the cheque. The term 'holder' is defined in s. 2 of the Act and includes a person who has possession of a bearer cheque (*Charles* v *Blackwell* (1877) 2 CPD 151). The position differs in the case of a cheque payable to the order of a specified person. Such an instrument can only be transferred by endorsement and delivery (s. 31(3)). If the payee's endorsement is forged on a cheque, any subsequent party does not become a holder of the instrument, and therefore cannot be a holder in due course. The holder of a bill is defined as 'the payee or endorsee of a bill . . . who is in possession of it . . .' (s. 2) but a forged endorsement is wholly inoperative. Furthermore, the instrument is not a bearer instrument since it was neither drawn payable to bearer nor has it become payable to bearer by reason of the inoperative endorsement. A person who takes a cheque under a forged endorsement is not a holder of the instrument and payment to such a person will not amount to a payment in due course so as to constitute a discharge under s. 59.

The bank not only has to conform to the Bills of Exchange Act 1882 but must also conform to the customer's mandate when making payment, for example, a person may be the holder of a cheque although payment on it has been countermanded. A cheque is a bill of exchange payable on demand and therefore the issue of maturity does not arise. However, a collecting bank will not receive a post-dated cheque for collection and if a post-dated cheque is presented for payment prior to its date, it should be dishonoured by the paying bank.

Protection under s. 60 of the Bills of Exchange Act 1882

As the use of cheques became more common the banks were faced with the increased problem of forged cheques. One of the commonest problems was forgery of the payee's endorsement. A paying bank has no means of knowing or verifying the payee's signature. Moreover, the cheque might have been negotiated several times prior to presentation for payment. Where a bank failed to discharge its obligation to make payment to the proper payee or endorsee because of a forged endorsement then, in the absence of some special rule to the contrary, the bank was required to make a second payment to the true owner of the cheque, and could not debit the customer's account in respect of the first payment. The burden on the paying bank was felt to be unreasonable and s. 19 of the Stamp Act 1853, which, in so far as it applied to cheques, was re-enacted in s. 60 of the Bills of Exchange Act 1882, was passed to protect the paying bank in respect of payments made on forged endorsements. Section 60 of the 1882 Act provides that where a bank in good faith and in the ordinary course of business pays a cheque on which an endorsement is subsequently found to be forged or unauthorised, the payment will be treated as having been made in due course. Thus, where s. 60 applies the bank is under no obligation to make a second payment out of its funds.

In order to be protected by s. 60, a payment must be made in 'good faith and in the ordinary course of business'. The good faith requirement is satisfied if the bank acts honestly, but it does not necessarily require the bank to act with care. The section does not specifically provide that a bank must act without negligence. In *Carpenters' Co.* v *British Mutual Banking Co. Ltd* [1938] 1 KB 511, at first instance, Branson J found that the defendant bank had paid cheques in good faith and in the ordinary course of business and was, therefore, protected by s. 60 notwithstanding its negligence in collecting them on behalf of the plaintiff's clerk, who had forged the payees' endorsements on them.

Whether a bank has acted in the 'ordinary course of business' for the purposes of s. 60 is to be determined by referring to banking practice rather than law (see Lord Halsbury LC in *Bank of England* v *Vagliano Brothers* [1891] AC 107 at 117). In *Carpenters' Co.* v *British Mutual Banking Co. Ltd* the learned judges of the Court of Appeal were divided on the issue whether negligence by the paying bank precludes the protection of s. 60 of the Bills of Exchange Act 1882. MacKinnon LJ, dissenting, said:

> A thing that is done not in the ordinary course of business may be done negligently; but I do not think the converse is necessarily true. A thing may be done negligently and yet be done in the ordinary course of business.

It is generally thought that the view of the majority in the case is more acceptable, so that provided the paying bank acts 'in the ordinary course of business' it is protected by s. 60 even though it is guilty of negligence. Similar views have been expressed in other jurisdictions in respect of their equivalent to s. 60. In the Australian case of *Smith* v *Commercial Banking Co. of Sydney Ltd* (1910) 11 CLR 667 the court was of the opinion that a bank may be negligent and yet act in the ordinary course of business. However, a bank which pays in obviously suspicious circumstances will lose the protection of the section. In *Auchteroni and Co.* v *Midland Bank Ltd* [1928] 2 KB 294 the court held that the bank was justified in paying over the counter a bill for £876 9s, but that a different course might have been adopted if a bill for a larger amount had been presented by, for example, an office boy or a tramp.

In *Questions on Banking Practice*, 11th ed. (London: Institute of Bankers, 1978), No. 503 at p. 170 it is stated that:

> The practical guidance is that when dealing with a negotiable instrument the banker does not need to view every presentation with suspicion. Business prudence in doubtful circumstances may demand care, but the need for enquiry arises only in exceptional cases. If the appearance of the presenter or the relevant facts, including the amount of the cheque, occasion suspicion, then the prudent course is to institute the necessary enquiries before effecting payment.

Such authority as exists would therefore appear to suggest that the requirement that payment be in the ordinary course of business is less stringent than the requirement that the bank act without negligence.

The situation which is not expressly provided for under s. 60 is whether the protection conferred to the paying bank is restricted to circumstances where the endorsement is used as a method of negotiating the cheque or is also available where an endorsement is merely placed as a receipt of payment by the bank. The dictum of Byles J in *Keene* v *Beard* (1860) 8 CB NS 372 would suggest that the signature of a person receiving payment of a cheque is not an endorsement but merely a receipt. However, the case was decided before the 1882 Act defined the term endorsement. In *Brighton Empire and Eden Syndicate* v *London and County Bank* (1904) *The Times*, 24 March 1904 the view was expressed that a signature written on the back of a cheque prior to payment in cash by the drawee bank is an endorsement under s. 60 of the Bills of Exchange Act 1882. Banks used to insist on the payee endorsing all cheques before paying them into an account or cashing them; one of the purposes of this was to confer protection on the paying bank under s. 60 with the collecting bank being treated as a holder of the cheque. This led to a considerable wastage of time and one of the objects of s. 1 of the Cheques Act 1957, was to reduce the need to check endorsements. Section 1 was drafted in such wide terms as to release a paying bank from any obligation to concern itself with endorsements on cheques and from any liability which might otherwise have arisen from the absence, invalidity or irregularity of an endorsement on a cheque, whether the bank was actually making payment to the named payee or some other person.

Many of the problems relating to forged endorsements have been solved by the Cheques Act 1992, which provides that the effect of the account payee crossing is to render the cheque non-transferable.

Section 80 of the Bills of Exchange Act 1882

Section 80 of the Bills of Exchange Act 1882 provides protection to the paying bank in addition to s. 60, although s. 80 is restricted specifically to crossed cheques. Section 80 should be read in conjunction with s. 79 of the Act, which sets out the duties of the bank in respect of payment of crossed cheques. Section 80 provides that where a crossed cheque has been paid in accordance with the tenor of the crossing, in good faith and without negligence, the paying bank is placed in the same position as if the cheque had been paid to the true owner. The requirement under s. 60 that the payment should be made in the ordinary course of business is replaced by the requirement that payment should be made in good faith.

As the paying bank is protected in respect of forged endorsements on cheques, whether crossed or uncrossed, by s. 60 of the Bills of Exchange Act 1882, the need for s. 80 is not apparent. The existence of the two sections is historical. Section 80 finds its origin in the form of s. 9 of the Crossed Cheques Act 1876, which, as the title of the Act implies, was concerned exclusively with crossed cheques. The 1876 Act was repealed by the Bills of Exchange Act 1882 although its provisions were re-enacted in the form of ss. 76–82 of the 1882 Act. Thus, s. 9 of the 1876 Act was re-enacted as s. 80 of the 1882. The need to have two separate provisions has been questioned by Milnes Holden, *History of Negotiable Instruments* (London: Pitman, 1955). However, s. 80, unlike s. 60, confers protection not only on the paying bank but also on the drawer whose cheque was received by the payee.

Modern line of authorities

To interpret the Bills of Exchange Act 1882, ss. 60 and 80, it is necessary to examine the authorities which have held that where there are surrounding circumstances known to the bank which put the bank on inquiry the bank must act with due care and it may not simply rely on the customer's mandate as expressed in the cheque (see *Selangor United Rubber Estates Ltd* v *Cradock (No. 3)* [1968] 1 WLR 1555 on the question of negligence). The *Selangor* case was approved and applied in *Karak Rubber Co. Ltd* v *Burden (No. 2)* [1972] 1 WLR 602 and *Rowlandson* v *National Westminster Bank Ltd* [1978] 1 WLR 798. The rationale behind these cases has been widely accepted (see *Ryan* v *Bank of New South Wales* [1978] VR 555). Consequently, a bank which insists on a duty of care from its customer when the latter issues his mandate must equally be under a reciprocal duty to the customer, especially when the bank is aware or ought to be aware that the customer's agent is acting unlawfully and dishonestly.

Section 1 of the Cheques Act 1957

Section 1 of the Cheques Act 1957 abolished the necessity for endorsements on cheques, with certain exceptions. The section provides that where a banker in good faith and in the ordinary course of business pays a cheque drawn on him which is not endorsed or is irregularly endorsed, he does not, in doing so, incur any liability by reason only of the absence of, or irregularity in, the endorsement, and is deemed to have paid in due course.

Sections 60 and 80 of the Bills of Exchange Act 1882 only protect the paying bank where the endorsement of an order cheque, which appears to be regular on its face, turns out to be forged. Where a payment is made for a cheque which is irregularly endorsed, that payment is made both negligently and outside the ordinary course of business. Thus, the protection conferred by s. 1 of the Cheques Act 1975 becomes important. A regular endorsement in the case of an individual is one which purports to be that of the payee or endorsee, by reproducing exactly the name as shown on the cheque. In *Slingsby* v *District Bank Ltd* [1932] 1 KB 544 Wright J said:

But I think the paying bank ought to require a signature indicating the position exactly as it is indicated by the mandate describing the payee.

Where a cheque is drawn 'John Smith' and is endorsed 'J Smith', that will be treated as a regular endorsement. If a company endorses a cheque and omits the words 'Ltd' or 'Co.' when they form part of its description, the endorsement will be irregular. A cheque may be endorsed by a person acting in a representative capacity. In such circumstances the endorsement is not regular if the representative capacity stated is not reasonably compatible with the authority to endorse (see *Gerald McDonald and Co.* v *Nash and Co.* [1924] AC 625). An endorsement is irregular when it differs materially from the description of the person endorsing it. The discrepancy in the endorsement renders the instrument irregular, although it may not affect its negotiability (*Arab Bank Ltd* v *Ross* [1952] 2 QB 216).

Section 1 of the Cheques Act 1957 applies to both crossed and uncrossed cheques and analogous instruments. The protection is not available where, e.g., the paying bank paid a crossed cheque in cash over the counter, since that would not be in the ordinary course of business.

Before 1957 a paying bank dishonoured any cheque that was irregularly endorsed or on which the endorsement was missing. This led to the paying bank having to reject substantial numbers of cheques and led the Mocatta Committee on Cheque Endorsement (Cmnd 3, 1956) to recommend that endorsements should no longer be required for cheques other than those presented for payment over the counter. This led to the enactment of s. 1 of the Cheques Act 1957. However, the Committee of London Clearing Banks took the view that the use of endorsements would be retained in certain circumstances. In a circular of 23 September 1957 the Committee stated that the paying bank would continue to insist on an endorsement in the following circumstances: (a) where cheques are presented for payment over the counter; (b) in respect of combined cheque and receipt forms marked 'R'; and (c) where cheques payable to joint payees are paid into an account which is not maintained in the name of all the payees.

Problems arising from the provisions of the 1882 and 1957 Acts

The Jack Committee on Banking Services (Cm 622, 1989) accepted that protection for the paying bank along the lines currently conferred is necessary. The existing statutory provisions are not wholly consistent. There is considerable overlap between the sections and their ambit and relationship is, at times, unclear. Even the prerequisites of ss. 60 and 80 of the Bills of Exchange Act 1882 and s. 1 of the Cheques Act 1957 are not consistent. Sections 60 and 1 require the bank to act in 'good faith' and 'in the ordinary course of business' whilst s. 80 requires the bank to act in 'good faith' and 'without negligence'. Moreover ss. 60 and 80 apply only to cheques, whilst s. 1 applies to cheques and other analogous instruments. Sections 60 and 1 require the paying bank to act 'in the ordinary course of business', whilst s. 80 does not impose that requirement. Section 80, unlike s. 60, applies to both order and bearer cheques.

Protection of the collecting bank

One of the most important functions of a bank is to collect the proceeds of cheques and other instruments on behalf of its customer; these instruments are payable either on the collecting bank itself or on other banks. Where a bank collects a cheque for payment it acts either as a collecting bank (where the bank acquires no proprietary title to the cheque) or as a discounting bank (*Re Farrow's Bank Ltd* [1923] 1 Ch 41). A cheque is discounted where the bank agrees to grant its customer an overdraft against the proceeds or actually allows the customer to draw against a cheque before the instrument is cleared. In *M'Lean* v *Clydesdale Banking Co.* (1883) 9 App Cas 95 it was held that the bank will also assume the role of a discounting bank where it reduces the customer's existing overdraft by the amount of a cheque pending clearance. Regardless of the capacity the bank acts in, it can be sued by the true owner of the cheque if the person for whom the bank acted for collection had a defective title and the remedies available to the true owner are identical.

Where a collecting bank acts as an agent for collection it may either be acting in a purely agency function, although (applying *Foley* v *Hill* (1848) 2 HL Cas 28) the collecting bank will acquire title to the deposits, or, if the customer is overdrawn, it will collect the proceeds in anticipation of reducing the amount of the overdraft. The bank may, therefore, be exposed to the danger that it collects the cheque for someone other than the true owner of the instrument. In such circumstances the customer is committing the tort of conversion and using the bank which acts in good faith merely as a vehicle for the misappropriation. The collecting bank, notwithstanding that it acts innocently, will also be liable in conversion and the true owner may find it worthwhile to sue the bank, rather than the fraudulent customer on whose behalf the bank has innocently acted. The bank converts the cheque by receiving the cheque for collection and by presenting it for payment (*Morison* v *London County and Westminster Bank Ltd* [1914] 3 KB 356). For the purposes of the action the cheque is deemed to have a value equal to its face value (i.e., the amount for which it is drawn: *Fine Art Society Ltd* v *Union Bank of London Ltd* (1886) 17 QBD 705; *Macbeth* v *North and South Wales Bank* [1908] 1 KB 13). In *International Factors Ltd* v *Rodriguez* [1979] QB 351 Sir David Cairns said that the conversion gives the person entitled to the cheque a right to damages measured by the face value of the cheque.

An alternative course of action is an action in quasi-contract, although this type of action has traditionally required a waiver of the right to pursue an action in conversion. In *Morison* v *London County and Westminster Bank Ltd* Lord Reading CJ explained the basis of the cause of action and stated that the plaintiff is entitled to waive the tort and sue for the same amount as money had and received to his use.

Although the true owner of the cheque has an alternative remedy, it is in reality of limited use because once the bank has paid over money to the customer, acting as an agent, it is no longer liable in an action for money had and received. Following the House of Lords decision in *Lipkin Gorman* v *Karpnale Ltd* [1991] 2 AC 548 an action may also be based on unjust enrichment on the basis that money has been paid under a mistake of fact.

Statutory protection conferred on the collecting bank

The tort of conversion is one of strict liability. The bank cannot plead, in its defence, that it acted in good faith and as an innocent agent for its customer in collecting a cheque to which the customer has no title or a defective title. The banks were given statutory protection against an action in conversion because of the very limited extent to which the customer's title could be verified. Furthermore, with the large number of cheques banks handle for collection any attempt to verify title would be insupportable.

Section 82 of the Bills of Exchange Act 1882 and s. 4 of the Cheques Act 1957

The case of *Ogden* v *Benas* (1874) LR 9 CP 513 highlighted the problems a collecting bank may face if it acts imprudently in collecting a cheque for its customer. Some protection was therefore given to the collecting bank under the Crossed Cheques Act 1876. Section 12 of the Act provided that a collecting bank was not liable in conversion where it acted in good faith and without negligence in collecting crossed cheques for a customer. The Act limited the protection conferred on collecting banks to a situation where payment was received on presentation of a crossed cheque and it was for the credit of a customer. No protection was given to a collecting bank where it collected an uncrossed cheque for someone other than the true owner of the cheque.

The provision was re-enacted in s. 82 of the Bills of Exchange Act 1882 without any substantial alteration. It thus preserved the anomaly that a bank was protected when it collected a crossed cheque for a customer 'in good faith and without negligence' but was given no protection when collecting open cheques. Further problems were caused by the decision in *Capital and Counties Bank Ltd* v *Gordon* [1903] AC 240 at p. 249, where the House of Lords held that a bank was not protected by s. 82 if the customer's account was credited before the cheque was actually cleared. Lord Lindley stated that so long as s. 82 remained unamended, banks which desired protection would have to be cautious and not place crossed cheques paid in for collection to the credit of their customers' accounts before they were paid. Consequently, the Bills of Exchange (Crossed Cheques) Act 1906 amended s. 82 so that a bank was deemed to receive payment of a cheque for a customer notwithstanding that the amount of the cheque had been credited to the customer's account before clearing. Section 82 was repealed by the Cheques Act 1957, which made new provisions in s. 4. Section 4 of the Cheques Act 1957 (like its predecessors) substitutes for the absolute common law duty a qualified duty to take reasonable care to refrain from taking any step which the bank ought reasonably to foresee is likely to cause loss or damage to the true owner. The section is wider in scope than the former s. 82 of the Bills of Exchange Act 1882 and applies both to crossed and uncrossed cheques (a change in the law recommended by the Mocatta Committee (Cmnd 3 (1956), para. 105)). The scope of s. 4 has been extended so that it applies to cheques which are not transferable (s. 81A of the Bills of Exchange Act 1882, as amended by s. 3 of the Cheques Act 1992) and other instruments which although not cheques serve a similar function, e.g., any document issued by a customer of a bank which, although not a bill of exchange, is intended to enable a person to obtain payment from a bank (in *Orbit Mining and Trading Co. Ltd* v *Westminster Bank Ltd* [1963] 1 QB 794 the Court of Appeal held that an instrument containing a 'pay cash or order' instruction was not a bill of exchange but it was a document to which s. 4(2) applied), or any document issued by a public officer which is not a bill of exchange but which is intended to enable a person to obtain payment from the Paymaster General or the Queen's and Lord Treasurer's Remembrancer, and bankers' drafts. Bankers' drafts fall outside the definition of a cheque because they are not drawn by one person on another (*Commercial Banking Co. of Sydney Ltd* v *Mann* [1961] AC 1). Section 4(3) goes on to provide that a bank is not to be treated as negligent merely because it does not concern itself with the absence of, or irregularity in, endorsement of an instrument. Subject to these changes and to some difference in the wording between s. 4 and the repealed provisions, cases decided under the former s. 82 of the 1882 Act are still relevant.

Prerequisites of s. 4(1) of the Cheques Act 1957

In order to obtain protection from s. 4 of the Cheques Act 1957 a collecting bank must satisfy a number of requirements namely: (a) it must have acted for a customer in collecting the instrument; (b) it must have 'received payment' for the customer, or it may collect the instrument for itself where it has already credited the customer's account; (c) it must act in good faith; and (d) without negligence.

The word 'customer' is not defined in either the 1957 or the 1882 Acts (see chapter 6). Section 4 applies to protect the bank where a cheque is collected for a customer who has 'no title, or a defective title'. These words must be construed by reference to s. 29(2) of the 1882 Act although the examples given in that subsection are not exhaustive. The protection extends also to cases where the customer has no title to the instrument, e.g., where the instrument has been stolen.

In order to claim the protection of s. 4 the collecting bank must show that it received payment in 'good faith and without negligence'. Section 90 defines good faith for the purposes of the Bills of Exchange Act 1882 and s. 6(1) of the Cheques Act 1957 provides that it is to be construed as one with the 1882 Act.

It is, however, the final requirement, i.e., the bank must act without negligence, which has resulted in considerable litigation. The burden of proof is on the bank and it must disprove negligence if it is to rely on s. 4 of the 1957 Act. In *Lloyds Bank Ltd* v *E.B. Savory and Co.* [1933] AC 201 Lord Wright said that 'as it is for the banker to show that he is entitled to this defence, the onus is on him to disprove negligence'.

Section 4(1) prescribes that the bank must observe a standard of care if it is to be protected by the section. Thus where the customer is in possession of a cheque at the time of delivery to the bank for collection, the collecting bank can assume that the customer is the true owner of the cheque. However, where the collecting bank has knowledge of facts or ought to have knowledge of facts which would cause a reasonable bank to suspect that the customer is not the true owner, the bank must take reasonable care. What will discharge this standard of care will depend on prevailing banking practice and for that reason cases decided before the Second World War, when banking facilities were less commonly used, may not be a reliable guide to the standard of care required for a collecting bank these days. Although it is not to be expected that bank officers should act as amateur detectives (*Lloyds Bank Ltd* v *Chartered Bank of India, Australia and China* [1929] 1 KB 40 at p. 73; *Penmount Estates Ltd* v *National Provincial Bank Ltd* (1945) 173 LT 344 at p. 346) the collecting bank cannot assume that every person who presents a cheque for collection is honest and the true owner of the instrument. The basis of the protection conferred on the collecting bank will therefore depend on what is considered reasonable in terms of general banking practice. The fact that the courts have adopted a variable standard is evident from the application of s. 4.

The Privy Council in *Commissioners of Taxation* v *English Scottish and Australian Bank Ltd* [1920] AC 683 (adopting the approach taken by the High Court of Australia in *Commissioners of the State Savings Bank of Victoria* v *Permewan, Wright and Co. Ltd* (1914) 19 CLR 457) stated the standard of care as follows:

> The test of negligence is whether the transaction of paying in any given cheque (coupled with the circumstances antecedent and present) was so out of the ordinary course that it ought to have aroused doubts in the bankers' mind, and caused them to make inquiry.

The negligence of the collecting bank, therefore, consists of a failure to make enquiry as to the customer's title (or lack of it) to a cheque where the surrounding circumstances would warrant a bank to make reasonable enquiries. In order to detect the possibility of fraud or forgery in relation to a cheque the bank must be aware of certain material information about its customer, e.g., the occupation and identity of the customer, whether cheques are likely to be drawn by an agent (although the bank will normally insist on such authority being confirmed in writing) etc. The bank is concerned with the identity and integrity of the customer so that it can determine his suitability to operate an account. The duty of care, therefore, commences immediately on the account being opened for a new customer and operates every time an item is collected for the customer. Lord Wright in *Lloyds Bank Ltd* v *E.B. Savory and Co.* explained that failure to undertake appropriate enquiries may well prevent the collecting bank from relying on s. 82 of the Bills of Exchange Act (the predecessor to s. 4).

The question of whether the collecting bank is liable in negligence in this context may involve a range of enquiries. It is not possible to give an exhaustive list of which acts or omissions will amount to negligence and deny the collecting bank the defence available under s. 4 of the Cheques Act 1957. These include:

(a)   precautions taken in opening an account;

(b)   collection of cheques payable to officials, companies or firms;

(c)   collection of cheques in favour of employers or principals for the account of an employee;

(d)   collection of cheques drawn by known employees in their own favour on the account of the employer or principal;

(e)   collection of employer's cheques in favour of third parties for the account of the employee;

(f)   the degree of scrutiny of an endorsement or order cheque;

(g)   account payee cheques collected for someone other than the named payee.

It is possible for a bank to show in all of the cases where negligence is alleged that it has exercised the necessary standard of care. The courts have examined the standard of care owed to the true owner of a cheque or other instrument in numerous cases and it is intended now to examine the application of s. 4.

Precautions in opening the account

In the majority of cases where a bank account is used to perpetrate a fraud some time will have lapsed since the opening of the account. It is therefore not always possible to safeguard the collecting bank against liability in conversion. However, the bank can take steps to verify the honesty and integrity of its customer by taking adequate precautions prior to opening an account. Indeed, the conduct of the bank prior to and during the opening of the account may be very relevant. The question of the conduct of the collecting bank at the time of opening the account and the subsequent collection of cheques obtained fraudulently by the customer was looked at in *Turner* v *London and Provincial Bank Ltd* (1903) 2 LDB 33 but the bank's duty to exercise reasonable care in this respect was not clearly established until *Ladbroke* v *Todd* (1914) 30 TLR 433. In that case Bailhache J held the bank negligent because it did not make enquiries about a prospective customer when such enquiry would have revealed that the man who opened the account was not whom he purported to be. However, it must be emphasised that it is not a question of negligence in opening the account but the circumstances connected with the opening of the account which are relevant to the issue of negligence

(*Commissioners of Taxation* v *English, Scottish and Australian Bank Ltd* [1920] AC 683). The failure to make an enquiry is not excused by the fact that even if the enquiry had been made it would not have revealed the true facts (*A.L. Underwood Ltd* v *Bank of Liverpool and Martins* [1924] 1 KB 775; *Thackwell* v *Barclays Bank plc* [1986] 1 All ER 676).

In opening an account, the bank must not only verify the customer's identity but also enquire, usually by requesting a referee's report, about the creditworthiness and integrity of the prospective customer and his circumstances in general. However, the collecting bank is not expected to be continuously aware of changes in the customer's lifestyle and this has been recognised by the courts. The decision in *Lloyds Bank Ltd* v *E.B. Savory and Co* [1933] AC 201 marked the extreme limits of the bank's obligations under s. 4 of the Cheques Act 1957. In that case the House of Lords held that the bank had, prior to opening two accounts, failed to undertake a full inquiry into the circumstances of its customers as required by the bank rule book and it had therefore acted negligently. Lord Wright said (p. 231) that where the new customer is employed in some position which involves his handling, and having the opportunity of stealing, his employer's cheques, the bank fails in taking adequate precautions if it does not ask the name of his employers. This is specially true, e.g., of a stockbroker's clerk; it may be different in the case of an employee whose work does not involve such opportunities.

In *Lloyds Bank Ltd* v *Chartered Bank of India, Australia and China* [1929] 1 KB 40 it was suggested that in addition to enquiries made when the customer's account is opened, the bank is under a duty to scrutinise the account from time to time to assure itself that everything appears regular. Moreover, the view has been expressed that the duty to enquire arises every time something occurs which appears to be out of the ordinary in respect of the account and the bank must at all times be cognisant of the customer's affairs (*Nu-Stilo Footwear Ltd* v *Lloyds Bank Ltd* (1956) 7 LDB 121; *Baker* v *Barclays Bank Ltd* [1955] 1 WLR 822). In order to comply with this obligation the bank would be required to keep the customer's account under constant review.

Lord Russell of Killowen, delivering a dissenting judgment, in *Lloyds Bank Ltd* v *E.B. Savory and Co.* was more cautious about the significance which should be placed on information relating to the customer's employment or that of the customer's spouse. In an age where mobility is common, the courts are likely to be more realistic about the bank's ability to remain constantly up to date about the customer's affairs. In *Orbit Mining and Trading Co. Ltd* v *Westminster Bank Ltd* [1963] 1 QB 794 it was held that the bank was not under a duty to keep an eye on changes in its customer's employment. Indeed, a request for certain types of information may actually cause a prospective customer offence, e.g., where a bank requires a successful and independent woman to give personal details of her partner's employers and income.

More recently, in *Marfani and Co. Ltd* v *Midland Bank Ltd* [1968] 1 WLR 956 Diplock LJ described the duty of the bank as 'a qualified duty to take reasonable care to refrain from taking any such step which he foresees is, or ought reasonably to have foreseen was, likely to cause loss or damage to the true owner'. His lordship pointed out that what enquiries ought to be made depends on current banking practice and cases decided over 30 years ago may not now be a reliable guide to the standard of care expected from a bank. Diplock LJ then formulated the following test for liability:

What the court has to do is to look at all the circumstances at the time of the acts complained of, and to ask itself were those circumstances such as would cause a reasonable banker, possessed of such information about his customer as a reasonable banker would possess, to suspect that his customer was not the true owner of the cheque.

The court in the *Marfani* case also took the view that it did not constitute any lack of reasonable care if before opening an account for an applicant the bank refrained from making enquiries which would probably fail to lead to the detection of the customer's dishonest purpose, if he were dishonest, and which would only offend him if he were not. The *Marfani* case is not to be treated as removing all the obligations placed on the banks to enquire by the *Savory* case. It recognises that negligence is to be measured by varying, current professional banking standards and every case must be considered on its merits.

In *Lumsden and Co* v *London Trustee Savings Bank* [1971] 1 Lloyd's Rep 114 Donaldson J gave extensive illustrations of the enquiries that a bank might make when opening an account. The facts of the case were that Blake, a dishonest employee, opened an account in the name of J.A.G. Brown with a cash deposit of £1. Blake then gave a reference for the fictitious 'J.A.G. Brown' stating that 'Brown' was of good character and probity. Blake signed the reference letter 'J. Blake, DSc, PhD', but failed to provide the name of his own bankers, as requested by the manager. The manager concluded that he was dealing with two professional men and failed to make any further enquiries. The plaintiffs drew a number of cheques in favour of Brown Mills and Co. in the abbreviated form 'Brown', with a space in front of the payee's name. Blake inserted the initials 'J.A.G.' in the space before the payee's name and paid the cheques into the account he had opened. In an action by the plaintiffs against the defendant bank it was argued that the bank had acted in good faith and without negligence and was therefore protected by s. 4 of the Cheques Act 1957. In giving judgment Donaldson J said that 'the crucial issue is whether the defendants have proved that they were not negligent in connection with the opening of the account'. The learned judge held that the 'defendants fell far short of any reasonable standard of care'.

Donaldson J made a point of the bank's failure to call for the customer's passport but in the *Marfani* case, Cairns J thought that a passport had not been thought of as necessary in any of the decided cases. A passport, where available, would, however, be invaluable in establishing identity.

Collection of cheques in favour of employers or principals for the account of an employee or agent

Particular questions arise in connection with the possible negligence of a collecting bank which collects cheques drawn payable 'to A for B', or to 'A on behalf of B', or 'to A for the account of B'. Probably the most important decision in this area is *Marquess of Bute* v *Barclays Bank Ltd* [1955] 1 QB 202 in which the plaintiff employed one McGaw as manager of certain sheep farms on the island of Bute. Government payment warrants, made payable to 'Mr D. McGaw, Kerrylamont, Rothesay, Bute', with the words 'for Marquess of Bute' inserted immediately after the payee's name were collected for McGaw's account by the defendant bank. In an action for conversion, the defendant bank was denied the statutory protection on the ground of its negligence. McNair J rejected the defences raised by the bank and said that in an action for conversion the claimant need only establish that at the material time he was entitled to immediate possession of the subject matter. His lordship observed that the warrants 'bore the clear indication at the lowest that McGaw was to receive the money as agent or in a fiduciary capacity, and it is elementary banking practice that such documents should not be credited to a personal account of the named payee without enquiry'. The court rejected the bank's argument that estoppel could apply to prevent an action against the bank. McNair J said that such an argument could only succeed if the documents were in a form that could reasonably be understood as an unequivocal representation that McGaw was entitled to the proceeds of the warrants.

Collection of cheques drawn by known employees or agents in their favour on the account of the employer or principal

In *Morison v London County and Westminster Bank Ltd* [1914] 3 KB 356 the plaintiff, an insurance broker, had an account with the National Provincial Bank Ltd. The bank had been authorised to honour cheques drawn on the account by H. Abbott, the plaintiff's clerk and manager. Without the plaintiff's knowledge, Abbott opened an account with the defendant bank and paid into this account approximately 50 cheques he had misappropriated between 1907 and 1911. All except two of the cheques were specially crossed to the defendant bank. The bank having collected the cheques was held liable in negligence. The fact that cheques were signed *per pro* and that Abbott was the manager for the plaintiff should have put the bank on enquiry but no such enquiry was made. The court, however, accepted the collecting bank's contention that if it was liable on the earliest of the 50 cheques, the fact that the plaintiff's bank had paid the cheques during 1907 and 1908 without being challenged made any enquiry on the later cheques unnecessary. Buckley LJ considered that 'the position after the end of 1907 was such that any suspicion which they ought to have had would have been lulled to sleep by the action of Morison himself'.

This theory of 'lulling to sleep' has been rejected in subsequent cases and in *Bank of Montreal v Dominion Gresham Guarantee and Casualty Co. Ltd* [1930] AC 659 the Privy Council said that 'neglect of duty does not cease by repetition to be neglect of duty' (see also: *Lloyds Bank Ltd v Chartered Bank of India, Australia and China* [1929] 1 KB 40).

The duty on the bank to enquire is not removed by the fact that an agent who draws cheques on his principal's account has a power of attorney under which he draws cheques to his own order (*Midland Bank Ltd v Reckitt* [1933] AC 1). However, there is no absolute rule that enquiry must be made in cases of this kind and that the collecting bank will be liable in negligence. In *Penmount Estates Ltd v National Provincial Bank Ltd* (1945) 173 LT 344) the defendant bank succeeded in its defence that it had not been negligent. In that case cheques payable to a principal were sent to his solicitor who forged the principal's endorsement and paid the cheques into his private account. The court held the collecting bank was not guilty of negligence in crediting the cheque to the solicitor's account since it was normal that a solicitor should pay into his account money belonging to the client.

It is submitted that this can only be true where client money is paid into a client account, and a bank which allows cheques drawn in favour of a third party to its customer's account will be liable in negligence (see also: *Australia and New Zealand Bank Ltd* v *Ateliers de Constructions Electriques de Charleroi* [1967] 1 AC 86).

Scrutiny of endorsements

In contrast to the paying bank when it pays to another bank, the collecting bank does have an obligation to scrutinise order cheques for the apparent regularity and sufficiency of endorsements. However, the Cheques Act 1992, s. 31 (amending the Cheques Act 1957, s. 4(2)(a)) provides that a collecting bank will not be denied the protection of s. 4 of the Cheques Act 1957 if it makes payment to the named payee contrary to a purported endorsement of the cheque.

Apart from this provision a collecting bank has always had a duty to scrutinise the regularity of endorsements and failure to do so would render the bank liable in negligence (*Bavins, Junr and Sims* v *London and South Western Bank Ltd* [1900] 1 QB 270).

Negligence in connection with crossed cheques

The effect of crossings on cheques has already been discussed. Caution needs to be exercised where cheques are marked 'account payee only'. The Cheques Act 1992 has rendered such instruments non-transferable although even at common law the collecting bank was placed under an obligation of enquiry.

Contemporary standards of negligence

Negligence on the part of the collecting bank may take place at any time during the course of handling the cheque. But it is rare that the collecting bank incurs a liability in negligence. However, recent cases have emphasised that cases which established the standards for negligence when the banking sector was smaller and its services available to limited customers may not be appropriate to establish current standards of negligence. Indeed, such cases should not be used to create impossible standards of care (see *Orbit Mining and Trading Co. Ltd* v *Westminster Bank Ltd* [1963] 1 QB 794; and *Marfani and Co. Ltd* v *Midland Bank Ltd* [1968] 1 WLR 956).

Defence of contributory negligence

In some cases the conversion of a cheque is facilitated by the carelessness of the true owner, for example, where a cheque is handed to a person in an incomplete form. In *Morison* v *London County and Westminster Bank Ltd* [1914] 3 KB 356 it was suggested that the true owner of a series of cheques converted by his employee and collected by the employee's bank could not succeed if his actions had lulled the bank into safety or alleviated its suspicion. It is very probable, however, that a bank will not be allowed to justify its negligence on the grounds that it was misled by the customer's carelessness.

An alternative defence of contributory negligence may be available to the bank. At one time the generally accepted view was that a collecting bank could not, when sued for damages for conversion, plead that the plaintiff had contributed to his own loss by his negligence. In *Lloyds Bank Ltd* v *E.B. Savory and Co.* [1933] AC 201 at 229 Lord Wright said it was 'immaterial averment' that the conversion was only possible because of want of ordinary prudence on the part of the true owner. An argument used to support this contention was that the true owner did not owe any duty of care to the bank.

In 1945 the Law Reform (Contributory Negligence) Act was passed and s. 1 of the Act provided that where a person suffered damage as a result of partly his own fault and partly that of any other person, a claim for damages will not be defeated by reason of the fault of the person who suffered the damage, but the damages recoverable will be reduced to the extent the court thinks just and equitable. In *Lumsden and Co.* v *London Trustee Savings Bank* [1971] 1 Lloyd's Rep 114 Donaldson J held that the collecting bank could successfully plead the contributory negligence of the true owner in reduction of the bank's liability. In that case damages awarded to the plaintiff were reduced by 10 per cent because of his contributory negligence. The court accepted the view first advanced by Milnes Holden that the Law Reform (Contributory Negligence) Act 1945 applied not only to actions for negligence but also to other torts, including the tort of conversion, so that if the plaintiffs are contributorily negligent in facilitating the fraud the amount of compensation awarded will be reduced.

Section 11(1) of the Torts (Interference with Goods) Act 1977 abolished contributory negligence as a defence in an action in conversion, but it was revived by s. 47 of the Banking Act 1979 and has survived the repeal of the rest of that Act.

However, the Australian courts have held that contributory negligence is not a defence available to the collecting bank. Samuels J in *Wilton* v *Commonwealth Trading Bank of Australia* [1973] 2 NSWR 644 refused to follow *Lumsden and Co.* v *London Trustee Savings Bank* and *Helson* v *McKenzies Ltd* [1950] NZLR 878 (see also *Day* v *Bank of New South Wales* (1978) 19 ALR 32; *Grantham Homes Pty Ltd* v *ANZ Banking Group Ltd* (1979) 26 ACTR 1).

Collection of cheques not endorsed by the holder

Prior to the Cheques Act 1957 in practically all cases where a bank received a cheque for collection the bank received the instrument as a holder. If a cheque was payable to bearer the mere delivery of the instrument to the collecting bank would suffice to constitute the bank the bearer (*Sutters* v *Briggs* [1922] 1 AC 1). If the cheque was payable to order, an endorsement would be required and the bank would become a holder of the instrument by negotiation (s. 31(1) of the Bills of Exchange Act 1882). As a holder the bank could sue on the instrument, except where the endorsement was forged or unauthorised. In that situation the bank would not be a holder of the cheque. However, s. 2 of the Cheques Act 1957 ensures that a bank which collects a cheque payable to order will not be prejudiced by the absence of an endorsement. It provides that a bank which gives value for, or has a lien on, a cheque payable to order which the holder delivers to the bank for collection without endorsing it, has such rights as it would have had if, upon delivery, the holder had endorsed the cheque in blank. The unendorsed cheque is therefore treated as payable to bearer in the hands of the collecting bank.

The section only applies where a cheque payable to order is delivered by the holder to a bank for collection. The effect of the section was examined in *Westminster Bank Ltd* v *Zang* [1966] AC 182, where it was argued that (a) the cheque was delivered to the bank, not as a holder under s. 2 but as an agent of the company; (b) the words in the section 'which the holder delivers . . . for collection' could not apply to an unendorsed cheque paid into an account which was not that of the payee; (c) the bank had not given value for the cheque; and (d) the bank had ceased to be a 'holder' of the cheque when it surrendered it. Both the first and second arguments were rejected by the House of Lords. The House held that the bank had failed to establish that it gave value for the cheque as it could not be shown that it had agreed to allow or had in fact allowed the company to draw against the cheque. Moreover, the bank lost its lien when it returned the cheques in order to enable legal action to be pursued.

THE COLLECTING BANK AS A HOLDER FOR VALUE, OR THE COLLECTING BANK'S LIEN

Where a collecting bank acts as an agent for its customer or receives payment in connection with a customer's account or is negligent, it may find itself liable in conversion. However, it is possible for the collecting bank, despite the fact that its customer did not possess a good title to the cheque in question, to acquire a good title to the instrument so that it can enforce the instrument in its own name. If the bank can show that it is a holder in due course, it can enforce the instrument despite any negligence on its part. The collecting bank becomes a holder for value, or even a holder in due course, and enjoys the protection normally conferred on such persons under s. 29 of the Bills of Exchange Act 1882. The position of the bank as a holder for value was examined in *Capital and Counties Bank Ltd* v *Gordon* [1903] AC 240. The House of Lords held that as the bank had credited the amount of the cheques to the customer's account before it received their value, the bank received payment as a holder for value, and not as an agent for the customer. Their lordships reasoned that as an agent for collection the collecting bank would not have credited the payee's account with the value of the cheques until payment had actually been received.

A bank may, therefore, collect a cheque either as the agent of its customer or as a holder for value on its own account. A bank may sue as a holder for value for part of the amount on a bill or as a mere holder (*Barclays Bank Ltd* v *Aschoffenburger Zellstoffwerke AG* [1967] 1 Lloyd's Rep 387). However, the two roles are not entirely mutually exclusive (see *Barclays Bank Ltd* v *Astley Industrial Trust Ltd* [1970] 2 QB 527).

Whether or not a collecting bank has given value has been discussed in a number of cases and a number of principles have been established (see *Barclays Bank Ltd* v *Harding* (1962) 83 Journal of the Institute of Bankers 109 and *Midland Bank plc* v *R. V. Harris* [1963] 2 All ER 685). The mere fact that the bank credits its customer's account with the amount of the cheque before clearance does not mean that it gives value for the cheque. In *A.L. Underwood Ltd* v *Bank of Liverpool and Martins* [1924] 1 KB 775 Atkin LJ said that to constitute value there must be in such a case a contract between banker and customer, i.e., that the bank will, before receipt of the proceeds, honour cheques of the customer drawn against the cheques.

This view is considered to represent the present law and has been accepted in a number of cases including *Importers Co. Ltd* v *Westminster Bank Ltd* [1927] 2 KB 297; *Baker* v *Barclays Bank Ltd* [1955] 1 WLR 822 and *Westminster Bank Ltd* v *Zang* [1966] AC 182.

In *Paget's Law of Banking*, 11th ed. (London: Butterworths, 1996) the authors conclude that a collecting bank will be a holder for value in the following circumstances, namely:

(a) where the collecting bank lends further on the strength of the cheque; or

(b) where the bank pays over the cheque or part of it in cash before the cheque is cleared; or

(c) where the bank agrees to an earlier drawing against the cheque than the normal course of business would permit; or

(d) where the bank accepts the cheque in reduction of an overdraft.

The collecting bank will give value if it expressly or implicitly agrees that it will, before receipt of the proceeds, honour cheques of the customer drawn against the cheque paid in for collection or if it does in fact allow the customer so to draw against the cheque. However, in *Westminster Bank Ltd* v *Zang* the defendant drew an order cheque in favour of a man called Tilley. Tilley paid the unendorsed cheque into the account of a company which he controlled, known as Tilley's Autos Ltd. The company's account was overdrawn at the time the cheque was deposited. The cheque was dishonoured and the bank returned the cheque to Tilley for the purposes of enabling him to bring an action against the drawer. The bank eventually brought an action to enforce payment, claiming that it was a holder in due course, or a holder for value, and could enforce payment. The question to be decided was whether there was an implied agreement between the bank and the company, arising out of a course of dealings between them, to allow drawings against uncleared cheques and whether the bank had accordingly given value for the cheque.

In the House of Lords, Viscount Dilhorne said that if there had been an implied agreement between the bank and the company to honour cheques drawn against uncleared effects, then the bank would have been obliged to pay cheques drawn against the uncleared cheque, even though the account was overdrawn. He considered that the extension of the overdraft could have been considered to be 'value' but in this case there was in fact no effective reduction of the overdraft in view of the fact that the bank charged interest on the amount of the cheque until it was cleared.

Viscount Dilhorne also held that no implied agreement could be read into the circumstances of the case in view of the fact that the printed words on the credit slip negatived such an agreement and no evidence was given that cheques drawn by the customer were honoured in consequence of the uncleared cheques being paid in. It must now be assumed that a bank can establish a claim to be a holder for value of a cheque paid in for collection only by proving an agreement of the kind envisaged by Atkin LJ or by showing that cheques were in fact honoured specifically against the uncleared effects.

On this reading of the law value is given by a bank for a cheque paid in by its customer if it can be shown that cheques drawn by the customer were paid which would otherwise have been dishonoured had the cheque in question not been paid in.

Lien of the collecting bank

Where a cheque is delivered by a customer to a bank for collection (whether the bank receives it as an agent for collection or on its own account), then, in the absence of an express or implied agreement, the bank has by implication of law a lien over the cheque to the extent of the customer's indebtedness (if any) to it at the time (*Johnson* v *Robarts* (1875) LR 10 Ch App 505; *Sutter* v *Briggs* [1922] 1 AC 1). By s. 27(3) of the Bills of Exchange Act 1882, where the holder of a bill has a lien on it, he is deemed to be a holder for value to the extent of the sum for which he has a lien. Under s. 2 of the Cheques Act 1957, a bank has a lien on a cheque payable to order which the holder delivers to it for collection without endorsing it and the bank becomes a holder notwithstanding the absence of an endorsement.

In *Barclays Bank Ltd* v *Astley Industrial Trust Ltd* [1970] 2 QB 527 Milmo J distinguished *Westminster Bank Ltd* v *Zang* [1966] AC 182 as being materially different on the facts. In particular, in *Westminster Bank Ltd* v *Zang* there was no question of the bank having a lien on the cheques paid in. In *Barclays Bank Ltd* v *Astley Industrial Trust Ltd* cheques were received by the bank for collection on behalf of a customer but were returned unpaid because payment had been countermanded. The bank had extended the customer's overdraft facility on the basis of the receipt of the cheques and was held entitled to sue the drawer as a holder in due course. Milmo J expressly rejected the defendant's argument that the bank could not be at once an agent for collection of a cheque and a holder for value of the cheque. The court held that the bank took the cheques within the meaning of s. 29(1)(b) of the Bills of Exchange Act 1882 and to the extent of the customer's overdraft, the bank acquired a lien over the cheques, and although the cheques were delivered for collection, the bank became a holder in due course under s. 27(3) of the Act.

He further rejected the argument that the fact of the bank charging interest on the uncleared effects prevented it from being a holder for value. However, this last finding is questionable in the light of Viscount Dilhorne's opinion in the *Zang* case.

Collecting bank as a holder in due course

If a collecting bank is a holder of a cheque and gives value, it may qualify as a holder in due course. Under s. 29(1) of the Bills of Exchange Act 1882, in order to be a holder in due course, the bank must take the bill complete and regular on the face of it, in good faith and without notice of any defect in the title of the person who negotiated it. The bank must have become a holder of it before it was overdue and without notice of any previous dishonour. Where a cheque is presented to the collecting bank without an endorsement, the lack of the endorsement is cured by s. 2 of the Cheques Act 1957. In *Midland Bank Ltd* v *R.V. Harris Ltd* [1963] 2 All ER 685 the plaintiff received for collection from its customer two cheques drawn by the defendants payable to the customer or order. The cheques were not endorsed by the customer. The bank gave value for the cheques but payment of them was countermanded by the defendants. The bank sued the defendants on the cheques claiming both as a holder for value and holder in due course. It was argued that s. 2 of the Cheques Act 1957 did not make the bank a holder but merely gave it certain rights of a holder. Consequently the bank could not be a holder in due course. Megaw J rejected this argument and held that the two cheques were effectively payable to bearer; the bank was to be treated as an endorsee of the cheques and a bearer as defined by s. 2 of the 1957 Act.

Where a bank has a lien on a cheque delivered to it by a holder for collection and is in consequence deemed to be a holder for value of the instrument to the extent of the sum for which it has a lien, the bank may qualify as a holder in due course. In *Barclays Bank Ltd* v *Astley Industrial Trust Ltd* [1970] 2 QB 527 Milmo J held that the plaintiff bank had a lien on the cheques delivered to it for collection and was deemed to have taken the cheques for value. As the other conditions in s. 29(1) of the Bills of Exchange Act 1882 were also satisfied, it qualified as a holder in due course.

13   Payment by Plastic Card

The use of plastic cards in the payment process has revolutionised the payment industry. The first charge card was started in America and was designed for businessmen to charge meals to their expense accounts. The Diners Card is still an important method of payment for business executives, although its use and function have been overshadowed by the credit card. Barclaycard was the first credit card to be launched in the UK, in 1966. However, it is only with increased competition, in particular by the American card giants, that interest rates have been marginally reduced. More recently, other benefits such as free travel insurance, a system of points which may be used to acquire a reduction in the purchase price of cars etc. have added a competitive edge to the credit card market. Other types of cards have also become popular, e.g., store cards and prepayment cards (e.g., the British Telecom card), and have reduced the need to carry large amounts of cash.

Plastic cards have developed considerably in their nature and function. They have moved from being cards capable of carrying out a single simple function to intelligent multifunctional cards used in routine banking transactions. Probably, the single most decisive factor in the development of the plastic card industry was the magnetic stripe which allows customer information to be stored and deciphered electronically so that the customer can be identified and that identity verified. The front of the card contains the name of the cardholder, his account number and details of his bank and branch (unless that is contained in the account numbering system) in embossed characters capable of OCR reading. The embossing enabled the necessary details of both the debtor's and creditor's accounts to be transferred to the sales slips of the original manual system of credit cards, leaving only the amount of the transaction to be entered manually. These days the entire payment voucher can be printed electronically so that the customer merely signs the payment mandate. The magnetic stripe on the back of the card contains the same information as that embossed on the front, and details of the personal identification numbers and the security devices. Although the magnetic card is almost universal in usage, other forms of card have been introduced. The 'smart card' has a microprocessor embedded in the card. The chip can process information, e.g., assess whether the PIN entered by the cardholder at the terminal tallies with the PIN carried by the card. The smart card can thus both identify the cardholder and authorise the transaction in off-line transactions. There are now several types of plastic card used in banking transactions.

CREDIT CARDS

The cardholder will use a credit card to purchase goods or services from dealers who display the card issuer's insignia. The ability to obtain cash advances against credit cards is also available. When goods or services are purchased, the supplier of such services will swipe the card in an electronic till or machine which will record the cardholder's name and number on a sales voucher. A description of the goods or services may also be imprinted on the voucher, together with the amount of the transaction. Alternatively, this information may be written on the voucher by the supplier. The cardholder will then sign the voucher and the supplier will then verify the signature on the voucher against the sample signature on the back of the card. The supplier will then send the voucher to the card issuer who will then pay the amount claimed on the voucher less an agreed service charge.

Alternatively, the cardholder may order goods and services by telephone and make payment by giving his card details over the telephone. In such circumstances the cardholder will not have an opportunity to sign the payment voucher presented against his account with the card-issuing company. There is, in such cases, a considerable opportunity for fraud.

A transaction which is above the supplier's pre-arranged limit has to be authorised before the card is accepted for payment. It is usual practice for the card issuer to send an itemised statement of account on a monthly basis. The cardholder is then given an interest-free period during which to make payment. The cardholder need only make the minimum payment specified on the statement; interest is then payable on the outstanding balance. Alternatively, the cardholder may pay the full amount shown on the statement and incur no liability for interest. In such a situation the cardholder actually gets interest-free credit.

Many credit cards bear a logo or insignia, e.g., 'VISA' or 'MasterCard'. The logo is usually owned by a corporation formed, either by banks or other card issuers, in order to sponsor and control the card. The scheme provider's primary role will be to hold the trade mark in respect of the card in question (including the logo) and to establish standards of membership and security. Thus, one of the primary objectives of the scheme provider is to ensure the effective interchange of payment card transactions in a secure and consistent manner. The scheme provider is therefore responsible for clearing and settlement procedures; card standards and technical specifications for cards, terminals etc.; licensing and trade mark services etc. In so far as possible, the rules of any scheme are not intended to interfere with competition between card issuers and/or acquirers. Each member must agree to abide by the rules of the scheme provider.

Scheme membership

The success of any payment system depends on its integrity and financial soundness and membership for card schemes reflects the need to avoid unnecessary risks. The supervision and regulation of members is to some extent left to the relevant supervisory body but scheme providers do not abdicate all responsibility for the financial soundness of the payment scheme. Members are monitored and, where necessary, are subjected to special conditions, e.g., a member can be required to establish a security deposit or provide letters of credit for the benefit of the scheme provider and other members. Any financial institution which qualifies for membership may apply. Once accepted the financial institution may issue cards to the public. The card issuer is responsible for establishing and implementing its own credit-approval requirements and for setting its own terms for providing credit, e.g., interest rates, annual fees, etc., the level of customer service and procedures for collecting debts. There are, however, detailed requirements in relation to card specification, production, delivery and security.

Analysis of transactions

Apart from agreements between the scheme provider and members, a credit-card transaction involves three contracts. The first contract is between the card issuer and the cardholder. The card issuer undertakes to pay for the purchases made by the cardholder within a specified credit limit. The issuer further agrees to settlement of the amounts outstanding from time to time by minimum payments to be made against monthly statements. In addition to the express contract entered into between the card issuer and the cardholder, the relationship is heavily regulated by statute. In the UK, it is the provision of credit that attracts consumer legislation and the protection applies to individual and unincorporated cardholders. Thus, the Consumer Credit Act 1974 permeates every aspect of the relationship between the cardholder and the card issuer. Provisions exist which affect the form and content of the credit agreement, the provision of information, liability for the misuse of the cards and the termination of agreements.

The second contract is between the card issuer and the dealer. It is based on a master agreement under which the issuer agrees to pay to the dealer amounts due from the cardholders. The dealer is required to authenticate the signature on the payment voucher against that appearing on the card. If the amount of the transaction is in excess of the floor limit set by the card issuer, the dealer must not enter into the sale transaction without having the transaction approved by the card issuer.

It has been suggested that a credit-card transaction amounts to an assignment by the dealer to the card issuer of the amount payable by the cardholder (S.A. Jones, 'Credit cards, card users and account holders' [1988] JBL 457). It is submitted that this is not so, since under the master agreement the card issuer will give a direct undertaking to reimburse the dealer provided the payment voucher signed by the cardholder is properly drawn. In *Re Charge Card Services Ltd* [1989] Ch 497 the court held that where payment is accepted by a dealer from a customer using a credit card then, in the first instance, that payment is due from the card issuer and not the cardholder.

The final agreement is between the dealer and the cardholder for the sale of goods or provision of services. It is under this contract that the payment becomes due and the credit card is accepted as the method of payment. The courts have had to examine the question whether, if the card issuer becomes insolvent, the dealer has a right to demand payment from the cardholder. The answer to the question depends on whether payment by means of a properly signed credit-card voucher by the cardholder amounts to an unconditional payment. Certainly, an analogy of the cases decided in accordance with rules relating to letters of credit would support the argument that the payment voucher signed by the cardholder constitutes only conditional payment (*Sale Continuation Ltd* v *Austin Taylor and Co. Ltd* [1968] 2 QB 849; *W. J. Alan and Co. Ltd* v *El Nasr Export and Import Co* [1972] 2 QB 189; *Maran Road Saw Mill* v *Austin Taylor and Co. Ltd* [1975] 1 Lloyd's Rep 156) and in the event of the card issuer's insolvency the cardholder would remain liable for the debt. However, this argument was rejected in *Re Charge Card Services Ltd* [1989] Ch 497, where the Court of Appeal (affirming Millett J at first instance) held that the relationship between the dealer and cardholder can be distinguished from the contract of sale requiring payment by means of a letter of credit. The buyer of goods under a letter of credit transaction has the opportunity to select the issuing bank. He can therefore be expected to bear the loss if the bank selected by him becomes insolvent. In cases involving credit cards, the parties agree to a specified procedure, i.e., payment by a specified issuer, but without the cardholder having the same freedom as the buyer under a letter of credit. Payment according to the specified procedure, therefore, discharges the cardholder and prevents the liability from reviving in the event of the card issuer's insolvency. The dealer accepts payment by credit card as an absolute discharge of the cardholder's personal liability to make payment.

CHARGE CARDS

The charge card (sometimes known as the travel and entertainment card), although not a credit card, has some similarities. The procedure is the same as described for a credit card except that under a charge card there is no agreement by the card issuer to extend credit to the cardholder. The cardholder is required to settle promptly the full amount outstanding on his statement. Charge cards fall into two broad categories namely: (a) charge cards issued by companies for use at a variety of outlets, e.g., Diners Club or American Express; and (b) store charge cards issued by stores to be used exclusively at those stores or stores of associated companies, e.g., John Lewis Partnership Chargecard. Accordingly, the Marks and Spencer Chargecard is misnamed since it allows cardholders credit. However, its limitation is that it is restricted to purchases from Marks and Spencer stores.

Information regarding charge cards is not regulated under the Consumer Credit Act 1974. Nor does the institution or person supplying the information have to be licensed as a credit-broker, unlike credit cards where the card issuer has to be licensed. Charge cards may come within the definition of a credit-token within the Consumer Credit Act 1974 but because the agreement under which they are issued stipulates that the number of payments to be made by the debtor in repayment of the whole amount outstanding on the card must not exceed one, such cards are exempted from the Act (Consumer Credit (Exempt Agreements) Order 1989 (SI 1989/869), art. 3(1)(a)(ii)).

CHEQUE GUARANTEE CARDS

Cheque guarantee cards developed as a result of the necessity to reduce the element of fraud in relation to cheque payments. To counter the threat of fraud in the payments industry a number of initiatives were undertaken in the early 1990s. The Plastic Fraud Prevention Forum (PFPF) was established, with a view to planning and executing a strategy to reduce fraud. The group reported to APACS. In 1991, the PFPF was incorporated within the structure of APACS. Additionally the Home Office commissioned a report on the *Prevention of Cheque and Credit Card Fraud (Crime Prevention Unit,* Paper 26, 1990 (Levi Report)).

The cheque guarantee card is issued by the clearing bank with whom the customer maintains a current account and the issuing bank undertakes to honour cheques drawn by the customer, if certain conditions are satisfied including that the cheque is backed by the guarantee card. Thus, a cheque backed by the cheque card is issued subject to any representations made by the drawer and the bank's promise to honour the cheque.

The bank's undertaking in respect of a cheque guarantee card was examined by Lord Diplock in *Metropolitan Police Commissioner* v *Charles* [1977] AC 177. His lordship concluded that it gives the payee a direct contractual right against the bank itself to payment on presentment, provided the card is properly used.

The bank's undertaking to honour a cheque backed by the cheque card is subject to the following conditions being satisfied, namely:

(a)   The cheque must be signed by the drawer in the presence of the payee and the signature on the cheque must correspond to that on the cheque card.

(b)   The cheque form must bear the same code number as that shown on the card. This number is the sorting code number of the bank and branch where the customer maintains his account.

(c)   The cheque must be drawn before the expiry date shown on the card.

(d)   The card number must be written on the back of the cheque by the payee or his authorised agent. This indicates the payee's reliance on the card and the bank's undertaking to make payment. It is not enough that the card number is written on the cheque by the drawer personally in the absence of the payee since that does not indicate reliance by the payee.

(e)   The cheque must be drawn for an amount not exceeding the amount for which the guarantee is given, usually £50 although cheque cards for £100 or £250 may be issued to customers on request.

(f)   Only one cheque for an amount not exceeding the limit of the cheque card can be issued in relation to a single transaction. This is to prevent the purchaser of goods from drawing several cheques all within the limit of the cheque card to pay for goods or services in excess of the limit.

Cheque cards, therefore, differ from credit cards in that the issuing bank undertakes to honour the negotiable instrument backed by the guarantee card, rather than to pay for transactions entered into by the customer or to extend credit. The primary payment obligation is, therefore, that evidenced by the cheque itself but, if payment is not forthcoming, the guarantee may be relied on to claim payment.

Cheque guarantee cards are not generally regulated by the Consumer Credit Act 1974. However, if credit is provided by the use of the cheque guarantee card because there is a formal overdraft agreement entered into with the customer, then that may be a credit agreement regulated by the 1974 Act, but it is not a credit-token agreement.

Where a cheque guarantee card is used to guarantee a cheque when there are insufficient funds to the credit of the customer's account and no formal arrangements have been, made this will not normally be regarded as credit for the purposes of the Consumer Credit Act 1974, because there is no formal agreement to provide credit between the bank and its customer.

If, under the cheque card arrangement, credit could be provided, the agreement may be regulated irrespective of whether the customer uses it to obtain credit. If the cheque guarantee card agreement is a regulated consumer credit agreement then it will need to comply with the formalities of the Consumer Credit Act 1974.

Since cheque cards are, generally, outside the scope of the Consumer Credit Act 1974, the courts will have to resolve issues relating to liability for misuse of cheques and cheque cards. The relationship is dependent on the rules of agency and contract law, so that if the bank is to be entitled to debit the customer's account, it must act in accordance with a valid payment mandate.

Where the terms of issue of the cheque card are reasonable, then such terms will be given effect by the courts. In practice banks tend to issue cheque cards under terms which impose liability on the customer for the full loss arising from the misuse of a cheque card if the customer has either been negligent or has deliberately failed to notify the bank of the misuse. Where, however, the cardholder notifies the bank of the loss of the card immediately he becomes aware of the loss, the cardholder's liability, if any, is likely to be restricted to £50. The issue of a forged cardholder's signature was considered in *First Sport Ltd* v *Barclays Bank plc* [1993] 1 WLR 1229, where a retailer accepted a cheque delivered to him by a fraudster, who pretended to be the rightful owner of the cheque and cheque card, and whose signature on the cheque corresponded to the signature on the cheque card. The retailer who accepted the cheque in good faith brought an action against the bank to enforce the promise given by the bank on the issue of cheques backed by a cheque card. The Court of Appeal held that as the retailer had acted in good faith he was entitled to payment. Evans LJ referred to the conditions which have to be satisfied if the payee is to be able to enforce payment; including the requirement that the specimen signature on the card and the cheque should correspond. Evans LJ concluded that the card had the effect of conveying to the retailer the bank's unilateral offer to enter into the contract. The genuine cardholder had the bank's authority to communicate the offer, whilst some other bearer, including a thief, had ostensible authority. The retailer, or other payee, did not have to communicate acceptance to the bank. It is enough that the retailer, or other payee, acts on that promise of the bank.

DEBIT CARDS

The debit or EFTPOS card may be used through an ATM or EFTPOS terminal. The holder may use the card in designated retail stores to purchase goods or to obtain services. A cardholder, who wishes to purchase an item, will hand his card to the retailer for payment. The card is then swiped through a card-reader attached to an EFTPOS terminal. The retailer will insert the amount of the transaction so that it is printed on the voucher. If the card is accepted, a till receipt, which identifies the terminal and sets out the time, date and amount of the transaction is printed. The cardholder will then sign the voucher. The retailer will then verify the signature executed on the voucher against the one on the card. One copy of the signed voucher is given to the cardholder and the other retained by the retailer. The transfer of funds from the cardholder's account to the retailer's account is executed electronically.

The main difference between the debit card and credit card is that the price of the goods or services is remitted to the retailer by means of a money transfer from the cardholder's bank account to the retailer's bank account. No credit is extended to the cardholder unless his bank account is overdrawn.

One of the most popular debit cards at present is the Switch Card. It was launched in 1988 by a network of banks consisting of the Midland, National Westminster and the Royal Bank of Scotland. Currently, its full membership includes the Royal Bank of Scotland, Barclays, Clydesdale Bank, Lloyds Bank, Halifax Building Society and a number of other banks.

The Switch clearing cycle involves three days (similar to the cheque clearing cycle when the instrument is physically presented). During the evening of the first day the retailer will collect all the vouchers for Switch-based transactions executed through his terminals. On the second day these are transmitted to the card issuer with settlement taking place on the third day. The issue of countermand, as with other forms of electronic payment, raises problems. Countermand is generally precluded once the payment voucher is signed by the cardholder.

CASHPOINT CARDS

A cashpoint or automated teller machine is an electronic funds transfer terminal that is capable of performing many of the roles traditionally undertaken by a bank cashier. Thus ATMs handle deposits, transfers between accounts, balance enquiries, cash withdrawals and payments of bills. Some ATM systems also deal with simple loan facilities. An ATM can be on-line or off-line. If the system is off-line the ATM card operates as a means of identification of the customer's personal identification number (PIN), which is encoded on the card itself. An on-line ATM verifies the customer's inserted PIN by comparing it with the customer's PIN in the computer's master file. The PIN is a numerical code which identifies the cardholder as an authorised account holder. There are serious problems with the possible misuse and abuse of ATM cards. Customers tend to forget their PIN numbers and to solve this problem may carry written records of them. If this written record falls into the wrong hands, together with the card, misuse may arise. Liability for misuse has to be examined both at common law and under the Consumer Credit Act 1974.

The American courts have dealt with the misuse of ATM cards in a series of cases. In *Judd* v *Citibank* (1980) 435 NYS 2d 210 the cardholder disputed the debiting of her account with the amount of $800, which was shown as having been made by the use of her cashpoint card. The cardholder could establish that at the time of the disputed withdrawal transaction she was at work, and that she had given neither her card nor her PIN to anyone. The Civil Court of the City of New York concluded that the cardholder had discharged the burden of proof and her account could not be debited. The court took into account that machines were subject to breakdown and malfunction. A similar decision was reached in *Porter* v *Citibank* (1984) 472 NYS 2d 582, where the cardholder had made a number of unsuccessful attempts to withdraw money on two separate days. Although the cardholder had notified the bank immediately on each occasion, the bank debited the account with the amounts of the unsuccessful withdrawals. The court gave judgment for the cardholder when the bank admitted that the ATM terminal in question was out of balance on several occasions each week.

Any terms imposed by a bank on its customer which seek to limit or restrict liability will be subject to both the Unfair Contract Terms Act 1977 and the Unfair Terms in Consumer Contracts Regulations 1994 (SI 1994/3159) (see chapter 8).

CONSUMER CREDIT ACT 1974

The Consumer Credit Act 1974 applies to 'credit-tokens' and 'credit-token agreements'. Section 14(1) of the Act defines the term 'credit-token' as a cheque, card, voucher or some other thing issued to an individual, by an issuer who carries on a 'consumer credit business', i.e., someone who enters into regulated credit agreements. By issuing the credit-token the issuer (the bank) undertakes that it will supply cash, goods or services on credit, or, where a third party supplies such things against the production of the token, the issuer will pay such third party.

The definition of a credit-token is fairly wide (Consumer Credit Act 1974, s. 14). It includes a book of vouchers that the debtor may use under a credit agreement in order to draw on the account, provided the issuer agrees to meet the vouchers. Whether or not credit has been given by the issuer will depend on the nature of the terms under which the voucher is issued and the use made of it. Cheque forms issued by banks are outside the definition of credit-token because the bank undertakes to its customer to pay against the instrument, and not for the supply of goods, services or cash (Guest and Lloyd, *Encyclopaedia of Consumer Credit Law*, para. 2–015). Credit cards do fall within the scope of s. 14 of the Consumer Credit Act 1974. They involve tripartite arrangements for the supply of cash, goods or services to the holder by dealers at the issuer's expense. Cashpoint cards will, normally, constitute credit-tokens. Cash is supplied to the customer, often even if the customer's account is overdrawn. Debit cards are also credit-tokens to the extent that credit is supplied when the third party supplies goods or services against the card and is then reimbursed by the card issuer. A charge card (or travel and entertainment card) will fall outside the scope of s. 14 if the agreement under which it is issued requires the account to be settled in full by a single payment. However, if such cards can be used for other functions, e.g., to obtain cash, then they are credit-tokens under s. 14 (see R. Goode, *The Consumer Credit Act: A Student's Guide* (London: Butterworths, 1979, p. 91).

Not every agreement involving the use of a credit-token falls within the scope of the Consumer Credit Act 1974. If the Act is to operate there must be a credit-token agreement for the provision of credit in connection with the credit-token. If the credit-token agreement only allows the cardholder to overdraw on a current account, the agreement is exempt from the formalities which must be complied with under the 1974 Act.

A credit-token agreement will only be regulated by the Consumer Credit Act 1974 if the issuer agrees to provide credit, or to pay for goods, services or cash provided on credit to an amount which does not exceed £15,000 (Consumer Credit (Increase of Money Limits) Order 1983 (SI 1983/1878)).

Form and content of the agreement

The Consumer Credit Act 1974 requires a credit-token agreement to be in writing and signed by both the prospective cardholder and card issuer (s. 61(1)).

Ordinarily, a copy of such an agreement must be sent by the card issuer to the cardholder within seven days following its execution (s. 63(2)). The Act also lays down detailed regulations on the form and content of the agreement. During the currency of the agreement and on payment of a nominal sum (50p), the cardholder is entitled to a copy of the executed agreement and to certain additional agreements. The agreement must give information in relation (Consumer Credit (Agreements) Regulation 1983 (SI 1983/1553)) to, e.g., the credit limit, the rate of interest and other charges payable and the timing of the repayments. Failure to comply with these requirements will render the agreement unenforceable, except by an order of the court. In order to decide whether or not to grant such an order, the court will have regard to whether the cardholder/debtor has suffered any hardship or prejudice as a result of the failure.

The Act requires seven days' notice to be given before any effective variation of a contract. Where the rate of interest is varied, notice can be given by publishing the variation in at least three national newspapers and, where reasonably practicable, through publicity in the card issuer's branches. In addition, under the Banking Code of Practice, card issuers have agreed to give reasonable notice to customers of changes to terms and conditions or interest rates. Where there are sufficient changes to warrant it, a consolidated agreement including all variations should be issued every 12 months.

A credit-token agreement may be cancelled in certain circumstances.

Unsolicited credit-tokens

The Consumer Credit Act 1974 makes it a criminal offence for a card issuer to supply unsolicited credit-tokens (Consumer Credit Act 1974, s. 51(1)). However, the prohibition against the supply of unsolicited cards does not apply where a credit-token agreement has been made and the card is supplied under that agreement (s. 51(3)(a)). Further, the prohibition does not apply where a replacement is sent, e.g., where an expired or lost card is replaced (s. 51(3)(b)).

The Act does not free the cardholder from any duty to reimburse the card issuer for the acceptance and use of an unsolicited card.

Liability for misuse

Section 83(1) of the Consumer Credit Act 1974 provides that a debtor under a consumer credit agreement is not liable to the creditor for any loss arising from the use of the credit facility by an unauthorised person. However, s. 84 allows the card issuer to insert a clause in the agreement which will make the cardholder liable for up to £50 for loss arising from misuse of the card when it was not his possession. Liability of the cardholder ceases in any event when notice is given to the card issuer, but the cardholder will be liable for the full loss accruing from the misuse of the card if the person responsible for the misuse acquired the card with the consent of the cardholder. However, the cardholder cannot be made liable unless the agreement entered into with the cardholder gives information concerning the person or body to be notified in the event of loss or theft of the card (s. 84(3) and (4)). The cardholder's liability will arise under s. 84 if the agreement imposes limited liability on the holder, but if the agreement is silent then the position is regulated by s. 83, which frees the holder from liability for loss in cases of misuse.

Under the voluntary Code of Banking Practice (3rd ed.) a general rule has been applied to all types of payment cards (other than prepayment cards) that the card issuer bears all loss (as between the cardholder and card issuer) for unauthorised transactions after the card issuer has been notified of the loss, theft or misuse of the card and the cardholder's liability is limited to £50 prior to such notification (para. 4.14). This limitation is unlikely to apply where the cardholder has been fraudulent or, possibly, where the cardholder has been guilty of gross negligence.

Connected lender liability

A cardholder may have the benefit of a claim against the card issuer for any breach of contract by the retailer (Consumer Credit Act 1974, s. 75). The section applies to credit-card agreements but it does not apply to purchases using a charge card or store card where any amounts outstanding on the account must be repaid in full in a single lump sum. The section provides that where the purchase price of the goods is between £100 and £30,000 the card issuer will be equally liable with the merchant for any misrepresentation or breach of contract on the part of the merchant. Thus, where goods purchased by a cardholder are faulty, the cardholder may claim reimbursement from either the merchant from whom he purchased the goods or alternatively from the card issuer. Where the merchant is still trading, the card issuer may then claim the loss sustained by an appropriate chargeback or by way of subrogation. However, where the cardholder has claimed against the card issuer it is often because the merchant has become insolvent and so is unable to reimburse for the defective goods. In such circumstances and in the absence of a deposit or security, the merchant acquirer or card issuer will suffer the loss. This liability is not limited to the amount of the credit advanced so that where the card is used only in part-payment for the goods the card issuer will be liable for the full amount of the cardholder's loss. Similarly, if the defective goods cause a loss in excess of their value, e.g., by damaging other property of the cardholder, the card issuer will be liable for the full amount of the loss.

Default and termination of agreements

Where a cardholder is in breach of his card agreement the card issuer may terminate the agreement and demand repayment of the outstanding balance on the card. The Consumer Credit Act 1974, s. 87, provides that prior to taking enforcement action the card issuer must first serve the cardholder with a default notice, notifying the cardholder of the breach. There are regulations governing the form and contents of the default notice. The cardholder must be given at least seven days from service of the notice to make good the breach or to pay compensation (s. 88). If the cardholder does so then the breach is treated as not having occurred (s. 89).

In addition to the requirement to serve default notices before commencing any proceedings to collect amounts due under consumer credit agreements, the general law also provides (Administration of Justice Act 1970, s. 40) that creditors must not harass anyone with demands for payment in respect of the frequency or the manner of payments so that the debtor or members of his family or household are subjected to alarm, distress or humiliation.

14   Credit Transfers and Direct Debits

GIRO SYSTEMS

Giro systems have operated throughout the world and have always displayed many variations in financial institutions and customs. There are, however, certain basic similarities in all the various kinds of giro systems which allow for a common explanation of the giro systems. The word 'giro' comes from the Greek '*guros*' meaning a ring, circle, revolution or circuit. The essential feature of giro is the rapid transmission and circulation of money to and from a single centre. The overriding function of giro is to create a payment system that is safe, quick and economical.

Development of giro in Continental Europe

Modern giro originated in Austria in 1833, as an improvement on the British Post Office Savings Bank system which had already been in existence for over 20 years. Although this innovation remained unnoticed internationally for many years, it was eventually Austria's example which led to a wave of giro systems being established. In 1906, both Japan and Switzerland set up giro systems, followed by Germany in 1908, Luxembourg in 1911 and Belgium in 1913. The start of the phase which led to all the major continental countries adopting a giro system may be dated from the municipal giro which the city of Amsterdam established in 1917. This paved the way for the Netherlands as a whole to establish its postal giro in 1918. The same year saw France and Italy put into operation their own giro systems which, but for the First World War, would have been introduced earlier. In 1920 Denmark and in 1925 Sweden both established giro systems.

By the mid 1920s, therefore, most of the richer Continental countries as well as Japan already had their postal giro systems. At the same time, strenuous demands were being made in Britain and a number of other countries for the provision of a giro system. There was, however, a long delay before further international progress was made and the UK finally introduced the National Giro in 1968.

Development of giro in Britain

The first attempt to introduce a giro system was made in 1926 when the Trades Union Congress adopted a resolution in favour of a postal cheque system. In 1928 a member of the General Council of the TUC gave evidence in favour of the establishment of a postal cheque system, to the committee of the Post Office Advisory Council set up to consider the possible introduction of such a system. The committee's report concluded that the committee was opposed to the introduction of a system based on the Continental model but that a tentative step should be made in the direction of offering cheque facilities for Post Office Savings Bank depositors.

The Royal Commission on the Working of the Monetary System (the Radcliffe Commission), in 1959, was the next to give a positive lead and concluded that in the absence of a move on the part of the existing institutions to provide the services there would be a case for investigating the possibility of instituting a giro system to be operated by the Post Office.

National Giro

After considerable debate the then government, in August 1965, issued a White Paper entitled *A Post Office Giro* (Cmnd 2751). The White Paper concluded that, in the light of various studies, a Post Office Giro, offering the usual facilities of the giro systems in European countries, would be a valuable addition to the existing methods of money transmission. In particular, for the general public with simple needs and especially no bank accounts, it would provide a simple, safe and efficient method of settling bills and sending money. Thus, National Giro was established in 1968 when the Postmaster General was empowered to operate 'a service of the kind commonly known as a giro system' (Post Office (Borrowing Powers) Act 1967, s. 2). Wider powers were subsequently given to offer 'banking services' under the Post Office (Banking Services) Act 1976. In 1978, the system was renamed the National Girobank and in 1985 the bank was incorporated as Girobank plc. In operating Girobank, the Post Office was deemed to be a bank and to be carrying on the business of banking. The Post Office was subject to supervision by the Treasury and was therefore exempted from the prohibition against carrying on a deposit-taking business under the Banking Act 1979. In 1989, the government announced that it wished to sell Girobank, and the Alliance & Leicester Building Society completed the purchase in 1990. It is proposed that when the building society converts to a bank that the undertaking Girobank plc will be transferred to Alliance & Leicester plc.

Girobank is a member of the London Bankers' Clearing House. It provides a wide range of normal banking services using the Post Office as its branches. It is a sponsoring bank in the Bankers' Automated Clearing Services (BACS), a settlement bank in the Clearing House Automated Payment System (CHAPS), a member of the Society for Worldwide Interbank Telecommunication (SWIFT) and a founder member of the Association for Payment Clearing Services (APACS).

The majority of accounts of Girobank customers are kept at a single centre at Bootle in Merseyside, which processes all transactions. However, two regional offices have been opened, in Birmingham for customers in the Midlands and Wales, and in Liverpool for customers in the North West and Northern Ireland. Instead of using cheques, payments between account holders can be made by sending transfer instructions to the centre, which will then inform both the transferee and transferor of the transfer and can inform the transferee of the purpose of the payment.

In 1985 Girobank introduced automated teller machines as part of a national ATM network known as 'Link'. This was subsequently merged with the 'Matrix' network and joined by a number of the banks.

Bank giro

Bank giro is the name adopted by the clearing banks to cover their money transfer services, namely, credit transfers and direct debits.

A debtor who has a bank account and chooses to settle his debt by drawing a cheque on his account in favour of the creditor has two options. He can send the cheque to the creditor, who will then present it to his bank, with an appropriate paying-in slip, so that the proceeds once collected from the debtor's account can be credited to his account. In exceptional cases the cheque may be negotiated to a third party. Alternatively, the debtor may use the bank giro credit system by presenting the cheque, together with an appropriate credit slip, at his bank or any branch of any bank. The credit, and if necessary the cheque, are passed through the clearing system and the debtor's bank debits its customer's account and transfers the amount to the beneficiary's bank. Pre-printed code numbers are used to identify the payer's and creditor's banks. A giro transfer, unlike a cheque, cannot be negotiated to a third party.

It is common for large concerns, especially public utility companies, insurance companies, rating authorities and major stores, to provide partly completed bank giro credit slips with, or as part of, their bills. Code numbers are frequently used to enable computers to effect a reconciliation of the amounts due and received. A customer may pay several such bills with one cheque, provided he makes the cheque payable to his own bank and utilises his branch for the service (see J. Kraa, 'Giro', *Journal of the Institute of Bankers*, vol. 81 (1960), pp. 262–71, where the author summarises the differences between payment by cheque and the giro payment).

Development of the credit transfer system

Payment by means of a cheque has a number of disadvantages, including the dangers of loss and misappropriation of the instrument. The credit transfer system avoids the disadvantages associated with payment by cheques. Within the system (a) standing orders, and (b) traders' credits need to be briefly mentioned.

Standing orders The system of making payments on behalf of customers by means of standing orders seems to have originated during the latter half of the nineteenth century. A standing order is a written order given by a customer to his bank to make a series of payments on his behalf. These are often used to make regular payments by customers, e.g., to insurance companies etc.

Traders' credits Traders' credits were designed to relieve the customer of the expense and inconvenience of drawing a large number of cheques to pay creditors. The procedure was for the debtor to draw a single cheque for the total of the bills to be paid, and to present that to his bank with a list of the payments and individually completed credit slips. One of the first organisations to use this system on a national basis was the Milk Marketing Board, which distributed large amounts of payments to farmers each month. Traders' credits are now more effectively made through BACS.

Credit clearing

In 1960, a clearing for the exchange and settlement of credit vouchers was added to the then cheque clearing system (see E.A. Young, 'The Bankers Clearing House', *Journal of the Institute of Bankers*, vol. 81 (1960), pp. 196–204). The new clearing was called the credit clearing. The procedure for the credit clearing is that the payer initiates the transfer of funds by giving written instructions to his bank on a credit transfer form. The instruction must authorise the payment of a specified amount to an identified person with the same or another bank. Where more than one payment is to be made, the debtor must list the details of each payment in a separate schedule and a separate credit transfer form must be made out for each transaction. A cheque for the total amount is drawn by the debtor and paid to his bank to cover the total payments made by the bank. If the debtor does not maintain an account with the bank he may be required to pay the equivalent amount in cash. On receipt of the credit transfer forms, the paying bank passes the vouchers through the credit clearing in London.

The credit transfer forms are sorted into bundles to be presented to each collecting bank, and are then delivered to the clearing house or directly to the collecting bank by 10.30 a.m. The dockets accompanying the bundles of credit transfer forms will list the amount of each credit transfer. The total of all dockets must be agreed between the paying and collecting banks on the day of delivery, although adjustments can be made on the following day in the event of errors. Any wrongly delivered vouchers must also be returned within a day of their receipt and a final agreement of in and out totals, including wrongly delivered vouchers returned the previous day. On the same day, a final settlement takes place. The payee's account is credited by the bank on the day after receiving the credit transfer voucher.

Direct debits

In 1967 the clearing banks, the Scottish banks and the Northern Irish banks introduced a new service, known as 'direct debiting'. The system may be used for the payment of fixed amounts due at regular intervals, or for varying amounts due at varying intervals. The payment is initiated by the payee or the creditor, who is normally a business or company. An application to participate in this system is made by the payee to his bank and consent obtained. All institutions using the direct debit system are given an identification number, which must be included in the details of all debits they initiate. The payee must obtain a direct debiting mandate from the debtor authorising the debtor's bank to honour debits initiated by the creditor, which is then sent to the debtor's bank. The form must contain the debtor's signature and indicate the name of the creditor, the amount to be debited (whether fixed or variable) and the dates upon which the payments are to be made, if they are periodic. The payee can receive payment under the direct debit either through BACS or by the payee sending a direct debit voucher to the London head office of the payer's bank.

Clearing of giro transfers

At present there are two methods of money transfer in operation. The manual transfer of credit vouchers involves the transmission of giro forms and is similar to the clearing process involved in cheque clearing. This requires the customer (the debtor) to deliver to his bank a bank giro credit voucher, accompanied by a cheque or a withdrawal form. The paying bank will transfer the relevant data from the bank giro credit form (e.g., clearing codes for the paying bank and the relevant branch, together with similar information about the recipient bank and branch, and information regarding the payer and payee and the amount to be transferred). The payer's account is debited by a message keyed into the computer terminal at his branch. The giro bank credit is then dispatched to the transferring bank's clearing office. On the following day, the clearing office delivers this form through the clearing house to the recipient bank's clearing office. In some cases the amount is then credited to the payee's account whilst on the same day the form is forwarded to the payee's branch. In other cases, the crediting of the payee's account is carried out at the branch and not at the head office of the recipient bank.

The procedure is somewhat different if the bank giro credit is delivered at a branch other than the one with which the payer maintains an account. In such a situation both the giro credit form and the attached cheque are transmitted through the clearing and the payer's cheque reaches his own branch.

The manual clearing system of money transfer orders is cumbersome and slow. The payment cycle takes three days, and may sometimes take an additional day.

Clearing through BACS

Bankers Automated Clearing Services Ltd (BACS) provides an alternative to the manual clearing of credit vouchers. In 1971, the London and Scottish clearing banks joined together to form a company (BACS) to provide a cost-effective automated clearing house service for inter-bank clearing of payments and collection transactions originating either from the sponsoring banks or from customers sponsored by member banks. There are currently 17 BACS members (in March 1996 the members were: Abbey National plc, Bank of England, Bank of Scotland, Barclays Bank plc, Clydesdale Bank, Co-operative Bank plc, Coutts & Co., Giro-bank plc, Halifax Building Society, Lloyds Bank plc, Midland Bank plc, National Westminster Bank plc, Nationwide Building Society, Northern Rock Ltd, the Royal Bank of Scotland plc, TSB Bank Ltd and Yorkshire Bank plc). Full participation entitles a bank to sponsor customers for direct input to BACS, in addition to entitling the full participating banks to input directly and receive output directly themselves. In 1992, there were some 50,000 companies able to input directly or through a bureau under the sponsorship of one of the member banks and building societies. The transfer of funds by BACS can be used for a variety of transactions, but the commonest use is by companies for the payment of wages and salaries. The insurance industry is a major user of the BACS clearing and relies heavily on it for an effective and cheap method of collecting premiums.

In order to make payment through BACS, the paying institution produces a magnetic disc or tape (although other methods of input are acceptable) containing details of each individual sum payable, including details of the payee and his bank account. The information required is similar to that found on a bank giro credit voucher. Transaction tapes are classified on the basis of the identity of the payer.

BACS has a retention facility and details of payments may be sent to it for processing up to 30 days prior to payment. On the specified day, the payment is credited to the payees' bank accounts, and the payer's account with the sponsoring bank is debited on the same day with the total amount of all payments made. The same process is followed if the amount is to be collected by direct debits initiated by a customer. A demand is made through BACS, and the creditor's bank issues a demand for payment. The computer discs or tapes will then be encoded with particulars of the amounts and the debtor's bank account to be debited. In addition to making payments, all items passing through BACS are recorded on microfilm so that if there is a query concerning any specific payment the BACS user has a record available.

Although BACS effects an immediate transfer of funds so that debits and credits are passed on the same day without retention of funds in the banking system, the payments involve a three-day processing cycle. The data has to be made available to BACS, at its premises in Edgware, by midnight on the first day. It may be communicated either electronically or by the manual delivery of prepared discs or tapes or by using BACSTEL, the BACS telecommunication link (BACSTEL now accounts for 86 per cent of all BACS input (APACS Annual Review 1995, p. 11). The discs or tapes received by BACS are processed so that new derivative discs or tapes are prepared for delivery to each recipient bank and will show the name and account number of each payee or in the case of direct debits the payer, and the amount payable. All BACS's work is completed by 3.00 a.m. on the second day and the discs or tapes prepared by BACS are sent by courier to the head offices of the recipients, or in the case of direct debits the paying banks involved (alternatively they may be transmitted electronically to each bank). Discs or tapes received from BACS are processed by the recipient bank's computer centre on the second day and at this stage banks merge the BACS payments with their other work. Each payment is credited to the amount of the respective customer, or debited to his account in the case of direct debits. On the third day of the payment process the information is made available to individual branches by head office. Where notification is required to be given to customers, that is done by the branch where the recipient maintains his account.

Where payment is made in error, countermand of the payment instruction may be possible if it reaches BACS before 11.00 a.m. on the second day of the clearing process. A customer who decides to cancel a payment will have to inform its sponsoring bank, which will then notify BACS of the countermand. It would obviously be inadvisable for the customer to request the sponsoring bank to cancel the whole file containing many payment instructions, since that may affect many unrelated payments. A cancellation or alteration of a payment will only be possible if all the parties involved in the process consent.

Where payment is instructed by a BACS sponsored client, a tape giving details of the payments to be made is prepared by the computer centre of the client or by a computer bureau. It is then delivered directly to BACS and the sponsoring bank merely features as a transferring bank so that the total value of the tape is debited to the client's account with its bank. In all other respects the payment process is as described above. The sponsoring bank receives the information it needs through BACS.

Traders' payments can now be settled through BACS, which enables a trader to settle accounts without having to make each individual payment by cheque. The trader will prepare an encoded disc or tape in respect of payments due to his suppliers and this will be processed through BACS. Where payments have to be made regularly, the same tape can be used to made repeated payments.

Clearing House Automated Payment System

The BACS payment, like the manual clearing of cheques, involves a three-day process and that is a major drawback. In order to avoid this delay in the payment process the Clearing House Automated Payment System was developed. It has superseded the Town Clearing which operated a same-day clearing system for certain paper-based payments.

In 1980, the UK banks decided to work towards an electronic inter-bank system for making guaranteed sterling payments from one clearing bank to another. The system, known as the Clearing House Automated Payment System Ltd (CHAPS), became operational in 1984. There are currently 16 settlement members of CHAPS (in March 1996 the members were Bank of England, Bank of Scotland, Barclays Bank plc, Citibank NA, Clydesdale Bank plc, Co-operative Bank plc, Coutts & Co., Crédit Lyonnais SA, Deutsche Bank AG, Girobank plc, Midland Bank plc, National Westminster Bank plc, Royal Bank of Scotland plc, Standard Chartered Bank and TSB Bank plc ('CHAPS Overview and Brief Description', issued by APACS)). The system operates on a nationwide basis through the head offices of each clearing bank, which are connected by computer terminals to the banks' principal branches throughout the country. The CHAPS system has been extended to non-settlement banks and corporate customers who can make and receive CHAPS payments through a direct link with their settlement banks. There are no minimum or maximum payment limits for a CHAPS payment.

The CHAPS system operates to make same-day electronic payments from one participating bank to another by the use of separate computer terminals maintained at the head offices and branches of the settlement banks. These terminals are connected through a central concentrator with the computer terminals of the head offices of other settlement banks by landlines belonging to British Telecom and through a central packet-switching unit to ensure that messages reach their intended destination. The computer terminals at the head offices of the settlement banks feed instructions through the concentrator, known as the CHAPS Gateway, which acts as a routing device for the transmission of instructions to the settlement banks. There is no single centralised computer into which the head offices of the participant banks can feed information so that the computer itself effects the payment. Although a payment mandate sent to the head office of a paying bank cannot be countermanded or recalled once it has entered the system (r. 2(b), CHAPS Clearing Rules, April 1996, provides that a CHAPS payment must be an 'irrevocable guaranteed unconditional sterling payment . . .'), it will not be released for transmission until it is checked and authenticated by a senior member of staff of the paying bank. The payment is then transmitted to the head office of the receiving bank whose own computer will immediately credit the payment to the payee's account; simultaneously, the receiving bank's computer will transmit the information contained in the payment instruction to its branch where the payee's account is held. The payment instruction comprises the name of the payee, the amount of the payment, the special sorting code number of the payee's bank and the branch to which payment is to be made, and the payee's account number. Similar information about the payer's account will be given so that his account may be debited on the computerised record of the accounts of the paying bank's customer.

Until 22 April 1996, when CHAPS became a real time gross settlement system (RTGS), settlement took place at the end of the CHAPS working day, when a special piece of software contained in the Bank of England CHAPS computer gateway interrogates the other CHAPS members for details of payments made and received during the course of the day. The Bank of England's system produced the settlement figure for each participating bank and the net difference was transferred between the settlement banks in accounts held with the Bank of England. However, settlement at the close of business introduces the risk of loss because a participating institution may become insolvent prior to settlement. Although netting reduces insolvency losses and leads to a payment for amounts sent less amounts received, for the right to survive set-off requires pre-insolvency mutuality; only the debts between the same counterparties can be set off against each other.

Since 22 April 1996 each CHAPS payment message is settled across members' accounts at the Bank of England before being sent to the receiving bank. The CHAPS Gateway Software has been altered so that a settlement request is initially sent to the Bank of England. If there are sufficient credit balances in the sending bank's account (r. 4 of the CHAPS Clearing Rules provides that each settlement member must ensure that payments are not entered into their Gateway unless there are sufficient funds in the member's settlement account with the Bank of England to settle the payment at the time entered. This rule does not apply if r. 13 operates) then the Bank of England will debit that account and credit the receiving bank's account, and then return a confirmation to the sending bank. On confirmation from the Bank of England, the payment message will be released automatically to the receiving bank by the sending bank's Gateway. The receiving bank will acknowledge receipt of payment by sending a logical acknowledgment message (LAK). To avoid gridlock a circles processing facility has been developed which allows the simultaneous settlement of payments queued on behalf of different banks (r. 13). If the Bank of England is unable to process RTGS, then CHAPS and the Bank of England can revert to net settlement at the Bank of England at the end of the business day (r. 14). A system of net bilateral receiver limits would then be brought into operation by the members.

Thus, the settlement does not rely on any set-off mechanism between participants, nor on any intra-day credit implicitly granted by other participants in the system. Each settlement is final and there is no unwinding the payment. Indeed Modern payment systems have practically eliminated any time lag between the transfer mandate and the settlement.

INTERNATIONAL MONEY TRANSFERS

The international transfer of money is an essential feature of free trade and has taken on a greater significance as financial markets have become more closely linked and dependent on each other by computers and technology. Almost all international money transfers are effected through banking channels and almost all transfers are carried through by means of the banker's draft, the mail transfer, the telegraphic transfer and the telecommunications networks, e.g., SWIFT, the Society for Worldwide Interbank Financial Telecommunications.

Society for Worldwide Interbank Financial Telecommunications

The financial communications system developed by SWIFT was a major step towards the application of electronic funds transfer to the international transfer of funds. Although SWIFT is not a funds transfer system, it facilitates the transfer of funds through the use of a secure and reliable international communications network.

SWIFT is a non-profit cooperative company organised under Belgian law, which is wholly owned by its members. All member banks hold shares which are reallocated each year in proportion to each member's usage of SWIFT. The shareholders elect a board of directors which chooses a general manager and has power to implement changes in provisions governing SWIFT's allocation of liability, to admit new members and to expel members. In order to become a member, an organisation must be engaged in banking and transmit international financial messages.

Originally, the system was operated through three main operating centres, located in Brussels, in Amsterdam and in Culpeper, Virginia, in the United States. These centres constituted the transmitting link between the banks. Subsequently, the Brussels centre was not retained, and in 1990, the entire system was restructured and renamed SWIFT II. The system now consists of a number of 'slices', each of which consists of a number of networks capable of independent function, and capable of receiving, transmitting and storing messages. At present there are two control 'slice processors' located at two of the original centres in Amsterdam and Culpeper, Virginia and these supervise the networks within the system.

Individual banks have access to SWIFT II through the regional centre known as SWIFT Access Point (SAP) and which in the UK is situated at BACS's premises in Edgware. Each country is assigned to such a centre, although in the USA there are eight such terminals. When a customer instructs the bank to carry out a money transfer transaction or other similar financial transaction, his instruction is conveyed by the bank's terminal to the regional SAP terminal by a special SWIFT link or by a telex message. The SAP will encode the message and dispatch it to the slice processor. As with other money transfers, the SWIFT message will set out all the relevant details of the transfer, including the name of a correspondent bank overseas which the transmitting bank wishes to use to complete the payment. The slice processor transmits the message, after verifying the encoded security numbers contained in it, to the appropriate SAP in the country of destination. The message is decoded and transmitted to the recipient direct, or through the agency of a correspondent bank to the recipient bank using the domestic transfer systems.

SWIFT II is a communications network and is not a clearing or settlement system. SWIFT II undertakes to transmit transaction instructions on the day they are received from the paying customer, although time zone differentials may have to be taken into account. Messages arriving at their destination after the close of business are stored at the SAP and processed on the next business day in the order in which they are received, except priority messages, which involve an extra cost, and are processed ahead of non-priority transactions. SWIFT deals with 2 million messages per day, 75 per cent of which relate to payment transactions, with an estimated value of US$2.5 trillion (SWIFT, 'Facilitating New Bank Products in Cross-Border Mass Payment', paper presented by Peter Scott at 1994 International Payment Systems Conference, London 25–6 April 1994).

SWIFT accepts limited liability for breach of certain duties. It undertakes responsibility for loss of interest arising out of a late payment due to its fault (SWIFT User Handbook, Pt V, s. 23.2.6). Although there is no limit for any individual claims, SWIFT's overall annual liability for loss of interest arising out of late payment may not exceed 50 million Belgian francs (SWIFT User Handbook, Pt V, s. 24.5.2). SWIFT is also responsible for direct loss or damage (i.e., loss of amount and interest stipulated in the message) due to:

(a) negligence by SWIFT in the performance of its obligations and security;
(b) fraud committed by its employees or contractors employed for operating the system; and
(c) fraud of third parties not employed by SWIFT, but within the responsibility of SWIFT (SWIFT User Handbook, Pt V, s. 24.4.2)

LEGAL OBLIGATIONS AND CONTRACTUAL RELATIONSHIPS WITHIN ELECTRONIC FUNDS TRANSFERS

There is considerable divergence between the methods of transferring funds. Each system is based on a complex mixture of contractual relationships devised between the parties, and the law of agency undoubtedly plays a major role in transfers of funds. Thus, a credit transfer is not a single process and in fact represents a number of distinct contractual relationships between, e.g., (a) the payer and the payer's bank; (b) the payer's bank and the payee's bank; (c) the payee and the payee's bank; and (d) the payer and payee. In addition to these relationships, there are numerous other potential relationships. Thus, if the payee's bank is not a settlement bank, it will have to clear through a bank which is a settlement bank. The situation may also be the same in reverse with the payee bank. Once the international dimension is brought into the picture and cross-border payments are made, other relationships are grafted on, e.g., correspondent banks and foreign clearings.

In the UK, money transfer methods have developed and responded to both consumer demand and banking practice. Money transfer systems have not been made subject to specific legislation and much of the current common law would serve merely as persuasive authority. Although the United Nations General Assembly approved the Report of the United Nations Commission on International Trade Law (UNCITRAL) and the Model Law on International Credit Transfers at UNCITRAL's 25th Session of 4–22 May 1992 (see UN General Assembly, Official Records, 4th Session, Supp. No. 17, UN Doc. A/47/17) and recommended that all States enact legislation on the Model Law, there is currently no indication of the UK government following that recommendation.

ROLE OF THE TRANSFERRING BANK

The paying or transferring bank will act as an agent of the payer when making credit transfers. In that capacity the bank is under a duty not only to conform to the customer's mandate but also to carry out the payment mandate with reasonable skill and care in accordance with current banking practice (*Selangor United Rubber Estates Ltd* v *Cradock (No. 3)* [1968] 1 WLR 1555; *Karak Rubber Co. Ltd* v *Burden No. 2* [1972] 1 WLR 602). The principle was vividly explained by Steyn J in *Barclays Bank plc* v *Quincecare Ltd* [1992] 4 All ER 363, where the learned judge said that prima facie every agent for reward is bound to exercise reasonable care and skill in carrying out the instructions of his principal. There is no logical or sensible reason for holding that bankers are immune from such an elementary obligation.

This key duty, to exercise reasonable skill and care, is replicated in s. 13 of the Supply of Goods and Services Act 1992. The obvious facets of this duty would appear to be as follows:

(a)   the bank must make payment with reasonable dispatch;
(b)   the bank must install and maintain reasonably efficient security systems; and
(c)   the bank must employ a reliable correspondent.

In the context of the agency relationship the paying bank's obligation is to make payment in strict conformity with the customer's mandate and a bank which fails to comply with the mandate is denied its right, as an agent, to reimbursement. The converse is that the instructions given by the customer must be clear and unambiguous (*Midland Bank Ltd* v *Seymour* [1955] 2 Lloyd's Rep 147). If its customer's instructions are ambiguous a bank will be justified in following a course of action that is reasonable and in accordance with prevailing banking practice.

The duty to exercise reasonable skill and care also requires the bank to take proper precautions and to organise its business so as to ensure that it provides and maintains an efficient payments system, with the necessary security (the Jack Committee proposed that banks should adopt the principle that an EFT system must meet certain minimum standards of security in its authorisation procedures, so as to provide an acceptable degree of protection for the customer against the consequences of unauthorised instructions (Cm 622 (1989), para. 10.15)). Where transfer is by means of a CHAPS payment, the transferring bank is under an obligation to ensure that, provided the customer's instructions are clear and unambiguous, same-day payment is effected. It seems that the transferring bank's obligations will be discharged if it acts with reasonable skill and care in executing the customer's mandate. If the failure to execute the payment is attributable to the receiving bank (e.g., a failure to acknowledge the receipt of the payment so that the message is not included in the settlement for that day) then the transferring bank cannot be held liable for non-payment. If the reason for non-execution of the payment is that the instructions received by the transferring bank have accumulated to such an extent that they cannot all be transmitted when the CHAPS payment messages close for the day, it is questionable whether the paying bank would be liable to the payer for failing to fulfil his instructions, provided the customer was warned of any possible delays in the system and provided that they are fulfilled with reasonable dispatch the following day. The transferring bank's obligations to the payer must be determined by each payment instruction separately, and the bank's duty to exercise skill and care must be ascertained with regard to the circumstances in which each instruction is given.

In addition to operating its equipment for making CHAPS payments efficiently, the transferring bank owes a duty to ensure that it exercises reasonable skill and care in relation to the adequacy of the payment and settlement systems and that the equipment is properly maintained. This duty is probably non-delegable so that it will not be sufficient for the bank to exercise reasonable care in appointing technical advisers and engineers if they do not exercise the appropriate skill and care (*Greaves and Co. (Contractors) Ltd* v *Baynham Meikle and Partners* [1975] 1 WLR 1095). The transferring bank will be liable to its customer if the failure to transmit a payment message is due to a defect or malfunction in the equipment caused by inadequate maintenance and supervision of the computer systems.

The transferring bank owes a duty to exercise reasonable skill and care in employing a correspondent bank. The transferring bank is vicariously liable for the acts of its correspondent and if a credit transfer is not executed because of the failure of the correspondent bank, it is not entitled to debit the customer's account (the point was trenchantly made in *Royal Products Ltd* v *Midland Bank Ltd* [1981] 2 Lloyd's Rep 194; see also *Equitable Trust Co. of New York* v *Dawson Partners Ltd* (1927) 27 Ll L Rep 49).

A transfer of funds made abroad may not necessitate the use of a correspondent bank, because a direct transfer may be possible. Where an intermediary bank is required to effect the transfer, the transferring bank may by express agreement seek to transfer the risk of loss occasioned by the intermediary to the paying customer. Any agreement which seeks to reallocate risk and liability will be subject to the Unfair Terms in Consumer Contracts Regulations 1994 (SI 1994/3159; see chapter 8). The Regulations provide that an unfair term is one which is contrary to the requirement of good faith and causes a significant imbalance in the parties' rights and obligations under the contract to the detriment of the consumer. The Banking Code of Practice sets out rules about liability for loss as between card issuers and customers but it does not extend to on-line banking services.

ROLE OF THE CORRESPONDENT BANK

A correspondent bank will be employed where the transferring bank is unable to transfer funds according to the customer's instructions directly to the payee. As it acts as an agent of the transferring bank in executing the original customer's instructions, there does not exist a direct contractual relationship between it and the original customer. The situation which exists between the parties is one where the agent appoints a sub-agent to carry out the principal's instructions. In *Calico Printers' Association* v *Barclays Bank Ltd* (1931) 36 Com Cas 71 Wright J observed that as a general rule there is no privity of contract between a principal and his agent's sub-agent. This view was reaffirmed by Webster J in *Royal Products Ltd* v *Midland Bank Ltd* [1981] 2 Lloyd's Rep 194 in connection with the absence of a relationship between the customer who gives a mandate to transfer funds and the correspondent bank.

The courts have, however, held that in exceptional cases they will recognise a contractual relationship between the original customer and the correspondent bank. Thus, in *Silverstein* v *Chartered Bank* (1977) 392 NYS 2d 296 the American court held the transferor did have a contract with his bank's correspondent as the latter had been expressly selected by the customer himself. In *Evra Corporation* v *Swiss*

Bank Corporation (1981) 522 F Supp 820 the United States District Court held that the correspondent was liable in damages for breach of contract and negligence. Although the decision was reversed on other grounds, the appellate court did not question the existence of privity between the charterers and the correspondent bank.

ROLE OF THE RECIPIENT BANK

The receiving bank will act on instructions received from the transferring bank or its correspondent and must credit the payee's account according to the instructions received. The receiving bank would appear to be under a duty to credit the named payee's account with the specified amount. Depending on the method of payment used, the payee's account must be credited either immediately or within a reasonable period. To that extent it is submitted that the receiving bank actually acts as an agent of the transferring bank. This view was adopted by the American court in *Shawmut Worcester County* v *First American Bank and Trust Co.* 731 F Supp 57, where the court held that the recipient bank acts as the agent of the transferring bank for such purposes. However, it must therefore follow that, once the payee's account is credited with the amount of the transfer, the payee bank acts not as an agent for the transferring bank but for the account holder (the payee to whose account the funds have been credited).

In the UK the courts have looked at the issue whether in credit transfer transactions the recipient bank is an agent of the payee. Chorley (*Law of Banking* 6th ed. (London: Sweet and Maxwell, 1974)), while generally suggesting that in credit transfer transactions the paying bank is to be regarded as the payer's agent and the collecting bank as the payee's agent, states: 'It is arguable, however, that on receipt of a credit transfer on behalf of his customer the banker receives the money as a borrower under the rule in *Foley* v *Hill*'. Chorley says that the view that the 'recipient banker — like the paying banker — is engaged as an agent is indisputable; it is less certain who is to be regarded as his principal'. The memorandum, *Bank Money Transfer Services*, published in 1967 by the clearing banks and the Scottish banks indicates that the participating banks are authorised to act for each other in giro transactions. Chorley concludes that the principal is the customer for whose credit the amount is received and this is also assumed in the cases. In *Mardorf Peach and Co. Ltd* v *Attica Sea Carriers Corporation of Liberia* [1976] QB 835; [1977] AC 850) in the Court of Appeal, Lord Denning MR and Lawton LJ held that payment of hire for a ship by the charterers of it had taken place when the payment order was handed to the receiving bank as agent for the owners and accepted by it without objection. This conclusion was arrived at through the argument that payment orders are treated as the commercial equivalent of cash and that after the payment order was handed over, the charterers were to be treated as having no control over the payment. The House of Lords allowed an appeal, although the assumption that the receiving bank was the agent of the owners was not questioned. However, the House accepted that the receiving bank, although an agent of the owners, had only a limited authority to accept payment and that authority extended only to an acceptance of a payment made punctually. In the light of the limited authority conferred on the receiving bank it is necessary to deal with the issue whether an agency relationship has to be imposed. On the authority of *Foley* v *Hill* (1848) 2 HL Cas 28 it could be argued that the bank receives the money in its own right and that it makes no difference whether the sum is paid to the bank by the customer himself or by a third party. However, it would appear to be inappropriate to say that the bank receives money paid by the customer into the account as agent for the customer. The bank receives money for the customer. This point was discussed in *Midland Bank Ltd* v *Conway Corporation* [1965] 1 WLR 1165, where the court held that in the circumstances the bank was not an agent for the purposes of the Public Health Act 1936. The bank gave no receipt for the money received, it had no right to refuse acceptance of it and was acting solely under its duty as a banker to receive any money paid in. It was therefore not proper to draw an inference that there is a special relationship between the bank and its customer which constitutes the bank an agent to receive the rent. Lord Parker CJ and Browne J did not express any view on whether the bank in receiving money for its customer might be an agent in the more limited sense in *Mardorf Peach and Co. Ltd* v *Attica Sea Carriers Corporation of Liberia*. Further support for this view is implicit in *Royal Products Ltd* v *Midland Bank Ltd* [1981] 2 Lloyd's Rep 194, where Webster J stated that it is implicit in the relationship of the customer and the bank that the bank should receive sums paid to it for the account of the customer. There is no question of a 'special relationship' to take the parties outside the principle in *Foley* v *Hill*. The completion of the instructions occurs when the customer of the receiving bank is enabled to draw on or otherwise use the sum transferred. If the bank is treated as agent of the customer for receipt of the sum transferred a difficulty arises as to when the bank ceases to hold the money as debtor. Webster J thought that after the customer was able to draw on or otherwise use the sum transferred, his remedy against the bank was as an unsecured creditor and not as owner of the property, thus indicating that prior to the bank actually crediting the sum to the account of the customer the bank is a debtor and not an agent.

Article 10 of the UNCITRAL Model Law states that the receiving bank is the agent of the transferring (or correspondent) bank until the recipient bank accepts the funds for the credit of the payee's account. The answer, however, is not so simple, especially where electronic systems of funds transfer are used. The position of the parties in such cases is settled by contract, and if the contractual terms are reasonable then the courts will give effect to them. Thus, in a CHAPS payment the receiving bank must be under an obligation to exercise reasonable care to ensure that its computer terminals, modem and computerised accounting system are in proper working order so as to be able to receive and transmit payment messages. Such a duty will be owed to its customer for whom the receiving bank undertakes to receive and credit to his account a CHAPS payment, but also to the transferring and correspondent bank, if used, under a master contract under which the CHAPS system is operated. Similarly, in SWIFT transfers, the master contract between the banks makes detailed provision concerning the allocation of losses in the event of a systems breakdown or where instructions are improperly executed.

COUNTERMAND

Does the transfer of funds amount to an assignment?

The question whether an instruction to effect a payment by EFT amounts to an assignment of funds has considerable significance. It is submitted that as the final result of a funds transfer by EFT is precisely that achieved through a paper-based system, i.e., the transfer of funds to the payee, the answer must be the same regardless of the method of payment. Therefore, regardless of the method of payment used, if the effect of a mere instruction to transfer funds operates by way of a legal assignment, the payment will become irrevocable immediately (Law of Property Act 1925, s. 136; see also *Hockley* v *Goldstein* (1920) 90 LJ KB 111). If the transfer mandate is treated as an equitable assignment, the transaction is completed when the debt is assigned. Thus, payment would be complete once the bank puts into motion the necessary steps for transferring the funds even though the debtor is not advised of the transfer (*William Brandt's Sons and Co.* v *Dunlop Rubber Co. Ltd* [1905] AC 454). In *Delbrueck and Co.* v *Manufacturers Hanover Trust Co.* (1979) 609 F 2d 1047 it was argued that amounts credited by a customer in an account with the transferring bank were a chose in action and therefore capable of being assigned. Moore J, however, stated that under American law in order for there to be a valid 'assignment of a chose in action, there must be a specific direction to transfer by the assignor and notice to the assignee'. The order to transfer funds having been given to the transferring bank, the court concluded that delivery of the credit slip to the receiving bank was sufficient notice of the transfer where the receiving bank acted as an agent of the payee.

However, it is submitted that the UK courts would take the view that instructing the transferring bank to make payment, through giro or other transfer system, would not amount to an assignment of part of the payer's credit balance to the payee. Section 136 of the Law of Property Act 1925 does not permit assignment of part of a debt. A customer who has a credit balance in his account with the transferring bank, although the balance is likely to have been built up over a period of time by a series of transactions (credit and debit), is owed a single debt by the bank. An instruction to transfer a part of the balance to a payee is therefore unlikely to fall under the 1925 Act. Moreover, an instruction to make payment on a specified future date (e.g., with a BACS payment) cannot be treated as an immediate assignment of future funds or even as an assignment on the day the payment instruction is to be executed.

Alternatively, the initiation of the EFT transaction could be argued to constitute an immediate transfer of funds to the payee if it could be shown that the transferring bank becomes a trustee for the benefit of the payee. However, this argument is unlikely to be sustainable and the courts have clearly held that the placing of money in a separate account by a bank, or the setting aside of money for a specific purpose in a bank account does not constitute a trust in favour of the intended payee (*Lister and Co.* v *Stubbs* (1890) 45 ChD 1; *Moseley* v *Cressey's Co.* (1865) LR 1 Eq 405). It is true, however, that more recently in *Barclays Bank Ltd* v *Quistclose Investments Ltd* [1970] AC 567 and *Re Kayford Ltd* [1975] 1 WLR 279 the courts have held that if money is placed in a separate account by a bank for the specific purpose of being returned to the creditor if the purpose for which it is lent is not satisfied, then the money is held on trust for the creditor (see also *Re Nanwa Gold Mines Ltd* [1955] 1 WLR 1080). However, these rules are likely to apply only in exceptional cases and cannot be followed generally.

If the instruction to the transferring bank to transfer money to the payee does not amount to an assignment of funds then the payer may have an opportunity to countermand payment. The issues which have to be resolved are when is payment complete and when does it become irrevocable?

Completion of payment and revocation

The issues relating to when payment is made and up until what stage a payment mandate can be countermanded are made complex by the diverse methods of money transfer that are available. The issues are made more complex by the fact that many of the money transfer methods operate within a framework established by the banks and rely on the law of contract with the result that many of the issues likely to cause legal problems have not been resolved. However, the very existence of these methods of transferring money anticipates the existence of suitable clearing systems and settlement takes place by striking net balances between the banks. As a general rule it would appear that a payment is complete when the transferring bank becomes irrevocably committed to making payment and once that happens countermand is impossible. Thus, the issues relating to completion of payment and countermand are inextricably linked. The answer to the two questions depends on the method of payment used, e.g., the point when payment is complete in the BACS system is not the same as in the CHAPS system. The time of payment may also vary depending on the parties involved, e.g., an international funds transfer using the SWIFT system may involve the transferring bank using the CHAPS gateway to send a payment message to the SWIFT slice processor in Edgware, which then transmits messages to the SWIFT slice processor in, e.g., the USA, where the payee is to receive payment and then using the CHIPS system (the American equivalent of the CHAPS system) to direct payment to the payee's bank and ultimately his account. The entire payment process is based on complex contractual arrangements and it may be that although some of the parties in the chain have received payment others have not.

The courts will have to resolve these issues on an individual basis and operate within the contractual framework developed by the banks if payment systems are to continue to operate as currently.

When is payment made?

This issue is especially important where payment has to be by a specified time or under the underlying contract between the parties a penalty clause or a forfeiture clause will apply. The cases where this has been examined have involved the right of a ship owner to withdraw a ship under a charterparty because the charterer has failed to pay the hire on time. The issue was examined in *The Brimnes* [1975] QB 929, where the charterer's bank, Hambros, was instructed to pay the hire to the shipowner's bank, Morgan Guaranty Trust (MGT) in New York. Hambros also had an account at the same branch of MGT. Accordingly, it instructed MGT by telex to transfer the appropriate amount from its own account to that of the shipowners. The Court of Appeal held that payment to the shipowners was effected, not when the telex was received, but some two hours later when the message had been processed and the decision to effect the transfer had been taken. Thus, a mere request or instruction by the transferring bank to the receiving bank to credit the payee's account does not itself constitute payment, but a commitment to transfer funds will be effective as soon as the bank is irrevocably committed to that decision. In the course of the judgment the court endorsed a statement of Brandon J (at first instance) that good payment can be considered made when the result of the transfer of funds is to give the transferee the unconditional right to the immediate use of funds.

This view was considered in *A/S Awilco* v *Fulvia SpA di Navigazioni* [1979] 1 Lloyd's Rep 367; [1980] 2 Lloyd's Rep 409; [1981] 1 WLR 314, where the position was more complicated. In that case Credito Italiano Genova (CIG), acting as agent for the charterers' bank, instructed the owners' bank by telex on 22 January 1976, to make the requisite payment to the owners' account as per the order of the charterers' bank. The Turin branch of the owners' bank was to receive a payment in respect of the same amount, valued at 26 January 1976, to the credit of its account at Chase Manhattan New York where CIG also had an account ('Telecover you value 26 through Chase Manhattan Bank New York account yours of Turin stop'). The arbitrator found as a fact that under Italian banking law and practice the credit transfer became irrevocable at about noon on 22 January. Despite this Robert Goff J held that 'payment in cash' had not been effected because interest did not accrue to the account of the owners until 26 January when payment was to be covered and interest would have to have been paid by the owners if the money had been withdrawn prior to that date.

The decision was reversed on appeal, although the view of Cairns LJ in *The Brimnes*, concerning 'value dated' credit transfers was treated as correct. The Court of Appeal, however, held that it followed from the arbitrator's finding that the credit transfer was irrevocable on 22 January and that the substantive part of the telex ordering the owners' bank to pay the sum to the account of the owners was capable of being an unconditional payment. The sentence in the telex 'Telecover you value 26 through Chase Manhattan Bank New York account yours stop' was merely an inter-banking direction or communication. The court also concluded that the fact that the owners might be required to pay interest if they withdrew the money from the bank did not affect the nature of the unconditional payment.

The House of Lords, in a unanimous judgment, reversed this decision. The judgment of Brandon J in the *The Brimnes* as to when payment was made was approved and the issue which had to be resolved was whether the word 'unconditional' used in the judgment was to be construed narrowly so as to refer to the absence of a condition which the courts would construe as being necessary to the performance of the contractual obligation or whether it was to apply to any obligation which would prevent the owners from using the funds. The House of Lords took the view that the latter construction was correct and because interest charges would be imposed if the money was withdrawn from the account the owners did not have the unconditional use of the funds. Further, the House took the view that the part of the telex which referred to 'value 26' was crucial because it informed the owners' bank of to whom the debt was to be made good.

Countermand of payment

Closely allied to the question of when payment becomes complete is the issue of the customer's right to countermand his original mandate to make payment. Obviously once the paying bank has become irrevocably committed to the payment the payer cannot countermand the payment instruction. The issue has been examined in two English cases. In *Momm* v *Barclays Bank International Ltd* [1977] QB 790 the plaintiffs and another bank, Herstatt, maintained separate accounts with the defendant bank. The plaintiffs and Herstatt concluded a currency transaction under which Herstatt were to transfer a sum of money to the plaintiffs' account at the defendant bank valued at 26 June 1974. On 25 June, Herstatt instructed the defendants to make the transfer. The defendants did this on receipt of the instruction on 26 June. At 4.15 p. m. on that day Herstatt announced that they were going into liquidation and on 27 June, the defendants reversed the entry to the plaintiffs' account as Herstatt's account was in a net deficit position. Kerr J held that the transfer was complete when the defendants would have refused to have accepted a countermand instruction from Herstatt, which would have been when the computer processes to credit the plaintiffs' account were set in motion. It made no difference that the defendants had notified neither the plaintiffs nor Herstatt of this prior to a purported revocation of the transfer. This decision must be contrasted with the Court of Appeal judgment in *Rekstin* v *Severo Sibirsko Gosudarstvennoe Akciomernoe Obschestvo Komseveputj* [1933] 1 KB 47. Rekstin had obtained judgment against Severo. In order to avoid execution Severo ordered the Bank for Russian Trade to transfer sums from its account at the bank to a Russian trade delegation with diplomatic immunity, which also had an account at the bank. After a clerk at the bank had made the necessary book entry to close the Severo account but before the corresponding credit entry in the delegation's account had been made Rekstin served a garnishee order *nisi* on the bank. The Court of Appeal held that the bank still held the sums to the account of Severo and that the garnishee order *nisi* was effective. The court treated as important that the trade delegation knew nothing of the proposed transfer and it had never consented to its account being credited. Kerr J in the *Momm* case distinguished the *Rekstin* case and said:

> In my view this decision should be treated as confined to its special facts . . . I think that it merely decided that payment by means of an in-house transfer has not taken place if the payee has not assented to it, and perhaps also if the transfer has not been completed.

It is worth noting that Kerr J in the *Momm* case treated the credit entry in the plaintiffs' account with the defendant bank as a final settlement or final payment, although there was no proof that the plaintiffs had authorised the defendant bank to receive payment. Kerr J emphasised that payment would be final if it stood undisturbed at the end of the 'value date'.

The issue of when payment becomes irrevocable was examined in another case resulting from the collapse of the German Herstatt bank. In *Delbrueck and Co* v *Manufacturers Hanover Trust Co* (1979) 609 F 2d 1047 the plaintiffs, a German bank, maintained an account with the defendant bank in the USA and entered into exchange contracts with the Herstatt bank. Under these contracts approximately US$12.5 million were payable by the plaintiffs to the Herstatt bank on 26 June. On 25 June the plaintiffs sent a telex message to the defendant bank requesting it to credit Herstatt bank's account with the Chase Manhattan bank with the requisite amount. At 10.30 a.m. on 26 June (Eastern Standard Time) Herstatt was closed down by the German Reserve Bank. At approximately 11.40 a.m. the defendant bank transferred to Chase the amount involved using the CHIPS (American equivalent to CHAPS) system. Within the next 30 minutes the plaintiffs gave an instruction to the defendant bank to countermand payment and then confirmed this by telex. At 9.00 p.m. on the same day, Herstatt's account with the Chase Manhattan was credited with the amount of the payment. The plaintiffs brought an action in negligence and claimed that the defendant bank had acted in breach of a duty of care when it failed immediately to act on the countermand. The District Court dismissed this action and the decision was affirmed by the Second Circuit Court of Appeals. Moore J reviewed the technology involved in a CHIPS transfer and held that a transfer executed through this autonomous network invariably reached the recipient bank almost instantaneously once it was released by the computer terminal of the transferring bank. Moreover, it was understood between the participating banks that the funds could be drawn on by the payee once the payment message had been received by the receiving bank. Thus, the payment was complete once it was effected by the defendant bank and the fact that the credit was not entered into Herstatt's account until 9.00 p. m. was merely a matter of internal book-keeping, which did not effect the completion of the payment. Moore J therefore concluded that once the payment message was executed by CHIPS the message could not be revoked or countermanded.

Although the conclusions reached in the *Momm* and *Delbrueck* cases would appear to be inconsistent, it is submitted that the two decisions can be justified on the basis that different transfer methods were used. The *Momm* case was based on the finding that banking practice made provision for the reversal of credit entries. The *Delbrueck* case, however, arose out of the use of a system which precluded revocation once the payment message was released through the paying bank's computer terminal. No doubt the possibility of a payment being countermanded will depend on the system being used and the relevant banking practice. The Jack Committee on Banking Services (Cm 622, 1989) was concerned that where instantaneous methods of money transfer are used, the customer may be denied the opportunity to countermand payment. The Committee concluded that banks should formulate their own contractual rules on countermand for each EFT system so, whenever possible, the customer is given an opportunity to countermand instructions. Further, customers should be notified of the steps necessary for an effective countermand to be given.

ELECTRONIC PAYMENT AND SETTLEMENT OF DEBT

There are fundamentally two types of payment and settlement systems, namely, gross settlement and net settlement systems. Where banks are involved in a continuous course of dealing and so make and receive payments regularly, for and on behalf of their customers, they will want to ensure that amounts owed to them will be paid and that they are safeguarded against the possibility of the transferring bank becoming insolvent.

The structure of the gross settlement systems is relatively simple and each individual payment is processed separately and (unless explicit credit is granted within the system) effected as soon as cover is available on the account of the clearing bank causing the payment to be made. Thus settlement does not rely on any set-off mechanism between participants (except in connection with the normal operation of the bank accounts), nor on any intra-day credit implicitly granted by other participants in the system. Furthermore, each settlement is final and there is no mechanism for unwinding the transaction, e.g., CHAPS where the use of modern technology has practically eliminated any time lag between the entry of the transfer and the settlement.

An alternative method of settling transfer of funds is through the net settlement systems. In a multilateral net settlement system, which is the traditional method used, the payment process can be divided into two phases: netting and settlement. During the netting phase, the various payment orders given by the participating clearing banks in favour of the other participants (or their customers) are transmitted to a netting agent, who calculates the net overall position of each participant at an agreed cut-off time. Unless there are special contractual arrangements providing for novation, such net positions are not legally binding, as they are the result of an accounting exercise. During the second phase, the participants with a net debit position must effect settlements in favour of the participants with a net credit position.

Risk control mechanisms employed by CHAPS (prior to 1996) were bilateral credit limits (for each counterparty, vis-à-vis another, a bilateral credit limit sets the maximum total received less sent that the other may extend to it at any point throughout the exchange) and net debit caps (a net debit cap measures the multilateral or overall debit position of a counterparty and may be established either on the basis of the total bilateral credit limits or under guidelines, which usually refer to capital adequacy standards).

BANK CONFIDENTIALITY, THE DATA PROTECTION ACT 1984 AND COMPUTERISED BANKING

A bank's duty of confidentiality has been long established. It is suggested that the obligation should not be affected by the methods of recording and keeping records about the bank's customers and their transactions. However, it is likely that breaches of this duty will be more common with increased computerisation. As a result of the increase of electronic funds transfers: (a) more banking records will be generated; (b) information will be easier to retrieve; (c) the number of institutions that may have access to such records will increase; and (d) the use of such records will enable the capture of more information about customers (National Commission on Electronic Funds Transfers in the USA, 'Electronic funds transfers systems — a survey of the legal issues', (1984) 58 Law Inst J 1200, 1202).

It is not merely the increased amount of information kept by banks about their customers that raises concerns in respect of the confidentiality aspects of the banker and customer relationship, but also the practical aspects of such transactions. Electronic funds transfers reveal more information about their customers than non-EFT transactions. The analysis of EFT transactions may more readily be used to create a comprehensive financial and personal profile. Such transactions may be used to monitor a customer's daily movements, e.g., by monitoring money withdrawals or other transactions from automated teller machines or by the use of EFTPOS systems.

The scope and extent of the duty of confidentiality has already been discussed (see chapter 8). The correctness of the principles of law stated by the majority in *Tournier* v *National Provincial and Union Bank of England Ltd* [1924] 1 KB 461 has not been doubted since the case was decided and has been affirmed in many decisions (e.g., see May LJ in *Lipkin Gorman* v *Karpnale Ltd* [1989] 1 WLR 1340, 1357).

Whilst there have been many inroads to the principles established in *Tournier* v *National Provincial and Union Bank of England Ltd* the idea of bank confidentiality has been given statutory recognition in somewhat unusual circumstances. Part V of the Banking Act 1987 contains six sections dealing with the confidentiality of information obtained under its provisions.

Data Protection Act 1984

The Data Protection Act 1984 was enacted to 'regulate the use of automatically processed information relating to individuals'. It is designed to allow the UK to ratify the Council of Europe's Convention for the Protection of Individuals with regard to Automatic Processing of Personal Data. The Act applies to banks, clearing houses and banks' customers. Automated clearing systems, such as CHAPS and BACS, keep a considerable amount of personal information about their participant customers. Although such clearing houses have no direct relationship with individuals about whom they keep information, they collect such information through their banks. A customer will instruct his bank to transfer funds from his account to a specified payee. His bank will carry out the instruction through a clearing house (e.g., BACS). The latter will credit the account of the payee's bank, debit the account of the payer's bank, and send messages to both banks informing them of the credit and debit of the relevant accounts. In undertaking this transaction, the clearing house will have available a considerable amount of information about the bank's customer and in such circumstances there is a need to protect the confidentiality of such information.

Section 1(6) of the Data Protection Act 1984 provides that CHAPS and other similar clearing houses are 'computer bureaux'. The participating banks which use the data in the clearing houses' computers are 'data users' within the meaning of s. 1(5). The customers of the participating banks, about whom the data is collected and stored, are 'data subjects' within the meaning of s. 1(4). Moreover, the type of information kept by banks and clearing houses is included in the definition of s. 1(2). Thus, there can be little doubt about the relevance of the Data Protection Act 1984 to information kept by banks and clearing houses through the use of computerised systems about individuals.

Section 5 of the Act prohibits a person who is registered either as a data user, or as a data user and a computer bureau, its servant or agent, from disclosing any information held by it, its servant or agent to any person not described in the relevant data-user entry. Those entries are likely to describe the other parties to the transaction, e.g., the payer, payee, the respective banks, a clearing house through which payment is directed and any other relevant party thought to be necessary to perform the transaction. Section 15 precludes computer centres and data users from disclosing confidential information without the prior authority of the person concerned. However, a disclosure of such information to computer centres' and banks' servants and agents who carry out relevant transactions is permitted. The disclosure of information is also permitted to the Data Protection Registrar or the Data Protection Tribunal if disclosure is necessary for the discharge of their functions under the Act (s. 17) and for other reasons specified by the Act.

272

The Data Protection Act will require amendment to bring the UK in line with the new EU Directive on Data Protection (95/46/EC, OJ No. 281/31, 23.11.95, p. 31). The Directive extends data protection to certain types of manual data (art. 3) and requires (in certain cases) the data subject's consent to the processing of personal data (arts 7(a) and 8(2)(a)). Member States are required to implement the Directive within three years of the date of adoption but there is a 12 year transitional period for compliance in respect of existing manual data (art. 32).

15   Remedies to Recover Money

A bank can only debit its customer's account if it makes payment against a valid mandate. In some instances the customer may be estopped from challenging the bank's right to debit his account, or the bank may have statutory protection under the Bills of Exchange Act 1882 entitling it to debit the customer's account. In some cases the bank does not enjoy the protection given by the common law or by statute and the bank may seek to recover the amount of the payment wrongfully made. The commonest instances of payments made under a mistake are where:

(a)   a customer has effectively countermanded payment on a cheque but due to an error the bank makes payment;

(b)   where the bank makes payment in the mistaken belief that the customer's signature is genuine, when in fact it has been forged;

(c)   because of a computer error, a payment made by bank giro is effected twice, instead of once.

In such a situation the bank may prefer to seek to recover the money from the payee, rather than enter into a dispute with its own customer over its right to debit his account.

RIGHT TO RECOVER FROM THE PAYEE

The word 'payee' has to be understood in a wide context. The amount paid usually involves payment by the paying bank to the collecting bank employed by the ultimate payee. If payment is made due to an error, recovery of the amount may be claimed either from the ultimate payee or from his agent bank. The money will be recoverable from the agent up until such time as the agent has paid it over to the principal or has otherwise disposed of it on behalf of the principal (see *Buller v Harrison* (1777) 2 Cowp 565). The principle was restated in *Gowers v Lloyds and National Provincial Foreign Bank Ltd* [1938] 1 All ER 766, where Greene MR said that money paid to an agent under a mistake of fact could be recovered from him so long as he had it in his possession. However, if the agent has paid the money away to the principal, then it cannot be recovered from the agent, and it can only be recovered from the principal. This issue has been examined in a number of cases. In *Continental Caoutchouc and Gutta Percha Co* v *Kleinwort Sons and Co* (1904) 90 LT 474 Collins MR distinguished between two types of cases, namely:

(a)   where a bank received payment as a mere agent, then any amount erroneously paid could not be recovered from the bank once it was paid to the principal; and

(b)   where the bank received payment for itself then it was in the same position as any other ultimate payee to whom payment is made under a mistake.

Support is found for this view in *Thomas* v *Houston Corbett and Co.* [1969] NZLR 151, where it was said that whether the amount is received by the payee as an agent or as a principal depends on his understanding of the transaction and the capacity in which he purports to act. Moreover, the court held that a defendant will not succeed in avoiding repayment by establishing that he was acting as an agent if:

(a)   he had notice of the plaintiff's claim before paying the money to the principal or otherwise disposing of it on his behalf;

(b)   in the course of the transaction he acted as the principal;

(c)   he received the money in consequence of some wrongdoing to which he was a party or of which he had knowledge.

The courts have established that where money is collected by a bank and transferred to the use of the principal then it can no longer be recovered from the bank as the agent. However, where the bank collects amounts to the credit of a current account (usually a running total is kept) a situation may arise where an amount erroneously paid to the credit of the account is actually paid out again before the error is discovered. It may also happen that further amounts have been credited to the customer's account and the question then is whether the money paid erroneously to the credit of the customer's account is paid over to the (principal) customer. A strict application of the rule in *Clayton's Case* (*Devaynes* v *Noble*, *Clayton's Case* (1816) 1 Mer 529) and the first in first out principle would indicate that the erroneous credit entry would be exhausted. However, it may be that the courts will hold that where the total credit balance does not fall below the amount of the erroneous credit the customer who is unjustly enriched is deemed to use that part of the credit balance to which he is properly entitled and the bank is required to restore the amount of the erroneous payment. In *Australia and New Zealand Banking Group Ltd* v *Westpac Banking Corporation* (1988) 164 CLR 662 ANZ, by mistake, sent a telegraphic transfer transferring approximately $114,000 instead of an intended transfer of approximately $14,000 to Westpac for the credit of J Pty Ltd, whose account at the time of transfer was overdrawn by about $68,000. By the time ANZ notified Westpac of the error, a series of transactions had taken place which resulted in all but about $17,000 of the amount of the erroneous payment having been utilised by J Pty Ltd. The court held that Westpac's liability to repay the amount of the erroneous transfer was limited to the $17,000. However, it was argued (although the argument was rejected) in that case that payments out should be regarded as utilising and exhausting the whole of the available overdraft facility before being treated as applying any funds representing the overpayment and that, to the extent that the available overdraft accommodation would not suffice, the funds representing the overpayment should be treated as replenished by subsequent payments in.

Support for this argument is also found in *Holland* v *Russell* (1861) 30 LJ QB 308, where Cockburn CJ suggested that the amount was to be regarded as paid over when it had been made the subject of a 'settled account' or an account stated. However, a bank statement does not constitute a settled account and the bank is only estopped from reversing a payment credited to the account if the customer has changed his position relying on the statement. Hence, so long as the credit entry remains capable of reversal, any money paid by mistake should be recoverable.

Who can bring the action?

Until recently, the view was that an action in quasi-contract or for money had and received could not be brought by the customer whose account has been wrongfully debited but had to be instituted by the paying bank. The argument in favour of this view was that, under *Foley* v *Hill* (1848) 2 HL Cas 28 once money was credited to the customer's account, title in that money passed to the bank, and a debtor and creditor relationship was established in respect of the credit fund standing in the customer's account. This reasoning has been reviewed in two recent cases (*Agip (Africa) Ltd* v *Jackson* [1990] Ch 265; [1991] Ch 547; and *Lipkin Gorman* v *Karpnale Ltd* [1991] 2 AC 548) which establish that the customer has a right to sue for the recovery of funds paid out under a mistake of fact. In *Agip (Africa) Ltd* v *Jackson* the plaintiff company sought to recover large amounts of money fraudulently transferred by its chief accountant to the credit of accounts held by the defendants. One of the defences raised was that, under *Foley* v *Hill*, the funds remitted were the paying bank's money, and the plaintiff company had no right to the money. At first instance, Millett J rejected this argument and said that 'by honouring the customer's cheque in favour of a third party and debiting his account, the bank acts as principal in repaying part of the debt to its customer and as the agent of the customer in paying his money to the third party'. The Court of Appeal affirmed the decision of Millett J. The Court of Appeal, whilst not rejecting the principle established under which money credited to a bank account becomes the bank's money, took the view that an application of the *Foley* v *Hill* principle 'only tells half the story'. Fox LJ said that:

> The banker's instruction is to pay from the customer's account. He does so by a payment from his own funds and a corresponding debit. The reality is a payment by the customer, at any rate in a case where the customer has no right to require a recrediting of his account. Nothing passes *in specie*. The whole matter is dealt with by accounting transactions partly in the paying bank and partly in the clearing process.

The Court of Appeal agreed with Millett J's conclusion that the position was not altered by the fact that the paying bank was deceived into paying on the basis of a forged instruction. Fox LJ observed that if the paying bank 'paid away Agip's money, Agip itself must be entitled to pursue such remedies as there may be for its recovery'.

In *Lipkin Gorman* v *Karpnale Ltd* Lord Goff of Chieveley held that the solicitors had a title which could be traced at common law into funds retained by the club.

He said that the relationship of the bank with the solicitors (its customers) was essentially that of debtor and creditor; and since the client account was at all material times in credit, the bank was the debtor and the solicitors, the creditors. Such a debt constitutes a chose in action, which is a species of property; and since the debt was enforceable at common law, the chose in action was legal property belonging to the solicitors at common law.

The cases clearly take the view that an action for recovery of money paid by the bank under a mistake of fact may be brought either by the bank itself or by the customer whose money has been misapplied. The customer, however, is unlikely to bring the action where he can compel the bank to restore the amount wrongfully debited to his account and the bank will probably be left to pursue the action. From a practical point, the view in the *Agip* case probably makes more commercial sense.

RECOVERY OF MONEY NOT INVOLVING A NEGOTIABLE INSTRUMENT

The three modern cases in this area are *Chase Manhattan Bank NA* v *Israel-British Bank (London) Ltd* [1981] Ch 105; *National Westminster Bank Ltd* v *Barclays Bank International Ltd* [1975] QB 654 and *Barclays Bank Ltd* v *W. J. Simms, Son and Cooke (Southern) Ltd* [1980] QB 677. Of these, which are all first instance, the *W. J. Simms* case is an appropriate starting point. The facts of the case were that the drawer countermanded the payment of a cheque but due to an error the bank paid the cheque on the day following its countermand. When the bank discovered its mistake, it recredited the drawer's account and demanded repayment from the payee. Robert Goff J held that the bank was entitled to recover. In a careful analysis of the authorities he said that the law relating to recovery of amounts paid under a mistake of fact could be summarised as follows:

> If a person pays money to another under a mistake of fact which causes him to make a payment, he is prima facie entitled to recover it as money paid under a mistake of fact.

The claim may, however, fail if the payer intends the payee to have the money in all events, or the payment is made for good consideration, in particular if the money is paid to discharge a debt owed to the payee by the payer or by a third party by whom he is authorised to discharge the debt, or the payee has changed his position in good faith, or is deemed in law to have done so.

Mistake must be one of fact, not of law

This principle can be traced back to *Kelly* v *Solari* (1841) 9 M & W 54, where Lord Abinger CB said:

> The safest rule however is that if the party makes the payment with full knowledge of the facts, although under ignorance of the law, there being no fraud on the other side, he cannot recover it back again.

Robert Goff J in *Barclays Bank Ltd* v *W. J. Simms, Son and Cooke (Southern) Ltd* [1980] QB 677 analysed earlier House of Lords decisions. In *Kleinwort Sons and Co.* v *Dunlop Rubber Co.* [1909] 2 KB 483 Kramrisch were rubber merchants who were financed by both Kleinwort and another merchant bank, Messrs Brandts. Kramrisch supplied Dunlop with rubber directing them to pay the price to Brandts who had a charge on it. By mistake Dunlop paid Kleinwort, who received the payment in good faith. Kramrisch failed and Dunlop were held liable to pay Brandts. Dunlop sought to recover the money paid as under a mistake of fact. The main question was whether Kleinwort had altered their position as a result of the payment and it was decided that they had not. In *Kerrison* v *Glyn Mills Currie and Co.* (1911) 81 LJ KB 465 a mining company drew bills of exchange on a New York bank. To facilitate payment, the plaintiffs, who had an interest in the company, remitted £500 to the defendant bank, who were London agents of the New York bank. The defendant bank credited the New York bank's overdrawn account with the amount involved. Neither the plaintiffs nor the defendant bank were aware that, at the time, the New York bank had just failed and was unable to meet the bills of exchange. The plaintiffs demanded repayment of the amount paid as money paid under a mistake of fact and the bank set up its right to set off. It was held that the plaintiffs were entitled to recover the amount paid. The mistake was operative as the plaintiffs had made the payment involved in anticipation of the completion of the transaction. In *R.E. Jones Ltd* v *Waring and Gillow Ltd* [1925] 2 KB 612; [1926] AC 670 a rogue named Bodenham obtained from the respondents furniture to the value of over £13,000 on hire purchase terms. Bodenham defaulted on the hire-purchase agreement, and the respondents repossessed the goods. Bodenham then approached the appellants informing them that he represented a firm of motor manufacturers called International Motors. He persuaded the appellants to accept an appointment as agents for International Motors under terms which included the payment of a deposit of £5,000. Bodenham through his falsity persuaded the appellants to draw two cheques in favour of the respondents and handed them to Bodenham, who then handed them to the respondents in respect of the deposit payable under the hire-purchase agreement. The respondents' accountant queried the cheques with the appellants since they bore the signature of only one director. The appellants, in good faith, substituted a single cheque for £5,000 properly signed. The cheque for £5,000 was cashed by the respondents, who then restored to Bodenham the furniture they had seized. When the fraud was discovered the respondents resumed possession of the furniture and the appellants claimed repayment of the £5,000 from the respondents. The Court of Appeal, referring to *Chambers* v *Miller* (1862) 13 CB NS 125 concluded that 'the plaintiffs and defendants were each of them under a misapprehension although each was influenced by different mistakes of fact'. The court, therefore, concluded that the plaintiffs could not recover the money as having been paid under a mistake of fact. On appeal, the House of Lords, however, unanimously concluded that the mistake of fact was sufficient to ground recovery, although a minority considered that the respondents had a good defence to the claim because they had changed their position in good faith.

Distinction between fact and law

In the banking law context a mistake of fact may take numerous forms, including payment on a forged cheque (*National Westminster Bank Ltd* v *Barclays Bank*

International Ltd [1975] QB 654) and payment of a cheque contrary to a countermand (*Barclays Bank Ltd* v *W.J. Simms, Son and Cooke (Southern) Ltd* [1980] QB 677. However, in exceptional cases the courts have allowed recovery of payments made under a mistake of law or where payment has been induced by the payee's fraud, oppression, undue influence or breach of fiduciary duty or received in bad faith. In *Kiriri Cotton Co. Ltd* v *Dewani* [1960] AC 192 it was held that a mistake of law does not by itself justify recovery of a payment, but if there is something more, e.g., something which shows that, of the two of them, the defendant is the one primarily responsible for the mistake, then it may be recovered (see also *Holt* v *Markham* [1923] 1 KB 504, in which misinterpretation of War Office orders was held to be a mistake of law; *Anglo-Scottish Beet Sugar Corporation Ltd* v *Spalding Urban District Council* [1937] 3 All ER 335, in which failure by a tenant to deduct the landlord's property tax was held to be a mistake of law). A mistake relating to foreign law is regarded by the English courts as a question of fact and the resultant payment would not be irrecoverable. Further, it has been suggested that where one party misleads another even inadvertently on a point of law, money paid in pursuance of such an error is recoverable if the recipient responsible for the error owed a fiduciary duty to advise the other correctly (see *Harse* v *Pearl Life Assurance Co.* [1904] 1 KB 558.

Mistake must have caused the payment

In order to recover money paid under a mistake of fact it must be proved that the mistake caused the payment and the burden of so proving is on the payer. In *Holt* v *Markham* [1923] 1 KB 504 Warrington LJ held that the onus of proving that there was a mistake lies on the plaintiffs and their claim will be defeated if the defendant can show that through their conduct he was led to believe that he was entitled to the money. The burden includes satisfying the court on the balance of probabilities that the relevant mistake was one of fact and not of law. It will normally be necessary to identify and call the person acting on behalf of the payer who was mistaken. Although this was not done in *Avon County Council* v *Howlett* [1983] 1 WLR 605 Slade LJ warned that it should be done in the future. Where payment is induced by a mistake about two separate issues, the dominant mistake must be one of fact (see *Trigge* v *Lavallee* (1862) 15 Moo P 270 at 298; *Home and Colonial Insurance Co. Ltd* v *London Guarantee and Accident Co. Ltd* (1928) 45 TLR 134).

Mistake must be that of the payer, but not necessarily that of the payee

At one time it was thought necessary for the mistake to be one made as between the payer and the party receiving payment. This was affirmed in *National Westminster Bank International Ltd* v *Barclays Bank Ltd* [1975] QB 654 where Kerr J stated:

> It is settled law that if a bank honours a cheque or bill in the mistaken belief that it has sufficient funds from its customer to do so, then the money cannot be recovered back, because a mistake of this nature only operates between the bank and its customer and not between the bank and the payee.

The uncertainty caused by this requirement is illustrated in *Weld-Blundell* v *Synott* [1940] 2 KB 107, where Asquith J remarked that it is extremely difficult to ascertain what the phrase mistake 'as between the parties' is intended to mean, since it is accepted that there is no requirement that the mistake must relate to the liability of the payer to the payee to make payment or that the mistake must be shared by both parties.

However, in *Barclays Bank Ltd* v *W.J. Simms, Son and Cooke (Southern) Ltd* [1980] QB 677 Robert Goff J took the view that the claim would not fail merely because the mistake had not been 'as between' the payer and payee or because the mistake had not induced the payer to believe that he was liable to pay money to the payee, or his principal. The learned judge analysed the earlier cases which were used to support the argument that no action will lie to recover money paid under a mistake of fact, unless the mistake was 'as between' the payer and the payee, in the sense that both were suffering under the same mistake. He said that the opinion of Erle CJ in *Chambers* v *Miller* (1862) 13 CB NS 125 had been misinterpreted and taken out of context. The learned judge also rejected views expressed in *Aiken* v *Short* (1856) 1 Hurl & N 210 and *Kelly* v *Solari* (1841) 9 M & W 54. His lordship observed that the supposed rule that payment must be 'between' the parties was inconsistent with the House of Lords decision in *R.E. Jones Ltd* v *Waring and Gillow Ltd* [1926] AC 670 and must have been rejected by the House in that case. Moreover, it was implicit in the speeches of their lordships that it is not a prerequisite of recovery that the plaintiff must have mistakenly believed that he was liable to the defendant to pay the money to him.

Consequently, Robert Goff J concluded that the supposed rule that the mistake must be as between the payer and payee means no more than that the mistake must have caused the payment (reformulating *Weld-Blundell* v *Synott* and *Porter* v *Latec Finance (Qld) Pty Ltd* (1964) 111 CLR 177) but that view is contrary to the statement of settled law expressed by Kerr J in *National Westminster Bank Ltd* v *Barclays Bank International Ltd*. Moreover, Robert Goff J emphasised that if the mistake is otherwise operative, it did not have to be between the bank, or payer, and the payee. It was adequate that it was a fundamental mistake which induced the payment. In *Commercial Bank of Australia Ltd* v *Younis* [1979] 1 NSWR 444 Hope JA (with whom Reynolds and Hutley JJA concurred) concluded that the bank's mistake was fundamental and that allowing Younis to retain the $3,000 of the countermanded cheque would have resulted in him being unjustly enriched. Further support for this proposition is found in the *Simms* case where the learned judge concluded that although the payee had not changed his position, the mistake was nevertheless fundamental. A mistake will also be fundamental if it leads the bank to believe that it is under a duty to make payment when it is not so obliged. However, there may be other types of mistake which result in payment being made but which the courts do not consider to be fundamental (e.g., *Porter* v *Latec Finance (Qld) Pty Ltd* (1964) 111 CLR 177).

Defence of change in position and of consideration for payment

The two defences which are, sometimes, raised where the payer seeks to recover money paid under a mistake of fact are:

(a) that the payee had changed his position in reliance on the payment; or
(b) that the payee had given consideration for the amount transferred to him.

The two defences are fundamentally different. A change in the payee's position occurs after the payment has been received and it could be argued that estoppel could apply to prevent the bank from recovering the money. This defence is based on considerations of common justice and it would be inequitable to insist that the money be repaid when the payee has relied on it to his detriment. However, the defence is limited to detriment suffered as a result of direct reliance and does not apply in the type of situation which occurred in *United Overseas Bank* v *Jiwani* [1976] 1 WLR 964, where the payee would have changed his position in any event. However, the defence, even in this restricted sense, was not generally available until recently. In *R.E. Jones Ltd* v *Waring and Gillow Ltd* [1926] AC 670 the majority of the House of Lords surveyed the earlier authorities and concluded that estoppel did not apply in that case to prevent the plaintiffs from recovering money paid under a mistake of fact. More recently, in *Lipkin Gorman* v *Karpnale Ltd* [1991] 2 AC 548 the House of Lords examined the defence of change of position. Lord Goff of Chieveley (at p. 579) said that where an innocent defendant's position is so changed that he will suffer an injustice if called upon to repay either in part or in full, the injustice of requiring him so to repay outweighs the injustice of denying the plaintiff restitution. Thus, not every alteration by the payee in his situation will allow the defence to be raised. The defence is not open to one who has changed his position in bad faith, as where the defendant has paid away the money with knowledge of the facts entitling the plaintiff to restitution; and it is accepted that the defence should not be open to a wrongdoer.

Lord Goff explained that the mere fact that the payee has spent the money does not of itself involve a change in position and that if the expenditure would have been incurred in any event then the defence will not apply (*United Overseas Bank* v *Jiwani* [1976] 1 WLR 964).

Consideration has to move on the formation of the contract and an exchange of promises will suffice. In the case of a negotiable instrument (s. 27(1) of the Bills of Exchange Act 1882), the consideration may be given before the payment involved is effected. A defence based on the provision of consideration involves the assertion that the payee has acquired title to the funds or the property. Whether or not the payee gave consideration for the cheque should make no difference to the bank's right to recover. In most cases this issue would not arise and the bank would not be aware whether or not the payee had given consideration. Further, where payment is countermanded, the drawer does not want payment to be made, although consideration is likely to have been given by the payee.

In *Lipkin Gorman* v *Karpnale Ltd* the House of Lords, reversing the judgment of the Court of Appeal, held that the supply of chips by the club's cashier did not amount to the furnishing of a separate lawful consideration and since C's debts with the club involved gambling the contracts made were void. The club had therefore not furnished value for the funds and the firm from whom the funds had been misappropriated could recover.

RECOVERY OF MONEY PAID UNDER A MISTAKE OF FACT INVOLVING A NEGOTIABLE INSTRUMENT

There are certain specific problems where the mistaken payment arises in connection with the discharge of a negotiable instrument. One of the issues which needs to be examined is whether negligence on the part of the payer will prevent him from recovering the mistaken payment. A second is whether recovery will be prevented if the payee has altered his position as a result of the payment.

Negligence on the part of the payer

In *National Westminster Bank Ltd* v *Barclays Bank International Ltd* [1975] QB 654 at 666 Kerr J indicated that special rules apply to bills of exchange which are not forgeries *in toto* but which contain at least one genuine signature and which have been negotiated to at least one innocent holder. These principles apply only to 'negotiable instruments proper' and not to forged cheques which are worthless pieces of paper and a nullity (*Imperial Bank of Canada* v *Bank of Hamilton* [1903] AC 49; *National Westminster Bank Ltd* v *Barclays Bank International Ltd*) nor to an unendorsed cheque on which payment is countermanded (*Barclays Bank Ltd* v *W.J. Simms Son and Cooke (Southern) Ltd* [1980] QB 677).

The earlier cases support the view that payment on a negotiable instrument caused by negligence cannot be recovered. In *Price* v *Neal* (1762) 3 Burr 1354 the plaintiff sued to recover two sums of £40 each, paid to the defendant on two bills of exchange of which the plaintiff was the drawee. The defendant, an endorsee for valuable consideration of the first bill presented it for payment on maturity and the plaintiff made payment. The plaintiff also accepted the second bill and endorsed it to the defendant for valuable consideration. Subsequently, payment was also made on this bill. In fact both bills had been forged by a third party and when this was discovered the plaintiff sought to recover the £80 he had paid to the defendant who had acted in good faith and without notice of the forgeries. Lord Mansfield held that in neither case could the plaintiff recover his money and that an acceptor should know the handwriting of the drawer, and that it is rather by his fault or negligence than by mistake if he pays on a forged signature. In *Smith* v *Mercer* (1815) 6 Taunt 76 it was held that payments made under a mistake of fact could not be recovered when, having discovered the mistake, there was a delay in informing the defendant. In *London and River Plate Bank Ltd* v *Bank of Liverpool Ltd* [1896] 1 QB 7 Mathew J considered that the principle applying to both these decisions was that if the plaintiff 'so conducted himself as to lead the holder of the bill to believe that he considered the signature genuine, he could not afterwards withdraw from that position', a principle independent of negligence.

However, in *Kelly* v *Solari* (1841) 9 M and W 54 the Court of Exchequer held that money paid by directors of an insurance company on a policy which had lapsed by reason of non-payment of premiums could be recovered even though the means of knowing that the policy had lapsed were available to the plaintiffs. Parke B said that if money 'is paid under the impression of the truth of a fact which is untrue, it may, generally speaking, be recovered back, however careless the party paying may have been, in omitting to use due diligence to inquire into the fact'.

This rule has been applied to negotiable instruments. In *Imperial Bank of Canada* v *Bank of Hamilton* [1903] AC 49 payment was made on a fraudulently altered cheque and it was contended that payment had been negligent. Lord Lindley, giving the judgment of the Privy Council held that the money was recoverable on the basis of *Kelly* v *Solari*. In *National Westminster Bank Ltd* v *Barclays Bank International Ltd and Another* [1975] QB 654 the second defendant, one Ismail, was a Nigerian businessman anxious to move funds out of Nigeria, contrary to strict exchange control regulations. He purchased, at a premium, a cheque for £8,000 drawn on the National Westminster Bank, in London. He sent the cheque to his own bank, Barclays Bank International, in London, for special collection. The cheque was duly presented and paid. A fortnight later it was discovered that the cheque form had been stolen and completed as a forgery. National Westminster brought an action for recovery of the money and the second defendant resisted the claim, arguing, *inter alia*, that a paying bank owes a duty of care to recipients in honouring cheques, and the plaintiffs had been negligent. Kerr J, while being prepared to assume in the defendant's favour that he had acted innocently, nevertheless held him liable to repay the plaintiffs, who had paid out the money in the belief that the cheque was genuine. A bank does not by paying a cheque make any representation to the recipient as to the genuineness of its customer's signature. However, it was evident that any negligence by the bank would have prevented recovery. Kerr J examined two conflicting Commonwealth authorities. In *Arrow Transfer Co. Ltd* v *Royal Bank of Canada* (1971) 19 DLR (3d) 420 cheque forms were misappropriated from the plaintiff company's cheque-book by an employee, who forged the signature of the authorised signing officer. The plaintiff company brought an action for conversion and money had and received against the paying and collecting banks. The Court of Appeal of British Columbia approved the judgment given by Seaton J, at first instance, who held that an action could not lie because there can be no conversion of an instrument on which the drawer's signature was a forgery.

The point was more directly raised in *Imperial Bank of India* v *Abeyesinghe* (1927) 29 Ceylon NLR 257, where the defendant received a cheque payable to himself in part payment of a fictitious transaction, which he had been instructed to handle on behalf of a supposed vendor of certain property. The cheque, in fact, was a complete forgery and the defendant, having presented it himself, received payment, which he then transferred to his principal. The bank brought an action to recover the money from the defendant. Fisher CJ distinguished the *London and River Plate Bank* case and held that the references in that case to representations made by the paying bank were not applicable to a case which involved an instrument which was a complete forgery. He rejected the view that a paying bank is under a duty to the recipient of the cheque to know its customer's signature. The bank has no time to make inquiries into the title of the person who presents the instrument for payment and it must either pay the instrument or dishonour it.

It has been accepted that there is no duty imposed on the paying bank toward the recipient to know the signature of a third party, e.g., the payee. If there is no duty owed to the payee or holder of the cheque to verify the drawer's signature then there can be no negligence on the part of the paying bank.

Recovery where the payee's position is prejudiced

In normal circumstances a holder who receives payment on a negotiable instrument is entitled to regard payment as final and in *Price* v *Neal* (1762) 3 Burr 1354 it was said that an action in restitution was barred once payment was made on the instrument. In *Cocks* v *Masterman* (1829) 9 B & C 902 the court explained the lack of right to recovery of the proceeds paid under a mistake of fact on the ground that the holder is entitled to give notice of dishonour on the very day on which a bill is dishonoured. The parties who pay the bill ought not to be able by their negligence to deprive the holder of any right or privilege. And in *London and River Plate Bank Ltd* v *Bank of Liverpool Ltd* [1896] 1 QB 7 Mathew J expressed the opinion that if a mistake was discovered rapidly, then the money paid may possibly be recovered. But if 'the money is paid in good faith, and is received in good faith, and there is an interval of time in which the position of the holder may be altered, the principle seems to apply that money once paid cannot be recovered back'. The reason for this view is not negligence or the bank's knowledge, but the right to an immediate answer to the fate of the cheque. The learned judge said that a change of position is bound to occur with the lapse of time. However, he did not exclude the possibility that a change of position could take place even where the mistake is drawn to the payee's attention on the same day.

Subsequent authorities have restricted this ruling and held that it cannot apply to a forged instrument. In *Imperial Bank of Canada* v *Bank of Hamilton* [1903] AC 49 the Privy Council refused to apply the rule established in earlier cases. Their lordships concluded that the collecting bank was not affected by the delay in giving notice of the forgery, that the instrument in that case was a complete forgery, and the person who presented the forgery was not entitled to notice of dishonour. The rule in *Cocks* v *Masterman* and *London and River Plate Bank Ltd* v *Bank of Liverpool Ltd*, whilst being applicable to negotiable instruments, does not apply to other cases where notice of the mistake is given within a reasonable time and loss is not occasioned by delay.

Imperial Bank of Canada v *Bank of Hamilton* was applied in both *National Westminster Bank Ltd* v *Barclays Bank International Ltd* [1975] QB 654 and *Barclays Bank Ltd* v *W.J. Simms Son and Cooke (Southern) Ltd* [1980] QB 677, where the learned judge held that the earlier rule invoked in *Price* v *Neal* and applied in *Cocks* v *Masterman* could not apply where notice of dishonour was not required, as in the case of a countermanded cheque.

BANK'S RIGHT TO TRACE THE PROCEEDS

A bank which seeks to recover money paid under a mistake may not only recover from the collecting bank or the person whose account was credited but it may also recover from anyone who holds the money by derivation from the recipient, provided it can still be identified. At common law, therefore, funds sought to be recovered must still be identifiable. In *Banque Belge pour l'Étranger* v *Hambrouck* [1921] 1 KB 321 H fraudulently obtained a number of cheques from his employer, which he paid into his own account, and his bank collected the amounts from his employer's bank. H then withdrew these sums by cheques in favour of his mistress, D, who paid the cheques into her own account. The bank sought to recover the amount from the mistress and further sought a declaration that the amount placed to her credit was the bank's property in equity. It was argued that D took the money without notice of H's wrongdoing and she acquired a valid title. The court rejected this argument since D was a volunteer, and said that the only person acquiring the property sought to be traced who is immune from the payer's claim is one who has given value. Atkin LJ's conclusion that the proceeds of the fraud could be traced at common law into a mixed fund is at variance with the judgments of Scrutton and Bankes LJJ. Atkin LJ's decision is also at variance with the judgment in *Sinclair* v *Brougham* [1914] AC 398. It is accepted at common law that once money is mixed with other funds (e.g., where it becomes part of the general balance in a current account or is transferred to a subsequent holder) it cannot be traced. However, a plaintiff who cannot trace at common law may be able to follow the assets in equity. This principle was clearly established in *Re Hallett's Estate, Knatchbull* v *Hallett* (1880) 13 ChD 696, where a solicitor instructed his bank to sell certain bonds, held by him on behalf of a client. The proceeds from the sale were paid to the credit of the solicitor's personal account. The solicitor withdrew amounts from this account so that the credit balance on the account was reduced to an amount smaller than the trust moneys wrongfully credited to the account. The client claimed to be entitled to follow the amount of the proceeds of the bonds against the credit balance on the solicitor's personal account. The solicitor's trustee in bankruptcy challenged this claim on the grounds that any credit balances held by the solicitor were exhausted. A strict application of the rule in *Clayton's Case* (*Devaynes* v *Noble, Clayton's Case* (1816) 1 Mer 529), under which amounts paid out were to be appropriated against the earliest credit entry, would have led to the conclusion that the trust moneys had been withdrawn, leaving the plaintiff without a remedy. The Court of Appeal, however, affirmed the judgment at first instance, and held that the rule in *Clayton's Case* was inapplicable. The solicitor was deemed to draw first on his own funds, and the credit balance remaining on the personal account was held by the solicitor in a fiduciary capacity. Jessell MR took the view that although the solicitor was not a trustee in the strict sense of the word the client was entitled to a tracing order.

The position was summarised in *Re Diplock* [1948] Ch 465, where it was said that money can be traced in equity into a mixed fund subject to three limitations, namely:

(a)   the relationship between the plaintiff and recipient (or other person who obtains the property) must be such as to give rise to a fiduciary relationship of some sort;
(b)   the plaintiff's money must be strictly identifiable; and
(c)   the equitable remedy, i.e., the grant of a tracing order, must not work an injustice.

The first of these three propositions was challenged in *Chase Manhattan Bank NA* v *Israel-British Bank (London) Ltd* [1981] Ch 105, where, by mistake, on 3 July 1974, the plaintiffs paid to the defendants approximately $2 million twice over. The defendants discovered the mistake two days later but made no attempt to correct it. In August, the defendants petitioned the court for a winding-up order, which was made at the beginning of December. In an action the plaintiffs sought to trace and recover in equity the sum paid under a mistake. Goulding J held that the defendants were constructive trustees of the money which they had received in consequence of the mistake. He concluded that there was a fiduciary relationship between the payer and the recipient, and that a 'person who pays money to another under a factual mistake retains an equitable property in it and the conscience of that other is subjected to a fiduciary duty to respect his proprietary right'. It is unfortunate that Goulding J had to conclude that a fiduciary relationship arose between the parties, who had entered into a commercial arrangement, by virtue of the mistaken payment and it is submitted that a solution ought to have been found on grounds of justice.

The plaintiffs' claim in the *Chase Manhattan* case had certain advantageous features. The defendants discovered the mistaken payment within two days, but made no attempt to return it. Unlike the defendants' general creditors, the plaintiffs had not advanced credit to the defendants and did not take the risk of the defendants' insolvency. In such circumstances, allowing the defendants to retain the money would result in the defendants' general creditors receiving a windfall. However, these arguments would not apply in every case where a mistaken payment is made.

The rules relating to the grant of an equitable tracing order were further clarified in *Agip (Africa) Ltd* v *Jackson* [1991] Ch 547, where for a number of years the plaintiff's dishonest chief accountant had misappropriated funds and had them transferred to accounts of nominee companies in London. The transaction which gave rise to the proceedings involved misappropriated funds being transferred to the Isle of Man and then to parties overseas. The Court of Appeal, affirming Millett J, held that the funds could be traced in equity. Such a tracing order is available if there is a fiduciary relationship which calls the equitable jurisdiction into operation. It was clear that the plaintiff's chief accountant owed them fiduciary duties as an employee. Further, Fox LJ expressed the view that a third party into whose hands the money was transferred would lose the defence that he acquired it in good faith if he had the type of knowledge that would impose liability on him as a constructive trustee.

More recently, in *Polly Peck International plc* v *Nadir (No. 2)* [1992] 4 All ER 769) Scott LJ concluded that the degree of knowledge that a plaintiff must establish on the part of a third-party recipient of funds in an equitable tracing claim must be such as to impose liability as a constructive trustee. He did not clarify whether the knowledge required was that applicable in respect of knowing assistance or of knowing receipt, but he distinguished between the remedies available. An action intended to impose liability as a constructive trustee would, as an action *in personam*, entail an order for the payment of compensation, whereas a tracing order, being an order *in rem*, would attach to the trust property itself.

Another recent case on tracing is *El Ajou* v *Dollar Land Holdings plc* [1993] 3 All ER 717, where a businessman sought to recover money misappropriated from him as a result of a massive share fraud perpetrated in Amsterdam by three Canadians. Ultimately, the misappropriated funds were used in a joint property venture entered into between the Canadians and the defendants, with the defendants eventually buying out the Canadians. One of the issues raised was whether the defendants' acquisition was made in good faith and for valuable consideration. Millett J dismissed the action and in respect of the remedy he said:

> The victims of a fraud can follow their money in equity through bank accounts where it has been mixed with other moneys because equity treats the money in such accounts as charged with the repayment of their money. If the money in an account subject to such a charge is afterwards paid out of the account and into a number of different accounts, the victims can claim a similar charge over each of the recipient accounts.

It would, therefore, appear that for an equitable tracing order to be granted a number of requirements must be satisfied:

(a) the misappropriation of the funds must have been carried out in circumstances involving a breach of fiduciary duty; and

(b) the funds must be identifiable as money misappropriated from the plaintiff.

Where the ultimate recipient can establish that he received the misappropriated funds for valuable consideration, without notice and in good faith (i.e., without actual or constructive notice of the misappropriation), an order to trace funds will not be granted.

PART 5

16 Bank Finance

BANK LOANS FOR GENERAL PURPOSES

The forms of bank and building society finance have undergone a revolution since the 1960s. Competition has resulted in a considerable extension in the lending activities of both banks and building societies. Nowhere has this been greater than in the area of mortgage lending for house finance: an area not long ago considered to be the exclusive domain of the building societies.

Before making a loan facility available a bank or building society manager will have to be satisfied about the viability of the project so as to make a sound business decision. For example, a banker will want to know what exactly the loan is to be used for. There are two main reasons for this, namely: (a) he must assure himself that the purpose is legal; and (b) that the intended use is reasonably likely to produce a profitable result. Banks are, in general, reluctant to provide 'standby' facilities except for the most reliable customers. Purely speculative projects will be avoided but it is not unreasonable for a bank to undertake 'a fair trade risk'. It should, however, be remembered that the extent of such a risk is likely to be narrower for a bank than for an entrepreneur.

The lending bank will also wish to know the source of repayment, so as to ensure that repayment proposals are clear and well planned and within the borrower's ability. If the lending is not self-liquidating, i.e., if the project financed does not generate sufficient funds to repay the borrowing within a reasonable time, then the lending bank must be satisfied that there are alternative sources of repayment.

The bank will have regard to the duration of the risk. Money which the bank is lending will, generally, be placed with the bank on short-term deposit, or in a current account. It is not, therefore, sensible for a bank to commit itself to long-term loans which cannot be repaid quickly if the need should arise. However, to some extent the bank will rely on the improbability that enough depositing customers will demand repayment of their deposit to cause any embarrassment.

Where the bank is lending on a long-term basis it must be aware of the possible effect of changing economic and political circumstances. This is especially true when lending on the international market, where a revolution or even a natural disaster may radically alter the chances of repayment.

The bank will want to make a profit on its lending and its calculations must be based on the cost of funds to it (i.e., the interest it pays to depositors) and the overheads of business. The specific costs of documentation and arranging a particular loan are likely to be covered by the arrangement fee, but the bank will rely on the interest differential to provide the major part of the profit. The actual interest charged will be determined by many factors, including the bank's policy. Different types of borrowing attract different formulae for calculating and charging interest and considerations such as loss of risk, risk of mismatching etc. are all relevant. Generally, the appropriate rates of interest will be determined by a bank's head office, although individual branch managers may be given some discretion.

OVERDRAFT

An overdraft is a traditional method of bank finance which represents a line of credit made available by a bank to its customer through the normal use of the customer's current account. Although an overdraft is considered to be a short-term facility, a lot of businesses operate on a continuous overdraft. Therefore, an overdraft facility is not, in reality, always short-term in terms of usage. Interest is calculated on a daily basis but is debited to the account only periodically. As the amount of the overdraft is likely to fluctuate on a daily basis, the method of charging interest daily on the amount overdrawn is significant.

Legal nature of the overdraft

The leading case of *Foley* v *Hill* (1848) 2 HL Cas 28 and other subsequent cases have clearly established the nature of the legal relationship which subsists between a bank and its customer. In normal circumstances when the customer has a credit balance on his account, it is the bank which is in the role of the debtor to its customer and it has 'contracted, having received that money, to repay to the principal, when demanded, a sum equivalent to that paid into his hands' (per Lord Cottenham LC in *Foley* v *Hill*). When the current account is overdrawn, the roles of the parties are reversed, and the customer becomes a debtor of the bank for the amount overdrawn.

An overdraft facility may be granted to a customer as a result of an express agreement entered into with the bank. In such a situation, the bank is likely to agree to the customer being authorised to draw against his account up to a specified ceiling. As amounts are paid into the credit of the customer they are set off against the amount overdrawn thereby giving the customer a larger balance on the overdraft against which amounts may be drawn. As further sums are drawn against the account so the amount of the overdraft facility available will be reduced. Alternatively, an overdraft facility may be implied to the banker and customer relationship from the circumstances. Thus, for example, where a customer draws a cheque for a sum which exceeds the credit balance on the account, that act of the customer is treated as a request for an overdraft facility, and if the cheque is honoured, the bank has extended an overdraft facility. In *Cuthbert* v *Robarts Lubbock and Co.* [1909] 2 Ch 226 the court held that the drawing of a cheque by a customer for a sum in excess of the amount standing to the credit of the current account is really a request for a loan, and if the cheque is honoured, the customer has borrowed money from the bank.

However, a bank is under no obligation to extend an overdraft facility to its customers. Once customers have availed themselves of the amount standing to the credit of their accounts the bank's indebtedness to the customer is discharged. If a bank agrees to allow the customer to overdraw in return for a consideration provided by the customer, then the customer is legally entitled to overdraw on the account up to any agreed overdraft limit. The bank will be liable in damages to the customer if it refuses to allow the customer to overdraw, or if it either erroneously, or otherwise, dishonours cheques drawn by the customer but which are within the agreed overdraft limit. The giving of a security by the customer to its bank has been held to be adequate consideration for the bank's commitment to extend an overdraft to the customer (*Fleming* v *Bank of New Zealand* [1900] AC 577). In such a situation the bank is effectively estopped from denying that the customer was entitled as against the bank to overdraw up to a specified amount. An alternative form of consideration is an undertaking by the customer to repay the amount overdrawn together with any interest and bank charges.

Withdrawal of the overdraft facility

An overdraft is repayable on demand unless the bank has otherwise agreed. The practice of treating overdrafts as repayable on demand, in the absence of different terms, has been accepted by the law. There is only one judicial decision which appears to impose an obligation on the bank to give its customer a reasonable length of notice prior to calling for repayment of an overdraft before issuing a writ to recover the amount owing (*Brighty* v *Norton* (1862) 3 B & S 305). The preponderance of judicial opinion is that a bank may demand immediate repayment of an overdraft at any time, and it owes no duty to the customer to ensure that the demand is made in sufficient time before it becomes effective so that the customer has a reasonable opportunity to raise money elsewhere, if necessary. However, the bank cannot treat the customer as being in default until it has given the customer sufficient time to obtain the money to repay the overdraft from a bank in the locality of his residence or business address (*Toms* v *Wilson* (1862) 4 B & S 442 per Cockburn CJ; *Moore* v *Shelley* (1883) 8 App Cas 285). In *Williams and Glyn's Bank Ltd* v *Barnes* [1981] Com LR 205 the bank granted its customer an overdraft facility in order to finance some transactions of a company of which the customer was the chairman and majority shareholder. When the company's financial position deteriorated further, the bank demanded immediate repayment of the amount outstanding on the overdraft. Ralph Gibson J expressed the view that in the absence of an express agreement providing for the duration of the overdraft facility, or for the date of repayment, the task of the court must be to consider whether, according to the ordinary rules for the implication of terms into commercial contracts, any term for the duration of the facility or the date of repayment is to be implied. If no such term is to be implied then the money lent under the facility is 'no more than money lent and is, therefore, repayable on demand'. The mere knowledge by the bank that a customer intends to spend all or part of the money in a business venture which will take a long time to come to fruition cannot itself give rise to an implied term requiring a period of notice for repayment calculated by reference to the probable duration of that business venture. More recently in *Bank of Baroda* v *Panessar* [1987] Ch 335 Walton J observed that a debtor who was required to pay money on demand was only entitled to such length of notice as was necessary to implement the mechanics of payment needed to discharge the debt. In view of the modern methods of communication and transfer of money available, the time needed may be exceptionally short.

The bank's right to immediate repayment of the overdraft should not be exercised so as to unduly prejudice the interests of the customer. In *Joachimson* v *Swiss Bank Corporation* [1921] 3 KB 110 it was said that in the absence of an express agreement reasonable time should be given to a customer to repay the overdraft.

In *Rouse* v *Bradford Banking Co. Ltd* [1894] AC 586 a partnership was reorganised and subsequently allowed to increase an existing overdraft granted to the original firm. The House of Lords rejected the argument that the new partnership had the right to expect to have the overdraft available for a specified period. However, Lord Herschell LC added that, although an overdraft arrangement may not in itself grant the customer an indefinite time in which he would be able to utilise the facility, neither of the parties would contemplate a withdrawal of the facility without notice shortly after its extension. Similarly, in *R.A. Cripps and Son Ltd* v *Wickenden* [1973] 1 WLR 944 Goff J held that, although an overdraft was repayable on demand, the customer must be given a reasonable notice before the facility is withdrawn. The bank's right to claim immediate repayment of the overdraft may be waived either by express or implied agreement. The court may decide that as a matter of necessity and to give efficacy to the contract, a term may be implied requiring the bank to give notice over a reasonable period of time before the right to repayment arises. In *Williams and Glyn's Bank Ltd* v *Barnes* [1981] Com LR 205, having explained the general right of a bank to demand immediate repayment of an overdraft, Ralph Gibson J held that the documentation in the case before him established that the lending bank agreed that the overdraft was not repayable on demand and the facility could not be cancelled at any time by the bank. The bank was required to give such notice as would permit the customer an opportunity to explore alternative sources of borrowing, or of selling part of its undertaking. Ralph Gibson J further concluded that a reference to the 'usual banking conditions' without stating what they were, and without clear language showing that such conditions were to prevail over any terms as to duration or termination, whether express or necessarily derived from the language used, could not negate a term which was otherwise part of the agreement.

However, an express clause that an overdraft is repayable on demand is not necessarily effective. In *Titford Property Co. Ltd* v *Cannon Street Acceptances Ltd* (22 May 1975 unreported, cited in Cresswell et al., *Encyclopaedia of Banking Law*) a facility letter was drawn up which granted the customer an overdraft for a 12-month period, but which included a clause providing for repayment at call. When the bank demanded repayment prior to the expiry of the 12-month period, the customer brought an action against the bank claiming that the overdraft was not repayable on demand. Goff J held that where a bank allows an overdraft facility for a fixed time, any clause requiring repayment of the same facility on demand is completely repugnant to the purpose of the facility and should be read as subordinate to the main clause, or alternatively completely ignored.

The decision in *Titford Property Co. Ltd* v *Cannon Street Acceptances Ltd* was considered by Ralph Gibson J in *Williams and Glyn's Bank Ltd* v *Barnes* where the learned judge expressed the view that if the judgment of Goff J is to be regarded as stating that in a contest for primacy between a term loan and a clause for repayment on demand, the provisions for the term loan must always prevail, then he should not feel able to follow it. Ralph Gibson J expressed the opinion that if the bank could not reasonably have supposed that the borrower would treat the clause for repayment on demand seriously, and the borrower could not sensibly be expected to have supposed that the bank did mean the term to be effective, the law both permits and requires the court to disregard the term. The approach adopted by Ralph Gibson J enables the court to reach its own conclusions and enforce the real intentions of the parties; for these reasons it must be submitted that it is correct.

Bank's right to withdraw an overdraft facility before the overdraft is utilised

Whether the bank can give notice to withdraw an overdraft facility for which the customer has given consideration (i.e., where there is a binding contract to provide an overdraft) will depend on the terms of the contract. If it is a term of the contract that the overdraft will be available for a fixed period, e.g., for three months, it would appear that the bank is bound to provide the overdraft facility within the stipulated period and up to any agreed limit. In the case where the bank is under no contractual obligation to provide the overdraft facility but has merely represented to its customer that the facility is or will be available, the position is not entirely clear. It is submitted that the bank will have committed itself to allow the facility by its representations to the customer (*Jorden* v *Money* (1854) 5 HL Cas 185; *Argy Trading Development Co. Ltd* v *Lapid Developments Ltd* [1977] 1 WLR 444). A closely related question which arises is whether the bank can refuse to honour cheques or drafts, within the limit of the agreed overdraft, before any notice of withdrawal has been given to the customer. Here again the position differs according to whether or not the bank has a contractual obligation to grant the overdraft but it is submitted that the customer must be given a reasonable opportunity to set his affairs in order (i.e., to arrange alternative financing facilities) (*Fleming* v *Bank of New Zealand* [1900] AC 577).

Bank's right to set off

There is one situation where the bank can recover the whole or part of an overdraft without first calling on the customer to repay it. This is where the bank has an immediate right to set off an item credited to the overdrawn account or to another account held by the same person against the amount which that person owes on the overdraft (*Garnett* v *M'Kewan* (1872) LR 8 Ex 10; see chapter 7). In this situation the bank does not seek to enforce its claim as a creditor against the customer and so no demand or notice of its intention to exercise a right of set-off is required. If the customer goes bankrupt, statute provides that the mutual indebtedness of the customer and the bank to each other, arising from the customer having two or more accounts, with some in credit and others in debit, will entitle the bank to set off so that only the remaining balance, if any, can be recovered (Insolvency Act 1986, s. 323(1), (2) and (4)). The statutory rule is mandatory and cannot be contracted out of (*National Westminster Bank Ltd* v *Halesowen Presswork and Assemblies Ltd* [1972] AC 785). Furthermore, the rule applies whether or not the amounts can be immediately set off, and so a set-off will be permitted even though the bank has agreed to allow the customer time to repay.

Interest on overdrafts

Interest will be calculated on overdrafts either at the agreed rate, or if there is no agreement, at the bank's currently published lending rate. This is fixed by reference to the bank's base rate (which tends to be uniform for all commercial banks) plus a number of percentage points over the minimum depending on the risk to the bank and the creditworthiness of the customer.

Overdraft interest is charged daily to the customer's account although not debited against the account until the end of the current quarterly or half-yearly period. Consequently, in calculating overdraft interest, account is not taken of amounts credited to the customer's account until the business day following that on which the bank receives the credit item. Where an account is continuously overdrawn a substantial part of the debit balance may actually represent interest.

The charging of interest is a matter of banking practice. It can be recovered on the basis of the implied contract or on the basis of a course of dealings or mercantile usage. Interest may be awarded by the court under s. 3 of the Law Reform (Miscellaneous Provisions) Act 1934, although the Act does not authorise charging compound interest. In *Yourell* v *Hibernian Bank Ltd* [1918] AC 372 Lord Atkinson considered charging compound interest 'a usual and perfectly legitimate mode of dealing between banker and customer'. In *National Bank of Greece SA* v *Pinios Shipping Co. No. 1* [1990] 1 AC 637 the House of Lords held that the usage under which banks are entitled to charge compound interest prevails generally as 'between bankers and customers who borrow from them and do not pay interest as it accrues'.

A point which is uncertain is whether the same method of calculation could be used in situations in which the original debt did not involve periodic repayments leading to the compounding of interest. In *Minories Finance Ltd* v *Daryanani* (1989) *The Times*, 14 April 1989 the repayment of certain loans, granted by a bank in London to a Nigerian company, was blocked by an embargo imposed by the Nigerian government. The bank served a demand in London on the guarantors. On the question of compound interest the Court of Appeal held that as the facility letter did not include an express provision entitling the bank to charge compound interest, the question of the bank's right to charge compound interest was a triable issue and leave to defend was granted. It should be remembered that in this case the issue arose only in respect of interest charged prior to the date on which the bank made its demand.

TERM LOANS

Although overdrafts are regarded as short-term finance, in reality many businesses operate on a permanent overdraft. However, it is commonly considered as more prudent to finance the purchase of fixed assets or long-term projects by a longer-term loan rather than an overdraft. During the early 1970s the banks expanded contractual term lending, with loans of up to five or seven years being available. Longer-term finance was made available through the merchant banks, many of which are owned by the clearing banks. The loans provided by merchant banks are usually repayable over a period exceeding 10 years, usually either at a fixed rate of interest or at a variable rate related to the corresponding current yields in the long-term gilt-edged market. It is normal for these loans to be secured on the existing fixed assets of the business.

Term-loan agreement

Term loans are almost invariably made under a written agreement which sets out in detail the terms of lending. Short-term loans are made on standard terms whilst others are tailored to the special needs of the borrower. A typical loan agreement is likely to contain specific provisions relating to repayment, conditions, representations and warranties, creditor protection, undertakings and events of default.

The advance

A term-loan agreement will invariably state the maximum amount of the loan. It will specify the method by which the loan is to be advanced, i.e., either by a single drawing of the whole amount at the option of the borrower or by successive instalments over a period of months or even years. Where the purpose of the loan is to provide finance for a specified project it is usual for the loan to be advanced in instalments; each instalment is advanced only on submission and approval of appropriate documentary evidence that the previous stages of the project have been satisfactorily completed. In the case of large loans (particularly syndicated loans) the borrowing company may be required to give notice to the lending bank or the agent bank before it can draw the amount of the next instalment on the next drawing date.

The loan agreement will provide that a charge will be levied on the undrawn balance of the maximum amount of the loan (a commitment fee). This fee is charged periodically at the time when interest payments fall due and it terminates when the maximum amount agreed has been advanced to the borrower. Where the loan is to be made in successive instalments, a charge will only be made if the amount drawn by the borrower is less than the maximum available under the instalment.

Duration of the loan

The agreement itself will specify the duration of the loan. Term loans of up to five or seven years are commonly advanced by the banks although longer-term loans of up to 10 years are increasingly agreed. The loan agreement is legally binding and the insertion of a term specifying the duration of the loan precludes any subsequent claim by the lending bank that the loan can be withdrawn at any time. Any demand for repayment made before the stipulated expiry term is ineffective unless there is default on the part of the borrower which entitles the bank under the terms of the loan agreement to call for immediate repayment, e.g., a failure to maintain the agreed payments of either capital or interest.

In the absence of a provision relating to the duration of the loan agreement, the loan will be repayable on the bank giving the borrower a reasonable length of notice demanding repayment (*Buckingham and Co* v *London and Midland Bank Ltd* (1895) 12 TLR 70), but it would appear that the borrower would be entitled to repay such a loan at any time without giving any notice in advance.

Repayment

The commencement and duration of the repayment period are a matter of negotiation. The agreed repayment terms are reciprocally binding on the borrower and the lending bank or banks. Consequently, the bank cannot require the borrower to repay the loan earlier than the date or dates agreed under the original agreement. The borrower cannot save interest by repaying the loan before the agreed date or dates, although it may make an early repayment if it also pays interest in advance calculated up to the agreed repayment dates.

A term-loan agreement may give an option to the borrower to repay the whole or part of the outstanding balance of the loan earlier than the date or dates agreed. In this way, the borrower saves interest. However, it is usual for the loan agreement to specify the earliest date on which prepayment may be made. Additionally, the loan agreement may also specify that the borrower must give the lending bank (or agent bank in the case of a syndicated loan) a specified notice before it can make prepayment and must pay interest on the amount prepaid for that period.

Where the loan is advanced for a specified purpose and the loan agreement does not deal with the issue of repayment, then the bank cannot withdraw the loan facility or claim repayment before the purpose is achieved (*Williams and Glyn's Bank Ltd* v *Barnes* [1981] Com LR 205), unless, of course, an event of default occurs which gives the bank an automatic right to immediate repayment.

Conversion into non-recourse loan

With some self-liquidating advances, the loan agreement may contain an option for the borrower to convert the outstanding balance of a loan into a non-recourse loan. A non-recourse loan is one under which a higher rate of interest is payable than under the initial loan, and the principal of the loan is repayable over a longer period than the initial loan period and is repayable only out of the profits or proceeds of the project financed. The importance of a non-recourse loan to the borrowing company is that repayment of the loan is made solely out of the generated profits from the financed projects. Consequently, any personal liability on the part of the borrowing company which could result in the company's insolvency is avoided. This liability is then exclusively charged on the assets comprised in the project which the loan was used to finance and the revenue arising from the project and its operation, and the lending bank cannot resort to the borrower's other assets if the loan is not fully repaid. Those other assets are therefore available for the company to sell, lease or otherwise dispose of free from any charge or security created under the loan agreement, and they are also available to be used as security for further borrowing by the company.

However, the lending bank does not take an equity participation in the project or development, and the bank is still a creditor of the borrower. It may recover any indebtedness (the outstanding balance of the loan with interest) in connection with the term loan out of the earnings or returns of the completed project. If the income of the project is not sufficient to discharge the outstanding principal sum and interest, the lending bank will have the power by the loan agreement to appoint a receiver to take over the management of the project or to sell the company's assets comprised in it.

Interest

Interest on term loans made by banks is charged at a rate which varies with market rates during the currency of the loan. Consequently, the risk of interest rates rising during the currency of the loan is borne by the borrower.

CONSUMER CREDIT ASPECTS OF OVERDRAFTS AND TERM LOANS

The Consumer Credit Act 1974 was passed to give effect to the recommendations of the Crowther Committee (Cmnd 4596) whose main concern was to stamp out sharp practices employed by certain financial institutions in respect of consumer credit and hire purchase. Banks were not amongst the institutions whose practices caused concern. However, it was felt that reform across the structure of the hire-purchase and consumer-credit industry was required. Nevertheless, banks did manage to obtain some important concessions, especially in respect of overdrafts.

The Consumer Credit Act 1974 applies certain protective measures to 'regulated credit agreements' and 'regulated hire agreements'. The debtor or hirer has to be a consumer, whilst the financier or credit provider may be 'any other person'. On the whole, banks and building societies enter into credit agreements.

The Consumer Credit Act 1974 applies to protect consumers (a term which extends to individuals, partnerships and unincorporated associations) in respect of transactions not exceeding £15,000.

Overdrafts

A bank overdraft falls within the definition of a regulated consumer credit agreement for unrestricted-use running account credit, even if extended without prior arrangement with the customer. Examples of an unrestricted-use credit agreement include the provision of an overdraft facility, cheque cards, and loans of money the use of which is at the free disposition of the borrower (even though the purpose of the loan may be known to the creditor).

Sometimes a bank will agree to extend an overdraft facility to its customer and a new maximum overdraft limit is agreed but its details are not finalised. For example, the customer does not take, or infrequently takes, advantage of the overdraft facility. In such a situation there is a multiple agreement within the Consumer Credit Act 1984, s. 18(1)(a), and on each occasion the customer takes advantage of the overdraft facility a separate agreement arises for the purposes of the Act (Goode, *Consumer Credit Act* (London: Butterworths, 1979), I, [558]).

Although overdrafts extended to individuals not exceeding £15,000 fall within the scope of the Consumer Credit Act 1974, its stringent requirements relating to entering into a credit agreement, its form and contents, and its cancellation, do not apply to bank overdrafts (Determination made on 21 December 1989 by Director General of Fair Trading; see Guest and Lloyd, *Encyclopaedia of Consumer Credit Law*, para. 4–4801).

The rate of interest charged is another area where regulations have been made under the Consumer Credit Act 1974. The Act requires the 'total charge for credit' to be disclosed in certain situations. Its calculation takes into account the rate of interest and also any other charges for the extension of the credit. In the case of an overdraft facility, however, the rate of interest alone is required to be disclosed and other charges (e.g., a commitment fee) may be disclosed separately. Further, banks extending overdraft facilities are not subject to regulations dealing with the form and content of the credit agreement. These exclusions from the scope of the Consumer Credit Act 1974 are of considerable importance to the banks.

Section 49 of the Consumer Credit Act 1974, makes it an offence to canvass or 'solicit' the entry of an individual (debtor) into a debtor-creditor agreement off trade premises. The offence of canvassing involves an individual soliciting by making oral representations that a relevant agreement should be entered into during a visit (s. 48). To constitute canvassing the oral representations must be made during the course of the visit and so telephone canvassing is not caught. However, s. 49(3) of the Act exempts the canvassing of entry into an overdraft arrangement if two conditions are satisfied, namely:

(a)   The exemption applies only to accounts covered by a determination of the Director General of Fair Trading. Current accounts operable by cheques have been the subject of such a determination (Determination of 1 June 1977; Guest and Lloyd, *Encyclopaedia of Consumer Credit Law*, para. 4–4800).

(b)   The person canvassed has to be an account holder; it is irrelevant whether the account is a current or deposit account.

The Act preserves the right of the bank to demand repayment of the overdraft on demand. Section 76, which requires the creditor to serve a written notice seven days prior to enforcing repayment, does not apply to overdrafts. Where an overdraft is granted for a specified period, the bank is required to give seven days' notice prior to enforcing the agreement. However, where repayment is demanded because of default, a default notice must be served on the customer.

Term loans

Part V of the Consumer Credit Act 1974, which does not apply in respect of overdrafts, will apply in respect of bank loans provided the loan is for not more than £15,000. The agreement is then subject to cancellation by the consumer within a prescribed period after it is entered into, if in the course of negotiations, oral representations were made by the other party. The cancellation provisions do not apply if the loan is secured over land or has been made for the purchase of land, or if the agreement is signed at the premises of the creditor (Consumer Credit Act 1974, s. 67). In reality few loans are cancelled by the borrower (consumer).

In the case of loans, however, s. 60 of the Act introduces more complex provisions. The Consumer Credit (Agreements) Regulations 1983 (SI 1983/1553) must be complied with if the agreement is to be enforceable. The Regulations require that the agreement must bear a heading stating that it is an agreement regulated under the Consumer Credit Act 1974; that it contains information advising the consumer about his or her rights under the Act, including the right of cancellation; and that the signature of the consumer must be executed in a signature 'box'. Information relating to the amounts and dates of repayment must clearly be given. The Regulations make provision for the cost of credit. Where the agreement involves fixed-sum credit, the contract has to disclose the total charge for the credit and rate of interest. In an agreement for running-account credit, the agreement has to show the maximum amount which may be outstanding or the manner in which it may be determined.

Where the loan agreement is secured on land, the Act requires the bank to send to the customer an advance copy of the agreement and mortgage or charge. The bank must then allow the consumer seven days to consider whether or not to withdraw from the transaction. At the end of that period, the bank will send a further copy of the agreement and mortgage or charge for signature. The customer then has a further seven days, during which the bank must not contact the customer except at his request, to peruse the document free from any pressure from the bank.

Where the bank has pre-signed the agreement only one copy need be given to the customer, otherwise two copies must be supplied.

The influence of the Consumer Credit Act 1974 continues after the agreement has been executed and the formalities complied with. The Act regulates certain aspects of the transaction during its currency, and the bank's duties of disclosure continue after the execution of the agreement.

LETTERS OF CREDIT

The commonest purpose for which banks issue commercial letters of credit is to finance import and export transactions in goods. In a letter of credit transaction, the seller requires a commitment by a creditworthy third party to pay the price of goods, together with any incidental costs of transportation and insurance. Once the bank gives an irrevocable commitment the seller is protected in the event of the buyer's insolvency and the issuing bank must make payment provided the proper shipping documents are presented by the seller.

On the presentation of the shipping documents, the bank will either credit an account for the benefit of the seller with an amount not exceeding that specified in the letter of credit and on which the seller may draw when payment falls due on the bill of exchange accepted by the bank, or the bank may make an immediate payment to the seller of the discounted value of the bill of exchange. In this way, the seller may obtain immediate cash payment under an acceptance credit after the issuing bank has accepted the bill of exchange.

A letter of credit may be issued on the basis that a second bank will confirm the credit and give its own independent undertaking to make payment against conforming shipping documents. In such circumstances the seller (beneficiary of the credit) gets the guarantee of two independent banks that payment will be made against proper documents.

Basic features of a letter of credit

It is not intended to discuss the law relating to commercial letters of credit in this book. However, some basic aspects of the law relating to letters of credit should be noted.

It is of the essence of a letter of credit that there is a pre-existing underlying contract for the sale of goods between the debtor and the beneficiary. However, once the letter of credit has been issued, it exists independently of the underlying contract of sale. It follows that the bank is not concerned with any disputes that arise between the parties to the underlying contract (*Hamzeh Malas and Sons* v *British Imex Industries Ltd* [1958] 2 QB 127). Only documents which are in strict compliance with the terms of the credit will be sufficient to invoke the bank's duty to make payment under the credit. In *Equitable Trust Co. of New York* v *Dawson Partners Ltd* (1927) 27 Ll L Rep 49 Viscount Sumner expressed the view that there is 'no room for documents which are almost the same, or which will do just as well'. There are two reasons underlying this rule, namely:

(a) for the issuing bank to be entitled to reimbursement by its customer for the sum paid under the credit, the documents must be in strict conformity with the customer's instructions; and

(b) the documents must be in order so that in the event of the goods being lost, damaged or destroyed, the bank and its customer can rely on the documents to found a claim.

Letters of credit as a means of extending credit

The issue or confirmation of a letter of credit may be used to finance either the buyer or the seller (or even both) in connection with an international sale transaction. The issuing bank incurs an immediate obligation to the seller upon issuing the letter of credit (although that obligation does not have to be satisfied until some time in the future) and if the buyer does not place the bank in funds to meet that obligation, then the bank will have to satisfy that obligation either by paying under the credit or negotiating the bill. The issuing bank, therefore, provides the buyer with a financial facility by issuing the credit; it may even advance funds to the buyer if it pays under the credit and then be reimbursed by the buyer. The confirming bank does not, however, provide any financial facility to the buyer and there is no direct contractual relationship between that bank and the buyer (*Calico Printers' Association* v *Barclays Bank Ltd* (1931) 36 Com Cas 71). Although the confirming bank enters into an obligation to the seller to honour the credit, it enters into contractual relations only with the issuing bank for whom it acts as an agent. Consequently, it must look to the issuing bank for reimbursement of amounts paid under the credit and only if it has accepted conforming documents (*Bank Melli Iran* v *Barclays Bank Dominion Colonial and Overseas*) [1951] 2 Lloyd's Rep 367).

The seller's right to receive payment under the credit is a right to future payment if he complies with the terms of the credit. This contractual right to payment or acceptance or negotiation of a bill of exchange may be assigned to a third party. The assignment enables the assignee, instead of the beneficiary of the credit, to receive payment following the beneficiary's performance of the underlying contract. Alternatively, the seller may create an equitable charge over any rights under the letter of credit, which shows that he intends to make the documents available as security for a debt which he owes to a third party.

However, the seller cannot transfer the credit to a second beneficiary unless the credit permits the use of the credit by a person other than the named beneficiary. Usually a transfer by a beneficiary is for cash which the beneficiary uses to buy the goods that are to be supplied under the credit. Once the credit has been transferred then the transferee can present documents under the credit, including his own invoice, and he will then be entitled to receive payment.

Issuing bank's right to reimbursement

The person who is financed by the issue of the letter of credit is the buyer who, unless the issuing bank is placed in funds at the time of the issue of the credit or unless the buyer authorises the issuing bank to debit the credit balance of his account, will rely on the bank giving him credit. The bank will usually enter into a written contract under which the buyer will agree to reimburse the bank for the amount advanced under the credit and any expenses. Where, however, the bank places itself in a position in which it will be unable to carry out its obligations under the letter of credit, the customer is not required to put the bank in funds. Thus where the bank becomes insolvent or goes into liquidation, the customer's obligation to put the bank in funds is terminated (*Sale Continuation Ltd* v *Austin Taylor and Co. Ltd* [1968] 2 QB 849). Where, in fact, the customer has already put the bank in funds prior to it going into liquidation, the bank holds the funds on trust to fulfil the purpose for which they were paid, e.g., to pay the beneficiary (*Re Kayford Ltd* [1975] 1 WLR 279).

Conditions for claiming reimbursement

The issuing bank will act as an agent for the buyer, and therefore in order to be entitled to reimbursement the bank must comply exactly with the instructions given to it. If the issuing bank or any of its agents (including a confirming bank) fails to act in conformity with the instructions, the bank loses its right to reimbursement, and will be liable in damages to the customer (buyer) for breach of contract (*Equitable Trust Co. of New York* v *Dawson Partners Ltd* (1926) 25 Ll L Rep 90; *South African Reserve Bank* v *Samuel and Co. Ltd* (1931) 40 Ll L Rep 291). Where the issuing or confirming bank takes up documents in good faith from the beneficiary and they appear to be complying documents which conform to the conditions of the letter of credit when in fact they include a forged or falsified document, the bank is entitled to be reimbursed (*Gian Singh and Co. Ltd* v *Banque de l'Indochine* [1974] 1 WLR 1234). However, where a bank accepts or negotiates a forged bill of exchange for which neither the beneficiary nor his agent may be held responsible, the bank acts without authority (*United City Merchants (Investments) Ltd* v *Royal Bank of Canada* [1983] 1 AC 168).

Trust letters and receipts and letters of hypothecation

The issuing bank may release the shipping documents to the buyer when the buyer has not yet reimbursed the bank under the terms of a trust letter or receipt. In such circumstances the buyer acknowledges that he holds the goods and the eventual proceeds of sale as an agent or trustee for the bank. In many cases the terms of the trust letter or receipt are incorporated in the written instructions given to the issuing bank on the issue of the letter of credit.

Alternatively, the buyer may deliver a letter of hypothecation or charge by which the goods and proceeds of sale will be charged with the amount owing to the bank. It is likely that the buyer will have delivered a general letter of hypothecation to the bank over all goods likely to be purchased by him in respect of which the bank issues letters of credit. The anticipatory charge attaches in equity to particular goods as and when the buyer purchases them (*Holroyd* v *Marshall* (1862) 10 HL Cas 191; *Re Bond Worth Ltd* [1980] Ch 228).

The effect of trust letters or receipts and letters of hypothecation is the same, i.e., they create an equitable charge in favour of the bank over the goods and the proceeds of sale. As an equitable charge it will have to be registered under the companies legislation.

17　Bankers' Securities

NATURE OF SECURITY

Whatever class of security a bank agrees to accept it should be remembered that the object of the security is to provide a source of satisfaction for the debt covered. The bank should, therefore, rarely advance up to the full market price, but should allow a margin to cover itself against certain risks, such as overvaluation, market fluctuations, and loss which may arise owing to a forced sale. The form of security should be appropriate to the property over which it is taken, e.g., where the value of the property derives from a business, the form of security should be such as will enable the bank to realise the business as a going concern. It is also imperative that during the lifetime of the loan and before the necessity to realise the security arises, the borrower is allowed to carry on his ordinary business without too many limitations.

When a bank takes security it does not become the absolute owner of the property, but it will have certain rights over the property until the debt is repaid.

Possessory securities are based on the acquisition by the creditor of the possession of the chattel which serves as security. In the case of a lien, the borrower remains the owner of the property, although the creditor is in actual or constructive possession of the property. The items which are subject to a banker's lien are those which the bank acquires in the ordinary course of business, e.g., cheques, bills of exchange or other instruments deposited with the bank for collection. Whether a particular instrument in the possession of the bank is acquired in the ordinary course of business will depend not only on the nature of the banking business, but also on the nature of the business relationship or course of dealings developed between the bank and its customer.

Under a pledge, the pledgee is entitled to the exclusive possession of the property until the debt is discharged, and the pledgee, in certain circumstances, will have a power of sale, although ownership in the property remains with the pledgor. Unlike a lien, it is not essential that the pledgor actually has ownership of the goods pledged, but he must pledge with the consent of the owner. The pledgee may sell the pledged property without recourse to the courts, but must account to the pledgor for any surplus remaining after repaying the debt. Items subject to pledge are usually goods and chattels and fully negotiable securities.

With proprietary securities the creditor has the right to seize the goods if the debtor defaults or becomes insolvent, and to satisfy the debt from the proceeds of their sale. During the existence of a loan arrangement the property is left in the possession of the debtor. Mortgages of chattels and land are illustrations of proprietary securities; so too are fixed and floating charges over assets comprised in a business. The mortgagee may enter into possession but will more likely exercise other remedies, e.g., appointment of a receiver or sale. The sort of items subject to a mortgage are likely to be title deeds, life policies, stocks and shares and other choses in action.

Guarantees are often called 'personal securities'; they are personal obligations undertaken by strangers to a transaction for the performance of the duties under it of one of the parties.

AVOIDANCE OF A SECURITY

The question of vitiating factors may arise in the context of real securities (i.e., securities charged to land) and guarantees. Many guarantors enter into commitments in good faith but without expecting to have to honour their obligation. In some cases, the guarantor may be able to assert that either the bank took advantage of him, or that the principal debtor has used undue influence against the guarantor, and the bank has become caught in the situation.

Avoidance by reason of undue influence

Equity will set aside contracts or gifts on the ground that a party has behaved unconscionably and has obtained a benefit by reason of the exercise of undue influence (*Allcard* v *Skinner* (1887) 36 ChD 145). Where a 'stronger' party obtains some benefit from a 'weaker' party, it is sometimes presumed that the relationship between the two is of the kind that requires proof that the benefit received by the stronger party was not received by the exercise of undue influence. Although such a relationship is not presumed between principal and agent (*Re Coomber* [1911] 1 Ch 723) or between husband and wife (*Howes* v *Bishop* [1909] 2 KB 390; *Bank of Montreal* v *Stuart* [1911] AC 120; *MacKenzie* v *Royal Bank of Canada* [1934] AC 468) the courts will intervene in some cases of 'inequality of bargaining power' and are cautious and watchful of any hints of the surety (wife) being subjected to undue influence (see *Yerkey* v *Jones* (1939) 63 CLR 649). Such a relationship of undue influence does exist between an elderly parent and emancipated child (*Bullock* v *Lloyds Bank Ltd* [1955] Ch 317) or between solicitor and client. There is a presumption of undue influence where the guarantor was persuaded to enter into the guarantee by someone in whom he placed his 'trust and confidence' (see *Lloyds Bank Ltd* v *Bundy* [1975] QB 326. There is no presumption of undue influence in the case of husband and wife, and the burden of proving undue influence lies on those who allege it (*Nedby* v *Nedby* (1852) 5 De G & Sm 377).

However, both the Court of Appeal and the House of Lords in *Barclays Bank plc* v *O'Brien* [1993] QB 109; [1994] 1 AC 180 concluded that the line of cases from *Turnbull and Co* v *Duval* [1902] AC 429 demonstrates a treatment of 'wives who have given security to support their husband's debts more tender than that which would have been applied to other third party sureties'. The Court of Appeal judgment of Scott LJ in the *Barclays Bank* case sought to give the wife who provides security for the personal and business debts of the husband extended protection by creating a 'protected class' of surety.

In a detailed survey of the law (see *Turnbull and Co.* v *Duval*; *Chaplin and Co. Ltd* v *Brammall* [1908] 1 KB 233; *Yerkey* v *Jones*) Scott LJ concluded that although the position of married women today is both generally and vis-à-vis their husbands very different from the time when the earlier cases were decided, the degree of emancipation of women is uneven. For that reason, and the fact that the earlier cases have not been overruled, Scott LJ, as 'a matter of policy', held that a 'protected class' of surety should be recognised. This 'protected class' would allow the protection of the married woman (*Yerkey* v *Jones*) and the vulnerable elderly who had agreed to provide security for the debts of their adult children (*Avon Finance Co. Ltd* v *Bridger* [1985] 2 All ER 281). It would also extend to 'all cases in which the relationship between the surety and the debtor is one in which influence by the debtor over the surety and reliance by the surety on the debtor are natural and probable features of the relationship'. In cases falling within the 'protected class', the security given by the surety would, in certain circumstances, be unenforceable, although the creditor had no knowledge of, and had not been responsible for, the 'vitiating feature of the transaction'. In such cases, equity would hold the security given by the surety to be unenforceable by the creditor if:

(i) the relationship between the debtor and the surety and the consequent likelihood of influence and reliance was known to the creditor; and (ii) the surety's consent to the transaction was procured by undue influence or material misrepresentation on the part of the debtor or the surety lacked an adequate understanding of the nature and effect of the transaction; and (iii) the creditor, whether by leaving it to the debtor to deal with the surety or otherwise, had failed to take reasonable steps to try and ensure that the surety entered into the transaction with an adequate understanding of the nature and effect of the transaction and that the surety's consent to the transaction was a true and informed one.

The House of Lords dismissed an appeal by the creditor, Barclays Bank plc, from the decision of the Court of Appeal. Lord Browne-Wilkinson held that if a wife was induced by the undue influence, misrepresentation or other legal wrong of her husband to stand surety for the husband's debt, the creditor would, in circumstances which should have put him on inquiry, be fixed with constructive notice of the wife's right to set aside the transaction, unless the creditor had warned the wife, at a meeting not attended by the husband, of the risks involved and had advised the wife to take independent action. Lord Browne-Wilkinson rejected the special equity theory established by Scott LJ in the Court of Appeal. He said that under the ordinary principles of equity, the wife's right to set aside the transaction will be enforceable against third parties (e.g., a creditor) if either the husband was acting as the third party's agent or the third party had actual or constructive notice of the facts giving rise to her equity. Although there may be cases where, without artificiality, it can properly be held that the husband was acting as an agent of the creditor, such cases will be rare. The main problem is to identify the circumstances in which the creditor will be taken to have had notice of the wife's equity to set aside the transaction.

The doctrine of notice lies at the heart of equity. Where there are two innocent parties, each enjoying rights, the earlier right prevails against the later right if the person acquiring the later right either has actual knowledge of the earlier right or can be deemed to have constructive notice (i.e., he would have discovered the earlier right if he had taken the proper steps). Consequently, where a wife has agreed to stand surety for her husband's debts as a result of undue influence or misrepresentation, the creditor will take subject to the wife's equity to set aside the transaction if the circumstances were such that the creditor should have been put on notice. It is at this stage that the 'invalidation tendency' or the law's 'tender treatment' of the married woman becomes relevant. This 'tenderness' of the law towards married women is due to the fact that, even today, many wives repose confidence and trust in their husbands in relation to their financial affairs. Moreover, the informality of business dealings between spouses may raise a substantial risk that the husband did not accurately state to the wife the nature of the liability she was undertaking. Lord Browne-Wilkinson held that a creditor is put on inquiry when a wife offers to stand surety for the husband's debts by a combination of two factors, namely:

(a)   the transaction is prima facie not to the advantage of the wife; and
(b)   there is a substantial risk in transactions of that kind (in inducing the wife to act as a surety) that the husband has committed a legal or equitable wrong that entitles the wife to set aside the transaction.

Unless a creditor who is put on inquiry takes reasonable steps to satisfy himself that the wife's consent to stand surety has been properly obtained, the creditor will have constructive notice of the wife's rights. Lord Browne-Wilkinson held that the creditor can reasonably be expected to take steps to bring home to the wife the risk she undertakes by acting as surety and to advise her to take independent advice. A creditor will be deemed to have taken reasonable steps if he insists that the wife attend a private meeting (in the absence of the husband) with a representative of the creditor at which she is told of the extent of her liability as surety, warned of the risk she is running and urged to take independent advice. If these steps are taken then the creditor will have taken such reasonable steps as are necessary to preclude a subsequent claim that it had constructive notice of the wife's rights. Where the creditor has knowledge of further facts which render the presence of undue influence not only possible but probable, the creditor will have to insist that the wife is separately advised.

Lord Browne-Wilkinson went on to hold that although the case before him concerned the wife who stands as surety for her husband's debts, the same principle would apply to cohabitees. The 'tenderness' shown by the law to married women is not based on the marriage ceremony but reflects the underlying risk of one cohabitee exploiting the emotional involvement and trust of the other.

In *National Westminster Bank plc* v *Morgan* [1985] AC 686 the House of Lords had held that in order for the presumption of undue influence to operate, it must be shown that the transaction was wrongful in the sense that it operated to the manifest disadvantage of the person influenced. Lord Scarman took the view that the Court of Appeal erred in holding that the presumption of undue influence arose because of the nature of the relationship between the parties. Evidence was also required that the transaction itself was wrongful and that it constituted an unfair advantage taken of the person subjected to the influence.

The *Morgan* case, therefore, held that a transaction will be set aside if the transaction results from the undue influence of one party over the other and the transaction is to the manifest disadvantage of that other. It also affirmed that the mere fact that the surety is a wife does not raise a presumption of undue influence, and neither will the presumption be raised where the relationship is that of banker and customer. Scott LJ in the Court of Appeal recognised an additional category of cases where the doctrine of undue influence will apply, namely (a) where the surety lacked an adequate understanding of the nature of the transaction; and (b) where the bank, knowing that the relationship between the surety and debtor was one where the surety was likely to be influenced by the debtor, failed to ensure that the surety obtained independent legal advice or to explain the effect of the document. To that extent, the House of Lords has affirmed the judgment of the Court of Appeal, although the 'protected class' of surety has been rejected.

Loan made jointly to husband and wife

More recently, however, the courts have held that the doctrine of undue influence will not protect a wife who creates a charge over the matrimonial home as security for a loan made to the husband and wife jointly. Consequently, the lender will not be affected by the undue influence of the husband, unless the husband was acting as the creditor's agent. In *CIBC Mortgages plc* v *Pitt* [1994] 1 AC 200 Lord Browne-Wilkinson held that where actual undue influence had been exercised and proved, 'manifest disadvantage' does not have to be established, but the claimant is entitled as of right to have the transaction set aside. However, if the transaction takes the form of a joint loan, as opposed to the wife acting as a surety, the third party will not be fixed with constructive notice of undue influence. Otherwise, on the purchase of a home in joint names, the building society or bank financing the purchase would have to insist on meeting the wife separately from her husband, advise her about the nature of the transaction and recommend that she seek separate legal advice from that of her husband.

What distinguishes the case of the joint-account advance from the surety is that, in the latter, there is not only the possibility of undue influence having been exercised, but also the added risk of it having been exercised because, prima facie, the guarantee by the wife of the husband's debts is not for her financial benefit.

Avoidance by reason of misrepresentation

Contracts of guarantee, unlike contracts of insurance, are not *uberrimae fidei* or contracts 'of the utmost good faith', under which one or both parties is under an obligation to disclose to the other all material facts known to him which may influence the decision of the other. Non-disclosure by the bank of facts which lead the bank to suspect that the principal debtor was defrauding the guarantor would not necessarily invalidate the guarantee (*National Provincial Bank of England Ltd* v *Glanusk* [1913] 3 KB 335). The test established in *Hamilton* v *Watson* (1845) 12 Cl & F 109 is whether there is any contract between the bank and the principal debtor which would mean that the position of the guarantor was not what might reasonably be expected. If there is, the guarantor is entitled to have this disclosed to him; but he must make his own specific inquiries if he is concerned about other points. The principle in *Hamilton* v *Watson* was applied in *Cooper* v *National Provincial Bank Ltd* [1946] KB 1, in which the bank did not disclose to the guarantor that the husband of the principal debtor, who was an undischarged bankrupt, had authority to operate the principal debtor's account and that the account had, previously, been operated in an irregular manner. The guarantee was nevertheless held to be enforceable, since there was nothing concerning the principal debtor's account which a guarantor might not reasonably have expected. Similarly, in *Lloyds Bank Ltd* v *Harrison* (1925) 4 LDB 12 it was held that the guarantee was enforceable even though the bank had not told the guarantor that the principal debtor was in difficulties and that the bank had insisted that the principal debtor should accept only such business as would reduce his stock.

If, however, the guarantor does make inquiries of the bank in respect of certain matters, and the bank, not being obliged to, decides to make the information available, it must act honestly and to the best of its abilities. Whilst the bank is not bound to disclose all that it knows about the principal debtor's dealings, it must not conceal from the guarantor any fact which may materially affect the transaction between the bank and the guarantor.

Avoidance by reason of mistake

A guarantor cannot claim to be relieved from his guarantee by reason of mistake on the ground that he did not understand some particular provision of the guarantee, or even the general drift of the guarantee. Where, however, a person signs a guarantee under a fundamental mistake as to the nature of the document he signs, the guarantee may be void by reason of mistake. The defence of *non est factum* ('it is not my act') is available when the guarantee was not in fact signed by the guarantor or his agent, but by some other person. The law has extended this principle to protect persons who, because of illiteracy or disability, e.g., blindness, have to trust other persons to explain the document to them. The principle protects persons who are permanently or temporarily unable, through no fault of their own, to understand the purpose of the document (see *Foster* v *Mackinnon* (1869) LR 4 CP 704). In *Saunders* v *Anglia Building Society* [1971] AC 1004 (affirming *Gallie* v *Lee* [1969] 2 Ch 17) the House of Lords decided that where a person signed a document, the plea of *non est factum* can only succeed if he can show that the document which he signed was not the document he intended to sign and that he acted with due care in signing it. It follows that the plea of *non est factum* will rarely succeed if the document was signed by an adult and literate person (see also *Credit Lyonnais* v *P. T. Barnard and Associates Ltd* [1976] 1 Lloyd's Rep 557).

GUARANTEES AS SECURITY

Guarantees are the simplest form of security. They are extremely important and widely used in dealings with individuals, traders, partnerships, limited companies etc., which have insufficient assets for real securities. Under a guarantee the guarantor undertakes to answer for the debt, default or miscarriage of another person known as the 'principal debtor'. The borrowing customer remains primarily liable on the debt; the guarantor's liability only arises if the person primarily liable defaults (see *Moschi* v *LEP Air Services Ltd* [1973] AC 331 at 348, where Lord Diplock described the nature of the guarantor's obligations).

A familiar example of a guarantee contract is where a parent guarantees a young customer's overdraft, or where a director guarantees a company's indebtedness to the bank.

A person who promises to pay another person's debt is not necessarily a guarantor and that obligation must be distinguished from, e.g., an indemnity.

There are a number of strict rules restricting the liability of the guarantor and giving him certain rights against the creditor and principal debtor. The Code of Banking Practice provides that in relation to guarantees and other types of third-party security, banks and building societies must advise private individuals proposing to give a guarantee that: (a) by giving the guarantee or third party security liability may be imposed on them instead of, or as well as, the other person (principal debtor); and (b) that the guarantor should seek independent legal advice before entering into the guarantee or third-party security. Certain other formal conditions have to be satisfied if the guarantee is to be enforceable, namely:

(a) *Writing.* A guarantee is unenforceable by action unless the agreement or some memorandum or note is executed in writing and signed by the guarantor or his agent (Statute of Frauds (1677), s. 4). Any writing by which the guarantor of a debt can be identified in a memorandum of guarantee, and which shows an intention to adopt the guarantee will suffice as a signature (*Decouvreur* v *Jordan* (1987) *The Times*, 25 May 1987). The guarantor's signature is usually witnessed but this is not strictly necessary. Where there is a written guarantee, objective intrinsic evidence is admissible to explain the terms used (*Perrylease Ltd* v *Imecar AG* [1987] 2 All ER 373 at 381).

(b) *Consideration.* A contract of guarantee must be supported by consideration, unless it is under seal or is expressed to take effect as a deed. The consideration need not be stated in the document but it must be proved. Where consideration is for 'further advances' against an existing overdrawn account, it must be shown that such further advances have been made (see *Provincial Bank of Ireland* v *Donnell* [1934] NI 33; *Bank of Montreal* v *Sperling Hotel Co. Ltd* (1973) 36 DLR (3d) 130). If the guarantee is in consideration of the bank continuing to afford banking facilities to the principal customer, and none are provided, then consideration may fail (*Royal Bank of Canada* v *Salvatori* [1928] 3 WWR 501; *National Bank of Nigeria Ltd* v *Awolesi* [1964] 1 WLR 1311). If guarantee refers to an existing account, opening a new account is not sufficient consideration.

(c) *Capacity.* Capacity to enter into a contract of guarantee is essential. Before 1987, a minor could not be bound by a guarantee given by him. Since the abolition of the *ultra vires* rule the capacity of a limited company to give a guarantee has not been in doubt, and any director may bind the company to that contract (Companies Act 1985, s. 35(A)(2)(b) provides that knowledge of the limitations on the powers of the directors to enter into the contract would not necessarily prove lack of good faith on the part of the bank).

Multi-party guarantees

Where two or more persons give a guarantee, their liability may be joint, or several, or joint and several. In a joint guarantee each co-guarantor is liable for the whole of the sum guaranteed and all should be sued together. However, if proceedings are taken against only one or some of the co-guarantors, the remaining co-guarantors not included in the action are no longer discharged from liability, and may subsequently be sued (Civil Liability (Contribution) Act 1978, s. 3). On the death or bankruptcy of a joint co-guarantor the estate of the deceased is freed from liability under the guarantee, and the bank must enforce the guarantee against the remaining co-guarantors. In a several guarantee each of the co-guarantors may be made liable separately for the whole of the guaranteed amount. An unsatisfied judgment against one of the several guarantors will not prevent an action against the remaining. The death or bankruptcy of one of the several co-guarantors does not of itself release the estate from liability for advances made before the bank receives notice of the event.

In practice, it is irrelevant to the bank whether the guarantee is expressed to be several, or joint and several. The guarantee, however, is usually made joint and several and this may be advantageous to the guarantors. The guarantee should also make provision entitling the bank to release or discharge or make any arrangements with any one or more of the guarantors without discharging the rest, thereby excluding the rule that the release of one or more of the guarantors releases the others (*Mercantile Bank of Sydney* v *Taylor* [1893] AC 317; *Barclays Bank Ltd* v *Trevanion* (1933) *The Banker*, vol. 27, p. 98).

When there are to be co-guarantors, the bank should ensure that all of them execute the contract and no advance should be made to the principal debtor until that is done. If one or more of the co-guarantors fails or refuses to sign the guarantee, then those co-guarantors who have already signed the guarantee and can show that they signed the document on the understanding of it being signed by all the relevant parties, will be discharged from liability (*National Provincial Bank of England* v *Brackenbury* (1906) 22 TLR 797). The same rule applies if the signature of one of the co-guarantors is forged.

Limited, specific and continuing guarantees

Most guarantees given to a bank are intended to cover a series of transactions (e.g., a fluctuating overdraft balance) spread over a period of time. The bank will generally seek a guarantee over the 'whole debt' and it should exercise care in making any amendment to the standard wording of a guarantee which seeks to restrict the extent of guarantee. Thus, a form of wording which limits the extent of the guarantee should be avoided if the bank is likely to make further advances. A single or specific guarantee will be exhausted by an advance which takes the total amount advanced up to the agreed limit, i.e., the guarantor will be liable for up to a specified amount, which might thereafter be reduced by the operation of the rule in *Clayton's* case on a current account. To avoid the operation of that rule any advances made under a specific guarantee should be made on a separate loan account. By contrast, a continuing guarantee will cover all debts on the same account and is not affected by any payments into the principal debtor's account, for it does not secure any particular advance to the principal customer but the final combined balance on all the principal debtor's accounts (see *Re Sherry* (1884) 25 ChD 692).

Where the principal debtor is not liable

A guarantee is an accessory contract and therefore presupposes that some other person is primarily liable. If the principal customer is not in fact liable, the guarantor too will not be liable under the guarantee. In *Coutts and Co* v *Browne-Leckey* [1947] KB 104 it was held that the guarantors of an infant's loan could not be sued since advances to minors were considered as absolutely void. Oliver J suggested this rule applied to cases where all the parties knew the facts (cf. *Yeoman Credit Ltd* v *Latter* [1961] 1 WLR 828).

Rights of the guarantor

From the moment a guarantee is entered into, the guarantor has certain implied rights against the bank, namely:

(a)   The guarantor has the right, at any time after the principal debt becomes due, to apply to the bank and pay it off. In practice this right is rarely exercised but on giving the bank a proper indemnity for costs, the guarantor may then sue the principal debtor in the bank's name (*Swire* v *Redman* (1876) 1 QBD 536 at 541).

(b)   The guarantor has the right to require the bank to call on the principal debtor to pay the debt at any time after it becomes due (*Rouse* v *Bradford Banking Co.* [1894] 2 Ch 32).

(c)   Whilst the guarantee is in force the guarantor has the right to require the bank at any time to give particulars of the extent of his liability and the bank is bound to give the necessary information. Whilst the bank must not disclose to the guarantor the details of its dealing with its customer, the principal debtor, because these are subject to the duty of confidentiality, it may inform the guarantor of the extent of his liability.

(d)   A guarantor has the right against the bank to any defence, or right of set-off, or counter-claim which is available to the principal customer prior to default (*Bechervaise* v *Lewis* (1872) LR 7 CP 372). The guarantor, after default by the principal customer, cannot set off against the debt any sums which fall due thereafter.

(e)   Once the guarantor has paid the amount of the guarantee, he has a right to be subrogated to all the rights of the bank against the principal debtor, unless such rights have been waived. Thus, if a bank was a preferential creditor, the guarantor will be able to exercise the same rights against the principal debtor.

(f)   On payment of the debt the guarantor has a right to any security given to the bank by the principal debtor (or by a co-guarantor) regardless of whether or not the guarantor knew of the security at the time of giving the guarantee (*Forbes* v *Jackson* (1882) 19 ChD 615).

(g)   Although the bank may (if the guarantee is properly worded) claim the full amount outstanding both from the principal customer and from each guarantor, the bank cannot make a profit out of the claim. In addition to handing over any securities to the guarantor, it must refund any surplus to the guarantor. The bank, however, is entitled to recover any outstanding interest from the guarantor which it may have been unable to recover from the principal customer.

Rights against the principal debtor

A guarantor has an implied right to an indemnity from the principal debtor if he gives a guarantee at the request of the principal debtor. The principal debtor may give the guarantor an express right of indemnity, in which case the guarantor's rights will be governed by that indemnity. However, if the guarantee is given without any request from the principal customer, the guarantor may not have any implied right to be reimbursed (*Owen* v *Tate* [1976] QB 402). Under the implied right of indemnity, the guarantor has, unless the guarantee provides otherwise, an immediate right against the principal debtor (*Davies* v *Humphreys* (1840) 6 M & W 153) on each occasion he pays on the guarantee, although he is not entitled to accelerate that right by paying the guaranteed debt before it falls due (*Coppin* v *Gray* (1842) 1 Y & C Ch 205).

Rights of co-guarantors

A co-guarantor has a right of contribution against the other co-guarantors of the same debt, each guarantor being liable proportionately to the amount he has guaranteed. If one of the guarantors is insolvent, any deficiency must be borne by the other guarantors rateably. The right of contribution against the other co-guarantors exists whether they are bound severally, or jointly and severally (see *Scholefield Goodman and Sons Ltd* v *Zyngier* [1986] AC 562 at 571).

There is no right of contribution if the co-guarantors are liable under separate contracts for equal portions of the same principal debt, e.g., where each guarantor has entered into a separate transaction with the bank (*Coope* v *Twynam* (1823) Turn & R 426). If the right of contribution does arise, then it applies whether or not the guarantor who has paid knew of the existence of the co-guarantors at the time he gave the guarantee (*Craythorne* v *Swinburne* (1807) 14 Ves Jr 160).

The right of contribution may arise either before or after the guarantor who seeks the contribution has paid the bank. Before making payment to the bank any co-guarantor can compel the other co-guarantors to contribute towards satisfying the common liability and apply to the court for a declaration of his right to contribution (*Wolmershausen* v *Gullick* [1893] 2 Ch 514). If a co-guarantor is sued by the bank for payment under the guarantee, he can assert his right of contribution by joining the other co-guarantors as defendants in the action, or by obtaining an order directing that, when he has paid his own share of the common liability, the co-guarantors should indemnify him from further liability.

The extent of the right of contribution depends on the number of solvent co-guarantors (*Ramskill* v *Edwards* (1885) 31 ChD 100) and on the amount for which each guarantor is liable. If co-guarantors are each liable for the whole of the principal debt or for equal amounts of the debt, each solvent co-guarantor is liable to contribute equally. If the co-guarantors are not liable for equal amounts, the right of contribution is calculated proportionately to the amount for which each is liable (*Wolmershausen* v *Gullick* [1893] 2 Ch 514).

Discharge of the guarantor

A guarantor is 'revocably' discharged from his obligations under the guarantee if the principal debtor pays the principal debt. The reason why the guarantor is only revocably discharged is that a payment made by the principal debtor could, in some exceptional cases, turn out to be a preference and may therefore have to be refunded to the liquidator. As the guarantor is only revocably discharged, the bank should not return the guarantee to the guarantor, nor write any words indicating that it has been cancelled. There are a number of events which may result in the discharge of the guarantor, namely:

(a) An express release of the principal debtor from all further liability will discharge the guarantor since such a release extinguishes the guaranteed debt (*Perry* v *National Provincial Bank of England* [1910] 1 Ch 464; *Clarke* v *Henty* (1838) 3 Y & C Ex 187). This principle will apply despite any express reservations (*Commercial Bank of Tasmania* v *Jones* [1893] AC 313), except where the principal debtor obtains the release by fraudulent means (*Scholefield* v *Templer* (1859) 4 De G & J 429).

(b) A binding agreement between the bank and the principal debtor to allow an extension of time to the principal debtor to repay the debt will discharge the guarantor from liability if made without his consent, whether or not he is in fact prejudiced by the agreement (*Ex parte Gifford* (1802) 6 Ves Jr 805). Such an agreement would necessarily prejudice the guarantor by preventing him from exercising his right to require the bank to call on the principal debtor to pay off the debts and then recover the amount from the principal debtor (see *Rouse* v *Bradford Banking Co.* [1894] 2 Ch 32). An agreement whereby the bank agrees not to demand due repayment in return for a promise by the principal debtor to pay a higher rate of interest is not an agreement to give time if the creditor retains a right to demand repayment at any time (*York City and County Banking Co* v *Bainbridge* [1880] 43 LT 732). The guarantor would appear not to be discharged if, when agreeing to give time to the principal debtor, the bank expressly reserves its rights against the guarantor even though the guarantor did not consent to or know of the reservation (*Kearsley* v *Cole* (1846) 16 M & W 128). The guarantor will not be discharged by an agreement to give time to the principal debtor if the agreement was made after the bank had obtained judgment against the principal debtor and the guarantor (*Re A Debtor (No. 14 of 1913)* [1913] 3 KB 11), or against the guarantor alone (*Jenkins* v *Robertson* (1854) 2 Drew 351), or if the guarantor agrees either in the guarantee or subsequently that time may be given to the principal debtor (*Midland Counties Motor Finance Co. Ltd* v *Slade* [1951] 1 KB 346).

The guarantor is not discharged from liability if the bank does not agree to give time to the principal debtor but merely refrains from taking steps to recover the principal debt, or refuses to take proceedings which are bound to be abortive (*Musket* v *Rogers* (1839) 5 Bing NC 728).

(c) A guarantor will be discharged if the bank agrees to any material variation of the principal contract without obtaining the guarantor's consent and without reserving its rights against the guarantor (*Ward* v *National Bank of New Zealand Ltd* (1883) 8 App Cas 755 at 765). Any material variation of the underlying contract will mean the guarantor would be bound to underwrite a different contract if he were not released. If the guarantor has agreed to guarantee several separate and distinct obligations, and if the principal debtor's liability in respect of the principal contract is then varied in respect of any one or more particular obligation, the guarantor will be discharged from liability in respect of that obligation, but not in respect of the other obligations (*Skillett* v *Fletcher* (1867) LR 2 CP 469). The same rule will apply to any other principal debt which is severable.

(d)   If the guarantor has guaranteed a number of separate obligations which are required to be performed under the principal contract, then the variation of the principal contract in respect of any one of them will discharge the guarantor in respect of that variation (*Skillett* v *Fletcher* (1867) LR 2 CP 469). However, if the bank accepts, or is compelled to accept, a breach of contract by the principal debtor, that does not amount to a material variation and the guarantor is not discharged. A breach of contract by the principal debtor should be treated as a breach of contract by the guarantor, because the guarantor has a duty to ensure that the principal debtor performs his obligations. The guarantor, therefore, becomes liable in damages to the extent of the principal debtor's debt to the bank (*Moschi* v *Lep Air Services* [1973] AC 331).

A bank will naturally want to retain the utmost freedom of action in its dealing with its customer, the principal debtor. The bank may therefore insert a 'time and indulgence clause' in its contract with the principal debtor. This will enable the bank to vary the terms of the loan to the principal debtor, or to grant further time to pay when the advances become repayable, or to take additional security or release an existing security. Any such variation will discharge the guarantor unless the guarantor agrees either in advance, or even subsequently, to the variation (*Perry* v *National Provincial Bank of England* [1910] 1 Ch 464).

(e)   A guarantor will be discharged if the bank materially departs from or varies the terms of the guarantee. Any such alteration will constitute an alteration in the guarantor's obligations, unless the alteration is quite insubstantial (*Holme* v *Brunskill* (1878) 3 QBD 495 quoted in *Egbert* v *National Crown Bank* [1918] AC 903). Thus, for example, if a guarantee stipulates that credit will be given for a certain period to the principal debtor, the stipulation must be complied with (*Bacon* v *Chesney* (1816) 1 Stark 192). A guarantor will be discharged if he executes the guarantee on the understanding that a specified number of guarantors will sign the document but one or more fail to do so (*National Provincial Bank of England* v *Brackenbury* (1906) 22 TLR 797).

Where there are co-guarantors, all of them will be discharged if the bank varies the terms of the guarantee in respect of one of them without obtaining the consent of the others and without reserving its rights against the others. Thus, all the co-guarantors will be discharged if one of them is released by the bank (*Mercantile Bank of Sydney* v *Taylor* [1893] AC 317).

(f)   A guarantor may be discharged if there is a change in the legal position of the parties, e.g., the guarantor of indebtedness by partners will be discharged if any existing partners leave the partnership or die or become bankrupt, or if a new partner enters the partnership (Partnership Act 1890, s. 18). Where a guarantee is given in relation to the debts of a company and that company either merges or amalgamates with another (*Bradford Old Bank* v *Sutcliffe* [1918] 2 KB 833), the guarantor is discharged. A guarantor of the debts of a company will not be discharged if the company merely changes its name.

Termination of the guarantee

Termination of a guarantee means only that the guarantor is excused from all further liability incurred by the debtor. The guarantor is not excused from liabilities which have already accrued (*Westminster Bank Ltd* v *Sassoon* (1926) *The Times*, 27 November 1926). However, where the guarantor guarantees the debit balance of a bank customer's current account the rule in *Clayton's* case will have the effect of gradually discharging the guarantor's liability if payments are made to the credit of the account, for the debts for which he became liable were 'fixed' at the time the guarantee was terminated. This may be prevented if the guarantee contains a term such as the 'guarantor's liability for the amount due from the debtor at the time when the guarantee is determined shall remain notwithstanding any subsequent payment into or out of the account by or on behalf of the debtor' (in *Westminster Bank Ltd* v *Cond* (1940) 46 Com Cas 60 such a clause was held to be effective). Alternatively, the bank may stop the principal customer's current account, and open another one for him. In practice, banks do include terms such as the one used in *Westminster Bank Ltd* v *Cond*, but also stop the account. In *Re Sherry* (1884) 25 Ch 692 it was held that the bank had a right, on the termination of the guarantee, to break the principal debtor's account, and that even on the death of the debtor, the breaking of the account was effective to protect against the discharge of the debt.

A guarantee may be determined in one of the following circumstances, namely:

(a) it is not entirely clear whether the death of the guarantor will determine the guarantee. If the guarantee specifically requires the personal representatives of the guarantor to terminate the guarantee by giving notice, then the guarantee will not be terminated by the death of the guarantor, since it contemplates that it may continue beyond the guarantor's death (*Egbert* v *National Crown Bank* [1918] AC 903). However, in no case is the guarantee determined until the bank has received notice of the death of the guarantor (*Ashby* v *Day* (1885) 52 LT 723);

(b) a guarantor who becomes mentally incapable is discharged in respect of future transactions of the principal debtor once the bank has received notice of the incapacity, but the guarantor will remain liable in respect of past transactions (*Westminster Bank Ltd* v *Cond* (1940) 46 Com Cas 60). The same rule applies in respect of a guarantor who is declared bankrupt. The bank should, therefore, once it has notice of the mental incapacity or bankruptcy of the guarantor, close the account and pass all future transactions through a new account. This was not done in *Bradford Old Bank Ltd* v *Sutcliffe* [1918] 2 KB 833 and consequently the liability of the mentally incapacitated guarantor was satisfied by subsequent payments into the account.

Letters of comfort

Statements which look like binding promises but which are in fact mere statements of intention have been of considerable concern. Letters of comfort are taken where a third party is unwilling to enter into a guarantee. Lenders and 'comfort givers' generally approach the matter from opposite directions; the lender will seek something like (or better than) a guarantee which imposes a secondary liability on the other person, whilst the 'comfort giver' may only be willing to acknowledge the existence of a transaction, but is not willing to undertake any legal responsibility if anything goes wrong. A lender may, therefore, turn to comfort letters when a third party is not prepared to assume formal liability, whether contingent or not, for the borrower's indebtedness. The commonest situations where comfort letters may be given are where, e.g., a parent company is asked to give an undertaking in respect of the obligations of its subsidiaries; or where a foreign government wishes to encourage inward investment; or in connection with international construction contracts. A parent company may prefer to give a letter of comfort rather than a formal guarantee for any one of a number of reasons, e.g., the parent company does not want to be legally committed.

If the letter of comfort is to be enforceable as a legally binding contract then all the essential elements of a contract must be present. The questions which are most likely to cause difficulty are whether or not there was an intention to create legal relations and whether the terms of the letter of comfort are sufficiently certain to form an enforceable contract. Whether a contract is sufficiently certain to bind the parties must be determined by an objective test although there is a presumption in the case of commercial agreements that the parties intended to create legal relations (see *Rose and Frank Co* v *J.R. Crompton and Brothers Ltd* [1925] AC 445).

The legal effect of a statement indicating that a transaction is binding in honour only is never likely to be tested in the courts. The recipient of the letter of comfort may consider that as a matter of commercial judgment it will be in the interests of the provider of the letter to abide by its terms, notwithstanding the fact that it is expressed to be binding in honour only. Letters of comfort falling in this category cause little difficulty and both parties are aware that it is only commercial pressure that will force the provider to fulfil the terms of the letter.

A letter of comfort which does not provide that it is intended to be binding in honour only will prima facie give rise to legal relations between the parties. However, depending on the nature of the wording used the letter of comfort may (or may not) give the party seeking to rely on it substantive rights. The courts have had to look at the effect letters of comfort are intended to have in order to determine whether the plaintiff is provided with any substantive rights. In *Chemco Leasing SpA* v *Rediffusion plc* [1987] 1 FTLR 201 the letter of comfort was held to confer substantive rights on the plaintiff which could be legally enforced.

The legal status of letters of comfort was re-examined in *Kleinwort Benson Ltd* v *Malaysia Mining Corporation Bhd* [1989] 1 WLR 379, where the Court of Appeal concluded that if the comfort letter merely indicates an 'intention' or evidences the 'policy' of the donor, i.e., to ensure that the subsidiary is in a position to meet its liabilities to the bank, it is likely that the letter simply constitutes a moral obligation rather than a legal liability. This is especially so where the bank charges a higher rate of interest as compensation for not having a full guarantee.

POSSESSORY SECURITIES

Goods

The very nature of goods means that they present a number of problems as security. Goods may be perishable, the price of commodities may fluctuate, storage may be expensive and goods manufactured for one purpose may be inappropriate for resale. It may be difficult for a bank to dispose of goods if the buyer defaults, without the assistance of the customer. This section of the chapter examines the rights which a bank may acquire over goods or documents which it has in its possession because of the default of its customer.

Banker's lien

A lien is a right to retain property belonging to a debtor until he has paid the debt due to the person retaining the property. A lien may arise as a result of a particular transaction connected with the property subject to the lien. A general lien arises not only out of the particular transaction but out of the general dealings between the parties. Thus, for example, an issuing or confirming bank under a letter of credit is entitled to hold the shipping documents which it receives from the beneficiary as security for the amount it has paid or committed itself to pay under the bills of exchange. The banker's lien arises by operation of law in consequence of the instructions given to the issuing bank to open the credit and the lien is independent of any other security the bank may take by express agreement. The ordinary right of the bank under its lien is a right merely to retain possession of the shipping documents but in the case of documents the lien carries with it the right to sell the goods represented by them. As such it approximates more closely to a pledge than to a common law lien. In the case of other documents over which a bank has a lien there is no implied power of sale or realisation. In *Brandao* v *Barnett* (1846) 12 Cl and F 787 Lord Campbell said that banks have a general lien on all securities deposited with them, as bankers, by a customer, unless there be an express contract, or circumstances that show an implied contract, inconsistent with lien. This was reinforced in *National Westminster Bank Ltd* v *Halesowen Presswork and Assemblies Ltd* [1972] AC 785, where the House of Lords distinguished between a lien and a right of set-off. The court accepted the view that a bank has a general lien on all documents deposited by its customer.

The essential factor in deciding whether documents are or are not subject to a lien is whether or not they came into the hands of the bank in the course of its business as a banker. The bank has a general lien or right of retention over all kinds of documents belonging to its customer over which it has possession and the bank can hold them until all the amounts owed to it in respect of loans and advances have been paid back to the bank. The lien extends to all documents under which money will be paid to the customer or by means of which money may be obtained, whether they are negotiable or not. Where documents relate to goods the lien extends to the goods themselves so that if the customer fails to reimburse the bank, it can sell the goods and so realise the advance it has made on the customer's behalf. The bank may exercise a lien over cheques payable to its customer (*Re Keever* [1967] Ch 182; *Barclays Bank Ltd* v *Astley Industrial Trust Ltd* [1970] 2 QB 527; *Bank of Credit and Commerce International SA* v *Dawson and Wright* 1987 FLR 342), bills of exchange, share certificates and investment securities generally. In *Sewell* v *Burdick* (1884) 10 App Cas 74 it was held that the securities over which a bank has a lien include bills of lading and other documents representing goods in transit. An issuing bank is therefore entitled to a lien over shipping documents taken up by it under a letter of credit as security for its right to reimbursement. In *Sewell* v *Burdick* the House of Lords stated that the endorsement and delivery of a bill of lading by way of a pledge was equivalent, and not more than equivalent, to a delivery of the goods themselves, but it then went further and held that the deposit of a bill of lading by way of security does not divest the shipper of his proprietary rights in the goods. A lien therefore gives the bank a security over the shipping documents but it does not transfer the ownership of the goods to the bank since no man can have a lien over his own property (*National Westminster Bank Ltd* v *Halesowen Presswork and Assemblies Ltd* [1972] AC 785).

In *Aschkenasy* v *Midland Bank Ltd* (1934) 51 TLR 34, it was held that a bank which instructs another bank to make a payment to a third party is itself a customer of the other bank. It follows that a confirming bank may claim a lien over shipping documents taken up by it to enforce its right to be indemnified by its immediate customer, the issuing bank, and the fact that the applicant for the credit has put the issuing bank in funds does not in any way affect the confirming bank's lien. The lien which a bank acquires over shipping documents delivered when it accepts or purchases a bill of exchange drawn by the beneficiary of a letter of credit must be distinguished from the lien of the endorsee of an unspecified bill of exchange drawn under a credit.

The lien acquired by the bank is only a security for obtaining the acceptance or negotiation of the bill of exchange by the issuing or confirming bank. In *Guaranty Trust Co. of New York* v *Hannay and Co.* [1918] 2 KB 623 the Court of Appeal held that once the bill of exchange has been accepted, the holder of the bill has to rely exclusively on the credit of the issuing or confirming bank; his lien on the shipping documents is extinguished, and a new and separate lien arises in favour of the bank giving the issuing or confirming bank security for its right of reimbursement.

Pledge

An applicant for a letter of credit may create different forms of security over the shipping documents and the goods in favour of the issuing or confirming bank. A banker's lien arises by operation of law, whereas a pledge will arise as a result only of express agreement of the parties and incidents of the pledge are likewise determined by agreement. The banker's lien is in addition to any security expressly created and is not superseded by any such express security. One of the forms of security available to the bank is a legal pledge of the goods in question and this is created by delivery of the subject matter to the bank as creditor, thereby giving it a legal right of possession until the debt to the bank under the letter of credit is discharged. The essence of a pledge is that the security vested in the pledgee consists exclusively of the possession of the goods in question and not any derivative proprietary interest in them. Consequently, if the goods are returned by the pledgee to the pledgor otherwise than as agent for the pledgee, the pledge comes to an end (*North Western Bank Ltd* v *John Poynter, Son and Macdonalds* [1895] AC 56). However, although the pledgee has no proprietary interest in the goods a pledge confers an implied right for the pledgee to realise the security by selling the goods. Shipping documents held by the pledgee may be used for this purpose.

At common law a pledge can be created by delivery to the pledgee of actual or constructive possession of the goods pledged. If the goods are in the hands of the pledgor, he can effect the pledge by actual delivery of the goods. In other cases he can give possession by some other sufficient act, e.g., handing over the keys of the warehouse where the goods are stored so as to vest control over them in the pledgee. If the goods are in the hands of a third party who holds them on behalf of the pledgor, a pledge may be effected by the pledgor instructing the third party to hold the goods for the account of the pledgee and by the third party attorning to the pledgee (i.e., acknowledging that he holds the goods on behalf of the pledgee and the latter has constructive possession). Where the goods are represented by documents, the mere delivery of the documents to the pledgee does not generally vest possession of the goods themselves in him unless the person who has custody of them is notified of the arrangements and agrees to hold the goods on behalf of the pledgee. In the absence of such an agreement the pledge of the goods is incomplete and ineffective. However, an exception was recognised in *Barber* v *Meyerstein* (1870) LR 4 HL 317, where it was held that a pledge of the goods by means of a deposit of documents relating to them is possible either if the document is a negotiable instrument or if it is a current bill of lading. Thus, the endorsement and delivery of a bill of lading while the ship carrying the goods represented by the bill is at sea operates in exactly the same way as the delivery of the goods themselves to the consignee or his endorsee after the arrival of the ship. Similarly, in *Sewell* v *Burdick* (1884) 10 App Cas 74 it was held that an endorsement and delivery of the bill of lading by way of pledge was equivalent, but not more than equivalent, to the delivery of the goods to the pledgee.

The rule has been recognised in subsequent cases, although its application has been somewhat restricted (see *Official Assignee of Madras* v *Mercantile Bank of India Ltd* [1935] AC 53).

In *Official Assignee of Madras* v *Mercantile Bank of India Ltd* it was held that the exception relating to bills of lading cannot be extended to railway consignment notes, warehouse warrants or other documents used in connection with the transport and storage of goods. Similarly, in *William M'Ewan and Sons* v *Smith* (1849) 2 HL Cas 309 it was held that the issue or transfer of a delivery order calling on a warehouse keeper to deliver goods to the person who presents the order is not, without an attornment by the keeper, sufficient to bring about a constructive delivery of the goods to which it relates. The court observed that a transfer or pledge of documents of title to goods does not amount to a transfer or pledge of the goods themselves; a pledge of the documents is merely a pledge of those documents regarded as physical objects, except in the case of a bill of lading. A delivery order does not transfer the ownership or possession of the goods and even if it is endorsed the transfer of a delivery order is not sufficient to estop the owner from asserting his rights in the goods. Similar dicta are to be found in *Official Assignee of Madras* v *Mercantile Bank of India Ltd* [1935] AC 53 and in *Inglis* v *Robertson* [1898] AC 616.

The common law, however, has been supplemented by legislation which has been enacted to protect banks which make advances to mercantile agents. Under the legislation a pledge of any document of title to goods, whether a bill of lading, rail or road consignment note, air waybill, dock or warehouse warrant or a delivery order, may create a valid pledge, but only if the pledgor is a factor (Factors Act 1889, s. 2(1)). This is supplemented by s. 3 of the Act, which provides that a pledge of the documents of title to goods is to be deemed a pledge of the goods and, for the purposes of the Act, the expression 'pledge' is to include 'any contract pledging, or giving a lien or security' on the goods (s. 1(5)). In *Lloyds Bank Ltd* v *Bank of America National Trust and Savings Association* [1938] 2 KB 147 the court held that the statutory exception in respect of a pledge by a factor applies whether the factor acts as a mercantile agent for a third person or on his own account.

A further statutory exception was created by s. 25(2) of the Sale of Goods Act 1893 (now s. 25(1) of the Sale of Goods Act 1979), which provides that a bank which makes an advance has a valid pledge if the buyer of goods has received the documents of title to them from the seller and has pledged the goods or the documents of title to them before the seller's lien or right of stoppage in transit for the price payable under the contract of sale has expired. However, the statutory exceptions raise uncertainties and therefore are rarely relied on in practice. Furthermore, the unpaid seller's lien is suspended if he takes a bill of exchange for the purchase price.

Where a bank is owed money advanced to pay the price of goods it will probably release the shipping documents to the buyer so that he can sell the goods and reimburse the bank. The question of importance for the bank is whether, having released the documents to the buyer, its charge or security over the goods is in any way affected. In *North Western Bank Ltd* v *John Poynter, Son and Macdonalds* [1895] AC 56 the House of Lords held that delivery of goods, either actual or constructive, to the debtor destroyed the possibility of a pledge continuing or subsequently arising. However, on the facts of the case the bank took a pledge of the goods by delivery of the bill of lading relating to them and gave the applicant only a limited authority to sell the goods as its agent. Consequently, the bank did not give up possession of the goods and its pledge continued so that it was entitled to the proceeds of the sale in priority to general creditors of the pledgor. The limited authority of the buyer of goods whose purchase is financed by a letter of credit to deal with the goods if the bank releases them to him so that he may sell them as the bank's agent does not in any way prevent the pledge in favour of the bank from continuing, even though the buyer has physical control of the goods for the purposes of the sale.

The logical consequences of this rule were worked out by the court in *Re David Allester Ltd* [1922] 2 Ch 211, where the court held that the bank was entitled to have the value of the goods realised by experts, in this case the pledgor. Consequently, handing over the bills of lading for the purpose of selling the goods did not deny the continuing rights of the pledgee, the bank.

North Western Bank Ltd v *John Poynter, Son and Macdonalds* and *Re David Allester Ltd* were approved by the Privy Council in *Official Assignee of Madras* v *Mercantile Bank of India Ltd*, where it was held that the respondents had merely parted with possession of the railway receipts to the insolvent merchants for a limited purpose, i.e., as agents for the respondents for the purpose of dealing with the goods.

A different situation may arise where the bank releases the documents of title (other than a bill of lading) to its customer, who undertakes to deal with the goods on behalf of the bank but who, in fraud of the bank, pledges the documents of title to a third party who acts in good faith. It has been held that in such a case the bank is not estopped as against the third party from setting up its title to the goods, even though the third party acts in good faith (see *Mercantile Bank of India Ltd* v *Central Bank of India Ltd* [1938] AC 287).

Letters of hypothecation, letters of trust and trust receipts

In order to overcome the difficulties of the pledge as a form of security over documents of title to goods, two other forms of security are usually resorted to by banks which finance a purchase of goods, namely the letter of hypothecation and the letter of trust (or trust receipt). A letter of hypothecation creates an equitable charge over the goods which ensures that if the goods are sold by the applicant the proceeds of sale are subject to a first charge in favour of the bank. Consequently, if the applicant becomes bankrupt, or in the case of a company, if it is wound up, the bank ranks as a secured creditor and is entitled to be paid first out of the proceeds of sale. The letter of hypothecation has largely been superseded by the letter of trust or trust receipt. The trust receipt evidences an agreement between the bank and the customer that the bank will hand the documents of title to the customer so that he can obtain delivery of the goods. In turn the customer holds the documents of title, the goods when they are received and eventually the proceeds of sale of the goods on behalf of the bank.

The letter of trust or trust receipt is either embodied in the application for the issue of a letter of credit by the bank, or is given separately by the applicant (buyer) when the shipping documents have been taken up by the issuing or confirming bank and they are delivered to the buyer so that he may collect the goods on arrival. Under the letter of trust, the buyer undertakes to hold the proceeds of sale as a trustee for the bank absolutely and to pay the whole of the proceeds of sale to the bank, which will retain what is owed and return the balance to the applicant of the credit. If the applicant departs from the authority given to him to deal with the goods he is guilty of a breach of trust. The trust relationship that arises is treated by the courts as creating a valid security interest in favour of the bank (see *Re David Allester Ltd* [1922] 2 Ch 211.

The courts have in fact given the bank even greater protection under letters of trust and trust receipts by holding that not only is the customer guilty of a breach of trust by wrongfully disposing of the goods, but that the bank may sue him and the disponee for conversion of the shipping documents in such a case. In *Midland Bank Ltd* v *Eastcheap Dried Fruit Co.* [1962] 1 Lloyd's Rep 359 the court held that the defendants were in breach of the contract constituted by the delivery of the documents to them with the collection note attached, and also that the defendants were guilty of conversion of the documents since they had interfered with the plaintiff's possessory right to the documents. In this situation a person to whom the purchaser of the goods wrongfully disposes of shipping documents which he has received under a trust receipt is guilty of conversion of the documents despite the fact that he gives value for them and acts in good faith so that in equity he has a good title to the goods themselves.

The equitable proprietary interest of the bank over the goods, and subsequently the proceeds of sale, subsists only so long as the bank is in a position to fulfil its obligations to its customer. If the bank repudiates these obligations either expressly or impliedly, e.g., if it becomes insolvent, it loses its proprietary interest. In *Sale Continuation Ltd* v *Austin Taylor and Co. Ltd* [1968] 2 QB 849 it was said that in those circumstances the bank's proprietary interest in the goods ceases automatically and the applicant may keep the shipping documents, the goods or the proceeds of sale for his own benefit.

CHOSES IN ACTION AS SECURITY

Credit balances as security

A balance standing to the credit of a customer's account is repayable on the terms it was made. Whilst the account is in credit the balance constitutes a debt owed by the bank to its customer. As such, the debt is an asset and the customer may utilise it as a security in respect of a transaction financed by a bank or other financial institution. However, using a credit balance as a security may cause difficulties, e.g., the credit balance may be reduced by the customer making withdrawals, or the credit balance may be made the subject of a garnishee order. Problems can arise if the customer becomes bankrupt or insolvent. Although these problems can be overcome, using a credit balance as security is likely to result in restrictions on the account holder's right to utilise the account. The method of granting security over the credit balance will depend on whether the security is given to the bank with whom the account is maintained or with a third party.

Where funds are deposited with the bank

Where a security is created in favour of a bank with which the credit balance is maintained the bank has a right to set off any amounts owed to it by the creditor (customer). The right to set off is a procedural right and does not confer on the party entitled to exercise it a proprietary right. Although the equitable right to set off is invaluable to banks (e.g., where a bank is required to make payment under a bank guarantee it can reimburse itself by exercising a set-off against the customer's credit balance), it is subject to several limitations. Thus, until such time as a bank can exercise the right of set-off the customer can make withdrawals against the credit balance thereby reducing the amount available for set-off. Further, a right of set-off is subordinate to the right of a judgment creditor who has served a garnishee order before the set-off is exercised.

When the customer is adjudicated bankrupt or becomes insolvent the bank's right to set off is governed by statute (Insolvency Act 1986, s. 323). The statutory right of set-off cannot be contracted out of, in the sense that the parties cannot by agreement limit its operation (*National Westminster Bank Ltd* v *Halesowen Presswork and Assemblies Ltd* [1972] AC 785). However, the statutory right to set off is considerably wider than the right to set off debits against credits that the bank can exercise under the general law. In particular, the bank is entitled to set off liabilities payable at a future date and unliquidated liabilities against the deposit. However, what was uncertain was whether a purely contingent liability could be set off, e.g., under a counter-indemnity taken in connection with the issue of a performance bond that has not yet been called. Some support can be found for the view that a contingent liability could not be set off against a present debt (see *Re Fenton* [1931] 1 Ch 85, which was decided on the basis of the rule against double proof in insolvency proceedings; *Re A Debtor (No. 66 of 1955)* [1956] 1 WLR 1226). However, since *Re Charge Card Services Ltd* [1987] Ch 150 the better view appears to be that contingent debts are capable of being set off provided that they satisfy the other requirements laid down. A significant requirement is that of mutuality, i.e., the debts must be between the same parties in the same right, with the result that only a liability owed to the bank by the depositor in the same capacity may be set off against the credit.

However, because of the limitation attached to the equitable and statutory rights of set-off, it has become the practice of banks to take a contractual right of set-off. This right may be subject to special agreement (letter of set-off) or may be created by means of specific clauses incorporated in the underlying financial agreement between the bank and its customer. The object of the clause is to enable the bank to set off against the credit balance any claims the bank has, whether such claims are existing, contingent, unconditional, liquidated or unliquidated. The purpose of the clause is to restrict the right of the customer to make withdrawals so long as the liability is contingent. However, the bank must ensure that the customer's need for liquidity in respect of his account is not hampered.

A variation to the set-off agreement is the 'flawed asset' arrangement. The arrangement imposes a 'flaw' on the customer's asset, i.e., the arrangement restricts the customer's right to utilise the credit balance. In its simplest form, the arrangement consists of the deposit of money under an agreement by which the depositor agrees that the deposit is not to become repayable until certain liabilities have been satisfied, or if the liabilities are contingent, are no longer capable of arising. Thus, the bank is entitled to freeze the bank balance until such time as the customer's liability is discharged. A number of problems arise in respect of set-off agreement, namely:

(a) A credit balance may be assigned in equity or under s. 136 of the Law of Property Act 1925. Regardless of the form of assignment, the assignee's rights are subject to equities available to the bank against the assignor. However, an equity could be set up only if it accrued before the debtor was given notice of the assignment.

(b) Does a contractual set-off take precedence over garnishee proceedings?

(c) Should a set-off agreement be registered as a charge if the customer is a company or, if made by an individual, as a bill of sale? A credit balance with a bank is not normally treated as a book debt and therefore the issue of registration should not normally arise (Goode, *Legal Problems of Credit and Security*, 1985, 2nd ed.). In the case of an unincorporated customer, the answer would be the same even if the balance constituted a book debt, since registration is not required where the debtor is specified in the instrument creating the assignment (Insolvency Act 1986, s. 344(3)(b)). The position differs where the customer is incorporated, since any charge on book debts will need to be registered under the Companies Act 1985, s. 396(1)(c).

(d) The final problem arises in respect of an incorporated customer, which enters into a set-off arrangement with the bank, and is being wound up. The Insolvency Act 1986 provides that all claims which are not given a special status (e.g., preferential creditors) rank *pari passu*. In *British Eagle International Airlines Ltd* v *Compagnie Nationale Air France* [1975] 1 WLR 758 the House of Lords held that a clearing arrangement which purported to oust the statutory rules on set-off was against public policy. The case is based on the rule that in the insolvency of a debtor under a multi-party set-off or a clearing agreement, the agreement cannot prejudice the rights of the other parties in the insolvency. It has been argued that on the same reasoning, the courts would invalidate a contractual set-off and a flawed-asset arrangement (Cresswell et al., *Encyclopaedia of Banking Law*, vol. 1, para. E2478).

Charges over bank balances

A credit balance standing in a customer's bank account is a chose in action and may be made the subject of a charge or mortgage, effected by means of an assignment. Where a charge is created over cash deposited with a bank, the bank seeks to become secured and to rank in the depositor's insolvency as a secured creditor. In ordinary circumstances, a security interest in a debt can either be created by mortgage or charge. The only method by which a debt can be mortgaged is by an absolute assignment under s. 136 of the Law of Property Act 1925. The assignment will be coupled with an express or implied equity of redemption in favour of the assignor (*Durham Brothers* v *Robertson* [1898] 1 QB 765). However, it has been suggested that the Act requires a tripartite transaction and that a deposit cannot be mortgaged in favour of the bank with which it is held, since, on assignment back to the debtor, the debt would cease to exist (Goode, *Commercial Law*, p. 721; *Legal Problems of Credit and Security*, p. 86). However, an assignment by way of charge (i.e., an equitable assignment) is an adequate security. An equitable charge is created when the chargor and chargee agree that a given liability shall be paid out of a chose in action belonging to the chargor. Where such a security is given to a third party (e.g., supplier of goods on credit) it is essential to include provisions preventing the depletion of the security by withdrawals. Whether a security over a bank balance can be given to the bank which itself maintains the account was considered in *Re Charge Card Services Ltd* [1987] Ch 150. Millett J in that case held a charge in favour of a debtor of his own indebtedness to the chargor is conceptually impossible. Although the case did not involve a charge over a bank deposit, the reasoning appears to apply to such a charge. The facts of the case were that Charge Card, which carried on the business of issuing credit cards used by holders for purchases made at petrol stations, assigned its receivables to Commercial Credit. The factoring agreement provided that the debts involved would be collected by Commercial Credit and paid to the credit of an account maintained by it in Charge Card's name. Under the agreement, Commercial Credit was granted the absolute discretion to retain money standing to the credit of the account in question as a security for any amount required to meet Charge Card's liabilities. An issue which arose upon Charge Card's insolvency was whether the clause was void against the liquidator as an unregistered charge over book debts. Millett J, giving judgment for Commercial Credit, held that the right of retention did not amount to a charge since money deposited with the bank became the bank's own money. The real effect of the clause was to grant Commercial Credit a contractual set-off, which was effective to the extent that it complied with s. 31 of the Bankruptcy Act 1914.

The views expressed by Millet J were reinforced in *Welsh Development Agency* v *Export Finance Co. Ltd* [1992] BCLC 148 where Dillon LJ expressed the view that a charge in favour of a debtor of his own indebtedness is conceptually impossible. In *Re Bank of Credit and Commerce International SA* (No. 8) [1996] Ch 245 a bank went into liquidation after making several loans to a number of companies. The loans had been secured by purported charges executed by third parties over their deposit accounts maintained at the bank. The liquidator applied for directions to determine whether in trying to recover the loans from the companies (principal debtors) he could set off the amounts standing to the credit of the third party deposit accounts. The Court of Appeal held that since the depositors had not given any express guarantee or personal covenant to repay the debts no sums could be recovered from the depositors to the bank within the meaning of r. 9.40 of the Insolvency Rules 1986 (which superseded the Bankruptcy Act 1914). Therefore, the companies had no right to set off the credit balance of the deposit accounts against the debts. The liquidator was entitled to recover the full amounts of the debts from the companies (for general discussion see Richard Calnan, 'Security over Deposits After Re BCCI (No)', *Journal of International Banking and Financial Law* vol. 11, no. 3 (March 1996), pp. 111–18).

Where a security given over a bank balance is merely a contractual right of set-off, it will not have to be registered under the companies legislation. Where such an arrangement is treated as a charge, it will need to be registered.

PROPRIETARY SECURITIES

Unregistered land as security

A mortgage has two essential features, namely:

(a)   the purpose of the transaction is to provide security for the performance of an obligation, which is usually the repayment of a loan and interest thereon; and

(b)   this purpose is attained by transferring to the creditor or mortgagee certain rights of property.

A legal mortgage of land under the Law of Property Act 1925 must be created by demise for a term of years or by a charge expressed to be granted by way of legal mortgage. Unless a legal charge is employed a legal mortgage must vest a term of years in the mortgage and any attempt by the mortgagor to convey the whole of his legal estate in the land to the mortgagee operates automatically as a grant of a term of years leaving a reversionary legal estate vested in the mortgagor (Law of Property Act 1925, s. 85(2)). The term of years granted to the mortgagee is subject to a termination on the redemption of the mortgage. The mortgagor retains the legal estate subject to the term of years, and this enables him to create further legal mortgages which take effect either as legal charges or as demises for a term of years longer by at least one day than the preceding mortgage.

The second method of creating a legal mortgage in land is by way of a legal charge (Law of Property Act 1925, s. 87(1)). The protection given to the mortgagee is identical to that given by a legal mortgage created by demise and the legal chargee has the same rights and remedies as a legal mortgagee. The difference between a legal mortgage and a legal charge is that the legal charge does not contain a conveyance of a legal estate to the mortgagee so that the mortgagor remains vested with his original legal estate instead of holding a reversionary interest. Instead of granting the chargee a legal estate the mortgagor or chargor charges the land by way of legal mortgage with the payment of the principal, interest and any other moneys secured by the charge. Furthermore, there is no provision for redemption in a legal charge, which simply determines on repayment of the amount secured by it. In all other respects the legal mortgage and the legal charge are precisely the same; the covenants entered into by the mortgagor and the powers of the chargee are identical.

The Law of Property Act 1925 provides that a first mortgagee of land has the same right to possession of the documents of title as if his security included the whole legal estate of the mortgagor (s. 85(1)). Failure to take possession of the title deeds may give priority to a subsequent mortgagee. The deposit of title deeds with the legal mortgagee protects the priority of his mortgage over any subsequent mortgages which may be created. A mortgage secured by a deposit of the title deeds can be created without all the deeds being deposited provided that those which are deposited include the instrument by which the legal estate was vested in the mortgagor. A mortgage protected by the deposit of the title deeds is not registrable as a land charge under the Land Charges Act 1972, either as a puisne mortgage or as a general equitable charge, since the distinguishing feature of such interests is that they are not accompanied by a deposit of the title deeds. A mortgage protected by the deposit of some of the title deeds including the conveyance to the mortgagor is therefore outside the category of puisne mortgages, since, under s. 2(4) of the Land Charges Act 1972 a mortgage is excluded if secured by 'a deposit of documents' (of title) not a deposit of all the documents.

An equitable mortgage is simply an agreement to create a legal mortgage and it is treated in equity as the equivalent of a legal mortgage so far as possible. This means that (a) equity will compel the mortgagor to execute a legal mortgage by deed and (b) will give the same remedies to the mortgagee as are available to a legal mortgagee except those which statute expressly reserves to legal mortgages, e.g., the statutory power of sale. An agreement to create a legal mortgage of land must be evidenced by a written memorandum of the agreement signed by the mortgagor or his agent in order to make it enforceable by action (Law of Property Act 1925, s. 85(2)). Further, the Law of Property (Miscellaneous Provisions) Act 1989 (s. 2) provides that all dispositions of interests in land must be in writing with the document containing all the terms which the parties have expressly agreed. Such a document must be signed by each party, or his agent. The effect of s. 2 was examined in *United Bank of Kuwait plc* v *Sahib* [1996] 3 WLR 272 where the Court of Appeal held that the old rule that a deposit of title deeds creates a valid equitable charge on the basis that it amounted to an act of part performance to create a mortgage, and was inconsistent with the requirements under the 1989 Act which requires that contracts for the disposition of interests in land had to be evidenced in writing.

An equitable charge over land is created by agreement or an instrument which treats it as security for a debt or other obligation without conferring on the chargee either a term of years as a security or charging the land expressly by way of legal mortgage. The remedies of an equitable chargee are in equity the same as those of an equitable mortgagee, except that he is not entitled to foreclose and acquire the mortgagor's estate in the land or to take possession of it. Like an equitable mortgage an equitable charge must be evidenced by a written memorandum of the agreement to create it or by a written instrument actually conferring the charge if the charge is to be enforceable by action but written evidence is dispensed with if the agreement to create the charge has been partly performed.

A legal or equitable mortgage or charge of a legal estate made after 1925 and not protected by a deposit of documents relating to that legal estate is registrable either as a puisne mortgage or as a general equitable charge. The Land Charges Act 1972, s. 4(5) provides that registrable mortgages are void as against a subsequent purchaser of land or of any interest in the land whether legal or equitable unless the mortgage is registered at the Land Charges Registry. In addition to this provision the Law of Property Act 1925, s. 97, provides that every legal or equitable mortgage of a legal estate in land which is not protected by the deposit of documents will rank in priority according to its date of registration as a land charge under the Land Charges Act 1925. This provision conflicts with the Land Charges Act 1972 in that it makes the priority of a second mortgage over a prior unregistered mortgage conditional on the second mortgage itself being registered.

The statutory rules governing the priorities between successive mortgages does not, however, affect the exceptional provisions of the Law of Property Act 1925, s. 94(1), when successive advances are made on the security of the same mortgage. Prior to the Act the rule was that where a mortgagee advanced money on an equitable mortgage or charge without at the time of the advance having notice (although notice to one of several joint mortgagees was notice to all of them: *Freeman* v *Laing* [1899] 2 Ch 355) of a prior equitable mortgage, he could afterwards by acquiring an existing legal mortgage which had priority over the equitable mortgage claim the same priority for his own equitable mortgage or charge as that which attached to the legal mortgage and in effect tack or add the amount advanced to him on his equitable mortgage or charge to the amount secured by the legal mortgage. If A, the legal mortgagee at the time of making a further advance, had no notice that subsequently to his legal mortgage a second mortgage had been created in favour of B, A was allowed to tack his second loan to the advance secured by his first legal mortgage and to claim priority for both advances over intervening mortgages of which he was unaware. In order to prevent A tacking the second advance to the first, B would have to prove that A had actual or constructive notice of B's mortgage at the time of his second advance (*Hopkinson* v *Rolt* (1861) 9 HL Cas 514), but if A had such notice, B's mortgage would rank before A's further advance even though A, the first mortgagee, had given a binding undertaking to make further advances on the same security (*West* v *Williams* [1899] 1 Ch 132).

The Law of Property Act 1925 abolished tacking except as expressly permitted by s. 94(1) of the Act, with the consequence that a later mortgagee cannot now gain priority over an intermediate mortgage by acquiring an earlier legal mortgage. The law governing the priority of a mortgage for further advances is now regulated in detail by s. 94. This serves a most useful purpose when securing loans by banks to their customers since when banks take security for overdrafts it is generally contemplated that variations in the customer's balances will occur during the subsistence of the security and when the overdraft facility is drawn on the bank will in effect make further advances.

The Law of Property Act 1925, s. 94(1), allows the tacking of further advances to a prior mortgage loan so as to ensure priority over intervening mortgages where 'an arrangement has been made to that effect with the subsequent mortgagees.' So if an intermediate mortgagee consents to the prior mortgagee having priority for advances made subsequently to the intermediate mortgagee's mortgage, the priority which his advance would normally have will be subordinated to payment in full of the amount owed to the first mortgagee.

If the first mortgage is not expressly given for securing a current account or further advances, the registration of a subsequent mortgage under the Land Charges Act 1972 is equal to actual notice to the first mortgagee (Law of Property Act 1925, s. 198(1)), and the first mortgagee could not tack further advances made after the date of registration of the subsequent mortgage. If this provision also applied to a mortgage securing a current account, the bank would have to search the land charges register before paying a cheque on the account to ensure that no intermediate mortgage had been registered. In order to solve this difficulty s. 94(2) provides that if the first mortgage was created expressly for securing a current account or further advances made by the mortgagee, the registration of a subsequent mortgage or charge does not amount to notice of that charge to the first mortgagee. A first mortgagee in this case may therefore tack further advances made after the registration of the later mortgage or charge, provided that at the time of the further advance the later mortgagee had not brought the charge to his attention by some positive act other than registration (the rule in *Hopkinson* v *Rolt* is thus confirmed). A mortgagee who takes a security to secure further advances must search the register for prior charges at the time of the original loan and is bound by any mortgages or charges then registered, but he is not required to search again when he makes further advances and can treat mortgages registered meanwhile as ineffective against him. This is, of course, an exception to the principle that registration is equivalent to actual notice and is of exceptional importance to banks to whom the taking of a mortgage for a customer's overdraft would be of little value if cheques drawn by the customer after the date of the mortgage could not be honoured without first making a search in the Land Charges Register. The exception applies to all mortgages where the contract contemplates further advances and not merely to mortgages securing current accounts.

If a subsequent mortgagee has given notice of his charge to the first mortgagee before a further advance is made, the first mortgagee cannot then tack further advances and if the mortgage secures an overdraft, the rule in *Clayton's Case* (*Devaynes* v *Noble, Clayton's Case* (1816) 1 Mer 529) will apply as regards subsequent payments into the account so as to reduce the debit balance at the date the bank receives notice of the subsequent mortgage. If, therefore, there is a reduction of the overdraft by the bank after it has notice of the subsequent mortgage, there will be a corresponding reduction of the debit balance at that date for which the bank has priority and if further advances are then made by the bank increasing the overdraft, the bank cannot tack them to the original loan and will be deferred to the amount owing to the subsequent mortgagee. In order to avoid the operation of the rule in *Clayton's Case* in this situation the bank should close the mortgagor's overdrawn account as soon as it receives notice of a subsequent mortgage and any future payments in or drawings by the mortgagor should be credited or debited to a separate account. The leading case in which the bank suffered by its failure to close the original account on receipt of the second mortgage is *Deeley* v *Lloyds Bank Ltd* [1912] AC 756, where a customer of Lloyds Bank mortgaged his business premises to the bank in 1893 to secure his overdraft on current account. In 1895 he created another mortgage in favour of a second mortgagee who gave notice of his mortgage to the bank. The bank failed to close the mortgagor's overdrawn account at that time or to open a separate account for further transactions. The mortgagor subsequently made payments into and out of the account, and under the rule in *Clayton's Case* the subsequent payments into the account had the effect of reducing the balance owing to the bank on the first mortgagee which had priority over the second mortgage. The House of Lords held that the second mortgage took priority over any advances made by the bank after notice of the charge had been brought to the bank's attention.

Section 94 provides that if by its contractual undertaking a bank or other mortgagee has placed itself under an obligation to make further advances, whether or not it has notice of an intermediate mortgage or charge, the first mortgagee has priority over that mortgagee or chargee for all advances made by it in fulfilment of its obligation. This rule reverses the decision of the court in *West* v *Williams* [1899] 1 Ch 132, where it was held that a mortgagee who was bound to make further advances on the security of a mortgage did not obtain priority for his later advances until they were actually made and accordingly he could not tack them to his original advance if he had notice of an intermediate mortgage when the further advance was made. By s. 94(1)(c), however, a first mortgagee now obtains priority for his further advances if he is obliged to make them and neither registration nor actual notice of an intermediate mortgage will prevent him from tacking them to his original advance. Banks rarely commit themselves contractually to making further advances when overdraft facilities are granted and so s. 94(1)(c) is likely to be of benefit to a bank only when it agrees to make a loan for a term of years on the security of a mortgage and the loan is to be made by instalments.

Registered land as security

It has been assumed up to the present that land mortgaged to a bank as security for its customer's indebtedness to it is unregistered land. Increasingly, however, land is registered under the Land Registration Acts 1925 to 1986. Loans on the security of registered land may be made and protected in one of the following ways, namely:

(a)   by a legal mortgage or legal charge created by a deed completed by the substantive registration of the lender as the proprietor of the mortgage or charge in the charges register of the title (the registered charge);

(b)   by a legal mortgage by deed protected by a mortgage caution on the proprietorship register of the title;

(c)   by a legal or equitable mortgage protected by a notice on the charges register of the title or by a caution against dealings entered on the proprietorship register; and

(d)   by an equitable mortgage or lien created by a deposit of the land certificate relating to the title and protected by a special notice of deposit entered on the charges register of the title.

Registered charges affecting a legal estate in registered land rank as between themselves according to the order in which they are entered in the charges register of the title and not according to the order in which they are created. Since they are registered dispositions of the title they rank for priority as regards all other dispositions for money or money's worth as from the date when they are registered in the charges register.

The provisions relating to the tacking of mortgages of unregistered land do not apply to registered charges of registered land (Law of Property Act 1925, s. 94(3)) but the provisions of s. 94(1) do apply as regards other mortgages and charges of registered land between themselves. When a registered charge is made for securing further advances or a current account the Chief Land Registrar will enter a notice to that effect on the charges register and before making a subsequent entry on the register which would affect the priority of the chargee for any further advance the Registrar gives notice of the intended entry to the proprietor of the charge (Land Registration Act 1925, s. 30(1)). The proprietor of a charge to secure further advances on a current account can tack advances subsequently made by him unless the advance is made after the date on which the notice of a proposed entry in the register should have been received by him from the Registrar (s. 30(1)). If, for example, a registered charge is created in favour of a bank to secure an overdrawn account, the honouring of cheques which increases the overdraft constitutes further advances for which the bank is entitled to priority unless it has received notice from the Land Registry of an intended entry protecting another mortgage or charge or unless such a notice has been sent to it and it should have received the notice before the further advance is made.

If the proprietor of a registered charge is under an obligation noted on the register to make further advances, all subsequently registered charges and other mortgages and charges of the registered land are subject to the right of the bank to claim priority in respect of such further advances (s. 30(3)). For the reasons given above, however, mortgages of land to a bank to secure further advances which it promises to make are rarely encountered in practice.

A legal or equitable mortgage of registered land by deed may be protected by a caution known as a mortgage caution. Section 106 of the Land Registration Act 1925 provides that registered land may be mortgaged in any manner which would have been permissible if the land had been unregistered, provided the instrument of mortgage describes the land either by reference to the register itself or so fully that the registrar is able to identify it without reference to any other document. The mortgage can be protected by entering a caution on the register in a prescribed form (this is known as a mortgage caution) and the mortgagee then has all the powers and remedies of the proprietor of a registered charge, but cannot sell the registered land until the mortgage has been converted into a registered charge. The effect of a mortgage caution is that dealings by the registered proprietor of land cannot be registered until notice has been served by the Chief Land Registrar on the mortgagee. The mortgagee may at any time require the mortgage to be registered as a registered charge and the mortgage caution is cancelled when this is done (Land Registration Act 1925, s. 106(5)). He then has priority in respect of the charge as of the date when the mortgage caution was entered. If an ordinary caution is entered to protect a mortgage, it merely gives the mortgagee a right to object to registration of later dispositions but does not preserve priority for the mortgage (Land Registration Act 1925, s. 20(1)).

A legal or equitable mortgage which is not created by deed but is in writing can take effect in equity as a contract and it may be protected on the Land Register by a caution in the ordinary form (Land Registration Act 1925, s. 54), so entitling the mortgagee to advance notice from the registrar of his intention to register any dealing with the land. Since the caution does not preserve priority for the mortgage or charge, however, it is more advisable to protect it by entering a notice of it on the charges register in respect of the registered land. This entitles the mortgagee to priority over other mortgages which are created later (Land Registration Act 1925, s. 54).

A mortgage by deposit of title deeds is a common method of securing a temporary loan. Section 66 of the Land Registration Act 1925 provides a method of mortgaging registered land by depositing the land certificate and banks often use this method for securing temporary loans on registered land. A mortgage by deposit of the land certificate (called in the Act a 'lien') may be made in one of two ways, namely:

(a) the proprietor of the land first deposits the land certificate with the mortgagee and the latter gives notice of the deposit to the Registrar; or

(b) before making the deposit the proprietor of the land gives notice to the Registrar of his intention to make a deposit of the land certificate. The registrar will enter this notice in the register and then send the land certificate to the chargee named.

The power to create a lien by deposit of the land certificate is subject to any restriction on the register, and the lien itself can only take effect subject to overriding interests and to any other rights and interests already protected on the register at the time of deposit. However, the entry of the notice of deposit in the charges register of the registered land preserves priority for the holder of the lien against other persons. Consequently an equitable charge which has been protected by a notice of deposit has priority over subsequent mortgages and charges. In *Re White Rose Cottage* [1965] Ch 940 a company, which was the proprietor of certain registered land executed, a memorandum of deposit of the land certificate with a bank to secure advances and undertook to hold the property as trustee for the bank to preserve its security. Notice of deposit of the documents was duly registered. Subsequently, judgment creditors of the company obtained charging orders and lodged cautions with the land registry in respect of them. The bank then applied to the land registry to enter a notice on the register of an equitable charge created by the memorandum. Notice of this was given to the judgment creditors, who objected to the notice being entered except on condition that their two charging orders were given priority over the bank's charge. A transfer of land was later executed by the bank under a power of attorney and in the transfer the bank released the land from moneys secured on it in favour of the purchaser. The court held that the bank's notice of deposit of the land certificate operated in the same way as an ordinary notice and the bank's security therefore took effect in priority to the subsequent charging orders. The judgment creditors were consequently not entitled to object to the registration by the bank of a notice in the ordinary form to protect its charge. But the transfer to the purchaser was to be construed as a sale by the company as mortgagor with the concurrence of the bank, and the transferee therefore took the same title as the company had, freed from the bank's mortgage but subject to the equitable charges conferred by the charging orders.

If a bank takes a mortgage or charge of registered land with a provision that its security shall extend to further advances made by it, s. 94(1) of the Law of Property Act 1925 applies because s. 94(4) only excludes from the operation of the section registered charges (Land Registration Act 1925, s. 30) created under the Land Registration Act 1925. By s. 94(2) of the Law of Property Act 1925 registered charges for the purpose of the section means a mortgage by deed registered as a registered charge and involving the issue of a charge certificate. The result of this is that a mortgagee or chargee of registered land who does not hold a registered charge but whose mortgage or charge extends to further advances obtains priority for such further advances over intermediate mortgages if he is unaware of their existence when the further advances are made.

FIXED AND FLOATING CHARGES

Trading company, trading stock and book debts often constitute the most valuable assets of a trading company. It would also be ideal if security could be created over future property acquired by the company. It was, however, impossible at common law to create a security over future assets without a new act of transfer at the time of acquisition. Nor was it practicable to create a mortgage over shifting assets like trading stock since it would mean that consent of the mortgagee would be required each time the mortgagor disposed of its trading stock in the ordinary course of its business.

Equity came to aid in two different ways. First, in *Holroyd* v *Marshall* (1862) 10 HL Cas 191 equity sanctioned the creation of a charge over future property which automatically attaches to the subject property on acquisition. The case involved an equitable mortgage of machinery under which the mortgagor had liberty to substitute new machinery which would become subject to the charge. The court upheld the validity of the mortgage and held that the mortgage had priority over the claims of an execution creditor. The second device used by equity was the floating charge.

The floating charge was first recognised in *Re Panama, New Zealand and Australian Royal Mail Co.* (1870) LR 5 Ch App 318, where it was held that the debenture holders had a charge upon all property of the company, past and future, and that they stood in a position superior to that of the general creditors who could touch nothing until the debenture holders were paid. Since the *Re Panama* case there have been a number of statements which describe the nature of the floating charge (see *Governments Stock and Other Securities Investment Co. Ltd* v *Manila Railway Co.* [1897] AC 81; *Re Yorkshire Woolcombers Association Ltd* [1903] 2 Ch 284; *Evans* v *Rival Granite Quarries Ltd* [1910] 2 KB 979).

Comparison with specific charge

A security must be either floating or specific. The terms are mutually exclusive. The floating charge is the antithesis of a specific charge. The point of distinction between the two is not that a floating charge covers present as well as future assets of the company. A specific charge can be created over the same. However, upon the creation of a specific charge, the charge fastens upon the charged assets either immediately or, in the case of future property, upon the company acquiring an interest in the charged property. The consent of the creditor would therefore be required before the company can deal with the charged property. The distinguishing feature of a floating charge is that the debtor company is left with the freedom to deal with charged assets in the ordinary course of business, without the need to obtain the consent of the holder of the floating charge (see *Re Panama* case). The presence of this feature has been examined by the courts in many cases.

If the debtor company is deprived of the right to deal with the charged assets in the ordinary course of business, the charge created is a specific charge (*Siebe Gorman and Co. Ltd* v *Barclays Bank Ltd* [1979] 2 Lloyd's Rep 142). In *Siebe Gorman and Co. Ltd* v *Barclays Bank Ltd* a company, in order to secure its present and future indebtedness to its bank, executed a debenture in favour of the bank, charging by way of a first fixed charge all book debts and other debts then and from time to time owing to the company. The provisions of the debenture obliged the company, during the continuance of the security, to pay all moneys received in respect of such debts into the company's account with the bank and not to charge or assign them in favour of any person without the prior written consent of the bank. The company later assigned a bill of exchange to the plaintiff and in proceedings brought by the plaintiff against the bank the plaintiff argued that the purported fixed charge was in reality a floating charge and was overridden by the assignment to the plaintiff. Slade J held that there is no reason why a specific charge cannot be created over book debts.

Crystallisation of floating charges

The term 'crystallisation' denotes the conversion of a floating charge into a specific charge. On crystallisation the debtor company's freedom to manage the charged assets ceases, the floating charge no longer floats over the subject of the charge but fastens on the assets owned by the debtor company comprised in the charge at the date of crystallisation and also on all such assets comprised in the charge which are subsequently acquired by the company (*N.W. Robbie and Co. Ltd* v *Witney Warehouse Co. Ltd* [1963] 1 WLR 1324).

Charge on future property versus purchase-money charge

In a typical situation a company, in order to secure an overdraft, may create a floating charge in favour of the bank over all its present and future assets. Subsequently, the company may borrow money from, say X, to purchase a piece of land upon terms that X should have a charge on the property so purchased. The question arises whether the bank's floating charge or X's purchase-money charge has priority. The law was uncertain how to determine this question. In *Re Connolly Brothers Ltd (No. 2)* [1912] 2 Ch 25 a company issued debentures creating a floating charge upon its undertaking and all of its property, present and future. The debentures contained a restrictive clause prohibiting the creation of any other mortgage or charge in priority to the debentures. Subsequently the company applied to O to advance money to enable the company to purchase certain real property and agreed to give O a charge upon the property so purchased. O consented to make the advance on those terms. On completion of the purchase the title deeds of the property were deposited with O and the company later executed a memorandum of deposit in favour of O. The issue of priority arose between the floating charge created by the debentures and the equitable mortgage of O. The Court of Appeal held that since the company had bound itself contractually to give an equitable mortgage to O before the purchase, it never became an unencumbered owner of the property, therefore the equitable mortgage had priority over the floating charge, which could attach to the property only in its encumbered form (see also *Church of England Building Society* v *Piskor* [1954] Ch 553.

The legal position has been clarified by the House of Lords decision in *Abbey National Building Society* v *Cann* [1991] 1 AC 56, where the House of Lords decided that the mortgagee had priority. It was held that, where a purchaser relied on a loan for the completion of his purchase, the transactions of acquiring the legal estate and granting the charge were one indivisible transaction, at least where there had been a prior agreement to grant the charge on the legal estate when obtained. The purchaser never acquired anything but an equity of redemption and there was no '*scintilla temporis*' during which the legal estate vested in him free from the charge. The legal estate was, from the outset, encumbered by the charge and could not be available to feed the estoppel free from it. *Church of England Building Society* v *Piskor* was overruled.

As a result of the decision in *Abbey National Building Society* v *Cann*, it is now clear that where money is advanced and relied on for the purchase of property against an agreement to charge the property as security, the mortgage has priority over an after-acquired property charge, whether fixed or floating.

Floating charge versus interests created before crystallisation

Subsequent specific charge   A specific charge, whether legal or equitable, has priority over an earlier floating charge. This is because the essence of the floating charge is that it is subject to the power of the debtor company to dispose of the charged assets in the ordinary course of business, and the creation of specific mortgages and charges is within the ordinary course of business (*Re Colonial Trusts Corporation, ex parte Bradshaw* (1879) 15 ChD 465). In *Wheatley* v *Silkstone and Haigh Moor Coal Co.* (1885) 29 ChD 715 North J held that the holder of a floating charge had priority over general creditors only.

A subsequent specific charge still has priority even if the specific mortgagee or chargee had notice of the earlier floating charge (*Re Hamilton's Windsor Ironworks* (1879) 12 ChD 707).

Restrictive clauses   Most floating charges contain restrictive clauses, commonly known as negative pledge clauses, prohibiting the creation of any mortgage or charge ranking in priority to or *pari passu* with the floating charge. However, it is well established that notice of the existence of a floating charge does not constitute constructive notice of the restrictive clause (*English and Scottish Mercantile Investment Co. Ltd* v *Brunton* [1892] 2 QB 700; *Re Valletort Sanitary Steam Laundry Co. Ltd* [1903] 2 Ch 654). In *Re Standard Rotary Machine Co. Ltd* (1906) 95 LT 829 it was held that notice of the floating charge itself did not constitute notice of the restrictive clause contained therein. In this case a company issued debentures by way of a floating charge over all its undertaking and property. The floating charge contained a restrictive clause prohibiting the creation of any mortgage or charge ranking in priority to or *pari passu* with the charge. The company subsequently created a specific charge over some of its fully paid shares in favour of the plaintiff. The court had to decide whether the later specific charge had priority over the earlier floating charge. The floating charge was duly registered. It was held that even assuming that the bank had notice of the floating charge, the bank did not have notice of the restrictive clause.

Subsequent floating charge   A floating charge has priority over a subsequent floating charge. In *Re Benjamin Cope and Sons Ltd* [1914] 1 Ch 800 Sargeant J said (at p. 806) that, although a floating charge can be displaced by a fixed charge, it does not follow that an earlier floating charge can be displaced by a subsequent floating charge. Nevertheless, where a floating charge expressly allows the debtor company to create a further floating charge over a specific portion of the charged assets, the subsequent floating charge has priority over the first (see *Re Automatic Bottle Makers* [1926] Ch 412).

Execution creditors   An execution creditor has priority over a holder of a floating charge if and only if the execution is completed before crystallisation of the floating charge (*Robson* v *Smith* [1895] 2 Ch 118).

As regards execution against goods, it is settled that the execution is not completed merely upon seizure of the goods. In *Re Standard Manufacturing Co.* [1891] 1 Ch 627 and in *Re Opera Ltd* [1891] 3 Ch 260 the court held that the holder of the floating charge was entitled to priority over the execution creditors.

Attachment of debts   It has been decided in *Robin* v *Smith* [1985] 2 Ch 118 that a garnishee order has priority over a floating charge where the garnished debt has been paid to the garnishee before the floating charge crystallises. In this case a garnishee order absolute was made against Smith ordering him to pay to the garnishor a debt owed by him to a company. Subsequently the plaintiff, holder of a floating charge, gave notice to the garnishee claiming that he was entitled to all debts of the company and required the garnishee not to pay others. The garnishee complied with the garnishee order and paid the debt to the garnishor. The plaintiff sued the garnishee, claiming that the latter had no right to pay to the garnishor after the receipt of the notice. Romer J held that the payment to the garnishor was good against the charge holder on the ground that the floating charge had not crystallised at the time the garnishee paid the debt. In *Norton* v *Yates* [1906] 1 KB 112 the question arose whether the execution creditor still had priority when the floating charge crystallised before the payment of the garnished debt. The court held that the garnishee order did not amount to a transfer of the debt, and the garnishor did not thereby become a creditor of the garnishee. Therefore the garnishee order *nisi* was subject to such rights and equities as already existed over the garnished debt. Since a receiver was appointed the holder of the floating charge had priority (see also: *Cairney* v *Back* [1906] 2 KB 746).

In the leading case of *Evans* v *Rival Granite Quarries Ltd* [1910] 2 KB 979 the Court of Appeal firmly established that the mere existence of a floating charge did not defeat or prevent executions by judgment creditors.

Debtor asserting right of set-off   A debtor can claim a right of set-off if the cross-claim arises before crystallisation, even if he has notice of the floating charge

at the time the cross-claim arises. In *Biggerstaff* v *Rowatt's Wharf Ltd* [1896] 2 Ch
93 Kay LJ treated the debentures as incomplete assignments which did not become
complete until such time as a receiver was appointed.

Floating charge versus interests created after crystallisation

Once a floating charge crystallises, it becomes a specific charge which fastens on
to the charged assets and the general rule is that it has priority over all subsequent
competing interests. There are however exceptions to this rule. Although the court
has sanctioned the validity of automatic crystallisation clauses, the question of
priority between a floating charge which has been converted into a fixed charge
under such a clause and a subsequent specific mortgage or charge remains open.
In other words, the effect of crystallisation on the debtor company must be
separated from its effect on other incumbrancers.

It has been argued by a number of learned authors (Gough, *Company Charges*,
pp. 104–5; Goode, *Legal Problems of Credit and Security*, 2nd ed., p. 90) that the
specific mortgage has priority over the floating charge despite its crystallisation;
the reason being that by creating a floating charge, the chargee has conferred
authority on the debtor company to sell or charge the charged assets in the ordinary
course of business. While automatic crystallisation or crystallisation by notice
terminates the company's actual authority to deal with the charged assets, the
company still has apparent authority to do so, and any dealing with the charged
assets within the ordinary course of business of the company must bind the holder
of the floating charge despite the fact of crystallisation. Therefore if the company
creates a specific charge over the charged assets after crystallisation and the
chargee has no notice of the fact of crystallisation, the specific charge must have
priority over the floating charge.

The same principle does not apply to unsecured creditors, their rights are subject
to any rights and equities as already existed over the company's assets; they are
unaffected by the company's actual or apparent authority to deal with the assets
subject to the floating charge. Hence as soon as the floating charge crystallises
before completion of execution, whether by automatic crystallisation clause or not,
the floating charge has priority over the execution creditors.

BOOK DEBTS AS SECURITY

Forms of security over book debts

Mortgage of book debts   A mortgage of book debts can take the form of statutory
assignment or equitable assignment. After the mortgagee has given notice to the
debtor, he is entitled to collect payment from the debtor.

Charge over book debts   A charge does not involve an assignment to the chargee:
it is a mere encumbrance on the charged debt. It follows that the chargor continues
to be the creditor and the debtor's obligation to pay the debt to the creditor, i.e.,
the chargor, remains unaffected by notice of the charge. However, a charge is to
be equated with an assignment for the purpose of set-off (see *Business Computers
Ltd* v *Anglo-African Leasing Ltd* [1977] 1 WLR 578; *N.W. Robbie and Co. Ltd* v

Witney Warehouse Co. Ltd [1963] 1 WLR 1324; *Rother Iron Works Ltd* v *Canterbury Precision Engineers Ltd* [1974] QB 1), and for the purpose of determining priority.

Floating charge over book debts

Ever since the floating charge was invented by Victorian lawyers, it has been customary for companies to create security over their book debts by way of floating charge, i.e., the chargor company is left free to dispose of the book debts and the proceeds of collection. Upon crystallisation of the floating charge, it fastens on all the existing and future book debts of the company (see *N.W. Robbie and Co. Ltd* v *Witney Warehouse Co. Ltd* [1963] 1 WLR 1324) and the receiver appointed by the holder of the floating charge will take control of the chargor company.

Fixed charge on book debts

The history of company liquidations has been such that lenders sought to strengthen their security by creating fixed charges over book debts, which have several advantages over the floating charge in terms of priority. Debts are peculiar because they cease to exist upon payment by the debtor. Therefore in order to create a fixed charge over debts, it is not enough to restrict the chargor company's right to dispose of the charged debt; there must also be a restriction on the way the chargor company is free to collect its debts and dispose of the proceeds.

In *Siebe Gorman and Co. Ltd* v *Barclays Bank Ltd* [1979] 2 Lloyd's Rep 142 the court decided that it was possible in law to create a fixed charge over book debts. There the debenture in question, in addition to restricting dealings with the charged debts, also required the chargor company to pay all proceeds of debts into the company's account with the chargee bank. Slade J held that a fixed charge had been created since on the construction of the debenture the bank would not have been obliged to allow the company to draw upon the account at a time when it still owed the bank money under the debenture.

In the Irish case *Re Keenan Brothers Ltd* [1986] BCLC 242 Keenan Brothers Ltd created in favour of its bank a charge over its present and future book debts. The instrument of charge referred to the charge as a 'fixed charge'. The charge obliged Keenan Brothers to pay all moneys it received in satisfaction of the book debts secured by the charges into a designated bank account with the chargee bank and withdrawals could only be made with the prior written consent of the bank. The Supreme Court of Ireland held that the charge created in favour of the bank was a fixed and not a floating charge.

Siebe Gorman and *Re Keenan Brothers* were distinguished in *Re Brightlife Ltd* [1987] Ch 200. In that case Brightlife, by a debenture, created, *inter alia*, a 'first specific charge' over 'all book debts now or at any time during the continuance of this security due or owing to the company'. The debenture required Brightlife not to sell, factor or discount debts without prior written consent of the debenture holder, but there was no provision restricting dealings with the proceeds of debts collected. The issue before the court was whether a first fixed charge had been created by the debenture. Hoffmann J held that the debenture, though expressed to create a 'first specific charge', operated to create a floating charge. The learned judge distinguished *Siebe Gorman* on the ground that there the debenture was in favour of a bank and not only prohibited the company from selling or charging its book debts but required that they be paid into the company's account with that bank and Slade J decided that as a matter of construction the bank would not have been obliged to allow the company to draw upon the account at a time when it still owed the bank money under the debenture. Hoffmann J also distinguished *Re Keenan Brothers* on the footing that there the company was obliged to pay the proceeds of all debts into a designated account with the bank and no withdrawals could be made without the prior consent of the bank.

Charge of debts in favour of a bank

The *Re Charge Card Services Ltd* [1987] Ch 150 it was decided that it is impossible in law to have a charge in favour of a debtor of his own indebtedness. Millett J said, at p. 176:

> The objection to a charge in these circumstances is not to the process by which it is created, but to the result. A debt is a chose in action; it is the right to sue the debtor. This can be assigned or made available to a third party, but not to the debtor, who cannot sue himself. Once any assignment or appropriation to the debtor becomes unconditional, the debt is wholly or partially released. The debtor cannot, and does not need to, resort to the creditor's claim against him in order to obtain the benefit of the security; his own liability to the creditor is automatically discharged or reduced.

Millett J derived support from the House of Lords decision in *National Westminster Bank Ltd* v *Halesowen Presswork and Assemblies Ltd* [1972] AC 785, where Viscount Dilhorne, Lord Simon of Glaisdale and Lord Cross of Chelsea endorsed the view expressed by Buckley LJ in the Court of Appeal that a bank could not have a lien on the credit balance in its customer's current account. The learned judge also distinguished *Re Hart, ex parte Caldicott* (1884) 25 ChD 716. There a partner of a firm deposited money with a bank by way of security for the indebtedness of his firm. The Court of Appeal held that the bank was not required to value its security before proving for its debt against the firm. Millett J distinguished it on the ground that it was not necessary to decide whether the deposit created a charge.

The implication of *Re Charge Card Services Ltd* to the banker is that it cannot have a charge over the credit balance in its customer's account. It may be able to set off against the credit balance any indebtedness due to it from the customer (see *Re Bank of Credit and Commerce International SA* [1996] Ch 245, discussed on p. 105).

Priorities

Equitable assignee (chargee) versus equitable assignee (chargee)   Priority between competing equitable assignees and chargees of book debts is governed by the rule in *Dearle* v *Hall* (1828) 3 Russ 1: priority goes to the first to give notice of his interest to the debtor unless he has notice of an earlier assignment at the time he acquires his interest. Notice of a prior assignment can be actual or constructive. Since a charge or mortgage of book debts by a company is registrable under the Companies Act 1985 and registration constitutes notice to a subsequent mortgagee or chargee (Companies Act 1985, s. 416), normally a subsequent encumbrancer will be bound with constructive notice of a prior encumbrance. However, registration is constructive notice only of matters appearing on the register at the time the subsequent encumbrancer acquires his interest, and constructive notice does not apply to subsequent purchasers of book debts. Thus a subsequent incumbrancer who acquires his interest before the registration of a prior interest does not have constructive notice of it, neither does a factor, whether he acquires his interest before or after registration of the prior interest. Moreover, assignment by way of sale, i.e., factoring, need not be registered under the Companies Act 1985. Notice of a prior floating charge does not affect priority because the essence of the floating charge is that the chargor company is free to dispose of the charged assets in the ordinary course of business, which includes the creation of mortgages or charges and the selling of book debts to a factor. Where the floating charge contains a negative pledge clause which forbids the company from assigning the charged book debts, a subsequent chargee or factor who has notice of the charge does not thereby have notice of the restriction since registration constitutes constructive notice of the required particulars only.

Equitable assignee versus legal assignee The interest of a chargee under a floating charge is necessarily equitable, s. 136 of the Law of Property Act 1925 expressly provides (see chapter 3). Some factors will, however, take legal assignments of book debts rather than rely on equitable assignments. The priority between the two is governed by the rule in *Dearle* v *Hall*.

STOCKS AND SHARES AS SECURITY

The types of stocks and shares likely to be offered to a bank as security for a loan are 'registered' stocks and shares and 'fully negotiable' stocks and shares. Where stocks and shares are registered, the names of the owners are recorded on a register, and no change of legal ownership can occur until the name of the old owner is removed from the register and the new name inserted. Where stocks and shares are in bearer form they are negotiable instruments and ownership vests generally in the bearer. The main types of registered stocks and shares are public authorities' loan bonds and stocks, and stocks and shares of companies.

Public authorities' loans

Public body stock is issued by governments, local authorities, nationalised industries and other public bodies as security for loans made to the public. The holder of a public authority's loan stock is usually entitled to receive a fixed rate of interest and repayment of capital at a fixed date. Some public authorities' stocks are 'listed' on the London Stock Exchange and these are better security for a loan made by a bank than stocks that are not listed. This is because listed stocks are readily marketable and it is possible to ascertain a market value for them at any given time. The registers of ownership for British government stocks are maintained by the Bank of England, although several British government stocks are also registered on the National Savings Register or the registers of the trustee savings banks. Ownership of government stock (marketable securities), British Savings Bonds and National Savings Income Bonds is recorded on the National Savings Stock Register.

Stocks and shares of companies

Fully paid shares may be converted into stock and vice versa. Some types of company stocks and shares are safer security for a loan than others. The safest security for a loan is 'debenture stock', which represents a loan made to the company. The holder of the debenture stock has a right to receive interest from the company, usually at a fixed rate, and is usually a secured creditor of the company. The nature of the security will depend on what assets are charged by the debenture trust deed.

Unsecured loan stock may also be given as security. The holder of unsecured loan stock is a creditor of the company and has a right to receive interest from the company. Preference shares may also be used as security for a loan. Although the preference shareholder is not a creditor of the company, he does have a right to receive a dividend on his shareholding prior to the ordinary shareholders.

The registers of both public and private companies are kept either by the company itself or by an outsider, e.g., a bank or chartered accountant. The register will show the names and addresses of the stockholders and/or shareholders and the quantity of shares and stock held. Holders are given a stock or share certificate and may transfer their holding by executing a stock or share transfer form and delivering it, with the certificate, to the transferee.

Creation of a legal mortgage of registered stocks and shares

A bank will take a legal mortgage of registered stocks and shares by obtaining from the registered holder a properly executed form of transfer, together with the stock or share certificate, and then have itself registered as the new registered holder of the stocks and shares. Where the registered holder is not the registered mortgagor himself but a nominee, the transfer form must be executed by the mortgagor's nominee and not by the mortgagor. The form of transfer cannot be registered unless a written instrument of transfer of the stock or shares is signed by the transferor.

When taking a legal mortgage of registered stocks and shares, the bank should give the mortgagor a 'facility letter' or formal 'loan agreement' describing the loan, the terms of repayment and the nature of the security. The bank should also take from the mortgagor a memorandum of deposit, containing details of the bank's powers in relation to the stocks and shares. The memorandum of deposit should list the mortgaged stocks or shares from time to time deposited with the bank.

The memorandum of deposit should state which debts owed to the bank are secured by the mortgage. If the mortgage is given to secure a fluctuating debt, e.g., an overdraft, the memorandum should state that the mortgage is given as a continuing security for the balance on the debtor's account with the bank so that the rule in *Clayton's Case* (*Devaynes* v *Noble, Clayton's Case* (1816) 1 Mer 572) will not have the effect of reducing the debt which is secured. The memorandum should also state (if that is the case) that the mortgage is being taken in addition to any other securities given to secure the same debt, not in substitution for them. The memorandum normally includes provision for the bank to sell the mortgaged stocks and shares if the mortgagor defaults. In the absence of an express provision in the memorandum, the bank will have an implied right of sale if the mortgagor defaults (*Deverges* v *Sandeman Clark and Co.* [1902] 1 Ch 579). Where no date for repayment is fixed, the courts have held the bank can enforce the security on giving reasonable notice to the mortgagor. In *Deverges* v *Sandeman Clark and Co.* a month's notice of the bank's intention to enforce the security was held to be reasonable.

A legal mortgagee of partly paid shares is liable for any calls on them and the memorandum should provide for the mortgagor to indemnify the bank in respect of any calls.

Creation of an equitable mortgage of registered stocks and shares

An equitable mortgage of registered stocks and shares is created when the mortgagor enters into a binding agreement to execute a proper form of transfer in favour of the bank or its nominees or where the bank (or its nominee) has not yet been registered as the new holder of the mortgaged stocks and shares. An equitable mortgage is created by the mortgagor depositing his stock and share certificates with the bank by way of security. In *Harrold* v *Plenty* [1901] 2 Ch 314 Cozens-Hardy J pointed out that such an act seems '. . . to amount to an equitable mortgage or, in other words, to an agreement to execute a transfer of the shares by way of mortgage'.

Deposit of the stock or share certificate will not amount to an equitable mortgage unless it can be shown that the deposit was by way of security. A bank may find it difficult to show that the deposit of the certificate was by way of security unless the mortgagor gives the bank a memorandum of deposit or a blank transfer form, with the intention that the mortgagee will, when necessary, fill the blank and perfect the security. The memorandum of deposit should contain essentially the same information as one made when a legal mortgage is created. Additionally, the memorandum should describe the circumstances in which the bank is permitted to complete the blank form of transfer in favour of itself or third party.

Whether a transfer of a company's shares may be written ('under hand') or must be in a deed is governed by the requirements of the company's articles of association, but fully paid-up shares may be transferred under s. 1 of the Stock Transfer Act 1963 by a signed instrument of transfer in the statutory form notwithstanding anything contained in the company's memorandum or articles.

A blank transfer cannot be by deed. If a person executes as a deed a document which is left in blank, it is void for uncertainty and cannot be perfected by completion after execution (*Markham* v *Gonaston* (1598) Cro Eliz 626; *Powell* v *London and Provincial Bank* [1893] 2 Ch 555).

A bank which has an equitable mortgage over British government stock or company stock or shares can further protect itself by means of a 'stop notice'. The effect of a stop notice is to prevent any dealings in securities or the payment of a dividend without notifying the person who served the stop notice to give him an opportunity to assert his claim. A bank which serves a stop notice on a company in respect of securities charged to it may obtain a restraining order or injunction to prevent payment of a dividend or dealings in the securities.

Fully negotiable stocks and shares as securities

Fully negotiable securities taken in good faith and for value may be retained by the purchaser (including a mortgagee) against the true owner. In that respect they are an excellent security. If a mortgagee takes them bona fide and for value and without notice of a defect in title, he can hold them against the true owner. Fully negotiable securities are charged by way of pledge rather than mortgage. Although the mere deposit of a fully negotiable security gives the bank a complete title, it is desirable to take a memorandum of deposit showing the purpose of the deposit.

A bank which takes fully negotiable instruments as security from a customer will acquire a valid title if it takes in good faith and for value, and without notice of any defect in the pledgor's title. Whether a bank takes the securities in good faith is a question of fact and mere negligence in taking the securities will not necessarily deprive the bank of its rights, but negligence or carelessness when considered in connection with the surrounding circumstances may be evidence of bad faith (see chapter 11).

LIFE POLICIES AS SECURITY

The assignment, legal or equitable, of a life assurance policy is a very general form of security for an advance up to the surrender value of the policy. Provided premiums continue to be paid, it is a security that increases in value. It is useful as a supplementary security, because in the event of the borrower's death, part or whole of the debt will be liquidated when the policy moneys are paid over by the insurance company.

A contract for life assurance is a contract *uberrimae fidei*, i.e., of the 'utmost good faith' and the assured must disclose all material facts within his knowledge affecting the life. Non-disclosure of a material fact may result in the policy being void. If the insurers are to avoid a policy on the grounds of non-disclosure, they must prove the fact to be material. A material fact is one which would influence the judgment of a prudent insurer in fixing the premium, or determining whether or not to take the risk and whether or not a fact is material is a question of fact. Examples of material facts are: failing to disclose convictions for dishonesty (material for house insurance) (*Woolcott* v *Sun Alliance and London Insurance Ltd* [1978] 1 WLR 493); failing to disclose that a number of other insurers had declined the risk of life assurance (*London Assurance* v *Mansel* (1879) 11 ChD 363) and failing to disclose doubts about the assured's mental health (which might have made him prone to suicide) (*Lindenau* v *Desborough* (1828) 8 B & C 586).

The assignment

The assignment is taken from the person entitled to the benefit which forms the security value, i.e., the person to whom the surrender value, or moneys are payable under the policy. This 'beneficiary' may or may not be the life assured. The beneficiary must be of full capacity or the assignment will be ineffective. A legal assignment must be in accordance with the Policies of Assurance Act 1867. The Act requires the assignment be witnessed and signed, although it need not be by deed. The insurer must be informed of the date and effect of the assignment.

The effect of a legal assignment of a life assurance policy is as follows:

(a)   after receiving notice, the insurer is bound to pay the assignee only, and is discharged by earlier payment to another;

(b)   the insurer is entitled to the defences of set-off or counterclaim existing between himself and the assured before notice;

(c)   the priorities between successive assignees are regulated by the order in which notice is received by the insurer (the rule in *Dearle* v *Hall* (1828) 3 Russ 1).

An equitable assignment may be made by an oral agreement, or by memorandum (*Myers* v *United Guarantee and Life Assurance Co.* (1855) 7 De G M & G 112) or by deposit of the policy with intent that it be security. A memorandum of deposit may be taken to explain the purpose of the deposit. Alternatively, the bank may take an irrevocable power of attorney, entitling it to sell in the name of the assignor.

18 Recovery of Bank Advances

The most obvious way in which a bank or other financial institution may recover
an advance it has made is to bring an action in debt for the amount of the advance,
together with any interest and commission and any other charges which become
payable. The bank or other institution may serve a writ when the loan falls due for
repayment if there is default, or it may instead issue a county court summons (the
£10,000 limit on the county court jurisdiction in contract was abolished by the
High Court and County Courts Jurisdiction Order 1991). If interest payments were
due during the currency of the loan and they are not paid, an action can be brought
to recover the interest payments as they become due. In such circumstances,
default on the interest payments may also result in the capital sum lent also
becoming due immediately.

Relatively few actions for the recovery of advances made by banks are defended.
Because the bank's claim will normally be for a liquidated sum which can be
arithmetically calculated, the bank can enter a final judgment against a defendant
who either fails to acknowledge service of a writ and give notice of his intention
to defend the bank's action, or, after service of the statement of claim, fails to serve
a defence on the plaintiff.

However, prior to an action to recover the amount due to the bank either from
the customer to whom the advance was made or from the guarantor, the bank may
seek to exercise a set-off. If the bank is itself indebted on another account to the
prospective defendant (whether a principal debtor of the bank or a guarantor), and
the bank's indebtedness is immediately due or is recoverable by the defendant on
demand (e.g., a credit balance on a current account), the bank may set off the
prospective defendant's indebtedness to it against its own indebtedness to the
prospective defendant, and thereby pay itself the whole or part of the amount which
is owed to it (*Garnett* v *M'Kewan* (1872) LR 8 Ex 10) (see chapter 7).

A bank which seeks to recover an advance or other outstanding amount will first
resort to any right of set-off which it may exercise. It will initiate litigation against the
borrower company and any guarantors only if the bank has no right of set-off, or if it is
unable to recover the full amount by exercising such a right. However, the bank may
also have a right to realise a security and/or to seek a bankruptcy order or seek an order
to have the borrowing company wound up. The various remedies will be examined in
this chapter, except the bank's right of set-off, which has already been examined.

ACTION FOR DEBT

An action brought by a bank to recover a loan made to its customer, or in the event of default by the customer, an action against any guarantor of the customer's indebtedness can be expeditiously pursued to judgment if the bank serves on the defendant a copy of its statement of claim at the same time as the writ which initiates the action, or if the bank endorses its statement of claim on the writ (RSC, Ord. 6, r. 2(1)). The statement of claim must specify the amount claimed as the principal amount, together with interest and other charges (RSC, Ord. 18, r. 8(4)), but if the particulars of the claim have already been delivered in writing to the defendant, the statement of claim need only state the total amount claimed and that the particulars have already been delivered. The statement of claim must also state that the action will be stayed if the defendant (or anyone on the defendant's behalf) pays the amount claimed to the bank or its solicitor, together with the bank's costs for issuing and serving the writ and statement of claim within 14 days of service (RSC, Ord. 6, r. 2(1)). The statement of claim should claim interest on the principal amount of the loan at the rate provided by the contract and calculated up to the date of issue of the writ. The statement of claim should also claim further interest at the same rate from that date until the date when judgment is entered but that amount will not be immediately quantifiable (RSC, Ord. 18, r. 8(4)).

The advantage to the bank of serving a statement of claim with its writ, or endorsing its statement of claim on the writ, is that if notice of intention to defend the action is given, the bank may apply to the court on a summons for summary judgment on the ground that the defendant has no defence to the action (RSC Ord. 14, r. 1(1)). The application must be supported by an affidavit sworn on behalf of the bank by one of its authorised officers or by its solicitor; the affidavit must verify the facts on which the bank's claim is based and conclude with a statement that the defendant has no defence to the action (RSC Ord. 14, r. 2(1) and (2)).

The defendant must be served with the summons for summary judgment and the supporting affidavit, and he may file and serve on the bank an affidavit in reply in which he may allege that he has a defence to the bank's claim, specifying it and setting out the facts which establish the defence (RSC, Ord. 14, r. 4(1)). A copy of the defendant's affidavit must be served on the bank or its solicitor, and it may then serve a further affidavit dealing with matters raised as a defence in the defendant's affidavit. In reality, it is rarely necessary for the bank to file a further affidavit in response to the defendant's affidavit since the original affidavits will establish the basis for the claim and the intended defence.

On the hearing of the summons the burden of establishing a *prima facie* defence to the bank's claim rests on the defendant, but the court will give leave to defend the action if the facts alleged in the affidavit filed by the defendant are plausible (i.e., not obviously unprovable), and would, if proved, establish a defence, or if the court considers there is a substantial question of fact to be tried (RSC, Ord. 14, r. 4(3)). The court may give the defendant leave to defend the bank's action conditionally or unconditionally.

REALISATION OF SECURITY

Only as a last resort and after the possibility of obtaining payment through other methods have failed will the bank rely on its right to realise any security it holds for a loan or advance made to the borrowing customer. If the borrowing customer is a company and clearly insolvent so that full recovery of the company's indebtedness is not possible, a bank will rely on its security. For this reason it is important for a bank to ensure that the value of the security is sufficient to cover the amount advanced when it makes its initial advance, and to check periodically to ensure that the advance and any further sums are covered by the security. The Insolvency Act 1986 contains several procedures intended to deal with situations where a company is in financial difficulties. Some of these procedures are intended as an alternative to putting a company into liquidation.

INSOLVENCY PRACTITIONERS

Only an authorised insolvency practitioner may act as a liquidator (or as a receiver, administrator, supervisor of a voluntary arrangement etc.). He must be an individual. To obtain authorisation the applicant must satisfy either a professional body to which the DTI has delegated its powers of authorisation in respect of its own members, or a competent authority (tribunal) appointed by the DTI that he is:

(a)   a fit and proper person; and
(b)   satisfies prescribed requirements in respect of education, practical training and experience.

The intention and effect of this system is to confine the functions of insolvency practitioners to members of certain prominent professional bodies, mainly account- ants, and among members of those bodies to authorise only those of their members who have specialised in insolvency work. The system, which was recommended by the Cork Committee in 1982, is designed to exclude a minority of unqualified persons of dubious character from continuing to act as insolvency practitioners. An authorised insolvency practitioner is required to obtain renewed authorisation at intervals, when his record will be taken into account.

The Company Directors Disqualification Act 1986, s. 7, contains 'reporting provisions' by which an insolvency practitioner who is acting in any of the capacities mentioned above in connection with a company will report to the DTI on certain aspects of the past performance of the directors. Indirectly, therefore, the restriction of insolvency work to authorised practitioners is a means of introducing much closer examination of the record of directors of companies which have become insolvent, possibly owing to the neglect of those directors.

However, the system of authorised insolvency practitioners is intended to go much further than restraining malpractice. Its purpose is to promote a stringent review by competent experts of the management of companies, which have become insolvent, with some pressure on them to be thorough in their investigations.

VOLUNTARY ARRANGEMENTS

The Insolvency Act 1986, ss. 1–7, sets out the scheme for company voluntary arrangements, which was introduced by the Insolvency Act 1985. The scheme allows a company which is either in liquidation, or the subject of an administration order, or even still a going concern, to enter into a scheme of arrangement or composition with its creditors with the minimum of formality. Where the company is a going concern the proposal will be made by the company's directors acting collectively (s. 1(1)). In such circumstances the directors retain their powers of management, and although the company does not benefit from a general moratorium under which creditors are prevented from enforcing their debts, the creditors who agree to be bound by the arrangement once it has been approved will be prevented from taking independent action for recovery of their debts.

The scheme is prepared under the supervision of a qualified insolvency practitioner, known as 'the nominee' (s. 1(2)). If the nominee is already the liquidator or administrator of the company, he can submit the proposals to the creditors as part of the liquidation or administration process. If the nominee is not the liquidator or administrator of the company, he must submit a report to the court stating whether, in his opinion, the scheme is viable, and whether a meeting of the creditors should be called (s. 2(2)). The purpose of the creditors' meeting is to decide whether or not to approve the proposal (s. 4). The creditors have considerable discretion in dealing with proposals before them; they are not restricted to simply approving or rejecting the scheme as presented, but they may modify it, provided that the fundamental characteristics of the scheme remain unaltered and provided that the debtor company agrees. The meeting cannot approve any proposal or modification which adversely prejudices the rights of any secured or preferential creditors to be paid in priority or to be paid *pari passu* with each other, unless those likely to be affected approve the arrangement (s. 4(3) and (4)). The outcome of the meeting must be reported by the chairman to the court (s. 4(6)). Once the proposals have been approved at the creditors' meeting, they become binding on every person who had notice and who was entitled to vote at the meeting, whether or not such persons actually attended (s. 4(6)).

If at the time the creditors consent to a voluntary arrangement there is an administration or a winding-up order in force, the court may decide to stay all proceedings in the administration or liquidation, or may give directions in respect of the order modifying the normal course of the administration or liquidation.

The court's involvement in a company voluntary arrangement is minimal and formal approval of the scheme by the courts is unnecessary. If, however, the scheme is challenged within 28 days of the court receiving the chairman's report of the creditors' meeting, it will be subject to a full scrutiny (s. 6(3)). A creditor of the company, or its liquidator, or administrator, or any insolvency practitioner may challenge the scheme on the grounds that it unfairly prejudices the interests of a creditor, member or contributory of the company; or that there was some material irregularity at or in relation to the meeting (s. 6(1)).

If a proposed scheme is approved or is not subject to challenge, the nominee then becomes the supervisor of the composition or scheme and assumes full responsibility for its implementation (s. 7(2)). The terms of the scheme must follow the requirements of s. 1 of the 1986 Act. The position of the secured and preferential creditors is protected by s. 1(3) and (4), but such creditors could choose to modify their rights under the arrangement.

ADMINISTRATION ORDERS

The Insolvency Act 1985 introduced another new procedure, under which the court is empowered to make an 'administration order' in regard to a company in financial difficulties with the result that the management of the company is placed in the hands of an administrator (s. 8). The administration procedure requires greater judicial involvement than a company voluntary arrangement and affords protection to the company's assets during the period of administration. The function of the administrator is to devise and implement a satisfactory rescue plan (s. 8(3)). The administrator will act on behalf of all the creditors, not merely the debenture holders, who, however, are given a right to veto the making of an administration order, if they are secured by a floating charge over the company's assets, and appoint an administrative receiver. The debenture holders, instead, can insist that a receiver be appointed to protect their interests.

The legislation on administration is now in the Insolvency Act 1986, ss. 8 to 27.

Section 8(1) of the Insolvency Act 1986 provides that two conditions must be satisfied before the court will exercise its power to make an administration order:

(a) the company must be unable to pay its debts, and
(b) there must be a likelihood that the purpose for which the administration order is sought will be attained.

The company's inability to pay its debts is determined by reference to the definition contained in s. 123 of the 1986 Act. The likelihood of attaining the purpose for which the order is sought is to be judged by reference to s. 8(3), which provides that the order can be made only for one or more of the following purposes:

(a) ensuring the survival of the company, and the whole or any part of its undertaking, as a going concern;
(b) the approval of a voluntary arrangement by the company's creditors under Part I of the Insolvency Act 1986;
(c) the sanctioning under s. 425 of the Companies Act 1985 of a compromise or arrangement between the company and its creditors or shareholders;
(d) achieving a more advantageous realisation of the company's assets than would be possible on a winding up.

The phrase 'likely to achieve' was held to mean that the court must be satisfied on the evidence put before it that the proposed purpose will more probably be achieved than not be achieved (*Re Consumer and Industrial Press Ltd* [1988] BCLC 177). Provided that s. 8 is satisfied the court will weigh up the advantages of granting an administration order. However, in *Re Harris Simons Construction Ltd* [1989] 1 WLR 368 Harman J held that the standard of probability established by Peter Gibson J was too high for the jurisdiction and the courts should more readily rely on their jurisdiction not to grant the order. Hoffman J's view was that s. 8 was satisfied if the court considers that there is a real prospect that one or more of the stated purposes may be achieved (see also *Re Primlaks (UK) Ltd* (1989) 5 BCC 710). In *Re SCL Building Services Ltd* [1989] 5 BCLC 746 Peter Gibson J again had the opportunity to review the circumstances in which the court may grant an order under s. 8. Referring to *Re Harris Simons* and *Re Primlaks* he applied the real prospect test.

An application for an administration order may be made to the court by the company or its directors, or by one or more of the company's creditors, or by a combination of these persons. Once a petition for an administration order has been presented the Act provides immediate protection of the company's assets, and any existing or pending legal action is stayed whilst the court considers whether or not to grant the order. Thus, whilst the court is considering whether or not to make an order the company cannot be put into liquidation; any security held by its creditors cannot be enforced without the consent of the court and goods held under a hire-purchase agreement or subject to any retention of title agreement cannot be repossessed without the leave of the court (s. 10(1)), but an administrative receiver may be appointed (s. 10(2)). Once the administration order has been granted, the restrictions on enforcing judgment or instigating an action against the company continue to apply, but a receiver can no longer be appointed.

Once an administration order is made the administrator must send to the company and publish in the prescribed manner a notice of the order. He must notify the Companies Registry within 14 days and the company's creditors within 28 days of the making of the order.

The company's business correspondence, including invoices and orders issued during the period of administration must indicate that an administration order has been made against the company.

On appointment, the administrator must take control of the company's assets (s. 14 and sch. I set out powers of the administrator). If the administrator is to carry out his functions and devise a rescue plan, there must be an exchange of information between him and the company's directors, who must prepare a statement of the company's affairs. The statement of affairs must be verified by affidavit and should include details of the company's assets, debts and liabilities, details of the creditors and the nature of securities held by them, together with any other necessary information.

The administrator has considerable powers to do such acts and enter into such transactions as are necessary for the management of the company's affairs and business and the achievement of the purpose for which the administration order was made. He has specific powers to carry on the business of the company; to raise or borrow money and to grant security over the company's property; to refer disputes to arbitration; to appoint a solicitor, accountant or other professionally qualified person to assist him in the performance of his functions; to present or defend a petition for the winding up of the company; to employ and dismiss employees; to do all things incidental to the exercise of these and other specific powers conferred on him (s. 14 and sch. I). Additionally, the administrator has authority to remove and appoint directors, and unless the administrator consents neither the company nor its officers can exercise any power so as to interfere with the administrator's functions.

In exercising his powers, the administrator is deemed to be acting as the company's agent. As such the administrator owes fiduciary duties to the company to act in good faith, to exercise his powers for proper purpose, not to make a secret profit or act in any way that his personal interests conflict with his duties as an administrator. A person dealing with him in good faith and for value is protected if the administrator exceeds his authority.

An administrator may be personally liable, if he acts outside his authority on any contracts made by him and any contracts of employment adopted by him. On vacating his office an administrator will normally be released from all liability for any acts or omissions unless he has misapplied company assets or acted in breach of duty.

RECEIVERSHIPS AND SALES

The powers of realisation given to mortgagees and chargees by the general law are never enough to meet the needs of the bank which has taken a charge over the business assets and undertakings of a company. A mortgagee or chargee, whether his security is legal or equitable, may obtain an order of the court that the property comprised in the security should be sold, or that a receiver be appointed either to receive the income or to sell or otherwise realise the property. The court will order a sale or a receivership only if the borrower has defaulted in paying the principal or interest under the loan agreement, or if the subject matter of the security is in jeopardy.

Statutory powers of realisation

A bank will not want the delay involved in seeking an order for sale or the appointment of a receiver by the court if the company is insolvent, or likely to become insolvent. Limited powers of sale and to appoint a receiver are conferred on mortgagees and chargees by the Law of Property Act 1925, ss. 101, 103, 104 and 109, but these powers are effective only if the security is executed as a deed, and may be exercised only in a limited range of circumstances, which are insufficient to protect a bank which has financed a trading company. Because of the inadequacy of the general law, documents creating a security over a company's business assets for bank advances invariably contain their own provisions defining the circumstances in which the bank may realise its security, the way in which the realisation may be carried out and the way in which the proceeds of the realisation may be applied. Such powers are exercisable immediately on default. When the bank's powers of realisation become exercisable, the document charging the company's assets will empower the bank to sell or otherwise realise all or any of the company's assets charged, and to exercise the powers of sale under the Law of Property Act 1925. More significantly, the bank will be empowered to appoint a receiver.

ADMINISTRATIVE RECEIVERS

(The following discussion is based on *Mayson, French and Ryan on Company Law*, 13th ed. (London: Blackstone, 1996).)

An administrative receiver is a receiver or manager of the whole or substantially the whole of a company's property (the term 'administrative receiver' appeared for the first time in the Insolvency Act 1988). He is appointed by the holders of a debenture secured by a floating charge over the whole or substantially the whole of a company's assets or by such a charge and one or more other securities. Where there is an express power to appoint a receiver, one cannot be appointed unless the event entitling the exercise of the power to appoint has occurred (*Kasofsky* v *Kreegers* [1937] 4 All ER 374).

The power to appoint a receiver will be exercisable on the occurrence of one of several specified events provided for in the debenture. The occurrence of these specified events usually indicates that the company is in financial difficulties. The most common event of non-compliance is a failure to meet a demand for payment of the secured debt, although the demand need not specify the exact amount being claimed (*Bunbury Foods Pty Ltd* v *National Bank of Australasia Ltd* (1984) 153 CLR 491).

From the time of appointment an administrative receiver of a company has sole authority to deal with the charged property. The directors are no longer authorised to deal with the charged property, although they continue in office and are still liable, e.g., to submit returns and documents to the registrar (*Newhart Developments Ltd* v *Co-operative Commercial Bank Ltd* [1978] QB 814, although doubt was cast on the *Newhart* case in *Tudor Grange Holdings Ltd* v *Citibank NA* [1992] Ch 53 in relation to other issues raised in the case).

The administrative receiver of a company is deemed to be an agent of the company unless and until the company goes into liquidation (Insolvency Act 1986, s. 44(1)(a)). As the administrative receiver is the agent of the company, and not of the chargee appointing him, the chargee avoids incurring the onerous duties of a mortgagee in possession. The debenture holder who appoints a receiver cannot, therefore, be made liable for a wrong committed by him during the course of his appointment (*Re Simms* [1934] Ch 1), nor will he be liable for debts incurred by the receiver (*Cully* v *Parsons* [1923] 2 Ch 512), nor will the receiver's remuneration be a liability of the debenture holder (Insolvency Act 1986, s. 60(1)). The chargee escapes all liability unless he meddles in the receivership, in which case he will become liable for the consequences of that meddling (*Standard Chartered Bank Ltd* v *Walker* [1982] 1 WLR 1410).

If an administrative receiver carries on the company's business then the business is nonetheless that of the company and not the receiver (*Gosling* v *Gaskell and Grocott* [1897] AC 575). The actions and conduct of the administrative receiver of a company are 'affairs' of the company which may be investigated by inspectors appointed by the Secretary of State for Trade and Industry under the Companies Act 1985 (*R* v *Board of Trade, ex parte St Martins Preserving Co. Ltd* [1965] 1 QB 603).

Where an administrative receiver is appointed, the property coming into the hands of the receiver is applied first to paying the company's preferential debts and only then to meeting the obligation owed to the chargee (Insolvency Act 1986, s. 40). However, the rights of any other persons to the company's property must be protected if they were acquired before crystallisation (*Re Morrison, Jones and Taylor Ltd* [1914] 1 Ch 50), e.g., if any property of the company is subject to a fixed charge ranking before the charge or charges in respect of which the administrative receiver has been appointed then the administrative receiver cannot utilise that property either to pay the debt secured by the floating charge or to pay preferential debts. However, any property subject to a prior floating charge can be used because its priority was lost when the appointment of a receiver crystallised the floating charge under which he was appointed and turned it into a fixed charge (*Griffiths* v *Yorkshire Bank plc* [1994] 1 WLR 1427).

Preferential creditors

A disadvantage of a floating charge is that if an administrative receiver is appointed, or if the company is wound up before an administrative receiver is appointed, then certain debts of the company, called preferential debts will be paid out of the assets subject to the floating charge in priority to the chargee's debts (Insolvency Act 1986, ss. 40 and 175(2)(b)). The preferential debts are defined in

s. 386 and sch. 6 and include money owed to the Inland Revenue for PAYE deductions in respect of employees' wages and salaries, VAT, betting and gaming duties, car tax (SI 1987 No. 2093) etc.

A further disadvantage of a floating charge is that any assets of a company in liquidation which are subject to a floating charge are assets from which the expenses of the liquidation (including the liquidator's remuneration) are payable in priority to any other claim (*Re Barleycorn Enterprises Ltd* [1970] Ch 465).

Duty of care

A mortgagee exercising a power of sale owes the mortgagor a duty of care to take reasonable care to obtain the 'true market value' or 'the proper price' of the property (*Cuckmere Brick Co. Ltd* v *Mutual Finance Ltd* [1971] Ch 949; *Tse Kwong Lam* v *Wong Chit Sen* [1983] 1 WLR 1349). A receiver who exercises a power of sale owes a similar duty (*Standard Chartered Bank Ltd* v *Walker* [1982] 1 WLR 1410). If the mortgagee or receiver is to discharge his duty, he must ensure that the proposed sale of the company's assets is fully advertised and he obtains professional advice about the best method of sale. If the sale is by auction then the appropriate reserve price must be fixed and matters such as the desirability of seeking planning permission etc. must be attended to (*American Express International Banking Corporation* v *Hurley* [1985] 3 All ER 564). However, a bank is allowed to sell promptly and does not have to delay the sale in the hope that a better price may be obtained at a later date (*Reliance Permanent Building Society* v *Harwood-Stamper* [1944] Ch 362; *Bank of Cyprus (London) Ltd* v *Gill* [1980] 2 Lloyd's Rep 51). The duty of care obliges the mortgagee not to fix a date for the sale so early that there is no time to advertise it properly. The duty requires that features which may tend to increase the value of the property are properly advertised. If the duty of care is satisfied, the receiver will be entitled to sell or otherwise enforce the security even though this is not in the interests of the mortgagor. In the Court of Appeal case of *Shamji* v *Johnson Matthey Bankers Ltd* [1991] BCLC 36 Oliver LJ adopted a passage from the *Cuckmere* case namely:

> If the mortgagee's interests, as he sees them, conflict with those of the mortgagor, the mortgagee can give preference to his own interests.

The duty of care is owed to the mortgagee, and also to any third party who has guaranteed the mortgage debt and will therefore have to pay more if the primary security realises less than it should (*Standard Chartered Bank Ltd* v *Walker*). However, in *Downsview Nominees Ltd* v *First City Corporation Ltd* [1993] AC 295) the Privy Council held that an administrative receiver of a company does not owe any duty of care to the company or to persons who have a charge over the company's property ranking after the one under which the administrative receiver was appointed.

LIQUIDATION OR DISSOLUTION OF COMPANIES

A company as an artificial person comes into existence when the registrar enters its name on the register of companies and issues a certificate of incorporation.

Before a company can be dissolved it must usually be wound up or 'liquidated'. Liquidation entails collecting the company's assets and converting them into money, using the money to pay its debts, and, if anything then remains, distributing the surplus to the members in accordance with their entitlement.

The first step is therefore to put the company into liquidation and appoint a liquidator or joint liquidators. When the liquidation is completed the liquidator gives notice of it to the registrar.

Types of liquidation

There are now three types of liquidation:

(a)   Compulsory liquidation by order of the court. The High Court, or, if the company's paid-up share capital does not exceed £120,000, the local county court, has jurisdiction to order that the company shall be wound up by the court.

(b)   Voluntary liquidation, which may be either:

(i)   members' voluntary liquidation (Insolvency Act 1986, ss. 84 and 86); or
(ii)   creditors' voluntary liquidation (Insolvency Act 1986, s. 98(1)).

The characteristic of a voluntary liquidation of either type is that it is begun by a resolution passed by a general meeting of members of the company.

Liquidation of solvent companies

Even if the company is believed to be able to pay its debts in full, its liquidator must be an insolvency practitioner. A members' voluntary liquidation is not under the control of creditors and it usually proceeds in a rather more relaxed manner.

Compulsory liquidation

Introduction   The majority of company liquidations are voluntary, and are therefore initiated by a resolution passed in general meeting. Even if the company is insolvent and under pressure from its creditors, it usually suits both the directors and the creditors to promote a creditors' voluntary liquidation which is a less expensive and less formal procedure than a compulsory winding up.

However, compulsory liquidation is the remedy of last resort for the creditor or member if a company refuses to satisfy its legitimate demands or is simply unresponsive, usually because it has been abandoned by the directors. In every case a petition to the court for compulsory liquidation must state, and be supported by evidence of, certain specified grounds upon which the court at its discretion may order compulsory liquidation.

Grounds for a winding-up order   A company may be wound up by the court on the following grounds specified in s. 122(1) of the Insolvency Act 1986:

(a)   the company has so resolved by special resolution;
(b)   default is made in delivering the statutory declaration of capital etc. in order to obtain the registrar's certificate that a public company may commence business;

(c) the company does not commence its business within a year from its incorporation or suspends its business for a whole year;

(d) the number of members is reduced below the statutory minimum (one for most companies (SI 1992/1699));

(e) the company is unable to pay its debts;

(f) the court is of the opinion that it is just and equitable that the company should be wound up;

(g) it is an old company, within the meaning of the Consequential Provisions Act.

Company's inability to pay debts A company is deemed to be unable to pay its debts if it defaults for three weeks or more in meeting a demand for a debt exceeding £750 (or such other limit as the Secretary of State may fix under the Insolvency Act 1986), or if it fails to satisfy execution for a judgment debt, or the court is satisfied that it is unable to pay its debts. The company's contingent and prospective liabilities can only be taken into account when determining whether the value of the company's assets is less than its liabilities (s. 123(2)). The fact that, for the time being, the company has insufficient liquid assets to pay its present debts where payment of those debts has not been demanded, is insufficient (*Re Capital Annuities Ltd* [1979] 1 WLR 170).

Who may petition Most petitions are presented either by one or more creditors on the ground that the company is unable to pay its debts in excess of £750, or by one or more contributories on the basis that deadlock or oppressive conduct in the management, or other grounds, make it just and equitable to wind up the company. However, the full list of those who may present a petition is longer. A petition may be presented by:

(a) The company;

(b) Any creditor or creditors who establish a prima facie case.

Generally the court ought not to deprive a petitioning creditor of his prima facie right to a winding-up order unless his petition is opposed by creditors with the majority in the value of their debts. Where the petitioning and supporting creditors belong to the same group of companies as the company sought to be wound up, the court should have regard to the nature of their debts (e.g., that they were 'domestic' (intra-group) debts owed to a member company). Furthermore, where the petitioning creditor was the parent company, it could control the activities of the company sought to be wound up (*Re Southard and Co. Ltd* [1979] 1 WLR 1198).

The court can and will restrain a petition which is an abuse of process. In *Re A Company (No. 001573 of 1983)* [1983] BCLC 492 it was held an abuse to petition for winding up on the same day that an order for costs was made against the company and the petitioner doubted its ability to pay.

If a debt is genuinely disputed, the court may restrain a winding-up petition. But the court will take due heed of potential difficulties in establishing a debt against, for example, a foreign company (in *Re Russian and English Bank* [1932] 1 Ch 663). Restraining petitions based on disputed debts is a rule of practice and the court will always consider whether there appears to be a substantial dispute (*Re Claybridge Shipping Co. SA* [1981] Com LR 107).

In *Re A Company (No. 0012209) of 1991)* [1992] 1 WLR 351 Hoffmann J granted an injunction to restrain the presentation of a winding-up petition by a creditor as the company was solvent and it appeared that its defence to the creditor's claim had a prospect of success. The creditor was ordered to pay the company's costs on an indemnity basis. His lordship added, however, 'that if the court comes to the conclusion that a solvent company is not putting forward any defence in good faith and is merely seeking to take for itself credit which it is not allowed under the contract, then the court would not be inclined to restrain presentation of the petition'.

(c) A contributory or contributories, when the number of members has fallen below the statutory minimum or if the contributory is an original allottee or has held shares for six months in the 18 months preceding the presentation of the petition or received them through devolution from a former member.

(d) The DTI after an investigation and on certain other grounds. The court may use a report of the inspectors as prima facie grounds for ordering a winding up (*Re Armvent Ltd* [1975] 1 WLR 1679).

(e) The official receiver, where a voluntary winding up cannot be continued with due regard to the interests of creditors or contributories. The power of the Secretary of State is not so limited (*Re Lubin, Rosen and Associates Ltd* [1975] 1 WLR 122).

The court may have regard to the wishes of creditors and contributories when hearing a petition and may order meetings to ascertain those wishes (Insolvency Act 1986, s. 195).

Procedure   The petitioner will present a petition supported by affidavit verifying the facts stated therein. Unless the petition is presented by the company itself a copy is supplied for service on the company, which is entitled to appear and oppose the petition at the hearing. The petition is advertised in the *London Gazette* at least seven business days in advance of the date fixed for the hearing. This is to enable creditors of the company, and other interested parties, to have notice in time to be represented at the hearing if they wish. The petition is heard in open court. On hearing the petition the court may: (a) dismiss it; or (b) adjourn the hearing; or (c) make an interim order; or (d) make any other order it thinks fit; or (e) make an order for compulsory winding up.

At any time after the presentation of the petition the court may appoint a provisional liquidator, usually to safeguard the assets of the company pending the outcome of the hearing of the petition (Insolvency Act 1986, s. 135). It is not normally necessary to take this precaution, however, as the order, if made, is retrospective to the date of presentation of the petition and dispositions of assets after the date are made void by the winding-up order.

The order when made leads to an investigation by the official receiver as liquidator into the causes of the company's failure and the general record of its management. The official receiver, like an administrative receiver, may call for a statement of affairs from company officers. He will report to the court and he may also apply to the court for the public examination of officers in open court. Such an examination of a director of a company in compulsory liquidation may be ordered irrespective of the nationality of the director and notwithstanding that he is resident abroad (*Re Seagull Manufacturing Co. Ltd* [1993] Ch 345).

A director of a company is not entitled to rely on the privilege against self-incrimination to refuse to answer questions put to him by the liquidator under ss. 235 and 236 of the 1986 Act, but such privilege is available to a fiduciary from whom the principal is seeking information about dealings with trust money under the general law (*Bishopsgate Investment Management Ltd* v *Maxwell* [1993] Ch 1).

Conduct of the liquidation   The official receiver is automatically appointed liquidator on the making of the order (Insolvency Act 1986, s. 136(2)) so that there is from the outset a liquidator in office. The official receiver resumes the office of liquidator if it later falls vacant.

The liquidator has 12 weeks in which to decide whether to convene meetings of creditors and contributories with a view to appointing someone else. If meetings are held, each meeting may nominate a liquidator but the nominee of the creditors automatically takes office, subject to a right of objection to the court, given to all creditors and contributories, to be exercised, if at all, within seven days. The same meetings, or subsequent meetings, may resolve to establish a liquidation committee, including representatives of creditors and of contributories, to work with the liquidator, who may obtain the sanction which he needs from a liquidation committee for the exercise of those of his statutory powers for which sanction is required. If there is no liquidation committee its functions are vested in the DTI.

As the liquidation progresses, the liquidator calls meetings as necessary, and in the end he will call a final meeting of creditors and of contributories.

Effect of the winding-up order   The winding-up is deemed to have begun at the time of presenting the petition (or the commencement of voluntary liquidation if that preceded compulsory liquidation) and the official receiver becomes the liquidator.

A standstill is imposed on the company's transactions with retrospective effect to the commencement of the winding up as follows:

(a)   any disposition of property of the company is void unless sanctioned by the court;

(b)   any transfer of shares or alteration of status of members is similarly void;

(c)   any attachment etc. of assets of the company is void;

(d)   no legal proceedings against the company may be commenced or continued except by leave of the court;

(e)   the employees of the company are dismissed but the liquidator may by mutual agreement retain them in the service of the company;

(f)   the management of the company and the control of its business and property is in the hands of the liquidator, who has wide statutory powers, and may apply to the court for an order vesting assets in him;

(g)   charges on company property may become void.

Voluntary winding up

Type of resolution required   A voluntary winding up is commenced by passing a resolution in general meeting. The type of resolution required varies according to the circumstances:

(a) If the articles fix the period of duration of the company or provide that upon the happening of an event it shall be dissolved and the period has expired or the event has occurred, it suffices to pass an ordinary resolution, referring to the articles, and resolving that the company be wound up accordingly. In practice articles rarely include any such automatic winding up provisions.

(b) The company may resolve to wind up by special resolution (which states no reasons). This is the normal method of winding up a solvent company.

(c) The company may by extraordinary resolution resolve that by reason of its liabilities the company is unable to continue its business and that it is advisable to wind up.

Any such resolution must be advertised in the *London Gazette* within 14 days of the meeting. A copy of it must also be delivered to the Registrar within 14 days.

Members' voluntary winding up Any voluntary winding up is a creditors' voluntary winding up unless the directors have made and delivered to the Registrar a declaration of solvency. It is not a question of whether the company is solvent, which may be uncertain when it goes into liquidation. It must be assumed to be insolvent unless the directors accept personal responsibility for stating that they believe the company is solvent.

The declaration, if made, is on a form which incorporates a statement of estimated assets and liabilities up to the latest practicable date. The directors must state that after making full inquiry they are of the opinion that the company will be able to pay its debts in full within a specified period, which may not exceed 12 months. If in the event the company is unable to pay its debts in full within the 12-month period, the directors are presumed to have made their declaration without having reasonable grounds for it, which is a criminal offence. The burden of showing that they did have reasonable grounds, as a defence, rests on them.

The creditors have no part in the liquidation because it is expected that they will be paid in full and they have no right to interfere with the company's conduct of its affairs.

If in the course of the liquidation the liquidator concludes that the company will after all be unable to pay its debts in full within the specified period he must call a meeting of creditors which is advertised in the *London Gazette* and in two local newspapers. The creditors may, before the meeting, demand information about the company's affairs. At the meeting, the liquidator will lay before the creditors a statement of affairs. Thereafter the liquidation proceeds as a creditors' voluntary winding up, as if the declaration of solvency had not been made.

At the end of each year of the liquidation, and within three months of the anniversary date, the liquidator is required to hold a general meeting of the company and lay before it a statement of his acts and dealings. When the liquidation has been completed the liquidator will call a final meeting, by advertisement in the *London Gazette*. He is required to lay before the meeting accounts of his dealings with the company's property. Within the week after the meeting the liquidator must send to the registrar a copy of his accounts and a return that the meeting has been held (or if there was no meeting due to lack of a quorum, a return that it was duly summoned). This leads on to the dissolution of the company.

Creditors' voluntary winding-up   There is no declaration of solvency and consequently the company is required to call a meeting of its creditors not later than the fourteenth day after it holds its own meeting to resolve to wind up. The meeting of creditors is called on seven days' notice and this is advertised in the *London Gazette*. The notice must either give the name and address of an insolvency practitioner from whom creditors may obtain information in advance or it must specify a place where, in the final two business days before the meeting, any creditor may obtain a list of all the creditors. No charge is to be made for these services.

At the creditors' meeting one of the directors will preside and lay before the meeting a statement of the company's financial affairs.

The members and the creditors at their respective meetings may nominate an insolvency practitioner to be appointed liquidator. If different persons are nominated, the creditors' nominee takes office, subject to a right of appeal to the court, given to directors, members and creditors, to be exercised within seven days.

As there may be an interval between the meeting of members and the meeting of creditors, any liquidator appointed by the members will take office until, if ever, a different person is appointed by the creditors. However, a liquidator appointed by the members has no power to dispose of the company's assets, except those which are perishable etc. and such as the court may sanction, until the meeting of creditors is held. Then if the creditors do not appoint a different liquidator the members' nominee has the usual powers conferred on a liquidator.

The creditors may resolve at their meeting to establish a liquidation committee with up to five representatives of each of the creditors and members. The function of such a committee, if established, is to work with the liquidator who may seek its sanction for the exercise of his statutory powers.

Effect of going into voluntary liquidation   The decision to go into liquidation is effective from the day on which the resolution is passed in general meeting. The directors remain in office but their powers cease except in so far as they may be authorised by the competent authority to continue.

The company's property must be applied in payment of its debts and any surplus may then be distributed to its members. The company, through the liquidator, may carry on its business but only for purposes of the beneficial winding up of the company, i.e., ultimate sale or closure. No transfer of shares or alteration of members' status may be made unless the liquidator sanctions it. There is no automatic restraint on legal action against the company or its property. However, the liquidator may apply to the court for an order to halt any action of that kind by a creditor.

Assets and liabilities in a compulsory or voluntary liquidation

The liquidator's duty is to convert the company's assets into money and apply it in payment of the company's debts before distributing what, if anything, remains to the shareholders. In the course of this programme the liquidator may take action to set aside recent company transactions or to recover contributions or compensation from company officers.

In the distribution of surplus assets to shareholders, the liquidator must conform to their respective rights. In principle they all participate equally, but if the company has issued preference shares, the holders of those shares usually (a) have a priority entitlement to repayment of capital but (b) have no right to participate in distribution of any surplus assets remaining after the repayment of capital on ordinary shares. If there are arrears of unpaid preference dividends, they lapse unless it is expressly provided that they shall be paid off (as capital) in liquidation.

In dealing with the assets the liquidator may have to take action against creditors or to disclaim burdensome assets which entail more outlay than they are worth.

Apart from considering the order of priority of debts of different kinds the liquidator must ensure that only legally enforceable claims are recognised. If, for example, a debt is statute-barred, he must refuse to pay it (*Re Art Reproduction Co. Ltd* [1952] Ch 89). It is the liquidator's duty to satisfy himself that a creditor has a valid claim and that the amount demanded is correct. There is a formal procedure for 'proof of debts' in compulsory liquidation. However, the liquidator would as a matter of course write to every creditor of whom there is a record in the books and invite him to give notice of the amount due to him, with supporting papers.

The liquidator has statutory power to pay any class of creditors in full and also to negotiate a compromise or arrangement, e.g., with debenture holders. However, these are powers which he may only exercise with the prescribed sanction, e.g., of the liquidation committee.

After dealing with any other problems the liquidator should follow the proper order of application of assets according to the priority of the company's debts. If he fails to pay a creditor out of assets available, in accordance with the proper order, the creditor may sue the liquidator (*Pulsford* v *Devenish* [1903] 2 Ch 625).

Assets in the hands of creditors A creditor who has obtained judgment against the company for a debt which the company still does not pay may then issue execution to attach property of the company. However, unless he has completed this process before the liquidation commences, he must hand back to the liquidator the property which he has attached. Execution is completed by seizure and sale of the attached property, or the appointment of a receiver or obtaining a charging order under the Charging Orders Act 1979. The method varies according to the type of property which is affected.

Although a voluntary liquidation commences on the passing of the resolution to wind up, a creditor who has notice that a meeting has been called for this purpose is affected by that notice as if it were the commencement of the liquidation.

In the course of the execution the sheriff (a county court officer) may have seized goods of the company with a view to sale. If before he has sold them, the sheriff has notice of an order for compulsory liquidation or of the passing of a resolution for winding up, he must return the goods to the liquidator. Moreover, if the judgment debt exceeds £500, he must after sale retain the proceeds (less expenses) for 14 days and account for the money to the liquidator, if within that period he has notice of an order for compulsory liquidation or of the issue of a notice to convene a meeting to wind up voluntarily.

If, however, the company pays its debt to the sheriff, after he has seized its goods, to avoid sale of the goods, this is not money paid in the course of execution and the creditor is entitled to retain it (*Re Walkden Sheet Metal Co. Ltd* [1960] Ch 170).

In a compulsory liquidation execution or distress by a creditor or landlord after the presentation of the petition is void. In voluntary liquidation the liquidator may apply to the court for an order to avoid execution or distress effected after the passing of the resolution to wind up. The order would be made unless the company had deceived the creditor in order to delay his action against its goods.

Disclaimer of assets The liquidator has a statutory power to disclaim 'onerous property' of the company. He is no longer required to obtain leave of the court for a disclaimer. Onerous property is defined to include unprofitable contracts and other property which it would be difficult to sell (Insolvency Act 1986, s. 178(3)).

The effect of the disclaimer is that the company's entire interest in the property ceases, but any person who thereby suffers a loss becomes a creditor of the company for the amount of his loss.

A liquidator may disclaim property although he has taken possession, exercised rights of ownership over it or tried to sell it. However, the other party who would be affected by a disclaimer may bring the liquidator to an immediate decision by serving a notice, requiring the liquidator to state whether or not he intends to disclaim. Unless he then within 28 days gives notice of disclaimer, he loses the right to do so.

Secured creditors A secured creditor has a dual relationship with the company. Like any other creditor he may claim from the company as its debtor payment of the amount due to him. In addition he is in the position of, or analogous to, a mortgagee with a limited interest in the property of the company over which he has security. He may enforce those proprietary rights, usually by appointing a receiver.

However, against a company in liquidation the secured creditor must opt for one remedy or the other. If he elects to prove his debt by notice to the liquidator, he is deemed to have surrendered his security. However, he is more likely to enforce the security and recover the debt by that means without making a claim against the liquidator. If the property which is the security has a realisable value which is less than the secured debt then the creditor may sell the property charged to him and claim as an unsecured creditor for the amount by which the proceeds of realisation fall short of the debt. If the creditor merely values his security, i.e., puts an estimated value on it, and claims the balance as an unsecured debt, the liquidator may redeem it at that value or have it sold.

If the security yields a surplus over the debt and expenses, the creditor accounts for the surplus to the liquidator.

Preferential unsecured debts It is often convenient to refer to 'preferential creditors' but strictly it is only the debt which can be preferential. It may happen, for example, that part of the same debt is preferential and the rest is not.

The categories of preferential debts were reduced by the insolvency legislation. The categories of preferential debts are defined in sch. 6 to the Insolvency Act 1986 as:

(a) income tax deducted or which should have been deducted by the company from the taxable pay of employees of the company under the PAYE system during the 12 months prior to the relevant date and not yet paid over to the Inland Revenue;

(b)   value added tax owed by the company in respect of the period of six months up to that date;

(c)   salaries or wages of company employees in respect of the period of four months ended on that date, subject to a maximum of £800 for each employee;

(d)   holiday pay and employer's contributions to occupational pension schemes.

In addition some other unpaid taxes such as car tax, taxes on gaming and betting, and social security contributions in respect of the 12 months before the relevant date are preferential.

Employees' pay is often the largest item amongst the list of preferential debts to be met. Loans to pay wages are preferential debts to the extent that the loan money, often lent by a bank, has been used to pay wages etc. which if unpaid would have been preferential. Alternatively, the Department of Employment has statutory power, within certain limits, to pay the wages of employees (otherwise unpaid) of an insolvent employer. If it does so, it becomes a creditor of the company for the amount it has paid out, and has the same preferential claims as the employees would have had.

Where a bank has provided a loan, it is a question of fact whether the money was used to pay wages which would otherwise be preferential debts. The banks usually insist that money advanced for this purpose shall be paid from a separate wages account. However, where a company borrowed from a bank through its main account and made transfers from that account to a specially designated wages account, which was not overdrawn at the commencement of liquidation, the bank was treated as a preferential creditor (through the overdraft on the main company account) of money paid out by the company in wages (*Re James R. Rutherford and Sons Ltd* [1964] 1 WLR 1211).

A director of a company is not as such an employee, so that his fees due under the articles cannot be a preferential debt. However, if he is also a working director, his arrears of unpaid salary as a manager are preferential within the usual limits indicated above.

Priority of preferential debts   A liquidator (and also a receiver or an administrator) is required to pay preferential debts, rateably between all debts in that category, in priority to debts secured by a floating charge on the company's assets and unsecured non-preferential debts.

If a secured creditor has more than one debt owing to him by the company, and covered by his security, and some are preferential and others are not, he is not required on realising his security to apply the money evenly in part payment of all the debts. Instead he may, since it improves his position, apply the money first to repayment of his non-preferential debts, so that he preserves the maximum entitlement as a creditor for preferential debts (*Re William Hall (Contractors) Ltd* [1967] 1 WLR 948).

Ordinary and deferred debts   After the preferential debts have been paid in full, the non-preferential, ordinary unsecured debts come next to be paid. These are usually sums owed to trade creditors for goods or services supplied to the company.

A secured creditor whose security has proved to be insufficient to discharge his debt in full and a creditor for a preferential debt in excess of the limits may claim the balance as an ordinary debt.

Voluntary payments to employees   As the word 'voluntary' indicates these are not debts at all, but it is convenient to deal with them here since they are payments which the liquidator may be authorised and bound to make, after payment of all debts, before distributing what remains to shareholders.

These are payments to employees of the company who have been made redundant by reason of the closure or sale of the company's business. A company has statutory power (Companies Act 1985, s. 719) to make such gifts subject to compliance with the proper internal procedure for authorisation. Before making any such payments the liquidator must ensure that he has paid all debts of the company and that he has authority to pay the employees.

Order of application of assets   Secured creditors normally recover their debts from the realisation of their security. Only if there is a surplus resulting from the security will any part of its value go to the fund from which unsecured creditors are paid. To that extent the secured creditors have an automatic priority over unsecured creditors, except that preferential unsecured debts are paid out of property subject to a floating charge.

The order of application of assets in the hands of the liquidator is:

(a)   *liquidation expenses*, including the cost of selling, preserving, collecting in assets etc., the liquidator's remuneration and the incidental expenses of the liquidation, such as the costs of a petition for compulsory liquidation if the court awards costs to the petitioner;

(b)   *preferential unsecured debts*, and the balance remaining is then used to pay the debt owing to the holder of a floating charge;

(c)   *ordinary unsecured debts*, including the claims of secured and preferential creditors for deficiencies remaining after they have taken their priority entitlement higher up the scale;

(d)   *deferred debts*;

(e)   *repayment of members' capital*, i.e., first, capital paid up on their shares and then any surplus remaining to members according to their entitlement (usually it goes to the ordinary shareholders alone).

Voidable transactions and compensation

Avoidance of floating charges   The basic rule is that the commencement of liquidation or the making of an administration order will automatically render void a floating charge on the company's property if created within the previous 12 months (Insolvency Act 1986, s. 245). However, unless the charge was created in favour of a person connected with the company, the charge is not void if the company was solvent at the time of creation of the charge. If the charge was created in favour of a connected person, the solvency of the company at the time is immaterial and the period over which s. 245 has retrospective effect is extended from 12 months to two years.

A charge is valid in so far as it is security for consideration given at the time or after the creation of the charge. The charge is therefore void only to the extent that it is to secure liabilities which existed before the charge was created. The subsequent consideration, for which the charge would be valid, may be money, goods or services supplied to the company or a reduction of its indebtedness, plus interest at the agreed rate (if any) on that consideration.

The term 'connected person' is elaborately defined by the insolvency legislation (ss. 249 and 435). In a typical, but by no means the only, case a connected person is a director or a shareholder who has control (alone or jointly with others).

The period of 12 months, or two years, prior to the petition for an administration order is also extended forward to cover the period between the petition and the making of the order, so that a charge created after the petition has been presented becomes void if an administration order is later made on it.

Although there are differences of detail, s. 245 is a reformulation of provisions found in the Companies Act 1986, s. 617, and some of the earlier cases continue to afford guidance. A loan to the company made after it had created a floating charge, but for the purpose of enabling the company to repay an existing loan from the same lender obtained before the charge, is a transparent evasion of the requirement that, to be valid, the loan must follow the charge and so the charge is not a valid security for the second (or the first) loan (*Re Destone Fabrics Ltd* [1941] Ch 319). In *Power* v *Sharp Investments Ltd* [1993] BCC 609 the words 'at the same time as, or after, the creation of the charge' in s. 245 were clearly included for the purpose of excluding from the exemption of moneys paid to the company before the creation of the charge, even though they were paid in consideration for the charge. The court also said that where no charge had been created by an agreement or the company passing a resolution prior to the execution of the debenture then any money paid before the execution of the debenture would not qualify under the subsection, unless the interval between the payment and execution was so short that it could be regarded as minimal and execution regarded as contemporaneous. The court refused to follow *Re Columbian Fireproofing Co. Ltd* [1910] 2 Ch 120 and *Re F. & E. Stanton Ltd* [1929] 1 Ch 180.

The banks rely on the decision in *Re Yeovil Glove Co. Ltd* [1965] Ch 148 in taking a floating charge as security for a current or running account. In the *Yeovil Glove* case the essential facts were that the company had a bank overdraft at the time when the charge was created and an overdraft of approximately the same amount at the commencement of liquidation. However, in the interval credits to the account exceeded the amount of the overdraft at the time of the charge. It was held that these credits (under the rule in *Devaynes* v *Noble, Clayton's Case* (1816) 1 Mer 572) should be treated as repayment of the earlier debt, and the subsequent drawings on the account were new loans subsequent to the charge, which was therefore a valid security for the overdraft resulting from them.

Voidable preferences The current rules on voidable preferences (Insolvency Act 1986, s. 239) are a revised version of the earlier law (Companies Act 1985, s. 615) on what was then called 'fraudulent preference'. The basic rule is that the court, on the application of a liquidator or administrator of a company, may make an order to set aside a preference given by a company to one of its creditors, or to a guarantor of its debts, at a time when the company was already (or became by reason of the preference) unable to pay its debts.

A preference is anything by which the person who benefits from it is placed in a better position, if the company went into insolvent liquidation, than he would otherwise have been. An obvious case is where the company reduces its bank overdraft, by suspending drawings to make payment of its debts to trade creditors, in order to reduce the liability of one of its directors as guarantor of the overdraft (*Re M. Kushler Ltd* [1943] Ch 248). However, new credit advanced to the company in exchange for security or terms which put the creditor in a better position than the other creditors does not amount to a preference to the extent that it is represented by new value provided by him. It is the putting in a better position of an existing creditor for existing debts that can amount to a preference.

In addition to demonstrating the advantage which the preference yields, it must be shown either that the person preferred was a 'connected person' or that in giving the preference the company was 'influenced . . . by a desire to produce' such a preference, i.e., it must be intentional. This is in accord with case law on the previous statutory provision (on 'fraudulent preference'), where the act was valid if it appeared that it was done for good commercial reasons and not in order to grant preference (*Re Paraguassu Steam Tramway Co., Adamson's Case* (1874) LR 18 Eq 670; see also *Re Beacon Leisure Ltd* [1992] BCLC 565).

If the person preferred is a connected person, he may still be able to resist an order to reverse the preference shown to him if he is a connected person solely by reason of being an employee of the company, or if he can show, i.e., the burden of proof is on him, that the company was not 'influenced by a desire' to prefer him.

The statutory formula (in s. 239) 'influenced by desire' is new and the test was applied in *Re DKG Contractors Ltd* [1990] BCC 903.

The other major limitation is that the preference must have occurred within 'the relevant time' (see, e.g., *Re DKG Contractors Ltd*). The standard period is six months before the commencement of liquidation or the date of the petition for an administration order (plus the subsequent interval between petition and making the order). But the period is two years if the person preferred is connected with the company, otherwise than merely as an employee.

If s. 239 is complied with and a fraudulent preference found to have occurred, the court is required to make whatever order it thinks fit to restore the position to what it would have been if there had been no preference.

Transactions at an undervalue   The court has a similar power under s. 238 of the Insolvency Act 1985 to make an order to neutralise a transaction at an undervalue into which the company entered at a time when it was unable to pay its debts. The application to the court may only be made by a liquidator or an administrator and certain limiting conditions restrict the court's powers.

A transaction is at an undervalue if it is an outright gift or is for significantly less in consideration received by the company than the value of the consideration which it gave. However, such a transaction may not be set aside if the company entered into it in good faith and for the purpose of carrying on its business (*Re Welfab Engineers* [1990] BCLC 833) and there were at the time reasonable grounds for believing that it would benefit the company.

The effect of these requirements is substantially to confine the scope of the avoidance power to artificial transactions. These criteria have something in common with those which are applied in determining what powers, if not expressed in the objects clause, may be implied.

A transaction at an undervalue may only be set aside under s. 238 if it occurred within the period of two years before the commencement of liquidation or of the petition for an administration order (with an extension forward to take in the interval between the petition and the making of the order). While s. 238 has unrestricted extraterritorial effect and allows service of process on a foreign bank not carrying on business in England, the court has an overall discretion not to make an order under the section, in particular if it is not satisfied that the foreign defendant is sufficiently connected with England for it to be just and proper to grant the relief sought (*Re Paramount Airways Ltd* [1993] Ch 223).

Fraudulent trading   If in the course of the liquidation of a company it appears to the court that its business has been carried on with intent to defraud its creditors or the creditors of any other person, or for a fraudulent purpose, the court may on the application of the liquidator declare that any persons who were knowingly parties to carrying on the business in this way shall make such contribution to the company's assets as the court may determine (Insolvency Act 1986, s. 213). Liability may be imposed on any person and in *Re White and Osmond (Parkstone) Ltd* (ChD 30 June 1960 unreported) the court took the view that a director who continued trading during difficult times in the hope that 'there was light at the end of the tunnel' could not be made liable under s. 213. This approach was disapproved in *R* v *Grantham* [1984] QB 675 where it was said that directors may be exposed to liability for fraudulent trading simply because they continued trading where the company could not pay its debts as and when they fell due or shortly thereafter. A single transaction will suffice to impose liability, although it is more likely that a series of transactions will together indicate fraud.

Only the liquidator can seek this remedy. It is no longer possible for a creditor to ask for an order for payment to be made to him, as occurred in *Re Cyona Distributors Ltd* [1967] Ch 889. Further, the court has a discretion as to the amount of the contribution which it may order. It is not a question of ordering payment of specific debts (see, e.g., *Re A Company (No. 001418 of 1988)* [1991] BCLC 197, where it was decided that the amount ordered to be paid would include a punitive element).

Fraudulent trading is also a criminal offence, which may be charged whether or not the company has gone into liquidation (Companies Act 1985, s. 458).

The Cork Committee (*Insolvency Law and Practice* (Cmnd 8558, 1982)) discussed this subject at length. The normal grounds for invoking the sanctions against fraudulent trading are that the directors have failed to take proper steps to avoid or to minimise the consequences of impending insolvency. Usually they have permitted the company to continue to trade at a time when there was no prospect that the company would be able to pay the debts incurred in the course of this trading.

A single transaction can constitute carrying on the business (*Re Gerald Cooper Chemicals Ltd* [1978] Ch 262). Payment of some debts but not all may also amount to carrying on business (*Re Sarflax Ltd* [1979] Ch 592). Section 458 of the Companies Act 1985 is designed to include those who exercise a managerial function or are 'running the business' (*R* v *Miles* [1992] Crim LR 657).

However, proceedings against directors under what is now s. 213 of the Insolvency Act 1986 have rarely been successful because it is necessary to prove fraud on their part. As fraudulent trading is also a criminal offence, the standard of proof required, even in civil actions, is demanding. Yet it is rarely possible to prove actual dishonest intent. It was once held that this intent would be inferred from the directors' decision to incur debts without any reasonable prospect that the company would be able to pay them (*Re William C. Leitch Brothers Ltd* [1932] 2 Ch 71). However, the same judge in another case said that it was necessary to show 'real dishonesty . . . involving moral blame' (*Re Patrick and Lyon Ltd* [1933] Ch 786). Evidence of that is not easy to get.

The Cork Committee therefore recommended a new basis of civil liability, i.e., liability for wrongful trading, which should impose an objective test. However, the possibility of both civil and criminal liability being imposed may serve as a deterrent for extreme cases.

Wrongful trading The Cork Committee's proposal for civil (only) liability for wrongful trading, with a less demanding standard of proof, has been adopted (Insolvency Act 1986, s. 214). But the basis of liability is defined in a different manner from that proposed by the Cork Committee. In framing what is now s. 214 the DTI decided that a wider test was desirable. The Cork formula would not, for example, apply to directors who did not let the company incur additional unpaid debts but who failed to take action, e.g., to sell off assets or retrench expenditure, which was a necessary remedial measure to avoid the likelihood of insolvency.

The substantive content of s. 214 has been heavily criticised both in Parliamentary debate and among bodies representative of business managers and the professions. It provides that liability for wrongful trading will be imposed if the following conditions are satisfied, namely:

(a)   the person to be made liable must be or have been a director of a company which has gone into insolvent liquidation (*Re DKG Contractors Ltd* [1990] BCC 903); and

(b)   at some time before the commencement of liquidation, he actually knew or 'ought to have concluded' that there was no reasonable prospect that the company would avoid going into insolvent liquidation (*Re Purpoint Ltd* [1991] BCLC 491); and

(c)   on reaching stage (b) he did not in the court's view take 'every step' which he ought to have taken 'with a view to minimising the potential loss to the company's creditors'. That he did take such steps is the defence open to him in any proceedings against him under s. 214.

In considering the conduct of a defendant director, he is to be judged by the standard of 'general knowledge, skill and experience' which might reasonably be expected of (a) any person in his position; and (b) of this individual in particular. The latter point means that the director's personal qualifications and experience, e.g., as an accountant, are to be taken into consideration as well as more general criteria, in deciding whether he acted correctly (*Norman v Theodore Goddard* [1991] BCLC 1028 (director absolved as he had taken expert professional advice).

Much of the argument about this involved formula relates to the words 'ought to have concluded'. The critics object that it tests the actual performance of an individual by reference to matters of which he may have been ignorant. The DTI argued that it imposed on directors, at all times, a duty to keep themselves informed of the financial position of the company, e.g., by insisting that management accounts of some sort should be laid before each board meeting.

The other main criticism is of the words 'every step' which are deliberately very vague. The Cork Committee's recommendation, relating to debts which might not be paid, is more precise and on that account less comprehensive.

A particular criticism is that these wide and uncertain provisions may make it difficult for major creditors of companies, such as banks, to arrange with a company that some experienced 'company doctor' shall join the board to improve its financial expertise in time of need.

In *Re Purpoint Ltd* [1991] BCC 121 Vinelott J explained that the purpose of a court order under s. 214 is to recoup the loss to the company so as to benefit the creditors as a whole. The court has no jurisdiction to direct payment to creditors or to direct that money paid to the company should be applied in payment of one class of creditors in preference to another.

Directors who seek to justify themselves must relate their defence to s. 214. Their defence will not succeed merely on the general grounds that they claim to have acted reasonably and ought fairly to be excused (*Re Produce Marketing Consortium Ltd* [1989] 1 WLR 745; see also *Re DKG Contractors Ltd* [1990] BCC 903).

Other bases of liability 'Misfeasance' proceedings may be brought under s. 212 of the Insolvency Act 1986. This section permits the liquidator, or a creditor, of a company in liquidation to apply to the court to examine the conduct of any officer of the company on the grounds that he has misapplied company property or been guilty of breach of fiduciary or other duty in relation to the company. If the court sees fit it may order the delinquent officer to return company property or to pay compensation. The proceedings are civil not criminal.

Misfeasance is a flexible, though rather uncertain, means of bringing to account officers of a company, notably its directors, if they have misused their position or failed seriously in their duties.

In addition there is a long list of specific offences for which officers of companies may be brought to account in the course of liquidation. There are also more general sanctions against dishonesty under general criminal law. Lastly, the DTI has power to appoint inspectors to conduct investigations, the official receiver may apply to the court for public examination of company officers and there is the elaborate system of review of the conduct of directors of companies with a view to their disqualification on various grounds which include participation in wrongful trading (Company Directors Disqualification Act 1985, s. 10).

INSOLVENT INDIVIDUALS

The provisions of the Insolvency Act 1986 relating to insolvent individuals apply to England and Wales. The law on personal insolvency in Scotland has been amended under separate legislation. The Insolvency Act 1986 makes provision for personal insolvency to be dealt with in different ways, namely:

(a) bankruptcy, and
(b) voluntary arrangements.

An individual who enters into a voluntary arrangement or becomes bankrupt is called a debtor.

Voluntary arrangements

The voluntary arrangement for individuals is similar to that for companies. Both the Cork Committee (Insolvency Law and Practice, Cmnd 8558, 1982) and the White Paper, A revised framework for Insolvency law (Cmnd 9175) stressed the need for a type of voluntary arrangement which could be used by individual debtors who wanted to come to terms with their creditors with the minimum of formality.

A debtor may make a proposal whether or not he is an undischarged bankrupt. In the case of an undischarged bankrupt, either he or the trustee of his estate or the official receiver may make an application. The debtor is responsible for preparing the proposal. A 'nominee' must be appointed to act as a trustee or otherwise to supervise the implementation of the arrangement. The proposals are those of the debtor and not the intended nominee. Care should be taken with the compilation of the proposal because it is an offence if the debtor 'makes any false representation or commits any other fraud for the purpose of obtaining the approval of his creditors to a proposal for a voluntary arrangement' (Insolvency Rules 1986 (SI 1986/1925), r. 5.30). For the sake of convenience a proposal approved by the court should:

(a)   cover after-acquired property;

(b)   give a charge over the assets to secure the arrangement;

(c)   give to the interested supervisor all the powers of a trustee in bankruptcy;

(d)   provide for the appointment of a creditors' committee from whom consent on behalf of all the creditors may be obtained;

(e)   include power to vary the arrangements without having to return to the court;

(f)   include power to apply for a bankruptcy order against the debtor if he fails to cooperate in the arrangement.

An application may be made to the court for an interim order which prevents or stays any bankruptcy proceedings against the debtor. Where the debtor is already an undischarged bankrupt, the application must be made to the court in which the bankruptcy proceedings are being conducted. Where the debtor is not a bankrupt, the application must be filed in the court in which the proposer could present his own petition.

The court will make an interim order where it will assist the consideration and implementation of the debtor's proposals. The purpose of an interim order is to protect the debtor's property or, in the case of an undischarged bankrupt, to provide for the conduct of the bankruptcy pending consideration of the proposals. The court, however, may make an interim order only if it is satisfied that the debtor intends to make a proposal and that on the day of making the application, he was an undischarged bankrupt or was in a position to be able to petition for his own bankruptcy. The debtor must not have made a previous application for an interim order during the 12 months ending with the day of the present application.

The effect of an interim order is that, while in force, no bankruptcy petition relating to the debtor may be presented or proceeded with and no other proceedings or execution may be commenced or continued without the leave of the court.

While the interim order is in force, the debtor must provide the nominee both with a statement of the terms of the proposed composition or scheme and a statement of his affairs containing details about his creditors, debts, liabilities and assets. If the debtor fails to comply with these requirements, the court may discharge the interim order. The information supplied will enable the nominee to prepare and submit his own report to the court stating whether, in his opinion, a meeting of the debtor's creditors should be summoned to consider the debtor's proposals. If for any reason, on an application by the nominee, the court is satisfied that it would be inappropriate to summon a meeting of the creditors, the court may discharge the interim order.

If the report recommends that a meeting of the creditors should be called, the person submitting the report will summon all the creditors of whose claims he is aware to a meeting. The creditors of the undischarged bankrupt include all those who are creditors in respect of bankruptcy debts and all those who would be such creditors if the bankruptcy had commenced on the day on which notice of the meeting is given. The meeting may approve the proposed composition or scheme, or may approve it with modifications assented to by the debtor. The meeting cannot approve any proposal or modification that affects the rights of any secured or preferential creditors to enforce their security or receive payment in priority to ordinary creditors unless they consent to this being done. The result of the meeting must be reported to the court.

Where the meeting approves a proposed composition or scheme, the approved scheme or composition will take effect as if made by the debtor at the meeting. Every person who had notice of, and was entitled to vote at, the meeting (whether or not he actually did so) is bound by the composition or scheme as if he were a party to the scheme. If the debtor is an undischarged bankrupt the court may either annul the bankruptcy order by which the debtor was adjudged bankrupt or give such directions as to the conduct of the bankruptcy and the administration of the bankrupt's estate as the court thinks appropriate to facilitate the implementation of the approved scheme.

Bankruptcy proceedings

The old concept of the acts of bankruptcy has been abolished and replaced by the simple notion that the petitioner must allege that the debtor appears either to be unable to pay or to have no reasonable prospect of paying the debt or debts specified in the petition. The inability to pay debts can be shown only by proving either that a statutory demand served on the debtor to pay, secure or compound for the debt to the petitioner's satisfaction has not been complied with within three weeks, or that enforcement proceedings on a judgment debt to the petitioner have been returned wholly or partly unsatisfied. A number of conditions must be satisfied if a petition is to be validly presented, namely:

    (a) the debtor must be domiciled or personally present in England or Wales when the petition is presented;

(b)   the debt or debts must amount to at least £750 (the bankruptcy level) and must be for a liquidated sum payable immediately;

(c)   the debt must be unsecured. A secured debtor can petition provided that he agrees to relinquish his security or he can value his security and petition on the unsecured balance (Insolvency Act 1986, s. 267(1), (2) and (4)).

A bankruptcy petition can be brought by a supervisor of a voluntary scheme or a person bound by such a scheme. The only ground for a petition by the debtor himself is that the debtor is unable to pay his debts and the petition must be accompanied by a statement of affairs giving details of the debtor's creditors, his debts, liabilities and assets. Such a petition cannot be withdrawn without the leave of the court. Whilst generally the court will make the bankruptcy order sought it must not do so where it finds:

(a)   that the unsecured debts are below a specified amount for small bankruptcies;

(b)   the value of the assets is at least of a 'minimum amount';

(c)   that during the five years before the presentation of the petition the debtor has not been adjudicated bankrupt or made a scheme or composition with his creditors; and

(d)   that it would be appropriate to obtain a report.

Where the court refuses to make a bankruptcy order it will appoint a qualified insolvency practitioner to inquire into the debtor's affairs and report on the debtor's willingness to propose a voluntary scheme of arrangement and/or whether the creditors should be summoned to consider such proposals.

Consequences of the presentation of a bankruptcy petition

Where a bankruptcy petition has been presented against a debtor who is then adjudged bankrupt, any disposition of property or payment of money made after the petition was presented is void unless the court approves the transaction either before or after it took place. In the absence of the court's approval the person to whom the property is transferred holds it as part of the debtor's estate. However, the Insolvency Act 1986 gives limited protection to a person who deals with the debtor during the period between the presentation of the petition and the making of the bankruptcy order if he acts in good faith, for value and without notice of the presentation of the petition.

When a bankruptcy petition is presented to the court, it may appoint an interim receiver for the protection of the debtor's estate. The official receiver will be the interim receiver except where the petition was presented by the debtor himself and a qualified insolvency practitioner has been appointed to report on the debtor's affairs. An interim receiver has such powers as the court decides to allow him and in the absence of any restrictions imposed by the court he will have all the powers available given to the official receiver when acting as receiver after the bankruptcy order has been made. These powers include the power to sell perishable goods, power to sell goods which are likely to diminish in value if not sold and power to take such steps as are necessary to protect the estate.

Effect of the bankruptcy order on the bankrupt

The effect of a bankruptcy order is that the debtor is an undischarged bankrupt and he is deprived of the ownership of his assets which vest in the trustee in bankruptcy. The bankrupt must give up possession of his estate, hand over all the books, papers and records in his possession which relate to his estate or affairs and he must undertake any steps which may reasonably be required to protect his estate or such assets as may be recovered. The bankrupt must make an inventory of his estate, and give such information as may reasonably be required by the Official Receiver.

Proceedings following a bankruptcy order

The official receiver has all the powers of a receiver and manager appointed by the High Court. Although he can take steps to protect the bankrupt's property, he must not incur expenditure without obtaining permission from the Secretary of State. However, when expenditure is incurred in selling assets of the bankrupt he has a lien in respect of expenses incurred.

At any time after the making of the bankruptcy order and before the bankrupt's discharge the official receiver can apply to the court for a public examination of the bankrupt.

Trustee in bankruptcy

The administration of a bankrupt's estate will be carried out by a trustee in bankruptcy. The functions, powers and duties of the trustee are contained in the Insolvency Act 1986. The trustee in bankruptcy must realise and distribute the bankrupt's estate.

Avoidance of dispositions after presentation of a petition

Any disposition by the bankrupt (including a payment of money), unless with the prior or subsequent consent of the court, is void if it is made between the date of presentation of the petition and the date when the bankrupt's estate vests in the trustee in bankruptcy. A person who takes property or money before the date of the bankruptcy order in good faith, for value and without notice of the presentation of a petition is protected against having the transaction set aside. Recipients who take from the bankrupt after the bankruptcy order are given no such protection and will have to obtain the sanction of the court. The validity of all dispositions and payments by the bankrupt between the presentation of the petition and the date of vesting is a discretionary matter for the court.

The bankrupt's estate vests in the trustee in bankruptcy by virtue of the Act and no conveyance, assignment or transfer is required. The trustee in bankruptcy has power to make the bankrupt execute any documents and comply with such procedures as may be required and if the bankrupt without reasonable excuse does not comply, the bankrupt commits a contempt of court.

Property belonging to the bankrupt which is available for distribution

The bankrupt's estate comprises all property belonging to, or vested in, the bankrupt at the commencement of the bankruptcy. Property is defined by s. 436 to include all 'money, goods, things in action, land and every description of property wherever situated and also obligations and every description of interest, whether present or future or vested or contingent, arising out of, or incidental to, property'.

Personal actions include actions for negligence resulting in personal injury, assault, false imprisonment, malicious prosecution, injury to credit and defamation. Those not personal include contracts to deliver goods, contracts of indemnity, negligence causing injury to property, and contracts of repair. The importance of the distinction is that, in the former case, the right of action does not vest in the trustee, whereas in the latter case rights do vest in the trustee.

The bankrupt's tools, books, vehicles and other items of equipment necessary to the bankrupt for use personally by him in his employment, business or vocation are excluded from the bankrupt's distributable estate. Also excluded are clothing, bedding, furniture, household equipment and such provisions as are necessary for satisfying the domestic needs of the bankrupt and his family. However, if it appears to the trustee in bankruptcy that any such item has a realisable value which exceeds the cost of a reasonable replacement, the trustee in bankruptcy can claim it (with a title which relates back to the commencement of bankruptcy) by serving a written notice on the bankrupt claiming the exempt asset, which then falls into the estate (Insolvency Act 1986, s. 308(1)).

Property not belonging to the bankrupt which is available

Preferences   If a debtor does anything or suffers anything to be done which puts the creditor or a surety or guarantor for any of his debts or other liabilities into a better position than would have been the case if that thing had not been done, then, provided the debtor was influenced by a desire to produce that effect upon the position of the creditor, surety or guarantor, the transaction amounts to a preference if the debtor was insolvent at the time or became insolvent in consequence of the transaction (Insolvency Act 1986, ss. 340 and 341(2)). The length of time during which transactions are vulnerable will vary according to a number of circumstances:

(a)   if the transaction is at an undervalue (i.e., a gift by the debtor or a transfer for no consideration or for a consideration significantly less in value than that provided by the vendor), five years prior to the presentation of the petition;

(b)   if the transaction is not at an undervalue and is entered into with an associate of the debtor, two years before the presentation of the petition;

(c)   where the person preferred is not an associate and the transaction is not at an undervalue, six months prior to the presentation of the petition.

An associate is defined as the bankrupt's spouse or a reputed spouse, and in relation to any of them or the bankrupt, a brother, sister, uncle, aunt, nephew, niece, lineal ancestor or lineal descendant. A company controlled by the bankrupt or any associates is defined as an associate.

In the case of preferences to associates, influence is presumed until disproved. A person is insolvent if he cannot from his own resources meet his debts and liabilities as they fall due taking into account contingent and prospective liabilities.

The phrase 'influenced by a desire' to put the creditor into a better position will undoubtedly cause problems. The trustee must prove not only that the debtor intended to make a preference but also that he or she wanted to improve the creditor's position. A further problem arises with regard to being 'influenced' and the question which has to be answered is: to what extent should the desire to prefer have influenced the debtor? Under the Bankruptcy Act 1914, the debtor had to act with 'a' view of preferring the creditor and in *Re Bird, ex parte Hill* (1883) 23 ChD 695 it was held that 'a' view meant 'the' view and it had to be the dominant or sole view of the debtor. It would be open to the court to take the same approach in connection with preferences under the Insolvency Act 1986, s. 342(4).

The court's power to remedy a preference is wide. The court can (a) require any property transferred to be vested in the trustee in bankruptcy; (b) follow transferred property into the proceeds of sale or follow a payment; (c) release or discharge any security given by the bankrupt; (d) require any person who has received a benefit from the bankrupt to pay such sums as the court may direct; (e) grant new (or revive) obligations upon any surety or guarantor who was released or discharged under the preference; (f) charge property or require security to be provided where any such security or property was released or discharged as a result of the preference; and (g) make any orders for the proof of debt in the bankruptcy by any person in respect of any debts or other liabilities which arose from the preference.

The making of these orders may affect property in the hands of a non-bankrupt party to the preference or even a third party and may impose obligations on them. However, a person who acquires property bona fide for value and without notice of the relevant circumstances will be protected. Further, any person receiving a benefit in good faith for value and without notice of the relevant circumstances will also be protected. However, in both these cases the protected person must not have been a party to the transaction which itself was a preference.

Transactions at an undervalue

If at any time during the five years before the presentation of the petition for a bankruptcy order the bankrupt has, at any time when he was insolvent, entered into a transaction at an undervalue, the court can remedy the matter on an application of the trustee in bankruptcy. A transaction is at an undervalue if:

(a)   it is a gift by the bankrupt; or
(b)   the bankrupt received no consideration; or
(c)   the bankrupt entered into the transaction in consideration of marriage; or
(d)   the bankrupt received consideration which in money or money's worth was significantly less in value than that provided by the bankrupt.

Where the transaction is said to be at an undervalue it may be dealt with by the court under the rules applicable to preferences. Although there is no need to prove dishonesty, the purpose must be a dominant one (*Chohan* v *Saggar* [1992] BCC 306).

Extortionate credit transactions

An undischarged bankrupt and his trustee in bankruptcy are both denied the right to reopen an extortionate credit transaction under the Consumer Credit Act 1974.

However, a trustee in bankruptcy can apply under the Insolvency Act 1986, s. 343, in respect of an extortionate credit transaction, i.e., one in which, having regard to the risk accepted by the credit provider, the terms of the transaction required grossly exorbitant payments for the provision of the credit or otherwise were contrary to the ordinary principles of fair dealing. The Insolvency Act 1986, however, does not contain an equivalent to s. 138(2) to (5) of the Consumer Credit Act 1974, which list the matters relevant to determine whether a bargain is extortionate, e.g., age, business capacity, experience and health of the debtor, degree and nature of financial pressures on the debtor, prevailing interest rates etc.

The transaction in respect of which an application is made is presumed to be extortionate unless the contrary is proved and the burden of proof, therefore, is on the credit provider. The application can only be made in respect of transactions entered into within three years before the date of the bankruptcy order. The court has wide powers similar to those contained in the Consumer Credit Act 1974. Thus, the court can set aside all or any obligations under the agreement, or vary the contract or any security, or order payments of money, or require the surrender of any security or direct accounts to be taken.

Bankruptcy and enforcement procedures

Where, before the commencement of bankruptcy a judgment creditor issues execution against the debtor's goods or land or attaches a debt due to the judgment debtor, the creditor cannot retain 'the benefit of the execution' or any sums paid to avoid it unless it was complete or the sums were paid before bankruptcy commenced. The 'benefit of the execution' means the charge on the bankrupt's property which the enforcement process gives the judgment creditor (*Re Caribbean Products (Yam Importers) Ltd* [1966] Ch 331).

Where the sheriff has taken goods in execution and, before completing the execution, is notified of the making of a bankruptcy order against the judgment debtor, he must, at the request of the trustee in bankruptcy or the official receiver, deliver up the goods, or money seized or recovered in satisfaction of the execution. Any sums paid to avoid seizure and sale are not regarded as in satisfaction of the execution and cannot, therefore, be taken by the trustee. The sheriff's costs are a first charge on the proceeds and the property taken.

The trustee in bankruptcy cannot claim goods from any person who has acquired them bona fide under a sheriff's sale.

19 Mortgage Finance by Building Societies for House Purchase

POWER OF BUILDING SOCIETIES TO LEND ON MORTGAGE

The law of mortgages is fundamental to building societies. For building societies this area of law has both a constitutional and practical significance. First, s. 5(1) of the Building Societies Act 1986 provides that the principal purpose of a building society is that of raising, primarily by subscription of the members, a stock or fund for making to them 'advances secured on land' for residential use. The term 'advances secured on land' is defined in relation to land in England and Wales as meaning advances to members 'secured by . . . a mortgage of a legal estate or . . . an equitable interest in land . . .'. Thus, the concept of mortgage lending is a primary function for every building society and 'advances' must be secured by a 'mortgage'. There is also the fundamental practical point that the requirements for the structure of commercial assets specified in s. 20 of the Act oblige building societies to ensure that the making of such advances accounts for the bulk of their business. This follows from the fact that the advances secured on land make up practically the whole of a building society's holding of class 1 and 2 assets. (Although charges introduced by the Building Societies Act 1997 will give building societies much greater freedom in respect of their trading functions their primary function must still continue to be that of lending for purchase of residential property.)

Advances secured on land

A building society is empowered by the Building Societies Act 1986, s. 10(1), to make 'advances secured on land' to its members. For an advance to qualify as an advance secured on land the following requirements must be satisfied, namely:

  (a) the land on which the advance is secured must be in the UK;
  (b) if the land is in England and Wales or Northern Ireland, the security must consist of a mortgage of (i) a legal estate or (ii) an equitable interest of the type described in s. 10(6); and

(c)   if the land is in Scotland, the security must be a heritable security.

Advances secured on land may be either fully or partly secured by the mortgage, and the land need not be for the residential use of the borrowing member. The latter provision is in contrast with the wording of s. 5 which provides that the making of an advance secured on land will only fall within the purpose or principal purpose of a society if the land is for the residential use of the borrowing member. In this respect the scope of s. 10(1) is wider than the purpose or primary purpose specified in s. 5.

TYPES OF MORTGAGE

Legal mortgages

A legal mortgage of land or of an interest in land must be made by deed. Where the mortgage is of a freehold estate, it must be either a demise for a term of years absolute, with a proviso for cesser or cessation of the term on redemption, or a charge by way of legal mortgage (Law of Property Act 1925, s. 85(1)). If the mortgage is of a leasehold estate, the deed must be either a sub-demise for a specified term of years being less than the term vested in the mortgage or a charge by way of legal mortgage (Law of Property Act 1925, s. 86(1)). The legal charge is the more modern form of deed, and in a majority of cases, the building society mortgage will be a legal charge (under the Building Societies Act 1986, s. 119(1), the term 'mortgage' is expressed to include 'charge'). An advance which is secured by a legal charge will constitute an advance secured by a mortgage of a legal estate within a building society's statutory powers.

Equitable mortgages

An equitable mortgage will not vest any legal estate or interest in the mortgagee. As a general rule, any property which can be the subject of a legal mortgage can also be the subject of an equitable mortgage. The Building Societies Act 1986 does not make specific reference to equitable mortgages. A building society may lawfully make an advance secured on land by way of an equitable mortgage of a legal estate, being a specifically enforceable agreement to create a legal mortgage. Any such agreement will only be valid if it satisfies the Law of Property (Miscellaneous Provisions) Act 1989, s. 2, which requires the agreement to be in writing and to be signed by the parties to it.

Index-linked mortgages

The power to make advances secured on land includes the power (Building Societies Act 1986, s. 10(10)) to make advances under which the amount of the capital element due to the building society (with or without similar provision in respect of interest) may be adjusted from time to time by reference to a public index of prices specified in the mortgage terms, or to a public index of housing prices. The nature of index-linked mortgages was discussed by Peter Gibson J in *Nationwide Building Society* v *Registry of Friendly Societies* [1983] 1 WLR 1226, where it was said that such advances would be made on terms designed to ensure that the real value of the advance is repaid to it by adjustments made to take account of inflation, but that the rate of interest charged would be substantially lower than the rates ordinarily charged by the society.

Equity mortgages

As an alternative to linking the capital element due under a mortgage to a specified public index, building societies may make an advance secured on land under which the capital element owing to the society at any time is determined by reference to a share in the open market value of the particular property at that time (Building Society Act 1986, s. 10(10)(c)).

Contributory mortgages

Under a contributory mortgage, several lenders all take security for the separate advances made by each of them. Building societies are not specifically empowered by the Building Societies Act 1986 to make advances on the security of a contributory mortgage. However, since such mortgages are valid under the general law, and are not expressly prohibited by the 1986 Act, it follows that a building society has power to make such mortgages.

CLASSIFICATION OF ADVANCES SECURED ON LAND

Section 10(11) of the Building Societies Act 1986 provides that advances secured on land are to be classified as class 1 or class 2 advances. This classification relates to the statutory requirements for the structure of a building society's commercial assets. Class 1 advances constitute class 1 assets and there is no limit on the proportion of a society's commercial assets which can be represented by such advances. Class 2 advances, by contrast, constitute class 2 assets and are therefore subject to the overall percentage limit imposed by s. 20 (or if it has class 3 assets, on a society's aggregate holding of class 2 and 3 assets).

An advance will be a class 1 advance if (Building Societies Act 1986, s. 11(2)), when the society makes the advance, it is satisfied:

(a) that the advance is an advance secured on land;

(b) that the borrower is an individual;

(c) that the land is for residential use of the borrower, or his dependant;

(d) that the amount advanced will not exceed the value of the basic security;

(e) that there is no other mortgage of the land outstanding in favour of a person other than the society; and

(f) that the mortgage is neither an equity mortgage nor one whose capital element is linked to a public index of housing prices.

A class 2 advance is made where the society, when it makes the advance, either is not satisfied that all of the class 1 requirements have been met or is satisfied that any of those requirements has not been met, and the society is satisfied:

(a)   that the advance is an advance secured on land;

(b)   that where the amount advanced will exceed the value of the basic security, the excess will be secured by taking a security of a prescribed description in addition to the basic security; and

(c)   that no, or no more than one, other mortgage of the land is outstanding in favour of a person other than the society.

The distinction between class 1 and class 2 advances has been drawn with two objectives in view. The first is to preserve the established character of building societies as lending institutions by ensuring that class 1 advances are typical of the type of mortgage lending traditionally undertaken by the building society movement. The second is to ensure that the riskier forms of secured lending are excluded from class 1 and placed in class 2.

Additional security

A building society may make an advance for the purchase of land secured by a first mortgage of the land and by additional security provided either by the borrower or a third party. The value of any additional security must be disregarded for the purpose of classifying the advance as a class 1 or a class 2 advance.

Although the taking of additional security cannot normally increase the amount of an advance secured on land to a sum which exceeds the value of the basic security, it should not be forgotten that the taking of additional security may lead to the society advancing more to the borrower than it would otherwise have been prepared to lend. The Building Societies Act 1986, when enacted, required the Building Societies Association and the Commission to agree to a Code of Practice dealing with the question of additional security taken from third parties and with the question of warranties of value of mortgaged property.

The Code of Practice only applies where a building society proposes to make an advance (but not a further advance) which will be secured by a first mortgage of land in the UK and the purpose of the advance is to facilitate the purchase of that land. The code provides that:

(a)   the borrower should be given written details of any form of security (including an unsecured personal guarantee) which is additional to the basic security, and which the society proposes to take from a third party; and

(b)   the borrower should be informed in writing whether or not the society gives any assurance that the price agreed to be paid for the land on which the advance is to be secured is reasonable. Any limitation on the scope of such an assurance should be specified.

VALUATION

Section 13(1) of the Building Societies Act 1986 provides that every director of a building society is under a duty to satisfy himself that the arrangements made for assessing the adequacy of the security for any advance by the society which is to be fully secured on land are such as may reasonably be expected to ensure that:

(a)   an assessment of the adequacy of the security will be made on the occasion of each advance, whether or not the previous assessment was made with a view to further advances or re-advances;

(b)   each assessment will be made by an officer or employee of the society who is competent to make the assessment and who is not disqualified under s. 13(3); and

(c) ˙ each person making the assessment will be supplied with a written report on the value of the land, and any factors likely to affect its value, made by a person who is competent to value the land.

A number of points arise in respect of these provisions. The duty imposed by s. 13(1) is placed on the directors individually. The duty does not oblige the directors in each individual case to ensure that the security has been properly assessed. The duty placed on the directors is simply to satisfy themselves that the arrangements for assessing the adequacy of the society's securities are such as may reasonably be expected to ensure that the requirements set out in (a), (b) and (c) are satisfied. In other words, the directors' task is to satisfy themselves that a proper system of assessment has been established. Although no specific sanctions are prescribed for a failure by the directors to discharge the duty imposed on them by s. 13(3), the adequacy of these arrangements may be taken into account in judging the prudent management criteria under s. 45(3) of the 1986 Act. A failure to observe these criteria may lead the Building Societies Commission to impose conditions on a society's authorisation.

The arrangements required to be made by s. 13(1) apply only to the assessment of the adequacy of securities for advances which are to be 'fully secured' on land. The arrangements will cover all class 1 and class 2 advances which are to be fully secured on the basic security.

In relation to any land which is to secure an advance, the following persons are disqualified from making a report on its value:

(a)   the directors of the society;

(b)   any officer or employee of the society who makes assessments of the adequacy of securities for advances secured on land, or who authorises the making of such advances;

(c)   any person paid by the society for introducing the proposed borrower;

(d)   any person with a financial interest in any sale or disposition of land; and

(e)   any person who receives a commission for introducing the parties to any disposition of the land which is followed by the making of the advance.

Where the advance is to be made following a disposition of the land, s. 13(3) disqualifies two categories of persons from making the assessment. These categories include: (a) any person (other than the society itself) who has a financial interest in the disposition; and (b) any person who receives a commission for introducing the parties to the disposition.

A building society valuer carrying out a valuation for mortgage purposes will owe a duty of care in tort to the applicant for the proposed advance (*Yianni* v *Edwin Evans and Sons* [1982] QB 438; *Smith* v *Eric S. Bush* [1990] 1 AC 831). If the valuer employed by the building society is negligent, the society will be vicariously liable for any loss caused to the applicant.

Advances secured on land overseas

The power conferred on building societies by s. 10 of the Building Societies Act 1986 to make 'advances secured on land' only authorises the making of advances secured on land in the UK. Section 14 of the Act makes provision for power to be conferred on building societies to make advances on the security of land overseas. Orders have been made under the provisions relating to the Isle of Man (SI 1987/1498), Jersey (SI 1987/1872), Guernsey and Alderney (SI 1988/1394) and Gibraltar (SI 1989/1817). The Building Societies (Member States) Order 1992 (SI 1992/1547) empowers building societies with a qualifying asset holding to make advances secured on land in a member State of the EU, other than the UK. The Order was made by the Treasury using the affirmative resolution procedure. The security which may be taken for an advance made under the order is defined in broad terms: it may be any form of security which acknowledges a debt and obliges the borrower to pay it, and which secures payment of that debt on land in a member State other than the United Kingdom. The provisions for classifying advances made under the Order as class 1 or class 2 are the same for Guernsey, Alderney and Gibraltar, and include the requirement that the society must be satisfied that any right of the borrower's spouse relating to the land on which the advance is to be secured will be subject to the security. Section 11(10) of the Building Societies Act 1986 is excluded in relation to advances on land in other member States.

TYPES OF BORROWER

Normally, the building society borrower will be an adult beneficial owner of residential property with legal capacity to borrow money and to give security for the money borrowed. A minor is capable of being a member of a building society unless the society's rules provide otherwise. However, a minor cannot hold a legal estate in land (Law of Property Act 1925, s. 1(6)) and cannot, therefore, execute a valid legal mortgage. Loans to minors present a further problem in that a loan contracted by a borrower during his minority will not normally be enforceable against him unless and until he ratifies it on attaining his majority. As a result of the Minors' Contracts Act 1987, the court has a discretion to order a minor to make restitution of property which has passed to him under an unenforceable contract. Where a building society is aware that the applicant for an advance is a minor, it should ensure that, before the advance is made, the property is vested in two adult trustees for sale. The society can then pay the advance to the trustees, who will be able to give a good receipt and create an effective mortgage or charge. If the society advances money to an applicant in ignorance of his minority, the society may be entitled to relief under the doctrine of subrogation. In *Nottingham Permanent Benefit Building Society* v *Thurstan* [1903] AC 6 a building society advanced money to a member who, unknown to the society, was a minor for the purchase of some freehold land, and to complete the construction of a number of houses. When the minor attained the age of majority the contract was repudiated. The House of Lords held that the minor was entitled to repudiate the contract on attaining majority, since the loan and the mortgage securing it were void under the Infants Relief Act 1874 (now repealed. See chapter 6). However, the House also affirmed the judgment of the Court of Appeal that, quite independently of the mortgage, the society, having paid off the vendor, was entitled to the remedies of the vendor, in respect of the money so paid. The society could assert an equitable charge over the property, by way of subrogation to the vendor's lien.

A personal representative may raise money for the purposes of the administration of the deceased's estate by borrowing from a building society (Administration of Estates Act 1925, ss. 39(1) and 36(8)). However, any such mortgage would only secure against the estate the principal sum borrowed, together with fines, interest etc., but not any liabilities of the personal representative incurred in any other capacity.

A building society can advance money to trustees for sale on the security of a mortgage (Trustee Act 1925, s. 14) and will be given statutory protection if the money is advanced to two or more trustees or a trust corporation. If the trustees for sale are not beneficially entitled, any security over the trust property will only cover the principal sum advanced, together with interest etc., and will not extend to any personal liabilities of the trustees to the society, unless the settlement contains express powers to the contrary.

The powers of a company to borrow funds and to give security for such advances will normally be contained in the memorandum of association, as will a power to become a member of a building society. However, a trading company, whether it has an express power or not, will have an implied power to give security for its borrowing. In addition, in favour of someone dealing with the company in good faith, the power of the board of directors to bind the company, or to authorise others to do so, is deemed to be free of any limitation under the company's constitution (Companies Act 1985, s. 35A). Advances by a building society to a company cannot be class 1 advances because the borrower is not an individual.

REPAYMENT SYSTEMS

There are two main systems for the repayment of advances generally used by building societies in respect of mortgage advances, namely:

  (a) the annuity repayment or flat-rate system; and
  (b) the endowment system.

Under the annuity repayment or flat-rate system, the borrower makes combined payments of capital and interest at monthly or other periodic intervals during an agreed repayment term. The term will be divided into yearly accounting periods corresponding to the society's financial year, and provision will be made for interest to be charged on the full amount of the mortgage debt at the end of the preceding year and any money advanced to or becoming owing from the borrower during the year.

In ordinary cases, the capital outstanding from the borrower will be at its highest in the first year of the term, and the repayment instalments will largely be used towards discharging the interest payable to the society, with perhaps a small balance being left to reduce the capital. However, the reduction in capital achieved during the first and subsequent years means that the amount on which interest will be charged in later years will be reduced, and more of the instalments applied in paying off the capital.

Under the endowment system, the borrower's obligation to make repayments of capital is suspended during the mortgage term, so that the payment instalments consist solely of interest. Since none of the capital is being repaid during the term, interest will be charged throughout on the full amount advanced by the borrower. The borrower, however, also maintains, and charges, in favour of the society, an endowment policy on his own life for a term of years equal to that for which the mortgage is granted; and the advance is paid off by the proceeds of the policy at maturity, or on the borrower's death.

Usually, the repayment period is about 25 years, although periods of between 10 and 20 years are also encountered, and mortgages have been extended for periods of as much as 40 years. There have been some innovations in the different forms of mortgages, e.g., the 'low start' or 'deferred payment' mortgages, the 'equity release mortgages' etc.

PROVISIONS OF THE MORTGAGE DEED

With the exception that a legal mortgage of land or of an interest in land must be made by way of deed (Law of Property Act 1925, s. 52), there are no statutory prescribed forms of mortgage or charge by way of legal mortgage to a building society. The rules of the society will rarely do more than stipulate that the deed contains certain specified provisions. Building societies generally have printed forms of mortgages drafted to cater for the different types of facilities they provide, with the detailed terms often being incorporated by reference to a facility letter or a separate booklet of mortgage conditions. It is intended now to deal with some of the provisions more commonly found in building society mortgages.

Membership of the society

Every borrower to whom a society makes an advance secured on land must be a member of the society, whether membership is constituted by holding shares or otherwise. It is desirable that the fact of membership is mentioned in the mortgage deed, even where membership is constituted by shareholding, or by some arrangement outside the mortgage deed itself. The fact that all advances are to persons who are members makes it easier to regulate the society and borrower relationship through the rules, rather than the mortgage deed.

Interest

Interest rates are of particular concern to building societies, since to a considerable extent the success of their business depends on lending money by way of mortgage at higher rates than the interest paid to investors. Interest rates will fluctuate considerably during the lifetime of a 25-year mortgage and a building society with an inflexible rate of interest on its long-term mortgage may be exposed to the risk of having to pay more to its investors than it is currently receiving from its borrowers. In most cases provision is made by building societies directly to permit a variation of the interest rate to be charged by giving notice, either generally or in order to bring the rate into line with the rate currently charged on new loans. Provided that there is nothing reprehensible about the way the power to vary interest rates is exercised (*Multiservice Bookbinding Ltd* v *Marden* [1979] Ch 84) and that the borrower is free to redeem the mortgage at any time, the building society will be entitled to exercise its power to vary interest rates charged to borrowers. Indeed, it is common for building society mortgages to provide that the interest rate can be varied without formality provided that any notice of a variation is given by advertising either in the society's offices, or by advertising in newspapers circulating nationally or locally in the area in which the society does its business (where the society is local). However, dispensing with written notice of a change in interest rates does not avoid the need to notify the borrower of any variation in the amount of the mortgage instalments. In practice the instalments payable by the borrower will be fixed annually and building societies avoid the necessity of having to notify the borrower of any variation in the amount of instalments payable after each variation in the interest rates.

Compound interest The law relating to mortgages does not allow compound interest to be charged, except on the evidence of a clear provision enabling the charging of such interest. In *Eastern Counties Building Society* v *Russell* [1947] 1 All ER 500 the court held that the practice of charging an element of compound interest where the borrower was in arrears could not be justified without express provision in the mortgage deeds. Consequently, the guarantor against whom the arrears were claimed escaped liability to the society.

Further advances

Further advances (including re-advances equal to the whole or part of the capital which the borrower has repaid since the original advance was made) are primarily matters for negotiation between the society and the borrower. Where it is intended that the further advance should rank as a class 1 or class 2 advance, the adequacy of the security must be assessed when the further advance is made, although a fresh valuation report will not be required if the previous report remains adequate for the purpose of the assessment. The society must be satisfied that the requirements of the Building Societies Act 1986, s. 11(2) or (4), are satisfied. If the mortgage deed is expressed to secure the original advance only, a deed of further charge will be necessary to secure any further advance subsequently made to the borrower. However, where the mortgage deed is expressed to secure all moneys from time to time owing to the society, or all moneys from time to time payable under the mortgage conditions, it is likely that further advances may be made on the security of the original mortgage. Where further advances are handled in this matter, the borrower simply signs a receipt which acknowledges that further advance, and that it is secured by the original mortgage.

Repairs

The mortgagor is not under any statutory duty to keep the mortgaged property in repair, and the mortgagee's only right at common law is to ensure that the property is preserved from deterioration while in the hands of a subsequent encumbrancer. Building society mortgages, therefore, always contain a covenant by the mortgagor to keep the property in good repair. This is usually coupled with a provision entitling the society to enter and inspect the property, and to remedy any lack of repair on the part of the mortgagor.

Insurance

Where the mortgage is by deed, the mortgagee has a statutory power to insure the mortgaged property against loss or damage by fire and to charge the premiums paid on the mortgaged property (Law of Property Act 1925, s. 101(1)(ii)). However, since this statutory right is restricted to fire insurance, and is subject to certain other restrictions, the right is of limited value to building societies which therefore make provision in the mortgage conditions for a wider range of risks to be covered. Following views expressed by the Office of Fair Trading, building societies have given some degree of freedom to the borrower in the selection of the insurer. This is done either (a) by allowing the borrower to choose the insurer from a list of at least three insurers approved by the society, but with the society effecting the insurance; or by (b) the society allowing the borrower to insure and that choice being approved by the building society. Where the latter method of insuring the property is selected the policy should be in the joint names of the borrower and the society.

Planning

The borrower must be informed of any activities in relation to the property which will affect its value. Although few property owners are likely to undertake work of a nature which will diminish the value of the property, the society must be aware of the planning characteristics of the property. Any unauthorised work may have the effect of reducing the marketable value of the property until planning permission is obtained or until the work is removed. It is reasonable for the building society to require that the society's consent be obtained before any work or change of user which needs planning permission, and that the borrower give prompt notice of any proposals, notices, orders etc. which affect or potentially affect the property under the planning law and require him to comply with such laws.

Leasing by the mortgagor

A mortgagor cannot, against the wishes of a mortgagee, create a relationship of landlord and tenant between the mortgagee and a third party, to whom he lets the property. However, the Law of Property Act 1925, s. 99, gives a mortgagor in possession, who complies with statutory requirements, the power to grant a lease which will bind not only himself, but also his mortgagee. Consequently, undesirable tenancies could affect the mortgaged property. Further, in respect of rent-controlled property the tenants, whether desirable or undesirable, could become entitled to protection. In order to avoid such situations building societies can, under s. 99(13), exclude or modify the mortgagor's power of leasing in the mortgage deed. However, the mortgagor may remain at liberty to create tenancies which will be binding on himself alone. After *Iron Trades Employers Insurance Association Ltd* v *Union Land and House Investors Ltd* [1937] Ch 313 the ability of a mortgagor to create tenancies binding on himself alone came to be referred to as 'the common law power of leasing'. As a result of the *Iron Trades* case, building societies often incorporate a mortgage clause which requires the society's consent before entering into a tenancy agreement which binds the mortgagor alone.

In order to reduce lettings of which building societies may disapprove mortgages normally contain an exclusion of the statutory power and a covenant against other lettings without consent. The exclusion of the statutory power to let will cover the question of protection under the Rent Acts or the Housing Acts, whilst the covenant against other lettings without the consent of the building society will cover all lettings regarded as undesirable for any reason.

Where a property has been let without the consent of the building society, mere knowledge of the letting, coupled with inaction on the part of the society does not amount to consent to or approval of the tenancy (*Taylor* v *Ellis* [1960] Ch 368).

Consolidation

Where there are two separate mortgages on two distinct properties, with separate legal rights of redemption, and the mortgages are vested in the same mortgagee, and the mortgage money has become due on both mortgages, the mortgagor may not be allowed to redeem one without similarly redeeming the other. The requirement that the mortgage moneys must have become due on both mortgages means that in reality the equitable right of consolidation is not of much value to building societies. The fact that both mortgages must have become due means that default, or some similar event, must have occurred on both of the mortgages.

Although under s. 93(1) of the Law of Property Act 1925 a mortgagor is entitled to redeem any one mortgage without having to pay money due under another separate mortgage, that subsection applies only if a contrary intention is not expressed in the mortgage deed.

Most building societies include in their rules or mortgage deeds an express provision that the mortgagor will not be entitled to redeem the security without at the same time redeeming every other security on any other property mortgaged to the society. A covenant in this form will be held effective although a right requiring both or all mortgages to be redeemed is independent of the equitable doctrine of consolidation. Where a mortgagor covenants to observe all the rules of the society and one of the rules provides that the right to redeem one mortgage is subject to the obligation to redeem all other mortgages or to obtain the consent of the board to the redemption of the one mortgage, the rule is binding as if it were expressly incorporated into each mortgage (*Hughes* v *Britannia Permanent Benefit Building Society* [1906] 2 Ch 607).

Power to transfer mortgage

A building society cannot accept the transfer of a mortgage made in favour of another person except on a merger of building societies, and in some cases, on the re-transfer of a mortgage to which the society was originally a party.

A mortgage in favour of a building society may, however, be transferred to another person where the borrower consents (*Re Rumney and Smith* [1897] 2 Ch 351) or if he directs the transfer (Law of Property Act 1925, s. 95(1)). If the mortgage deed contains the power, the mortgage debt and any security for it, can be transferred without the consent of the mortgagor, but no other rights and advantages such as those derived from statute and the society's rules (*Sun Permanent Benefit Building Society* v *Western Suburban and Harrow Road Permanent Building Society* [1921] 2 Ch 438 at 458–9).

Under statute (Law of Property Act 1925, s. 114(1); Land Registration Act 1925, s. 33(1)) a building society may be able to transfer a mortgage without the consent of the borrower and without any express power being included in the mortgage document, and such a transfer would be effective to transfer the mortgage debt, the right to sue on the mortgage covenants and the right to enforce the security, but not certain other rights of the transferor society (e.g., the right to enforce the society's rules).

Costs and expenses

Under the general law of mortgages, a mortgagee is allowed to reimburse out of the mortgaged property all costs, charges and expenses reasonably and properly incurred in enforcing or preserving his security (*Parker-Tweedale* v *Dunbar Bank plc (No. 2)* [1991] Ch 26). However, it is desirable for a number of reasons that the issue of costs should be dealt with expressly in the mortgage, for example, (a) the society has an express power if any particular expenditure is challenged; (b) costs can be charged on an indemnity basis; and (c) the building society will have a right to charge costs incurred in proceedings which arise from the need to protect title to the mortgage against a third party.

INCIDENTS OF THE MORTGAGE

The rules of a building society must include provisions dealing with the manner in which advances are to be made and repaid, and conditions on which the borrower may redeem the amount due from him before the end of the period for which the advance was agreed (Building Societies Act 1986, s. 5(8)). The general law of mortgages in respect of redemption applies to building society mortgages. The general law can be summarised as follows:

(a)   The right of redemption can be postponed (unless ss. 94, 113 and 173 of the Consumer Credit Act 1974 apply), but it cannot be excluded or rendered illusory (*Knightsbridge Estates Trust Ltd* v *Byrne* [1939] Ch 441).

(b)   The mortgage cannot reserve any right to the mortgagee which is inconsistent with the mortgagor's right to redeem. For example, it cannot give the mortgagee an option to purchase the mortgaged property, because if the option were exercised, the mortgagor's right to redeem would be gone (see *Samuel* v *Jarrah Timber and Wood Paving Corporation Ltd* [1904] AC 323).

(c)   A collateral advantage which forms part of the mortgage transaction will not be valid after redemption. It will only be valid prior to redemption if it is not (i) unfair or unconscionable; (ii) in the nature of a penalty clogging the equity of redemption; or (iii) inconsistent with the equitable and contractual right to redeem.

Where a building society mortgage provides that it will only be redeemable on payment of a sum larger than the amount originally advanced that will constitute a collateral advantage and will only be enforceable if it does not fall foul of rule (c) above. However, a borrower will not be able to redeem the mortgage except on the payment of sums due as premiums, redemption fees etc. which are due under the mortgage.

TRANSFER OF THE EQUITY

The borrower's interest in the mortgaged property, including the right of redemption, is a marketable asset, and can be sold by the member. The rules sometimes specify the procedure to be followed on a sale of this kind, and that must be complied with. A building society may be willing to facilitate such a sale provided it is satisfied that the proposed purchaser can be relied on to pay the instalments due under the mortgage and to keep the property in good repair. In these circumstances, the building society will release the vendor member and substitute the purchaser as a borrowing member of the society.

DISCHARGE OF A MORTGAGE

There are two statutory powers under which a receipt may be given which will operate as a discharge of the property mortgaged to the building society. The general statutory powers are conferred by the Law of Property Act 1925, s. 115(1), in respect of unregistered land, and in the Land Registration Act 1925, s. 35, in respect of registered land. A special power is conferred by the Building Societies Act 1986, s. 17(3).

Under the Law of Property Act 1925, s. 115(1), the receipt must state the name of the person paying the money, be executed by the mortgagee or the person in whom the mortgaged property is vested and who is legally entitled to give a receipt for the mortgage money, and should be endorsed on the mortgaged document. If the receipt is for all the money secured by the mortgage, the receipt operates as a reconveyance or surrender or release. This discharges the mortgaged property from both the principal debt and the interest secured by the mortgage and from all claims under the mortgage.

Under the Land Registration Act 1925, s. 35, the registration of an instrument of discharge is required to be given under the seal of the society and countersigned by its secretary, or signed or executed by an authorised person.

Additionally, a society may discharge a mortgage by executing a reconveyance or surrender in favour of the owner of the equity of redemption or the reversion expectant on the determination of the mortgage term.

Alternatively, when all the money intended to be secured by a mortgage given to a building society has been fully repaid or discharged, the society may endorse on or annex to the mortgage: (a) a receipt in the prescribed form under the society's seal, countersigned by any person acting under the authority of the board of directors; (b) a reconveyance of the mortgaged property to such person of full age, and on such trusts (if any) as the mortgagor may direct.

Except where the charge is registered under the Land Registration Act 1925, such a receipt will operate as a surrender of the term created by the mortgage, or a reconveyance to the person who immediately before the execution of the receipt was entitled to the equity of redemption.

A statutory receipt is a final discharge and after it has been given no claim can be made by the society in respect of any sum secured by the mortgage, even if the receipt was given under a mistake (*London and County United Building Society* v *Angell* (1896) 65 LJ QB 194).

ENFORCEMENT OF A MORTGAGE

Where the borrower defaults a building society has the same remedies as any other type of lender, but the building society will normally recover possession of the mortgaged property and then sell it in the exercise of the statutory power of sale.

Recovery of possession

The mortgagee's right to take possession of the mortgaged property does not depend on the mortgagor being in default under the terms of the mortgage. The right arises by virtue of the mortgagee's estate in the mortgaged property (*Four-Maids Ltd* v *Dudley Marshall (Properties) Ltd* [1957] Ch 317 at 320). Moreover, the right to possession is not affected by the existence of any counterclaim by the mortgagor.

In practice, the exercise of the right to take possession by a building society will be affected by both the terms of the mortgage and by statute. Usually the terms of a building society mortgage provide that the society may not take possession unless and until some event occurs which makes the whole mortgage debt payable immediately.

The main statutory restriction which may affect the right of the building society to take possession of the mortgaged property is s. 36 of the Administration of Justice Act 1970, which gives the court power to adjourn the mortgagee's application for possession, or to stay or suspend the execution of a possession order made on such an application. If the power under s. 36 is to be exercised then:

(a) the mortgaged land must consist of or include a dwelling house;

(b) the action in which the mortgagee claims possession must not be merely an action for foreclosure in which a claim for possession is also made;

(c) the court must be satisfied that the mortgagor is likely to be able within a reasonable period to pay any sums due under the mortgage.

Power of sale

The Law of Property Act 1925 draws a distinction between the mortgagee's power of sale arising and the power becoming exercisable. The power arises when the mortgage money becomes due but it does not become exercisable until additionally one of the events specified in s. 103 of the Act has occurred. Once the power has arisen, the mortgagee can usually pass a good title to a purchaser, but he may then be liable to the mortgagor for any loss suffered.

A mortgagee who exercises a power of sale under the mortgage owes the borrower a duty to take reasonable care to obtain a proper price (*Cuckmere Brick Co. Ltd* v *Mutual Finance Ltd* [1971] Ch 949). The duty only arises if the mortgagee decides to realise his security but he is not under any duty either to realise the security at any particular time or at all (*China and South Sea Bank Ltd v Tan Soon Gin* [1990] 1 AC 536). If the mortgagee decides not to sell the mortgaged property, the borrower may apply to the court for an order that the property should be sold under s. 91(2) of the Law of Property Act 1925. Although the court will not normally order a sale against the mortgagee's wishes, where the net proceeds are unlikely to cover the mortgage debt, it may do so in exceptional circumstances. In *Palk* v *Mortgage Services Funding plc* [1993] Ch 330 the court concluded that it was just and equitable to order a sale of the property in the exercise of its discretion under s. 91(2) where the borrowers were faced with an open-ended and indefinitely increasing loss in the event that the building society were not allowed to exercise its power of sale.

Building societies are unique in being placed under a specific statutory duty 'to take reasonable care to ensure that the price at which the land is sold is the best price that can reasonably be obtained' (Building Societies Act 1986, sch. 4, para. 1(1)(a)). In *Reliance Building Society* v *Harwood-Stamper* [1944] Ch 362 Vaisey J took the view that the effect of a similar statutory provision then in force (Building Societies Act 1939, s. 10) was to place a building society in the position of a fiduciary vendor, although subject to three qualifications, namely:

(a) that the society was at liberty to sell when it thought proper;

(b) that it had a wide discretion as to the mode of sale under s. 101 of the Law of Property Act 1925; and

(c) that it enjoyed the protection from liability for involuntary loss conferred by s. 106(3) of that Act.

However, in view of the general duty of care established in the *Cuckmere Brick* case, it is thought unlikely that the statutory duty set out in the Building Societies Act 1986 would be regarded as placing building societies in a position different from that of mortgagees under the general law.

Proceeds of sale

On the exercise of a power of sale a society is entitled to retain out of the proceeds of sale all instalments payable up to the time of completion of the sale and any sum which represents the balance of the principal sum remaining owing at that time but not any extra charges which redemption would have involved. A mortgagee exercising his power of sale will hold the money arising from such a sale (after discharging any prior encumbrances to which the sale is not made subject, or after payment into court of a sum to meet any prior encumbrance) in trust to apply first in payment of the costs, charges and expenses properly incurred by him incidental to the sale, and secondly, in discharge of the mortgage money, interest and costs due under the mortgage with the residue being paid to the person entitled to the mortgaged property, or authorised to give receipts for the proceeds of the sale (Law of Property Act 1925, s. 105).

APPENDIX 1

Changes to the Powers of the Bank of England

Changes announced by the Chancellor of the Exchequer, Gordon Brown, in May 1997 will have an unprecedented effect on the powers of the Bank of England. The changes will bring the Bank of England more in line with the Bundesbank and the Federal Reserve Bank. The Bank of England's future role will be to focus on fighting inflation. At the same time the supervisory functions of the Bank of England will be transferred to an expanded Securities and Investments Board. This restructuring will reduce the contact the Bank will have with individual commercial banks as the guardian of the banking sector. Instead, the Bank will be driven by economic analysis and forecasting. However, the Bank will still be concerned with systemic failure and continue to exercise significant influence on the commercial banks and financial sector.

Scope of the changes

On 6 May 1997 the Chancellor announced that the Government was transferring to the Bank of England operational responsibility for setting interest rates. The Bank's monetary policy objective will be to deliver price stability and, without prejudice to this objective, support the Government's economic policy. The Government will set the inflation target for the Bank which will have the operational responsibility of achieving this target. Any decisions or action needed to achieve the inflation target will be undertaken by the Monetary Policy Committee of the Bank of England.

The Committee includes the Governor and two deputy Governors nominated by the Government, together with two senior Bank of England officials responsible for the management of monetary policy and market operations (The Chancellor's Statement to the House of Commons on the Bank of England, 20 May 1997, Document 49/97). The Committee also includes four other expert members appointed by the Government from outside the Bank of England. The Committee will be responsible for taking into consideration regional and sectorial information in its monetary policy decisions. All decisions of the Committee on interest rates will be announced immediately.

The Monetary Policy Committee's performance will be reviewed by the Court of the Bank of England. The Court will be reformed so that it can take account of the full range of industrial and business views.

The Government will retain the right to override the operational independence of the Bank of England in extreme economic circumstances for a limited period. This will enable it to retain clear responsibility to Parliament for monetary policy goals and the Bank of England will be required to account for the operation of monetary policy.

Prudential supervision

The Bank of England has been, formally and informally, at the core of banking supervision (see chapter 3). Indeed, there are many arguments for involving the central bank in the supervision of the financial system. Firstly, the Bank of England, through its role in the payments system, handles the accounts of the clearing banks and has an unrivalled knowledge of the structure of their assets and liabilities. It should, therefore, be in a position to spot the danger signals. Secondly, as lender of last resort the Bank of England is in touch with the UK (and other overseas banks although it may not act as lender of last resort to them) commercial banks and even if the Bank of England does not itself provide the resources to assist an ailing bank it may be able to broker a deal.

Whilst the Bank of England has had supervisory powers in relation to the banking sector other areas of the financial sector (e.g., securities firms and insurance companies) have been regulated under a separate regime. In his Statement to the House of Commons on 19 May 1997, the Chancellor announced that a regulatory structure which distinguishes between different types of financial institutions, e.g., banks, securities firms and insurance companies, can no longer be justified in a financial sector which is becoming more integrated. Indeed, the two-tier system of supervision and investor protection introduced by the Financial Services Act 1986 which splits responsibility between the Securities and Investments Board (SIB) and the Self Regulatory Organisations (SROs), together with the Recognised Professional Bodies, lacks a clear allocation of responsibilities and leads to confusion for investors. A simpler system of regulation will deliver a more effective system of supervision.

Further, in order to attain transparency and to separate the regulatory function from a Bank of England which has been given a greater economic function (independence over monetary policy) responsibility for banking supervision will be transferred from the Bank of England to a new and strengthened Securities and Investments Board which will also take direct responsibility for the regulatory regime covered by the existing Financial Services Act.

The strengthened Securities and Investments Board will become the single regulator with statutory responsibility for prudential supervision of the banks and other financial institutions. The new system of regulation is intended to place public interest first and to increase public confidence.

The Government intends to introduce legislation to give statutory effect to the reforms announced. Although the Monetary Policy Committee has already been established and announced, changes in interest rates legislation will be necessary to give the Bank of England operational independence over monetary policy. It is expected that this will be done under a new Bank of England Act which will also transfer banking supervision from the Bank of England to the new Securities and Investments Board. Further, a new Financial Services Act will be necessary to bring the plethora of different supervisors under a new regime with a strengthened Securities and Investments Board.

APPENDIX 2

The Banking Code

(Published with the kind permission of APACS.)

THE BANKING CODE

British Bankers' Association
Pinners Hall
105–108 Old Broad Street
London EC2N IEX
Telephone: 0171 216 8800
Fax: 0171 216 8811

The Building Societies Association
3 Savile Row
London WIX 1AF
Telephone: 0171 437 0655
Fax: 0171 734 6416

Association for Payment Clearing Services
Mercury House
Triton Court
14 Finsbury Square
London EC2A 1BR
Telephone: 0171 711 6200
Fax: 0171 256 5527

This is a voluntary Code followed by banks and building societies in their relations with personal customers in the United Kingdom. It sets standards of good banking practice which are followed as a minimum by banks and building societies subscribing to it. As a voluntary Code, it allows competition and market forces to operate to encourage higher standards for the benefit of customers.

The standards of the Code are encompassed in the 11 key commitments found at the beginning. These commitments apply to the conduct of business for all products and services provided to customers.

Mortgages are covered in more detail in the Council of Mortgage Lenders' Code of Mortgage Lending Practice. Not all subscribers to the Banking Code are members of the Council of Mortgage Lenders.

The Code provides valuable safeguards for customers. It should help them understand how banks and building societies are expected to deal with them. Customers should check who subscribes to it by contacting the Associations shown opposite [see p. 391].

The Independent Review Body for the Banking and Mortgage Codes monitors compliance by banks and building societies with the Code and also oversees its review from time to time.

Copies of the Code are available from banks and building societies and the Associations shown opposite [see p. 391].

Within the Code, 'you' means the customer and 'we' means the bank or building society the customer deals with.

It is effective from 1 July 1997 unless otherwise indicated.

CONTENTS

1. KEY COMMITMENTS

1. KEY COMMITMENTS

1.1 We, the subscribers to this Code, promise that we will:

- act fairly and reasonably in all our dealings with you;
- ensure that all services and products comply with this Code, even if they have their own terms and conditions;
- give you information on our services and products in plain language, and offer help if there is any aspect which you do not understand;
- help you to choose a service or product to fit your needs;
- help you to understand the financial implications of:
  - a mortgage;
  - other borrowing;
  - savings and investment products;
  - card products.
- help you to understand how your accounts work;
- have safe, secure and reliable banking and payment systems;
- ensure that the procedures our staff follow reflect the commitments set out in this Code;
- correct errors and handle complaints speedily;
- consider cases of financial difficulty and mortgage arrears sympathetically and positively;
- ensure that all services and products comply with relevant laws and regulations.

2. INFORMATION

Information available

2.1 When you become a customer and at any time you ask, we will give you:

Key features

- clear written information explaining the key features of our main services and products;

Your account

- information on how your account works, including:
  - stopping a cheque or other types of payment;
  - when funds can be withdrawn after a credit has been paid into your account and when funds begin to earn interest;
  - unpaid cheques;
  - out of date cheques;
  - when your account details may be passed to credit reference agencies;

Tariff

- a tariff, covering basic account services. This will also be available in branches;

Interest rates

- information on the interest rates which apply to your account(s), when interest will be deducted or paid to you and the basis on which interest is calculated.

ATM charges
2.2   We will give you details of any charges we make for using Automated Teller Machines (ATMs) when we issue the card.

Overdrafts and fixed term products
2.3   We will tell you of any additional charges and interest you may have to pay if:

- your account becomes overdrawn without agreement;
- you exceed your overdraft limit;
- your loan falls into arrears;
- you change your mind about a fixed term product.

Mortgage tariff
2.4   Before you take out a mortgage and at any time you ask, we will give you a tariff covering the operation and repayment of your mortgage, including charges and additional interest costs payable should you fall into arrears.

Other charges
2.5   We will tell you the charges for any other service or product before or when it is provided or at any time you ask.

Terms & conditions

Plain language
2.6   All written terms and conditions will be fair in substance and will set out your rights and responsibilities clearly and in plain language, with legal and technical language used only where necessary.

Joint accounts
2.7   If you have a joint account, we will give you additional information on your rights and responsibilities.

Closure
2.8   We will not close your account without giving you reasonable notice.

Keeping you informed of changes

Terms & conditions
2.9   Occasionally terms and conditions may have to be changed. We will tell you how you will be notified of these changes and will give you reasonable notice before any change takes effect. If there have been significant changes in any one year, we will give or send you a copy of the new terms and conditions or a summary of the changes.

Charges
2.10   If we increase a charge for basic account services, we will give you reasonable notice.

Interest rates
2.11   The interest rates which apply to your accounts may change from time to time. When we change the interest rates we will tell you about the changes at the earliest opportunity by either:

- letter/other personal notice; or
- notices/leaflets in branches and press advertisements. If this option is used, we will tell you the interest rate applicable to your account at least once a year, unless you have a type of account which has a passbook. If this is the case, you can collect this information from us whenever you update your passbook (which you are encouraged to do at least once a year).

Superseded accounts

2.12   If you have a type of savings or investment account, other than a fixed rate account, which is no longer available to customers, we will send you, once a year, a summary of all our interest rates. To help you compare interest rates and to consider whether or not to switch your money into another account, those accounts no longer available to customers will be clearly marked.

Marketing of services

2.13   Occasionally we will bring to your attention additional services and products which may be of benefit to you.

   However, when you become a customer, we will give you the opportunity to say that you do not wish to receive this information.

2.14   We will remind you, at least once every three years, that you can ask not to receive this information.

Consent to marketing

2.15   Unless you specifically request it, or give your express consent in writing, we will not pass your name and address to any company, including other companies in our group, for marketing purposes. You will not be asked to give your permission in return for basic banking services.

Host mailing

2.16   We may tell you about another company's services or products and, if you respond positively, you may be contacted directly by that company.

Minors

2.17   We will not send marketing material indiscriminately and, in particular, we will be selective and careful if you are under eighteen years old or where material relates to loans and overdrafts.

Advertising

2.18   We will ensure that all advertising and promotional material is clear, fair, reasonable and not misleading.

Helping you to choose a mortgage

2.19   Choosing a mortgage may be your most important financial commitment. There are three levels of service which may be provided and we will tell you which we offer at the outset. These are:

   (a)   **advice and a recommendation** as to which of our mortgages is most suitable for you. When giving advice, we will take care to help you to select a mortgage to fit your needs by asking for relevant information about your circumstances and objectives. Our advice will also depend on your particular needs and requirements and on the market conditions at the time. The reasons for the recommendation will be given to you in writing before you complete your mortgage. If we plan to offer this service, we will do so by 31 March 1998;

(b) **information on the different types of mortgage products** we offer so that you can make an informed choice of which to take;

(c) **information on a single mortgage product only,** if we offer only one mortgage product or if you have already made up your mind.

Before you take out your mortgage, we will confirm, in writing, the level of service given.

2.20   Mortgages are covered in more detail in the Council of Mortgage Lenders' Code of Mortgage Lending Practice.

Helping you to choose savings & investment accounts

2.21   We will take care to give you clear and appropriate information on the different types of savings and investment accounts available from us to help you to make an informed choice on the product to fit your needs. We will help you understand how your savings and investment accounts work, including any additional charges or loss of interest for withdrawal or cancellation.

2.22   We will give you information on a single savings or investment account if you have already made up your mind.

3.   ACCOUNT OPERATIONS

Running your account

Statements
3.1   To help you manage your account and check entries on it, we will give you regular account statements. These are normally provided monthly, quarterly or as a minimum annually, unless this is not appropriate for the type of account (for example on a passbook account). You may ask for account statements to be sent more frequently than normally available on your type of account.

3.2   If you have a type of account which is accessible by card, and you have a card, we will introduce systems by 1 July 1999 to send you account statements at least quarterly if there have been any card transactions on that account. This does not apply to passbook accounts.

3.3   If your statement or passbook has an entry which seems to be wrong, you should tell us as soon as possible so that we can resolve matters.

Pre-notification
3.4   If charges and/or debit interest accumulate to your current or savings account during a charging period, you will be given at least 14 days' notice of the amount before it is deducted from your account. The 14 days start from the date of posting the notification.

Cheques

3.5   We will keep original cheques paid from your account or copies for at least six years except where these have already been returned to you.

3.6   If, within a reasonable period after the entry has been made, there is a dispute with us about a cheque paid from your account, we will give you the cheque or a copy as evidence (except where the cheque has already been returned to you). If there is an unreasonable delay we will recredit your account until the matter is resolved.

3.7   If you already have your paid cheques returned, we will continue to return your cheques or copies to you and we will tell you our charges for this service.

3.8   When we need to tell you that one of your cheques or other items has been returned unpaid, we will do this either by letter or by other private and confidential means.

Cards & Pins

3.9   We will send you a card only if you request it or to replace one which has already been issued.

3.10   Your PIN (Personal Identification Number) will be advised only to you and will be issued separately from your card.

PIN self-selection
3.11   We will tell you if you can select your own PIN and, if so, you will be encouraged to do so carefully. This should make it easier for you to remember your PIN.
   We will have systems in place to allow you to select your own PIN by 1 July 2000.

3.12   You can ask not to be issued with a PIN.

Lending

Financial assessment
3.13   All lending will be subject to our assessment of your ability to repay. This assessment may include:

* taking into account your income and commitments;
* how you have handled your financial affairs in the past;
* information obtained from credit reference agencies and, with your consent, others, for example employers, other lenders and landlords;
* information supplied by you, including verification of your identity and the purpose of the borrowing;
* credit assessment techniques, for example credit scoring;
* your age;
* any security provided.

Guarantees
3.14   If you want us to accept a guarantee or other security from someone for your liabilities, you may be asked to consent to the disclosure, by us, of your

confidential financial information to the person giving the guarantee or other security or to their legal adviser. We will also:

- encourage them to take **independent legal advice** to make sure that they understand their commitment and the potential consequences of their decision. All the documents they will be asked to sign will contain this recommendation as a clear and prominent notice;
- advise them that by giving the guarantee or other security they may become liable instead of or as well as you;
- advise them of what the limit of their liability will be. An unlimited guarantee will not be taken.

Foreign exchange services

3.15   We will give you an explanation of the service, details of the exchange rate and an explanation of the charges which apply to any foreign exchange transactions which you are about to make. Where this is not possible, we will tell you the basis on which these will be worked out.

3.16   If you wish to transfer money abroad, we will tell you how this is done and will give you, at least, the following information:

- a description of the services and how to use them;
- an explanation of when the money you have sent abroad should get there and any reason for potential delays;
- any commission or charges which you will have to pay, including a warning where a foreign bank's charges may also have to be paid by the recipient.

4.   PROTECTION

Confidentiality

4.1   We will treat all your personal information as private and confidential (even when you are no longer a customer). Nothing about your accounts nor your name and address will be disclosed to anyone, including other companies in our group, other than in four exceptional cases permitted by law. These are:

- where we are legally compelled to do so;
- where there is a duty to the public to disclose;
- where our interests require disclosure;
  This will not be used as a reason for disclosing information about you or your accounts (including your name and address) to anyone else including other companies in our group for marketing purposes.
- where disclosure is made at your request or with your consent.

Credit reference agencies
4.2   Information about your personal debts owed to us may be disclosed to credit reference agencies where:

- you have fallen behind with your payments; and
- the amount owed is not in dispute; and

- you have not made proposals satisfactory to us for repayment of your debt following formal demand; and
- you have been given at least 28 days' notice of our intention to disclose.

4.3 We will not give any other information about you to credit reference agencies without your consent.

Data protection
4.4 We will explain that you have a right of access under the Data Protection Act 1984 to your personal records held on our computer files.

Bankers' references
4.5 We will tell you if we provide bankers' references. If a banker's reference about you is requested, we will require your written consent before it is given.

Protecting your accounts

Identification
4.6 When you first apply to open an account, we will tell you what identification we need to prove identity. This is important for your security and is required by law. We will also tell you what checks we may make with credit reference agencies.

4.7 If we record telephone conversations, our terms and conditions will explain this.

Taking care
4.8 The care of your cheque book, passbook, cards, electronic purse, PINs, passwords and selected personal information is essential to help prevent fraud and protect your accounts. Please ensure that you:

- **do not keep your cheque book and cards together;**
- **do not allow anyone else to use your card, PIN and/or password;**
- **always take reasonable steps to keep your card safe and your PIN, password and selected personal information secret at all times;**
- **never write down or record your PIN on the card or on anything kept with or near it;**
- **never write down or record your PIN, password or selected personal information without disguising it, for example, never write down or record your PIN using the numbers in the correct order;**
- **destroy the notification of your PIN and/or password as soon as you receive it.**

4.9 It is essential that you tell us as soon as you can if you suspect or discover that:

- **your cheque book, passbook, card and/or electronic purse has been lost or stolen;**
- **someone else knows your PIN, password or your selected personal information.**

Loss – what to do
4.10 The fastest method of notifying us is by telephone, using the numbers previously advised or in telephone directories.

4.11   Once you have told us that a cheque book, passbook, card or electronic purse has been lost or stolen or that someone else knows your PIN, password or selected personal information, we will take immediate steps to prevent these from being used to access your accounts.

Responsibility for losses
4.12   We will refund you the amount of any transaction together with any interest and charges:

- where you have not received your card and it is misused by someone else;
- for all transactions not authorised by you after you have told us that someone else knows your PIN, password or selected personal information;
- if additional money is transferred from your account to your electronic purse after you have told us of its loss, theft or that someone else knows your PIN;
- where faults have occurred in the ATMs, or associated systems used, which were not obvious or subject to a warning message or notice at the time of use.

Electronic purse
4.13   You should treat your electronic purse like cash in a wallet. You will lose any money left in the electronic purse at the time it is lost or stolen, in just the same way as if you lost your wallet. However, if your electronic purse is credited by unauthorised withdrawals from your account before you tell us of its loss, theft or misuse, your liability for such amounts will be limited to a maximum of £50, unless you have acted fraudulently or with gross negligence.

Cards
4.14   If your card is misused before you tell us of its loss or theft, or that someone else knows your PIN, your liability will be limited to a maximum of £50, unless you have acted fraudulently or with gross negligence.

4.15   Where a card transaction is disputed, we have the burden of proving fraud or gross negligence or that you have received your card. **In such cases we would expect you to co-operate with us and with the police in any investigation.**

Fraud and gross negligence
4.16   If you act fraudulently you will be liable for all losses. If you act with gross negligence which has caused losses you may be liable for them. This may apply if you fail to follow the safeguards set out in section 4.8.

5.   DIFFICULTIES

Financial difficulties

5.1   We will consider cases of financial difficulty sympathetically and positively. Our first step will be to try to contact you to discuss the matter.

How we can help
5.2   If you find yourself in financial difficulties, you should let us know as soon as possible. We will do all we can to help you to overcome your difficulties. The sooner we discuss your problems, the easier it will be for both of us to find a solution. The more you tell us about your full financial circumstances, the more we may be able to help.

5.3   With your co-operation, we will develop a plan with you for dealing with your financial difficulties, consistent with both our interests and yours.

5.4   If you are in difficulties you can also get help and advice from debt counselling organisations. At your request and with your consent, we will liaise, wherever possible, with debt counselling organisations that we recognise, for example:

- Citizens' Advice Bureaux; or
- Money advice centres: or
- The Consumer Credit Counselling Service.

Complaints

Internal procedures

5.5   We have internal procedures for handling complaints fairly and speedily and we will tell you what these are. These will include establishing a set time for an initial acknowledgement to your complaint. We will tell you how long it might take us to respond more fully.

5.6   If you wish to make a complaint, we will tell you how to do so and what to do if you are not happy about the outcome. Staff will help you with any queries.

Ombudsmen

5.7   Banks and building societies have separate independent ombudsmen or arbitration schemes. The ombudsmen or arbitrators are available to resolve certain complaints made by you if the matter remains unresolved through our internal complaints procedures.

5.8   All building societies must belong to the Building Societies Ombudsman Scheme.

5.9   All banks subscribing to this Code must belong to the Banking Ombudsman Scheme or, where appropriate, to one of the arbitration schemes listed overleaf.

5.10   We will display a notice in a prominent position in all our branches stating which Ombudsman or arbitration scheme we belong to and that copies of the Code are available on request.

5.11   We will give you details about which Ombudsman or arbitration scheme is available to you. You can also get information by contacting the appropriate Ombudsman or arbitration scheme at the addresses listed overleaf:

The Office of the Banking Ombudsman
70 Gray's Inn Road
London WCIX 8NB
Tel: 0171 404 9944
Enquiries only – LO-call Tel: 0345 660902

The Office of the Building Societies Ombudsman
Millbank Tower
Millbank
London SWIP 4XS
Tel: 0171 931 0044

The Finance and Leasing Association Arbitration Scheme
18 Upper Grosvenor Street
London W1X 9PB
Tel: 0171 491 2783

The Consumer Credit Trade Association Arbitration Scheme
Tennyson House
159/163 Great Portland Street
London WIN 5FO
Tel: 0171 636 7564

Monitoring & compliance

5.12   We will comply with the law and follow relevant codes of practice or similar documents as members of the British Bankers' Association (BBA), The Building Societies Association (BSA) and the Association for Payment Clearing Services (APACS). The main codes include:

- BBA, BSA, FLA Code of Practice on the Advertising of Interest Bearing Accounts;
- BBA Guide to Bankers' References (Status Enquiries);
- BSA Code of Practice on Linking of Services;
- CML Code of Mortgage Lending Practice;
- CML Statement of Practice on Handling Arrears and Possessions;
- CML Statement of Practice on the Transfer of Mortgages;
- Association of British Insurers (ABI) General Business Code of Practice;
- British Codes of Advertising and Sales Promotion;
- ITC (Independent Television Commission) Code of Advertising Practice;
- Guide to Credit Scoring.

5.13   We have a 'Code Compliance Officer' and our internal auditing procedures monitor compliance with the Code.

Review body
5.14   The Code is monitored by the Independent Review Body for the Banking and Mortgage Codes comprised of representatives from the banks and building societies and independent consumers. The address is:

Pinners Hall,
105–108 Old Broad Street,
London EC2N 1EX.
Tel: 0171 216 8800.

Complaints concerning the general operation of the Code can be made to them.

5.15   We complete a 'Statement of Compliance' every year which is signed by our Chief Executive and sent to the Independent Review Body for the Banking and Mortgage Codes.

6. HELP SECTION

Sponsoring associations
Enquiries about the Code and requests for copies of it can be addressed to the British Bankers' Association, The Building Societies Association and the Association for Payment Clearing Services. The addresses and telephone numbers are shown at the front of this booklet.

Copies of the Code
All institutions subscribing to the Code will make copies of it available to customers. Copies of the CML Code of Mortgage Lending Practice are available from the Council of Mortgage Lenders (CML), 3 Savile Row, London W1X 1AF, recorded help line telephone number 0171 440 2255.

Additional information
Additional information on a variety of banking and mortgage matters is available in the form of 'Bank Facts' from the BBA, 'Fact Sheets' and information leaflets from the BSA and the CML and 'Pay Points' from APACS. In addition, the Associations operate customer information lines or 'help lines'.

Useful definitions

These definitions explain the meaning of words and terms used in the Code. They are not precise legal or technical definitions.

ATM (Automated Teller Machine)
A cash machine or free standing device dispensing cash and providing other information or services to customers who have a card.

Banker's reference
A banker's reference is an opinion about a particular customer's ability to enter into or repay a financial commitment.

Basic banking service
The opening, maintenance and operation of accounts for money transmission by means of cheque and other debit instruments. This would normally be a current account.

Cards
A general term for any plastic card which may be used to pay for goods and services or to withdraw cash. For the purposes of this Code, it excludes electronic purses.

Credit reference agencies
Organisations, licensed under the Consumer Credit Act 1974, which hold information about individuals which is of relevance to lenders. Banks and building societies may refer to these agencies to assist with various decisions, e.g. whether or not to open an account or provide loans or grant credit. Banks and building societies may give information to or seek information from these agencies.

Credit scoring
A system which banks and building societies use to assist in making decisions about granting consumer credit. Credit scoring uses statistical techniques to measure the likelihood that an application for credit will be a good credit risk.

Electronic purses
Any card or function of a card which contains real value in the form of electronic money which someone has paid for in advance, some of which can be reloaded with further funds and which can be used for a range of purposes.

Guarantee
An undertaking given by a person called the guarantor promising to pay the debts of another if that other person fails to do so.

Out of date cheque
A cheque which has not been paid because its date is too old, normally more than six months.

Password
A word or an access code which the customer has selected to permit them access to a telephone or home banking service and which is also used for identification.

Personal customer
A private individual who maintains an account (including a joint account with another private individual or an account held as an executor or trustee, but excluding the accounts of sole traders, partnerships, companies, clubs and societies) or who receives other services from a bank or building society.

PIN (Personal Identification Number)
A number provided on a strictly confidential basis by a bank or building society to a card holder. Use of this number by the customer will allow the card to be used to withdraw cash and access other services from an Automated Teller Machine (ATM).

Security
A word used to describe items of value such as title deeds to houses, share certificates, life policies, etc. which represent assets used as support for a loan. Under a secured loan the lender has the right to sell the security if the loan is not repaid.

Selected personal information
A selection of memorable facts and information of a private and personal nature chosen by the customer (the sequence of which is known only to the customer) which can be used for identification and to verify identification when accessing accounts.

Tariff
A list of charges for services provided by a bank or building society.

Unpaid cheque
This is a term for a cheque which, after being paid into the account of a person to whom it is payable, is subsequently returned 'unpaid' ('bounced') by the bank or building society whose customer issued the cheque. This leaves the person to whom the cheque is payable without the money in his/her account.

Third Edition: March 1997
Published by BBA Enterprises Limited

APPENDIX 3

APACS Sample Forms

(Published with the kind permission of APACS.)

**NOTE: This is an example. Dimensions must be taken
from the text and not measured off this page.**

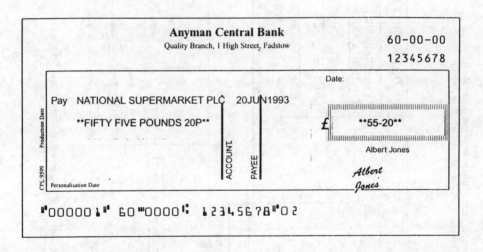

NOTE 1: The amount in figures is centred about the horizontal mid-line of zone C.

NOTE 2: This figure is an example of a cheque that complies with the requirements of this standard
and does not exclude other arrangements that may comply with the provisions of the main text.

PRE-PRINTED CREDIT

NOTE: This is an example. Dimensions must be taken from the text and not measured off this page.

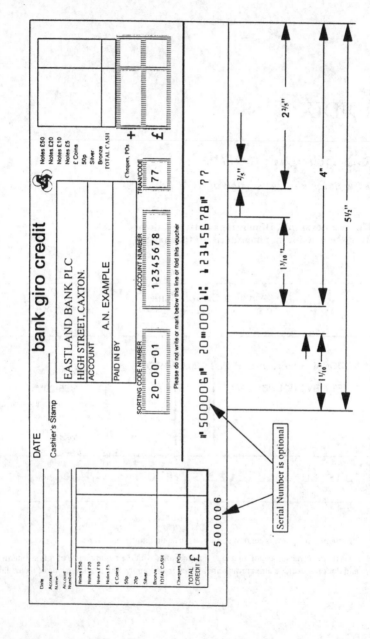

NOTE: The Sorting Code Number, Account Number and Transaction Code boxes shall always be centred vertically on the same axis as the Total Amount Box

COUNTER CREDIT

NOTE: This is an example. Dimensions must be taken from the text and not measured off this page.

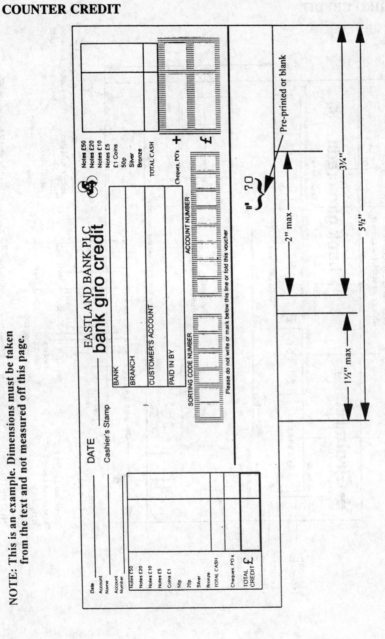

NOTE: The Sorting Code Number and Account Number boxes shall always be centred vertically on the same axis as the Total Amount Box

JOINT GIRO CREDIT

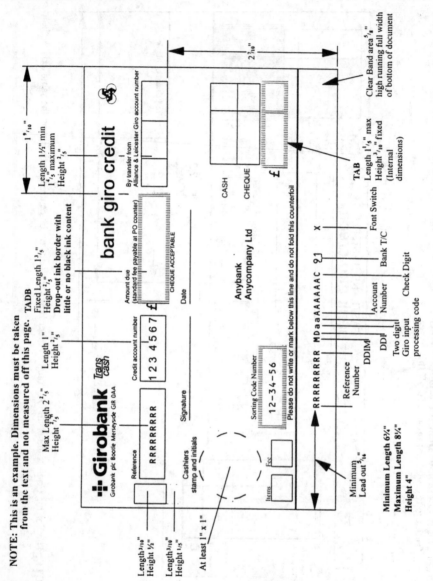

NOTE: This is an example. Dimensions must be taken from the text and not measured off this page.

NOTE: The Sorting Code Number box (and where applicable, the Account Number and Transaction Code boxes shall always be centred vertically on the same axis as the Total Amount Box

DIRECT DEBIT MANDATE

<table>
<tr>
<td>SPACE FOR COMPANY
OR TRADE MARK</td>
<td><h3>Instruction to your
Bank or Building Society
to pay by Direct Debit</h3></td>
<td>DIRECT
Debit

Originators Identification Number</td>
</tr>
</table>

Please fill in the whole form and send it to:
AN Company, Any Street, Any Town, Anywhere.

1. Name and full postal address of your Bank or Building Society

To The Manager

Bank or Building Society

Address

Postcode

2. Name(s) of Account Holder(s)

5. Reference Number

3. Branch Sort Code (from the top right hand corner of your cheque)

6. Instruction to your Bank or Building Society

Please pay A N Company Direct Debits from the account detailed in this Instruction subject to the safeguards assured by the Direct Debit Guarantee. I understand that this Instruction may remain with the (name of Company) and, if so, details will be passed electronically to my Bank/Building Society.

4. Bank/Building Society account number

Signature(s)

Date

Bank and Building Societies may not accept Direct Debit Instructions for some type of accounts.

12/96/01

DETACH HERE

The Direct Debit Guarantee

■ This Guarantee is offered by all Banks and Building Societies that take part in the Direct Debit Scheme. The efficiency and security of the Scheme is monitored and protected by your own Bank or Building Society.

■ If the amounts to be paid or the payment dates change, you will be told of this in advance by at least 14 days or as agreed.

■ If an error is made by AN Company or your Bank or Building Society, you are guaranteed a full and immediate refund from your branch of the amount paid.

■ You can cancel a Direct Debit at any time by writing to your Bank or Building Society. Please also send a copy of your letter to us.

DIRECT
Debit

Recommended Direct Debit Instruction

Index